COMPUTATIONAL INTERACTION

Computational Interaction

Edited by

ANTTI OULASVIRTA

Associate Professor
Aalto University

PER OLA KRISTENSSON

University Reader in Interactive Systems Engineering
University of Cambridge

XIAOJUN BI

Assistant Professor
Stony Brook University

ANDREW HOWES

Professor and Head of School at the School of Computer Science
University of Birmingham

OXFORD
UNIVERSITY PRESS

OXFORD
UNIVERSITY PRESS

Great Clarendon Street, Oxford, OX2 6DP,
United Kingdom

Oxford University Press is a department of the University of Oxford.
It furthers the University's objective of excellence in research, scholarship,
and education by publishing worldwide. Oxford is a registered trade mark of
Oxford University Press in the UK and in certain other countries

First Edition published in 2018

Impression: 1

Published in the United States of America by Oxford University Press
198 Madison Avenue, New York, NY 10016, United States of America

British Library Cataloguing in Publication Data
Data available

Library of Congress Control Number: 2017949954

ISBN 978–0–19–879960–3 (hbk.)
ISBN 978–0–19–879961–0 (pbk.)

Printed and bound by
CPI Group (UK) Ltd, Croydon, CR0 4YY

CONTENTS

PART IV HUMAN BEHAVIOUR

LIST OF CONTRIBUTORS

Aditya Acharya University of Birmingham, UK

Leif Azzopardi Strathclyde University, UK

Nikola Banovic Carnegie Mellon University, USA

Xiaojun Bi Stony Brook University, USA

Duncan P. Brumby University College London, UK

Paul Cairns University of York, UK

Xiuli Chen University of Birmingham, UK

Jessie Chin University of Illinois, USA

Anind K. Dey Carnegie Mellon University, USA

Alan Dix University of Birmingham, UK

Hyo Jin Do University of Illinois, USA

Camille Fayollas Université de Toulouse, France

Wai-Tat Fu University of Illinois, USA

Mingkun Gao University of Illinois, USA

Otmar Hilliges Advanced Interactive Technologies Lab, ETH Zürich, Switzerland

Andrew Howes University of Birmingham, UK

Takeo Igarashi University of Tokyo, Japan

Christian P. Janssen Utrecht University, The Netherlands

Andreas Karrenbauer Max-Planck-Institut für Informatik, Germany

Yuki Koyama National Institute of Advanced Industrial Science and Technology, Japan

Per Ola Kristensson University of Cambridge, UK

Tuomo Kujala University of Jyväskylä, Finland

Richard L. Lewis University of Michigan, USA

Q. Vera Liao IBM Thomas J. Watson Research Center, New York, USA

Jennifer Mankoff Carnegie Mellon University, USA

Célia Martinie Université de Toulouse, France

Roderick Murray-Smith University of Glasgow, UK

Antti Oulasvirta Aalto University, Finland

Tom Ouyang Google, Inc., USA

Philippe Palanque Université de Toulouse, France

Dario D. Salvucci Drexel University, USA

Brian Smith Columbia University, USA

Harold Thimbleby Swansea University, UK

John Williamson University of Glasgow, UK

Shumin Zhai Google, Inc., USA

Guido Zuccon Queensland University of Technology, Australia

Introduction

XIAOJUN BI,
ANDREW HOWES,
PER OLA KRISTENSSON,
ANTTI OULASVIRTA,
JOHN WILLIAMSON

This book is concerned with the design of interactive technology for human use. It promotes an approach, called computational interaction, that focuses on the use of algorithms and mathematical models to explain and enhance interaction. Computational interaction involves, for example, research that seeks to formally represent a design space in order to understand its structure and identify solutions with desirable properties. It involves building evaluative models that can estimate the expected value of a design either for a designer, or for a system that continuously adapts its user interface accordingly. It involves constructing computational models that can predict, explain, and even shape user behaviour.

While interaction may be approached from a user or system perspective, all examples of computational interaction share a commitment to defining computational models that gain insight into the nature and processes of interaction itself. These models can then be used to drive design and decision making. Here, computational interaction draws on a long tradition of research on human interaction with technology applying human factors engineering (Fisher, 1993; Hollnagel and Woods, 2005; Sanders and McCormick, 1987; Wickens et al., 2015), cognitive modelling (Payne and Howes, 2013; Anderson, 2014; Kieras and Hornof, 2017; Card, Newell, and Moran 1983; Gray and Boehm-Davis, 2000; Newell, 1994; Kieras, Wood, and Meyer, 1997; Pirolli and Card, 1999), artificial intelligence and machine learning (Sutton and Barto, 1998; Brusilovsky and Millan, 2007; Fisher, 1993; Horvitz et al., 1998; Picard, 1997; Shahriari et al., 2016), information theory (Fitts and Peterson, 1964; Seow, 2005; Zhai, 2004), design optimization (Light and Anderson, 1993; Eisenstein, Vanderdonckt, and Puerta, 2001; Gajos and Weld, 2004; Zhai, Hunter and Smith, 2002), formal methods (Thimbleby, 2010; Dix, 1991; Harrison and Thimbleby, 1990; Navarre et al., 2009), and control theory (Craik, 1947; Kleinman, Baron, and Levison, 1970; Jagacinski and Flach, 2003; Sheridan and Ferrell, 1974).

Computational Interaction. Antti Oulasvirta, Per Ola Kristensson, Xiaojun Bi, Andrew Howes (Eds).
© Oxford University Press 2018. Published 2018 by Oxford University Press.

Computational interaction is a science of the artificial (Simon, 1996), where the object of research is the construction of artefacts for stated goals and function. Herbert Simon took up construction as the distinctive feature of disciplines like medicine, computer science, and engineering, distinguishing them from natural sciences, where the subject is natural phenomena, and from arts, which may not share interest in attaining goals: 'Engineering, medicine, business, architecture, and painting are concerned not with the necessary but with the contingent, not with how things are but with how they might be, in short, with design' (Simon, 1996, p. xiii).

Simon made three important observations, which we share, about sciences of the artificial. First, he distinguished the 'inner environment' of the artefact, such as an algorithm controlling a display, and the 'outer environment', in which the artefact serves its purpose. When we design a user interface, we are designing how the outer and the inner environments are mediated. Both the human and the technology also have invariant properties that together with the designed variant properties shape the process and outcomes of interaction (see Figure I.1). The final artefact reflects a designer's implicit theory of this interplay (Carroll and Campbell, 1989). When we design computational interaction, we are designing or adapting an inner environment of the artefact such that it can proactively, and appropriately, relate its functioning to the user and her context. In computational interaction, the theory or model, is explicit and expressed in code or mathematics. Second, Simon elevated simulation as a prime method of construction. Simulations, or models in general, allow 'imitating' reality in order to predict future behaviour. Simulations support the discovery of consequences of premises which would be difficult, often impossible, to obtain with intuition. In computational interaction, models are used offline to study the conditions of interaction, and they may be parameterized in a real-time system with data to infer user's intentions and adapt interaction. Third, Simon pointed out that since the end-products are artefacts that are situated in some 'outer environments', they can and should be subjected to

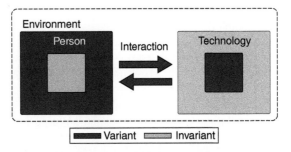

Figure I.1 Interaction is an emergent consequence of both variant and invariant aspects of technology and people. Technology invariants include, for example, current operating systems that provide an ecosystem for design. Technology variants include programmed interfaces that give rise to apps, visualizations, gestural control, etc. A person's invariants include biologically constrained abilities, such as the acuity function of human vision. A person's variants consist of the adaptive behavioural strategies. To design interaction is to explain and enhance the variant aspects given the invariants (both human and technology). In computational interaction, variant aspects are changed through appropriate algorithmic methods and models.

empirical research. Design requires rigorous empirical validation of not only the artefact, but also of the models and theories that created it. Since models contain verifiable information about the world, they have face validity which is exposed through empirical observations. They do not exist as mere sources of inspiration for designers, but systematically associate variables of interest to events of interaction.

However, computational interaction is not intended to replace designers but to complement and boost the very human and essential activity of interaction design, which involves activities such as creativity, sensemaking, reflection, critical thinking, and problem solving (Cross, 2011). We hold that even artistic and creative efforts can greatly benefit from a well-articulated understanding of interaction and mastery of phenomena captured via mathematical methods. By advancing the scientific study of interactive computing artefacts, computational interaction can create new opportunities and capabilities in creative and artistic endeavors. We anticipate that the approaches described in this book are useful in the interaction design processes of ideating, sketching, and evaluating, for example. Computational interaction can also be studied and developed in broader contexts of socio-technical systems, where power, labour, and historical settings shape interaction.

The fundamental ideas of computational interaction have been present for many years. However, there is now strong motivation to collect, rationalize, and extend them. In the early days of interaction design, design spaces were relatively simple; input devices, for example, were explicitly designed to be simple mappings of physical action to digital state. However, computer systems are now vastly more complex. In the last two decades, interaction has broken out from the limited domains of workstations for office workers to pervade every aspect of human activity. In the current mobile and post-PC computing era, new technologies have emerged that bring new challenges, for which the traditional hand-tuned approach to design is not well equipped. For example, wearable computing, augmented and virtual reality, and customizable interactive devices, pose increasingly wicked challenges, where designers must consider a multiplicity of problems from low-level hardware, through software, all the way to human factors. In these increasingly complex design spaces, computational abstraction and algorithmic solutions are likely to become vital.

Increasing design complexity motivates the search for a scalable interaction engineering that can complement and exceed the capabilities of human designers. A contention of this book is that a combination of methods from modelling, automation, optimization, and machine learning can offer a path to address these challenges. An algorithmic approach to interaction offers the hope of scalability; an opportunity to make sense of complex data and systematically and efficiently derive designs from overwhelmingly complex design spaces. This requires precise expression of interaction problems in a form amenable to computational analysis.

This book is part of an argument that, embedded in an iterative design process, computational interaction design has the potential to complement human strengths and provide a means to generate inspiring and elegant designs. Computational interaction does not exclude the messy, complicated, and uncertain behaviour of humans. Neither does it seek to reduce users to mechanistic caricatures for ease of analysis. Instead, a computational approach recognizes that there are many aspects of interaction that can be augmented by an algorithmic approach, even if algorithms are fallible at times and based on approximations of human life. Furthermore, computational interaction has the potential to reduce the design errors that plague current interactive devices, some of which can be life ending. It can dramatically reduce the iterations cycles required to create high-quality interactions that other approaches might write off as impossible to use. It can specialize and tailor general interaction techniques such as search for niche tasks, for instance, patent searches and systematic reviews. It can expand the design space and enable people to interact more naturally with complex machines and artificial intelligence.

In parallel with the increased complexity of the interaction problem, there have been rapid advances in computational techniques. At the fundamental level, rapid strides in machine learning, data science, and associated disciplines have transformed the problem space that can be attacked, generating algorithms and models of transformative power. At the practical level, affordable high-performance computing, networked systems, and availability of off-the-shelf libraries, datasets, and software for computational methods, make it feasible to analyse and enhance the challenging problems of interaction design. These are developments that should not be ignored.

This book sets out a vision of human use of interactive technology empowered by computation. It promotes an analytical, algorithmic, and model-led approach that seeks to exploit the rapid expansion in computational techniques to deal with the diversification and sophistication of the interaction design space. As noted by John Carroll (1997), and by others many times after, research on human-computer interaction has had problems assimilating the variety of methodologies, theories, problems, and people. The implementation of theoretical ideas in code could become a substrate and a nexus for computer scientists, behavioural and social scientists, and designers alike. If this promise is to be fulfilled, then serious effort must be made to connect mainstream search in human-computer interaction to computational foundations.

I.1 Definition

Defining a field is fraught with dangers. Yet there are two reasons to attempt one here: (i) to provide a set of core objectives and ideas for like-minded researchers in otherwise disparate fields to coalesce; (ii) to help those not yet using computational methods to identify the attributes that enable those methods to be successful and understand how this way of thinking can be brought to bear in enhancing their work. While any definition is necessarily incomplete, there is a strong sense that there is a nucleus of distinctive and exciting ideas that distinguish computational from traditional human-computer interaction research. The goal of our definition is to articulate that nucleus.

Definition Computational interaction applies computational thinking—that is, abstraction, automation, and analysis—to explain and enhance the interaction between a user (or users) and a system. It is underpinned by modelling which admits formal reasoning and involves at least one of the following:

- a way of updating a model with observed data from users;
- an algorithmic element that, using a model, can directly synthesize or adapt the design;

- a way of automating and instrumenting the modelling and design process;
- the ability to simulate or synthesize elements of the expected user-system behaviour.

For example, the design of a control panel layout might involve first proposing an abstract representation of the design space and an objective function (for example, visual search performance and selection time) for choosing between variants. It might then involve using an optimization method to search the space of designs and analysing the properties of the proposed design using formal methods. Alternatively, explaining observed user behaviour given a specific design might be explained by first proposing abstract representations of the information processing capacities of the mind (for example, models of human memory for interference and forgetting), then building computer models that automate the calculation of the implications of these capacities for each particular variant across the distribution of possible users, and then analysing the results and comparing with human data.

As in engineering and computer science, the hallmark of computational interaction is mathematical—and often executable—modelling that connects with data. However, while computational interaction is founded on fundamental theoretical considerations, it is constructive in its aims rather than descriptive. It calls for empirical rigour in evaluation and model construction, but focuses on using computationally powered models to do what could not be done before, rather than describing what has been done before. To this end, it emphasizes generating constructive conceptual foundations and robust, replicable and durable methods that go beyond point sampling of the interaction space.

I.2 Vision

The overarching objective of computational interaction is to increase our capacity to reliably achieve interactions with desirable qualities. A generic capacity is preferable over point solutions, because we need to deal with diverse users, contexts, and technologies. By seeking shared, transferable solution principles, the long-term aim shall be to effect the runaway 'ratcheting' of a body of research that builds up constructively and composition-ally; something that research on human-computer interaction has struggled to achieve in the past.

This motivates several defining qualities of computational interaction: verifiable, mathe-matical theory that allow results to generalize; scalable, theory-led engineering that does not require empirical testing of every variant; transparency and reproducibility in research; and the concomitant requirement for reusable computational concepts, algorithms, data sets, challenges, and code. In machine learning, for example, the pivot to open-source libraries, large state-of-the-art benchmark datasets, and rapid publication cycles has facilitated both the uptake of developments and progress rate of research.

This vision opens up several possibilities to improve the way we understand, design, and use interactive technology.

Increase efficiency, robustness, and enjoyability of interaction Models of interaction, informed by often large-scale datasets, can enable the design of better interactions. For instance, interactions can demand less time; reduce the number of errors made; decrease frustration; increase satisfaction, and so on. In particular, computational approaches can help quantify these abstract goals, infer these qualities from observable data, and create mechanisms through which interfaces can be optimized to maximize these qualities. A computational approach aims to create an algorithmic path from observed user-system interaction data to quantifiably improved interaction.

Proofs and guarantees A clear benefit of some approaches, such as formal, probabilistic, and optimization methods is that they can offer guarantees and even proofs for some aspects of solution quality. This may be valuable for designers who seek to convince customers, or for adaptive user interfaces, that can more reliably achieve desired effects.

Develop user-centred design Computational interaction not only supports but can re-envision user-centred design, where techniques such as parametric interfaces, data-driven optimization, and machine-learned input recognition create direct data paths from usage and observations to design and interaction. Computation allows interfaces to be precisely tailored for users, contexts, and devices. Structure and content can be learned from observation, potentially on a mass scale, rather than dictated in advance.

Reduce the empirical burden Models can predict much of expected user-system behaviour. Interaction problems can be defined formally, which increases our ability to reason and avoid blind experimentation. Computational methods should reduce the reliance on empirical studies and focus experimental results on validating designs based on sound models. Strong theoretical bases should move 'shot-in-the-dark' point sampling of designs to informed and data efficient experimental work.

Reduce design time of interfaces Automation, data, and models can supplant hand-tweaking in the design of interfaces. It should be quicker, and less expensive, to engineer complex interactions if the minutiae of design decisions can be delegated to algorithmic approaches.

Free up designers to be creative In the same vein, algorithmic design can support designers in tedious tasks. From tuning pose recognizers at public installations to choosing colour schemes for medical instrument panels, computational thinking can let designers focus on the big picture creative decisions and synthesize well-designed interactions.

Harness new technologies more quickly Hardware engineering is rapidly expanding the space of input devices and displays for user interaction. However, traditional research on human-computer interaction, reliant on traditional design-evaluate cycles, struggles to tackle these challenges quickly. Parametric interfaces, predictive, simulatable models, crowdsourcing, and machine learning offer the potential to dramatically reduce the time it takes to bring effective interactions to new engineering developments.

I.3 Elements

Computational interaction draws on a long history of modelling and algorithmic construction in engineering, computer science, and the behavioural sciences. Despite the apparent diversity of these disciplines, each provides a body of work that supports explaining and enhancing complex interaction problems. They do so by providing an abstract, often mathematical, basis for representing interaction problems, algorithms for automating the calculation of predictions, and formal methods for analysing and reasoning about the implications of the results.

These models differ in the way they represent elements of interaction: that is, how the properties, events, processes, and relationships of the human and technology are formally expressed and reasoned with. They may represent the structure of design, human behaviour, or interaction, and they may represent some tendencies or values in those spaces. They allow the computer to reason and test alternative hypotheses with the model, to 'speculate' with possibilities, and to go beyond observations. This can be achieved analytically, such as when finding the minima of a function. However, in most cases, the models are complex and permit no analytical solution, and an algorithmic solution is needed, in which case methods like optimization or probabilistic reasoning can be used. Such computations may give rise to predictions and interpretations that are emergent in the sense that they are not obvious given lower-level data. Another property shared by these approaches is that the involved models can be parameterized by some observations (data) that represent the problem at hand.

We have collected a few key concepts of interaction and design, which can be identified behind the many formalisms presented in this book. This is *not* meant to exhaustively list all concepts related to computational interaction and we invite the reader to identify, define, and elaborate additional concepts central to computational interaction, such as dialogues, dynamics, game theory, biomechanics, and many others.

Information Information theory, drawing from Shannon's communication theory, models interaction as transmission of information, or messages, between the user and the computer. Transmission occurs as selection of a message from a set of possible messages and transferring over a degraded (noisy, delayed, intermittent) channel. The rate of successful transmission, and the complexity of the messages that are being passed, is a criterion for better interaction. For instance, to use a keyboard, the user communicates to the computer system via the human neuromuscular system. A user can be seen as a source communicating messages in some message space over a noisy channel in order to transmit information from the user's brain into the computer system. Importantly, throughput and similar information theoretical constructs can be taken as objectives for design, modelled using human performance models such as Fitt's law and the Hick–Hyman law, and operationalized in code to solve problems. Applications include input methods, interaction techniques, and sensing systems.

Probability The Bayesian approach to interaction is explicit in its representation of uncertainty, represented by probability distributions over random variables. Under this viewpoint, interaction can be seen, for example, as the problem of inferring intention via evidence observed from sensors. Intention is considered to be an unobserved random variable existing in a user's mind, about which the system maintains and updates a probabilistic belief. An effective interaction is one that causes the belief distribution to converge to the user's true intention. This approach allows informative priors to be specified across potential actions and rigorously combined with observations. Uncertainty about intention can be propagated through the interface and combined with utility functions to engage functionality using decision-theoretic principles. As a consequence of proper representation of uncertainty, Bayesian approaches offer benefits in terms of robustness in interaction.

One major advantage of the probabilistic view is that many components at multiple levels of interaction can be integrated on a sound basis, because probability theory serves as a unifying framework; for example, linking probabilistic gesture recognizers to probabilistic text entry systems. Tools such as recursive Bayesian filters and Gaussian process regression can be used directly in inferring user intention.

Learning Machine learning equips a computer with the ability to use data to make increasingly better predictions. It can transform static data into executable functionality, typically by optimizing parameters of a model given a set of observations to minimize some loss. In computational interaction, machine learning is used to both predict likely user behaviour and to learn mappings from sensing to estimated intentional states. Supervised machine learning formulates the problem as learning a function $y = f(x)$ that transforms observed feature vectors to an output space for which some training set of observations are available. After a training phase, predictions of y can be made for unseen x. Estimation of continuous values such as, for instance, intended cursor position, is regression, and estimation of discrete values such as, for example, distinct gesture classes, is classification. Supervised machine learning can replace hand-tweaking of parameters with data-driven modelling. There are many high-performing and versatile tools for supervised learning, including support vector machines, deep neural networks, random forests, and many others. Unsupervised learning learns structure from data without a set of matching target values. Techniques such as manifold learning (learning a simple smooth low-dimensional space that explains complex observations) and clustering (inferring a set of discrete classes) have potential in exploring and eliciting interactions. Unsupervised learning is widely used in recommender systems and user-modelling in general, often with an assumption that users fall into distinct clusters of behaviour and characteristics.

Optimization Optimization refers to the process of obtaining the best solution for a defined problem. For example, a design task can be modelled as a combination of elementary decisions, such as which functionality to include, which widget type to use, where to place an element, and so on. Optimization can also use constraints to rule out infeasible designs. Several approaches exist to modelling design objectives, ranging from heuristics to detailed behavioural, neural, cognitive, or biomechanical models. The benefit of formulating a design problem like this is that powerful solution methods can be exploited to find best designs automatically, rooted on decades of research on optimization algorithms for both offline and online setups.

States State machines are a powerful formalism for representing states and transitions within an interface. This model of interaction captures the discrete elements of interfaces and represents states (and their groupings) and events that cause transitions between states. Formalisms such as finite-state machines (FSMs), and specification languages such as statecharts, allow for precise analysis of the internal configurations of interfaces. Explicit modelling permits rigorous analysis of the interface properties, such as reachability of functionality, critical paths, bottlenecks, and unnecessary steps. Graph properties of FSMs can be used to model or optimize interfaces; for example, outdegree can be used to study the number of discrete controls required for an interface. State machines offer both constructive approaches in rigorously designing and synthesizing interfaces and in analysing and characterizing existing interfaces to obtain quantifiable metrics of usability.

Control With roots in cybernetics and control engineering, control theory provides a powerful formalism for reasoning about continuous systems. In applications to human-technology interaction, the user is modelled as a controller aiming to change a control signal to a desired level (the reference) by updating its behaviour according to feedback about the system state. The design of the system affects how well the user can achieve the goal given its own characteristics. Control theory views interaction as continuous, although a computer may register user behaviour as a discrete event. Modelling interaction as a control system with a feedback loop overcomes a fundamental limitation of stimulus–response based approaches, which disregard feedback. The control paradigm permits multi-level analysis, tracing the progression of user-system behaviour over time (as a process) to explain eventual outcomes to user. It allows insight into consequences of changing properties of the user interface, or the user.

Rationality Rational analysis is a theory of human decision-making originating in behavioural economics and psychology of decision-making. The assumption is that people strive to maximize utility in their behaviour. Bounded rationality is the idea that rational behaviour is constrained by capacity and resource limitations. When interacting, users pursue goals or utility functions to the best of their capability within constraints posed by user interfaces, environments, and tasks. The idea of bounded rationality is explored in information foraging theory and economic models of search.

Agents Bounded agents are models of users that take action and optimally adapt their behaviour to given constraints: environments and capabilities. The bounds include not only those posed by the environment, which includes the interface, but limitations on the observation and cognitive functions and on the actions of the agent. These bounds define a space of possible policies. The hypothesis is that interactive behaviour is rationally adapted to the ecological structure of interaction, cognitive and perceptual capacities, and the intrinsic objectives of the user. The interactive problem can be specified, for example, as a reinforcement learning problem, or a game, and behaviour emerges by finding the optimal behavioural policy or program to the utility maximization problem. The recent interest in computationally implemented agents is due to the benefit that, when compared with classic cognitive models, they require no predefined specification of the user's task solution, only the objectives. Increasingly powerful representations and solution methods have emerged for bounded agents in machine learning and artificial intelligence.

The chapters of this book present further details on the assumptions, implementation, applications, as well as limitations of these elementary concepts.

I.4 Outlook

The chapters in this book manifest intellectual progress in the study of computational principles of interaction, demonstrated in diverse and challenging applications areas such as input methods, interaction techniques, graphical user interfaces, information retrieval, information visualization, and graphic design. Much of this progress may have gone unnoticed in mainstream human-computer interaction because research has been published in disconnected fields. To coalesce efforts and expand the scope of computationally solvable interaction problems, an exciting vista opens up for future research.

Both the potential of and the greatest challenge in computational interaction lies in mathematics and algorithms. A shared objective for research is mathematical formulation of phenomena in human use of technology. Only by expanding formulations can one devise new methods and approaches for new problems. On the one hand, mathematics and algorithms are the most powerful known representations for capturing complexity. On the other hand, the complexity of a presentation must match the complexity of the behaviour it tries to capture and control. This means that the only way out of narrow applications is via increasingly complex models. The challenge is how to obtain and update them without losing control and interpretability.

A significant frontier, therefore, is to try to capture those aspects of human behavior and experience that are essential for good design. Whether users are satisfied with a design is determined not only by how much time they spend to accomplish the task, but also by its aesthetic aspect, the ease of learning, whether it fits the culture of certain regions, etc. Interaction is also often *coupled* with the environment and the situated contexts of the user. For example, a user's typing behaviour is dependent on whether a user is walking, if the user is encumbered, and the way the user is holding the device. The system itself is also often coupled to the environment. Also, computational interaction should not be restricted to model a single user's interaction with a single a computer system. A single user may interact with many devices, many users may interact with a single computer system, or many users may interact with many computer systems in order to for instance carry out a shared task objective. These challenges call for collaboration with behavioural and social scientists.

This increasing scale and complexity will pose a challenge also for algorithms. Algorithms underpin computational interaction and for systems implementing principles of computational interaction it is important that the underlying algorithms scale with increasing complexity. For example, naive optimization is often infeasible due to the complexity of the optimization problem. However, it is often relatively straight-forward to search for an approximately optimal solution. Complexity is multifaceted in computational interaction and may, for instance, concern the expressiveness of a system (for instance, the number of gestures recognized by the system), the ability of a solution to satisfy multi-objective criteria, or manage a complex and constantly changing environment. To increase our ability to deal with complex real-world phenomena implies that we need to search for more efficient ways to update models with data. Some computational models are heavily reliant on representative training data. A challenge in data collection is to ensure the data is accurately reflecting realistic interaction contexts, which may be dynamic and constantly changing, and that it captures the variability of different user groups. Moreover, data may not be available until the particular user has started adopting the design. Such a 'chicken and the egg' dilemma has long been a problem in computational interaction: the interaction data is needed for designing interface or interactive systems; yet the data will not be available until the design or system is available and the user starts adopting it. These challenges call for collaboration with computer and computational scientists.

Finally, there's the human. Computational interaction can be viewed as a continuation of the long history of automation, which has undergone a series of victories and setbacks due to complexity causing the loss of agency, deskilling, demotivation, and so on. Once a computational interaction technique is operating there is a risk the user is losing agency as a consequence of an overly complex system aiding or overriding the user. Such problems are exacerbated when the system fails to correctly infer the user's intention, in particular, if the system fails in an unexpected way, or if it fails to offer suitable controls and interpretability. Computational interaction should offer appropriate degree of transparency that allows users to at understand the mechanisms leading to a particular system prediction or suggestion at such a level that they can achieve their goals. To do so effectively either requires understanding users' existing workflows and practices, users to adapt to new ways of interaction tailed for computational interaction design, or a combination of both. From the perspective of algorithms, even the design problem is centered around mathematics: the central problem for user interface design for algorithmic systems is to assist users in understanding and shaping control, learning, and optimization functions and guiding a system-informed exploration of the decision space. What is the best user interface to mathematics? When this problem is successfully solved, computers can support users' creativity by assisting them in effectively exploring high-dimensional decision spaces. By modelling a domain-specific creative process, it is possible to optimize the creative process itself and help identify suitable solutions that are better according to some criteria, such as speed, aesthetics, novelty, etc. These challenges call for collaboration with designers and design researchers.

....

REFERENCES

Anderson, J. R., 2014. *Rules of the mind*. Hove, UK: Psychology Press.

Brusilovsky, P., and Millan, E., 2007. User models for adaptive hypermedia and adaptive educational systems. In: P. Brusilovsky, A. Kobsa, and W. Nejdl, eds. *The Adaptive Web: Methods and Strategies of Web Personalization*. Berlin: Springer, pp. 3–53.

Card, S. K., Newell, A., and Moran, T. P., 1983. The psychology of human-computer interaction. New York, NY: Lawrence Erlbaum.

Carroll, J. M., 1997. Human-computer interaction: psychology as a science of design. *Annual Review of Psychology*, 48(1), pp. 61–83.

Carroll, J. M., and Campbell, R. L., 1989. Artifacts as psychological theories: The case of human-computer interaction. *Behaviour and Information Technology*, 8, pp. 247–56.

Craik, K. J. W., 1947. Theory of the human operator in control systems: 1. the operator as an engineering system. *British Journal of Psychology General Section*, 38(2), pp. 56–61.

Cross, N., 2011. *Design thinking: Understanding how designers think and work*. Oxford: Berg.

Dix, A. J., 1991. Formal methods for interactive systems. Volume 16. London: Academic Press.

Eisenstein, J., Vanderdonckt, J., and Puerta, A., 2001. Applying model-based techniques to the development of UIs for mobile computers. In: *Proceedings of the 6th International Conference on Intelligent User Interfaces*. New York, NY: ACM, pp. 69–76.

Fisher, D. L., 1993. Optimal performance engineering: Good, better, best. *Human Factors*, 35(1), pp. 115–39.

Fitts, P. M., and Peterson, J. R., 1964. Information capacity of discrete motor responses. *Journal of Experimental Psychology*, 67(2), pp. 103–12.

Gajos, K., and Weld, D. S., 2004. SUPPLE: automatically generating user interfaces. In: *Proceedings of the 9th International Conference on Intelligent User Interfaces*. New York, NY: ACM, pp. 93–100.

Gray, W. D., and Boehm-Davis, D. A., 2000. Milliseconds matter: An introduction to microstrategies and to their use in describing and predicting interactive behavior. *Journal of Experimental Psychology: Applied*, 6(4), pp. 322–35.

Harrison, M., and Thimbleby, H., eds., 1990. *Formal methods in human-computer interaction*. Volume 2. Cambridge: Cambridge University Press.

Hollnagel, E., and Woods, D. D., 2005. *Joint cognitive systems: Foundations of cognitive systems engineering*. Columbus, OH: CRC Press.

Horvitz, E., Breese, J., Heckerman, D., Hovel, D., and Rommelse, K., 1998. The Lumiere project: Bayesian user modeling for inferring the goals and needs of software users. In: *UAI '98: Proceedings of the Fourteenth Conference on Uncertainty in Artificial Intelligence*. San Francisco, CA: Morgan Kaufmann, pp. 256–65.

Jagacinski, R. J., and Flach, J. M., 2003. *Control Theory for Humans: Quantitative approaches to modeling performance*. Mahwah, NJ: Lawrence Erlbaum.

Kieras, D. E., and Hornof, A., 2017. Cognitive architecture enables comprehensive predictive models of visual search. *Behavioral and Brain Sciences*, 40. DOI: https://doi.org/10.1017/S0140525X16000121

Kieras, D. E., Wood, S. D., and Meyer, D. E., 1997. Predictive engineering models based on the EPIC architecture for a multimodal high-performance human-computer interaction task. *ACM Transactions on Computer-Human Interaction (TOCHI)*, 4(3), pp. 230–75.

Kleinman, D. L., Baron, S., and Levison, W. H., 1970. An optimal control model of human response part I: Theory and validation. *Automatica* 6(3). pp. 357–69.

Light, L., and Anderson, P., 1993. Designing better keyboards via simulated annealing. *AI Expert*, 8(9). Available at: http://scholarworks.rit.edu/article/727/.

Navarre, D., Palanque, P., Ladry, J. F., and Barboni, E., 2009. ICOs: A model-based user interface description technique dedicated to interactive systems addressing usability, reliability and scalability. *ACM Transactions on Computer-Human Interaction (TOCHI)*, 16(4). <doi:10.1145/1614390.1614393>.

Newell, A., 1994. *Unified Theories of Cognition*. Cambridge, MA: Harvard University Press.

Payne, S. J., and Howes, A., 2013. Adaptive interaction: A utility maximization approach to understanding human interaction with technology. *Synthesis Lectures on Human-Centered Informatics*, 6(1): pp. 1–111.

Picard, R. W., 1997. *Affective Computing*. Volume 252. Cambridge, MA: MIT Press.

Pirolli, P., and Card, S. K., 1999. Information Foraging. *Psychological Review*, 106(4), pp. 643–75.

Sanders, M. S., and McCormick, E. J., 1987. *Human Factors in Engineering and Design*. Columbus, OH: McGraw-Hill.

Seow, S. C., 2005. Information theoretic models of HCI: a comparison of the Hick-Hyman law and Fitt's law. *Human-Computer Interaction*, 20(3), pp. 315–52.

Shahriari, B., Swersky, K., Wang, Z., Adams, R. P., and de Freitas, N., 2016. Taking the human out of the loop: A review of Bayesian optimization. *Proceedings of the IEEE*, 104(1), pp. 148–75.

Sheridan, T. B., and Ferrell, W. R., 1974. *Man-machine Systems: Information, Control, and Decision Models of Human Performance*. Cambridge, MA: MIT Press.

Simon, H. A., 1996. *The Sciences of the Artificial*. Cambridge, MA: MIT press.

Sutton, R. S., and Barto, A. G., 1998. *Reinforcement learning: An introduction.* Volume 1, Number 1. Cambridge, MA: MIT Press.

Wickens, C. D., Hollands, J. G., Banbury, S., and Parasuraman, R., 2015. *Engineering Psychology & Human Performance.* Hove, UK: Psychology Press.

Thimbleby, H., 2010. *Press on: Principles of Interaction Programming.* Cambridge, MA: MIT Press.

Zhai, S., 2004. Characterizing computer input with Fitts' law parameters—the information and non-information aspects of pointing. *International Journal of Human-Computer Studies,* 61(6), pp. 791–809.

Zhai, S., Hunter, M., and Smith, B. A., 2002. Performance optimization of virtual keyboards. *Human–Computer Interaction,* 17(2–3), pp. 229–69.

PART I
Input and Interaction Techniques

1

Control Theory, Dynamics, and Continuous Interaction

RODERICK MURRAY-SMITH

1.1 Introduction

What do we really mean when we talk about Human–Computer Interaction(HCI)? It is a subject with few firm, agreed foundations. Introductory textbooks tend to use phrases like 'designing spaces for human communication and interaction', or 'designing interactive products to support the way people communicate and interact in their everyday lives' (Rogers , Sharp, and Preece, 2011). Hornbæk and Oulasvirta (2017) provides a recent review of the way different HCI communities have approached this question, but only touches briefly on control approaches. Traditionally, HCI research has viewed the challenge as *communication of information* between the user and computer, and has used information theory to represent the bandwidth of communication channels into and out of the computer via an interface: 'By interaction we mean any communication between a user and a computer, be it direct or indirect' (Dix , Finlay, Abowd, and Beale, 2004), but this does not provide an obvious way to measure the communication, or whether the communication makes a difference.

The reason that information theory is not sufficient to describe HCI is that in order to communicate the simplest symbol of intent, we typically require to move our bodies in some way that can be sensed by the computer, often based on feedback while we are doing it. Our bodies move in a continuous fashion through space and time, so any communication system is going to be based on a foundation of continuous control. However, inferring the user's intent is inherently complicated by the properties of the control loops used to generate the information—intention in the brain becomes intertwined with the physiology of the human body and the physical dynamics and transducing properties of the computer's input device. In a computational interaction context, the software adds a further complication to the closed-loop behaviour (Figure 1.1). Hollnagel (1999) and Hollnagel and Woods (2005) make a compelling argument that we need to focus on how the *joint* human–computer system performs, not on the communication between the parts.

Computational Interaction. Antti Oulasvirta, Per Ola Kristensson, Xiaojun Bi, Andrew Howes (Eds).
© Oxford University Press 2018. Published 2018 by Oxford University Press.

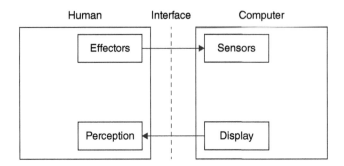

Figure 1.1 Human–Computer Interaction as a closed-loop system.

Another reason that control theory can be seen as a more general framework is that often the purpose of communicating information to a computer is to control some aspect of the world, whether this be the temperature in a room or the volume of a music player,[1] the destination of an autonomous vehicle or some remote computational system. This can be seen in Figure 1.2, which illustrates the evolution of human–machine symbiosis from direct action with our limbs, via tools and powered control. Over time this has led to an increasing indirectness of the relationship between the human and the controlled variable, with a decrease in required muscular strength and an increasing role for sensing and thought (Kelley, 1968). The coming era of *Computational Interaction* will further augment or replace elements of the perceptual, cognitive, and actuation processes in the human with artificial computation, so we can now adapt the original figure from Kelley (1968) to include control of *computationally enhanced systems*, where significant elements of:

1. the information fed back to the human,
2. the coordination of control actions and
3. the proposals for new sub-goals

are augmented computationally as shown in Figure 1.3. This computational augmentation is intended to achieve a similar decrease in the complexity of human cognition, perception and actuation that earlier generations achieved over muscle strength. In some cases this will decrease the human interaction with some tasks, in order to be able to apply more attention and cognitive resources to other, currently more important, aspects of their environment. For example, computationally enhancing the music player in a car allows the driver to have an acceptable degree of control over the style of music played while, more importantly, being able to concentrate on driving safely. A further step, completely automating driving itself would allow the human to shift their resources to focus on engaging with family members or preparing for an upcoming business meeting.

---

[1] One might think the reference here is the loudness of the music, but in many social contexts it is probably the inferred happiness of the people in the room that is actually being controlled, and any feedback from volume indicators are just intermediate variables to help the user.

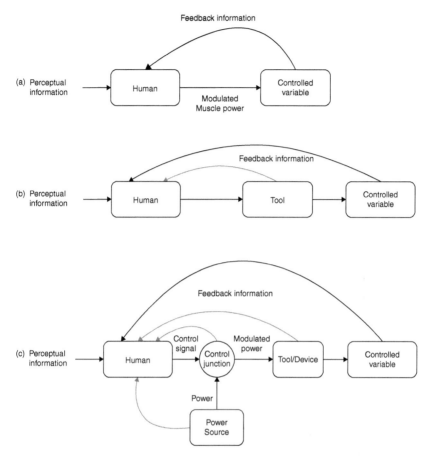

Figure 1.2 The evolution of human control over the environment from (a) direct muscle power via (b) use of specialised tools for specifhc tasks and (c) externally powered devices, potentially regulated by automatic controllers. Adapted from (Kelley, 1968). Grey lines indicate optional feedback connections.

1.1.1 Related Work

Few modern researchers or practitioners in HCI have had any training in *control theory*, which has been an interdisciplinary branch of engineering and mathematics for 70 years. It deals with the behaviour of dynamic systems with inputs, and how their behaviour is modified by feedback. The specific area of control systems relating to human users became a major area of activity from the 1950s. This chapter aims to introduce human–computer interaction researchers with a computing science background to the basics concepts of control theory and describe a control perspective of some common interaction models.

Manual control theory (McRuer and Jex, 1967; Costello, 1968) seeks to model the interaction of humans with machines, for example, aircraft pilots or car drivers. This grew

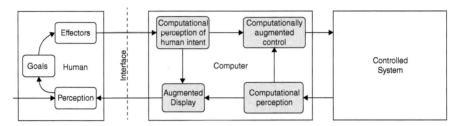

Figure 1.3 The next step in evolution–control with power- and computationally-enhanced devices. Grey blocks indicate computational intelligence enhancement.

from Craik's (1947, 1948) early, war-related work, and became more well known in the broader framing of Wiener's *Cybernetics* (1948). As observed by Wickens and Hollands (1999), the approach to modelling human control behaviour came from two major schools: the skills researchers and the dynamic systems researchers. The 'skills' group often focused on undisturbed environments, while the 'dynamics', or 'manual control theory' approach (e.g., Kelley, 1968; Sheridan and Ferrell, 1974) tended to seek to model the interaction of humans with machines, for example, aircraft pilots or car drivers, usually driven by engineering motivations and the need to eliminate error, making it a closed-loop system. The 'skills' group tended to focus on learning and acquisition while the 'dynamics' group focused on the behaviour of a well-trained operator controlling dynamic systems to make them conform with certain space-time trajectories in the face of environmental uncertainty. This covers most forms of vehicle control, or the control of complex industrial processes. Poulton (1974) reviews the early tracking literature, and an accessible textbook review of the basic approaches to manual control can be found in Jagacinski and Flach (2003). Many of the earlier models described here were based on frequency domain approaches, where the human and controlled system were represented by Laplace transforms representing their input/output *transfer function*. Optimal control theoretic approaches used in the time domain are described in (Kleinman, Baron, and Levison, 1970, 1971). The well-established field of *human motor control theory*, e.g., (Schmidt and Lee, 2005), which seeks to understand how the human central nervous system controls the body, is an important component of using control theory in HCI, but this chapter focuses on the basic role of control concepts in HCI.

1.2 The Control Loop

1.2.1 The Classical Control Loop

Figure 1.4 shows a representation of the classical control loop. It is a general representation of many possible control or tracking tasks, covering car driving, mouse movement, or the control of a chemical process. It represents a dynamic system, so the output of each block is time varying.

The *Goal* is also called the *reference*. It describes the desired *state* of the controlled system. The state is a real vector which describes the condition of the controlled system, a position in

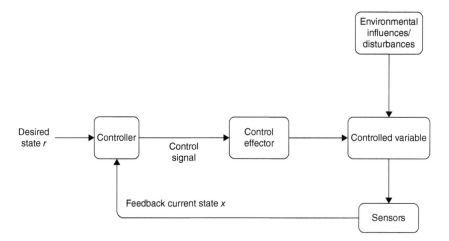

Figure 1.4 Classical control loop.

the *state space*. The concepts of state variable, state, and state space are important tools which can help designers understand the problem. The *choice of state variables* for your model is a statement about the important elements of the system. The state dimensions combine to form the *state space*. Behaviour is visualized as movement through this space, and the values of state reflect the position compared to important landmarks such as the goal.[2] Problem constraints can be represented as boundaries in the state space and qualitative properties of the system can be described as regions in the state space (Bennett and Flach, 2011).

Inputs and Outputs: The controller generates control inputs to the controlled system. Transformations of the system state are observed, i.e., the *outputs*. The concepts of *controllability* and *observability* are important, as they describe the degree to which a control system can observe and control the states of a particular system.

Open/Closed Loop: If an input is transformed in various ways but the control variable does not depend on feedback from the system state, the system is described as *open loop*. *Closed loop* systems have feedback from the state to the controller which affect the input to the controlled system.

Disturbances: External or unpredictable effects which affect the system state. In an open-loop system, the controller is unable to compensate for these, while a closed-loop controller can observe the error and change its control variable to compensate.

Stability: In technical control systems, stability is a key aspect of design. This has been less of an issue in modern HCI, but is important in automotive and aircraft control, where interactions between the human operator and technical control systems can lead to instability, and 'pilot-induced oscillations'. Stability is relevant not only for equilibria, but also for period motions. For example, a pendulum is typically stable to minor perturbations around its normal limit cycle.

Feedback: The display is to provide the user with information needed to exercise control; i.e. predict consequences of control alternatives, evaluate status, and plan control actions, or

---

[2] Note that for dynamic systems *position* in a state space can describe a rapidly changing situation.

better understand consequences of recent actions. We can augment displays or controls. If we augment the display, we improve the input to the human to simplify their control task. If we augment the control, we change the effective dynamics between control input and system output. For example, most mouse drivers apply nonlinear filters to the raw data from the mouse sensors.

'*Dynamics*': how a system responds over time. Investigation of the behaviour of a controlled system requires us to observe its change of state, and in physical systems this requires transfers of energy or mass. An instantaneous change of state in such a system would require an infinitely large flow of energy or mass, but in real systems we have a transition which takes place over time, and we call such systems *dynamic systems*.

In HCI, because the human effectors (e.g., an arm in pointing) have mass, and systems with mass cannot instantaneously achieve high velocity, the rate at which velocity or position builds up depends on the force applied to the limb, and its mass, resulting in an acceleration $a = \frac{F}{m}$ which then has to integrate up over time to have an impact on measured velocities or positions.

Information states in a computer can change instantaneously, from a human perspective. However, it is not only the physical limitations of our effectors that matter. Powers builds on Gibson's work in (Powers, 1973, 1989, 1992) to highlight that humans (and other animals) evolved to control their perceptions, to generate their behaviour. The human and the computer create a coupled dynamic system. As the human has perceptual bandwidth limitations, he or she requires time to process their sensory feedback and to act on it (again subject to bandwidth limitations), a well-designed system should not make changes in state at a rate faster than the human can follow—otherwise they cannot control the system.

In the case of a human controlled system, the control block might be split between a 'human operator' block and a 'control' block, where elements of the technical system which have a control function are conceptually separated from the process being controlled (see Figure 1.5). In the case of computer user interfaces this may represent different layers of software.

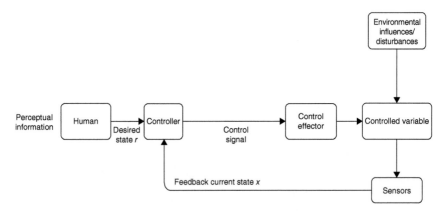

Figure 1.5 Human–Computer control loop where the 'control' element is partitioned into human-controlled and system controlled elements.

1.3 Classes of Continuous Interaction and Examples

Modern graphical user interfaces on personal computers controlled by mice are primarily spatial in nature, using targeting of position over stationary regions for communication of intent. The widespread use of touchscreen smartphones has increased the use of dynamic gestures where a variable is measured over *time*, such as swipes, flicks, and taps, but the methods used have not tended to scale well to more complex cases with richer sensor systems, where a lot of interaction potential is disregarded. Being able to use dynamic state changes to control interaction and infer context could open up new styles of interaction, but our current analytic tools, such as Fitts' law, are not sufficient. If we can identify a continuous signal loop between the user and interface, such that the user is, at times, continuously minimizing the error between his or her intention and the system state, we can say the user is interacting in a continuous fashion with the system. We say 'at times', because there will usually be a de-clutching mechanism, such as letting go of the mouse, such that the interaction is *intermittently continuous*.

The fields of physiology, cognitive science, and ergonomics provide us with models of human aspects of interaction, e.g., low-level perception, motor control, short-term memory, and attention. Computing science is full of models of aspects of machine behaviour, e.g., inference algorithms, finite state machines (FSMs), statecharts, etc., but there is less theoretical support in the area of *interaction*. Manual control theory provided the first steps, with aircraft and automobile control, and models were often implemented on analogue computers. At that time digital computers involved essentially discrete interaction, but now that improvements in sensing, simulation tools, speed, and memory mean that important elements of the computer side have become essentially continuous again, we need to look at ways of analysing the joint system.

1.3.1 Hitting a Fixed Spatial Target with a Pointer

The graphical user interface involves spatial representations of actions in graphical user interfaces. In a simple 1-from-N case, the N possible actions are laid out as N shapes in two dimensions, and the user has continuous control of a cursor via e.g., a mouse. The control task for the user is then to recognize the target (often via a visual prompt such as an icon) and to move the cursor towards it, clicking once within the boundary of the target shape. If the chosen target has a position (x_r, y_r), and the current cursor state is (x, y) then there is an 'error'

$$ e = \left\| \begin{bmatrix} x_r \\ y_r \end{bmatrix} - \begin{bmatrix} x \\ y \end{bmatrix} \right\|, $$

which describes the distance between cursor and target, and the control task is to minimize this error as fast as the human effector dynamics allow, bringing the cursor x, y towards (x_r, y_r). In control theory, we describe this as a *step response* because the change of target position looks like a step in the time-series representation. The process of spatial targeting was examined in detail from the control perspective, for one-dimensional pointing in Müller, Oulasvirta, and Murray-Smith (2017).

One important issue is that for most interaction tasks you are moving a cursor towards an *area*, not a *point*, so the conditions for selection are met before the error is brought to zero. As the size of the area increases relative to the distance travelled (a decreasing *index of difficulty* in Fitts' terminology), this becomes more significant. Müller, Oulasvirta, and Murray-Smith (2017) found that users tended not to minimize the error in the final endpoint and used different control behaviours when faced with larger targets. We will discuss this again in Section 1.6.1.

1.3.1.1 Control Order

The control action *u* for mouse input typically measures the velocity of the mouse over a surface, and feeds that through to the cursor via a nonlinear *transfer function*.[3] Casiez and Roussel (2011) develop a framework for comparing pointing transfer functions. However, the sensed input from the human could also be position (as in touchscreens) or acceleration from accelerometers such as those on a smart watch or mobile phone. The *control order* refers to the number of integrations between control input to a plant and output of a plant. Higher order systems are harder to control. Zero order control is position control, and the gain level will affect accuracy and speed in target space. First order control, velocity control, has one integration between position and velocity, and works well for systems with a well-defined null or zero position (like a spring-loaded joystick). The main advantage is that the range of motion in the space is not limited to the range of moment in input space. The limits on input constrain the velocity, not the range of space. With second order, acceleration control, a return to the null position zeros the acceleration but not the velocity – you need to counteract the velocity by decelerating, so it is more difficult than first- or second-order control, but reflects real-world activity. Higher order control systems are much more difficult to learn (pilots need to deal with third- and fourth-order elements in fixed wing flight). If making comparisons between different input devices, it is important to compare the same dynamics, e.g., a comparison of a position mouse input with a velocity joystick input might lead to misleading conclusions.

An interesting trend in the evolution of interfaces has been to reduce the control order, moving from joysticks to mice to direct touch. Direct interaction can be cognitively simpler, but also has disadvantages associated with the size of workspace. Zero-th order position input makes the input space the same size as the display, whereas higher order inputs can change the gain to trade-off speed of movement with end target precision. Direct interaction usually means that an extra navigation layer which allows the user to move between smaller canvases needs to be added to the interaction design. A direct mapping also makes it harder to 'slide in intelligence' to flexibly modulate the user input with computational models of anticipated behaviour, whereas this is easier when the input evidence integrates up over time.

---

[3] Note that in control theory the term *transfer function* tends to refer to a linear time-invariant (LTI) system in Laplace or Fourier transform representation.

1.3.2 Variability

Sources of variability in human action include noise, trajectory planning and delays in the feedback loop. In some tasks motor planning can be complex, but with most interfaces being designed to have simple dynamics, and human limbs being typically well controlled over the range of motions used, most user interface (UI) interaction is still relatively simple. The variability is therefore dominated by the human's predictive control interacting with delayed feedback, and the variability in defining the timing of changes of motion. If the user moves extremely slowly then the effects of human lags and delays are negligible.

Will control models do a better job of representing user variability? Most of the historical applications of manual control models did not focus on variability but the intermittent predictive control models have done a better job of this. (Gawthrop, Lakie and Loram, 2008) demonstrate that a simple predictive controller can be consistent with Fitts' law, while non-predictive controllers cannot. The same paper also presents the link between *intermittent control*, predictive control and human motor control, and further develops this in Gawthrop, Loram, Lakie and Gollee, 2011; Gawthrop, Gollee, and Loram, 2015).

We can see the interaction of difficulty of the targeting task with the speed and variability of human movement, even in simple one-dimensional spatial targeting tasks (Müller, Oulasvirta, and Murray-Smith, 2017). These experiments make clear the anticipatory, or predictive element in human action, as the behaviour for different levels of difficulty changes well before the user reaches the target.

Quinn and Zhai (2016) describe the challenges associated with understanding user behaviour when performing gestural input, focusing on gesture keyboards. They highlight how users are not tightly constrained, but are attempting to reproduce a prototype shape as their goal. Earlier models assumed that the motor control process was similar to serial aiming through a series of landmarks. They used a minimum-jerk model of motor control to model human behaviour and describe the variability in user control in gesture keyboards, which includes some general issues, including an inclination to biomechanical fluidity, speed–accuracy trade-offs, awareness of error tolerances in the algorithms, visual online feedback from the interface, and the errors due to sensorimotor noise and mental and cognitive errors.

1.3.3 Tracking a Moving Target with a Pointer

A generalization of hitting a stationary spatial target is to allow the target to move, forcing the user to track the target (Crossman, 1960; Poulton, 1974). The control models which are optimized for this task will have different parameters, structures, and qualitative properties from those suited to the static case in Section 1.3.1. The quality of the control will depend on the frequency range of the target movements and the delay and lag inherent in the user response. The most common application of this is in gaming. It may have further application in detecting attention and for selection in virtual or augmented reality situations.

An important element of the research in target pursuit is the amount of trajectory preview the human user has, as this changes the amount of information that can be communicated

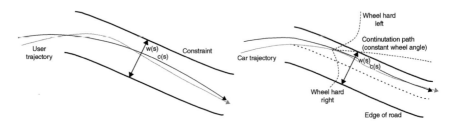

Figure 1.6 Two-dimensional 'tunnel' task (left). A classical automotive steering task (right).

(see Crossman, 1960) in part by making it easier for the user to use prediction to plan the exact timing of their actions, and avoid the impact of delays.

1.3.4 Driving a Pointer Through a Spatial Continuum of Constraints

In hitting a spatial target, it did not matter how you got to the target, the system just has a simple mapping of click location to actions. In other cases, the selection is dependent on the user generating a trajectory that fits particular spatial constraints. This is sometimes described as a 'tunnel' task (see Figure 1.6). The *Steering law* proposed by Accot and Zhai (1997, 2002) is an example of a generalization of Fitts' results to trajectory tasks. In this case we have a reference trajectory, $C_r(s)$, which describes a series of (x_r, y_r) values at arc length s. This can be accompanied by a varying constraint, or width $W(s)$.[4]

Most of the existing research has avoided the use of dynamic control models, preferring to generalize the task as an infinite series of spatial constraints (although the steering task was a staple of early work, e.g. Car steering (Rashevsky, 1959, 1960), or pencil line-drawing tasks (Drury, 1971)). In recent years there has been increasing awareness of the mismatch between human behaviour and the simple early steering models. Pastel (2006) examines performance in steering tasks with sharp turns, and Yamanaka and Miyashita (2016a, 2016b) examine the impact of narrowing or widening tunnels on user performance, despite these notionally having the same index of difficulty.

This can be reformulated as a control task, where an agent has to progress along the tunnel within the constraints of the tunnel 'walls'. If we factor in typical human delays and lags in a tracking model such as the McRuer model (Jagacinski and Flach, 2003), then with standard frequency response analysis we can analytically show that sharp turns in the tunnel will lead to larger deviations from the central path, and will require a reduction in speed, compared to a lower curvature trajectory, if the user is to stay within the tunnel constraints. This also highlights the important element of user 'look ahead' where a predictive or feedforward element comes into play. Users can see the trajectory ahead, with its constraints, and adjust their velocity and plan their directional control behaviour accordingly. The impact of a given amount of timing uncertainty is greater for larger curvature in the tunnel, or tighter width constraints. Accot and Zhai's initial 1997 work did not incorporate curvature into the ID,

---

[4] The analysis of boundary crossings in (Accot and Zhai, 2002) is closely related, especially if there is a sequence of multiple crossings needed to achieve a specific goal. This can be seen as a discretization of the steering law task, with intermittent constraints.

but did hypothesize a likely relationship of the tangential velocity $v(s) \propto \rho(s)W(s)$, where $\rho(s)$ is the local radius of curvature. The goal here is to create a model of the probability density function from the current state (x, v) at t_n for the user's future behaviour t_{n+1}, $t_{n+2} \ldots$, etc. Because of motor variability, this will naturally spread out spatially over time in areas of high curvature, returning close to the optimal path in easier areas. The nature of the trade-off between spread of trajectories and variation in speed will depend on the implicit cost function the user is performing to. Are they being cautious and never breaching the constraints, or more risk-taking and increasing speed?

Appropriately identified models of human tunnel-following behaviour would allow us to create a more appropriate function for inferring intent than simply detecting that a user had exited the tunnel. Predicting the likely dynamic behaviour for a user attempting the tunnel at a given speed could allow us to infer which of N targets was most likely. An interesting extension of this is instead of speed-accuracy trade-offs, we could look at effort-accuracy trade-offs, where users might choose to provide less precision in the location or timing of their actions. (The techniques can link closely to methods used for filtering noisy inputs).

Feedback during the process can change closed-loop performance significantly. For example, when examining touch trajectories associated with the 'slide to open' on an iPhone, we could view it as a response to a spatially constrained trajectory following task, but because of the visual metaphors the user typically perceives it as dragging the slider (which in itself is a direct position control task) to activate the device. The physical metaphor might make sense for a new user, but as the user becomes more skilled and confident, they may be keen to have faster or more sloppy movements to achieve the same end. For example, the actual constraints on the touch input need not correspond to the limit of the drawn object, depending on the context and design trade-offs. For example, if the system sensed that the user was walking while using the slide–to–open feature, it could be more forgiving on the constraints than in a stationary context, or a confident, cleanly contacting, fast swipe might be allowed to unlock the device, even if it were at the wrong angle.

1.3.4.1 Phase space tunnels

An interesting generalisation of the spatial tunnel is to define tunnels in phase space which include spatial coordinates and their time derivatives (e.g. $(z, \dot{z})$). This allows us to define not only a spatial trajectory but also the way that unfolds over time. An example of data collected from a finger moving above a capacitive touch screenplay sensitive to 5cm above the device is shown in Figure 1.7.

1.3.5 Gestures

Gestures can be viewed as generating a spatial trajectory through time, and can therefore be represented by differential equations, and tolerances around a prototypical gesture. For a review of gestures in interaction, see (Zhai, Kristensson, Appert, Andersen and Cao, 2012). The underlying control task then, is almost identical to that of Section 1.3.4, although typically in gestures there is no visual guide for the user to follow – they are expected to have memorized the gestures, and implicit constraints, such that they can be generated in an open–loop fashion. In some cases, a rough reference framework is provided for the gesture.

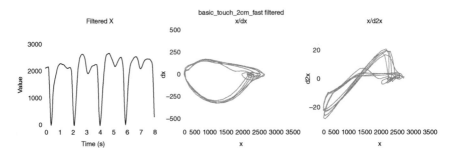

Figure 1.7 Examples of time-series (left) and phase space plots in velocity (middle) and acceleration (right) against position for a finger moving above a touch screen. Note how the particular style of movement corresponds to a constrained region of the phase space.

For example, the Android gesture lock screen provides a grid of points as a framework for users' gestures. This reduces the possible gesture prototypes to a discrete set, as the gesture passes through these subgoals, and helps normalize the users' spatial performance and transparently removes the variability factor of timing.

A differential equation representation of gestures is used by Visell and Cooperstock (2007). A specific example of differential equations for gesture is that of generating controlled cyclic behaviour as discussed in Lantz and Murray-Smith (2004). The advantage of rhythmic gestures is that they can be repeated until the system recognizes them, whereas ballistic gestures are more frustrating to repeat from scratch if the system fails to recognize them.

Handwriting can be viewed as a specific case of gesture system, but one which leaves a visible trace, and which most humans have spent years learning. Recent developments in handwriting recognition based on the use of recurrent neural networks to learn the dynamic systems required to both generate and classify handwriting (Graves, 2013) could be generalized to other areas of gestural input. This work made progress by not requiring the training data for the handwriting task to be broken down into individual letters, but to work at a word level, letting the machine learning cope with the variability, and co-articulation effects from neighbouring letters. This might be of interest in analysis of interactions 'in the wild' where it can be difficult for a human to label when exactly a user changed their goal to a particular target or task.

1.3.6 Panning, Scrolling, Zooming and Fisheye-style Distortions

When the information space a user is interacting with is too large to fit on the display, the user needs to be able to control their (x, y) location in the space via panning and scrolling, and their zoom level z. These can be independently controlled, or can be automatically coupled to cursor movements. In many systems the continuous dynamics of transitions are not defined as differential equations, but are programmed as a series of transitory 'effects'.

In Eslambolchilar and Murray-Smith (2008) we created a simple 'flying brick' model which gave the panning and zooming inertia, and used state-space equations which coupled the zoom level with the velocity,

$$\dot{x}_1(t) = v(t) = x_2(t) \tag{1.1}$$

$$\dot{x}_2(t) = a(t) = \dot{v} = -\frac{R}{m}x_2(t) + \frac{1}{m}u(t) \tag{1.2}$$

$$\dot{x}_3(t) = z(t) = -\frac{b}{m}x_2(t) - \frac{R'}{m}x_3(t) + \frac{c}{m}u(t), \tag{1.3}$$

which can then be more conveniently represented in the state space form $\dot{x} = Ax + Bu$,

$$\begin{bmatrix} \dot{x}_1 \\ \dot{x}_2 \\ \dot{x}_3 \end{bmatrix} = \begin{bmatrix} 0 & 1 & 0 \\ 0 & -\frac{R}{m} & 0 \\ 0 & -\frac{b}{m} & -\frac{R'}{m} \end{bmatrix} \begin{bmatrix} x_1 \\ x_2 \\ x_3 \end{bmatrix} + \begin{bmatrix} 0 \\ \frac{1}{m} \\ \frac{c}{m} \end{bmatrix} u. \tag{1.4}$$

This shows how a single degree-of-freedom (DOF) input can control both velocity and zoom-level. The non-zero off-diagonal elements of the A matrix indicate coupling among states, and the B matrix indicates how the u inputs affect each state. Note that you can change from velocity to acceleration input just by changing the values of the B matrix. This example, could be represented as having zoom as an output equation, rather than state, and the coupling between zoom and speed comes only primarily the B matrix.

We can create a control law such that $u = L(x_r - x)$ and write new state equations, $\dot{x} = Ax + Bu = Ax - BLx + BLr = (A - BL)x + BLr$, which shows how the control augmentation has changed the closed loop dynamics. The user input can then be linked to the x_r value so that this could then be linked to a desired velocity, or a desired position in the space. It is also possible to have a switched dynamic system which changes the dynamics depending on the mode the user is in, supporting their inferred activity, and Eslambolchilar and Murray-Smith (2008) describe examples with different regimes for exploration, cruising and diving modes. The stability and control properties of such systems are examined in Eslambolchilar and Murray-Smith (2010).

This approach was further developed in Kratz, Brodien, and Rohs (2010), where they extended the model to two-dimensions and presented a novel interface for mobile map navigation based on Semi-Automatic Zooming (SAZ). SAZ gives the user the ability to manually control the zoom level of a Speed-Dependent Automatic Zooming (SDAZ) interface, while retaining the automatic zooming characteristics of that interface at times when the user is not explicitly controlling the zoom level.

1.3.6.1 Dynamic Systems as Canonical Representations of Interface Dynamics

Taking a dynamic systems approach has the potential to give a cleaner underlying structure, and makes the comparison of performance between different design decisions easier to document and analyse. Research in HCI can also be slowed by the lack of transparency of many of the systems we interact with. Commercial software is often only available as a 'black box', where we can interact with it, but cannot see the underlying code. This is an area where systematic approaches to identify the dynamics of system transitions can allow us to create a canonical representation of the dynamics as a differential equation which is independent of how it was implemented. An example of this is the work on exposing scrolling transfer functions by Quinn, Cockburn, Casiez, Roussel and Gutwin (2012). Quinn and Malacria (2013) used robots to manipulate various touch devices to infer the scrolling dynamics. A differential equation approach provides a universal representation of the different implementations, even if they did not originally use that representation internally. This could have a role in intellectual property disputes, where more objective similarity measures could be proposed, which are independent of trivial implementation details. The differential equation approach can also be applied to other mechanisms for presenting large data spaces, e.g., fisheye lenses (see Eslambolchilar and Murray-Smith, 2006).

1.3.7 Homeostasis- and Tracking-based Interaction

Interfaces can infer the user's intent based on detection of controlling behaviour, as developed in Williamson and Murray-Smith (2004); Williamson (2006) and built on by Fekete, Elmqvist, and Guiard (2009). These models can either be set up as pursuit/tracking tasks or as homeostatic tasks, where the goal is to stabilize the system. These can be used in security-sensitive interactions to make the visibility of a user's actions irrelevant without knowing the state of the display. It can also be used with unconventional sensing configurations, and has recently been further developed as a promising approach for eye tracking and gestural interaction based on body tracking (see, e.g., Clarke, Bellino, Esteves, Velloso, and Gellersen, 2016; Velloso, Carter, Newn, Esteves, Clarke, and Gellersen, 2017).

1.4 Fitts' Law Results from a Control Perspective

The speed/accuracy trade-off has been a staple topic for the HCI community, with much of the attention focussed on Fitts' law (Fitts, 1954; Fitts and Peterson , 1964). Chapter 7 of (Schmidt and Lee, 2005) and (MacKenzie , 1992) provide good reviews. Fitts proposed that the time (MT) to move to a target area is a function of the distance to the target (A) and the size of the target (W),

$$MT = a + bID, \qquad (1.5)$$

where ID is the Index of Difficulty

$$ID = \log_2 \left(\frac{2A}{W} \right). \qquad (1.6)$$

Movement times and error rates are important aspects of human interaction, but they do not provide a complete picture.

A feedback control based explanation was provided in 1963 by Crossman and Goodeve, reprinted in (Crossman and Goodeve 1983), where they suggested that Fitts' Law could be derived from feedback control, rather than information theory. They proposed that there would be a ballistic, open-loop phase followed by a closed-loop homing-in phase. This is sometimes called the iterative-correction model. kinematic records of subject movements, however, tended to only have one or at most two corrections, so an alternative was proposed in Meyer's optimised-submovment model (Meyer, Keith-Smith, Kornblum, Abrams and Wright, 1990). Meyer et al. proposed that the time (MT) to move to a target area is a function of the distance to the target (A) and the size of the target (W), $MT = a + bID$, where the index of difficulty, $ID = (\frac{A}{W})^{\frac{1}{n}}$, where n relates to the upper limit on submovements. $n = 2.6$ minimised the RMS error. A number of authors have already related Fitts' Law to basic control models, including (Cannon, 1994; Connelly , 1984). Here, we follow the presentation in (Jagacinski and Flach, 2003) to demonstrate that Fitts' law results can be derived from first-order control behaviour. They propose that the change in position from the home position to a target be viewed as a step change in reference variable r. They use a simple first order controller composed of a gain k and integrator. $\dot{x} = Bu$, where the control signal $u = r - x$, and $B = k$. If we imagine a step change, r from initial state $x = 0$, then the response of the first order lag will be an exponential response

$$x(t) = r(1 - e^{-kt}).$$

For a target sized w, centered on r, the time taken to get within $\frac{1}{2}w$ of r is

$$x(t) = r - \frac{1}{2}w$$
$$r(1 - e^{-kt}) = r - \frac{1}{2}w$$
$$e^{-kt} = \frac{w}{2r}$$
$$-kt = \ln \frac{w}{2r}$$
$$t = -\frac{1}{k} \ln \frac{w}{2r}$$

which, after converting to a base 2 logarithm, via $\log_a x = \frac{\ln x}{\ln a}$, is

$$t = \frac{\ln 2}{k} \log_2 \frac{2r}{w}, \qquad (1.7)$$

which is similar in form to Fitts' ID, in equation (1.6). The gain k affects the speed of acquisition – the time constant for such a first order lag is $\frac{1}{k}$, the time it takes to reach 63% of the steady state response.

1.5 Models

Models can be used to create the controllers, or can be directly incorporated into the controller. In some cases, the controller can be seen as an implicit model of the system and environment (Conant and Ross Ashby, 1970; Eykhoff , 1994). In many areas of HCI research we need to compare user behaviour to some reference behaviour. How similar are two trajectories? Use of simple Euclidean distance measures between two time series can be quite misleading. However, if we can identify model parameters for a specific user, we can calculate the likelihood of model parameters given the observed data, which can be more robust in some cases.

1.5.1 Models of the Human–Human Limitations

Models of the capabilities and limitations of humans in interaction loops are well established in the research literature. From a control perspective, key elements relate to the *bandwidth* a user can control, *delays* due to cognitive processing time, and neuro-physiological response times. A more challenging area for HCI researchers is that of *prediction* or *anticipation*, as it can be more difficult to measure and control for in experiments.

1.5.1.1 Prediction/Anticipation by the Human

Humans can look ahead from their current state, and predict how their current state and constraints between them and their target will affect their ongoing behaviour. There will, however, be uncertainty in these predictions. The uncertainty will depend on user skill, sensing uncertainty, external disturbances, and context. The prediction horizon is typically associated with the *time* needed to process the information and act such that problems at the prediction horizon are avoided, rather than being a fixed *distance* ahead, akin to the stopping distance for a car increasing with increasing speed.

Can predictive control models explain, e.g., the change in steering task performance when the constraints are widening or narrowing? A model-predictive control with state uncertainty and a prediction uncertainty increasing with the prediction horizon will typically have a distribution of future trajectories, and if a certain probability threshold of breaching the constraints is crossed, then the user needs to change behaviour by reducing speed, or changing direction. For example, Figure 1.8 shows that, in the case of a widening tunnel, the predictions are all within the tunnel, whereas a narrowing one has some breaching the constraints, forcing the user to slow down. Similarly, if the curvature of the reference trajectory increases, for a fixed tunnel width, then we would expect an impact on performance because of the impact of uncertainty in timing on control actions being greater in high-curvature, narrow regions.

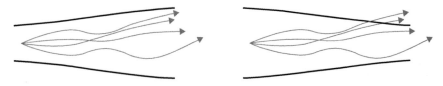

Figure 1.8 Impact of prediction horizon and narrowing straight tunnel. The same variability that can be contained in a widening tunnel will breach the constraints of a narrowing one.

The ability to adapt can depend on whether the task is one of *forced* or *unforced* reference following. In unpaced tasks, users can increase speed and accuracy, as their preview increases. In forced pace tasks, their speed cannot change, but their accuracy improves if their preview increases (Poulton, 1974).

1.5.1.2 Speed/Accuracy/Effort Trade-offs

A further key area is how humans typically make trade-offs when they are asked to maximize different aspects of a cost function. *Speed*, *accuracy* and *effort* are typically mutually conflicting objectives. Azzopardi's chapter in this volume, on the use of economics models in information retrieval describes examples of users making trade-offs between effort and performance. (Guiard and Rioul, 2015) explore the tradeoffs between speed and accuracy in pointing. (Shadmehr, Huang and Ahmed, 2016; Apps, Grima, Manohar, and Husain, 2015; Rigoux and Guigon, 2012) explore the role of effort in human performance. (Lank and Saund, 2005) consider sloppiness in interaction.

1.5.2 Models of the Computer

The block diagram representation of control loops in engineering is intended to indicate their modularity and independence. It shows how groups of components in a feedback loop can be exchanged with others. An important assumption here is that when we change one block, other blocks remain the same. Such independence would be very valuable for system designers, as if an input device were changed from, e.g., a mouse to a joystick, we could then predict the overall change to the system behaviour. With human controllers, however, this is often not the case because of the human ability to predict and adapt.

Part of the rationale for taking a control perspective is that we want to get away from the notion that behaviour is a simple response to a stimulus. In reality, the actions shape the environment, and agents often seek out stimulation. A problem with the reductionist approach is that it separates perception and action (in experiments and in theories). This often happens in HCI, where people will treat inputs and outputs separately.

Treating the system as a 'Black box' in a behaviourist manner means just looking at inputs and outputs, or the process can be broken into stages – the information-processing perspective. If feedback is considered, it is often treated in a peripheral manner, and does not affect the experiment design. The key issue is that, in Figure 1.9, the 3rd and 4th diagrams are essentially the same—the circular perspective shows how the boundaries between elements become blurred and the emergent dynamics become the focus of interest. This becomes even more tricky to disentangle once we bring human predictive ability into the analysis.

The *Joint Cognitive Systems* approach examines the behaviour of the whole closed–loop system, and (Hollnagel and Woods, 2005) criticize the information theoretic approach. They point out that decomposition of block-diagrams, as used with engineering systems, can be problematic when humans are involved, because humans are not fixed technical

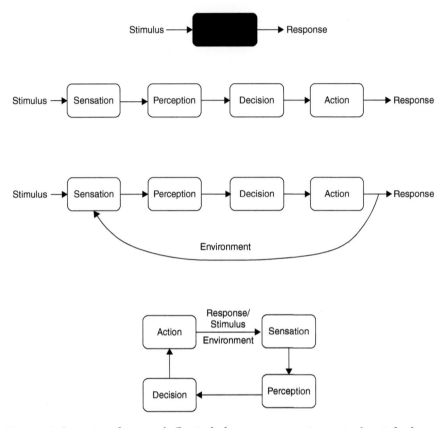

Figure 1.9 Separation of cause and effect in the human–computer interaction loop is fundamentally problematic. (Adapted from Jagacinski and Flach, 2003).

subsystems: rather, they will adapt their behaviour to take into account the change in the computer system around them. This is well documented in McRuer et al.'s *crossover model*, described in (Sheridan and Ferrell, 1974; Jagacinski and Flach, 2003; McRuer and Jex, 1967), where pilots would adapt their behaviour Y_H so that even with unstable controlled dynamics, the overall closed-loop behaviour near the 'crossover frequency' ω_c remained close to a 'good' servo reference behaviour

$$Y_H Y_C \approx \frac{\omega_c \exp(-j\omega\tau_\epsilon)}{j\omega},$$

despite changes in the aircraft dynamics (Y_C). τ_ϵ represents the effective time delay, combining reaction delay and neuromuscular lag. Young (1969) provides a wide-ranging review on how the human can adapt in manual control contexts, highlighting the challenges in understanding human adaptation in complex failure settings (Young, 1969).

1.5.3 Adapting the Interface Dynamics

The dynamics of the computer can be adapted to try to make the task easier for the user. This includes 'sticky mouse' dynamics, magnification effects, inertia, fisheye lenses, and speed-dependent zooming.

Attractors, in dynamic systems can be used to describe or implement sticky mouse dynamics, or bounce-back on images (Cockburn and Firth, 2004). (Cho, Murray-Smith, and Kim, 2007) used dynamic attractors to implement a tilt-based photo browser for mobile phones. Control–display ratio adaptation (Blanch, Guiard, and Beaudouin-Lafon, 2004; Casiez, Vogel, Balakrishnan, and Cockburn, 2008) can be viewed as having spatially varying dynamics. Resizing the area around the target (Grossman and Balakrishnan, 2005) provides different feedback to the user and alters the effective dynamics. Enhancing pointing (Balakrishnan, 2004). Negative inertia (Barrett, Selker, Rutledge, and Olyha, 1995) can be described as adding a lead term to the the the system dynamics. Accelerating touchpad (Yun and Lee, 2007). (Shadmehr, 2010) looks at the temporal discounting of rewards in effort trade-offs.

1.6 Shared Control

The control representation is well suited to making clear how different control elements, whether human or automatic, can be combined to shape the closed-loop behaviour.

The contribution from different controllers can be separated out in time, via switching processes, or by frequency, via hierarchical structures, or blending mechanisms. One approach is the *H-metaphor* (Flemisch, Adams, Conway, Goodrich, Palmer, and Schutte, 2003) which proposes designing interfaces which allow users to have flexibility to switch between 'tight-reined' or 'loose-reined' control; in other words, increasing the control order and allowing variable levels of autonomy in different contexts.

1.7 Limitations of the Control Perspective for HCI

Although almost any HCI task has a control interpretation, the natural question remains whether the gain in using the concepts and tools of control theory provides a significant advantage. There are key differences from the traditional control domain, where most of the dynamic complexity was in the controlled system and disturbances applied to it, whereas with HCI most of the complexity is in the human controller. The human is a complex hierarchical controller, rapidly changing goals and working at a range of levels on a range of activities in any given period of time, and subject to a wide range of external disturbances and internally generated variability.

The focus on feedback control has often overshadowed the strong feedforward/predictive effects apparent in human behaviour on typical tasks. Humans are proactive and in realistic settings they tend to anticipate issues, rather than being purely response-driven. As (Kelley,

1968) discusses, mathematical models of human control behaviour often underplayed the richness of human sensing. Will the recent developments in agents which can learn to link rich visual perception to action via deep convolutional networks Mnih *et al.* (2015) change the nature of these models?

1.7.1 User Heterogeneity and Task Uncertainty

A lot of the early work in manual control was focused on well-trained pilots or drivers of vehicles which were already highly constrained in terms of viable state spaces. How much of this can we translate to the modern world of human-computer interaction, where designers need to design for a wide range of user skill levels, and where the control tasks are being used primarily to transmit information, and are subject to rapid changes of reference, as the user changes their goals with exposure to new information.

A key difference between human and automatic control is that the human controller is continually going through a process of goal conception and selection (Kelley, 1968), whereas automatic control systems tend to have stable goals and cost functions. A further difference is that traditional control theory tends to have fairly simple cost functions and simple sensing. Given the complexity of human behaviour, we can also question whether the complexity is in the control algorithm, the body dynamics, perception, or the cost function in the brain.

1.8 Conclusions and Future Research Challenges

This chapter argues that all fundamental building blocks in human–computer interaction have a control loop component to them—all information transfer in HCI is via control loops.

Control theory provides theoretical concepts which can provide HCI researchers and practitioners with different ways of conceiving and framing interaction problems, e.g., control elements such as state, input, order, feedback, prediction, and goal, as well as practical tools for analysing, designing, measuring and documenting working interactive systems.

This gives researchers new formal analytic tools for research into the details of interaction. It also prompts contemplation on the foundations of human–computer interaction. A key challenge, however, is the care that needs to be taken with translation of control concepts from engineering contexts, where the control is predominantly automatic, to the HCI contexts, where the control is predominantly human. The human ability to learn, predict, and adapt control behaviour means that many of the modular representations of control blocks from engineering are no longer valid. For researchers in computational interaction, the control loop perspective reminds us that the important thing is the closed-loop dynamic behaviour. Breaking parts of the process down and analysing these in detail in a stimulus–response manner can give a false impression of rigour, as once the overall context changes, or as the user's skill level increases, or the computer interface changes, their behaviour will also change.

1.8.1 Future Research Challenges

Coping with high-dimensional input: A recent challenge to HCI has been how to use sensed human motion as the basis for useful interaction. Recent improvements in sensor technology support the availability of high-dimensional sensor streams which could enable *natural user interfaces*, but designers have struggled to convert this to usable interaction. At the core of any successful mapping of rich, high-dimensional data to user-controllable systems will be the creation of mappings to low-dimensional spaces that users can control. This process has a lot in common with concepts which recur in the chapters of this edited volume: *distance measures, cost functions, inverse problems* and *optimization*. Using computationally complex systems such as deep convolutional neural nets to analyse a series of images and classify these into different perceived behaviours is an example of dimensionality reduction. To become *useful* interaction, however, we need to be able to take these and turn them into control loops with appropriate feedback and associated decision logic for state transitions in the system.

Embedding control tools in development environments: An important practical challenge is to enhance the support for control-theoretic design tools and visualisations within the typical development environments used by HCI researchers and developers.

Control models are not just analytic, they are *generative* models which can create the behaviour in real-time – we can create control agents that can be released in the testing phase to predict performance (time and error rates) on a given interface. This fits well with recent developments in instrumented interaction and simulation environments for AI systems, such as OpenAI's *Gym*[5] or Google Deepmind's *Lab*.[6] These will potentially allow us to acquire large amounts of natural interaction behaviour, and use machine learning tools to learn and test dynamic systems which replicate human control behaviour which includes the impact of visual perception.

....

REFERENCES

Accot, J., and Zhai, S., 1997. Beyond Fitts' Law: models for trajectory-based HCI tasks. In: *CHI '97: Proceedings of the SIGCHI conference on Human factors in computing systems*. New York, NY: ACM, pp. 295–302.

Accot, J., and Zhai, S., 2002. More than dotting the i's — foundations for crossing-based interfaces. In: *CHI '02: Proceedings of the SIGCHI conference on Human factors in computing systems*. New York, NY: ACM, pp. 73–80.

Apps, M. A. J., Grima, L. L., Manohar, S., and Husain, M., 2015. The role of cognitive effort in subjective reward devaluation and risky decision-making. *Scientific reports*, 5, 16880.

Balakrishnan, R., 2004. 'Beating' Fitts' law: virtual enhancements for pointing facilitation. *International Journal of Human-Computer Studies*, 61(6), pp. 857–74.

[5] https://gym.openai.com/
[6] https://deepmind.com/research/open-source/open-source-environments/

Barrett, R. C., Selker, E. J., Rutledge, J. D., and Olyha, R. S., 1995. Negative inertia: A dynamic pointing function. In: *CHI '95: Conference Companion on Human Factors in Computing Systems*, New York, NY: ACM, pp. 316–17.

Bennett, K. B., and Flach, J. M., 2011. *Display and interface design: Subtle science, exact art*. Cleveland, OH: CRC Press.

Blanch, R., Guiard, Y., and Beaudouin-Lafon, M., 2004. Semantic pointing: Improving target acquisition with control-display ratio adaptation. In: *CHI '04: Proceedings of the SIGCHI Conference on Human Factors in Computing Systems*. New York, NY: ACM, pp. 519–26.

Cannon, D. J., 1994. Experiments with a target-threshold control theory model for deriving Fitts' law parameters for human-machine systems. *IEEE Trans Syst Man Cybern*, 24(8), pp. 1089–98.

Casiez, G., and Roussel, N., 2011. No more bricolage!: Methods and tools to characterize, replicate and compare pointing transfer functions. In: *UIST '11: Proceedings of the 24th Annual ACM Symposium on User Interface Software and Technology*. New York, NY: ACM, pp. 603–14.

Casiez, G., Vogel, D., Balakrishnan, R., and Cockburn, A., 2008. The impact of control-display gain on user performance in pointing tasks. *Human–computer interaction*, 23(3), pp. 215–50.

Cho, S.-J., Murray-Smith, R., and Kim, Y.-B., 2007. Multi-context photo browsing on mobile devices based on tilt dynamics. In: *MobileHCI '07: Proceedings of the 9th International Conference on Human Computer Interaction with Mobile Devices and Services*. New York, NY: ACM, pp. 190–7.

Clarke, C., Bellino, A., Esteves, A., Velloso, E., and Gellersen, H., 2016. Tracematch: A computer vision technique for user input by tracing of animated controls. In: *UbiComp '16: Proceedings of the 2016 ACM International Joint Conference on Pervasive and Ubiquitous Computing*. New York, NY: ACM, pp. 298–303.

Cockburn, A., and Firth, A., 2004. Improving the acquisition of small targets. In *People and Computers XVII - Designing for Society*. New York, NY: Springer, pp. 181–96.

Conant, R. C., and Ross Ashby, W., 1970. Every good regulator of a system must be a model of that system. *International Journal of Systems Science*, 1(2), pp. 89–97.

Connelly, E. M., 1984. Instantaneous Performance Evaluation with Feedback can Improve Training. In: *Proceedings of the Human Factors and Ergonomics Society Annual Meeting*. New York, NY: Sage, pp. 625–8.

Costello, R. G., 1968. The surge model of the well-trained human operator in simple manual control. *IEEE Transactions on Man–Machine Systems*, 9(1), pp. 2–9.

Craik, K. J. W., 1947. Theory of the human operator in control systems: 1. the operator as an engineering system. *British Journal of Psychology. General Section*, 38(2), pp. 56–61.

Craik, K. J. W., 1948. Theory of the human operator in control systems: 2. man as an element in a control system. *British Journal of Psychology. General Section*, 38(3), pp. 142–8.

Crossman, E. R. F. W., 1960. The information-capacity of the human motor-system in pursuit tracking. *Quarterly Journal of Experimental Psychology*, 12(1), pp. 1–16.

Crossman, E. R. F. W., and Goodeve, P. J., 1983. Feedback control of hand-movement and fitts' law. *The Quarterly Journal of Experimental Psychology*, 35(2), pp. 251–78.

Dix, A., Finlay, J., Abowd, G., and Beale, R., 2003. *Human-computer interaction*. Harlow: Pearson Education Limited.

Drury, C. G., 1971. Movements with lateral constraint. *Ergonomics*, 14(2), pp. 293–305.

Eslambolchilar, P., and Murray-Smith, R., 2006. Model-based, multimodal interaction in document browsing. In: *Machine Learning for Multimodal Interaction, LNCS Volume 4299*. New York, NY: Springer, pp. 1–12.

Eslambolchilar, P., and Murray-Smith, R., 2008. Control centric approach in designing scrolling and zooming user interfaces. *International Journal of Human-Computer Studies*, 66(12), pp. 838–56.

Eslambolchilar, P., and Murray-Smith, R., 2010. A model-based approach to analysis and calibration of sensor-based human interaction loops. *International Journal of Mobile Human Computer Interaction*, 2(1), pp. 48–72.

Eykhoff, P., 1994. Every good regulator of a system must be a model of that system. *Modeling, identification and control*, 15(3), pp. 135–9.

Fekete, J.-D., Elmqvist, N., and Guiard, Y., 2009. Motion-pointing: Target selection using elliptical motions. In: *CHI '09: Proceedings of the SIGCHI Conference on Human Factors in Computing Systems*. New York, NY: ACM, pp. 289–98.

Fitts, P. M., 1954. The information capacity of the human motor system in controlling the amplitude of movement. *Journal of Experimental Psychology*, 47(6), pp. 381–91.

Fitts, P. M., and Peterson, J. R., 1964. Information capacity of discrete motor responses. *Journal of experimental psychology*, 67(2), pp. 103–12.

Flemisch, F. O., Adams, C. A., Conway, S. R., Goodrich, K. H., Palmer, M. T., and Schutte, P. C., 2003. The H-Metaphor as a guideline for vehicle automation and interaction. *Control* (December), pp. 1–30.

Gawthrop, P., Gollee, H., and Loram, I., 2015. Intermittent control in man and machine. In: M. Miskowicz, ed. *Event-Based Control and SignalProcessing*. Cleveland, OH: CRC Press, pp. 281–350.

Gawthrop, P., Lakie, M., and Loram, I., 2008. Predictive feedback control and Fitts' law. *Biological Cybernetics*, 98, pp. 229–38.

Gawthrop, P., Loram, I., Lakie, M., and Gollee, H., 2011. Intermittent control: A computational theory of human control. *Biological Cybernetics*, 104(1–2), pp. 31–51.

Graves, A., 2013. Generating sequences with recurrent neural networks. *CoRR*, abs/1308.0850.

Grossman, T., and Balakrishnan, R., 2005. The bubble cursor: Enhancing target acquisition by dynamic resizing of the cursor's activation area. In: *CHI '05: Proceedings of the SIGCHI Conference on Human Factors in Computing Systems*. New York, NY: ACM, pp. 281–90.

Guiard, Y., and Rioul, O., 2015. A mathematical description of the speed/accuracy trade-off of aimed movement. In: *Proceedings of the 2015 British HCI Conference*. New York, NY: ACM, pp. 91–100.

Hollnagel, E., 1999. Modelling the controller of a process. *Transactions of the Institute of Measurement and Control*, 21(4-5), pp. 163–70.

Hollnagel, E., and Woods, D. D., 2005. *Joint cognitive systems: Foundations of cognitive systems engineering*. Cleveland, OH: CRC Press.

Hornbæk, K., and Oulasvirta, A., 2017. What is interaction? In: *Proceedings of the SIGCHI Conference on Human Factors in Computing Systems*. New York, NY: ACM, pp. 5040–52.

Jagacinski, R. J., and Flach, J. M., 2003. *Control Theory for Humans: Quantitative approaches to modeling performance*. Mahwah, NJ: Lawrence Erlbaum.

Kelley, C. R., 1968. *Manual and Automatic Control*. New York, NY: John Wiley and Sons, Inc.

Kleinman, D. L., Baron, S., and Levison, W. H., 1970. An optimal control model of human response part i: Theory and validation. *Automatica*, 6(3), pp. 357–69.

Kleinman, D. L., Baron, S., and Levison, W. H., 1971. A control theoretic approach to manned-vehicle systems analysis. *IEEE Transactions Automatic Control*, 16, pp. 824–32.

Kratz, S., Brodien, I., and Rohs, M., 2010. Semi-automatic zooming for mobile map navigation. In: *MobileHCI '10: Proc. of the 12th Int. Conf. on Human Computer Interaction with Mobile Devices and Services*. New York, NY: ACM, pp. 63–72.

Lank, E., and Saund, E., 2005. *Computers and Graphics*, 29, pp. 490–500.

Lantz, V., and Murray-Smith, R., 2004. Rhythmic interaction with a mobile device. In: *NordiCHI '04, Tampere, Finland*. New York, NY: ACM, pp. 97–100.

MacKenzie, I. S., 1992. Fitts' law as a research and design tool in human–computer interaction. *Human-computer interaction*, 7(1), pp. 91–139.

McRuer, D. T., and Jex, H. R., 1967. A review of quasi-linear pilot models. *IEEE Trans. on Human Factors in Electronics*, 8(3), pp. 231–49.

Meyer, D. E., Keith-Smith, J. E. Keith, Kornblum, S., Abrams, R. A., and Wright, C. E., 1990. Speed-accuracy trade-offs in aimed movements: Toward a theory of rapid voluntary action. In: M. Jeannerod, ed. *Attention and Performance XIII*. Hove, UK: Psychology Press, pp. 173–226.

Mnih, Volodymyr, Kavukcuoglu, Koray, Silver, David, Rusu, Andrei A., Veness, Joel, Bellemare, Marc G., Graves, Alex, Riedmiller, Martin, Fidjeland, Andreas K., Ostrovski, Georg *et al.*, 2015. Human-level control through deep reinforcement learning. *Nature*, 518(7540), 529–33.

Müller, J., Oulasvirta, A., and Murray-Smith, R., 2017. Control theoretic models of pointing. *ACM Transactions on Computer Human Interaction*. Vol. 24, Issue 4, September, P27:1–27:36.

Pastel, R., 2006. Measuring the difficulty of steering through corners. In: *Proceedings of ACM CHI 2006 Conference on Human Factors in Computing Systems*, 1(2), pp. 1087–96.

Poulton, E. C., 1974. *Tracking skill and manual control*. New York, NY: Academic Press.

Powers, W. T., 1973. *Behavior: The control of Perception*. New York, NY: Routledge.

Powers, W. T., 1989. *Living Control Systems: Selected papers of William T. Powers*. New York, NY: Benchmark.

Powers, W. T., 1992. *Living Control Systems II: Selected papers of William T. Powers*. Bloomfield, NJ: Control Systems Group.

Quinn, P., Cockburn, A., Casiez, G., Roussel, N., and Gutwin, C., 2012. Exposing and understanding scrolling transfer functions. In: *Proceedings of the 25th annual ACM symposium on User interface software and technology*, New York, NY: ACM, pp. 341–50.

Quinn, P., Malacria, S., and Cockburn, A., 2013. Touch scrolling transfer functions. In: *Proceedings of the 26th Annual ACM Symposium on User Interface Software and Technology*. New York, NY: ACM, pp. 61–70.

Quinn, P., and Zhai, S., 2016. Modeling gesture-typing movements. *Human–Computer Interaction*. http://dx.doi.org/10.1080/07370024.2016.1215922.

Rashevsky, N., 1959. Some remarks on the mathematical aspects of automobile driving. *Bulletin of Mathematical Biology*, 21(3), pp. 299–308.

Rashevsky, N., 1960. Further contributions to the mathematical biophysics of automobile driving. *Bulletin of Mathematical Biology*, 22(3), pp. 257–62.

Rigoux, L., and Guigon, E., 2012. A model of reward-and effort-based optimal decision making and motor control. *PLoS Comput Biol*, 8(10), e1002716.

Rogers, Y., Sharp, H., and Preece, J., 2011. *Interaction Design: Beyond Human Computer Interaction*. 4th ed. New York, NY: Wiley & Sons.

Schmidt, R. A., and Lee, T. D., 2005. *Motor Control and Learning*. Champaign, IL: Human Kinetics.

Shadmehr, R., 2010. Control of movements and temporal discounting of reward. *Current Opinion in Neurobiology*, 20(6), pp. 726–30.

Shadmehr, R., Huang, H. J., and Ahmed, A. A., 2016. A representation of effort in decision-making and motor control. *Current biology*, 26(14), pp. 1929–34.

Sheridan, T. B., and Ferrell, W. R., 1974. *Man-machine Systems: Information, Control, and Decision Models of Human Performance*. Cambridge, MA: MIT Press.

Velloso, E., Carter, M., Newn, J., Esteves, A., Clarke, C., and Gellersen, H., 2017. Motion correlation: Selecting objects by matching their movement. *ACM Transactions on Computer-Human Interaction (ToCHI)*, 24(3), Article no. 22.

Visell, Y., and Cooperstock, J., 2007. Enabling gestural interaction by means of tracking dynamical systems models and assistive feedback. In: *ISIC. IEEE International Conference on Systems, Man and Cybernetics*, pp. 3373–8.

Viviani, P., and Terzuolo, C., 1982. Trajectory determines movement dynamics. *Neuroscience*, 7(2), pp. 431–7.

Wickens, C. D., and Hollands, Justin G., 1999. *Engineering psychology and human performance*. 3rd ed. New York, NY: Prentice-Hall.

Wiener, N., 1948. *Cybernetics: Control and communication in the animal and the machine*. Cambridge, MA: MIT Press.

Williamson, J., and Murray-Smith, R., 2004. Pointing without a pointer. In: *ACM SIG CHI*, New York, NY: ACM, pp. 1407–10.

Williamson, J., 2006. Continous uncertain interaction, Ph.D thesis, School of Computing Science, University of Glasgow.

Yamanaka, S., and Miyashita, H., 2016a. Modeling the steering time difference between narrowing and widening tunnels. In: *CHI '16: Proceedings of the 2016 CHI Conference on Human Factors in Computing Systems*. New York, NY: ACM, pp. 1846–56.

Yamanaka, S., and Miyashita, H., 2016b. Scale effects in the steering time difference between narrowing and widening linear tunnels. In: *NordiCHI '16: Proceedings of the 9th Nordic Conference on Human-Computer Interaction*. New York, NY: ACM, pp. 12:1–12:10.

Young, L. R., 1969. On adaptive manual control. *IEEE Transactions on Man-Machine Systems*, 10(4), pp. 292–331.

Yun, S., and Lee, G., 2007. Design and comparison of acceleration methods for touchpad. In: *CHI'07 Extended Abstracts on Human Factors in Computing Systems*. New York, NY: ACM, pp. 2801–12.

Zhai, S., Kristensson, P. O., Appert, C., Anderson, T. H., and Cao, X., 2012. Foundational issues in Touch-Surface Stroke Gesture Design - An Integrative Review. *Foundations and Trends in Human Computer Interaction*, 5(2), pp. 95–205.

2

Statistical Language Processing for Text Entry

PER OLA KRISTENSSON

2.1 Introduction

Text entry is an integral activity in our society. We use text entry methods for asynchronous communication, such as when writing short messages and email, as well as when we compose longer documents. For nonspeaking individuals with motor disabilities, efficient text entry methods are vital for everyday face-to-face communication.

Text entry is a *process* and a text entry method is a system for supporting this process. Fundamentally, the objective of a text entry method is to allow users to transmit the intended text from the user's brain into a computer system as fast as possible. Many transmission methods are possible, including speech, cursive handwriting, hand printing, typing and gesturing.

The primary objective when designing a text entry method is to maximise the *effective* text entry rate—the entry rate achievable when the error rate is within a reasonable threshold. Entry rate is typically measured as either characters per second (cps) or words per minute (wpm), where a word is defined as five consecutive characters, including space.

Error rate can be defined over characters, words or sentences. Character error rate is defined as the minimum number of insertion, deletion and substitution character edit operations necessary to transform a user's response text into the stimulus text. Word error rate is defined as the minimum number of insertion, deletion and substitution word edit operations necessary to transform a user's response text into the stimulus text. Sentence error rate is the ratio of error-free response sentences to the total number of stimulus sentences.

Intelligent text entry methods (Kristensson, 2009) are text entry methods which infer or predict the user's intended text. Such methods aim to amplify users' ability to communicate as quickly and as accurately as possible by exploiting redundancies in natural languages.

This chapter explains the role of computational interaction in the design of text entry methods. It present three interlinked modelling approaches for text entry which collectively

Computational Interaction. Antti Oulasvirta, Per Ola Kristensson, Xiaojun Bi, Andrew Howes (Eds).
© Oxford University Press 2018. Published 2018 by Oxford University Press.

allow the design of probabilistic text entry methods. Such methods open up a new design space by *inferring* the user's intended text from noisy input.

We begin by explaining how language can be viewed as information (bits) in a framework provided by information theory. Information theory allows the quantification of information transmitted between a user and a computer system and provides a mathematical model of text entry as communication over a noisy channel. Although this model is limited in several ways, certain design decisions can be informed by this model.

The fundamentals of information theory reveal that natural languages are highly redundant. Such redundancies can be exploited by probabilistic text entry methods and result in a lower error rate and potentially a higher entry rate. However, to exploit the redundancies in natural languages it is necessary to model language. For this purpose the chapter introduces the principles of language modelling and explains how to build effective language models for text entry.

Having built a language model, the next step is to infer the user's intended text from noisy input. There are several strategies to achieve this. This chapter focuses on the token-passing statistical decoder, which allows a text entry designer to create a generative probabilistic model of text entry that can be trained to efficiently infer user's intended text. In addition, it can be adapted to perform several related functions, such as merging hypothesis spaces generated by probabilistic text entry methods.

We then review how probabilistic text entry methods can be designed to correct typing mistakes, enable fast typing on a smartwatch, improve predictions in augmentative and alternative communication, enable dwell-free eye-typing, and intelligently support error correction of probabilistic text entry.

Finally, we discuss the limitations of the models introduced in this chapter and highlight the importance of establishing solution principles based on engineering science and empirical research in order to guide the design of probabilistic text entry.

2.2 Language as Information

As observed by Claude Shannon in his seminal paper that led to the foundation of information theory (Shannon, 1948), quantifying the information content in messages provides an understanding of the properties of languages and text entry methods.

A message m in some message space $\mathbb{M}$ is sent from a sender to a receiver. Importantly, for a message m to carry information $I(m)$ from the sender to the receiver, the information must not already be known to the receiver. If the information is already known $I(m) = 0$. $I(m)$ measures the amount of new information, or surprisal, there is in receiving a message. The more surprising the message is to the receiver, the more information content in the message.

$I(m)$ is called self-information and is defined as:

$$I(m) = \log_2\left(\frac{1}{P(m)}\right) = -\log_2\left(P\left(m\right)\right), \tag{2.1}$$

where $P(m)$ is the probability of the message in the message space $\mathbb{M}$.

The above equation is better understood by considering a message as communicating an event, such as the outcome of a flipping a fair coin. Let information about one event m_1 be $I(m_1)$ and another event m_2 be $I(m_2)$. Then, assuming these events are independent, the information about both these events is $I_{both} = I(m_1 \cap m_2) = I(m_1) + I(m_2)$.

The probabilities of these events are $P(m_1)$ and $P(m_2)$ and $P_{both} = P(m_1 \cap m_2) = P(m_1) \cdot P(m_2)$.

In other words, self-information of independent events *adds* while the probabilities of the events *multiply*. This is exactly how log probabilities operate, which explains the logarithm in the above equation. Since logarithms scale with a constant factor, this constant factor has to be negative in order to ensure information is a positive quantity. The base of the logarithm determines the unit. By convention the base is usually 2 ($\log_2$) and thus the unit is in bits.

For example, consider a Bernoulli trial involving flipping a fair coin. The probability of either outcome is 0.5. To communicate the specific outcome of an individual event to the sender is the equivalent of sending a message m with $I(m) = \log_2 \left(\frac{1}{0.5} \right) = \log_2(2) = 1$ bit. Now, consider communicating the outcome of having flipped a fair coin four times as either m_{4h} (four heads in a row) or $\overline{m_{4h}}$ (*not* observing four heads in a row). The probability $P(m_{4h})$ of observing four heads in a row is $\frac{1}{16}$ and $I(m_{4h}) = -\log_2 (P(m_a)) = -\log_2 \left(\frac{1}{16} \right) = 4$ bits. Communicating the other possible outcome, $\overline{m_{4h}}$, we first find the probability $P(\overline{m_{4h}}) = 1 - P(m_{4h}) = 1 - \frac{1}{16} = \frac{15}{16}$. Then $I(\overline{m_{4h}}) = -\log_2 \left(\frac{15}{16} \right) \approx 0.093$ bits.

The average self-information of all messages in a message space is known as entropy. Entropy H is a measure of the uncertainty in the message space $\mathbb{M}$:

$$H(\mathbb{M}) = \sum_{m \in \mathbb{M}} P(m)I(m) = - \sum_{m \in \mathbb{M}} P(m) \log_2 (P(m)) \tag{2.2}$$

Entropy measures disorder. An entropy of zero means there is no disorder and everything is completely predictable. Entropy is the average bits required to communicate a message, assuming an optimal coding scheme. The difference between the average bits actually used for communication and the optimal bits truly necessary to encode all messages is a measure of redundancy.

A measure related to entropy is perplexity, PP, which measures how well a probability model is at prediction. Perplexity is defined as $PP = 2^H$, where H is the entropy of the model. Perplexity is the weighted average number of choices a random variable has to make.

For example, consider the following source alphabet Ω (with associated probabilities for ease of notation): $\Omega = \left\{ A = \frac{1}{2}, B = \frac{1}{4}, C = \frac{1}{8}, D = \frac{1}{8} \right\}$. The entropy H for this source alphabet is: $H(\Omega) = -\sum_{i=1}^{4} P_i \log_2 (P_i) = \frac{1}{2}(-1) + \frac{1}{4}(-2) + \frac{1}{8}(-3) + \frac{1}{8}(-3) = 1.75$ bits. The entropy $H(\Omega) = 1.75$ bits is the lower-bound on the number of bits required required to communicate the alphabet Ω. It is possible to construct such a communication scheme by assigning the code 0 to A, the code 10 to B, the code 110 to C and the code 111 to D (the last two codes are interchangeable as their probabilities of occurrence are identical). By multiplying the bit length of each symbol with its probability of occurrence we can see that this variable-length coding scheme will require 1.75 bits, on average. Since this is identical to the entropy of the source alphabet, this coding scheme is optimal. In contrast, a naïve implementation which assigned every symbol in Ω the same 2-bit code length would require 2 bits. The difference of 0.25 bits between the naïve implementation and the optimal implementation is the redundancy. The perplexity $PP(\Omega)$ of the optimal coding scheme is $PP(\Omega) = 2^{H(\Omega)} \approx 3.4$. In contrast, the perplexity of the naïve coding scheme is 4. However, if all four symbols in Ω were equally likely, then the perplexity of the optimal coding scheme would also be 4.

Information theory enables a model of text entry as communication over a noisy channel (Shannon, 1948). Using this model it is possible to calculate the bitrate of a text entry method. Assuming the random variable $\mathbb{I}$ is a distribution over the set of words the user is intending to write, and the random variable $\mathbb{O}$ is a distribution over the set of words the user is writing, then the rate R (in bits) is:

$$R = \frac{I\,(\mathbb{I}; \mathbb{O})}{t}, \tag{2.3}$$

where $I\,(\mathbb{I}; \mathbb{O})$ is the mutual information[1] and t is the average time it takes to write a word in $\mathbb{O}$. Since $I\,(\mathbb{I}; \mathbb{O}) = H(\mathbb{I}) - H(\mathbb{I}|\mathbb{O})$, where $H(\mathbb{I}|\mathbb{O})$ is the conditional entropy[2], the rate can be rewritten as:

$$R = \frac{H(\mathbb{I}) - H(\mathbb{I}|\mathbb{O})}{t}. \tag{2.4}$$

If the probability of error is zero, that is, all words in $\mathbb{I}$ can always be inferred from $\mathbb{O}$, then the conditional entropy $H(\mathbb{I}|\mathbb{O})$ will disappear and $R = H(\mathbb{I})/t$.

Information theory can be used to guide the design of text entry methods. Inverse arithmetic coding (Witten et al., 1987), a near-optimal method of text compression based on language modelling, inspired the text entry method Dasher (MacKay et al., 2004; Ward et al., 2000; Ward and MacKay, 2002). Unlike most other text entry methods, in Dasher a user's gesture does not map to a particular letter or word. Instead, text entry in Dasher involves continuous visually-guided closed-loop control of gestures via, for example, a mouse or eye gaze. A user writes text by continuously navigating to a desired sequence of letters in a graphical user interface laid out according to a language model (MacKay et al., 2004).

Dasher has an information-efficient objective in the following sense. If the user writes at a rate R_D (in bits) then Dasher attempts to zoom in to the region containing the user's intended text by factor of 2^{R_D}. If the language model generates text at an exchange rate of R_{LM} then the user will be able to reach an entry rate of R_D/R_{LM} characters per second (MacKay et al., 2004).

Dasher can also be controlled by discrete button presses in which timing is disregarded. Assuming the button pressing is precise, and therefore without errors, the capacity C of the communication channel is then:

$$C = \frac{\log_2(n)}{t}, \tag{2.5}$$

---

[1] The mutual information $I(\mathbb{A}; \mathbb{B})$ of two discrete random variables $\mathbb{A}$ and $\mathbb{B}$ is $I(\mathbb{A}; \mathbb{B}) = \sum_{a \in \mathbb{A}} \sum_{b \in \mathbb{B}} P(a,b) \log_2 \left(\frac{P(a,b)}{P(a)P(b)} \right)$.

[2] The conditional entropy $H(\mathbb{B}|\mathbb{A})$ of two discrete random variables $\mathbb{A}$ and $\mathbb{B}$ is $\sum_{a \in \mathbb{A}, b \in \mathbb{B}} P(a,b) \log_2 \left(\frac{P(a)}{P(a,b)} \right)$.

where n is the number of buttons and t is the average time to switch buttons. If the process is noisy, such that the wrong button is pressed a fraction f of the time, then the capacity is:

$$C = \frac{\log_2(n)}{t} \left(1 - H_2(f)\right), \quad f \in \left[0, \frac{1}{2}\right],$$ (2.6)

where H_2 is the binary entropy function[3] MacKay et al. (2004). Critically, even a rather low error rate of $f = 1/10$ scales C by approximately 0.53, and thus reduces the channel capacity by approximately a factor of two.

2.3 Language Modelling

Natural languages are highly redundant. A striking example of language redundancy is Zipf's law (Zipf, 1949), which estimates the probability P_r of occurrence of a word in a corpus to be $P_r \propto \frac{1}{r^\alpha}$, where r is the statistical rank of the word in decreasing order and α is close to unity. As an example of this relationship, the 100 most frequently used words in the British National Corpus comprise close to 46 per cent of the entire corpus (Zhai and Kristensson, 2003).

There is no compelling complete explanation for Zipf's law, although it has been observed that certain simple random processes generate text with Zipfian properties (Miller, 1957; Witten and Bell, 1990). Alternatively, Zipf's law may be due to the evolution of how words are mapped to concepts with respect to both speaker and listener demands (i Cancho and Solé, 2003).

Since natural languages are highly redundant it follows that the vast majority of letter and word combinations are improbable. We can capture probable sequences of letters and words by counting their occurrences in some large representative dataset—a corpus. A language model assigns probabilities to sequences of letters and words. The vocabulary $\mathbb{V}$ is the set of words in the language model.

Let $W = w_1, w_2, ..., w_m$, where w_m is the mth word in a word sequence. Then $P(W)$ is the probability of this word sequence and the objective of the language model is to estimate this probability, regardless of how unlikely it might be.

Language models are evaluated by computing the perplexity of the language model on a test set of words. For a test set of words $T = t_1, t_2, ..., t_m$, the perplexity is (Jurafsky and Martin, 2000):

$$PP(T) = P(t_1, t_2, \ldots, t_m)^{-\frac{1}{m}}$$ (2.7)

$$= \sqrt[m]{\frac{1}{P(t_1, t_2, \ldots, t_m)}}$$ (2.8)

$$= \sqrt[m]{\prod_{i=1}^{m} \frac{1}{P(t_i | t_1, \ldots, t_{i-1})}}.$$ (2.9)

---

[3] $H_2(p) = -p \log_2(p) - q \log_2(q)$, where p is a probability and $q = 1 - p$.

The above derivation shows that the perplexity is minimized when the conditional probability of the word sequence is maximized.

If the probability of observing a word is independent of all previous words, then the entropy for a vocabulary $\mathbb{V}$ is:

$$H = - \sum_{i=1}^{|\mathbb{V}|} P(w^i) \log_2 (P(w^i)), \tag{2.10}$$

where $w^i \in \mathbb{V}$ is the ith word in the vocabulary $\mathbb{V}$.

If the probability of observing all words in the vocabulary is the same then the entropy is $H = -\sum_{i=1}^{|\mathbb{V}|} (1/|\mathbb{V}|) \log_2 (1/|\mathbb{V}|) = \log_2 (|\mathbb{V}|)$ and the perplexity is $PP = 2^H = 2^{\log_2 (|\mathbb{V}|)} = |\mathbb{V}|$. If we can only observe one word then the entropy is 0 and the perplexity is 1.

In general, a language model estimates a probability $P(w_m | w_1, w_2, ..., w_{m-1})$. This does not scale as the number of words increases. Therefore, language models make a Markov assumption and restrict the number of previous words to $n - 1$. This results in an n-gram language model, which estimates $P(w_m | w_1, w_2, ..., w_{m-1})$ as $P(w_m | w_{m-n+1}, ..., w_{m-1})$. Commonly used models are unigram ($n = 1$), bigram ($n = 2$), and trigram ($n = 3$).

The fundamental process of training a language model is by frequency estimation: counting instances of n-grams in corpora. These counts have to be normalized in order to create a probabilistic model. For example, to estimate a particular trigram probability we calculate:

$$\hat{P}(w^c | w^a, w^b) = \frac{c(w^a, w^b, w^c)}{c(w^a, w^b)}, \tag{2.11}$$

where, again, $w^i \in \mathbb{V}$ is the ith word in the vocabulary $\mathbb{V}$ and $c(\cdot)$ is the counts (frequency of occurrence) in the data.

This is an example of maximum likelihood estimation (the likelihood of the training set given the model is maximized). Typically language models use log probabilities to prevent numerical underflow.

A problem with n-gram language models is to robustly estimate the probabilities of word sequences: a vocabulary size of $|\mathbb{V}|$ requires the estimation of $|\mathbb{V}|^n$ parameters. In practice, many n-grams will never be observed in the training text and thus result in zero probability estimations, which is clearly incorrect, as every word sequence has *some* probability of occurrence. In other words, the n-gram language model is overestimating the probabilities for observed word sequences and underestimating the probabilities for unobserved word sequences. To mitigate this problem, language models are smoothed using smoothing methods.

One solution is to redistribute some probability mass from observed word sequences to unobserved word sequences. This is known as discounting, and several discounting methods have been proposed in the literature (see Chen and Goodman, 1999). Another solution is to rely on a more general distribution, such as an $(n-1)$-gram model instead of an n-gram model. This is known as back-off. The most appropriate smoothing method depends on the requirements imposed by a particular system (Chen and Goodman, 1999).

2.4 Decoding

A *decoder* infers users' intended text from noisy data. Such a decoding process can be achieved in a number of ways, although the objective is usually framed within a relatively simple probabilistic model.

The user wishes to transmit a message y via some form of signal x. For instance, a user may want to transmit the signal "a" (the character a) by touching in the vicinity of the A key on a touchscreen keyboard. Assuming an error-free input channel, this objective may be trivially achieved by implementing a lookup table that maps certain pixels on the touchscreen keyboard (for instance, all pixels occupying a visual depiction of the letter key A on the touchscreen keyboard) to the character a. The advantage of this method is simplicity in its implementation. The disadvantage is an implicit assumption of error-free input, which is a false assumption as this process is inherently noisy. Noise arises from several sources, such as users themselves (neuromuscular noise, cognitive overload), the environment (background noise), and the device sensors. Due to these noise sources the process is inherently *uncertain*.

As a consequence, a decoder models this process probabilistically. The objective is to compute the probability of the message y in the some message space $\mathbb{Y}$ given an input signal x. This conditional probability $P(y|x)$ can be computed via Bayes' rule:

$$P(y|x) = \frac{P(x|y)P(y)}{P(x)}. \tag{2.12}$$

The most probable message $\hat{y} \in \mathbb{Y}$ is then:

$$\hat{y} = \arg\max_{y \in \mathbb{Y}} \left[\frac{P(x|y)P(y)}{P(x)} \right]. \tag{2.13}$$

However, since the decoder is only attempting to identify the message that maximizes the posterior probability, the denominator is just a normalization constant and will be invariant under the search. It can therefore be ignored:

$$\hat{y} = \arg\max_{y \in \mathbb{Y}} \left[P(x|y)P(y) \right]. \tag{2.14}$$

$P(x|y)$ is the likelihood of the input signal x given a particular hypothesis for y. $P(y)$ is the prior probability of the message y without taking the input signal into account.

Various decoding strategies can be used to find the most probable message $\hat{y}$, including hidden Markov models and deep neural networks. A particularly flexible framework is token-passing (Young et al., 1989), which has primarily three advantages. First, it is straight forward to model sequence decoding problems using token-passing, which will become evident later in this chapter. Second, it is easy to control the search using beam pruning, which is crucial when the search space grows exponentially or becomes infinite. Third, token-passing makes it relatively easy to parallelize the search as global memory access can be minimized.

Assume the system receives an observation sequence $O = \{o_1, o_2, \ldots, o_n\}$. These observations can, for instance, be a series of touch coordinates on a touchscreen keyboard. The objective of the decoder is now to identify the most probable hypothesis for the observation sequence.

In the token-passing paradigm, the system searches for the best hypothesis by propagating tokens. A token is an abstract data structure tracking at least three pieces of information: 1) the generated sequence of output symbols; 2) the associated accumulated probability; and 3) the current observation index.

We decode an observation sequence of length n by starting with a single initial token, which predicts the empty string ϵ with 1.0 probability for observing zero observations.

The process now works as follows. We take any token at observation index $i \in [0, n)$ and propagate k tokens to observation index $i + 1$, where k is, for instance, the number of keys on the keyboard (possible output symbols). This is repeated for all tokens until a token is in the last observation and can no longer propagate any tokens as there are no more observations. These final tokens represent all complete hypotheses that explain the entire observation sequence. The final token with the highest probability contains the hypothesis which best explains the observation sequence.

Every time a token is propagated, the system explores a new state. The accumulated probability of the token for the new state is computed by combining a likelihood model estimate with a prior probability, as explained above. The exact formulation depends on the specific implementation, which may include additional terms. Figure 2.1 shows a search trellis for an observation sequence with three observations.

The previous model essentially propagates tokens which consume observations and in return generate letter sequence hypotheses. The probabilities of these hypotheses depend on the language model context (previously generated letters) and the observations themselves (for example, how close or far away touch point observations are to certain letter keys).

A limitation with this model is that it only substitutes observations for letters. In practice, it is common for users to omit typing certain letters or accidentally typing additional letters. Transposition errors, where two letters are interchanged, are also common. To handle such situations we need to extend the decoder to handle insertions and deletions of observations in the observation sequence.

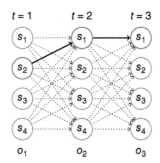

Figure 2.1 Trellis of an observation sequence $O = \{o_1, o_2, o_3\}$. The thick arrows indicate an example highest probability path.

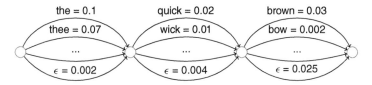

Figure 2.2 An example of a word confusion network.

A deletion of an observation corresponds to ignoring an observation. This is straight-forward to model by adding an ϵ-transition state to each observation index that allows a token to propagate to the next observation index without generating a corresponding letter.

An insertion of an observation in the observation sequence corresponds to adding an additional letter to a hypothesis without consuming an observation. This can be modelled by allowing tokens to propagate to the current observation index. If this operation is unrestricted it results in an infinite search space as it is possible for a search path to keep exploring a progressively increasing letter sequence without ever exploring the next observation index.

A substitution-only decoder results in an exponential search space. If we also allow an arbitrary number of insertions of observations then the search space is infinite. However, most search paths are unlikely and the search complexity can be dramatically reduced by beam pruning. Using beam pruning we can store the highest probability for each observation index and only permit tokens to propagate which have an accumulated probability that either exceeds this probability or is only below it by a certain threshold amount determined by the beam width.

Several extensions are possible. For example, for an auto-correcting keyboard it may be beneficial to reassess the probability of a letter sequence hypothesis under an n-gram word language model when the hypothesis has generated a letter sequence followed by a word delimiter. Also, insertion, deletion or substitution of observations can carry penalties, which may be encoded as either constants or functions.

The decoder search results in a search graph and it is possible to use it to construct word confusion networks (Mangu et al., 2000). A word confusion network is a time-ordered series of connected word confusion clusters. Each word confusion cluster represents the word hypotheses between two time steps, see Figure 2.2. Word confusion networks are a useful representation of the hypothesis space of a search graph. This hypothesis space can be used in various ways, for instance it can be used to provide users with an ability to choose among alternative hypotheses if the first hypothesis is incorrect.

2.5 Example Applications and Design Tactics

Statistical language modelling for text entry has many applications in human-computer interaction. Here we review a few selected application areas to demonstrate how probabilistic text entry allows us to use the computational models introduced earlier in this chapter to design new interaction techniques that solve non-trivial user interface problems.

2.5.1 Correcting Typing Mistakes

A mainstream touchscreen keyboard provides optional additional robustness to the text entry process by automatically correcting the user's typing. An auto-correcting touchscreen keyboard achieves this by statistically decoding the user's intended text given a series of noisy touchscreen point observations. The performance of an auto-correcting keyboard is a function of primarily three components: the decoder, the language model (the prior), and the touchpoint distribution model (the likelihood).

A typical strategy is to assume touchpoint distributions follow a two-dimensional Gaussian distribution and use a character-based n-gram language model to automatically correct every key when it is typed (Goodman et al., 2002). It is possible to refine this model in several ways. First, the touchpoint distribution model can be made more accurate using Gaussian Process regression. A study revealed that Gaussian Process regression significantly reduced the character error rate by 1.0 per cent when participants are standing still when typing and by 1.3 per cent when participants are walking when typing (Weir et al., 2014).

Second, users tend to make insertion and deletion errors (typing additional keys or failing to type required keys) in addition to substitution errors, which tends to break simplistic substitution-only models (Kristensson and Zhai, 2005). This observation suggests that the decoding model needs to be flexible enough to handle such errors to provide a performance gain (Kristensson and Zhai, 2005). In addition, a variety of strategies can be used to auto-correct users' typing. For example, one design decision is to only auto-correct the last inputted letter key and keep all previous letters fixed. A second possibility is to allow the decoder to change previous letters in addition to the last inputted letter key. A third possibility is to only auto-correct an entire word when the user types a word delimiter. Finally, a fourth possibility is to both auto-correct the last inputted letter key and keep all previous letters fixed and auto-correct the entire word when the user types a word delimiter. A user study showed that all four strategies perform about the same with the exception of the first strategy, which only corrects the last inputted letter key. A likely explanation is the inability of such a model to correct transposition errors (Weir et al., 2014).

Third, the quality of the language model affects performance. For instance, the smoothing method affects the performance of the language model (Chen and Goodman, 1999). It is also critical to train the language model on in-domain training text representative of the text users are intending to write.

Fourth, adapting the language model to the user improves performance. While the frequency in which we use individual words follows a heavily skewed Zipfian distribution that can be easily predicted, individual users' active vocabularies will be different. Even simple linear interpolation language model adaptation (Bellegarda, 2004) reduces word error rates substantially (Fowler et al., 2015).

Fifth, allowing users to regulate the auto-correct process improves performance. A study showed that users are generally able to identify words that will be auto-corrected correctly. However, users are less able to identify words where auto-correction fails. In other words, users tend to overestimate the ability of auto-correction algorithms. On the other hand, users appear to have a reasonable model for identifying when auto-correction fails, which motives a system for allowing users to guide the auto-correction process (Weir et al., 2014).

One solution is to introduce another modality, such as pressure, to allow users to signal to the decoder whether a particular observation (touchscreen point) is likely to be on the intended letter or not. By modelling the likelihood as a 2D Gaussian distribution, the system can allow the user to modulate their uncertainty in a key press by pressure by adjusting the standard deviation for a touch point by computing $\sigma_t = C/\omega_t$, where ω_t is the pressure of the touch t and C is an empirically determined parameter, which needs to be calibrated on data to ensure the standard deviation is reasonable for moderate pressure (Weir et al., 2014). A study revealed that this system significantly reduced the need for users to manually correct their text and significantly increased entry rates (Weir et al., 2014).

2.5.2 Fast Typing on a Smartwatch

Probabilistic text entry can not only improve an existing interface. It can also enable new interfaces, which would be impossible to design without statistical language processing. One simple example is the problem of typing efficiently on a smartwatch. Since a smartwatch has a very limited form factor it is non-trivial to support typing on the watch itself. Several techniques have been proposed in the literature which rely on redesigning the keyboard typing process. For example, ZoomBoard (Oney et al., 2013) or disambiguation with a smaller set of keys (Komninos and Dunlop, 2014) rely on multi-step selection. However, all such methods tend to be slow as they rely on multi-step selection or other additional articulation effort (such as a series of strokes) to input a letter.

An alternative approach is to simply transplant the existing mobile phone touchscreen QWERTY keyboard users are familiar with and make it available on a smartwatch. This is possible by using, for instance, a token-passing statistical decoder to infer users' typing from noisy touch points, which are often in the vicinity of the intended letter key, but not on it (Vertanen et al., 2015). An evaluation of such a system revealed that users typed 35–38 wpm with a 40 mm- and 25 mm-wide touchscreen QWERTY and 40 wpm with a standard-size 60 mm-wide mobile phone touchscreen keyboard (the differences in entry rate were not statistically significant). The character error rate was about the same for the 40 mm- and 60 mm-wide keyboards (3 per cent vs. 4 per cent). The 25 mm-wide keyboard resulted in a significantly higher character error rate of 10.7 per cent (Vertanen et al., 2015). Tuning the decoder on training data from typing on the 25 mm-wide keyboard and then testing the re-tuned decoder on held-out test data from the experiment reduced the character error rate down to 6.4 per cent. A longer study with a single expert user also revealed that this expert user could type at 37 wpm with a character error rate of 3.6 per cent, which suggests user performance, in particular error rate, improves with practice.

Since the above system is performing decoding it can provide additional flexibility for signalling spaces between words compared to a plain touchscreen keyboard. The system above allows users to either type a space, swipe left-to-right (which is a more certain signal compared to touching the space key), or simply omit spaces altogether. The latter is possible because the decoder can insert spaces automatically. In the evaluation above, study participants chose to use different delimiters, which suggest providing such flexibility is sensible.

The above system suggests that the instinct to redesign a user interface to fit within additional constraints, in this case the size of the touchscreen display, may not always be the optimal approach. Here the redundancies in natural languages allowed an efficient decoder to accurately correct users' typing patterns, even when the typing was very noisy.

2.5.3 Language Models for Augmentative and Alternative Communication

Augmentative and alternative communication (AAC) provides alternative communication methods for non-speaking individuals with motor disabilities, such as motor neurone disease (also known as amyotrophic lateral sclerosis) or cerebral palsy. Users unable to speak rely on AAC devices to communicate via speech synthesis. Literate AAC users typically rely on either a predictive keyboard, which can be either a physical keyboard or a touchscreen keyboard, or eye-tracking, or switch-systems.

Regardless of input device, the communication rate is much lower compared to the rate people speak. Bridging this communication gap necessitates some form of additional support. One strategy is to provide word predictions, which is an effective strategy if the user is severely rate-limited. The quality of word predictions depends on the text used to train the language model. In-domain training data should closely model the everyday face-to-face communications an AAC user will engage in with the help of the AAC device. If the data is out-of-domain, such as newswire text or transcriptions of telephone conversations, the word predictions are unlikely to be as useful to the user.

However, it is difficult to collect domain-appropriate data for AAC. An alternative approach is to crowdsource a small set of AAC-like sentences by asking crowd workers to imagine themselves being an AAC user (Vertanen and Kristensson, 2011). This results in a relatively small set of sentences in the order of thousands. Next, by using this surrogate dataset as a seed corpus it is possible to select similar sentences from a large open dataset, such as messages from the microblog Twitter. The most effective data selection method for this task (in terms of minimizing perplexity) is cross-entropy difference selection (Moore and Lewis, 2010). Compared to a baseline, this crowdsourcing/social media method of generating an AAC-like dataset resulted in a reduction of perplexity in the language model by 60–82 per cent relative and improved keystroke savings in a prediction interface by 5–11 per cent (Vertanen and Kristensson, 2011).

2.5.4 Dwell-free Eye-Typing

Some non-speaking individuals with motor disabilities are only able to communicate effectively with their eyes. The communication solution is to integrate an eye-tracker into a display and mount the display in a convenient area in front of the user's face. Typically a mounting device is used to secure the eye-tracking display to a wheelchair, the floor, or a wall.

The traditional method for typing using eye gaze is called eye-typing. An eye-typing system presents the user with a graphical keyboard. The user writes text by gazing at each letter key in succession. Unlike a touchscreen keyboard there is typically no obvious method of signalling to the system when a key has been typed and the system will need to disambiguate whether the user intended to type a letter key or merely happened to look at it. This is known as the Midas touch problem (Jacob and Karn, 2003). Eye-typing solves this problem using a dwell-timeout. If the user fixates at a letter key for a set amount of time (typically 800–1000 ms) then the system infers that the user intended to type the letter key. The dwell-timeout is usually indicated to the user graphically, for instance, via an animated clock.

While eye-typing does provide a method of communication, there are several negative aspects to the process. First, the dwell-timeouts impose a hard performance bound since the user is forced to fixate at every letter key in a word for a fixed timeout. Second, eye-typing breaks the flow of writing as every word is broken up into a series of saccades followed by fixations that must be longer in duration than the dwell-timeout. Third, the eyes are sensory organs, not control organs. It requires conscious effort to keep fixating at a specific area of the display.

As a consequence of the above limitations, traditional eye-typing is rather slow, typically limited to about 5–10 wpm (e.g., Majaranta and Räihä, 2002; Rough et al., 2014). A possible improvement is to let the user set their own dwell-timeout, with the hope that users will be able to adjust lower dwell-timeouts and hence writer faster. Experiments with such systems show that able-bodied participants in front of well-calibrated eye-trackers can reach an entry rate of about 7–20 wpm (Majaranta et al., 2009; Räihä and Ovaska, 2012; Rough et al., 2014).

An alternative interface is Dasher, which we introduced earlier in this chapter. However, Dasher entry rates are limited to about 12–26 wpm (Ward and MacKay, 2002; Tuisku et al., 2008; Rough et al., 2014).

In summary, traditional gaze-based text entry methods are limited to about 20 wpm. It is also important to remember that nearly all the above studies have been conducted with able-bodied users positioned in front of a desk with a well-calibrated eye-tracker for an experimental session.

In practice, at least two design considerations are critical when designing a text entry method using eye gaze for users with motor disabilities. First, the precision of eye gaze varies dramatically among different users. Some users can move quickly and precisely from letter key to letter key and are primarily limited by the dwell-timeout. In practice, such users tend to rely heavily on word prediction when eye-typing. Other users have difficulty due to various noise sources, such as an inability to keep the head positioned in the centre of the eye-tracker's virtual tracking box, an experience of pain or other issues resulting in sleep deprivation, or jerky uncontrolled movements of the head and body causing the head and/or display (if mounted on, for example, a wheelchair) to move.

Second, the tolerance for errors varies depending on the application. In speaking mode, the tolerance for errors is higher as the primary objective is to ensure understanding. In other applications, such as email or document writing, it is more important that the text does not contain obvious errors.

Dwell-free eye-typing (Kristensson and Vertanen, 2012) is a technique that mitigates these issues. The main principle behind dwell-free eye-typing is that it is possible to eliminate the need for dwell-timeouts by inferring users' intended text. In dwell-free eye-typing a user writes a phrase or sentence by serially gazing at the letter keys that comprise the phrase or sentence (gazing at the spacebar is optional). When the phrase or sentence is complete the user gazes at the text area. The system uses a statistical decoder to automatically infer the user's intended text.

A human performance study using an oracle decoder, which always infers the intended text correctly, showed that users can in principle reach an average entry rate of 46 wpm (Kristensson and Vertanen, 2012). By modelling traditional eye-typing as a combination of dwell-timeout and overhead time (the time to transition between keys, etc.) it becomes apparent that for every conceivable operating point of eye-typing, dwell-free eye-typing will be faster. For example, a study with record eye-typing rates (Majaranta et al., 2009) had an eye-typing entry rate which corresponds to roughly a dwell-timeout and an overhead time of approximately 300 ms each (Kristensson and Vertanen, 2012). This is roughly half the empirical average entry rate observed for dwell-free eye-typing using an oracle model (Kristensson and Vertanen, 2012).

Dwell-free eye-typing has been implemented as a probabilistic text entry method and is now a component of the AAC communication suite Communicator 5 by Tobii-Dynavox[4]. The system is designed based on a token-passing statistical decoder and can decode word sequences of any length and there is no need to type any spaces (Kristensson et al., 2015).

2.5.5 Error Correction

An often overlooked bottle-neck in text entry is error recovery. In practice, errors are inevitable due to spelling mistakes, noise in the neuromuscular system, distractions and incorrect model assumptions in the system. It can be very expensive to ignore errors. Early studies of desktop dictation systems found that users suffered from cascading errors, where every time the user attempts to correct a speech recognition error by speech repair, the resulting text becomes even more problematic (Karat et al., 1999).

One strategy to mitigate such cascades is to provide users with a possibility to explore the hypothesis space of the original utterance via an alternative modality, which can be achieved by generating a word confusion network from the search graph and then display the most probable words in the word confusion network to the user (Kurihara et al., 2006). To improve performance further, an additional ϵ-word can be added to the word confusion network to allow the user to delete the word represented by the cluster (Vertanen and Kristensson, 2009b). A user study has indicated that such alternative error correction interfaces can substantially improve performance when error rates are high. For example, a word error rate as high as 40 per cent can be corrected down to 0 per cent while maintaining an entry rate of approximately 15 wpm (Vertanen and Kristensson, 2009b).

An alternative version of the same strategy is Speech Dasher (Vertanen and MacKay, 2010). Speech Dasher allows users to correct speech recognition errors by using Dasher, which was described previously in this chapter, to navigate the hypothesis space of the speech recognizer for the original utterance. A small study indicated that users could write

---

[4] https://www.tobiidynavox.com/globalassets/downloads/leaflets/software/tobiidynavox-communicator-5-en.pdf

corrected text at an entry rate of 40 wpm despite an original word error rate of 22 per cent in the speech recognizer (Vertanen and MacKay, 2010).

An orthogonal approach to error correction is to allow the user to repeat the misrecognized words, and optionally also include some surrounding context (McNair and Waibel, 1994; Vertanen and Kristensson, 2009a).

In particular, if the user's initial observation sequence generated a word confusion network and the user's error repair observation sequence generated another word confusion network, then it is possible to find the hypothesis with the highest probability that takes both word confusion networks into account (Kristensson and Vertanen, 2011). Figure 2.3 shows two word confusion networks, not necessarily generated by the same probabilistic text entry method. The solid transitions show the original transitions between the word confusion clusters. By taking some of the probability mass from the original word confusion clusters we can soften these networks by connecting each cluster with additional wildcard and ϵ-transitions and by adding wildcard self-loops to each cluster, shown in dotted lines in Figure 2.3. The ϵ-transition allows the search to proceed to the next cluster without generating a word. A wildcard-next transition allows the search to proceed to the next cluster and generate any word. A wildcard self-loop allows the search to generate any word while remaining in the same cluster.

The end result is a representation of a combined search space for both word confusion networks. A merge model based on the token-passing paradigm can now search for the most probable joint path through both word confusion networks. Each token tracks the position in each of the word confusion networks, an accumulated probability, and the previous few words of language-model context. The search starts with an initial token in the first cluster of both networks. The search ends when the token leaves the last cluster in each of the networks. The search selects a token active in the search and, based on the token's position in each word confusion network, identifies all possible moves that can either generate a real

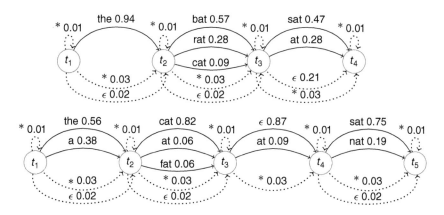

Figure 2.3 Two example word confusion networks that could be generated from the same, or a different, probabilistic text entry method's search graphs for the same intended text. The original word confusion networks have been softened by additional dotted transitions.

word or a wildcard word. The search then computes the cross-product between all candidate moves in each word confusion network subject to two rules. First, if both word confusion networks generate real words then these words must match. In other words, the model does not believe in a world in which a user would intend to write two different words at the same time. Second, only one of the word confusion networks is allowed to generate a wildcard word. Every move is assessed by a language model, which is the same as the language model used to generate the word confusion networks. The search space is infinite but beam pruning can be used to keep the search tractable (Kristensson and Vertanen, 2011).

Initial results indicate that this merge model can reduce a word error rate of 27 per cent for speech recognition and 14 per cent for gesture keyboard down to 6.6 per cent by merging the word confusion networks generated for the same sentence by both modalities. It is also possible to allow spotty correction. In spotty correction the user does not re-write or re-speak the entire phrase or sentence. Instead the user merely re-writes or re-speaks the words in the original phrase or sentence that have been recognized incorrectly. The system automatically locates the erroneous words and replaces them. Initial results indicate that spotty correction of misrecognized speech utterances can reduce an initial error rate of 48.5 per cent by approximately 28 per cent by allowing users to use the gesture keyboard modality to re-write the incorrect words in the original speech recognition result.

The conclusion is that a probabilistic text entry method does not only provide a means to infer the user's intended text. The process outcome of the search itself can be used to design interaction techniques that mitigate additional problems in the text entry process.

2.6 Discussion

There is no doubt that statistical language processing techniques have been critical in the design of several text entry methods, such as auto-correcting touchscreen keyboards. Decades of speech recognition research have been invaluable as a driving force for the discovery of effective methods for training and smoothing language models and designing efficient decoding strategies. Speech recognition is a rapidly evolving discipline, and recent progress in deep neural networks outperforms classical speech recognition approaches (Hinton et al., 2012). Thus, while the principles and techniques in this chapter remain relevant, in practice, the precise modelling requirements of a complex task may suggest using a more advanced decoder than the token-passing model briefly explained in this chapter.

2.6.1 Modelling Limitatons

The models presented in this chapter and elsewhere for probabilistic text entry all have limitations. For example, earlier we introduced communication over a noisy channel as one model of text entry (Shannon, 1948). However, such a model is making a range of simplifying assumptions. A good overview can be found in the literature on determining the communication rate of brain-computer interfaces (Speier et al., 2013).

The language model acts as a prior in the decoder, and it is often a critical component in a successful probabilistic text entry method. However, the language model is limited by a wide range of simplifying assumptions, and as a statistical model it is reliant on training text being representative of unseen text. It is easy to identify examples which make such assumptions dubious, for instance—as pointed out by Witten and Bell (1990)—Ernest Vincent Wright wrote a 260-page novel in English without ever using the letter *e*. As another example, an *n*-gram language model assumes that the probability of occurrence of a word only depends on the last few (typically two) previous words, which is a false assumption. There is also an implicit assumption that the training text is fully representative of the text the user is intending to write, which, again, is nearly always false. Finally, smoothing is necessary in order to be able to estimate probabilities over unseen sequences of characters or words.

The likelihood model in a decoder can be designed in various ways. For a touchscreen keyboard, the typical choice is 2D Gaussian distributions (Goodman et al., 2002; Vertanen et al., 2015), although there is evidence that a slight performance improvement can be achieved using Gaussian Process regression Weir et al. (2014).

In addition, there are other potential sources of information that are usually not taken into account. Users' situational context, for example, if they are walking or encumbered when typing, is typically not modelled or taken into account. However, there is research that indicates that sensing users' gait and modelling this additional information source into the auto-correction algorithm can improve performance (Goel et al., 2012). In practice, it is difficult to model context as it relies on accurate and practical sensing technologies and sufficient amounts of relevant training data.

Finally, the design of a decoder involves making a range of assumptions. As previously discussed, a statistical decoder can, among other things, substitute, delete, or insert observations, and there are numerous other modifications and additional applications, for instance, the merge model for word confusion networks which was explained previously. The type of decoder, the precise model, and the selection and setting of parameters will all affect performance. In practice, it can be difficult to implement and train a statistical decoder with complex modelling assumptions.

2.6.2 Solution Principles

Addressing the modelling limitations discussed here is important ongoing and future work. However, while modelling addresses a particular objective, such as reducing an error rate under certain conditions, modelling alone cannot guide the design of future probabilistic text entry methods.

There is also a need to discover solution principles—principles that can guide the design of a range of probabilistic text entry methods. Such principles should be underpinned by evidence, such as results from empirical studies or modelling. Solution principles used in tandem with an understanding of limitations and capabilities of computational models of interaction help shape a design space. This design space can then enable the discovery of designs that are otherwise difficult to conceive.

For example, consider the problem of enabling fast typing on a smartwatch. As discussed earlier, there is no need to redesign the user interface layer. On the contrary, statistical decoding enables us to transplant the standard touchscreen QWERTY keyboard to the tiny screen and infer users' intended text with a low error rate. At the same time we know, in particular for text entry, that there is resistant to change due to the amount of effort invested in learning to be proficient with typing on a QWERTY layout. This suggests a solution principle of *path dependency* (David, 1985; Kristensson, 2015)—user interfaces are familiar to users for a reason and unless there is a good reason for redesign, it may better to design a system that supports existing user behaviour. In the case of text entry design, statistical decoding allows us to present users with a miniature version of a mobile phone keyboard for a smartwatch, and have it support the typing behaviour and patterns users are already familiar with.

Another example discussed in this chapter covered the limitations of language models, which in turn affect the efficacy of touchscreen keyboard auto-correction algorithms. Earlier we saw that allowing users to modulate the uncertainty of their input to the auto-correction algorithm reduces error rate. This suggests a solution principle of *fluid regulation of uncertainty*. In other words, when an interactive system is interpreting noisy data from a user it may be worthwhile to investigate if it is possible to design a method that enables users to express their own certainty in their interaction. This additional information can be encoded into a statistical decoder or other computational model of interaction. It allows users to guide the system's inference in situations when the system's model may have incomplete information. Thus it enables users to preempt errors, increasing efficiency and reducing frustration by preventing an error recovery process.

Finally, another solution principle suggested by the applications presented in this chapter is *flexibility*—allow users to optimize their interaction strategy based on situational constraints. For example, consider the system we described earlier, which allows users to repair erroneous recognition results by re-speaking or re-writing the intended text, and optionally include some surrounding context to maximize the probability of success. Such a system could potentially allow users to flexibly combine multiple modalities, such as speaking and typing in thin air with an optical see-through head-mounted display. In such a scenario, both text entry methods are probabilistic and the user's interaction is inherently uncertain. A user may, for instance, adopt a strategy of speaking first and then opt to fix errors by re-typing the intended text in thin air.

The solution principles we have sketched above are examples of systematic design insights, which, if underpinned by engineering science or empirical research, allow computational interaction designers to explore a richer design space where the fabric of design also includes taking into account behavioural aspects of users interacting with inherently uncertain intelligent interactive systems.

2.7 Conclusions

This chapter has explained how methods from statistical language processing serve as a foundation for the design of probabilistic text entry methods and error corrections methods. It has reviewed concepts from information theory and language modelling and explained how to design a statistical decoder for text entry, which is using a generative probabilistic model based on the token-passing paradigm. It then presented five example applications of statistical language processing for text entry: correcting typing mistakes, enabling fast typing on a smartwatch, improving prediction in augmentative and alternative communication, enabling dwell-free eye-typing, and intelligently supporting error correction of probabilistic text entry. Future developments are likely to focus on discovering improved computational models and investigating solution principles for probabilistic text entry design.

....

REFERENCES

Bellegarda, J. R., 2004. Statistical language model adaptation: review and perspectives. *Speech Communication*, 42(1), pp. 93–108.

Chen, S. F., and Goodman, J., 1999. An empirical study of smoothing techniques for language modeling. *Computer Speech and Language*, 13, pp. 359–94.

David, P. A., 1985. Clio and the economics of qwerty. *The American Economic Review*, 75(2), pp. 332–7.

Fowler, A., Partridge, K., Chelba, C., Bi, X., Ouyang, T., and Zhai, S., 2015. Effects of language modeling and its personalization on touchscreen typing performance. In: *Proceedings of the 33rd Annual ACM Conference on Human Factors in Computing Systems*. New York, NY: ACM, pp. 649–58.

Goel, M., Findlater, L., and Wobbrock, J., 2012. Walktype: using accelerometer data to accomodate situational impairments in mobile touch screen text entry. In: *Proceedings of the SIGCHI Conference on Human Factors in Computing Systems*. New York, NY: ACM, pp. 2687–96.

Goodman, J., Venolia, G., Steury, K., and Parker, C., 2002. Language modeling for soft keyboards. In: *Proceedings of the 7th international conference on Intelligent user interfaces*. New York, NY: ACM, pp. 194–5.

Hinton, G., Deng, L., Yu, D., Dahl, G. E., Mohamed, A.-r., Jaitly, N., Senior, A., Vanhoucke, V., Nguyen, P., Sainath, T. N., and Kingsbury, B., 2012. Deep neural networks for acoustic modeling in speech recognition: The shared views of four research groups. *Signal Processing Magazine, IEEE*, 29(6), pp. 82–97.

i Cancho, R. F., and Solé, R. V., 2003. Least effort and the origins of scaling in human language. *Proceedings of the National Academy of Sciences*, 100(3), pp. 788–91.

Jacob, R., and Karn, K. S., 2003. Eye tracking in human-computer interaction and usability research: Ready to deliver the promises. In: Fagerberg, J., Mowery, D. C., and Nelson, R. R., eds. *The Mind's Eye: Cognitive and Applied Aspects of Eye Movement Research*. Amsterdam: Elsevier Science, pp. 573–606.

Jurafsky, D., and Martin, J. H., 2000. *Speech & language processing*. Upper Saddle River, NJ: Prentice-Hall.

Karat, C.-M., Halverson, C., Horn, D., and Karat, J., 1999. Patterns of entry and correction in large vocabulary continuous speech recognition systems. In: *Proceedings of the SIGCHI conference on Human Factors in Computing Systems*. New York, NY: ACM, pp. 568–75.

Komninos, A., and Dunlop, M., 2014. Text input on a smart watch. *Pervasive Computing, IEEE*, 13(4), pp. 50–8.

Kristensson, P. O., 2009. Five challenges for intelligent text entry methods. *AI Magazine*, 30(4), p. 85.

Kristensson, P. O., 2015. Next-generation text entry. *Computer*, (7), pp. 84–7.

Kristensson, P. O., and Vertanen, K., 2011. Asynchronous multimodal text entry using speech and gesture keyboards. In: *Twelfth Annual Conference of the International Speech Communication Association*.

Kristensson, P. O., and Vertanen, K., 2012. The potential of dwell-free eye-typing for fast assistive gaze communication. In: *Proceedings of the Symposium on Eye Tracking Research and Applications*. New York, NY: ACM, pp. 241–4.

Kristensson, P. O., Vertanen, K., and Mjelde, M., 2015. Gaze based text input systems and methods. US Patent App. 14/843,630.

Kristensson, P. O., and Zhai, S., 2005. Relaxing stylus typing precision by geometric pattern matching. In: *Proceedings of the 10th international conference on Intelligent user interfaces*, pp. 151–8.

Kurihara, K., Goto, M., Ogata, J., and Igarashi, T., 2006. Speech pen: predictive handwriting based on ambient multimodal recognition. In: *Proceedings of the SIGCHI conference on human factors in computing systems*. New York, NY: ACM, pp. 851–60.

MacKay, D. J., Ball, C. J., and Donegan, M., 2004. Efficient communication with one or two buttons. In: *AIP Conference Proceedings*, 735(1), pp. 207–18.

Majaranta, P., Ahola, U.-K., and Špakov, O., 2009. Fast gaze typing with an adjustable dwell time. In: *Proceedings of the SIGCHI Conference on Human Factors in Computing Systems*. New York, NY: ACM, pp. 357–60.

Majaranta, P., and Räihä, K.-J., 2002. Twenty years of eye typing: systems and design issues. In: *Proceedings of the 2002 symposium on Eye tracking research & applications*. New York, NY: ACM, pp. 15–22.

Mangu, L., Brill, E., and Stolcke, A., 2000. Finding consensus in speech recognition: word error minimization and other applications of confusion networks. *Computer Speech & Language*, 14(4), pp. 373–400.

McNair, A. E., and Waibel, A., 1994. Improving recognizer acceptance through robust, natural speech repair. In: *Third International Conference on Spoken Language Processing*. New York, NY: ACM, pp. 1299–1302.

Miller, G. A., 1957. Some effects of intermittent silence. *The American Journal of Psychology*, 70(2), pp. 311–14.

Moore, R. C., and Lewis, W., 2010. Intelligent selection of language model training data. In: *Proceedings of the ACL 2010 conference short papers*. Red Hook, NY: Curran Associates, pp. 220–4.

Oney, S., Harrison, C., Ogan, A., and Wiese, J., 2013. Zoomboard: a diminutive qwerty soft keyboard using iterative zooming for ultra-small devices. In: *Proceedings of the SIGCHI Conference on Human Factors in Computing Systems*, pp. 2799–802.

Räihä, K.-J., and Ovaska, S., 2012. An exploratory study of eye typing fundamentals: dwell time, text entry rate, errors, and workload. In: *Proceedings of the SIGCHI Conference on Human Factors in Computing Systems*. New York, NY: ACM, pp. 3001–10.

Rough, D., Vertanen, K., and Kristensson, P. O., 2014. An evaluation of dasher with a high-performance language model as a gaze communication method. In: *Proceedings of the 2014 International Working Conference on Advanced Visual Interfaces*. New York, NY: ACM, pp. 169–76.

Shannon, C., 1948. A mathematical theory of communication. *The Bell System Technical Journal*, 27(3), pp. 379–423.

Speier, W., Arnold, C., and Pouratian, N., 2013. Evaluating true bci communication rate through mutual information and language models. *PloS One*, 8(10):e78432.

Tuisku, O., Majaranta, P., Isokoski, P., and Räihä, K.-J., 2008. Now dasher! dash away!: longitudinal study of fast text entry by eye gaze. In: *Proceedings of the 2008 Symposium on Eye Tracking Research & Applications*. New York, NY: ACM, pp. 19–26.

Vertanen, K., and Kristensson, P. O., 2009a. Automatic selection of recognition errors by respeaking the intended text. In: *Automatic Speech Recognition & Understanding, 2009. ASRU 2009*. New York, NY: IEEE Press, pp. 130–5.

Vertanen, K., and Kristensson, P. O., 2009b. Parakeet: A continuous speech recognition system for mobile touch-screen devices. In: *Proceedings of the 14th international conference on Intelligent user interfaces*. New York, NY: ACM, pp. 237–46.

Vertanen, K., and Kristensson, P. O., 2011. The imagination of crowds: conversational aac language modeling using crowdsourcing and large data sources. In: *Proceedings of the Conference on Empirical Methods in Natural Language Processing*. Red Hook, NY: Curran Associates, pp. 700–11.

Vertanen, K., and MacKay, D. J., 2010. Speech dasher: fast writing using speech and gaze. In: *Proceedings of the SIGCHI Conference on Human Factors in Computing Systems*. New York, NY: ACM, pp. 595–98.

Vertanen, K., Memmi, H., Emge, J., Reyal, S., and Kristensson, P. O., 2015. Velocitap: Investigating fast mobile text entry using sentence-based decoding of touchscreen keyboard input. In: *Proceedings of the 33rd Annual ACM Conference on Human Factors in Computing Systems*. New York, NY: ACM, pp. 659–68.

Ward, D. J., Blackwell, A. F., and MacKay, D. J., 2000. Dasher—a data entry interface using continuous gestures and language models. In: *Proceedings of the 13th annual ACM symposium on User interface software and technology*. New York, NY: ACM, pp. 129–37.

Ward, D. J., and MacKay, D. J., 2002. Fast hands-free writing by gaze direction. *Nature*, 418(6900), pp. 838–8.

Weir, D., Pohl, H., Rogers, S., Vertanen, K., and Kristensson, P. O., 2014. Uncertain text entry on mobile devices. In: *Proceedings of the SIGCHI Conference on Human Factors in Computing Systems*. New York, NY: ACM, pp. 2307–16.

Witten, I. H., and Bell, T. C., 1990. Source models for natural language text. *International Journal of Man-Machine Studies*, 32(5), pp. 545–79.

Witten, I. H., Neal, R. M., and Cleary, J. G., 1987. Arithmetic coding for data compression. *Communications of the ACM*, 30(6), pp. 520–40.

Young, S. J., Russell, N., and Thornton, J., 1989. *Token passing: a simple conceptual model for connected speech recognition systems*. Cambridge: University of Cambridge Engineering Department.

Zhai, S., and Kristensson, P.-O., 2003. Shorthand writing on stylus keyboard. In: *Proceedings of the SIGCHI conference on Human factors in computing systems*. New York, NY: ACM, pp. 97–104.

Zipf, G. K., 1949. Human behavior and the principle of least effort.

3

Input Recognition

OTMAR HILLIGES

3.1 Introduction

Sensing and processing of user input lies at the core of Human-Computer Interaction (HCI) research. In tandem with various forms of output (e.g., graphics, audio, haptics) input sensing ties the machine and the user together and enables interactive applications. New forms of input sensing have triggered important developments in the history of computing. The invention of the mouse by Douglas Engelbart in the early 1960s and its mainstream adaptation in the late 1980s and early 1990s have played a significant role in the transition from the mainframe computer to the personal computing era. Similarly, the perfection of capacitive multi-touch input by Apple with the introduction of the iPhone in 2007 has dramatically changed the computing landscape and has brought computing to entirely new parts of the population.

Notably the timeframes from invention of a input paradigm to its mainstream adoption can be very long, sometimes lasting up to thirty years. This process can be explained by the intrinsic connection between input recognition and user experiences. Humans are remarkably good at detecting isolated events that are not inline with their expectation, which gives us the evolutionary advantage of detecting and reacting to potentially life-threatening events. However, this also implies that any input recognition mechanism has to work accurately almost 100 per cent of the time or a user will very quickly get the impression that 'it does not work' (even when 95 per cent of the time it does). This implies that any input paradigm has to undergo many iterations of invention, design, and refinement before it reaches the necessary accuracies. Furthermore, any time we touch the input stack, we also alter how the user interacts with the machine and thus impact the user experience. Hence, the design and engineering of input recognition techniques is a crucial part of HCI research and is fundamental in bringing more alternative and complementary input paradigms closer to end-user adoption, enabling new forms of post-desktop interaction and hence new forms of computing.

This chapter provides an overview of the general approach to input sensing processing of the data produced by a variety of sensors. In particular, we focus on the extraction

Computational Interaction. Antti Oulasvirta, Per Ola Kristensson, Xiaojun Bi, Andrew Howes (Eds).
© Oxford University Press 2018. Published 2018 by Oxford University Press.

of semantic meaning from low-level sensor data. That is, the chapter provides a general framework for the processing of sensor data until it becomes usable as input mechanism in interactive applications. Typically, sensors collect physical signals, such as pressure or motion, and convert them into electrical signals. These signals are then streamed to a machine, which is programmed to recognize, process, and act upon them.

3.2 Challenges

Much research in HCI is dedicated to the questions *what* humans can do with computers and *how* they interact with them. So far we have seen three dominant waves in computer interfaces: purely text-based interfaces (e.g., the command line, 1960s), graphical interfaces based on mouse and keyboard (1980s), and direct-touch based interfaces on mobile phones and tablet computers (2000s). As digital technology moves further away from the desktop setting, it is becoming increasingly clear that traditional interfaces are no longer adequate means for interaction and that the traditional computing paradigm will be replaced or complemented by new forms of interaction.

It is no longer hard to predict that we are heading towards a future where almost every man-made object in the world will have some form of input, processing, and output capabilities. This implies that researchers in HCI need to explore and understand the implications as well as the significant technological challenges of leveraging various sensors to facilitate and enhance interaction. Some researchers seek to expand and improve the interaction space for existing devices (e.g., augmented mice or keyboards Taylor et al.). Others try to develop entirely novel interactive systems, forgoing traditional means of input entirely. Such developments are often explored alongside the emergence of new sensing modes and interaction paradigms (e.g., depth cameras for natural user interfaces Hilliges et al. "Holodesk").

Together these emerging technologies form the basis for new ways of interaction with machines of all kinds and can, if carefully designed, lay the foundations for a diverse set of future application domains, including smart home and health support appliances, intelligent living and working spaces, interactive devices such as mobile and wearable devices, automobiles and robots, smart tutoring systems, and much more. However, for such benefits to materialize many challenges in input recognition have to be overcome. These can be categorized as follows:

3.2.1 Emerging Sensing Modalities

There is already a wide range of sensors available that one can employ in order to sense user input, including cameras, acceleration sensors, capacitive and resistive sensing, sensing in the electromagnetic spectrum, and many more. Choosing a particular sensor for a certain type of application is never a trivial task, and it often requires a careful design-space exploration and often trade-offs between sensing fidelity and user or environmental instrumentation. For instance, consider adding gesture recognition capabilities to a mobile device without taking the device out of the pocket. Such an input mechanism could allow the user to control the phone menus and to answer incoming calls. However, there is no existing 'hand-gesture recognition' sensor that could simply be added to a portable device. Instead, a variety of solutions have to be considered. One could base the detection on colour images (Song, Sörös, Pece, Fanello, Izadi, Keskin, and Hilliges, 2014), motion sensors and magnetometers (Benbasat and Paradiso 2002), radar waves (Song, Wang, Lein, Poupyrev, and Hilliges, 2016) or piggy-backing on existing WIFI infrastructure (Pu, Gupta, Gollakota, and Patel 2013). Each of these technologies come with intrinsic advantages and drawbacks, e.g., a camera requires line-of-sight and incurs high computational cost, leveraging IMUs or radio-frequency signals limits the fidelity of inputs that can be recognized. Clearly, a complex and difficult-to-navigate design space ensues. Unfortunately, there exists no one-size-fits-all solution to this problem. However, understanding the characteristics of various sensing modalities and their implications for input sensing can inform the design process and finally determines the usability of a system.

3.2.2 Signal Processing and Input Recognition

In parallel to the question of which sensing modality to choose, many technical issues relating to the recognition of input arise. For instance, what is the mapping between the sensor output and the presumed gesture? Can this be established a prori and if so, does this mapping hold true for all users? How is the sensor affected by noise, and to what extent this affects the classification results? Is the sensor response characteristic enough to be discernible across different inputs, and if so how many? Are the inputs to be classified 'general', or do they depend on a particular task? Can we combine the sensor with already existing sensing capabilities in the device? All these issues need to be tackled by a developer wanting to build an interactive, sensor-based system. While there exists a wide variety of hardware and software support to attain data from sensors, there is much less infrastructure available in supporting HCI researchers and engineers to answer the questions around how to process the data once it has arrived on the host machine. This chapter discusses the technical foundations of this process.

3.2.3 Human Factors

The ultimate goal of sensing-based input work is to understand the implicit intention the user had in mind by observing the user's non-verbal actions and motion. This is a challenging task since the human face and body exhibit complex and rich dynamic behaviour that are entirely non-linear, vary over time (at different time scales), and are drastically subject to the context of interaction. For example, consider the case of motion-controlled gaming (e.g., Nintendo's Wii console). Beginners can be observed to fully mimic real-world motions in typical games for the platform such as sport simulations (e.g., golf, bowling). However, very quickly the majority of the users figures out that the controller only measures relative motion and that the real magnitude of motion does not impact the input recognition. Therefore, users quickly adopt a more efficient form of interaction consisting of small flicks of the wrist rather than performing the full golf-swing as intended by the designer. This energy minimization strategy is inherent to human motion and needs to be considered when designing motion-based interfaces, implying that there is a need for sensing technology and input recognition algorithms that can detect and discriminate subtle and very low-magnitude motions in order to reduce fatigue and effort of use. In terms of context dependency speech-based interfaces are a prime example. Where speaking to a machine may be perfectly acceptable and potentially even the preferred mode of interactions in some settings such as the home, it may be entirely unacceptable in other, more social, settings, such as on a train or in an elevator. Thus, research in computer vision, signal processing, and machine learning for sensing and modelling of multimodal human machine interaction to recognize spatiotemporal activities, to integrate multiple sensor sources and learning individual- and context- dependent human-behaviour models are all important research directions.

3.2.4 Personalization

Many HCI research prototypes have employed non-standard forms of input such as gestures where the exact mapping between human action and system response is created by system designers and researchers. Although such gestures are appropriate for early investigations, they are not necessarily reflective of long-term user behaviour. Therefore, a juxtaposition of the user learning how to operate a system, and how the user would want to operate the system, arises. This issue has been highlighted first by (Wobbrock, Morris, and Wilson 2009) in a so-called gesture elicitation study in which users are first shown the effect of an input and are then asked to perform a matching gesture. The resulting user-defined gesture sets often vary drastically from 'expert' designed gesture sets. Similar findings have been replicated in many follow-up studies and a pattern emerges in which there is high agreement only for a small set of system functionalities (often those that leverage some physically inspired metaphor) and a large number of functionalities that elicit almost no agreement across users. These results indicate a need for personalization of input recognition systems (and gesture sets). However, there is very little technical research on how to implement such personalized recognition systems.

Some of these challenges have known solutions, which we aim to address in this chapter, whereas others such as online adaptation of input recognition systems and their personalization remain largely unaddressed and open up directions for future research.

Due to the mentioned issues, modern multi-modal interfaces leverage sophisticated machine learning models to recover user intent and input from often noisy and incomplete sensor data. In the following sections we provide a brief overview over a general framework that applies such machine-learning models to the interaction tasks.

3.3 Sensor-based Input Recognition

Figure 3.1 summarizes the general procedure now common practice in many interactive systems and applications (Song, Sörös, Pece, Fanello, Izadi, Keskin, and Hilliges, 2014; Song, Pece, Sörö, Koelle, and Hilliges, 2015; Taylor, Keskin, Hilliges, Izadi, and Helmes, 2014; Le Goc, Taylor, Izadi, and Keskin, 2014; Sato, Poupyrev and Harrison, 2012; Harrison, Tan, and Morris, 2010). From low-level signals (e.g., images, audio, acceleration data) relevant

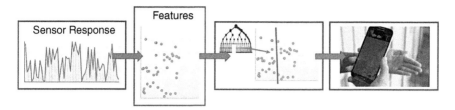

Figure 3.1 General data-driven input recognition pipeline. A sensor signal produces a certain feature set, which can be used to classify a predictive model. This model can then be deployed on computing devices to enable interaction.

information is extracted via signal transformations. This transformed representations are called features. Subsequently, the features are labeled (often manually) and from this training data a statistical model is fitted to the data.

Such models can either be generative (i.e., they learn a hypothesis about how the data was generated) or discriminative (i.e., the model can distinguish between samples from different underlying distributions). Furthermore, one can distinguish two related but separate tasks: regression and classification. Regression describes the process of predicting the (continuous) value of an underlying (unknown) function. For example, based on the model year and mileage, one could predict a car's resale value. Classification describes the process of predicting a class or category label. For example, in the context of interactive systems a model could be trained to predict different types of gestures.

After training, such a model can be used to predict values or class labels on *unseen* data. That is, we can now feed live data through the feature extraction process and then feed these (unlabelled) feature vectors through the model to attain a class label (e.g., gesture type). In practice, no machine learning model will always predict the correct label and therefore it is often necessary to further process the predictions via some temporal filtering or smoothing procedure. This processed stream of data can then be used as input in an interactive application. For example, one may map certain gestures to particular event handlers in a graphical interface.

In the context of non-desktop user interfaces, an additional interesting challenge arises in that the information from multiple streams of data needs to be integrated. This process is also known as *sensor fusion*. Here, the goal is to merge the different information sources in an optimal way so that they can be complementary to each other and so that they can lead to better decision-making about the user's intent. In this context probabilistic filtering techniques such as the Kalman Filter, Hidden-Markov-Models and Particle Filters are commonly applied. However, a discussion of these would go beyond the scope of this chapter.

3.4 Machine Learning for HCI

Machine learning (ML) is a vast sub-field of computer science and a complete treatment not only exceeds the scope of this subject, but also the scope of this book. However, many excellent resources are available that give good introductions to the core concepts and a good overview of the many machine-learning algorithms (e.g., Mohri, Rostamizadeh, and Talwalkar, 2012; Bishop, 2006). Nonetheless, it is important to understand the basics of machine learning in order to build intelligent and robust interactive systems that ideally are flexible enough to work well across different users and user groups, as well as being capable of adapting to individual user preferences and capabilities.

To the uninitiated the sheer number of algorithms that have been proposed can be bewildering and hence many HCI researchers treat machine learning as a 'magic black box'. However, to the unique settings and requirements of HCI it is not only beneficial but perhaps even mandatory to go beyond this view and to open up the black box in order to adjust it's workings for the specific needs of interactive systems. In this spirit we attempt to summarize the most important aspects of machine learning and illustrate how many important concepts map onto HCI and input recognition problems. We summarize our discussions by highlighting were the HCI settings go beyond the typically considered problem definition and thus identify fruitful areas for future work.

Mitchell (1997) provides the most compact, formal definition of machine learning: 'A computer program is said to learn from experience E with respect to some class of tasks T and performance measure P if its performance at tasks in T, as measured by P, improves with experience E.'

Whereby the task T refers to the type of skill that the algorithm is supposed to learn (not the learning itself). This is typically decomposed into supervised, unsupervised, and reinforcement learning tasks. For the purpose of this discussion we limit ourselves to the supervised case. Machine learning tasks are usually described in terms of how the system should process an example. In our context, an example is typically a collection of features extracted from low-level sensor signals. The most prominent task is then that of classification—that is the algorithm is supposed to decide to which of k categories a input sample belongs to. Other tasks (that we don't treat in more depth) include regression, transcription, machine translation, clustering, denoising, and infilling of missing data.

The performance measure P is a quantitative measure of the systems ability to perform the task. Normally the measure is specific to the task T. In classification, one often measures the accuracy of the model, defined as the proportion of examples for which the model produces the correct output (i.e., assigns the correct label).

The categorization of ML tasks is broadly aligned with the type of experience they are allowed to have during the learning process. Most of the learning algorithms in this chapter can be understood as experiencing an entire (labelled) dataset. A dataset itself is a collection of many examples, often also called data points or feature vectors.

3.4.1 Example: Linear Regression

To make the above definitions clearer, we quickly review a standard example of a machine learning algorithm: linear regression. While not specific to HCI or input recognition, the linear regression setting should be familiar to almost any HCI researcher and practitioner since it falls into the same category of linear models that are frequently used in statistical analysis of experimental data. In regression, the task is to take a vector $x \in \mathbb{R}^n$ as input and predict the value of a scalar $y \in \mathbb{R}$ as output. In linear regression, the estimated output $\hat{y}$ is a linear function of the inputs:

$$\hat{y} = \boldsymbol{w}^T \boldsymbol{x}, \tag{3.1}$$

where $\boldsymbol{w} \in \mathbb{R}^n$ is a vector of parameters that we seek to learn from data. One can think of $\boldsymbol{w}$ as set of weights that determine how much each feature affects the prediction of the value of y. This then formally defines the task T which is to predict y from $\boldsymbol{x}$ by computing $\hat{y} = \boldsymbol{w}^T \boldsymbol{x}$.

Now we need a definition of the performance measure P. In the 2D case linear regression can be thought of fitting a line into a collection of 2D data points. The standard way of measuring performance in this setting is to compute the mean squared error (MSE) of the model on a (previously unseen) test set. The MSE on the test data is defined as:

$$MSE_{(\text{test})} = \frac{1}{m} \| \hat{y}^{(\text{test})} - y^{(\text{test})} \|_2^2. \tag{3.2}$$

Intuitively, one can see that the error decreases to 0 exactly when $\hat{y}^{(\text{test})} = y^{(\text{test})}$. Figure 3.2, left schematically illustrates that the error (the area of the green squares, hence the name of the metric) decreases when the Euclidean distance between the predictions and the true target values decreases.

We now need an algorithm that allows the quality of the predictions to improve by observing a training set $(\boldsymbol{X}^{(train)}, \boldsymbol{y}^{(train)})$. In this case the learning procedure entails adjusting the set of weights $\boldsymbol{w}$. This is done via minimization of the MSE on the training set. To minimize $MSE_{(train)}$, we can simply solve for where its gradient is 0, given by $\nabla_{\boldsymbol{w}} MSE_{(train)} = 0$ which can be solved for $\boldsymbol{w}$ in closed form via the normal equations:

$$\boldsymbol{w} = (\boldsymbol{X}^{(train)^T} \boldsymbol{X}^{(train)})^{-1} = \boldsymbol{X}^{(train)^T} \boldsymbol{y}^{(train)}. \tag{3.3}$$

Intuitively, solving Equation 3.3 will 'move' the line in Figure 3.2, left around until the sum of the areas of the hatched squares is smallest. In practice one often uses a slightly more sophisticated model that also includes an intercept term b so that the full model becomes

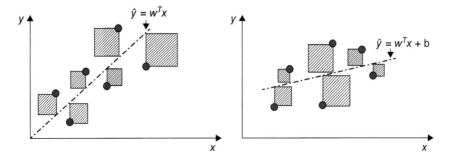

Figure 3.2 Illustration of linear regression and the mean-square error. Left: Simple model fits line through the origin and tries to minimize the mean area of the green squares. Right: More complex model with intercept parameter can fit lines that do not have to pass through the origin.

$\hat{y} = \boldsymbol{w}^T\boldsymbol{x} + b$. This additional parameter removes the requirement for the line to pass through the origin (cf. Figure 3.2, right).

Linear regression is a simple yet powerful model and it provides an almost complete example of how to build a learning algorithm.

3.5 Building a Machine Learning Algorithm

We can now attempt to generalize the above example to attain a generic recipe under which almost all machine learning algorithms fall. Such algorithms contain the following aspects: a dataset, a cost function to be minimized to find model parameters, an optimization procedure, and a model.

In our example of linear regression we combine data $\boldsymbol{X}$ and $\boldsymbol{y}$ use the MSE as cost and solve for the best model parameters by setting the gradient to zero and solving for $\boldsymbol{w}$, often in closed form via the normal equations. Realizing that we can exchange and replace any of these components mostly independently from each other we can construct a wide variety of algorithms.

Cost functions used in machine learning often include at least one term that causes the learning process to perform statistical estimation of some of the model parameters.

3.5.1 Maximum Likelihood Estimation

The central goal of machine learning is for a model to perform well on unseen data (this is called generalization). So far we have talked about learning as an optimization problem performed on the test data. The difference between regular optimization and machine learning is that we need to find model parameters (by observing training data) that produce low testing error. One typically estimates generalization error of a model by measuring its performance on a test set of examples that were collected independently and separately from the training set. The field of statistical learning theory provides a number of useful concepts and tools to predict generalization performance (and in consequence to optimize it). A full discussion of related concepts such as generalization, variance-bias trade-off, model capacity, over- and underfitting, cross-validation as well as parameter, and function estimation goes beyond this chapter and we refer the reader to excellent resources on this topic (e.g., Vapnik, 1998; Mohri, Rostamizadeh, and Talwalkar, 2012; James, Witten, Hastie, and Tibshirani, 2013).

An important concept in machine learning is that of bias and variance which are two inherent sources of error in any estimator. Bias measures deviations from the true value of the function or parameter whereas variance describes the expected deviation from the true value caused by any particular sampling strategy of the data. The statistical learning theory and machine learning literature have proposed many different estimators. If we are given the choice between several such estimators, how are we going to choose between them? If we know that one produces higher bias whereas the other suffers from high variance, which one should we choose? Rather than picking an estimator at random and then analysing the bias and variance we can leverage the maximum likelihood principle to derive specific functions that are good estimators for a particular model. Consider the set of m examples $\mathbb{X} = \{(x^1, \ldots, (x^m)\}$ drawn from the true (but unknown) data generating distribution $p_{data}(\boldsymbol{x})$. We then let $p_{model}(\boldsymbol{x}; \Theta)$ be a parametric family of probability distributions over the same space indexed by Θ. Intuitively speaking p_{model} maps any $\boldsymbol{x}$ to a numerical value that estimates the true probability p_{data}. The maximum likelihood estimator (MLE) for Θ is then given by:

$$\Theta^* = \arg\max_{\Theta} p_{model}(\mathbb{X}; \Theta) \tag{3.4}$$

$$= \arg\max_{\Theta} \prod_{i=1}^{m} p_{model}(\boldsymbol{x}^{(i)}; \Theta). \tag{3.5}$$

This product of probabilities has a number of numerical inconveniences and is therefore substituted by the more well behaved but equivalent formulation leveraging the observation that taking the logarithm of the likelihood does not change the value of the objective function but allows us to rewrite the equation as a sum:

$$\Theta^* = \arg\max_{\Theta} \sum_{i}^{m} \log p_{model}(\boldsymbol{x}^{(i)}; \Theta). \tag{3.6}$$

Dividing m gives a version of the objective expressed as an expectation wrt to the empirical distribution $\hat{p}_{data}$ given by the m training data samples:

$$\Theta^* = \arg\max_{\Theta} \mathbb{E}_{\boldsymbol{x} \sim \hat{p}_{data}} \log p_{model}(\boldsymbol{x}; \Theta). \tag{3.7}$$

One way of interpreting this is to think of MLE as a minimization process of dissimilarity between the empirical distribution $\hat{p}_{data}$ and the model distribution p_{model}. In other words, we want the model to predict values that are as close as possible to the samples in the training data. If the model would predict exactly all samples in the training data the two distributions would be the same. This dissimilarity can be measured by the KL divergence:

$$D_{KL}(\hat{p}_{data} \| p_{model}) = \mathbb{E}_{\boldsymbol{x} \sim \hat{p}_{data}} [\log \hat{p}_{data}(\boldsymbol{x}) - \log p_{model}(\boldsymbol{x})]. \tag{3.8}$$

To minimize the KL divergence we only need to minimize (since the remaining terms do not depend on the model):

$$-\mathbb{E}_{\boldsymbol{x} \sim \hat{p}_{data}} [\log p_{model}(\boldsymbol{x})]. \tag{3.9}$$

to obtain the same result as via maximizing Equation 3.7. This process is referred to as minimizing the cross-entropy between the two distributions. Any loss consisting of a negative log-likelihood forms such a cross-entropy between training and model distribution. In particular, the previously used mean-squared error is the cross-entropy between the empirical distribution and a Gaussian model distribution. We will use this aspect shortly to model linear regression in the MLE framework.

It is straightforward to generalize the MLE principle to cases where we wish to estimate conditional probabilities $P(y|x;\Theta)$. That is, if we wish to predict y given x. This setting is the basis for most supervised learning algorithms, which are very prominent in input recognition and other areas of HCI. With X denoting all inputs and Y denoting all target values, the conditional maximum likelihood estimator can be written as:

$$\Theta^* = \arg\max_{\Theta} P(Y|X; \Theta). \tag{3.10}$$

in the case of the data being independently sampled and identically distributed (i.i.d.) then we can rewrite this in a per sample decomposed form:

$$\Theta^* = \arg\max_{\Theta} P(y^{(i)}|x^{(i)}; \Theta). \tag{3.11}$$

3.5.2 MLE Properties

While maximum likelihood estimators give no optimality guarantees for finite, small sets of training samples, they do poses a number of appealing properties in the limits of the number of samples $m \rightarrow \infty$. As the sample size increases to infinity, the ML estimate of a parameter converges to the true value being estimated. This is known as the consistency property of an estimator. Other estimation principles are also consistent but differ in their efficiency (wrt to statistical considerations). ML estimators achieve the Cramér-Rao lower bound (Radhakrishna Rao, 1945; Cramir, 1946) when the sample size tends to infinity. This means that no consistent estimator has lower asymptotic mean squared error than the MLE. For example, in linear regression this corresponds to the MLE finding model parameters such that the estimated values of y have the lowest mean-squared error compared to the true value. Due to the consistency and statistical efficiency properties of the MLE principle, it is the preferred estimation approach in machine learning. However, when the sample size is low, overfitting may become an issue and often requires regularization to attain good generalization behavior.

3.5.3 Linear Regression as MLE

Let us now revisit linear regression in the MLE framework. Instead of estimating a single scalar $\hat{y}$, we now assume the model produces a conditional distribution $p(y|x)$. If the training dataset is very large, there may well be several samples with the same values of x, but different values of y. The learning goal then is to fit the conditional probability distribution to all different values of y that are compatible with x. We define $p(y|x) = \mathcal{N}(y; \hat{y}(x; w), \sigma^2)$, where the function $\hat{y}(x; w)$ returns the prediction of the mean of the Gaussian. The variance σ^2 here is fixed and can be chosen by the user to be some constant. The conditional log-likelihood is then:

$$\sum_{i=1}^{m} \log p(y^{(i)}|x^{(i)}; \Theta) = -m \log \sigma - \frac{m}{2} \log(2\pi) - \sum_{i=1}^{m} \frac{\|\hat{y}^{(i)} - y^{(i)}\|}{2\sigma^2}, \tag{3.12}$$

where $\hat{y}^{(i)}$ is the output of the linear regression for the ith input and m is the number of training samples. Recalling that m and σ are constants, we can see from the RHS that the above equation will have a different value than the mean-square error, defined in Equation 3.2, but will have the identical location of the optimum. In other words, optimizing Equation 3.12 wrt to the model parameters w will produce exactly the same parameters as minimizing the mean-squared error.

We now have a framework with desirable properties in the maximum-likelihood estimation principle. We have also seen that it produces the same result as optimizing MSE in the case of linear regression and, due to the MLE properties, this justifies the (previously arbitrary) choice of MSE for linear regression. Assuming that sufficient training samples m are given, MLE is often the preferred estimator to use for a wide variety of machine learning problems. Generalizing the MLE principle to conditional probabilities provides the basis for most machine learning algorithms, in particular, those that fall into the supervised learning category.

3.5.4 Cost Functions and Numerical-optimization

Recall that nearly all ML algorithms can be seen as instances of the dataset, cost function, model, and optimization procedure. Numerical optimization is an entire research field in itself and we will only provide some high-level directions here and refer to the literature for details about the optimization algorithms themselves.

Equation 3.9 can be used to write the linear regression algorithm that combines the dataset (X, y) and the cost function

$$C(w, b) = -\mathbb{E}_{x \sim \hat{p}_{data}} \log p_{model}(y|x) \tag{3.13}$$

to be minimized to find the best parameters w, b. This can be solved in closed form via the normal equation. We've also discussed that typically cost functions will contain at least on term where parameters have to be estimated and that MLE is the preferred principle of doing so in many instances.

Even if we add additional terms to the cost function $C(w, b)$ such as a regularization term $\lambda \|w\|_2^2$ it can still be solved in closed form. However, as soon as the model becomes non-linear most cost functions can no longer be solved in closed form. This requires the use of iterative numerical optimization procedures such as gradient descent (Cauchy, 1847) or, more commonly, stochastic gradient descent (SGD). In some cases, especially if the cost function is non-convex, in the past gradient descent methods were considered a bad choice. Today we know that SGD often converges to very low values of the cost function especially for models with very large numbers of parameters and training datasets of increasing size. The most prominent example of such ML models are the currently very successful class of Deep Neural Networks.

In order to make cost functions amenable to optimization via SGD we can decompose it as a sum of per-example loss terms such that $L(x, y, \Theta) = -\log p(y|x; \Theta)$ is the per-example loss in the case of cross-entropy:

$$C(\Theta) = \mathbb{E}_{x,y \sim \hat{p}_{data}} L(x, y, \Theta) = \frac{1}{m} \sum_{i=1}^{m} L(x^{(i)}, y^{(i)}, \Theta) \tag{3.14}$$

to perform gradient descent we need to compute

$$\nabla C(\Theta) = \frac{1}{m} \sum_{i=1}^{m} \nabla L(\boldsymbol{x}^{(i)}, y^{(i)}, \Theta). \tag{3.15}$$

The core idea here is that the gradient itself is an expectation and that it can be approximated by using a small set of samples. Hence, in every step of the SGD algorithm a minibatch of samples is drawn at random from the training data to compute the gradient in which direction the algorithm moves. The size $m\prime$ of the minibatch is typically held constant to a few hundred samples, even if the total training data contains millions of samples. This gradient approximation is performed as follows:

$$\mathbf{g} = \frac{1}{m'} \nabla \sum_{i=1}^{m'} L(\boldsymbol{x}^{(i)}, y^{(i)}, \Theta). \tag{3.16}$$

The parameter update is then simply:

$$\Theta := \Theta - \mu \mathbf{g}, \tag{3.17}$$

where μ is the learning rate and has to chosen by the user.

While SGD is the work-horse of Deep Learning it has many uses outside of this sub-field of ML. SGD is the de-facto standard to train even linear models, especially if the training dataset size is large or if the model has many parameters.

3.6 Supervised Learning

In machine learning, the term supervised learning refers to the process of constructing a predictive model that infers an underlying function from *labelled* training data (Mohri, Rostamizadeh, and Talwalkar, 2012; Bishop, 2006). Importantly, each sample in the training data is a pair of input samples (typically a feature vector) and a output value most often called the label. Many learning algorithms exist that analyze the training data and that construct a model that maps between the inputs and the desired outputs. An important aspect in this context is generalization, meaning that the model should be able to predict correct labels even for samples that are not in the training data (unseen samples). A model that yields low error on the training data but high error on unseen data is said to display poor generalization capability and is most likely over fitting to the training data.

More formally, given a set $\mathbf{D}$ of $\mathcal{M}$ training samples $\mathbf{D} = \{(\boldsymbol{x}^1, \boldsymbol{y}^1), ..., (\boldsymbol{x}^m, \boldsymbol{y}^m)\}$, where $\boldsymbol{x}^i$ is the ith feature vector and $\boldsymbol{y}^i$ is its label (for example the gesture class). The learning goal then becomes to find a function $\mathbf{g}{:}X{\rightarrow}Y$ that maps a sample $\boldsymbol{x}$ from the input space X to the output space Y. The function $\mathbf{g}$ is an element of the so-called hypothesis space that contains all possible functions $\mathbf{G}$. In some algorithms, $\mathbf{g}$ is represented by a scoring function $\mathbf{f} : X \times Y \rightarrow \mathbb{R}$ so that $\mathbf{g}$ returns the highest value of $\mathbf{f}$: $\mathbf{g}(\boldsymbol{x}) = \arg\max_y \mathbf{f}(\boldsymbol{x}, \boldsymbol{y})$. While $\mathbf{G}$ and $\mathbf{F}$ can be an arbitrary space of functions, many machine learning algorithms are probabilistic in nature and hence the function $\mathbf{g}$ often is either a conditional probability model $\mathbf{g}(\boldsymbol{x}) = \mathbf{p}(\boldsymbol{y}|\boldsymbol{x})$ or a joint probability model $\mathbf{f}(\boldsymbol{x}, \boldsymbol{y}) = \mathbf{p}(\boldsymbol{x}, \boldsymbol{y})$. For example, naïve Bayes (which we will not discuss in this chapter) is a joint probability model and Decision Trees and Random Forests (which we will discuss in this chapter) are conditional probability models. However, there are successful and widely applied non-probabilistic models, most notably the Support Vector Machine (SVM).

As we have seen before in many cases maximum likelihood estimation is the preferred approach to optimize many supervised learning models, in particular those that are based on estimating a conditional probability distribution $p(y|x)$. This learning goal is then achieved via MLE of the parameter vector Θ for a parametric family of distributions $p(y|x;\Theta)$. As discussed above linear regression corresponds to this family of supervised learning algorithms.

3.7 Popular Approaches in HCI

After briefly introducing the general supervised learning framework we now discuss a small selection of machine learning algorithms that are of particular importance to HCI and multi-modal user interfaces. There are, of course, many more models and algorithms and many are applicable to various HCI problems and tasks. However, exhaustively discussing all of these is not only beyond the scope of this chapter but also beyond the scope of this book, and many excellent resources exist (for example, Bishop, 2006).

3.7.1 Logistic Regression

We have visited linear regression many times to illustrate various aspects of the machine learning basics. However, in HCI we're more often interested in the classification task rather than regression of scalar values. It is straightforward to extend the probabilistic linear regression framework parametrized as $p(y|x; \Theta) = \mathcal{N}(y; \Theta^T x, I)$. If we change the family of probability distributions so that we attain probabilities for two different classes then we can leverage this framework for binary classification, for example, to discriminate two different inputs based on the current value of a sensor or input device.

For the binary case we really only need to predict the value for one of the classes. Since the probabilities have to sum up to 1, the probability of the first class determines the probability of the second class. The predicted value in linear regression is the mean of a normal distribution, which can take any value. However, probabilities must fall in the range of $[0, 1]$. One way to address this problem is to re-map the predicted value to the $[0, 1]$ range via the logistic sigmoid function and to interpret the output of the function as the class probability:

$$p(y = 1|x; \Theta) = \sigma(\Theta^T x). \tag{3.18}$$

Note that we now compute the conditional probability of the output y being one (i.e., the first class), given the inputs x. This model is (somewhat confusingly) known as logistic regression, although it describes an approach to binary classification. Moreover, note that the model is now non-linear due to the sigmoid function and hence can no longer be solved via the normal equation but instead we must find the optimal parameters via maximum likelihood estimation, for example, by minimizing the negative log-likelihood via SGD.

3.7.2 Support Vector Machines

Arguably one of the most successful algorithm in machine learning so far has been the Support Vector Machine (SVM) (Vapnik, 1998) and by extension it has also had significant impact on HCI research. The algorithm and its many variants are extremely well studied and documented so that an in-depth treatment here is not necessary. We refer the interested reader to the many excellent books on the topic (Vapnik, 2013; Bishop, 2006; Steinwart and Christmann, 2008) and revert to only providing an intuition and to showcasing it's applicability to HCI research.

In its most basic form the SVM is a non-probabilistic, linear binary classifier. In other words, the algorithm tries to separate point samples (i.e., feature vectors) into two distinct classes (positive and negative samples) and does this by drawing a linear hyperplane (i.e., a straight line in 2D, a plane in 3D, and so forth) that separates the two classes. In contrast to fully probabilistic algorithms, the SVM algorithm only computes a score or distance function from the hyperplane but does not naturally provide an uncertainty estimate for its output. However, extensions exist to compute probabilities from the basic classification score.

An important aspect in the SVM framework is that of max-margin classification; based on the annotated training samples, the algorithm learns to draw a hyperplane that separates the two classes by the widest margin or gap so that no other hyperplane would result in a larger distance to any of the positive or negative samples in the training set (see Figure 3.3, left). At classification time, unseen test samples are projected into this space and fall either into the positive or negative region, and are hence assigned the corresponding label.

Slightly more formally speaking, the SVM training algorithm constructs a hyperplane in high dimensional spaces. The hyperplane can be used for classification (and regression, but

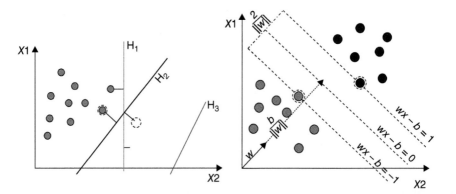

Figure 3.3 Left: Illustration of the max-margin property. Hyperplane $H3$ does not correctly separate classes. Hyperplanes $H1$ and $H2$ both separate correctly but $H2$ is the better classifier since it is furthest from all sample points. Right: Schematic overview of the SVM algorithm. Dotted lines indicate decision surface and margins. Support vectors are marked with dotted circles.

this topic is not treated here). The goodness of the classifier is parametrized as the distance to the nearest training data points of any class. Intuitively this could be seen as quality metric of the classification since a large distance to the decision surface, again intuitively, implies low generalization error or chance of misclassification. Given a training set $\mathbf{D} = \{(\mathbf{x_i}, \mathbf{y_i})\} \mid \pmb{x}_i \in \mathbb{R}^p,\ y_i \in \{-1, 1\}_{i=1}^n$, again with $\pmb{x}_i$ being the **p**-dimensional feature vectors and $\pmb{y}_i$ their categorical labels we want to construct the max-margin hyperplane that separates the samples with $\pmb{y}_i = 1$ from those with $\pmb{y}_i = -1$. A hyperplane is parametrized as the set of points that satisfy:

$$\pmb{w}^T \pmb{x} - b = 0, \tag{3.19}$$

where $\pmb{w}$ is a vector that is perpendicular to the hyperplane (i.e., a surface normal) and the distance off the hyperplane from the origin is given by $\frac{b}{||w||}$. The learning task is then to find the parameters b and w that maximize the margin to the closest training samples. Intuitively (and in 2D) this can be seen as a street where the middle line in is the decision hyperplane and the curbs are two parallel hyperplanes which we wish to push as far away from the centre line. These two parallel hyperplanes can be written as $\pmb{w}^T \pmb{x} - b = 1$ and $\pmb{w}^T \pmb{x} - b = -1$ respectively. Via geometric consideration we can show that the distance between these two curbs is $\frac{2}{||w||}$. Maximizing this distance is equal to minimizing $||w||$. In order to prevent any training samples to fall within this street we add the constraints $\pmb{w}^T \pmb{x}_i - b \geq 1 | \forall \pmb{x}_i$ with $y_i = 1$ and $\pmb{w}^T \pmb{x}_i - b \leq -1 | \forall \pmb{x}_i$ with $y_i = -1$. This can be written more compactly as:

$$y_i(\pmb{w}^T \pmb{x}_i - b) \geq 1, \forall\, 1 \leq i \leq n, \tag{3.20}$$

Using this constraint, the final optimization criterion is then:

$$\underset{w,b}{\arg\min} ||w||,\ \text{s.t.}\ y_i(\pmb{w}^T \pmb{x}_i - b) \geq 1, \forall\, 1 \leq i \leq n. \tag{3.21}$$

This optimization problem can solved efficiently and is provably convex (given a linearly separable training set). Evaluating the classifier at runtime is also efficient as it only depends on a dot product between the test sample and w. For an illustration of the various terms, see Figure 3.3, right.

The original SVM algorithm as discussed so far is a linear classifier. However, for the task of handwritten digit recognition, Boser, Guyon, and Vapnik (1992) extended the algorithm to also deal with non-linearly separable data by introducing the so-called kernel trick (Schölkopf, Burges, and Smola, 1999). The algorithm remains almost the same with the only difference that the dot product is replaced by a (non-linear) kernel function, which allows for fitting of the hyperplane in a transformed, higher-dimensional space. This so-called non-linear or kernelized SVM is the most frequently found version in practice. The SVM algorithm has been implemented and is available as a black box classifier in many frameworks and toolkits (including Weka, scikit-learn, and OpenCV; see Witten, Frank, Hall, and Pal, 2016; Pedregosa, Varoquaux, Gramfort, Michel, Thirion, Grisel, Blondel, Prettenhofer, Weiss, Dubourg, Vanderplas, Passos, Cournapeau, Brucher, Perrot, and Duch-esnay, 2011; Bradski, 2000). Due to the ease of training, runtime efficiency, and availability of high-quality implementations alongside a generally good out-of-bag performance on many different tasks, this classifier has been extremely popular tool in the HCI literature.

3.7.3 Random Forests

With ever more sensors and sensing technologies becoming available to HCI researchers, we face increasingly difficult challenges in extracting meaningful information from these low-level sensors. At the same time, we want to push the fidelity of interaction as far as possible, and hence there is a great need for powerful machine learning models in HCI research. One class of algorithms that have been successful in many tasks, both in computer vision and in HCI, are random forests (RF) (Breiman, 2001), which have been used, for example, in body pose estimation (Shotton, Sharp, Kipman, Fitzgibbon, Finocchio, Blake, Cook and Moore, 2013) and hand pose and state estimation (Keskin, Kıraç, Kara, and Akarun, 2012; Tang, Yu and Kim, 2013) using depth cameras, but also in HCI using different sensing modalities (Le Goc, Taylor, Izadi, and Keskin, 2014; Kim, Izadi, Dostal, Rhemann, Keskin, Zach, Shotton, Large, Bathiche, Niessner, Butler, Fanello, and Pradeep, 2014; Taylor, Keskin, Hilliges, Izadi, and Helmes, 2014). It is important to note, though, that decision trees and random forests are an exception to the general MLE principle we have been following so far. This is due to the fact that the learning algorithm for decision trees is not directly compatible with gradient descent optimization since the energy contains many flat regions. Therefore, a custom optimization algorithm is necessary. In the case of RF, this is a greedy algorithm that maximizes information gain in either a depth-first or breadth-first fashion (cf. Breiman, 2001; Russell and Norvig, 2010).

A RF is an ensemble of decision trees T (Russell and Norvig, 2010), each tree in the ensemble produces a noisy classification result. However, accurate classification results can be attained by averaging the results from multiple, non-biased classifiers together. Each tree consists of split nodes and leaf nodes; the split nodes themselves can be seen as very primitive classifiers consisting of a split function f_θ and a learned threshold τ. At each split node the algorithm will evaluate the split function, designed to be computationally inexpensive, and as a result forward the currently evaluated datum (often a pixel) to its left or right child until the datum reaches one of the leaf nodes. Recent work based on RFs (e.g., Keskin, Kıraç, Kara and Akarun, 2012; Shotton, Sharp, Kipman, Fitzgibbon, Finocchio, Blake, Cook and Moore, 2013; Tang, Yu and Kim, 2013) leverages highly descriptive depth images and complementary depth-invariant features for classification. These approaches use continuous valued features (typically simple depth differences Shotton, Sharp, Kipman, Fitzgibbon, Finocchio, Blake, Cook, and Moore, 2013), of the form:

$$f_\theta(I, x) = d_I\left(x + \frac{u}{d_I(x)}\right) - d_I\left(x + \frac{v}{d_I(x)}\right), \qquad (3.22)$$

where I is an image and x a pixel location, d_I is a function that returns the depth value at a given pixel location and u and v are offsets from that original pixel location. This feature response is then compared against the threshold τ. This basic idea has since been extended to also work with intensity data (Taylor, Keskin, Hilliges, Izadi, and Helmes, 2014), 2D binary images (Song, Sörös, Pece, Fanello, Izadi, Keskin, and Hilliges, 2014) and capacitance measurements (Le Goc, Taylor, Izadi, and Keskin, 2014).

The split nodes can be seen as simple questions where each answer adds a little more information, or in other words, reduces the uncertainty about the correct class label for the particular pixel. The leaf nodes of tree t contain learned (from training data) probability distributions $P_t(c|I, x)$ over per-pixel class labels c. These probability distributions describe the likelihood with which a pixel belongs to any of the classes in the label space. The distributions of individual trees are then averaged together over all trees in the forest to attain the final class probability:

$$P(c|I, x) = \frac{1}{T} \sum_{1}^{T} P_t(c|I, x).$$
(3.23)

These per-pixel probabilities are then often pooled across the image and a simple majority vote is used to decide the class label for a given frame (or image) I.

An important aspect is that the order in which the split functions are concatenated (the tree structure), the tresholds τ and the probability distributions stored in the leaf nodes are learned from annotated training data. In the case of RFs this is done by randomly selecting multiple split candidates and choosing the one that splits the data best. The quality metric for the split thereby is typically defined by the information gain I_j at node j:

$$I_j = H(C_j) - \sum_{i \in L,R} \frac{|C_j^i|}{|C_j|} H(C_j^i).$$
(3.24)

where H is the Shannon entropy of C. Decrease in entropy, denoted by I_j, means increase in information, or in other words, that the uncertainty about the decision boundary goes down. At training time we exhaustively enumerate all possible splits (θ, τ) and select the one maximizing I_j (for more details, see Breiman, 2001; Shotton, Sharp, Kipman, Fitzgibbon, Finocchio, Blake, Cook, and Moore, 2013).

One particularly interesting aspect of RFs is that they are extremely efficient to evaluate at runtime. As outlined above, evaluating such a classifier essentially boils down to traversing a binary tree which can be done in real-time even on resource constraint embedded devices (Song, Sörös, Pece, Fanello, Izadi, Keskin, and Hilliges, 2014). This, together with the ample discriminative power, makes RFs a compelling framework for HCI work and a large number of examples can be found in the literature (Song, Sörös, Pece, Fanello, Izadi, Keskin, and Hilliges, 2014; Song, Pece, Sörö, Koelle, and Hilliges, 2015; Chan, Hsieh, Chen, Yang, Huang, Liang and Chen, 2015; Yeo, Flamich, Schrempf, Harris-Birtill, and Quigley, 2016; Taylor, Keskin, Hilliges, Izadi, and Helmes, 2014; Le Goc, Taylor, Izadi, and Keskin, 2014; Lien, Gillian, Karagozler, Amihood, Schwesig, Olson, Raja and Poupyrev, 2016).

3.8 Feature Extraction

So far we have rather abstractly spoken of data points or samples, of inputs and outputs. We haven't discussed yet what these data points actually are. As illustrated in Figure 3.1, the first step in ML-based pipeline is that of feature extraction. In other words, we are pre-processing the low-level signal such that we extract the most informative bits of information given the final goal. For example, if we look where to detect jums from MU data, then extracting peaks in the signal or looking for drastic changes in the acceleration profile (maybe even specifically in the direction opposing gravity) might be the most informative.

The quality (information content) of the extracted features is a decisive aspect in the overall achieved accuracy of a recognition system. The process of feature extraction derives values from and hence summarizes the raw data in a way that, ideally, the resulting feature vectors are informative and non-redundant and so that they facilitate the subsequent learning and generalization steps. Often an attempt is made to extract features that also provide a human intuition or that allow to bring domain knowledge about the signal and it's interpretation into the otherwise generic machine learning process.

A further benefit of this data reduction step is that it reduces the amount of computational resources needed to describe a large set of data. Analysis with a large number of variables generally requires a large amount of memory and computation power and hence reducing the number of variables to the most important ones can drastically speed-up both training and testing times.

Furthermore, training an ML model on the raw data may lead to overfitting to contextual information in the training data. For example, a model trained to recognize human activity may learn to 'recognize' activities such as Tai-Chi (which is often performed in parks and hence on grass) purely based on the green colour of the background if it was trained using the entire image. This issue then causes poor generalization to new samples (in which the context may be different).

3.8.1 Feature Selection

The raw signal often contains redundant information – for example, a non-moving camera measures the static background of an observed scene repeatedly whereas only few pixels in the image carry information (e.g., moving foreground objects). Related to the process of feature extraction is that of *feature selection*, in other words, the process of selecting the most informative subset of signal transformations for the given task at hand. For example, if the task is to predict whether a patient is likely to develop cancer, only few genes will be carrying useful information. Therefore, it would not be beneficial nor efficient to look at the entire genome information.

The basic premise is that a lot of data in the raw stream is redundant or uninformative and can hence be removed. A large number of feature selection techniques exist, but generally speaking, they attempt to maximize *relevance* of the selected features and to minimize *redundancy* between features. More precisely, the goal is to select features that serve as good predictors for the outcome variable and to select only complementary features since one relevant (highly correlated) feature may be redundant in the presence of another highly correlated feature. Feature selection plays an important role in many machine learning problems including handwriting recognition, object detection, and speech recognition.

Feature selection can be seen as a search problem where an algorithm proposes subsets of features and evaluates their quality with respect to the models performance (e.g., prediction accuracy). For any but the smallest feature sets, it is prohibitive to apply exhaustive search using error rate as evaluation metric. In consequence, a number of approaches have been proposed for this problem and they can be categorized by the evaluation metric they apply into wrapper, filter, and embedded methods (Guyon and Elisseeff, 2003).

Wrapper methods use the final machine learning model to score feature subsets. Each new subset is used to train a model, which is tested on a hold-out set and counting correct predictions against groundtruth labels is used as scoring functions. Due to the need to train many different models, such algorithms can be inefficient.

Filter methods use a so-called proxy measure to score the different feature subsets. Popular metrics are often based on mutual information (Peng, Long, and Ding, 2005) or correlation measures (Senliol, Gulgezen, Yu, and Cataltepe, 2008; Hall and Smith 1999). While filter methods are more efficient than wrapper methods, they are not tuned to any particular machine learning model and hence a high-scoring feature subset may still perform poorly in combination with some predictive models.

Embedded methods is a bucket term applied to various techniques that embed the feature selection process in the predictive model construction step. For example, training multiple versions of support vector machines (SVM) and then iteratively removing features with low weights. Such methods are often somewhere in between filter and wrapper methods in terms of computational complexity, but can result in better matchings between feature set and predictive model.

3.9 Case Studies

Here we briefly summarize some of the recent interactive systems, effectively building on the methodology outlined previously and, in particular, leveraging RLs as ML-model.

3.9.1 Natural User Interfaces for Productivity

Mechanical keyboards have remained the preferred method for text entry. However, there are areas where augmenting keyboards with additional input capabilities, such as touch or gestures, can make sense; prior studies have shown the benefits of doing so. (Taylor, Keskin, Hilliges, Izadi, and Helmes, 2014) propose a new type of augmented mechanical keyboard, sensing rich and expressive *motion gestures* performed both *on* and directly *above* the device (see Figure 3.4). The hardware design allows for the mechanical qualities of the keyboard to be preserved, but provides the ability to sense motion above the keys at very high frame-rates (325Hz). However, the sensor, comprising of a matrix of IR proximity sensors, produces a low-resolution (spatially) signal. The coarse but high-speed sensor data generated by the sensor requires a new approach to gesture recognition based on randomized decision forests (RF). One limitation of standard RFs is that they operate on single images and therefore are not well suited for temporal data. Given the sensor speed, the temporal domain is a rich source of information. The work introduces the use of *motion signatures*, extending the RF framework to natively support temporal data. Our method robustly recognizes a large corpus of static, dynamic, and hover gestures on and above the keyboard (cf. Figure 3.4).

3.9.2 Mobile Gesture Recognition

Song, Sérés, Pece, Fanello, Izadi, Keskin and Hilliges, (2014) proposes a novel ML-based algorithm to extend the interaction space around mobile devices by detecting rich gestures

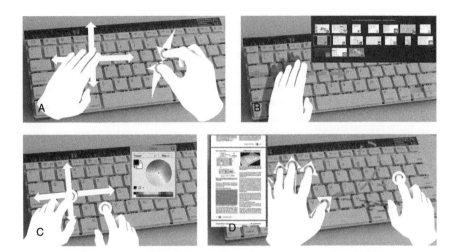

Figure 3.4 Gestures recognized by a RF-based classifier allow users to combine typing and gesturing to (A) navigate documents (B) for task switching (C+D) control of complex applications that require frequent mode-changes (Taylor Keskin, Hilliges, Izadi, and Helmes, 2014).

Figure 3.5 Song, Sérés, Pece, Fanello, Izadi, Keskin and Hilliges, (2014) propose an ML-based algorithm for gesture recognition, expanding the interaction space *around* the mobile device (B), adding in-air gestures and hand-part tracking (D) to commodity off-the-shelf mobile devices, relying only on the device's camera (and no hardware modifications). The paper demonstrates a number of compelling interactive scenarios, including bi-manual input to mapping and gaming applications (C+D). The algorithm runs in real time and can even be used on ultra-mobile devices such as smartwatches (E).

performed behind or in front of the screen (cf. Figure 3.5). The technique uses *only* the built-in RGB camera, and recognizes a wide range of gestures robustly, copes with user variation, and varying lighting conditions. Furthermore, the algorithm runs in real-time entirely on off-the-shelf, unmodified mobile devices, including compute-limited smartphones and smartwatches. Again, the algorithm is based on random forests (RF), which trade discriminative power and run-time performance against memory consumption. Given a complex enough problem and large enough training set, the memory requirement will grow exponentially with tree depth. This is, of course, a strong limitation for applications on resource-constrained mobile platforms. The main contribution is a general approach, dubbed cascaded forests, to reduce memory consumption drastically, while maintaining classification accuracy.

3.10 Deep Learning

Most of the models we have discussed in this chapter fall into the category of linear models. These models are appealing because they can be fit to data efficiently and reliably, often in closed form or via convex optimization (which provides convergence guarantees). However, such models have the obvious limitation that they can only model linear functions and can therefore not capture the interactions between any two inputs. The traditional approach to extend linear models is to apply the model not directly to x but to transform it first via a non-linear mapping function $\phi(x)$. For example, the kernel trick discussed in Section 3.7.2 implicitly applies such a non-linear mapping ϕ to the inputs which allows for linear classification in the transformed space. We can think of this step as ϕ providing a set of features describing the original inputs x, or, in other words ϕ provides a new representation of x (see Figure 3.6, left). The question then becomes how to choose ϕ.

In traditional ML approaches, two popular strategies are to either use a very generic kernel such as the RBF kernel, but in difficult problems generalization performance can be poor. A second approach is to integrate domain knowledge into manually designed mappings; this was the dominant approach for a long time, but requires deep domain knowledge, and there has been little transfer across different domains such as speech-recognition or computer vision.

The strategy applied by deep learning is then to apply deep neural network architectures to learn ϕ itself. This is appropriately called representation learning. In this setting we can parametrize the learning task as $y = f(x;\Theta, w) = \phi(x;\Theta)^T w$. One can then learn the parameters Θ from a broad class of function families ϕ, and learn parameters w that map from $\phi(x)$ to the desired output (see Figure 3.6). This can be realized by a deep feed-forward network where ϕ is defined by a hidden layer. Such feed-forward networks sacrifice convexity in the optimization, but can learn more complex interactions between inputs and outputs and learn to approximate arbitrary, non-linear functions.

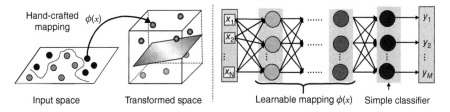

Input space   Transformed space   Learnable mapping $\phi(x)$ Simple classifier

Figure 3.6 Comparison of traditional and deep-learning approaches. Left: a had-designed mapping from low- to high-dimensional spaces is used to transform feature vectors. Right: in deep-learning the mapping $\phi(x)$ and its parameters are learned from a broad family of functions in order to transform the feature representation. A simple classifier can be used in both cases to separate the data in the high-dimensional space. In deep neural network training only the desired output of the top-most (output) layer is specified exactly via the cost function. The learning algorithm needs to find out how to best utilize model capacity of these layers by itself.

A feed-forward network approximates a function by learning the parameters that yield the best mapping between inputs and outputs. They are called feed-forward because information flows strictly forward from x and no feedback mechanisms exist (unless the models are put into recurrence as discussed in the example below). The name network stems from the fact that the function is decomposed into many different functions and a DAG describes how information flows through the different functions. Each function is typically modelled by a layer and the total number of layers determines the depth of the network (hence the name deep learning). One important aspect here is that there are different types of layers, namely the input layer, and the output layer, with hidden layers in between. During training of the network (typically via SGD), we constrain the optimization such that the output layer must produce estimates $\hat{y}$ that are close to the training labels y. However, for the hidden layers, no such specification is given and, loosely speaking, the network must figure out on its own how to use the model capacity these layers provide. Therefore, the training algorithm must decide how to use these layers so that overall the network produces an as-good-as-possible approximation of the true function. Because the output of these intermediate layers isn't shown or used directly, they are called hidden layers.

A further important aspect is that deep learning models use non-linear activation functions to compute the values of the hidden layers, allowing for non-linearity in the approximated functions. The general principle in designing deep learning models is the same as with linear models discussed in this chapter: one needs to define a cost function, an optimization procedure, and provide a training and test dataset. At the core of the success of deep learning techniques lies the back-propagation algorithm that computes gradients for the parameters of the various layers and hence makes the approach amenable to optimization via gradient-based approaches, and SGD in particular.

Currently deep learning approaches are of tremendous importance to applied ML since they form the most successful platform for many application scenarios, including computer vision, signal processing, speech-recognition, natural language processing, and, last but not least, HCI and input recognition. A complete treatment of the subject is not nearly feasible in the context of this chapter and we refer the reader to Goodfellow, Bengio and Courville, (2016) for an in-depth treatment. While HCI is not a 'natural' application domain for deep learning, in the sense that it is more expensive to collect and label data than in many other domains, it is still an extremely powerful tool in many aspects of input recognition. In part motivated by difficulties in finding good hand-crafted features, deep neural network approaches have been successfully applied to various tasks in video-based action recognition (Simonyan and Zisserman, 2014) and speech recognition (Hinton, Deng, Yu, Dahl, rahman Mohamed, Jaitly, Senior, Vanhoucke, Nguyen, Kingsbury and Sainath, 2012). Similarly (Neverova, Wolf, Taylor and Nebout, 2015) use convolutional neural networks (CNNs) for sign language recognition based on combined colour and depth data. In (Song, Wang, Lien, Poupyrev and Hilliges, 2016) deep learning is applied to dynamic gesture recognition using high-frequency radar data. Furthermore, significant improvements in human activity recognition based on accelerometers or gyroscopes have been demonstrated (Ordonez and Roggen, 2016).

3.10.1 RF-based Dynamic Input Recognition

Here we discuss one exemplary application of deep-learning in HCI, highlighting the potential but also the need for original research overcoming some of the domain specific difficulties.

Song and colleagues (2016) propose a deep learning architecture, specifically designed for radio-frequency based gesture recognition. The work leverages a high-frequency (60 GHz), short-range radar based sensor (Google's Soli sensor (Lien, Gillian, Karagozler, Amihood, Schwesig, Olson, Raja, and Poupyrev, 2016)). The signal has unique properties such as resolving motion at a very fine level and allowing for segmentation in range and velocity spaces rather than image space. This enables recognition of new types of inputs but poses significant difficulties for the design of input recognition algorithms. The proposed algorithm is capable of detecting a rich set of dynamic gestures and can resolve small motions of fingers in fine detail.

This particular project is interesting because it highlights the previously mentioned difficulties in finding hand-crafted features. The sensor used produces data with very specific characteristics and many traditional approaches (that have been designed for other sensor modalities) are not applicable one to one. In particular, many such algorithms rely on spatial information (e.g., Kim, Hilliges, Izadi, Butler, Chen, Oikonomidis, and Olivier, 2012; Sharp, Keskin, Robertson, Taylor, Shotton, Kim, Rhemann, Leichter, Vinnikov, Wei, Freedman, Kohli, Krupka, Fitzgibbon and Izadi, 2015; Taylor, Keskin, Hilliges, Izadi and Helmes, 2014), whereas Soli resolves dynamics (i.e., finger motion) at a fine-grained level but does not resolve the spatial configuration of objects in front of the sensor directly (cf. Figure 3.7).

The paper reports on experiments with manual feature extraction and use of several classifiers such as SVMs and RFs. However, achieving acceptable accuracies is reported to remain elusive and would have required deep domain knowledge about the radar signal

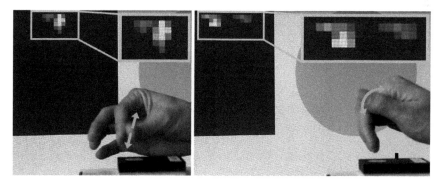

Figure 3.7 Soli signal properties. The sensor does not resolve spatial properties of objects but is very sensitive to fine-grained motion. Pixel intensity corresponds to reflected energy; horizontal axis is velocity; vertical axis is range (Song, Wang, Lien, Poupyrev, and Hilliges, 2016).

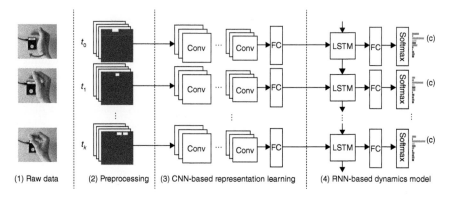

Figure 3.8 (1) Data produced by the sensor when sliding index finger over thumb. (2) Preprocessing and stacking of frames. (3) Convolutional Neural Networks. (4) Recurrent Neural Networks with per-frame predictions.

itself. Furthermore, the paper highlights the need for modelling of temporal dynamics, which is inherently difficult with frame-by-frame classification approaches.

In response to these difficulties, a deep learning architecture, schematically shown in Figure 3.8, is proposed that combines the steps of *representation learning* and *dynamic modelling* into a single end-to-end trainable model.

More specifically, the network learns a feature representation function $f(I_t, \Theta)$ that maps inputs I_t (i.e., Range-Doppler images) to outputs x_t, where Θ contains the weights of the network. During learning, the classification error of the overall pipeline is used as optimization criterion. Designing CNN architectures is a complex task involving many hyperparameters such as the number of layers and neurons, activation functions, and filter sizes. In the experiments section, the paper reports on different CNN variants. Most saliently, a comparison with a network adapted from computer vision (Simonyan and Zisserman, 2014) shows the need for a custom network architecture. This aspect of the work illustrates the flexibility that is gained from the modular, network-like properties of deep learning. With a relatively small number of ingredients one can design custom architectures for different use-cases and problem settings quickly.

3.10.1.1 Modelling Gesture Dynamics with RNNs

Since CNNs alone can not exploit the temporal information embedded in the RF data a long short-term memory (LSTM) recurrent neural network (RNN) is used for the modelling of dynamics.

Recurrent neural networks differ from feed-forward networks in that they contain feedback loops, encoding contextual information of a temporal sequence. Given an input sequence $x = (x_1, ..., x_T)$, where in our case the x_t is the feature vector extracted by the CNN at time t, the hidden states of a recurrent layer $h = (h_1, ..., h_T)$ and the outputs $q = (q_1, ..., q_T)$ can be attained:

$$h_t = H(\Theta_{ih} x_t + \Theta_{hh} h_{t-1} + b_h) \qquad (3.25)$$

$$\mathbf{q}_t = \Theta_{ho}\mathbf{h}_t + \mathbf{b}_o \tag{3.26}$$

where Θs are weight matrices connecting input, hidden, and output layers, $\mathbf{b}$ are bias vectors, and H is the hidden layer's activation function. Crucially, the hidden states $\mathbf{h}_t$ are passed on from timestep to timestep while the outputs $\mathbf{q}_t$ are fed to a softmax layer (a straightforward multi-class extension of the binary loss we introduced in the logistic regression example in Section 3.7.1), providing per-frame gesture probabilities $\hat{\mathbf{y}}_t$.

$$\hat{\mathbf{y}}_t = \text{softmax}(\mathbf{q}_t) \tag{3.27}$$

When learning over-long sequences, standard RNNs can suffer from numerical instabilities known as the vanishing or exploding gradient problem. To alleviate this issue LSTMs use memory cells to store, modify, and access internal state via special gates, allowing for better modelling of long-range temporal connections (see Figure 3.9). Very loosely speaking this means a more involved computation of the hidden layers outputs $\mathbf{h}_t$ For each unit, the relation between input, internal state, and output is formulated as follows:

$$\begin{aligned}
\mathbf{i}_t &= \sigma\left(\Theta_{xi}\mathbf{x}_t + \Theta_{hi}\mathbf{h}_{t-1} + \Theta_{ci}\mathbf{c}_{t-1} + \mathbf{b}_i\right) \\
\mathbf{f}_t &= \sigma\left(\Theta_{xf}\mathbf{x}_t + \Theta_{hf}\mathbf{h}_{t-1} + \Theta_{cf}\mathbf{c}_{t-1} + \mathbf{b}_f\right) \\
\mathbf{c}_t &= \mathbf{f}_t\mathbf{c}_{t-1} + \mathbf{i}_t \tanh(\Theta_{xc}\mathbf{x}_t + \Theta_{hc}\mathbf{h}_{t-1} + \mathbf{b}_c) \\
\mathbf{o}_t &= \sigma\left(\Theta_{xo}\mathbf{x}_t + \Theta_{ho}\mathbf{h}_{t-1} + \Theta_{co}\mathbf{c}_t + \mathbf{b}_o\right) \\
\mathbf{h}_t &= \mathbf{o}_t \tanh(c_t)
\end{aligned} \tag{3.28}$$

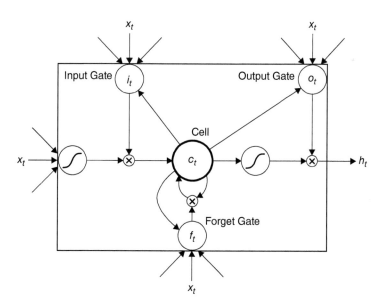

Figure 3.9 Illustration of LSTM input, output, cell, and gates and their connections. Computations are listed in Equation 3.28.

where σ is the logistic sigmoid function, and the input gate, forget gate, output gate, and cell activation are respectively represented by i, f, o, and c. The indices on the weight matrices Θ represent for input-to-hidden, hidden-to-output, and hidden-to-hidden connections, respectively.

Notably, the whole network is trained in an end-to-end fashion. That is, RNN and CNN are trained together. For this purpose the total loss for a given sequence of x values paired with a sequence of y values would then be just the sum of the losses over all the time steps. For example, if $L_{(t)}$ is the negative log-likelihood of $y_{(t)}$ given $(x_1, \ldots, x_T)$, then

$$L((x_1, \ldots, x_T), (y_1, \ldots, y_T)) = \sum_t L_{(t)} = - \sum_t \log p_{\text{model}}(y_t | (x_1, \ldots, x_T)), \quad (3.29)$$

where $p_{model}(y_t|(x_1, \ldots, x_T))$ is attained by reading the entry for y_t from the (model) output vector $\hat{\boldsymbol{y}}_t$. Computing the gradient for this loss is an expensive operation since for each time step a forward-pass is necessary at the end of which the softmax layer in the RNN predicts a gesture label for which we compute a loss value and then use back-propagation to compute the gradient of the network's weights Θ. Gradients and loss values are then summed over time and finally the network's parameters are optimized, minimizing the combined loss. This training procedure is known as backpropagation through time Werbos (1990).

3.11 Discussion

This chapter has discussed a principled and unified framework to input recognition that leverages state-of-the-art methods and algorithms from machine learning. Following the techniques outlined here enables implementation of sensing-based input recognition algorithms that are both efficient and robust to sensor noise and variation across users and across instances of the action being performed by the user. We conclude with a discussion on the limitations of current approaches and interesting directions for future work.

3.11.1 Not Just Applied ML—Unique Challenges in the HCI Setting

We have also discussed several cases in which input recognition goes beyond black box applications of existing methods in ML. To date such cases are often limited to specializations of ML algorithms to fit a particular need in the application domain. For example, both case studies discussed in Section 3.9 and the deep-learning approach discussed in Section 3.10.1 required changes to the model architecture or the representations used itself. While solving the application domain problem would not have been possible without these changes, little of this work is so general that it could be fed back into the ML literature. However, there are many aspects of HCI and input recognition in particular that require deeper engagement with the technical aspects of ML and at the same time open up interesting directions for original research.

We have mentioned in the beginning of this chapter that the design of interaction paradigms is a dynamic process, i.e., sensing technology evolves, user expectations and behaviour evolves, and even if the interface remains fixed, users will change their behaviour over time. All of these aspects are at odds with the traditional ML setting, where typically datasets remain fixed, and once a model has been optimized on this dataset, it too remains fixed. This is especially true for deep learning approaches that require large training data sets and perform training in an iterative stochastic fashion. This results in models that are fairly rigid once trained. Technically speaking once the optimizer has found a local but deep minima there is not much incentive for the algorithm to move. Therefore, a single sample, or a even a small number of new examples provided by the user after training has finished, won't change the weights of the model much and hence won't change the behaviour of the system. This calls for new approaches that allow for updating of already exiting models via a small number of additional training samples. Recent approaches enabling so-called one-shot learning in image classification tasks may be an interesting starting point.

Furthermore, (training) data in general is a problem in HCI in several ways. First, collecting data and the associated labels is an laborious and expensive process. In many areas this can be partially automated via crowd-sourcing or by providing users with additional value in exchange of their labelling work (e.g., online CAPTCHA verification, tagging friends in social networks). Unfortunately this is seldomly possible in the HCI context since normally data collection requires users to physically be present in the lab, to wear special equipment, and to perform input-like tasks in a repetitive fashion. Furthermore, due to the proliferation of and fast-paced evolution of sensing technologies, the lifetime of collected datasets is limited by the lifetime of the underlying acquisition technology. Especially emerging sensors and their signals can change drastically over short time horizons. Finally, changes in user behaviour and usage patterns need to be reflected in such datasets, which would require constant updating and curation of datasets. Finally, currently the most successful models in ML require large amounts of data for training and have significant memory and runtime consumption once trained. This means that such models are not directly applicable for mobile and wearable use since such devices are often much more constrained in memory and computational resources.

Together these issues call for innovation both algorithmically and in terms of tools and procedures. First, there is an opportunity for algorithms that combine the discriminative power and model capacity of current state-of-the art techniques with more flexibility in terms of online adaptation and refinement using a small number of sample points. Furthermore, advancements in terms of computational and memory efficiency would be necessary to fully leverage the power of ML in mobile and wearable settings. Second, we currently often use recognition accuracy as optimization criterion. However, this is sometimes merely a poor surrogate for the ultimate goal of usability. Therefore, finding ways of more directly capturing the essence of what makes for a 'good' or 'bad' UI and using this information to adjust the parameters of underlying ML models would be a hugely fruitful direction for research. Finally, HCI could contribute novel approaches and tools in terms of data-collection, labelling, and long-term curation of datasets. Moreover, there lie opportunities in tools and methods that allow technically untrained users and developers without an ML background to understand the behaviour of these algorithms more intuitively and to enable them to make predictions about the impact of changing a classifier or providing additional data (or labels).

3.12 Conclusions

In summary, this chapter has discussed the area of sensor-based input recognition. it is an area of research that lies at the heart of HCI and that has the potential to change the face of the computing landscape by altering how humans interact with machines at a fundamental level. This area is full of interesting technical and conceptual challenges and we hope to have been able to provide a useful summary of the various contributing aspects.

....

REFERENCES

Benbasat, A. Y., and Paradiso, J. A., 2002. An inertial measurement framework for gesture recognition and applications. In *Revised Papers from the International Gesture Workshop on Gesture and Sign Languages in Human-Computer Interaction*, GW '01, London, UK: Springer-Verlag, pp. 9–20.

Bishop, C. M., 2006. *Pattern Recognition and Machine Learning (Information Science and Statistics)*. Springer-Verlag New York, Inc., Secaucus, NJ, USA.

Boser, B. E., Guyon, I. M., and Vapnik, V. N., 1992. A training algorithm for optimal margin classifiers. In *Proceedings of the Fifth Annual Workshop on Computational Learning Theory*, COLT '92, New York, NY: ACM. pp. 144–52.

Bradski, G., 2000. The Open CV library. *Dr. Dobb's Journal of Software Tools*, 25(11), pp. 120–6.

Breiman, L., 2001. Random forests. *Machine Learning*, 45(1), pp. 5–32.

Cauchy, A., 1847. Méthode générale pour la résolution des systemes d'équations simultanées. *Comptes rendus de l'Académie des Sciences*, 25(1847), pp. 536–8.

Chan, L., Hsieh, C.-H., Chen, Y.-L., Yang, S., Huang, D.-Y., Liang, R.-H., and Chen, B.-Y., 2015. Cyclops: Wearable and single-piece full-body gesture input devices. In: *CHI '14: Proceedings of the 33rd Annual ACM Conference on Human Factors in Computing Systems*. New York, NY: ACM. pp. 3001–9.

Cramir, H., 1946. Mathematical methods of statistics. Princeton, MA: Princeton University Press.

Goodfellow, I., Bengio, Y., and Courville, A., 2016. *Deep Learning*. MIT Press. http://www.deeplearningbook.org.

Guyon, I., and Elisseeff, A., 2003. An introduction to variable and feature selection. *Journal of Machine Learning Research*, 3, pp. 1157–82.

Hall, M. A., and Smith, L. A., 1999. Feature selection for machine learning: Comparing a correlation-based filter approach to the wrapper. In: *Proceedings of the Twelfth International Florida Artificial Intelligence Research Society Conference*. Palo Alto, CA: AAAI Press. pp. 235–9.

Harrison, C., Tan, D., and Morris, D., 2010. Skinput: Appropriating the body as an input surface. In *Proceedings of the SIGCHI Conference on Human Factors in Computing Systems*, CHI '10, New York, NY: ACM. pp. 453–62.

Hinton, G., Deng, L., Yu, D., Dahl, G., rahmanMohamed, A., Jaitly, N., Senior, A., Vanhoucke, V., Nguyen, P., Kingsbury, B., and Sainath, T., 2012. Deep neural networks for acoustic modeling in speech recognition. *IEEE Signal Processing Magazine*, 29, pp. 82–97.

James, G., Witten, D., Hastie, T., and Tibshirani, R., 2013. *An Introduction to Statistical Learning: with Applications in R*. New York, NY: Springer.

Keskin, C., Kiraé, F., Kara, Y. E., and Akarun, L., 2012. Hand pose estimation and hand shape classification using multi-layered randomized decision forests. In: *European Conference on Computer Vision*. Berlin: Springer. pp. 852–63.

Kim, D., Hilliges, O., Izadi, S., Butler, A. D., Chen, J., Oikonomidis, I., and Olivier, P., 2012. Digits: Freehand 3D interactions anywhere using a wrist-worn gloveless sensor. In: *Proc. ACM UIST*, New York, NY: ACM, p. 167.

Kim, D., Izadi, S., Dostal, J., Rhemann, C., Keskin, C., Zach, C., Shotton, J., Large, T., Bathiche, S., Niessner, M., Butler, D. A., Fanello, S., and Pradeep, V., 2014. Retrodepth: 3d silhouette sensing for high-precision input on and above physical surfaces. In: *CHI'14: Proceedings of the 32nd Annual ACM Conference on Human Factors in Computing Systems*. New York, NY: ACM, pp. 1377–86. ACM.

LeGoc, M., Taylor, S., Izadi, S., and Keskin, C., 2014. A low-cost transparent electric field sensor for 3d interaction on mobile devices. In: *CHI '14: Proceedings of the 32nd Annual ACM Conference on Human Factors in Computing Systems*. New York, NY: ACM. pp. 3167–70.

Lien, J., Gillian, N., Karagozler, M. E., Amihood, P., Schwesig, C., Olson, E., Raja, H., and Poupyrev, I., 2016. Soli: Ubiquitous gesture sensing with millimeter wave radar. ACM Transactions on Graphics, 35(4), pp. 142:1–142:19.

Mitchell, T. M., 1997. *Machine learning*. Burr Ridge, IL: McGraw Hill.

Mohri, M., Rostamizadeh, A., and Talwalkar, A., 2012. *Foundations of Machine Learning*. Cambridge, MA: MIT Press.

Neverova, N., Wolf, C., Taylor, G. W., and Nebout, F., 2015. *Hand Segmentation with Structured Convolutional Learning*. Cham, Switzerland: Springer. pp. 687–702.

Ordonez, F., and Roggen, D., 2016. Deep convolutional and lstm recurrent neural networks for multimodal wearable activity recognition. *Sensors*, 16(1), pp. 1–25.

Pedregosa, F., Varoquaux, G., Gramfort, A., Michel, V., Thirion, B., Grisel, O., Blondel, M., Prettenhofer, P., Weiss, R., Dubourg, V., Vanderplas, J., Passos, A., Cournapeau, D., Brucher, M., Perrot, M., and Duchesnay, E., 2011. Scikit-learn: Machine learning in Python. *Journal of Machine Learning Research*, 12, pp. 2825–30.

Peng, H., Long, F., and Ding, C., 2005. Feature selection based on mutual information criteria of max-dependency, max-relevance, and min-redundancy. *IEEE Transactions on Pattern Analysis and Machine Intelligence*, 27(8), pp. 1226–38.

Pu, Q., Gupta, S., Gollakota, S., and Patel, S., 2013. Whole-home gesture recognition using wireless signals. In: *MobiCom '13: Proceedings of the 19th Annual International Conference on Mobile Computing & Networking*. New York, NY: ACM, pp. 27–38.

Radhakrishna Rao, C., 1945. Information and the accuracy attainable in the estimation of statistical parameters. *Bulletin of Calcutta Mathematical Society*, 37, pp. 81–91.

Russell, S. J., and Norvig, P., 2010. *Artificial Intelligence: A Modern Approach*. Discovering great minds of science. New York, NY: Prentice Hall.

Sato, M., Poupyrev, I., and Harrison, C., 2012. Touché: Enhancing touch interaction on humans, screens, liquids, and everyday objects. In: *CHI '12: Proceedings of the SIGCHI Conference on Human Factors in Computing Systems*. New York, NY: ACM, pp. 483–92.

Schélkopf, B., Burges, C. J. C., and Smola, A. J., eds. 1999. *Advances in Kernel Methods: Support Vector Learning*. Cambridge, MA: MIT Press.

Senliol, B., Gulgezen, G., Yu, L., and Cataltepe, Z., 2008. Fast correlation based filter (fcbf) with a different search strategy. In: *ISCIS 08: 23rd International Symposium on Computer and Information Sciences*. New York, NY: IEEE, pp. 1–4.

Sharp, T., Keskin, C., Robertson, D., Taylor, J., Shotton, J., Kim, D., Rhemann, C., Leichter, I., Vinnikov, A., Wei, Y., Freedman, D., Kohli, P., Krupka, E., Fitzgibbon, A., and Izadi, S., 2015. Accurate, Robust, and Flexible Real-time Hand Tracking. In: *CHI '15 Proceedings of the 33rd Annual ACM Conference on Human Factors in Computing Systems*. New York, NY: ACM, pp. 3633–42.

Shotton, J., Sharp, T., Kipman, A., Fitzgibbon, A., Finocchio, M., Blake, A., Cook, M., and Moore, R., 2013. Real-time human pose recognition in parts from single depth images. *Communications of the ACM*, 56(1), pp. 116–24.

Simonyan, K., and Zisserman, A., 2014. Two-stream convolutional networks for action recognition in videos. *CoRR*, abs/1406.2199.

Song, J., Pece, F., Sérés, G., Koelle, M., and Hilliges, O., 2015. Joint estimation of 3d hand position and gestures from monocular video for mobile interaction. In: *CHI '15: Proceedings of the 33rd Annual ACM Conference on Human Factors in Computing Systems*. New York, NY: ACM, pp. 3657–60.

Song, J., Sörös, G., Pece, F., Fanello, S. R., Izadi, S., Keskin, C., and Hilliges, O., 2014. In-air Gestures Around Unmodified Mobile Devices. In: *UIST '14: Proceedings of the 27th Annual ACM Symposium on User Interface Software and Technology*. New York, NY: ACM, pp. 319–29.

Song, J., Wang, S., Lien, J., Poupyrev, I., and Hilliges, O., 2016. Interacting with Soli: Exploring Fine-Grained Dynamic Gesture Recognition in the Radio-Frequency Spectrum. In: *UIST '16: ACM Symposium on User Interface Software and Technologies*. New York, NY: ACM, pp. 851–60.

Steinwart, I., and Christmann, A., 2008. Support vector machines New York, NY: Springer-Verlag.

Tang, D., Yu, T. H., and Kim, T. K., 2013. Real-time articulated hand pose estimation using semi-supervised transductive regression forests. In: *2013 IEEE International Conference on Computer Vision*. New York, NY: IEEE, pp. 3224–31.

Taylor, S., Keskin, C., Hilliges, O., Izadi, S., and Helmes, J., 2014. Type-hover-swipe in 96 bytes: A motion sensing mechanical keyboard. In: *CHI '14: Proceedings of the 32nd Annual ACM Conference on Human Factors in Computing Systems*. New York, NY: ACM, pp. 1695–704.

Vapnik, V. N., 1998. *Statistical learning theory*, Volume 1. New York, NY: Wiley.

Vapnik, V. N., 2013. *The nature of statistical learning theory*. New York, NY: Springer Science & Business Media.

Werbos, P. J., 1990. Backpropagation through time: what it does and how to do it. *Proceedings of the IEEE*, 78(10), pp. 1550–60.

Witten, I. H., Frank, E., Hall, M. A., and Pal, C. J., 2016. *Data Mining: Practical machine learning tools and techniques*. Burlington, MA: Morgan Kaufmann.

Wobbrock, J. O., Ringel Morris, M., and Wilson, A. D., 2009. User-defined gestures for surface computing. In: *Proceedings of the SIGCHI Conference on Human Factors in Computing Systems* New York, NY: ACM, pp. 1083–92.

Yeo, H.-S., Flamich, G., Schrempf, P., Harris-Birtill, D., and Quigley, A., 2016. Radarcat: Radar categorization for input & interaction. In: *UIST '16: Proceedings of the 29th Annual Symposium on User Interface Software and Technology*. New York, NY: ACM, pp. 833–41.

PART II
Design

4

Combinatorial Optimization for User Interface Design

ANTTI OULASVIRTA,
ANDREAS KARRENBAUER

4.1 Introduction

Combinatorial optimization offers a powerful yet under-explored computational method for attacking hard problems in user interface design. 'The science of better', or optimization and operations research, has its roots in mathematics, computer science, and economics. *To optimize* refers to the act and process of obtaining the best solution under given circumstances, and *combinatorial optimization* a case where solutions are defined as combinations of multiple *discrete* decisions (Rao, 2009). To design an interactive system by optimization, a number of discrete decisions is made such that they constitute as good whole as possible.

The goal of this chapter is to advance applications of combinatorial optimization in user interface design. We start with a definition of *design task* in combinatorial optimization:

$$\max_{d \in D} f(d)$$

where d is a design in a set of *feasible designs D*, and f is the *objective function*. In plain words, the task is to find the design that yields the highest value of this function. For example, we might be looking for the design of a web form that maximizes user performance in filling it in. However, this definition does not expose the structure of the design problem.

The following definition makes that explicit Rao (2009):

$$\text{Find } \boldsymbol{x} = \begin{pmatrix} x_1 \\ x_2 \\ \vdots \\ x_n \end{pmatrix} \in \boldsymbol{X} \text{ which maximizes } f(\boldsymbol{x}),$$

where $\boldsymbol{x}$ is an n-dimensional *design vector*, each dimension describing a *design variable*, $\boldsymbol{X}$ is the set of feasible designs (all to-be-considered design vectors), and $f(\boldsymbol{x})$ is the objective function.

Computational Interaction. Antti Oulasvirta, Per Ola Kristensson, Xiaojun Bi, Andrew Howes (Eds).
© Oxford University Press 2018. Published 2018 by Oxford University Press.

This revised task definition exposes the design space and its structure in X. The design space X is contained in the Cartesian product of the domains X_i of the design variables x_i. Formally $X \subseteq X_1 \times \ldots \times X_n$, where X_i is the domain of the i-th design variable, e.g., $X_i = \{0, 1\}$ for a binary decision variable, such as whether to select a feature or not. A design variable can address any open decision that can be defined via boolean, integer, or categorical variables. In a real design project, many properties of a interface would be preassigned, but some are open and treated as variables. Examples include sizes and colours and positions of an element and their types. In many combinations they have to satisfy functional and other requirements. These are collectively called *design constraints*. For example, when designing a Web layout, we should not place elements such that they overlap.

The first insight we can make is that some problems in design are exceedingly large, too large for trial-and-error approaches in design. For instance, to design an interactive layout (e.g., menu), one must fix the types, colours, sizes, and positions of elements, as well as higher-level properties, such as which functionality to include. The number of combinations of such choices easily gets very large. For example, for n functions there are $2^n - 1$ ways to combine them to an application, which for only fifty functions means 1,125,899,906,842,623 possibilities. Further, assuming that fifty commands have been selected, they can be organized into a hierarhical menu in $100! \approx 10^{158}$ ways.

The definition also exposes evaluative knowledge in $f(x)$. The objective function[1] encodes this evaluative knowledge. Technically, it is a function that assigns an *objective score* to a design candidate. It formalizes what is assumed to be 'good' or 'desirable', or, inversely, undesirable when the task is to minimize. The design candidate (a design vector) that obtains the highest (or lowest, when minimizing) score is the *optimum design*.

In applications in HCI, a key challenge is to formulate objective functions that encapsulate goodness in end-users' terms. This can be surface features of the interface (e.g., visual balance) or expected performance of users (e.g., 'task A should be completed as quickly as possible'), users' subjective preferences, and so on. It is tempting but naive to construct objective function based on heuristics. Those might be easy to express and compute, but they might have little value in producing good designs. It must be kept in mind that the quality of a interface is determined not by the designer, nor some quality of the interface, but by end-users in their performance and experiences. An objective function should be viewed as a predictor of quality for end users. It must capture some essential tendencies in the biological, psychological, behavioural, and social aspects of human conduct. This fact drives a departure from traditional application areas of operations research and optimization, where objective functions have been based on natural sciences and economics.

Another challenge is the combination of multiple objectives into an objective function:

$$f(x) = \omega_1 f_1(x) + \cdots + \omega_q f_q(x) \tag{4.1}$$

---

[1] Also called loss function, error function, energy function, merit function, criteria function, reward function, evaluative function, utility function, goodness function, or fitness function.

where q is the number of objectives considered, $f_i(x)$ is the function for objective i, and ω_i is the weight[2] attributed to i. Linearization is one way to deal with multiple criteria, and many methods have been presented to capture designers' intentions (Rao, 2009). While formulating and calibrating of multi-objective tasks is challenging, it must be remembered that designers solving design problems similarly make assumptions about the way in which the objectives are traded off. Combinatorial optimization can expose the assumptions and their consequences.

When a task has been defined, including the feasible set and an objective function, algorithmic solvers can attack it. This is the basis of benefits for practical efforts in design. Solvers can be used to find the optimal design, or surprising solutions, or designs with distinct tradeoffs, or solutions that strike the best compromise among competing objectives, or are robust to changes in conditions. A designer can identify how far a present interface is from the best achievable design. Modern optimization methods offer a higher chance of finding good or optimal solutions and, in certain conditions, mathematical guarantees (bounds) can be computed. Moreover, all choices are documented and scrutinable and can support knowledge sharing in design teams. In this regard, a combinatorial optimization task naturally incorporates a form of *design rationale* that is not only descriptive, but executable (Carroll, 2000).

Notwithstanding the relatively high cost of defining a tractable design task, combinatorial optimization is not only compatible with user-centred design but can facilitate it by assisting designers in problem-solving and automating certain tasks entirely. Instead of a designer generating designs and having them evaluated with users, the designer defines a task and lets the computer solve it. In one-shot optimization, this is done once (think about keyboards). However, advances in algorithms and hardware have made it possible to consider integration of optimization into design tools. In interactive optimization, computation is steered by the designer in the loop.

Prior to this chapter, there has been no attempt to elaborate and discuss the assumptions and principles of combinatorial optimization in user interface design. The goal of the chapter is to lay out the principles of formulating design tasks for combinatorial optimization. We focus on two obstacles: (1) definition of a design task, and (2) encoding of design and research knowledge in an objective functions.

First, mathematical definition of interface design problems has been difficult and became an impediment to applications. How can we present mathematically design problems that consist of multiple interrelated decisions and several objectives? In the absence of task definitions, applications in HCI were long limited to mainly keyboards. To expand the scope of optimizable design problems in HCI, it is thus necessary to research the mathematical definition of design.

Second, what goes in $f(x)$ is pivotal to the quality of designs. In essence, defining f 'equips' the search algorithm with design knowledge that predicts how users interact and experience. Therefore, in the design of objective functions one should favor predictive models rooted in well-tested theories. With increasing understanding of how to formulate

---

[2] Alternatively: tuning factor, calibration factor, scaling factor, or importance factor.

objective functions gauging design goals such as usability and user experience, new applications have been made possible, for example, in menu systems, gestural input, visualizations, widget GUIs, web layouts, and wireframe designs (Oulasvirta, 2017).

4.2 Interface Optimization: A Brief History

The idea of designing interfaces by means of optimization is not new. It has been invented, revisited, and developed over the course of several decades and across multiple fields, including not only computer science, but also human factors and HCI. August Drovak, the psychologist who invented the Dvorak Simplified Keyboard (DSK), can be considered an early pioneer. Dvorak manually explored better layouts for an improved typewriter design, challenging the predominant Qwerty layout. To inform design decisions, he referred to statistics of English language and novel experimental findings on typing performance (Dvorak, Merrick, Dealey, and Ford, 1936). While the design of DSK turned out to be better than Qwerty in empirical tests, it ultimately failed to replace it, perhaps due to insufficient gains in typing performance. However, Dvorak set an enduring example for systematic modelled design.

In the history of research that followed Dvorak, four discoveries have been made to advance combinatorial optimization methods in user interface design:

1. The decomposition of design problems into constituent decisions represented with decision variables;

2. The expression of design heuristics and psychological models in objective functions;

3. The modelling of technical constraints of devices and interfaces; and

4. The inclusion of human designer in the loop with interactive optimization.

The idea of defining a complex design problem via its constituent design variables is rooted in Fritz Zwicky's 'morphological analysis' (Zwicky, 1948). Zwicky proposed breaking down core decisions to obtain a finite solution space called the 'Zwicky cube'. While it primarily targets understanding of problems, and not their solution, it was the basis of the central HCI concept of *design space* (e.g., Card, Mackinlay and Robertson, 1991). Herbert Simon and colleagues proposed the first structured representation of complex human activities that permitted algorithmic solutions. They pioneered the concept of a search tree (Simon, 1973). Human activities that appear complex at surface, such as chess, could be broken down to smaller decisions that form a decision structure in the form of a tree. Problem-solving activities, then, are about traversing this tree. This idea informed the development of engineering design methods (Cross & Roy, 1989). While applications in user interfaces remained distant, it put forward the idea that complex design problems can be algorithmically solved if decomposed in the right way.

The foundations of combinatorial optimization methods were laid during the two decades following World War II (Rao, 2009). While optimization revolutionarized management, engineering, operations research, and economics, it was in the late 1970s when it was first applied to interface design. Rainer Burkard and colleagues formulated the design of typewriter layouts as *a quadratic assignment problem* (QAP) (Burkard and Offermann, 1977). However, the objective function used unrealistic estimates of finger travel times. Nevertheless, Burkard's work permitted the use of known solvers for QAP. Their definition also placed the problem in the context of other problems in computer science, exposing it as an NP-complete problem. Many other problems in user interface design would fall to this same class. It was more than a decade later, however, when data from empirical studies of typists were used to form a more realistic objective function (Light and Anderson, 1993). A milestone was reached in the late 1990s, when Fitts' law, weighted by bigram frequencies in English, was introduced as the objective function optimizing for typing performance (Zhai, Hunter, and Smith, 2002). Emerging epirical evidence suggested superiority of performance-optimized keyboard layouts over the Qwerty layout.

The idea of using models of human performance and cognition to inform the choice of interface designs is rooted in Stuart Card and colleagues' seminal work in the early 1980s (Card, Newell, and Moran, 1983). Card and colleagues referred to operations research as a model for organizing HCI research and proposed a cognitive simulation of a user, called GOMS, to replace expensive user studies and to be able to predict the consequences of design choices. A designer could now evaluate an interface by simulating how users perceive, think, and act when completing tasks. While subsequent work extended modelling to factors like errors, memory functioning, and learning, cognitive simulations became difficult to use and fell out of pace with the rapid development of technology. To aid practitioners, mathematical simplifications and interactive modelling environments were developed, yet these were not combined with algorithmic search. The models were not used to *generate* designs.

A decade later, human factors researchers noted that ergonomics researchers should not be content with studies and theories, but should actively seek to identify optimal conditions for human performance (Fisher, 1993; Wickens and Kramer, 1985). The first applications concerned the arrangement of buttons on menus and multi-function displays. As objective functions, they developed analytical models of visual search, selection time, and learning (Francis 2000; Liu, Francis, and Salvendy, 2002). This work extended the use of predictive models from Fitts' law to consider aspects of attention and memory. However, since little advice was given on how to formulate more complex design tasks, or how to solve them efficiently, designs were still limited to parameter optimizations and simple mappings.

Within the last two decades, these advances have been integrated into what can be called *model-based interface optimization*: using models of interaction and technology in the objective function (Eisenstein, Vanderdonckt, and Puerta, 2001; Gajos and Weld 2004; Oulasvirta, 2017). Three milestones can be distinguished in this space. The first is the formal definition of a user interface technology as the object of optimization. Software engineers proposed formal abstractions of user interfaces (UIDLs) to describe the interface and its properties, operation logic, and relationships to other parts of the system (Eisenstein, Vanderdonckt, and Puerta, 2001). UIDLs can be used to compile interfaces in different languages and to port them across platforms. However, since an UIDL alone does not contain information about the user, their use was limited to transformations and retargetings instead of complete redesigns. The second milestone was the encoding of design heuristics in objective functions. For example, Peter O'Donovan and colleagues have formulated an energy minimization approach to the design of page layouts using heuristics like alignment, visual importance, white space, and balance (O'Donovan, Agarwala, and Hertzmann, 2014). The approach improves the visual appeal of optimized layouts. However, such heuristics are surface characteristics and they may lack substantive link with objectives that users consider important, such as task completion time or aesthetics. For example, the amount of white space may or may not predict aesthetic experience. Moreover, resolving conflicts among multiple conflicting heuristics became a recognized issue. The third milestone is the direct use of predictive models and simulations of users in objective functions, extending the work that started in computer science and human factors. For example, Krzystzof Gajos and colleagues explored model-based approaches in the design of widget layouts, considering models of motor performance in conjunction with design heuristics for visual impairments (Gajos and Weld, 2004). This approach has been extended to the design of menu systems, gestural inputs, information visualization, and web page layouts (Oulasvirta, 2017).

A parallel thread of research has looked at exploitation of optimization methods in design tools. *Interactive optimization* is the idea of a human designer specifying and steering the search process. The key motivation is the fact that the standard 'fire and forget' paradigm of optimization methods is a poor fit with design practice. Designers cannot be expected to provide point-precise input values a priori. By contrast, they are known to constantly refine the problem definition, mix activities like sketching and evaluation and reflection, and draw from tacit knowledge. Techniques for interactive optimization can be divided according to four dimensions: (1) interaction techniques and data-driven approaches for specification of a design task for an optimizer; (2) control techniques offered for steering the search process; (3) techniques for selection, exploration and refinement of outputs (designs) and (4) level of proactivity taken by the tool, for example in guiding the designer toward good designs (as determined by an objective function). Some illustrative examples include DesignScape, which supports rapid exploration of alternative layouts with an energy minimization scheme (O'Donovan, Agarwala, and Hertzmann, 2015), MenuOptimizer, which provides a high level of control for specifying a task and actively visualizes usability-related metrics to guide the designer to choose better designs (Bailly, Oulasvirta, Kötzing, and Hoppe, 2013), and SketchPlorer, which tries to automatically recognize the design task and explores the design for diverse designs to serve as the basis of design exploration (Todi, Weir, and Oulasvirta, 2016).

4.3 Integer Programming Approach

We take up *integer programming* (IP) as the formalism to expose and discuss user interface design problems. For a practitioner, it offers a powerful tool for modelling and solving optimization problems using modern IP solvers. For an academic, it offers a rigorous basis for understanding the structure of design tasks, even if the problem would be solved by other methods than exact methods like IP. The key decisions, constraints, and objectives are expressed in an accessible way that is natural for interface design. Even if black box methods would be used for solving, they instantiate a problem formulation that can be expressed with IP.

The benefit of IP is universality: all problems in the complexity class NP admit concise formulations as integer programming problems. They can be cast as linear optimization problems over binary variables. To sum up, the benefits of IP in interface design are three-fold (Karrenbauer and Oulasvirta, 2014): (1) it offers a universal framework to define and compare design tasks, (2) powerful solvers are available that are not only fast but use exact methods to compute bounds for solutions, and (3) several relaxations are known that can boost performance.

The general structure of design task consists of decision variables, objective functions, calibration factors (or functions), and constraints. For the sake of presentation, we here restrict ourselves to binary variables and linear constraints. Binary variables are used to model decisions, e.g., in a selection problem $x_i = 1$ means that item i is selected and $x_i = 0$ if it is not. Suppose that we have n decision variables that we combine in an n-dimensional vector $x \in [0, 1]^n$ in the unit hypercube where each extreme point represents a configuration. Configurations that are infeasible are excluded by constraints, i.e., linear inequalities. For example, $x_i + x_j \leq 1$ implies that items i and j are mutually exclusive. Given weights for each decision/item, we can ask for the feasible solution with maximum total weight by maximizing

$$\sum_{i=1}^{n} w_i x_i$$

subject to

$$Ax \leq b$$
$$x \in \{0, 1\}^n$$

where the comparison between the left-hand side vector Ax and the right-hand side b is meant component-wise such that each row of the matrix A together with the corresponding entry in b represents a linear constraint.

In general, it is NP-hard to solve such integer linear optimization problems. This can be easily seen in the following example for the famous NP-hard INDEPENDENTSET problem where we are given an undirected graph $G = (V, E)$ and are supposed to compute a set of nodes that does not induce an edge:

$$\max \left\{ \sum_{v \in V} x_v : \forall \{v, w\} \in E : x_v + x_w \leq 1, \forall v \in V : x_v \in \{0, 1\} \right\}.$$

However, these optimization problems become polynomial-time solvable if we relax the integrality constraint.

We provide a first example next before turning into more general definitions in user interface design.

4.3.1 Introductory Example: Menu Design

To illustrate the approach for a reader unfamiliar with integer programming, we look at the design of a *linear menu* as an example. A linear menu organizes commands in an array. All commands are immediately visible and selectable on display, unlike in, say, a hamburger menu or hierarchical menu. This menu type is one of the most common user interfaces. Normally, a designer designing such a menu would sketch alternative designs relying on experience and heuristics such as 'place frequently used commands closer to the top' or 'place elements that belong together next to each other' or 'make the menu consistent with other menus'. The outcomes would be evaluated using inspection methods or usability testing, and the process would be repeated until a satisfactory design is attained.

Combinatorial optimization offers a way to mathematically describe such objectives and algorithmically solve the resulting design problem. Two core requirements are illustrated in the following:

1. Definition of the design space (feasible set of designs).

2. Definition of an objective function.

From a combinatorial perspective, the task is to assign n commands to n slots in a menu. The simplest version is called a *linear assignment task*. It can be formulated using a *binary decision variable* $x_{i\ell}$, which is 1 if command i is assigned to slot ℓ and 0 otherwise. This leads to a formulation:

$$\min \sum_{i=1}^{n} \sum_{\ell=1}^{n} c_{i\ell} x_{i\ell}$$

subject to

$$\forall l : \sum_{i=1}^{n} x_{i\ell} = 1 \qquad (4.2)$$

$$\forall i : \sum_{\ell=1}^{n} x_{i\ell} = 1$$

$$\forall i, l : x_{i\ell} \in \{0, 1\}$$

where $c_{i\ell}$ is a design objective capturing the cost (to user) for accessing command when assigned to slot ℓ. The two constraints, respectively, state that each slot must be filled by exactly one command, and that each command must be assigned to exactly one slot. In plain words, the optimal menu design is an assignment of all n commands such to the menu such that it yields lowest expected cost to user. This formulation exposes how the number of commands is linked to the size of the design space: there are $n!$ possible designs for n commands. However, this definition is not yet operational, because we lack a definition of the objective function $c_{i\ell}$.

To that end, let us consider optimizing the menu for *selection time*: the expected time for selecting a command. Assuming a novice user who scans menu options linearly from top to bottom, the optimal design should have the most important (e.g., most frequently accessed) items on top. For this purpose, we introduce a frequency-based score for each command: $f_i \in [0, 1]$. When this is multiplied by the position of the item (counting from the top), we get an objective function that serves as a proxy model for selection time: $c_{i\ell} = f_i \cdot l$. Note that this objective is similar to a linear regression model of novice search performance in menu selection (Cockburn, Gutwin, and Greenberg, 2007; Liu, Francis, and Salvendy, 2002). These models compute selection time as the number of fixations required when starting search from the top of the menu. Multiplication with a positive scalar, nor addition (or subtraction), does not change the optimal solution. Thus, the free parameters of the models do not affect the outcome of optimization and can be ignored.

However, this objective function does not determine how quickly a command can be selected once it has been found. To that end, we need a model of motor performance. Assuming that a single end-effector (e.g., a cursor or fingertip) is used for selection, selection time is governed by the time that it takes to move it across distance on top of the slot. Movement time in this case is given by Fitts' law:

$$MT = a + b \log_2 \left(\frac{D}{W} + 1 \right) \tag{4.3}$$

where D is distance of cursor to target centre and W is its width. Now, because all targets in a linear menu are of equal height, our objective function (Eq. 4.2) can be rewritten as a twofold objective function:

$$\min \sum_{i=1}^{n} \sum_{\ell=1}^{n} \omega f_i \log_2(\ell) x_{i\ell} + (1 - \omega) f_i \ell x_{i\ell} \tag{4.4}$$

where $\omega \in [0, 1]$ controls the relative importance of expert users whose performance is dominated by motor performance. Similarly, $1 - \omega$ denotes the relative importance novices, who spend more time scanning the menu one item at a time. With $\omega = 1$ the design task collapses to that of minimizing expected log-travel distance. However, in practice, no matter what the ω is set to, the problem can be solved by assigning commands from top to bottom in the order of decreasing frequency.

The task gets more challenging when commands should be grouped according to a semantic relationship (e.g., Bailly, Oulasvirta, Kötzing, and Hoppe, 2013). For example, in many application menus 'Open' and 'Save' are close to each other. To this end, we need define an association score: $a(i, j) \in [0, 1]$. It represents the strength of semantic relationship between two commands i and j, and could represent, for example, collocation in previous designs, word association norms, or synonymity. For instance, association between 'Open' and 'Save' should be high, and lower between 'Bookmark' and 'Quit'. To decide how commands should be grouped, we need another instance of the decision variable x: let x_{jk} be 1 when j is assigned to slot k and 0 otherwise. Considering visual search only, we now reformulate the objective function as:

$$\min \sum_{i=1}^{n} \sum_{\ell=1}^{n} \sum_{j=1}^{n} \sum_{k=1}^{n} (1 - a_{ij}) f_i f_j \ell k x_{i\ell} x_{jk} \tag{4.5}$$

We can collapse the first part of the objective to a four-dimensional cost matrix $c'(i, j, k, \ell)$, which tells the cost of assigning i to ℓ when j is assigned to k:

$$\min \sum_{i=1}^{n} \sum_{\ell=1}^{n} \sum_{j=1}^{n} \sum_{k=1}^{n} c'(i, j, k, \ell) x_{i\ell} x_{jk} \tag{4.6}$$

Technically, the problem is now quadratic, because of presence of the product of two decision variables. It is harder to solve than the linear version, because the optimum design is defined by how elements are in relation to each other, not only by an element's position in the menu. However, this definition is operationable and could be solved by black box optimizers.

4.4 Interface Design Problems

To define a design problem as a combinatorial optimization problem consists of three main steps:

1. *Decision variables:* The first step consists of setting up design variables as decision variables. Though this set of variables may be extended and modified in later iterations, the initial setup is the corner stone of the modelling process.

2. *Constraints:* Given the decision variables along with their respective domains, the next step deals with the exclusion of infeasible designs by linear constraints.

3. *Objective function:* The objective function is modelled in the third step. It may consist of several parts that are linked together.

In addition, calibration factors or functions may need to be added to trade off the objective terms.

This section describes the creation of the feasible set in the two first steps. Our goal is to illustrate the expression of design challenges in graphical user interface design, including how functionalities are selected, widget types determined, chosen elements organized on a layout, and their temporal behaviour decided. Instead of providing ready-made solutions, our goal is to illuminate the logic of expressing interface design tasks in IP.

To this end, this section introduces four types of combinatorial optimization problems for interface design, illustrating how they are defined using decision variables and constraints:

- Selection: a set of functionalities, elements, or their properties is to be selected from a larger set.
- Ordering: a set of elements must be ordered.
- Assignment: a set of elements is to be assigned on a limited size canvas or grid.
- Scheduling: messages need to be scheduled for presentation to the user.

4.4.1 Selection Problems

In selection problems, a set of elements must be chosen for some requirements and objectives. Consider the selection of functionalities, contents, or features (here: elements). This problem type is further broken down to three subtypes.

In a *covering problem*, we are given a set of elements $U = \{u_1, ..., u_n\}$ and a set of attributes $A = \{a_1, ..., a_m\}$ where each element is equipped with one or more attributes. Let A_i denote the subset of attributes associated with element u_i. Moreover, we are given positive requirements, say r_j, for each attribute a_j. The task is to select a subset of U that satisfies all requirements, i.e., the number of selected elements with attribute a_j is at least r_j for each attribute. The goal is to find a selection that minimizes the total costs, i.e., the sum of the costs for each selected element. Sometimes an element may have an attribute with some multiplicity, e.g., for the attribute *cost* we would be given values associated with each element. Moreover, it may or may not be allowed to select an element multiple times.

Consider the selection of widget types for a graphical interface, for example. Here a designer sets a minimum set of requirements to a interface, and there are multiple widgets to select from, each with distinct properties. For example, there may be a requirement that the user must select one option out of many. This may be implemented as a menu, drop-down list, etc., each with its associated 'costs' in terms of learnability, usability, use of display space, etc. A good solution to this problem covers all the requirements with minimum cost.

Prototypical covering problems are set-covering problems, where all requirements are 1 and in its cardinality version all costs are 1 as well. The term *set* refers to the different subsets of elements that share a common attribute. A special case of the set-covering problem is vertex cover where the elements are the nodes of a given graph and the attributes are the edges, i.e., we are asked to select a subset of the nodes of minimum cardinality that contains at least one node of each edge.

Packing problems are similar to covering problems: again, we are given a set of elements $U = \{u_1, ..., u_n\}$ and attributes $A = \{a_1, ..., a_m\}$. However, instead of requirements, we now have positive capacities c_j for each attribute a_j and only those subsets of U are feasible that do not exceed the capacity for each attribute. Analogously, a backpack has a certain volume and a total weight limit over all packed items. The attributes are volume and weight. Typically, the elements are also associated with a valuation, say p_i for element u_i, that can be considered as a profit. Hence, the goal is to find a selection of the elements that does not exceed the capacities and maximizes the total profit. Again, it may or may not be allowed to select an item multiple times.

As an HCI example, consider again the widget selection problem: not all available widgets might fit in a canvas of limited size. If an individual reward is associated with each widget, it is natural to ask for a fitting selection that yields the highest reward.

Packing problems are in some sense dual to covering problems: when we switch the role of elements and attributes, the role of capacities and costs as well as the role of profits and requirements, we obtain the associated dual covering problem. An important fact that follows from optimization theory is that the profit of any solution for the packing problem can not exceed the costs of any solution for the associated dual covering problem. In particular, this holds for the maximum profit and the minimum costs. The dual problem of the vertex cover problem mentioned earlier is the so-called matching problem where we asked to find a maximum cardinality subset of the edges such that each node is incident to at most one edge in the matching. Other well-known packing problems are the independent set problem, the set packing problem, and the knapsack problem. The independent set problem often appears as a subproblem for modelling mutually exclusive choices.

Network design problems are a special type of selection problems in connection with graphs. Typically, we are given a graph and are supposed to select a subset of the edges such that certain connectivity constraints are satisfied. A basic example is the so-called Steiner

Tree problem: for a given undirected graph $G = (V, E)$ and a set of *terminals* T, i.e., $T \subseteq V$, we shall select edges, say $E' \subset E$, such that each pair of terminals is connected by a path consisting only of edges from E'. Observe that at least one edge in a cycle can be removed while connectivity is still maintained, and hence, every optimum solution is a tree. The nodes of the selected edges that are not terminals are called Steiner nodes. For the Directed Steiner Tree problem, we are given a directed graph $G = (V, A)$, a designated root node $r \in V$, and a set of terminals $T \subseteq V \setminus \{r\}$, and our task is to select arcs such that there is a directed path from r to each terminal consisting only of selected arcs. Typically, a cost is associated with each arc, and we are supposed to find a feasible selection of minimum costs. Sometimes only the root and the terminals are given explicitly and the remaining nodes are only given implicitly, e.g., we could have a Steiner node associated with each subset of the terminals. A feasible solution would then define a hierarchical clustering of the terminals.

This problem appears for instance, in the context of the design of a hierarchical menu structure. The terminals are the actions that should be available as menu items. To achieve quick access times it makes sense to avoid clutter by grouping related actions together in a submenu. The root node represents the menu bar and an arc determines a parent-child relation, i.e., selecting an arc from the root to a menu item means to put this item directly into the menu bar, and hence it is accessible via one click.

4.4.2 Ordering Problems

In ordering problems, we are asked to provide a permutation of a given ground set such that traversal costs are minimized, i.e., there is a cost associated with the transition from an element to its successor in the designated order.

A famous example of this problem class is the Traveling Salesman Problem (TSP). We are given a set of locations $P = \{p_1, ..., p_n\}$ and distances d_{ij} for each pair of locations i, j. The goal is to find the shortest tour that visits every location and returns to the starting point at the end. That is, find a permutation $\pi : [n] \to [n]$ of the locations such that $d_{\pi(n), \pi(1)} + \sum_{i=1}^{n-1} d_{\pi(i), \pi(i+1)}$ is minimized.

In HCI, consider the task of grouping items in a linear menu. The goal here is to order a given set of menu items such that skimming the menu is done as fast as possible. Two items, when placed adjacent to each other, have an associated reading time such that the first primes the other. For example, reading 'Save' after 'Open' is faster than after 'Bookmarks'.

4.4.3 Assignment Problems

Assignment problems generalize ordering problems and can be considered as a combination of covering and packing problems. A basic instance consists of a set of n items and n locations. The goal is to find a one-to-one correspondence between the items and the locations. Assignment problems can be further broken down to two subtypes.

Linear problems: Here we simply search for the assignment such that the sum of the costs of the selected correspondences is minimized, i.e., the sum of c_{ij} over all pairs i, j whenever item i is assigned to location j. This type of problem can be solved in polynomial time.

Quadratic problems: In addition to the costs of assigning item i to location j, also consider the costs of dependencies between two selections, i.e., $c_{ijk\ell}$ determines the costs of assigning item i to location j conditioned on the choice of also assigning item k to location ℓ.

The Quadratic Assignment Problem (QAP) appears, for example, in the Keyboard Layout Problem, a.k.a. the Letter Assignment Problem: a set of n letters is supposed to be mapped to n slots on the keyboard. The objective is to maximize the typing speed or, equivalently, to minimize the inter-key intervals. To this end, we set $c_{ijk\ell} = p_{ik} \times t_{jl}$ where p_{ij} denote the bigram probabilities and t_{jl} the movement times. In general, QAP can be used to model mutual dependencies between pairs of selected elements. These occur whenever the interface is expected to support task sequences where one subtask is followed by another. However, this modelling power comes at the expense of efficiency of finding optimum solutions.

4.4.4 Scheduling Problems

A scheduling problem is a problem where jobs are assigned to resources at particular times. In the classic job shop scheduling problem, given n jobs $J_1, J_2, ..., J_n$ of varying resource use, they need to be scheduled on m machines with different processing capabilities in order to minimize the total time needed to finish processing all jobs. In the dynamic version of the problem, incoming jobs are not known in advance, but the algorithm must decide how to schedule them as they occur.

In the design of dynamic events in a notification system, jobs are incoming events (messages, system notifications) and resources are resources of the user. The problem of notification systems can be formulated as a scheduling problem. Here, given incoming messages with different priorities (e.g., messages from the OS, social media, news, etc), the task is to decide where and when to show them in the interface, for example, as a pop-up notification, or a notification tray, or whether to postpone it to some later point in time. The goal is to minimize distraction or overloading a user working on something else.

4.5 Objective Functions for Interactive Tasks

An objective function maps a design candidate $x \in X$ to a real-valued predictor of design quality: $f : X \rightarrow \mathbb{R}$. To be relevant in interaction design, this function should quantify an aspect related to usability, enjoyability, ergonomics, or errors.

A key issue we face in defining objective functions for interface design is the emergent nature of 'interaction': the way the properties of the design and the user affect outcomes in interaction unfolds dynamically over a period of time in the actions and reactions of the user. Numerous metrics and models presented in HCI research, neuroscience, and the behavioral sciences are potentially available for this end. The choice of modelling approach is not without issues.

The goal in constructing an objective function should be to maximize the optimizer's capacity to reliably find designs that meet the desired outcomes in interaction. There are two outstanding goals:

- *Predictive validity*: Prediction of desired outcomes in interaction
- *Computational efficiency*: Per-evaluation computation time in optimization

Because the most realistic models are expensive to compute, the designer weighs the quality of estimates against computational efficiency.

4.5.1 Choice of Model Class

The choice of modelling formalism is central, as it determines how design knowledge is encoded and executed, and how interaction is represented. It also affects computational efficiency. Four modelling formalisms distinguish from this perspective. They are here introduced in increasing order of complexity.

Heuristics   are rules of thumb used in design, such as 'white space should be minimized'. Several design guidelines are presented in interaction and graphic design literature. Mathematically, the simplest type is a binary-valued function yielding 1 if the design is part of the set H that fulfils this heuristic, and 0 otherwise. Many heuristics are real-valued.

A recognized problem with heuristics-driven optimization is how to weigh multiple of them. Since most heuristics are 'weak' (have little information), multiples of them are needed to refine or generate a good design. This leads to the problem of how to weigh the contribution of one heuristic against another.

Another issue of heuristics is their validity. As legacy of tradition rather than scientific inquiry, many heuristics are subjective and their predictive validity questionable.

Regression   models offer an expressive yet quickly computable mathematical form to link design factors with outcomes to users:

$$y = f(\mathbf{x}, \beta) + \epsilon \tag{4.7}$$

where
y is a dependent variable of interest,
x is a vector of design variables,
β is a vector of unknown (free) parameters, and
ϵ is variance unexplained by model f.

For example, Search-Decide-Point (SDP) is a regression model predicting task completion time in menu selection. It postulates a term for decision and search time, which is a linear interpolation between decision and visual search. As the user becomes more experienced with a menu, there is a shift from serial visual search to decision among competing elements. Regression models like SDP provide a stronger link between design variables and predicted user behaviour. However, most models are specialized to a single task or sub-task of interaction. Hence, multiple regression models may be needed, leading to the same issues as heuristics have in multi-objective optimization, although to a lesser degree.

Computational quality metrics   are programs that output some property of a design linkedto empirically verified effects on users. An example of an aesthetic-related metric is that of harmonic colours. It defines a set of colours that combine to provide a pleasant visual perception. Harmony is determined by relative position in colour space rather than by specific hues. Templates are provided to test any given set of colours against the harmonic set. The templates consist of one or two sectors of the hue wheel, with given angular sizes. They can be arbitrarily rotated to create new sets. The distance of a interface from a template is computed using the arc-length distance between the hue of element and the hue of the closest sector border, and the saturation channel of the element. Several perception- and aesthetics-related metrics are available (Miniukovich and De Angeli, 2015).

Simulators are step-wise executed functions M that map the model parameters θ to behavioral data. In HCI, the parameters θ capture both parameters of the user and those of the task, design, or context. If random variables are involved in the simulator, the outputs of the simulator can fluctuate randomly even when θ are fixed. Simulators are implemented as programs where parameters are provided as input. Simulators can be implemented in many ways, for example, as control-theoretical, cognitive, biomechanical, or computational rationality models, as discussed elsewhere in this book.

In contrast to heuristics, computational metrics, and regression models, simulators are *generative models* that predict not only the outcomes of interaction but intermediate steps, or the process of interaction. This is valuable in design, as one can output not only predictions for aggregates, but also examine predicted interaction in detail.

For example, visual search from graphical 2D-layouts is complex cognitive-perceptual activity driven by the oculomotor system and affected by task as well as incoming information. The Kieras-Hornof model of visual attention (Kieras and Hornof, 2014) is a simulator predicting how fixations are placed when looking for a given target on a given graphical layout. It bases on a set of *availability functions* that determine how the features of a target are perceivable from the user's current eye location. The availability functions are based on the eccentricity from the current eye location and angular size s of the target. Additive Gaussian random noise with variance proportional to the size of the target is assumed. For each feature, a threshold is computed and the probability that the feature is perceivable. These determine where to look next on the layout. Simulation terminates when a fixation lands on the target.

Another benefit of simulators over regression models is their high fidelity, which allows capturing the relationship between multiple parameters and structures describing the human mind. Some simulation models are Turing-strong formalisms with memory and ability to execute programs. A simulator can address multiple design objectives in a coherent manner that does not require tuning. However, they are significantly more expensive to execute. Certain optimization methods, especially exact methods (e.g, integer programming), are practically ruled out.

4.5.2 Choice of Unit of Analysis

Although not commonly recognized, UI optimization is not limited to Fitts' law and other classic cost functions. There are numerous options from cognitive and neurosciences and HCI research. These allow us to go beyond performance aspects to optimize for learnability, choices and decision-making, and even user experience. These models offer a rich toolbox for attacking complex and realistic design problems.

Considering the design of a graphical user interface as an example, cost functions can be distinguished based on how they relate candidate designs to user-related objectives and the different timescales of interaction. We present some salient categories with examples and discuss their relative merits.

Surface features   Surface metrics and heuristics are functions that capture properties of an interfaces that may correlate with user-related qualities. To optimize a surface-level cost function is to reorganize the UI's visual or spatial features to increase this correlation. Examples include optimizing a menu system for consistency, a scatterplot design to avoid overplotting, and a layout for minimum whitespace (Oulasvirta, 2017). A concrete example of an aesthetic metric used in wireframe optimization (Todi, Weir, and Oulasvirta, 2016) is grid quality (Miniukovich and De Angeli, 2015). It calculates the distance to the closest symmetrical layout and was shown to correlate with user aesthetic preferences. Computation starts with the layout vertex set, rescaled such that the x-axis coincides with the axis of symmetry and the y-axis contains the centre of mass of the x_i. This is mapped to the complex plane to obtain a set $z_i = x_i + Iy_i$. These points are horizontally symmetrical if they consist only of real values and complex conjugate pairs. The asymmetry for a layout is obtained by constructing a polynomial of involved coefficients and averaging the size of the imaginary parts of the coefficients. Vertical symmetry is scored in the same way, after a simple coordinate transformation.

Actions   Action or operation level objectives capture user performance in individual actions like visual search or selection. To the extent they correlate with task-level performance or user experience, they may be good surrogates that are easier to model and quicker to evaluate. Examples include optimization of wireframe sketches for visual search performance, widget layouts for individual motor capabilities, and gesture sets for learnability (Oulasvirta, 2017). For instance, consider the optimization of a keyboard layout for aimed movement performance (Zhai, Hunter, and Smith, 2002). In aimed movements, an end-effector, such as the tip of a finger or a cursor, is brought on top of a spatially expanded target to *select* it. Selection forms the basis of communicating intent with all visuo-spatially organized UIs, such as menus, keyboards, web pages, and GUIs. To optimize a UI for selection means that the speed and accuracy of selections is optimized. Fitts' law provides a well-known regression model that links movement time MT and task demands. optimization using Fitts' law minimizes distances and maximizes sizes of selectable elements, such as keys.

Tasks   Task-level models predict users' performance or success in completing activities with an interface, thus directly addressing usability-related concerns such as task completion time and errors. They assume some structure in the task, consisting of sequential or parallel steps. An example is the Search-Decide-Point (SDP) model used to optimize menus (Bailly, Oulasvirta, Kötzing, and Hoppe, 2013).

Experience   Models of experience predict how users might learn, experience, or stress about interaction. For example, the Rosenholtz model offers a way to minimize experience of *visual clutter*. It operates by choosing colours, sizes, and shapes of elements such that *feature congestion* is minimized. The layout elements have some distribution of features such as colour, contrast, orientation, and size. With few targets, the distribution is small compared to the overall size of the feature space. As the feature distribution occupies more of the available space, the feature space becomes congested. One first computes the mean and covariance of given feature vectors. The clutter of the display is defined as the determinant of the covariance matrix.

4.6 Choice of Optimization Method

After a task definition is in place, a combinatorial optimization method can search the set of candidate designs. Modern methods in combinatorial optimization can be divided into two main classes: (i) heuristics such as simulated annealing and (ii) exact methods such as integer programming. The latter offers mathematical guarantees for solutions but insists on analysis of the objective function for revealing simplifications and links to known tasks in the optimization literature. However, nonlinearities in an objective function may rule out application. Black box methods, in contrast, can attack any design problem but typically demand empirical tuning of the parameters and offer only approximate optimality. In this section, we discuss the main ideas and trade-offs of both approaches.

If the evaluation of the objective function for a given configuration is inexpensive, then randomized heuristics are often an effective way to obtain solutions of good quality. However, it requires some parameter engineering to find appropriate parameters (e.g., cooling schedule in simulated annealing) for the problem under consideration. If there is an analytical description of the objective function, then integer programming can offer a useful toolbox for the design processs. This is not only due to its modelling power, but also because of the availability of solvers that are efficient in practice (e.g., CPLEX and Gurobi).

4.6.1 Heuristics

Black box methods do not make any explicit assumptions on the objective function they are going to optimize, but rather they consider it as a black box or an oracle that tells them the objective value of a given candidate. There are deterministic and randomized black box methods (see e.g., Rao, 2009). Though it is possible to randomly try out candidates and return the best solution after a certain time, it is often more efficient to apply a more systematic approach. We here outline some well-known approaches. The reader is pointed to any of the many textbooks for more comprehensive reviews.

Greedy   Greedy algorithms divide the construction of a solution into multiple subsequent decisions. These decisions are taken in a certain order and are not revoked later. Typical examples are packing problems: the solution is picked item by item until further items cannot be picked anymore. It is natural to proceed by choosing the next item among those that still fit and that yields the largest growth of the profit w.r.t. the current selection.

Local search   The main ingredient of local search is the definition of a neighborhood of a given configuration. For example, the neighboring layouts of a keyboard layouts could be those that differ by swapping one pair of letters. Starting from an initial configuration, local search proceeds by chosing a neighboring configuration with an objective value that is at least as good as the current one. These choices could be, for example, greedy or randomized.

Simulated annealing   Simulated annealing can be considered as a special case of local search using randomness to control exploration/exploitation behaviour. The main difference is that a neighboring configuration is not only chosen when it yields to a better objective value, but also with a certain probability when it is worse. This probability decreases with the extent of the detoriation of the objective value. Typically this probability is $\exp(-\beta\Delta)$, where Δ is the difference in the objective value and β a parameter called *inverse temperature*. Simulated annealing belongs to the class of randomized search heuristics. Further members of this class are *evolutionary algorithms, ant colony optimization,* etc. Common to these is that they implement some logic to control the use of heuristics over the progression of search.

4.6.2 Exact Methods

The main characteristic of exact methods is that they are guaranteed to find the optimum solution in finite time. However, it is not surprising that this time may be exponential in the size of the instance because they are capable of solving NP-complete problems. The simplest exact method is *explicit enumeration,* where the objective value of each element of the solution space is evaluated, and the current best solution—the so-called *incumbent*— is updated. In contrast, *implicit enumeration* makes use of relaxations that can be solved efficiently, i.e., only a subset of the constraints is considered such that the problem becomes tractable.

This enables us to obtain information about a whole subset of the solutions, e.g., by a partial assignment of the variables, and compare it with the incumbent. If the best objective value of the relaxation restricted to a subset of solutions is worse than the objective value of the incumbent, we can safely discard all solutions from this subset at once, because none of them can replace the incumbent. Moreover, if the relaxation of a subset is already infeasible, we infer that the subset under consideration actually must be empty. In any of the two cases, we conclude that the negation of the conditions that qualified the subset must hold for all potential new incumbents. This additional information may be particularly helpful to strengthen further relaxations. Moreover, relaxations deliver guarantees for the quality of the incumbent, e.g., if the optimum objective value of the incumbent is only 1 per cent away from the optimum objective value of the relaxation, we know that it can also be at most 1 per cent away from the optimum of the original problem. A very popular form of implicit enumeration is called *Branch & Bound,* wich is one of the standard methods for solving integer (linear) programs.

4.6.3 Dealing with Multi-Objective Functions

Almost all real design tasks in HCI must address multiple objectives, because most user interfaces must support more than one user task and fulfil more than one objective. As objectives are often conflicting, the optimization task becomes that of finding the best compromise (or, 'the least worst compromise'). Multi-objective optimization is in the end about optimizing a single function into which the multiple objectives have been collapsed.

Tuning an objective function refers to setting of weights (ω). A designer decides how to trade each objective, for example how to exchange for example one 'unit of usability' for one unit of security. In HCI, the choice of ω is not only an empirical decision (what do users want?) but a strategic decision at the same time (what should they want?). For empirical tuning, one may run an experimental study to find the set of weights that best predicts some variable of interest. Statistics or logs from a live system can be used to weigh parameters. Strategic tuning refers to goals set outside optimization itself, for example, by marketing.

Despite its simplistic appeal, the weighted sum approach has some recognized issues. optimization literature proposed several advanced methods. They offer alternatives to weighing to express a designer's goals. General formulations and their pros and cons are summarized by Marler and Arora (2004).

4.7 Appraisal and Outlook

Combinatorial optimization contributes to HCI research a methodology that permits algorithmic solution of design problems. It provides an actionable definition for the over-used term 'optimal'. To say that a design is optimal is to say that in the defined set of candidate designs, there is no better design (global optimum has been identified). A design is *approximately* optimal means that either its objective value is within a defined margin of the optimal design or there is a high chance that only marginally better designs exist. Three important points are thus made about optimality: (1) optimality is only defined for a set of candidates and design objectives; when those are not defined, optimal design is unidentifiable; (2) to claim that a design has a chance to be optimal, it is essential to analyse the probability that the given search process has had to find it; (3) optimality, ultimately, refers to outcomes afforded by users; to claim 'optimality' is to make an empirically falsifiable prediction about interaction. This argumentation points out that combinatorial optimization can be a useful tool for understanding design even if not used as an algorithmic tool.

To 'design interaction' is about improving design decisions algorithmically in the light of best information on what makes interaction good, even if the global optimum is never reached. Furthermore, a combinatorial formulation of a design problem can be used to inform decisions: by using exact optimization methods, one can estimate the distance of a present design from the global optimum; by setting a distance metric in the design space, one can ask how far one's present design is from the optimum, or what is the minimum sequence of changes to get there; by introducing several objective functions, one for each user group, a designer can find the best compromise design for a diverse set of user group; by using methods of robust optimization, one can find the design that is the best compromise even if assumptions about use change.

It is the exact formulation of a design task that allows an algorithm to search for the best combinations of design decisions like this. Exact formulation is a double-edged sword, however. On the one hand, it is a call for deriving solutions from first principles, similarly as in engineering sciences. This promotes proper formulation of problems and analysis of conditions in which good outcomes can be reached. For practitioners, algorithmic approaches to concrete, hard design tasks could help improve usability and user experience. More broadly, optimization could promote a change of culture in design by encouraging the explication, scrutinization, and accumulation of design knowledge.

On the other hand, the limits of formal expression are the limits of optimization. Perhaps the most significant obstacle to progress in this space is, after all, not posed by algorithms, but rather by modelling of tasks and design knowledge. We end with a discussion of seven challenges for future work in this area that stem from this issue.

Challenge 1. Defining and cataloguing design tasks. While we presently have a reasonable handle of some design tasks in graphical layouts, the space has by no means been exhausted. Defining and cataloguing design tasks is necessary not only for making this approach more readily actionable, but also for understanding what interaction design is about. One of benefits of the optimization approach is that any 'oracle' that can produce feasible designs can be used. However, to exploit the benefits of exact optimization methods, we need to be able to define more tasks with integer programming. This helps us link known problems in UI design with known problems in computer science and build on existing knowledge on efficient solutions.

Challenge 2. Approximations of user simulations. Presently the state-of-the-art models of interactive tasks (think ACT-R) are simulators that are expensive to evaluate when optimizing. Evaluation time of simple simulator like KLM may take a few tens of milliseconds. However, for more realistic models of attention, they take a second or so due to neural or stochastic computations involved. Assuming models that learn or have a larger infrascture to cover, evaluation can take hours. What the field needs are methods to precompute, approximate, or simplify such simulators. In the absence of feasible models, our approach has been to relax the modelling requirements: instead of using a comprehensive model of a user, each case recruits models from a pool of basic models case by case, on the basis of which objectives are most important.

Challenge 3. Methods for multi-objective functions. One of the benefits of the white box approach to objective functions is that assumptions about what makes a design 'good' are made explicit. The designer can thus understand exactly what the optimizer is doing when searching. However, already in the case of a graphical layout, 'goodness' starts to involve a larger number of human aspects to consider, from perception to attention to aesthetics and motor control. The field needs to develop methods that allow a designer to understand how such objectives are implemented and how they work together. We also need mature optimization methods that avoid the issues of the weighted sum approach.

Challenge 4. Assisted calibration of objective functions. Multi-objective functions involve weights (or tuning factors) to quantify the relative importance of each objective. In addition, objectives can be normalized or otherwise transformed to ensure that advances in one does not overshadow advances in the other. Unfortunately, multi-objective optimization can be 'brittle' in the sense that small changes in these factors may radically change the results. The field needs methods that could obtain tuning factors empirically with a designer or from data. Such methods could, for example, use crowdsourcing to evaluate a large number of designs against human ground truth. Alternatively, they could be based on mining of existing designs, or inferred from user behaviour in logs.

Challenge 5. Efficient methods that allow real-time optimization. With some notable exceptions, the field has thus far worked on proofs-of-concepts using 'one shot' optimization. With increasing need for real-time adaptation and integration with design tools, it will become important to develop methods specifically targetting getting good results fast.

Challenge 6. Concepts for interactive definition and steering of optimization. To seriously re-envision UI design with an optimizer in the loop, the field needs to go beyond the 'fire and forget' paradigm. It is irreconcilable with design practice. A designer cannot be asked to provide all inputs to an optimizer to a decimal point and come back after a while for an answer. Designers constantly change the problem definition and the design space. How might design task be defined for an optimizer, its search process steered, and how could the optimizer positively encourage the designer to adopt better designs without choking creativity?

Challenge 7. Critical evaluation against model-predictions. It is fair to ask if optimized designs are actually usable, and how they compare with those of human-designed interfaces. Empirically verified improvements have been reported for keyboards, widget layouts, gesture controls, and menu design (Oulasvirta, 2017). In addition, one of the most significant benefits of the approach is that each design comes with model-based predictions about its use. Empirical data that is being collected is thus a direct assessment of the objective function that was used.

Over and beyond such challenges, perhaps the most exciting academic prospect of combinatorial optimization is that it offers a multi-disciplinary yet principled solution to one of the most profound questions in HCI research: how to solve a problem using available empirical and theoretical knowledge (Card, Newell, and Moran, 1983; Carroll, 2000; Gaver, Beaver, and Benford, 2003; Höök and Löwgren 2012; Nielsen 1994; Norman and Draper 1986; Oulasvirta and Hornbæk 2016; Winograd and Flores 1986; Zimmerman, Forlizzi, and Evenson, 2007). Combinatorial optimization invites computer scientists to define what 'design' means and psychologists, cognitive scientists, and designers to define what 'good' means in interaction.

· ·

REFERENCES

Bailly, G., Oulasvirta, A., Kötzing, T., and Hoppe, S., 2013. Menuoptimizer: Interactive optimization of menu systems. In: *UIST'13: Proceedings of the 26th annual ACM symposium on User Interface Software and Technology.* New York, NY: ACM, pp. 331–42.

Burkard, R. E., and Offermann, J., 1977. Entwurf von schreibmaschinentastaturen mittels quadratischer zuordnungsprobleme. *Zeitschrift für Operations Research,* 21(4), pp. B121–32.

Card, S. K., Mackinlay, J. D., and Robertson, G. G., 1991. A morphological analysis of the design space of input devices. *ACM Transactions on Information Systems (TOIS),* 9(2), pp. 99–122.

Card, S. K., Newell, A., and Moran, T. P., 1983. *The psychology of human-computer interaction.*

Carroll, J. M., 2000. *Making Use: Scenario-Based Design of Human–Computer Interactions.* Cambridge, MA: MIT Press.

Cockburn, A., Gutwin, C., and Greenberg, S., 2007. A predictive model of menu performance. In *Proceedings of the SIGCHI conference on Human factors in computing systems.* New York, NY: ACM, pp. 627–36.

Cross, N., and Roy, R., 1989. *Engineering design methods.* Volume 2. New York, NY: Wiley.

Dvorak, A., Merrick, N. L., Dealey, W. L., and Ford, G. C., 1936. *Typewriting behavior.* New York, NY: American Book Company.

Eisenstein, J., Vanderdonckt, J., and Puerta, A., 2001. Applying model-based techniques to the development of uis for mobile computers. In: *Proceedings of the 6th international conference on Intelligent user interfaces.* New York, NY: ACM, pp. 69–76.

Fisher, D. L., 1993. Optimal performance engineering: Good, better, best. *Human Factors: The Journal of the Human Factors and Ergonomics Society,* 35(1), pp. 115–39.

Francis, G., 2000. Designing multifunction displays: An optimization approach. *International Journal of Cognitive Ergonomics,* 4(2), pp. 107–24.

Gajos, K., and Weld, D. S., 2004. Supple: automatically generating user interfaces. In: *Proceedings of the 9th international conference on Intelligent user interfaces.* New York, NY: ACM, pp. 93–100. ACM.

Gaver, W. W., Beaver, J., and Benford, S., 2003. Ambiguity as a resource for design. In: G. Cockton and P. Korhonen. eds. *CHI 2003: Proceedings of the SIGCHI Conference on Human Factors in Computing Systems.* New York, NY: ACM, pp. 233–40.

Höök, K., and Löwgren, J., 2012. Strong concepts: Intermediate-level knowledge in interaction design research. *ACM Transactions on Computer-Human Interaction (TOCHI),* 19(3), p. 23.

Karrenbauer, A., and Oulasvirta, A., 2014. Improvements to keyboard optimization with integer programming. In: *Proceedings of the 27th annual ACM symposium on User interface software and technology.* New York, NY: ACM, pp. 621–6.

Kieras, D. E., and Hornof, A. J., 2014. Towards accurate and practical predictive models of active-vision-based visual search. In: *Proceedings of the 32nd annual ACM conference on Human factors in computing systems.* New York, NY: ACM, pp. 3875–84.

Light, L., and Anderson, P., 1993. *Designing better keyboards via simulated annealing.* San Francisco, CA: Miller Freeman Publishers.

Liu, B., Francis, G., and Salvendy, G., 2002. Applying models of visual search to menu design. *International Journal of Human-Computer Studies,* 56(3), pp. 307–30.

Marler, R. T., and Arora, J. S., 2004. Survey of multi-objective optimization methods for engineering. *Structural and Multidisciplinary optimization,* 26(6), pp. 369–95.

Miniukovich, A., and DeAngeli, A., 2015. Computation of interface aesthetics. In: *Proceedings of the 33rd Annual ACM Conference on Human Factors in Computing Systems,* New York, NY: ACM, pp. 1163–72.

Nielsen, J., 1994. *Usability engineering.* Mountain View, CA: Academic Press.

Norman, D. A., and Draper, S. W., 1986. User centered system design. *New Perspectives on Human-Computer Interaction.*

O'Donovan, P., Agarwala, A., and Hertzmann, A., 2014. Learning layouts for single-pagegraphic designs. *IEEE Transactions on Visualization and Computer Graphics,* 20(8), pp. 1200–13.

O'Donovan, P., Agarwala, A., and Hertzmann, A., 2015. Designscape: Design with interactive layout suggestions. In: *Proceedings of the 33rd Annual ACM Conference on Human Factors in Computing Systems.* New York, NY: ACM, pp. 1221–4.

Oulasvirta, A., 2017. User interface design with combinatorial optimization. *IEEE Computer,* 50(1), pp. 40–7.

Oulasvirta, A., and Hornbæk, K., 2016. HCI research as problem-solving. In: J. Kaye, A. Druin, C. Lampe, D. Morris, and J. P. Hourcade, eds. *Proceedings of the SIGCHI Conference on Human Factors in Computing*. New York, NY: ACM, pp. 4956–67.

Rao, S., 2009. *Engineering optimization: Theory and Practice*. New York, NY: John Wiley & Sons.

Simon, H. A., 1973. The structure of ill structured problems. *Artificial intelligence*, 4(3–4), pp. 181–201.

Todi, K., Weir, D., and Oulasvirta, A., 2016. Sketchplore: Sketch and explore with a layout optimiser. In: *Proceedings of the 2016 ACM Conference on Designing Interactive Systems*. New York, NY: ACM, pp. 543–55.

Wickens, C. D., and Kramer, A., 1985. Engineering psychology. *Annual Review of Psychology*, 36(1), pp. 307–48.

Winograd, T., and Flores, F., 1986. *Understanding Computers and Cognition: A New Foundation for Design*. Reading, MA: Addison-Wesley.

Zhai, S., Hunter, M., and Smith, B. A., 2002. Performance optimization of virtual keyboards. *Human–Computer Interaction*, 17(2–3), pp. 229–69.

Zimmerman, J., Forlizzi, J., and Evenson, S., 2007. Research through design as a method for interaction design research in HCI. In: *CHI 2007: Proceedings of the SIGCHI Conference on Human Factors in Computing Systems*. New York, NY: ACM, pp. 493–502.

Zwicky, F., 1948. The morphological method of analysis and construction. In: *Studies and Essays. Courant Anniversary Volume*. New York, NY: Interscience.

5

Soft Keyboard Performance Optimization

XIAOJUN BI,
BRIAN SMITH,
TOM OUYANG,
SHUMIN ZHAI

5.1 Introduction

Text entry is one of the most basic, common and important tasks on touchscreen devices (e.g., smartphones and tablets). A survey reported by time.com (McMillan, 2011) shows that the top three most common activities on smartphones are texting, emailing, and chatting on social networks: all of them involve intensive text input. According a study from Nielsen (2010), a teenager, on average, sends over 3,000 messages per month, or more than six texts per waking hour. Given the popularity of mobile text entry, any improvement on the text entry technology will likely have a big impact on the user experience on mobile devices.

A soft keyboard (i.e., virtual keyboard, or on-screen keyboard) is a graphical presentation of keyboard on touchscreen. It is now the major text method on touchscreen devices. A user can enter text by either tapping keys (referred as tap typing), or gesture typing in which a user enters a word by gliding finger over letters. Despite its wide adoption, entering text on soft keyboards is notoriously inefficient and error prone, in part due to the keyboard layout design, and in part the ambiguity of finger input.

First, it is widely known that Qwerty is suboptimal for entering text on mobile devices. Invented in the nineteenth century, one of the rationales of the Qwerty design was to minimize typewriter mechanical jamming by arranging common digraphs on the opposite sides of the keyboards (Yamada, 1980). Such a design has long been understood as inefficient as a single movement point (finger or stylus) keyboard. When used with a single stylus or a single finger, back and forth lateral movement is more frequent and over greater distance than necessary. Although some users tap a soft keyboard with two thumbs on a relatively large touchscreen devices, one-finger text entry is also very common for phone-size touchscreen devices, especially when the other hand is unavailable or when the user is performing gesture typing.

Computational Interaction. Antti Oulasvirta, Per Ola Kristensson, Xiaojun Bi, Andrew Howes (Eds).
© Oxford University Press 2018. Published 2018 by Oxford University Press.

In addition to its inefficiency, Qwerty is notoriously known as being error-prone for gesture typing. This problem occurs in part because when gesture typing, the input finger must inevitably cross unintended letters before reaching the intended one. However, the Qwerty layout itself further exacerbates ambiguity. Because common vowels such as 'u,' 'i,' and 'o' are arranged together, on Qwerty, many pairs of words (such as 'or' and 'our') have identical gestures, and many others (such as 'but' and 'bit') have very similar gestures. For example, the gestures for 'or' and 'our'—their superstrings 'for' and 'four'—also have identical gestures. In fact, our analysis over a 40,000-word lexicon showed that 6.4% of words have another word with an identical gesture on Qwerty.

Second, the imprecision of finger touch and the small key sizes exacerbate the challenge of mobile text entry, especially for tap typing. Compared with mouse or stylus input, finger touch is less precise as an input tool due to the large contact area. Recent research by Bi, Azenkot, Partridge, and Zhai (2013) shows if we only use the key boundaries to determine whether a key is accurately typed, 50% of the output words will be incorrect. Although modern 'smart' keyboards are augmented to correct user's erroneous input (i.e., correction) and complete a word based on partial input (i.e., completion), mis-correction and mis-completion often happen (e.g., examples at, resulting in unpleasant and annoying user experience.

This chapter reviews the research on using computational approaches to improve keyboard performance (Bi, Smith, and Zhai, 2012, Bi, Ouyang, and Zhai, 2014, Smith, Bi, and Zhai, 2015), especially by optimizing the keyboard layout and the correction & completion abilities of the decoder. The computationally designed layouts show big improvements over the existing Qwerty in both efficiency and accuracy; the optimized decoder has improved both the correction and completion ability, and struck a great balance between them. This chapter introduces the research on layout optimization for tap typing (Bi, Smith, and Zhai 2012), and discusses the layout optimization research for gesture typing (Smith, Bi, and Zhai, 2015). Finally, it introduces the work on optimizing the correction and completion abilities of a keyboard decoder (Bi, Ouyang, and Zhai, 2014).

5.2 Layout Optimization for Tap Typing

5.2.1 Qwerty Layout

Qwerty, designed by Christopher L. Sholes and colleagues in 1867 (Yamada, 1980), is the de facto standard for physical keyboards. Although designed for English input, it is also used to input other languages. In some countries, Qwerty is slightly modified to suit their languages. In French-speaking countries, the Azerty layout, on which A and Q, Z and W are switched from their Qwerty positions, is commonly used. The Qwerty keyboard, on which Y and Z are switched, is used in Germany and much of central Europe.

One of the rationales of the Qwerty layout is to minimize typewriter mechanical jamming by arranging common digraphs on the opposite sides of the keyboards (Yamada, 1980). Although it facilitates the two-hand typing, it is suboptimal as a single movement point (finger or stylus) keyboard. The input finger or pointer often needs to travel back and forth between two sides of the Qwerty layout for entering a word, resulting in long travel distances.

Starting from at least as early as Getschow, Rosen, and Goodenough-Trepagnier's (1986) optimization work for increasing efficiency for the motor impaired (Lewis, Kennedy, and LaLomia, 1999), researchers and developers have tried to find various ways to design more efficient alternatives, first using simple algorithms (Getschow, Rosen, and Goodenough-Trepagnier, 1986; Lewis, Kennedy, and LaLomia, 1999) or heuristics (MacKenzie and Zhang, 1999), eventually to more rigorous mathematical optimization (Zhai, Hunter, and Smith, 2000; 2002).

5.2.2 Optimization Objectives

Quantitative optimization is only possible with a well-defined objective function. Interweaved with thinking, composition, and visual search or visual verification, text entry is a complex task involving cognitive, perceptual and motor components. However after a sufficient amount of learning, typing performance is limited primarily by hand movement on the keyboard. Touchscreen keyboard optimization work has therefore focused on movement time reduction (MacKenzie and Zhang, 1999; Soukoreff and MacKenzie, 1995). This could be achieved by statistically minimizing either the movement time (MT) or movement distance (D).

Let D_{ij} be the centre to centre distance from letter key i to letter key j on a given keyboard layout and P_{ij} be the frequency of the digraph letter j following letter i among all digraphs in a given language corpus (i.e., P_{ij} is the ratio between the number of $i - j$ digraphs and the total number of digraphs). One can calculate the average distance (d) traveled for tapping a character on that layout:

$$d = \sum_{i=1}^{26} \sum_{j=1}^{26} P_{ij} D_{ij} \qquad (5.1)$$

D_{ij} and d can be measured in any distance unit. Assuming all keys have the same size, an informative distance unit will be simply the key width (diameter if the key is round) so that the distance measure is normalized against key size and counted as the number of keys travelled.

Equation 5.1 is a reasonable but underused optimization objective function. It means arranging the letter keys in such a way so the average movement distance is the lowest. For example, if the average travel distance to tap on a letter on QWERTY is 3.3 keys, a good result of optimization will be to lower that number to, for example, 1.5 keys. There are two advantages to such an optimization objective. First, it is simple and direct, involving no models or parameters that may be subject to debate. Second, it is also very meaningful: distance is literally and linearly related to 'work' in physics terms. Minimizing the amount of work is a reasonable goal of optimization.

An alternative and more commonly used optimization metric is the average movement time (MT) taken to reach a key. Since movement time cannot be manipulated directly, it has to be related to layout in some way. One approach, taken for example by Hughes, Warren, and Buyukkokten (2002), is to empirically measure T_{ij}, the average movement time between every pair of unlabelled keys on a grid. From there it was possible to obtain the average movement for a given layout with letters assigned on that grid.

A more common approach to movement time optimization uses a human movement model to compute movement time from distance. It is well known that movement time and travel distance are related in a simple equation known as Fitt's (1954) law. According to Fitt's law, the time to move the tapping stylus from key i to key j for a given distance (D_{ij}) and key width (W_{ij}) is:

$$MT_{ij} = a + b\log_2\left(\frac{D_{ij}}{W_{ij}} + 1\right), \tag{5.2}$$

where a and b are empirically determined coefficients. In other words, the more distant a key is from the movement starting point, or the smaller the key is in width, the longer the movement time will be.

It is possible to estimate the average text entry speed on a given touchscreen keyboard layout by summing up Fitt's law movement times between every pair of letters, weighted by the transitional frequency from one letter to another. Lewis and colleagues (Lewis, 1992; Lewis, Kennedy, and LaLomia, 1999; Lewis, Potosnak, and Magyar, 1997) were probably the first to use this calculation as a model of touchscreen keyboard performance. This model was more thoroughly and rigorously studied by MacKenzie and colleagues (MacKenzie and Zhang, 1999; Soukoreff and MacKenzie, 1995). Formally, it predicts the speed limit of tapping on a touchscreen keyboard as follows.

Let P_{ij} be the frequency of the ordered character pair i, j from N number of characters (typically but not necessarily 26 Roman letters); the mean time (t) for tapping a character is

$$t = \sum_{i=1}^{N}\sum_{j=1}^{N} P_{ij}MT_{ij} \tag{5.3}$$

Or,

$$t = a\sum_{i=1}^{N}\sum_{j=1}^{N} P_{ij} + b\sum_{i=1}^{N}\sum_{j=1}^{N} P_{ij}\log_2\left(\frac{D_{ij}}{W_{ij}} + 1\right) \tag{5.4}$$

Since

$$\sum_{i=1}^{N}\sum_{j=1}^{N} P_{ij} = 1,$$

$$t = a + b\sum_{i=1}^{N}\sum_{j=1}^{N} P_{ij}\log_2\left(\frac{D_{ij}}{W_{ij}} + 1\right) \tag{5.5}$$

t has the unit of seconds. t can be converted to input speed (V) in characters per minute (CPM): $V = 60/t$. Equation 5.5 has been called the Fitts-digraph model (Zhai, Hunter, and Smith, 2002).

There are two main advantages to use movement time as the objective function. First, time might be what users are most concerned about in entering text. Second, movement time as the objective function can be converted to the conventional typing speed units of characters per minute (CPM) or words per minute (WPM). For example, if the conventional typing speed standard for an office worker on a typewriter is 60 WPM, an optimization result of 40 WPM for a touchscreen keyboard would give us a good idea how good the result is. From CPM to WPM is a simple arithmetic conversion given 1 minute = 60 seconds and 1 word = 5 characters. The latter is simply a convention and it includes the space character after each word. The average number of characters in a word depends on the text corpus. Our calculation from the American National Written Text Corpus is 4.7 characters per word, excluding the space after the word. We choose to use CPM in the rest of this paper to avoid confusion.

On the other hand, there are disadvantages to using Fitt's law, primarily because there is a wide range of values of Fitt's law parameters (a and b in Equation 5.2) reported in the literature. Based on results from the more general Fitt's reciprocal tapping tasks, previous researchers have selected values such as $a = 0$, $b = 0.204$ (MacKenzie and Zhang, 1999; Zhai, Hunter, and Smith, 2002). Specifically in the context of touchscreen keyboarding, more appropriate estimates were made at $a = 0.083$ s and $b = 0.127$ s (Zhai, Sue, and Accot, 2002). We employed these parameters in this chapter. The accuracies of these values were subsequently verified by an empirical study to be reported later in this chapter. If we assumed $a = 0$, as it had been mistakenly done in the literature (MacKenzie and Zhang, 1999; Zhai, Hunter, and Smith, 2000), the percentage of time improvement estimated would tend to be exaggerated. Here, a reflects 'non-informational aspect of pointing action' (Zhai, 2004). Non-informational aspects of pointing here could include activation of muscles and key press actions that are independent of the distance to the targeted letter, and hence, not influenced by keyboard layout.

Fitt's law also suggests that movement time might be saved by giving greater size to the more commonly used letters. Although not a settled topic, previous work on key size optimization has been unsuccessful due to a number of reasons, including the difficulty of tightly packing keys with varying size and the conflict between central positions and size (Zhai, Hunter, and Smith, 2002).

Given the pros and cons of each approach, this chapter uses movement time as calculated in Equation 5.5 as the primary objective function, but we also simultaneously report the mean distance calculated according to Equation 5.1.

While the methods are general and, to a large extent, independent of the scope of keys included, we chose to first optimize only for the 26 Roman letters, excluding all auxiliary keys. Previous research in this area tended to include the space key in optimization because it is the most frequent character (MacKenzie and Zhang, 1999; Zhai, Hunter, and Smith, 2000). The choice of excluding the space key in this chapter is made for three reasons. First, on almost all the existing keyboards, including QWERTY and the keypad on a cell phone, the 26 Roman letters tend to be grouped together, while all other keys are arranged in the periphery. To ease the access of frequently used auxiliary keys, they are usually assigned different shapes and positioned at distinct positions (e.g., the spacebar on QWERTY). We keep this layout style when designing new keyboards to leverage users' familiarities and the possible cognitive advantages. Second, it is debatable what the best way to enter space is. Besides assigning the space key a distinct shape and position, previous research (Kristensson and Zhai, 2005) has argued that it is better to use a stroke gesture on the keyboard, such as a slide over more than one key-width distance to enter a space because such an action can be done anywhere on the keyboard (saving the time to travel to a specific location) and it is also a more robust word segmentation signal for word-level error correction. In the case of gesture keyboards, i.e. using stroke gestures approximately connecting letters on a keyboard as a way of entering words (Zhai and Kristensson, 2006), the space is automatically entered. Furthermore, the same optimization methodology used in this chapter can also be applied if a space key is included in the optimization process. Including it will not change the essence and main conclusions of this study.

Many languages use diacritics. It is possible to include letters with diacritics in the optimization process or to arrange them separately. We deal with this topic later in the chapter.

To establish reference points, we first calculated the average tapping time and distance on two existing layouts (QWERTY and ATOMIK) as a touchscreen keyboard for English, using English digraph frequencies obtained from a modern, large-scale English corpus: the American National Corpus (ANC) containing 22,162,602 words. Pervious research has shown that layout optimization is not sensitive to corpus source within the same language (Zhai, Hunter, and Smith, 2002). By applying Equation 5.5, the English input speed $V_{English}$ of the QWERTY keyboard is estimated at 181.2 CPM.

5.2.3 Optimization Method

Various approaches can be applied to optimize soft keyboard layouts, including using random search algorithms [2] and integer programming [6]. Each method has its pros and cons. We introduce the research of using one of random search algorithms. Borrowing from physical scientists' methods in understanding material or molecule structures as determined by the lowest energy state, Zhai, Hunter and Smith proposed to view the Fitts-digraph model as a 'virtual energy' function and apply the Metropolis random walk algorithm to search for optimized touchscreen keyboards (Zhai, Hunter, and Smith, 2000). They obtained the Metropolis/ATOMIK family of touchscreen keyboard layouts (Zhai, Hunter, and Smith, 2000; 2002) in this approach.

This approach consists of a finite number of iterations. In each iteration, the Metropolis algorithm picks up two random keys on the keyboard and swaps their positions to reach a new configuration. The input speed of a new configuration is then estimated based on the Fitts-digraph model (Bi, Smith, and Zhai, 2010). Whether the new configuration is kept as the starting position for the next iteration depends on the following Metropolis function:

$$W\,(O - N) = e^{\frac{-\Delta t}{kT}} \; if \, \Delta t > 0$$
$$= 1 \quad if \, \Delta t \leq 0 \tag{5.6}$$

In Equation 5.6, $W\,(O - N)$ is the probability of changing from configuration O (old) to configuration N (new); $\Delta t = t_{new} - t_{old}$, where t_{new} and t_{old} are mean times for typing a character on the new and old keyboard configurations, estimated by Equation 5.5; k is a coefficient; T is 'temperature', which can be interactively adjusted. Key to the algorithm is the fact that the search does not always move toward a lower energy state. It occasionally allows moves with positive energy changes to be able to climb out of a local minimum. We use the same basic optimization process in this chapter.

The conventional QWERTY keyboard lays the 26 English letters in a rectangle shape with three rows and ten columns, which is well suited for two-handed typing. Such a constraint is not necessary for touchscreen keyboards. If the keyboard is not constrained to any particular shape, the objective function of minimizing one point travel (by a stylus or a single finger) would tend to result in a rounded keyboard (Zhai, Hunter, and Smith, 2000). Our experience is that a more practical square shape (or near square such as a five rows by six columns grid) is more practical for graphic design and still gives sufficient flexibility for optimization (Zhai, Hunter, and Smith, 2002). As shown in Figure 5.2, in practical product designs the keys on the edge unused by the alphabet letters can be filled with auxiliary characters and functions.

5.2.3.1 Optimization for Multiple Languages

The possible compatibility across different languages and the flexibility of the keyboard optimization space observed in the previous layout optimization research give hope to the goal of simultaneously optimizing for multiple languages. The basic methodology used in the present study is to average the mean time of tapping a character across multiple languages, and minimize it by the Metropolis algorithm. Given m different languages, the mean time t of tapping a character across these m languages is calculated as:

$$t = \sum_{i=1}^{m} \frac{t_i}{m} \tag{5.7}$$

where t_i represents the mean time of inputting a character in language i, which is estimated by the Fitts-digraph model (Equation 5.5). Then, t is regarded as the objective function and minimized by the Metropolis algorithm. The optimization process is similar to previous work (Zhai, Hunter, and Smith, 2002), except that the 'virtual energy' (t_{new} and t_{old}) is estimated by Equation 5.7.

The average in Equation 5.7 can be possibly weighted according to each language's speaker population or some other criteria. Although any weighting scheme can be controversial, the same methodology and procedure presented in this paper should still apply. We stay with Equation 5.7 as the objective function in the present work.

5.2.4 Results

5.2.4.1 English and French

We start with optimizing a keyboard for both English and French. These two languages are commonly used in the world: it is estimated that over 470 million people speak English and more than 250 million people speak French. The keyboard optimized for these two languages could benefit many English-French speakers.

As shown in Figure 5.1 and 5.2, although English and French vary in many aspects, their letter and digraph frequency distributions are strongly correlated, with correlation coefficients 0.88 (letter) and 0.75 (digraph) respectively. These high correlations are

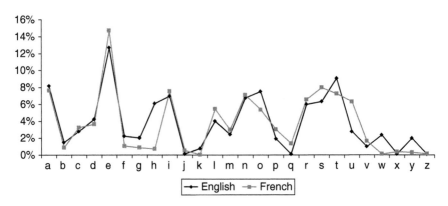

Figure 5.1 Letter Frequency of English and French.

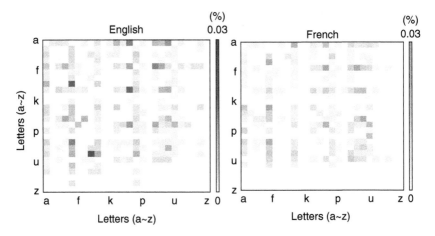

Figure 5.2 Heat maps of English (left) and French (right) digraph distribution. The shade intensity reflects each digraph cell's frequency.

encouraging for our optimization objective. Note that the English corpus is obtained from ANC, and corpora of other languages are from http://corpus.leeds.ac.uk/list.html.

According to Equation 5.7, the mean time of typing a character t is then calculated as:

$$t = 0.5t_{Eng} + 0.5t_{Fren} \tag{5.8}$$

where t_{Eng} is the mean time of typing an English letter, and t_{Fren} a French letter.

Using the Metropolis algorithm, we obtained a variety of keyboards with similar performance. Figure 5.3 shows one of them, which is denoted by K-Eng-Fren.

We also used the Metropolis method to optimize solely for English and French, obtaining K-English and K-French respectively (Figure 5.3). Figure 5.4 shows the performance of all three optimization results, as well as the performance of QWERTY. The calculated English input speed for K-English, K-Eng-Fren, and QWERTY are 230.1, 229.4, and 181.2 CPM

K-Eng-Fren

	g	v	k	z	
j	d	n	a	c	
f	o	i	t	h	w
q	u	r	e	s	y
x	p	m	l	b	

K-English

	z	j	d	g	k	
	y	l	n	i	c	
	f	o	a	t	h	w
	b	u	r	e	s	
	q	p	m	v	x	

K-French

	h	f	v	w	
	c	t	a	p	k
y	o	n	i	r	g
q	u	s	e	l	b
	x	m	d	j	z

Figure 5.3 The layout of K-Eng-Fren, K-English, and K-French.

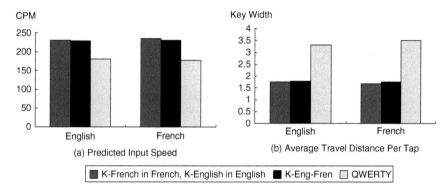

Figure 5.4 Predicted input speed and average travel distance per tap of K-English, K-French, and K-Eng-Fren and QWERTY.

respectively, and French input speed for K-French, K-Eng-Fren and QWERTY are 235.0, 230.8, and 177.8 CPM respectively. As one would expect, since K-Eng-Fren takes into account two languages simultaneously, it is inferior to K-English in English inputting speed ($V_{English}$). However, K-Eng-Fren is only 1 CPM lower than K-English in speed. Such a tiny performance drop should be negligible in real use. A similar relationship exists between K-Eng-Fren and K-Fren. Compared to the standard QWERTY layout, K-Eng-Fren is superior in both English and French input: K-Eng-Fren improves the English inputting speed by 48.2 CPM, and French by 53.0 CPM.

If we look at the average travel distance per tap (Figure 5.4b) on these layouts for English and French respectively, we can draw similar conclusions. For English, the average travel distance per key press on K-English, K-French, and K-Eng-Fren and QWERTY are 1.76, 1.93, 1.78, and 3.31, respectively. K-Eng-Fren is 46% shorter than QWERTY but only 1% longer than K-English. For French, the average travel distance per key press on K-English, K-French, and K-Eng-Fren and QWERTY are 1.85, 1.68, 1.76, and 3.51, respectively. K-Eng-Fren is 50% shorter than QWERTY but only 5% longer than K-French.

In summary, it is somewhat surprising, and quite encouraging, that it is possible to simultaneously optimize a keyboard layout for both English and French input efficiency.

The resulting layout has little loss for English from a keyboard specifically optimized for English and little loss for French from a keyboard specifically optimized for French.

5.2.4.2 English, French, German, Spanish and Chinese

We have shown that it is possible to optimize movement time simultaneously for at least two languages, English and French, without a practical loss in efficiency for each. This is certainly good news for optimizing keyboard design between a pair of languages. Bilingual optimization is a possible strategy since most multilingual users are likely to be bilingual. However optimizing for two languages at a time can also be a problem due to the large number of combinations (e.g., English-French, English-Chinese, English-German, Chinese-French, Chinese-German, German-French ...). The large number of combinations would impose configuration burdens on software and device makers, distributors, and users. Configuration simplicity can be one reason to maintain the status quo legacy of QWERTY for touchscreen keyboarding. This led us to tackle the next challenge—optimizing for five major languages: English, French, German, Spanish, and Chinese (pinyin) at the same time.

We can attribute the positive results of K-Eng-Fren to the flexibility of the touchscreen keyboard optimization space and the high correlation in digraph distributions between these two languages. The question now is whether these same factors can still allow for simultaneously optimized keyboards for four large European languages plus Chinese *pinyin*. Spanish and German share some common words with English and French, and all use the basic Latin alphabet. However, Chinese is different. It is logographic and shares few commonalities with the other four languages. Optimizing a keyboard for all five of these languages will help us understand how flexible the touchscreen keyboard optimization space is.

Moreover, these five languages are widely used in the world. Chinese, Spanish, and English are the top three most-spoken languages. The layout optimized for these five languages would benefit a large number of multilingual speakers.

Although Chinese is logographic, the most common approach to inputting Chinese on computers is based on *pinyin*, a phonetic spelling system also based on the Latin alphabet. Using *pinyin* to enter Chinese characters consists of two steps. First, the *pinyin* letters representing the pronunciation of the Chinese character is entered. As one *pinyin* string may correspond to many Chinese characters, the target character is then selected from the many homophonic candidates in the second step. Predictive techniques are usually used in this step: the ranking or even automatic selection of the corresponding logographic characters can be based on the proceeding characters in addition to the *pinyin* input. The first step involves typing letters, so keyboard layout could significantly affect its input speed. The second step is independent of the keyboard layout. To improve the input speed of Chinese via *pinyin*, keys should be arranged to improve *pinyin* input speed.

By analysing language corpora, greater deviation was observed of Chinese from the other four languages (see Figure 5.5. for letter frequency). For example, the most frequent letter in English, French, Spanish, and German is 'e', while 'i' is the most frequently used one in Chinese *pinyin*. Inconsistencies also exist in digraph distribution. For example, 'zh' is frequently used in Chinese *pinyin*, while it rarely occurs in English.

Figure 5.6 shows the correlation coefficients across these five languages. As shown, Chinese is loosely correlated with other four languages. In letter frequency distribution, the

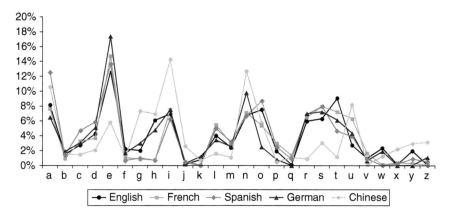

Figure 5.5 Letter Frequency in English, French, German, Spanish, and Chinese.

	English	French	Spanish	German	Chinese
English		0.75	0.74	0.69	0.36
French	0.88		0.86	0.70	0.30
Spanish	0.86	0.92		0.66	0.24
German	0.88	0.90	0.81		0.33
Chinese	0.48	0.44	0.46	0.51	

Figure 5.6 Correlation coefficients of letter (bottom-left) and digraph frequency distributions (top-right).

Pearson product-moment correlation coefficients between Chinese with other languages are all below 0.51, while those across the other four languages are all above 0.8. In digraph distribution, correlation coefficients between Chinese with other four languages are all below 0.4. In one case, between Spanish and Chinese, the digraph correlation is only 0.24. These low correlations impose a challenge to simultaneous optimization. If the positive result in Section 5.2.5.1 was largely due to the strong digraph correlation between English and French, the current goal of optimizing for five languages, including Chinese, would have to place greater hope on the flexibility of the optimization space itself.

Following the proposed multilingual optimization methodology, each of the five languages is weighted equally in the optimization process. The mean time of inputting a character is represented as:

$$t = 0.2t_{Eng} + 0.2t_{Fren} + 0.2t_{Spanish} + 0.2t_{German} + 0.2t_{Chn} \tag{5.9}$$

$t_{Eng}, t_{Fren}, t_{Spanish}, t_{German}$ and t_{Chn} are the mean times of typing a character in the corresponding languages, which are predicted by the Fitts-digraph model (Equation 5.5). By means of the Metropolis algorithm, we obtained the K5 layout, which was simultaneously optimized

K5					
	k	j	z	x	
	f	c	h	t	w
q	u	o	i	s	p
y	m	a	n	e	r
	b	l	g	d	v

K-English					
	z	j	d	g	k
	y	l	n	i	c
	f	o	a	t	h	w
	b	u	r	e	s
	q	p	m	v	x

K-French					
		h	f	v	w
		c	t	a	p	k
	y	o	n	i	r	g
	q	u	s	e	l	b
		x	m	d	j	z

K-Spanish					
	q	x	f		
	u	n	t	c	k
g	s	e	d	i	v
j	o	r	a	l	h
y	p	m	b	z	w

K-German					
		f	m	p		q
	z	u	a	s	c	y
	w	n	i	t	h	x
	j	d	e	r	o	v
		b	g	l	k	

K-Chinese					
		r	m	l	p
	w	e	d	j	x	v
	f	n	a	i	h	s
	k	g	o	u	z	c
		t	y	b	q	

Figure 5.7 The layouts of K5, and optimized layout for each individual language.

for inputting English, French, Spanish, German, and Chinese. We also obtained optimized layouts and their performances for each of the five languages (See Figure 5.7). Figure 5.8 summarizes these results in V (calculated input speed) and d (average distance in the unit of key width for entering a character) metrics.

Let us first examine the individual results when optimized specifically for each of the five languages, summarized in bold numbers in the diagonal cells of Figure 5.8. The first interesting observation is that after optimization for each language, the average travel distance per tap fell into a relatively narrow range: 1.76, 1.68, 1.76, 1.63, and 1.5 keys for English, French, Spanish, German, and Chinese, respectively. Greater differences between these languages may have been expected, given their different phonology. In comparison, QWERTY is somewhat equally bad for all: 3.31, 3.51, 3.7, 3.26, and 3.85 keys for English, French, Spanish, German, and Chinese respectively. The ratio between the average travel distance per tap on QWERTY and the average travel distance per tap on the keyboards individually optimized for each language are large: 1.88, 2.09, 2.10, 1.99, and 2.57 for English, French, Spanish, German, and Chinese, respectively. Figure 5.8 illustrates the travel distance difference among the various layouts. Although English has been the primary target language used in touchscreen keyboard optimization work (8, 14, 15, 16, 17 Zhai, Hunter, and Smith, 2000, 25), English in fact has the least to gain and Chinese has the most to gain from touchscreen keyboard optimization. These results and observations are new to our knowledge.

When the five languages are considered simultaneously, the optimization effect is still strong. As shown in Figure 5.8, the average distance d for tapping a character on K5 are 1.88, 1.86, 1.91, 1.77, and 1.68 keys for English, French, Spanish, German, and Chinese respectively, much shorter than QWERTY's 3,31, 3.51, 3.7, 3.26, and 3.85 keys, and close to the results obtained specifically for each language (1.76, 1.68, 1.76, 1.63, and 1.5 keys for

	English		French		Spanish		German		Chinese	
	v	d	v	d	v	d	v	d	v	d
K-English	**230.7**	**1.76**	226.5	1.85	221.2	1.9	224.5	1.87	220.3	1.95
K-French	221.7	1.93	**235**	**1.68**	224.1	1.85	225.9	1.84	207.8	2.25
K-Spanish	217.4	2.02	229.2	1.78	**229.9**	**1.76**	223.9	1.89	201.3	2.37
K-German	221.5	1.94	221.2	1.95	218	1.97	**237.8**	**1.63**	211.9	2.12
K-Chinese	205.1	2.34	207.6	2.27	204.3	2.31	213.1	2.14	**244.9**	**1.5**
K5	**225.1**	**1.88**	226.2	1.86	221.6	1.91	230.6	1.77	233.4	1.68
ATOMIK	221.5	1.94	221.2	1.96	215.9	2.05	222	1.93	212.8	2.1
QWERTY	181.2	3.31	177.8	3.51	173	3.7	181.9	3.26	168.7	3.85

Figure 5.8 Calculated input speed (CPM) and average travel distance per tap (keys) of various layout optimized for English, French, Spanish, German, Chinese, all five, and two previous layouts (ATOMIK and QWERTY).

	English	French	Spanish	German	Chinese
Individual optimization/QWERTY	0.53	0.48	0.48	0.50	0.39
K5/QWERTY	0.57	0.53	0.52	0.54	0.44
Individual optimization/K5	0.94	0.90	0.92	0.92	0.89

Figure 5.9 The ratios of travel distance between layouts for the five languages.

English, French, Spanish, German, and Chinese, respectively.) The ratios in travel distance between K5 and QWERTY, and between the individually optimized layouts and K5, are summarized in Figure 5.9.

As discussed earlier, the digraph correlations among the five languages are relatively weak, so optimizing for only one language provides no guarantee that the resulting layout would also be good for other languages. Note that the optimization process uses a stochastic method, so each layout obtained is just one instance of many possibilities. The specific instance of layout we obtained for English happened to be also quite good for the other four languages (see Figure 5.10), although not as good as K5. On the other hand, the specific instance of Spanish layout was relatively poor for Chinese. Interestingly, the layout optimized for Chinese was not very good for any of the other four languages (Figure 5.10).

The computational study and analysis thus far have not only produced optimized layouts for French, Spanish, German, and Chinese that have not been previously reported in the literature, but also demonstrated that it is possible to accommodate at least these five languages in one optimized layout, with about a 10% travel distance increase from individually optimized layouts (See Figure 5.9).

Having examined the layouts in terms of travel distance, let us now evaluate the calculated input speeds of all languages as shown in Figure 5.11 and in Figure 5.8. K5 is faster than

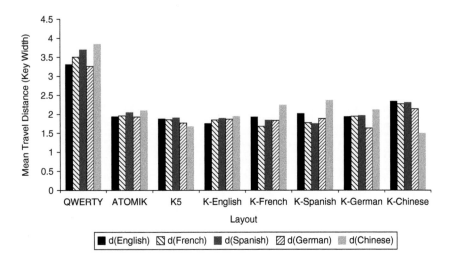

Figure 5.10 The average travel distance per tap for English, French, Spanish, German, and Chinese on various optimized and QWERTY layouts.

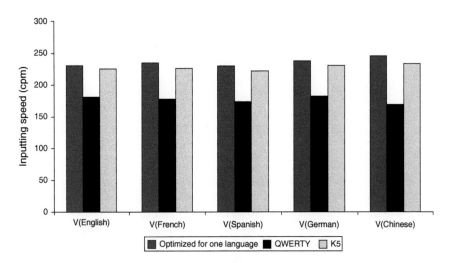

Figure 5.11 Calculated input speed of K5, QWERTY, and single-language optimization keyboards.

QWERTY for all the five languages. As an example, in English, K5 improves the input speed by 24% over QWERTY, from 181.2 CPM to 225.1 CPM. To compare with a past optimization effort, the performance metrics (V and d) of K5 for English are better than those of the revised ATOMIK, as currently used in ShapeWriter ($V = 221.5$ CPM, $d = 1.94$ keys).

Fortunately, considering five languages simultaneously caused only minimal performance decreases to the optimization results: the input speed of K5 is very close to K-English, K-French, K-Spanish, K-German, and K-Chinese, separately optimized for each language. The biggest decrease occurs in Chinese entry, in which K5 is 11.5 CPM, or around 5%, slower than K-Chinese.

The five popular languages investigated in this chapter are from diverse groups: English and German are Germanic languages, and Spanish and French are from the Romance language group. Although all four of these languages belong to the Indo-European family, Chinese is from the Sino-Tibetan language family. Despite the diversity, our results show that there are near-optimal layouts that can accommodate all of them, which demonstrates the flexibility of the touchscreen optimization space. While these five languages together are spoken by nearly two-thirds of the world's population, they are a small fraction of the total number of languages spoken. Furthermore, all of the five investigated, including Chinese *pinyin*, are based on the Latin alphabet. How much more we may expand this common optimization approach to cover even more languages, particularly those that are not Latin alphabet-based, remains an open question.

5.3 Layout Optimization for Gesture Typing

5.3.1 Qwerty for Gesture Typing

Gesture typing has gained large-scale adoption on mobile devices since its conception in the early 2000s (Kristensson and Zhai, 2004). Today, gesture typing can be found on all major mobile computing platforms in products such as ShapeWriter, Swype, SwiftKey, SlideIT, TouchPal, and Google Keyboard. Compared to touch typing (tapping), gesture typing offers several advantages. It supports a gradual and seamless transition from visually guided tracing to recall-based gesturing, allows users to approximate words with gestures rather than tapping each key exactly, and mitigates one major problem plaguing regular touchscreen typing: the lack of tactile feedback.

Despite these benefits, gesture typing suffers from an inherent problem: highly ambiguous word gestures. Bi, Azenkot, Partridge, and Zhai (2013) showed that the error rate for gesture typing is approximately 5–10% higher than for touch typing. This problem occurs because when gesture typing, the input finger must inevitably cross unintended letters before reaching the intended one. The Qwerty layout itself further exacerbates this problem. Because common vowels such as 'u,' 'i,' and 'o' are arranged together on Qwerty, many pairs of words have identical or very similar gestures. For example, the gestures for 'or' and 'our'— their superstrings 'for' and 'four'—have identical gestures. In fact, our analysis over a 40,000-word lexicon showed that 6.4% of words have another word with an identical gesture on Qwerty.

Given Qwerty's obvious problems, rearranging the keys to make word gestures more distinct should reduce the error rate when gesture typing. This section, we introduces the research on optimizing the keyboard layout for gesture typing.

5.3.2 Optimization Objectives

A gesture typing keyboard layout is optimized for three metrics: gesture clarity, gesture speed, and similarity to Qwerty.

5.3.2.1 Gesture Clarity

The gesture clarity metric is the most important metric in our optimization. The purpose of this metric is to measure the uniqueness of the word gestures on a keyboard layout. We based the metric on the location channel in SHARK2 (Kristensson and Zhai, 2004) and represent each word's gesture as its ideal trace, the polyline connecting the key centres of the word's letters. We define the nearest neighbour of a word w to be the word whose ideal trace is closest to w's ideal trace. This is the word that is most likely to be confused with w when gesture typing, independent from the language model. The closer a word is to its nearest neighbour, the more likely its gesture will be misrecognized. The gesture clarity metric score for a given keyboard layout is simply the average distance (weighted by words' frequencies) between each word and its nearest neighbour on that keyboard layout:

$$\text{Clarity} = \sum_{w \in L} f_w d_w,$$
$$\text{where } d_w = \min_{x \in L - \{w\}} d(w, x) \text{ and } \sum_{w \in L} f_w = 1. \tag{5.10}$$

L is a 40,000-word lexicon, f_w is the frequency of w, and d_w is the distance between w and its nearest neighbour. We compute the distance between two ideal traces w and x via proportional shape matching. Each gesture is sampled into N equidistant points, and the distance is simply the average of the distance between corresponding points:

$$d(w, x) = \frac{1}{N} \sum_{i=1}^{N} \|w_i - x_i\|_2 \tag{5.11}$$

Since the gesture clarity metric compares the gestures of every pair of words to find each word's nearest neighbour, its time complexity is $\Theta(N \cdot |L|^2)$. Here, L is the number of words in the lexicon and N is the number of sample points in each word gesture. Its quadratic time complexity with respect to L stands in stark contrast to the time complexities of earlier optimization metrics (which are exclusively linear with respect to L), making optimization using it intractable. For our 40,000-word lexicon, there are nearly 800 million pairs of word gestures to compare for each keyboard layout that we examine during the optimization process.

To make the metric more tractable, we made two key algorithmic refinements. First, when searching for the nearest neighbour for each word, we only considered prospective neighbours that started and ended with characters that were located within one key diagonal of the word's starting and ending character, respectively. This is similar to the initial template-pruning step employed in SHARK2 (Kristensson and Zhai, 2004), where the distance threshold in this case is the diagonal length of a key. Second, we used a small number of gesture sample points N to represent each word's gesture. If N were too large, the computation would be very expensive. If N were too small, word gestures (especially longer ones) might not be represented properly, leading to incorrectly chosen nearest neighbours.

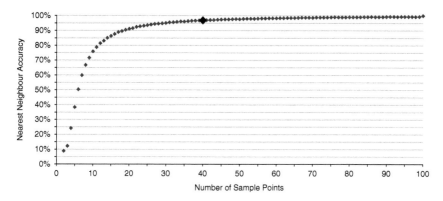

Figure 5.12 Word gesture neighbour sensitivity. The nearest neighbour that we find for a word depends on how finely the word gestures are sampled. Here, we show the percentage of nearest neighbours that are the same as when 100 sample points are used. The darker dot signifies 40 points, the amount used.

In order to see how small we could make N without affecting the integrity of our results, we performed a small experiment. First, we found each word's nearest neighbour on Qwerty using very fine sampling ($N = 100$). Then, we repeated this step for smaller values of N down to $N = 20$ and counted the number of nearest neighbours that were identical to the $N = 100$ case. Figure 5.12 shows the results. When the number of sample points is reduced to 40, 96.9% of the nearest neighbours are the same as they were before. We used this value for N in our algorithm.

5.3.2.2 Gesture Speed

The gesture speed metric estimates how quickly users can gesture type on a keyboard layout. We based this metric on the CLC model by Cao and Zhai (2007). The model (which stands for 'curves, line segments, and corners') stems from human motor control theory, and was designed to predict the amount of time it takes for a person to make an arbitrary pen stroke gesture. To do this, the model partitions the gesture into segments, where each segment is a curve (with a constant radius of curvature), a straight line, or a corner (whose interior angle does not need to be $90°$). The time that it takes for a person to gesture each type of segment is modelled with a different function. For line segments, the time is modelled with a power function that echoes how people tend to gesture faster with longer lines:

$$T\left(\overline{AB}\right) = m \cdot \left(\|\overline{AB}\|_2\right)^n. \tag{5.12}$$

Here, $\overline{AB}$ is a line segment, the output T is in milliseconds, $\|\overline{AB}\|_2$ is the length of $\overline{AB}$ in millimeters, and both m and n are constants (found to be 68.8 and 0.469 respectively in Cao and Zhai's original formulation (2004).

A polyline gesture is simply a collection of individual line segments. The time to complete this type of gesture is modelled as simply the sum of the individual line segments' functions:

$$T(P) = \sum_{\overline{AB} \in P} T(\overline{AB}), \tag{5.13}$$

where P is the polyline and $\overline{AB}$ is a segment in the polyline. Although Cao and Zhai found that the angles between polyline segments (that is, of a polyline's corners) have an effect on gesture entry time, the magnitude of the effect was small: less than 40 ms per corner compared to 200–700 ms per segment. Hence, the model uses corners to delineate segments but omits their 40 ms contribution.

As with the gesture clarity metric, each word in the lexicon is represented as its ideal trace. To help compute the metric, we store a table of the weighted number of occurrences of each bigram in our lexicon. The weighted number of occurrences $o(i-j)$ of a bigram $i-j$ (for letters i and j) is calculated as follows:

$$o(i-j) = \sum_{w \in L} f_w \cdot (\# \text{ occurrences of } i-j \text{ in } w) \tag{5.14}$$

Here, L is the lexicon, w is a word in the lexicon, and f_w is the frequency of word w in L. Each bigram is represented by a different line segment in the CLC model. Hence, to estimate G, the average time it takes to complete a word gesture, we calculate the following:

$$G = \sum_{i,j \in \alpha} o(i-j) \cdot T(\overline{K_i K_j}) \tag{5.15}$$

Here, i and j are both letters in alphabet α, the set of lowercase letters from 'a' to 'z.' K_i and K_j are the key centers of the i and j keys, respectively, $\overline{K_i K_j}$ is the line segment connecting the key centres, and the function T is defined in Equation 5.12. Hence, G is measured in milliseconds.

The last step is to convert the gesture duration G into words per minute (WPM), a measure of typing speed. Doing so gives us our gesture speed metric score:

$$\text{Speed} = \frac{60,000}{G} \tag{5.16}$$

60,000 represents the number of milliseconds in one minute. When calculating the gesture typing speed of a keyboard layout, we do not consider the effects of the space bar or capitalization (and the Shift key). One of the key contributions of gesture typing is the fact that spaces are automatically added between word gestures, eliminating the need for one in approximately every 5.7 characters typed (Zhai and Kristensson, 2003). Moreover, most of today's gesture-typing systems apply capitalization and diacritics automatically.

We should also note that, because the CLC model omits the cost of gesturing corners and the cost of travelling from the end of one gesture to the beginning of the next, the calculated speeds generally overestimate the speeds at which users would actually type. Rick (2010) proposed an alternative to the CLC model that is also based on Fitt's law, and although we ultimately chose to use the CLC model for our metric, we implemented Rick's model (without key taps for single-character words) to compare the models' behaviours. We found that Rick's model consistently output lower speed estimates than the CLC model, but that they both followed the same overall trend. More specifically, the mean (std. dev.) ratio between Rick's model's predicted speeds and the CLC model's predicted speeds for our final set of optimized layouts is 0.310 (0.004). After normalizing the metrics as described in Section 5.3.3.1, the mean (std. dev.) ratio becomes 0.995 (0.016).

5.3.2.3 Qwerty Similarity

As existing studies show (Yamada, 1980; Zhai, Hunter, and Smith, 2002; Rick, 2010), the key obstacle to the widespread adoption of optimized layouts is the arduous process of learning the new layouts. The Qwerty similarity metric measures how similar a given keyboard layout is to Qwerty. By making a new layout more similar to Qwerty (and hence less alien to longtime users of Qwerty), we hope to bridge the gap between the short-term frustration of learning the new layout and the long-term benefits that the layout provides.

The metric is based on the constraint that Bi, Smith, and Zhai (2010) used when creating the Quasi-Qwerty layout. In that optimization (which was for typing speed only), keys were not allowed to move more than one slot away from their Qwerty locations. Dunlop and Levine (2006) later relaxed this constraint in their multi-objective keyboard optimization by using the total squared Euclidean distance between keys' positions and their Qwerty locations instead. Since a keyboard layout is essentially a grid of keys, we use the total Manhattan distance between keys' positions and their Qwerty locations to measure Qwerty similarity. Like Dunlop and Levine's metric, this allows more freedom than the hard constraint used by Quasi-Qwerty. However, unlike Dunlop and Levine's metric, individual keys are not punished so severely if they move far from their Qwerty locations. This allows us to consider layouts in which a few keys move very far from their Qwerty locations.

The Qwerty similarity metric for a given keyboard layout is computed as follows:

$$\text{Similarity} = \sum_{i \in \alpha} \left(|k_{i_x} - q_{i_x}| + |k_{i_y} - q_{i_y}| \right) \tag{5.17}$$

where i is a letter in alphabet α, the set of lowercase letters from 'a' to 'z,' and k_{i_x} and q_{i_x} are the x-indices of the i key on the given keyboard layout and Qwerty, respectively. Unlike K_i and K_j in Equation 5.15, which are points with units of millimetres, k_i and q_i are unit-less ordered pairs of integers that represent the 2D index of key i's slot in the keyboard grid. In most of today's touchscreen keyboard layouts, the second and third rows are offset from the first row by half of a key width. Hence, in order to properly calculate the Manhattan distance for this metric, we treat the second and third rows as if they are shifted to the left by another half of a key width, so that the second row is left-aligned with the first row. The resulting representation of keyboard layouts is actually identical to the one used for creating Quasi-Qwerty (Bi, Smith, and Zhai, 2010). The Qwerty similarity metric is the only one that uses this modified keyboard representation.

5.3.3 Optimization Method

We frame the problem of designing a touchscreen keyboard for gesture typing as a multi-objective optimization, where the three objectives are improving (a) gesture clarity, (b) gesture speed, and (c) Qwerty similarity. There are multiple ways of judging how well a layout meets these objectives. One way is to create a simple objective function that somehow combines the objectives' associated metric scores (for example, by summing the scores in a linear combination). However, such an approach would force us to decide how much each metric should count for in deriving a single optimal layout, when, in fact, we are more interested in understanding the behaviour of each of the metrics and the inherent tradeoffs between them.

As a result, although we still employ a simple objective function as part of our optimization's second phase, we use another approach called Pareto optimization for the optimization at large. Pareto optimization has recently been used to optimize both keyboard layouts (Dunlop and Levine, 2006) and keyboard algorithms (Bi, Ouyang, and Zhai, 2013). In this approach, we calculate an optimal set of layouts called a Pareto optimal set or a Pareto front. Each layout in the set is Pareto optimal, which means that none of its metric scores can be improved without hurting the other scores. If a layout is not Pareto optimal, then it is dominated, which means that there exists a Pareto optimal layout that is better than it with respect to at least one metric, and no worse than it with respect to the others. By calculating the Pareto optimal set of keyboard layouts, rather than a single keyboard layout, we can analyse the tradeoffs inherent in choosing a keyboard layout and give researchers the freedom to choose one that best meets their constraints.

Our optimization procedure is composed of three phases, described in detail in the next subsections.

5.3.3.1 Phase 1: Metric Normalization

In the first phase, we perform a series of optimizations for each metric individually to estimate the minimum and maximum possible raw values for each metric. We then normalize each of the metric's scores in a linear fashion so that the worst possible score is mapped to 0.0 and the best possible score is mapped to 1.0. Normalizing the scores allows us to weight the metrics appropriately in Phase 2.

We use local neighbourhood search to perform the optimizations. In order to more reliably find the global extrema instead of local extrema, we incorporate a simulated annealing process similar to the Metropolis random walk algorithm (Hastings, 1970; Zhai, Hunter, and Smith, 2000). Each optimization starts with a random keyboard layout using the same footprint as Qwerty and runs for 2,000 iterations. At each iteration, we swap the locations of two randomly chosen keys in the current layout to create a new candidate layout. If the new layout is better than the current layout, we keep the new layout with 100% probability. Otherwise, we only keep the new layout with a probability specified by a user-controlled 'temperature.' Higher temperatures increase this probability, and allow us to escape from local extrema.

In total, we performed 10–30 optimizations for each metric. We found that the range for the raw gesture typing clarity metric scores was [0.256 key widths, 0.533 key widths], that the range for the raw gesture typing speed metric scores was [50.601 WPM, 77.929 WPM], and that the range for the raw Qwerty similarity metric scores was [0, 148]. Qwerty's raw scores for the three metrics are 2.390 mm, 62.652 WPM, and 0, respectively.

5.3.3.2 Phase 2: Pareto Front Initialization

In this phase, we generate an initial Pareto front of keyboard layouts by performing even more local neighbourhood searches. The searches are identical to the ones we perform in Phase 1, except this time we seek to maximize the score from linear combinations of all three metric scores. We use twenty-two different weightings for the linear combinations and perform roughly fifteen full 2000-iteration local neighbourhood searches for each weighting. The purpose is to ensure that the Pareto front includes a broad range of Pareto optimal keyboard layouts.

The Pareto front starts out empty at the very beginning of this phase, but we update it with each new candidate keyboard layout that we encounter during the searches (at each iteration of each search). To update the front, we compare the candidate layout with the layouts already on the front. Then, we add the candidate layout to the front if it is Pareto optimal (possibly displacing layouts already on the front that are now dominated by the candidate layout). The candidate layout is added whether it is ultimately kept in the particular local neighbourhood search or not.

5.3.3.3 Phase 3: Pareto Front Expansion

In the last phase, we perform roughly 200 passes over the Pareto front to help 'fill out' the front by finding Pareto optimal layouts that are similar to those already on the front. In each pass, we swap two keys in each layout on the front to generate a set of candidate layouts, then update the front with any candidate layouts that are Pareto optimal. This phase is similar to the optimization used by Dunlop and Levine (2006). However, by including Phase 2, we can ensure that all possible solutions are reachable without the need to swap more than two keys at a time.

We based our optimization's keyboard representation on dimensions of the Nexus 5 Android keyboard. Since most of today's touchscreen keyboards have very similar profiles, our results should be applicable to any touchscreen keyboard. Each key is represented by its entire touch-sensitive area (with boundaries placed between the centre points of neighbouring keys) and is 109×165 px (6.22×9.42 mm) in size.

Our lexicon consists of 40,000 words. Before starting the optimization, we converted words with diacritics to their Anglicized forms ('naïve' to 'naive,' for example), removed all punctuation marks from words (such as 'can't'), and made all words completely lowercase. Since gesture typing systems automatically handle diacritics, capitalization, and punctuation marks within words, this should not hurt the integrity of our optimization.

Due to the complexity and scope of our work, it took four machines (with 32 threads apiece) running continuously over the course of nearly three weeks to obtain the results presented below.

5.3.4 Results

Figure 5.13 shows the final Pareto front of keyboard layouts optimized for gesture typing. Overall, the front is composed of 1,725 keyboard layouts chosen from the 900,000+ candidate layouts that we examined in all. No single layout on the front is better than all of the others—each layout is better than the others in some way, and the tradeoffs that are inherent in choosing a suitable layout from the front are reflected in the front's convex shape.

More specifically, the front can be viewed as a 3D design space of performance goals that one can choose from for different usage scenarios. Layouts with high gesture clarity scores,

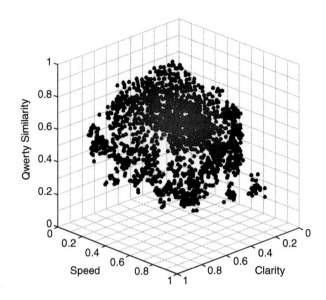

Figure 5.13 D Pareto front. The keyboard layouts with lighter shades are farther from the origin.

gesture speed scores, and Qwerty similarity scores are more apt to exhibit lower error rates, expert-level gesture entry times, and initial gesture entry times (respectively) than those with low scores. However, since each layout on the front represents a compromise between these three goals, the choice of layout for a particular user or usage scenario depends on the relative importance of each goal. For example, a fast but less accurate user may prefer a layout biased towards clarity, while a user who gesture types very accurately may prefer a layout biased toward speed. Nevertheless, if we know nothing about users' preferences or wish to choose a layout that can best accommodate a wide variety of preferences, it is reasonable to use one that is in the middle of the convex surface (serving each goal on a roughly equal basis) as Dunlop and Levine (2006) did.

We now highlight layouts optimized for each of the three metrics as well as layouts that serve roughly equal combinations of metrics. These layouts may serve as useful references to researchers and designers, and later (in the user study) help us test the effectiveness of our optimization and its associated metrics.

Figure 5.14(a) shows GK-C ('Gesture Keyboard—Clarity'), the layout optimized exclusively for gesture typing clarity. Figure 5.14(b) shows GK-S, which was optimized exclusively for speed. The layout optimized for Qwerty similarity is simply Qwerty itself.

Figure 5.14(c) shows GK-D (where the 'D' stands for 'double-optimized'). This keyboard offers a roughly equal compromise between gesture typing clarity and gesture typing speed without regard to learnability (Qwerty similarity). To find this layout, we projected the 3D Pareto front onto the clarity–speed plane to derive a 2D Pareto front between clarity and speed, then chose the layout on the 2D front that was closest to the 45° line. Figure 5.5 shows the 2D Pareto front and GK-D.

Figure 5.14(d) shows GK-T, where the 'T' stands for 'triple optimized.' This keyboard offers a roughly equal compromise between all three metrics: gesture typing clarity, gesture

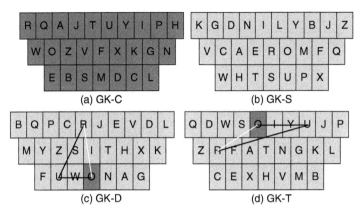

(a) GK-C

(b) GK-S

(c) GK-D

(d) GK-T

Figure 5.14 Single-optimized keyboard layouts. (a) Our GK-C keyboard ('Gesture Keyboard—Clarity') is optimized for gesture typing clarity only. (b) Our GK-S keyboard ('Gesture Keyboard—Speed') is optimized for gesture typing speed only.

Table 5.1 Keyboard metric score comparison. Shaded rows signify previous layouts.

Layout	Gesture Typing Clarity		Gesture Typing Speed		Qwerty Similarity	
	Normalized	Raw (key widths)	Normalized	Raw (WPM)	Normalized	Raw (key slots)
Qwerty	0.489	0.391	0.441	62.653	1.000	0
Sath Trapezoidal (6)	0.568	0.413	0.704	69.843	0.730	40
GK-C	1.038	0.543	0.317	59.256	0.554	66
GK-S	0.283	0.334	1.000	77.940	0.311	102
GK-D	0.743	0.462	0.739	70.793	0.324	100
GK-T	0.709	0.452	0.704	69.830	0.716	42
Square ATOMIK (25)	0.362	0.356	0.878	74.591	N/A	N/A
Square OSK (19)	0.381	0.361	0.979	77.358	N/A	N/A

typing speed, and Qwerty similarity. It is the one on the 3D Pareto front that is closest to the 45° line through the space. As Figure 5.5 illustrates, it is possible to accommodate the extra dimension of Qwerty similarity without a big sacrifice to clarity and speed.

Table 5.1 shows the metric scores for our optimized layouts as well as previous optimized layouts. Together, these optimized layouts give us a good understanding of what is possible in the optimization space for gesture typing.

First, we can improve gesture clarity by 38.8% by optimizing for clarity alone: GK-C's raw metric score is 0.543 key widths, while Qwerty's is 0.391 key widths. Likewise, we also see that we can improve gesture speed by 24.4% by optimizing for speed alone (resulting in GK-S).

Second, the 2D Pareto front for gesture clarity and gesture speed (Figure 5.15) shows that these two metrics conflict with each other. It forms a roughly −45° line, indicating

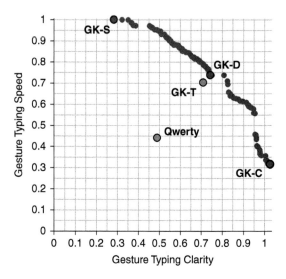

Figure 5.15 2D Pareto front for gesture typing clarity and gesture typing speed. GK-D, our double-optimized layout, is the point on the front nearest the 45° line. Note that Qwerty is far worse in both dimensions than GK-D, and that GK-T (which accommodates yet another dimension) is only slightly worse on these two dimensions than GK-D.

that optimizing for one leads to the decrease in the other. As GK-C and GK-S illustrate, the clarity metric tends to arrange common letters far apart in a radial fashion while the speed metric clusters common letters close together.

However, despite the conflict, it is possible to arrange common letters close together while keeping word gestures relatively distinct, achieving large improvements in both clarity and speed. In GK-D (our double-optimized keyboard), letters in common n-grams such as 'the,' 'and,' and 'ing' are arranged together, while the n-grams themselves are spaced apart. This arrangement offers a 17.9% improvement in gesture clarity and a 13.0% improvement in gesture speed over Qwerty.

Third, accommodating Qwerty similarity (as GK-T does) does little harm to gesture clarity or gesture speed. GK-T's gesture clarity is only 0.01 key widths lower than GK-D's, and GK-T's predicted speed is only 1 WPM lower than GK-D's. Meanwhile, GK-T's Manhattan distance from Qwerty is just 42 key slots, while GK-D's is 102 key slots.

5.4 Decoding Algorithm Optimization

5.4.1 Decoding Algorithm

Text entry on touch keyboards can be viewed as an encoding and decoding processes: the user encodes the intended word w into a series of touch points $(s_1, s_2, s_3 \ldots s_n)$, and the keyboard algorithm acts as the decoder, retrieving w from the spatial signals.

At an abstract level, the decoder selects a word w_i from the keyboard's lexicon and calculates its probability of being the intended word based on the information from the following three sources:

1) The proximities of letters in w_i to the touch points $(s_1, s_2, s_3 \ldots s_n)$.
2) The prior probability of w_i from a language model.
3) The possibilities of spelling errors (e.g., inserting/omitting/transposing/ substituting letters).

Pruning out the improbable ones, a list of the most probable words is then ranked and suggested to the user.

While many modern keyboard algorithms may work similarly at this abstract level, the actual implementations of industrial modern keyboards may be rather complex and vary across products. Since most of the commercial keyboard algorithms are not published, it is impossible to develop a general model representing all of them. Fortunately, we could conduct the present research on open source keyboards.

We developed a keyboard, referred as $P_{Baseline}$ hereafter, based on the latest version (Android 4.3_r3) of the Android Open Source Project (AOSP) Keyboard, which is open-sourced and broadly deployed in Android mobile devices. $P_{Baseline}$ shared the similar algorithm as the AOSP keyboard which can be read and analysed by any researcher or developer. The lexicon composed of around 170,000 words was stored in a trie data structure. As the algorithm received spatial signals $(s_1, s_2, s_3 \ldots s_n)$, it traversed the trie and calculated the probabilities for nodes storing words, based on the aforementioned three sources.

A critical part of the algorithm is to calculate the probabilities of word candidates by weighting information from three sources. Same as the AOSP keyboard, the weights of different sources are controlled by 21 parameters (Bi, Ouyang, and Zhai, 2014). These parameters are pertinent to the performance of $P_{Baseline}$. Altering them adjusts the relative weights of information from different sources, leading to different correction and completion capabilities. For example, reducing the cost of un-typed letters (i.e., lowering COST_LOOKAHEAD) would make the keyboard in favour of suggesting long words, but it might be detrimental to the correction ability. $P_{Baseline}$ is implemented based on the AOSP keyboard, and the parameters in $P_{Baseline}$ shared the same values as those in the AOSP keyboard, which serves as the baseline condition in the current research.

5.4.2 Optimization Objectives

The 'smartness' of the modern soft keyboard is usually measured by correction and completion abilities. The former refers to the ability to correct user's erroneous input, while the latter refers to the ability of completing a word based on partial input. For example, the Google keyboard on Android corrects 'thaml' to 'thank', and completes the word 'computer' after a user types 'comput'. Both correction and completion take advantage of the information regularities in a language, matching users' input signals against words from a lexicon. However, they cast the language regularities for different purposes. Correction uses the language regularities for correcting errors due to the imprecision of the finger touch or spelling errors such as inserting/omitting/substituting/transposing letters, while completion uses the language regularities for predicting unfinished letters based on partial (either correct or erroneous) input to offer keystroke savings.

Our goal is to optimize the decoding algorithm for both correction and completion abilities. Formally, these two abilities were defined as follows.

5.4.2.1 Correction

Correction is measured in word score, which reflects the percentage of correctly recognized words out of the total test words. The word score (W) is defined as:

$$W = \frac{\text{the number of correctly recognized words}}{\text{the number of words in test}} \times 100\% \qquad (5.18)$$

5.4.2.2 Completion

Completion is measured in keystroke saving ratio (S). Given a data set with n test words, S is defined as:

$$S = \left(1 - \frac{\sum_{i=0}^{n} S_{min}(w_i)}{\sum_{i=0}^{n} S_{max}(w_i)}\right) \times 100\% \qquad (5.19)$$

$S_{max}(w_i)$ is the maximum number of keystrokes for entering a word w_i. In the worst scenario where the keyboard fails to complete w_i, the user needs to enter all the letters of w_i and presses the space bar to enter it. Therefore,

$$S_{max}(w_i) = \text{length of } w_i + 1 \qquad (5.20)$$

$S_{min}(w_i)$ is the minimum number of keystrokes needed to enter w_i. Assuming that users fully take advantage of the completion capability, w_i will be picked as soon as it is suggested on the suggestion bar. Therefore, $S_{min}(w_i)$ is the least number of keystrokes needed to bring w_i on the suggestion bar plus one more keystroke for selection. The number of the slots on the suggestion bar may vary across keyboards. The keyboard used in this work provides three suggestion slots, the same as the AOSP keyboard.

Note that the measure defined here is the maximum savings offered to a user by the keyboard algorithm. If and how often the user takes them depends on the UI design, the users preference and bias in motor, visual, and cognitive effort trade-offs, which are separate research topics.

Typical laboratory-based studies demand intensive labour and time to evaluate keyboards and may still lack the necessary sensitivity to reliably detect important differences amid large variations in text, tasks, habits, and other individual differences. Bi, Azenkot, Partridge, and Zhai (2013) proposed using remulation—replaying previously recorded data from the same group from the same experiment in real time simulation—as an automatic approach to evaluate keyboard algorithms. We adopt a similar approach in the present research: we evaluated a keyboard algorithm against previously recorded user data to measure its performance. Unlike the Octopus tool (Bi, Azenkot, Partridge, and Zhai, 2013) which evaluated keyboards on devices, we simulated the keyboard algorithm and ran tests on a workstation. Octopus evaluates keyboards in a 'black box' fashion without access to their algorithms and source code. The off-device approach in this work is limited to the keyboards whose algorithm and source code are accessible, but is much faster than Octopus.

5.4.2.3 Datasets

We ran studies to collect data for optimization and testing. The data collection studies were similar to that in Bi, Azenkot, Partridge, and Zhai (2013). To avoid data collection's dependencies and limitations on keyboard algorithms, a Wizard of Oz keyboard was used in the study by Bi and colleagues (2013), which provided users with only asterisks as feedback when they were entering text. The collected data was segmented into words in evaluation. After the segmentation, the development dataset included 7,106 words, and the test dataset had 6,323 words.

5.4.3 Optimization Method

This section introduces a method for optimizing a keyboard algorithm for correction and completion, and apply it to $P_{baseline}$. In brief, we conceptualize the keyboard algorithm design as a multi-objective optimization problem with two objectives: a) correction and b) completion. For $P_{baseline}$ particularly, it is equivalent to optimizing the 21 parameters (Table 1 in (Bi, Ouyang, and Zhai, 2014)) for these two objectives.

To solve a multi-objective optimization problem, a simple approach is to convert the multiple objectives into one objective function, where each objective is a component in a weighted sum. However, the challenge of this approach is choosing an appropriate weight for each objective. Also, this method returns only one solution, which might not be the most desirable solution.

Instead of returning a single solution, we performed a Pareto optimization, which returns a set of Pareto optimal solutions. A solution is called Pareto optimal or non-dominated, if neither of the objective functions can be improved in value without degrading the other. A solution that is not Pareto optimal is dominated: there is a Pareto optimal solution which is better than it in at least one of the criteria and no worse in the other. Analysing the Pareto optimal solutions reveals the trade-off between multiple objectives. Additionally, the Pareto set provided a range of optimal solutions, allowing keyboard designers and developers to pick the desirable one according to their preferences.

We adopted the Metropolis optimization algorithm (Zhai, Hunter, and Smith, 2000) to search for the Pareto set. The process was composed of multiple sub processes. Each sub process started from a random set of the 21 parameters in the range $[0, 5]$, the estimated range of the parameter values based on the analysis of the algorithm. The sub process then optimized the 21 parameters for the objective function (Equation 5.21) based on the collected development dataset:

$$Z = \alpha W + (1 - \alpha) S \qquad (5.21)$$

which is a sum of word score (W) and keystroke saving ratio (S) with a weight α ($0 \leq \alpha \leq 1$). α was randomized at the beginning of each sub process and remained unchanged during the sub process; α changed across sub processes. Our purpose was to ensure that the Pareto set covered a broad range of Pareto optimal solutions.

In each iteration of a sub process, the 21 parameters moved in a random direction with a fixed step length (0.01). We then evaluated the keyboard algorithm with the new parameters against the development dataset according to the objective function (Equation 5.21). Whether the new set of parameters and search direction were kept was determined by the Metropolis function:

$$W(O \rightarrow N) = \begin{cases} e^{\frac{\Delta Z}{kT}} & \text{if } \Delta Z < 0 \\ 1 & \text{if } \Delta Z \geq 0 \end{cases} \quad (5.22)$$

$W(O \rightarrow N)$ was the probability of changing from the parameter set O (old) to the parameter set N (new); $\Delta Z = Z_{new} - Z_{old}$, where Z_{new}, and Z_{old} were values of objective functions (Equation 5.21) for the new and old set of parameters respectively; k was a coefficient; T was 'temperature', which can be interactively adjusted.

This optimization algorithm used a simulated annealing method. The search did not always move toward a higher value of objective function. It occasionally allowed moves with negative objective function value changes to be able to climb out of a local minimum.

After each iteration, the new solution was compared with the solutions in the Pareto set. If the new solution dominated at least one solution in the Pareto set, it would be added to the set and the solutions dominated by the new solution would be discarded.

5.4.4 Results

After 1000 iterations, the sub process restarted with another random set of parameters and a random α for the objective function Equation 5.21. We ensured that there was at least one sub process for each of the following three weights: $\alpha = 0, 0.5$, and 1. The optimization led to a Pareto set of 101 Pareto optimal solutions after 100 sub processes with 100,000 iterations in total, which constituted a Pareto frontier illustrated in Figure 5.16.

The Pareto frontier shows that the Pareto optimal solutions distribute in a small region, with keystroke saving ratio ranging from 30% to 38% and word score ranging from 81% to 88%. As shown in Figure 5.16, the Pareto frontier forms a short, convex, L-shaped curve, indicating that correction and completion have little conflict with each other and the algorithm can be simultaneously optimized for both with minor loss to each. Among the 101 Pareto optimal solutions, we are particularly interested in three solutions, illustrated in darker dots in Figure 5.16:

1) The solution with the highest word score (W), denoted by P_W. It is the solution exclusively optimized for correction.

2) The solution with the highest keystroke saving ratio (S), denoted by P_S. It is the solution exclusively optimized for completion.

3) The solution with highest $0.5W + 0.5S$, denoted by P_{W+S}. It is the solution optimized for both correction and completion, with 50% weight for each objective.

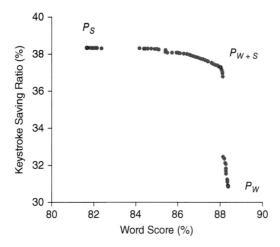

Figure 5.16 The Pareto frontier of the multi-objective optimization. The three darker dots were solutions with the most word score (P_w), the most keystroke savings (P_S), and the highest $0.5W+0.5S$ (P_{W+S}), respectively.

P_w and P_S reveal the highest correction and completion capabilities a keyboard can reach, while P_{W+S} is the most balanced solution with equal weights for correction and completion.

The optimization results showed the default parameter set taken from the AOSP keyboard in Android 4.3 (16 September 2013) was sub-optimal in both correction and completion according to the criteria, and the development dataset used in this study P_w, P_S, and P_{W+S} all improve the word score and keystroke saving ratio by at least 10% over $P_{Baseline}$.

It is more illuminating to compare the three Pareto optimal solutions P_w, P_S, and P_{W+S}, since they are all optimized under identical conditions with the same dataset. Figure 5.16 shows that P_{W+S} is close to P_S in keystroke saving ratio, and close to P_w in word score. It indicates simultaneously optimizing for both objectives causes only minor performance degradation for each objective. These results were later verified with the separate test dataset.

Parameters moved in various directions after the optimization. For such a complex optimization problem with twenty-one free parameters, it was difficult to precisely explain why each parameter moved in such a direction after the optimization. However, we observed some distinct patterns of parameter value changes, which partially explain the performance differences across keyboards.

For examples, the parameters pertinent to the cost of proximity of touch points to letters (i.e., PROXIMITY_COST, FIRST_PROXIMITY_COST) decreased substantially from $P_{Baseline}$ to P_w, P_S, and P_{W+S}, indicating that the optimized algorithms tend to be more tolerant to errors in spatial signals. The cost of untyped letters in a word (i.e., COST_FIRST_LOOKAHEAD) also decreased, indicating that the optimized algorithms were more likely to predict untyped letters as the user's intention, especially after typing the first letter, to save keystrokes.

5.5 Summary and Future Work

This chapter introduces the research of using computational methods to design keyboard layouts and optimize the correction and completion abilities of a keyboard decoder. We firstly introduces the research of using the Metropolis algorithm to optimize the layout for tap typing. The optimization led to layouts that substantially improved the expert input speed over Qwerty for five languages (English, French, German, Spanish, and Chinese). Our research also showed that it is possible to simultaneously optimize a touchscreen keyboard for multiple languages at the same time, with only a small compromise for each language's input optimality. We then introduces the research of optimizing the layout for gesture typing. The optimized layout improved the gesture speed and clarity over Qwerty, and still maintained similarity to Qwerty. Finally, we introduces the research on optimizing a keyboard decoder. The optimization method significantly improved the correction and completion ability of the decoder.

The research introduced in this chapter focused on the expert mode of typing, where the typing behaviour can be robustly modelled by well-established motor control models (e.g., Fitt's Law), and other factors, such as visual search and cognitive effort, play less of a role. Challenges arise when applying these methods to situations where the effects of other factors are non-negligible (e.g., in novice mode).

One result is about the learnability of the optimized layouts. To reach the expert mode and fully enjoy the benefit of the optimized layout, users need to spend a large amount of time practising. They also suffer from a short-term performance loss when they initially switch to a new layout (Bi, Smith, and Zhai, 2010; Zhai, Hunter, and Smith, 2000), due to the steep learning curve. Only a few users are willing to make such an effort. We have explored a variety approaches to address it, including minimizing the disparity from Qwerty (Bi and Zhai, 2016), and introducing Qwerty-like constraints (Bi, Smith, and Zhai, 2010). Although they alleviate the problem to various degrees, more research is needed to fully address it. One possible approach is to include maximizing learnability as an objective in the layout optimization. Jokinen, Sarcar, Oulasvirta, Silpasuwanchai, Wang, and Ren (2017) have proposed a model that can predict the learnability of a keyboard layout, which paves the path for implementing this approach.

The optimization method substantially improves the correction and completion ability of a keyboard decoder, which maximizes the decoding power a keyboard algorithm can offer. However, to what degree a user will take advantage of the decoding power depends on a variety of factors, including UI designs, personal bias towards using the suggestion bar, etc. Based on the success of popular mobile and, for example, CJK (Chinese, Japanese, Korean) text input methods, it is safe to say both correction and completion are desirable features. However, more research is needed to understand how and to what degree the correction and completion power of the keyboard decoder will translate to the improvement of overall user experience of a soft keyboard.

REFERENCES

Bi, X., Azenkot, S., Partridge, K., and Zhai, S., 2013. Octopus: evaluating touchscreen keyboard correction and recognition algorithms via. In: *Proceedings of the SIGCHI Conference on Human Factors in Computing Systems*. New York, NY: ACM, pp. 543–52.

Bi, X., Smith, B. A., and Zhai, S., 2010. Quasi-Qwerty soft keyboard optimization. In: *Proceedings of the 2010 CHI Conference on Human Factors in Computing Systems*. New York, NY: ACM Press, pp. 283–6.

Bi, X., Smith, B. A., and Zhai S., 2012. Multilingual Touchscreen Keyboard Design and Optimization, Human-Computer Interaction, Human-Computer Interaction, 27(4), pp. 352–82.

Bi, X., Ouyang, T., and Zhai, S., 2014. Both complete and correct? Multiobjective optimization of a touchscreen keyboard. In: *Proceedings of the ACM CHI Conference on Human Factors in Computing Systems*. Toronto, Canada, 26 April–1 May 2014. New York, NY: ACM Press, pp. 2297–306.

Bi, X., and Zhai, S., 2016. IJQwerty: What Difference Does One Key Change Make? Gesture Typing Keyboard Optimization Bounded by One Key Position Change from Qwerty. In: *Proceedings of the 2016 CHI Conference on Human Factors in Computing Systems*. New York, NY: ACM, pp. 49–58.

Cao, X., and Zhai, S., 2007. Modeling human performance of pen stroke gestures. In: *Proceedings of the ACM CHI Conference on Human Factors in Computing Systems*. San Jose, California, 28 April–3 May 2007. New York, NY: ACM, pp. 1495–504.

Dunlop, M. D., and Levine, J., 2012. Multidimensional Pareto optimization of touchscreen keyboards for speed, familiarity, and improved spell checking. In: *Proceedings of the ACM SIGCHI Conference on Human Factors in Computing Systems*. Austin, Texas, 5–10 May 2012. New York, NY: ACM, pp. 2669–78.

Fitts, P. M., 1954. The information capacity of the human motor system in controlling the amplitude of movement. *Journal of Experimental Psychology*, 47, pp. 381–91.

Getschow, C. O., Rosen, M. J., and Goodenough-Trepagnier, C., 1986. A systematic approach to design a minimum distance alphabetical keyboard. In: *Proceedings of the 9th Annual Conference on Rehabilitation Technology*. Minneapolis, Minnesota, 23–26 June 1986. Washington, DC: AART, pp. 396–8.

Hastings, W. K., 1970. Monte Carlo sampling methods using Markov chains and their applications. *Biometrika*, 57(1) pp. 97–109.

Hughes, D., Warren, J., and Buyukkokten, O., 2002. Empirical bi-action tables: a tool for the evaluation and optimization of text-input systems, applications I; stylus keyboard. *Human-Computer Interaction*, 17(2, 3), pp. 271–309.

Jokinen, P. P., Sarcar, S., Oulasvirta A., Silpasuwanchai, C., Wang, Z., and Ren, X., 2017. Modelling Learning of New Keyboard Layouts. In: *Proceedings of the 2017 CHI Conference on Human Factors in Computing Systems*. New York, NY:ACM, pp. 4203–15.

Kristensson, P.-O., and Zhai, S., 2004. SHARK2: a large vocabulary shorthand writing system for pen-based computers. In: *Proceedings of the 17th Annual ACM Symposium on User Interface Software and Technology*. New York, NY: ACM, pp. 43–52.

Kristensson, P. O., and Zhai, S., 2005. Relaxing stylus typing precision by geometric pattern matching. In: *Proceedings of ACM International Conference on Intelligent User Interfaces*. New York, NY: ACM, pp. 151–8.

Lewis, J. R., 1992. Typing-key layouts for single-finger or stylus input: initial user preference and performance (Technical Report No. 54729). Boca Raton, FL: International Business Machines Corporation.

Lewis, J. R., Kennedy, P. J., and LaLomia, M. J., 1999. Development of a Digram-Based Typing Key Layout for Single-Finger/Stylus Input. In: *Proceedings of The Human Factors and Ergonomics Society 43rd Annual Meeting*, 43(20), pp. 415–19.

Lewis, J. R., Potosnak, K. M., and Magyar, R. L., 1997. Keys and Keyboards. In: M. G. Helander, T. K. Landauer & P. V. Prabhu, eds. *Handbook of Human-Computer Interaction (2nd ed.)*. Amsterdam: Elsevier Science, pp. 1285–315.

MacKenzie, S. I., and Zhang, S. X., 1999. The design and evaluation of a high-performance soft keyboard. In: *Proceedings of the SIGCHI Conference on Human Factors in Computing Systems (CHI '99)*, New York, NY: ACM, pp. 25–31.

McMillan, G., 2011. Study: Fewer than 50% of Smartphone Users Make Calls. Time.com. Available at: techland.time.com/2011/07/21/study-fewer-than-50-of-smartphone-users-make-calls/

The Nielsen Company, 2010. U.S. Teen Mobile Report Calling Yesterday, Texting Today, Using Apps Tomorrow. Available at: nielsen.com/us/en/newswire/2010/u-s-teen-mobile-report-calling-yesterday-texting-today-using-apps-tomorrow.html

Rick, J., 2010. Performance optimizations of virtual keyboards for stroke-based text entry on a touch-based tabletop. In: *Proceedings of the ACM Symposium on User Interface Software and Technology*. New York, NY: ACM Press, pp. 77–86.

Soukoreff, W., and MacKenzie, I. S., 1995. Theoretical upper and lower bounds on typing speeds using a stylus and keyboard. *Behaviour & Information Technology*, 14, pp. 370–79.

Yamada, H., 1980. A historical study of typewriters and typing methods: from the position of planning Japanese parallels. *Information Processing*, 2(4), pp. 175–202.

Zhai, S., 2004. Characterizing computer input with Fitt's law parameters—The information and non-information aspects of pointing. *International Journal of Human-Computer Studies: Fitts' Law 50 Year Later: Applications and Contributions from Human-Computer Interaction*, 61(6), pp. 791–809.

Zhai, S., Hunter, M., and Smith, B.A., 2000. The metropolis keyboard—an exploration of quantitative techniques for virtual keyboard design. In: *Proceedings of the 13th Annual ACM Symposium on User Interface Software and Technology*. New York, NY: ACM Press, pp. 119–28.

Zhai, S., Hunter, M., and Smith, B. A., 2002. Performance optimization of virtual keyboards. *Human-Computer Interaction*, 17(2, 3), pp. 89–129.

Zhai, S., and Kristensson, P. O., 2003. Shorthand writing on stylus keyboard. In: *Proceedings of the SIGCHI Conference on Human Factors in Computing Systems*. New York, NY: ACM Press, pp. 97–104.

Zhai, S., and Kristensson, P. O., 2006. Introduction to Shape Writing: IBM Research Report RJ10393, and Chapter 7 of I. S. MacKenzie and K. Tanaka-Ishii, eds. *Text Entry Systems: Mobility, Accessibility, Universality*. San Francisco: Morgan Kaufmann Publishers, pp. 139–58.

Zhai, S., Sue, A., and Accot, J., 2002. Movement Model, Hits Distribution and Learning in Virtual Keyboarding. In: *Proceedings of the ACM Conference on Human Factors in Computing Systems*. New York, NY: ACM Press, pp. 17–24.

6

Computational Design with Crowds

YUKI KOYAMA,

TAKEO IGARASHI

6.1 Introduction

Computational design is the emerging form of design activities that are enabled by computational techniques. It formulates design activities as mathematical optimization problems; it formulates design criteria as either objective functions or constraints, design space as the search space (or the choice set), and design exploration, which can be performed by either systems, users, or their combination, as the process of searching for solutions. This viewpoint provides an opportunity to devise new ways of utilizing computational techniques (i.e., mathematical tools developed in computer science that leverage machine processing power). The main goal of computational design research is to enable efficient design workflow or sophisticated design outcomes that are impossible in traditional approaches relying purely on the human brain.

The quality of designed objects can be assessed using various criteria according to their usage contexts. Some criteria might work as conditions that should be at least satisfied (i.e., constraints); other criteria might work as values that should be maximized (i.e., objectives). These design criteria can be classified into two groups: *functional* criteria and *aesthetic* criteria. Functional criteria are the criteria about how well the designed object functions in the expected contexts. For example, a chair is expected to be 'durable' when someone is setting on it; in this case, durability can be a functional criterion that should be satisfied. In contrast, aesthetic criteria are about how perceptually preferable (or pleasing) the designed object looks. A chair might look 'more beautiful,' for example, if its shape is smooth and the width and height follow the golden ratio rule; in this case, beauty in shape performs the role of an aesthetic criterion that is desired to be maximized. Note that, in practical design scenarios, these two criteria are sometimes simultaneously considered by designers.

Computational Interaction. Antti Oulasvirta, Per Ola Kristensson, Xiaojun Bi, Andrew Howes (Eds).

6.1.1 *Challenges in Aesthetic Design*

Design with aesthetic criteria is especially difficult for computers alone to handle. The objective of a design problem is defined based on human perception, and it exists only in the brains of designers. It is generally difficult to represent this perceptual objective using a simple equation or a rule that can be calculated by machine processors. Thus, if one tries to devise a computational design method aiming at supporting or automating aesthetic design, it is inevitable for the framework to involve humans somewhere in the computation, which is non-trivial. Another notable challenge is that humans, even designers, cannot consistently answer the goodness value for a certain design without being familiar with the design space (or the possible alternatives). For example, suppose that you are shown a certain design and asked to provide its goodness score without knowing other possibilities; the answer should be almost random. However, if you are shown a certain design along with a baseline design, you could more reasonably provide its score by taking relative goodness into account. This means that it is also non-trivial how to effectively query humans in the computation.

6.1.2 *A Solution: Crowd-Powered Methods*

A possible solution is to build computational design methods based on a *human computation* paradigm, especially utilizing *crowdsourcing* to involve *crowd workers* in the design processes. Crowdsourcing, especially in the form of *microtask-based crowdsourcing*, enables computational systems to make use of the human perceptions of many people in a structured and algorithmic manner. This idea allows researchers to devise new frameworks for supporting or even automating design processes that are otherwise difficult. Crowdsourcing is superior to a single user or a small group in that the result is an average of many people, and thus it is less sensitive to individual variability and provides a reliable indicator of 'people's choice.' It is also useful when the designer wants to design visuals optimized for a specific target audience with a cultural background different from that of the designer himself; crowdsourcing platforms provide a convenient way for getting inputs from people with the target background.

The goals of this chapter are to discuss how to divide a task between human and computer, how to interact with crowds in the context of aesthetic design (i.e., microtask design), how to extract mathematical information from the responses by crowds, how to utilize the information using computational techniques, and how to enhance design activities using computation (i.e., interaction design).

This chapter specifically deals with *parametric design* (i.e., tweaking parameters for finding the best configuration) as a representative problem of aesthetic design. For example, photo colour enhancement (also referred to as tonal adjustment or colour grading) is one of such design scenarios (Figure 6.1); when a designer enhances the colour of a photograph, he or she has to tweak multiple design parameters, such as 'brightness' or 'contrast,' via a slider interface to find the most aesthetically preferable enhancement for the target photograph.

In the following sections, we first provide the background and definitions of the concepts related to this chapter. Then, we detail the discussion on computational design with crowds. Next, we describe two illustrative examples of crowd-powered computational

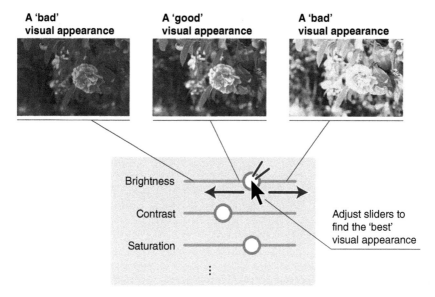

Figure 6.1 An example of design parameter tweaking, in which aesthetic preference is used as a criterion. Photo colour enhancement is one of such design scenarios, in which designers tweak sliders such as 'brightness' so that they eventually find the parameter set that provides the best preferable photo enhancement.

design methods. Finally, we conclude this chapter with additional discussion on the remaining challenges and future directions.

6.2 Background and Term Definitions

This chapter provides discussions on *computational design* methods for *parametric design* problems by taking advantage of *crowdsourced human computation*. We first provide the definition of these terms and a short literature review.

6.2.1 Computational Design

We defined the term *computational design* at the beginning of this chapter. While we believe that our definition well explains this research field, we do not argue that ours is the sole definition. As the term *design* can be defined in many ways, computational design can also be defined in many ways. Here, we review this field from the viewpoint of two design criteria: functional criteria and aesthetic criteria.[1]

---

[1] Interested readers are referred to Oulasvirta and Karrenbauer, this volume, for a detailed discussion on design criteria for UI design.

6.2.1.1 Functional Criteria

Recently, many computational design methods for designing functional objects have been investigated, especially for digital fabrication applications. So far, a variety of functional criteria have been formulated by researchers; Umetani, Koyama, Schmidt, and Igarashi (2014) formulated the functional criterion of paper airplanes (i.e., *fly-ability*) and used it for optimizing airplane designs by maximizing this criterion. Koyama, Sueda, Steinhardt, Igarashi, Shamir, and Matusik (2015) formulated the *hold-ability* and *grip strength* of 3D-printed connectors and then presented an automatic method for designing functional connectors. Several computational design methods consider the functionalities of objects' mass properties (e.g., *standing stability*, see Prévost, Whiting, Lefebvre, and Sorkine-Hornung, 2013). *Structural strength* of objects is also an important design criterion, and some computational design methods take this into consideration (e.g., Stava, Vanek, Benes, Carr, and Měch, 2012).

Another notable domain of computational functional design is graphical user interface (GUI) generation. In this context, the *user performance* of the generated interface is often considered the functional criterion that should be optimized. For example, Gajos and Weld (2004) presented an automatic GUI design method, in which they formulated *required user efforts* for manipulating GUI elements as the objective function to be minimized. Bailly, Oulasvirta, Kötzing, and Hoppe (2013) presented MenuOptimizer, an interactive GUI design tool that utilizes an optimizer to support designers to design effective menus.

It is notable that these functional criteria are often 'computable' by computers alone. This is because these criteria are basically not subjective nor perceptual, in contrast to aesthetic criteria.

6.2.1.2 Aesthetic Criteria

The goal of computational design for aesthetic criteria is to support or automate the maximization of the perceptual aesthetic quality of designs. Such aesthetic preference is closely tied to human perception, and thus it is difficult to quantify using simple rules. Yet, by focusing on very specific design domains, it is possible to handle and optimize aesthetic criteria by rule-based approaches. For example, Miniukovich and Angeli (2015) presented executable metrics of GUI aesthetics and showed its validity with a user study. Todi, Weir, and Oulasvirta (2016) applied similar metrics for optimizing GUI layout design. However, rule-based approaches require careful implementation and tuning of heuristic rules in limited scopes.

Data-driven approaches can ease the limitations of purely rule-based approaches. Most data-driven methods rely on heuristic rules but can derive optimal weights or model parameters for the rules by learning them from training data. For example, O'Donovan, Agarwala, and Hertzmann (2014) presented a data-driven method of predicting and optimizing aesthetic quality of layouts of two-dimensional graphic designs. Their aesthetic criterion is formulated by combining several heuristic rules (e.g., *alignment* and *white space*), and machine learning techniques are used to learn the weights and the model parameters. Other examples deal with colour palette aesthetics (O'Donovan, Agarwala, and

Hertzmann, 2011), 3D viewpoint preference (Secord, Lu, Finkelstein, Singh, and Nealen, 2011), and photo colour enhancement (Bychkovsky, Paris, Chan, and Durand, 2011).

Talton, Gibson, Yang, Hanrahan, and Koltun (2009) presented a method for supporting preference-driven parametric design by involving many people. Their method constructs a so-called *collaborative design space*, which is a subset of the target design parameter space consisting of aesthetically acceptable designs, based on the design history of many voluntary users. Then, the collaborative design space supports new users' design exploration. Their method takes roughly one year to obtain the necessary design history and needs many volunteers to engage exactly the same design space. In contrast, more recent crowdsourcing platforms have enabled *on-demand* generation of necessary data, which has opened new opportunities for computational aesthetic design.

6.2.2 *Human Computation and Crowdsourcing*

Human computation and crowdsourcing are often used for gathering human-generated data that are difficult for machines to generate (e.g., perceptual or semantic labels for images). We utilize this approach for formulating our crowd-powered methods for gathering perceptual preference data. We encourage readers to refer to the comprehensive survey and discussions on these terms by Quinn and Bederson (2011). Here, we briefly review these two terms from the viewpoint of our attempt.

6.2.2.1 Human Computation

Human computation is a concept of enabling difficult computations by exploiting humans as processing powers. This term was described by von Ahn (2005) as follows:

> ... a paradigm for utilizing human processing power to solve problems that computers cannot yet solve.

For example, human processors are much better at perceiving the semantic meanings of visual contents than machine processors; thus, for building a system that requires perceptive abilities, it is effective to incorporate human processors as well as machine processors. Such problems that are difficult for machine processors but easy for human processors, including visual design driven by preference, are observed in many situations. However, human processors also have critical limitations, such as that they are extremely slow and expensive to execute compared to machine processors. Therefore, it is important to carefully choose how to employ such human processors.

How to Employ Human Processors. A possible solution for employing many human processors is to implicitly embed human computation tasks in already existing tasks. reCAPTCHA (von Ahn, Maurer, McMillen, Abraham, and Blum, 2008) takes such an approach; it embeds optical character recognition (OCR) tasks to web security measures. Unfortunately, this approach is not easy for everybody to take. Another solution to motivate many ordinary people to voluntarily participate in human computation tasks is to do 'gamification' of tasks so that people do tasks purely for entertainment purpose (von Ahn and Dabbish, 2008). For example, ESP game (von Ahn and Dabbish, 2004) is a game in which players provide semantic labels for images without being aware of it. Recently, since the emergence of large-scale crowdsourcing markets, it has become increasingly popular to employ human processors using crowdsourcing. As we take this approach, we detail it in the following subsections.

6.2.2.2 Crowdsourcing

The term *crowdsourcing* was first introduced by Howe (2006b) and later more explicitly defined in (Howe, 2006a) as follows.

> Crowdsourcing is the act of taking a job traditionally performed by a designated agent (usually an employee) and outsourcing it to an undefined, generally large group of people in the form of an open call.

Today, many online marketplaces for crowdsourcing are available for researchers, such as Upwork,[2] Amazon Mechanical Turk,[3] and CrowdFlower.[4] Since 2006, crowdsourcing has been a more and more popular research topic in computer science. The forms of crowdsourcing are roughly categorized into the following categories.

Microtask-Based Crowdsourcing is a form of crowdsourcing where many workers are employed to perform a *microtask*–a task that is very small (usually completed in a minute) and does not require any special skills or domain knowledge to be performed. One of the most attractive features of this form is that anyone can stably employ a large number of crowd workers even for small tasks on demand with minimum communication cost. Recent crowdsourcing marketplaces, including Amazon Mechanical Turk, have enabled this new form. Although crowd workers in these platforms are usually non-experts, they do have full human intelligence, which enables many emerging applications.

One of the popular usages of microtask-based crowdsourcing is to outsource data-annotation tasks (e.g., Bell, Upchurch, Snavely, and Bala, 2013) for machine learning purposes. Another popular usage is to conduct large-scale perceptual user studies (e.g., Kittur, Chi, and Suh, 2008). Microtask-based crowdsourcing also enables *crowd-powered systems*, which are systems that query crowd workers to use their human intelligence in run time. For example, Soylent (Bernstein, Little, Miller, Hartmann, Ackerman, Karger, Crowell, and Panovich, 2010) is a crowd-powered word processing system that utilizes human intelligence to edit text documents.

Expert Sourcing is a form of crowdsourcing in which skilled experts (e.g., web developers, designers, and writers) are employed for professional tasks. Some online marketplaces (e.g., Upwork) provide an opportunity for researchers to reach experts. However, asking professional designers takes significant communication costs and

---

[2] https://www.upwork.com/
[3] https://www.mturk.com/
[4] https://www.crowdflower.com/

large variances between individuals' skills. An expert with the required skill is difficult to find and not always available. Compared to microtask-based crowdsourcing, expert sourcing may be less suitable for employing human processors and for designing crowd-powered systems that work stably and on demand.

Volunteer-Based Crowdsourcing is a form of crowdsourcing in which unpaid crowds voluntarily participate in the microtask execution (Huber, Reinecke, and Gajos, 2017; Morishima, Amer-Yahia, and Roy, 2014). One challenge in this form is to motivate crowd workers; crowds would do not tend to perform tasks unless the task execution provides certain values other than monetary rewards (e.g., public recognition for the efforts).

Researchers on crowdsourcing have investigated many issues. For example, Bernstein, Brandt, Miller, and Karger (2011) proposed a technique for reducing the latency of responses from crowds for enabling real-time crowd-powered systems. *Quality control* of workers' responses (Ipeirotis, Provost, and Wang, 2010) is also an important issue because crowd workers might make poor-quality responses because of cheating, misunderstanding of tasks, or simply making mistakes. In this chapter, we do not discuss these issues and instead focus on the mechanism of how crowds can contribute to design activities.

6.2.2.3 Crowdsourced Human Computation

We define *crowdsourced human computation* as a form of human computation in which human processors are employed via microtask-based crowdsourcing. This means that programmers can query 'oracles' requiring human intelligence into their codes as function calls. Little, Chilton, Goldman, and Miller (2010) presented *TurKit Script*, a programming API for developing algorithms using crowdsourced human computation (which they call *human computation algorithms*).

Gingold, Shamir, and Cohen-Or (2012) proposed several methods for solving long-standing visual perceptual problems using crowdsourced human computation, including the extraction of depth and normal maps for images and the detection of bilateral symmetries in photographs. Their image-understanding algorithms are designed to *decompose* the original difficult problem into a set of easy perceptual microtasks, *solve* the perceptual microtasks using crowdsourcing, and then *recompose* the responses from crowds using some computational techniques.

6.2.3 Parametric Design

In this chapter, we take *parametric design* as a representative task in aesthetic design. We use the term *parametric design* to represent a design paradigm in which visual contents are solely controlled by a set of (either continuous or discrete) parameters. Also, in parametric design, the number of parameters is often reasonably small so that designers can manually tweak them. For example, to adjust the tone of a photograph, designers tweak several sliders, such as 'brightness' and 'contrast,' rather than tweaking the RGB values of every pixel one by

Figure 6.2 Example scenarios of parameter tweaking for visual design, including photo colour enhancement, image effects for 3D graphics, and 2D graphic designs, such as web pages, presentation slide.

one; it is considered that the design space here is parametrized by several degrees of freedom mapped to sliders, and thus it is considered a parametric design.

Parametric designs can be found almost everywhere in visual design production. Figure 6.2 illustrates a few examples in which the visual content is tweaked so that it becomes aesthetically the best. For example, in Unity[5] (a computer game authoring tool) and Maya[6] (a three-dimensional computer animation authoring tool), the control panels include many sliders, which can be manipulated to adjust the visual nature of the contents.

Finding the best parameter combination is not an easy task. It may be easily found by a few mouse drags in a case in which the designer is familiar with how each parameter affects the visual content and is very good at predicting the effects without actually manipulating sliders. However, this is unrealistic in most cases; several sliders mutually affect the resulting visuals in complex ways, and each slider also has a different effect when the contents are different, which makes the prediction difficult. Thus, in practice, it is inevitable that a designer explores the *design space*—the set of all the possible design alternatives—in a trial-and-error manner, to find the parameter set that he or she believes is best for the target content. This requires the designer to manipulate sliders many times, as well as to construct a mental model of the design space. Furthermore, as the number of design parameters increases, the design space expands exponentially, which makes this exploration very tedious.

Computer graphics researchers have investigated many methods for defining reasonable parametric design spaces. For 3D modelling, the human face (Blanz and Vetter, 1999) and body (Allen, Curless, and Popović, 2003) are parametrized using data-driven approaches. The facial expression of characters is often parametrized using *blendshape* techniques (Lewis, Anjyo, Rhee, Zhang, Pighin, and Deng, 2014). For material appearance design, Matusik, Pfister, Brand, and McMillan (2003) proposed a parametric space based on measured data, and Nielsen, Jensen, and Ramamoorthi (2015) applied dimensionality reduction to the space. Procedural modelling of 3D shapes (e.g., botany, see Weber and

5 https://unity3d.com/
6 https://www.autodesk.com/products/maya/overview

Penn, 1995) is also considered parametric design in that the shapes are determined by a set of tweakable parameters. One of the recent trends is to define parametric spaces based on semantic attributes for facilitating intuitive exploration; this direction has been investigated for shape deformation (Yumer, Chaudhuri, Hodgins, and Kara, 2015), cloth simulation (Sigal, Mahler, Diaz, McIntosh, Carter, Richards, and Hodgins, 2015), and human body shape (Streuber, Quiros-Ramirez, Hill, Hahn, Zuffi, O'Toole, and Black, 2016), for example.

6.3 Computational Design with Crowds

6.3.1 Problem Formulation

We consider a design exploration in which multiple design parameters have to be tweaked such that the aesthetic preference criterion is maximized. This can be mathematically described as follows. Suppose that there are n real-valued design variables

$$\mathbf{x} = \begin{bmatrix} x_1 & \cdots & x_n \end{bmatrix} \in \mathcal{X}, \tag{6.1}$$

where $\mathcal{X}$ represents an n-dimensional design space. We assume that

$$\mathcal{X} = [0, 1]^n; \tag{6.2}$$

that is, each variable takes a continuous value and its interval is regularized into $[0, 1]$ in advance. In the case that a variable is manipulated by a slider, we suppose that the slider's lowest and highest values correspond to 0 and 1, respectively. Using these notations, a parameter-tweaking task can be formulated as a continuous optimization problem:

$$\mathbf{x}^* = \arg\max_{\mathbf{x} \in \mathcal{X}} g(\mathbf{x}), \tag{6.3}$$

where the objective function

$$g : \mathcal{X} \to \mathbb{R} \tag{6.4}$$

returns a scalar value representing how aesthetically preferable the design corresponding to the argument design variables is. We call this function as *goodness function*. A designer usually tries to solve this optimization problem by exploring $\mathcal{X}$ by manipulating sliders in a trial-and-error manner without any computational support. This exploration ends when the designer believes that he or she finds the optimal argument value $\mathbf{x}^*$ that gives the best preferable design. Figure 6.3 illustrates this problem setting. The goal of this chapter is to provide discussions on methods for solving this optimization problem either automatically or semi-automatically using computational techniques.

Assumptions and Scope. We focus our discussions on parametric design and put several assumptions on this problem setting to clarify the scope in this discussion. First, we assume that the target parameters are continuous, not discrete. We also assume that when a design parameter changes smoothly, the corresponding visual also changes smoothly. From these assumptions, the goodness function $g(\cdot)$ is considered to be a continuous, smooth function. Note that the goodness function can have multiple local maximums,

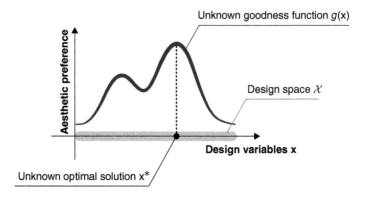

Figure 6.3 Problem formulation. We discuss computational design methods to solve the optimization problem described in Equation 6.3 or to find the optimal solution x^* that maximizes the aesthetic preference of the target design.

ridges, or locally flat regions around maximums. Also, we assume that the goodness function is constant with respect to time. The design space is expected to be parameterized by a reasonable number of parameters as in most commercial software packages; parametrization itself will be not discussed in this chapter. We handle the design domains in which even novices can assess relative goodness of designs (for example, given two designs, they are expected to be able to answer which design looks better); but importantly, they do not need to know how a design can be improved. Though we narrow down the target problem as discussed earlier, it still covers a wide range of practical design scenarios including photo enhancement, material appearance design for computer graphics, and two-dimensional graphic design (e.g., posters).

6.3.2 Where to Use Computational Techniques

To provide computational methods for solving the design problem described as Equation 6.3, there are two possible approaches with respect to the usage of computational tools as follows.

> **Estimation of the Objective Function.** The first approach is to estimate the shape of the goodness function $g(\cdot)$ by using computational tools. In other words, it is to compute the regression of $g(\cdot)$. Once $g(\cdot)$ is estimated, it can be used for 'guided' exploration: supporting users' free exploration of the design space $\mathcal{X}$ for finding their best favorite parameter set x^* through some user interfaces. One of the advantages of this approach is that even if the estimation quality is not perfect, it can still be effective for supporting users to find x^*. To implement this approach, there are two important challenges: how to compute this regression problem that deals with human preference and how to support the users' manual exploration using the estimated $g(\cdot)$. We discuss this approach further in Section 6.4.

Maximization of the Objective Function. The second approach is to compute the maximization of the goodness function $g(\cdot)$ by using computational optimization techniques so that the system can directly find the optimal solution $\mathbf{x}^*$. In other words, the system searches the design space $\mathcal{X}$ for the maximum of $g(\cdot)$. The found solution $\mathbf{x}^*$ can be used as either a final design or a starting point that will be further refined by the user. Implementing this approach requires several non-trivial considerations, for example, which optimization algorithms can be used and how it should be adapted for this specific problem setting. We discuss this approach further in Section 6.5.

For both approaches, human-generated preference data are necessary for enabling computation. In this chapter, we focus on the use of human computation to generate necessary preference data. Such human processors can be employed via crowdsourcing. By this approach, systems can obtain crowd-generated data on demand in the manner of function calls. Here we put an additional assumption: a common 'general' preference exists that is shared among crowds; though there might be small individual variation, we can observe such a general preference by involving many crowds.

6.3.3 What and How to Ask Crowds

It is important to ask appropriate questions to the crowds to obtain meaningful results. We discuss two possibilities in terms of the query design as follows.

Query about Discrete Samples. A typical approach is to ask crowds about the aesthetic quality of some discrete samples. The simplest task design is to present a sample in the parameter space and ask crowd workers to answer its goodness score directly. An interface for crowd workers could be a slider, a text box (for putting the score value), or an n-pt Likert questionnaire. From a mathematical viewpoint, this can be modelled as follows: given a parameter set $\mathbf{x}$ that the system is inspecting, crowds provide the function value

$$g(\mathbf{x}). \tag{6.5}$$

However, this does not work well in general. It requires crowd workers to be familiar with the design space; otherwise, it is difficult for crowd workers to make answers consistently (as also discussed at the beginning of this chapter).

A solution is to present multiple samples to crowds and to ask them to evaluate their 'relative' goodness. For example, it is easy for crowds to choose the better design from two options (i.e., a pairwise comparison). The interface for this task could be a simple radio button. Figure 6.4 (Left) illustrates this microtask design. This can be mathematically modelled as follows: given two sampling points, say $\mathbf{x}_1$ and $\mathbf{x}_2$, crowds provide the information of their relative order

$$g(\mathbf{x}_1) < g(\mathbf{x}_2), \tag{6.6}$$

or its opposite. This task is easy to answer even for non-experts because it does not require the crowds to know the design space or other design possibilities. A

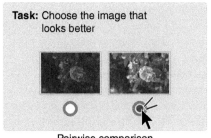 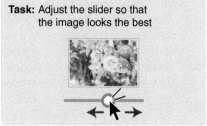

Figure 6.4 Microtask design. (Left) Pairwise comparison microtask. (Right) Single-slider manipulation microtask.

possible variant of this task is to provide relative scores by an n-pt Likert scale (the standard pairwise comparison is the special case with $n = 2$). A/B testing also belongs to this category. This pairwise comparison microtask is popular in integrating crowds' perceptions into systems (e.g., O'Donovan, Lībeks, Agarwala, and Hertzmann, 2014; Gingold, Shamir, and Cohen-Or, 2012). We discuss this approach further in Section 6.4.

Query about Continuous Space. An alternative approach is to ask crowd workers to explore a continuous space and to identify the best sample in the space. This requires more work by crowds, but the system can obtain much richer information than an evaluation of discrete samples. Asking crowds to directly control all the raw parameters (i.e., explore the original search space $\mathcal{X}$) is an extreme case of this approach. Mathematically speaking, given a high-dimensional parametric space $\mathcal{X}$, crowds provide the solution of the following maximization problem:

$$\underset{\mathbf{x} \in \mathcal{X}}{\arg\max} \; g(\mathbf{x}). \tag{6.7}$$

However, an exploration of such a high-dimensional space is highly difficult for crowd workers. Note that this task is difficult even for designers. Also, as this task is no longer 'micro,' it is less easy to stably obtain reliable quality responses. A solution is to limit the search space to a lower-dimensional subspace. For example, by limiting the space into a one-dimensional subspace, crowd workers can efficiently explore the space with a single slider. Figure 6.4 (Right) illustrates this microtask design. This is mathematically formulated as the following maximization problem:

$$\underset{\mathbf{x} \in \mathcal{S}}{\arg\max} \; g(\mathbf{x}), \tag{6.8}$$

where $\mathcal{S}$ is a (one-dimensional) continuous space that can be mapped to a single slider. We discuss this approach further in Section 6.5.

These microtask designs and their mathematical interpretations enable computational systems to access human preferences in the algorithms and to incorporate them into the mathematical formulations. In the following sections, we introduce two such crowd-powered systems from our previous studies as illustrative examples.

6.4 Design Exploration with Crowds

In this section, we illustrate a crowd-powered method to facilitate parametric design *exploration* (Koyama, Sakamoto, and Igarashi, 2014). To gather the necessary preference data, the system asks crowds to perform pairwise comparison microtasks. The system then analyses the data to estimate the landscape of the goodness function. The estimated goodness function is used to enable novel user interfaces for facilitating design exploration.

6.4.1 Interaction Design

The system provides the following two user interfaces to support design exploration leveraging the goodness function obtained by inputs from crowds.

Suggestive Interface. The system has a suggestive interface called Smart Suggestion (Figure 6.5). It generates nine parameter sets that have relatively high goodness values and displays the corresponding designs as suggestions. This interface facilitates design exploration by giving users a good starting point to find a better parameter set for the visual design. This implementation takes a simple approach to generate quality suggestions: the system generates 2,000 parameter sets randomly and then selects the nine best parameter sets according to their goodness values. This simple algorithm interactively provides suggestions of an adequate quality, which enables

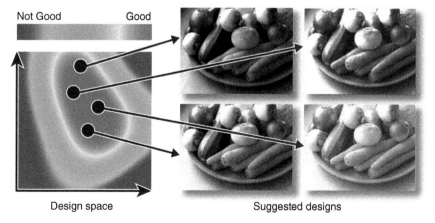

Figure 6.5 A suggestive interface enabled by the estimated goodness function. The user can obtain appropriate parameter sets as suggestions, which are generated considering the goodness of designs.

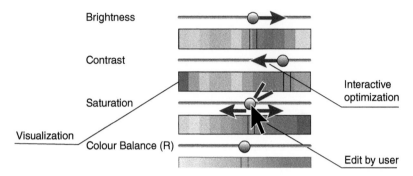

Figure 6.6 A slider interface enabled by the estimated goodness function. The user can adjust each parameter effectively by the visualization (Vis) near the slider and the optimization (Opt), which gently guides the current parameters toward the optimal direction.

users to regenerate suggestions quickly enough for interactive use if none of the suggestions satisfy them.

Slider Interface. The system has a slider interface called VisOpt Slider (Figure 6.6). It displays coloured bars with a *visualization* of the results of a crowd-powered analysis. The distribution of goodness values is directly visualized on each slider using colour mapping, which navigates the user to explore the design space. Note that when the user modifies a certain parameter, the visualizations of the other parameters change dynamically. This helps the user not only to find better parameter sets quickly but also to explore the design space effectively without unnecessarily visiting 'bad' designs. When the *optimization* is turned on, the parameters are automatically and interactively optimized while the user is dragging a slider. That is, when a user starts to drag a slider, the other sliders' ticks also start to move simultaneously to a better direction according to the user's manipulation.

These two interfaces are complementary; for example, a user can first obtain a reasonable starting point by the suggestive interface and then interactively tune it up using the slider interface.

6.4.2 Estimating the Objective Function

The system employs crowdsourcing to analyse parameters to support the exploration of visual design. The goal of the analysis is to construct the goodness function $g(\cdot)$. The process to obtain a goodness function consists of four steps, as shown in Figure 6.7.

Sampling Parameter Sets. First, the system samples M parameter sets $x_1, \ldots, x_M$ from the parameter space $\mathcal{X}$ for the later process of crowdsourcing. To do this, we simply choose a random uniform sampling; the system randomly picks a parameter set from the parameter space and repeats this process M times.

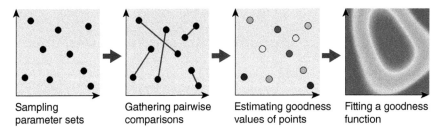

Sampling parameter sets → Gathering pairwise comparisons → Estimating goodness values of points → Fitting a goodness function

Figure 6.7 Overview of the crowd-powered algorithm for estimating the goodness function.

Gathering Pairwise Comparisons. The next step is to gather information on the goodness of each sampling point. We take the pairwise comparison approach; crowd workers are shown a pair of designs and asked to compare them. As a result, relative scores (instead of absolute ones) are obtained. For the instruction of the microtask for crowd workers, we prepare a template:

> *Which of the two images of [noun] is more [adjective]? For example, [clause]. Please choose the most appropriate one from the 5 options below.*

In accordance with the purpose and the content, the user gives a noun, an adjective such as 'good' or 'natural,' and a clause that explains a concrete scenario to instruct crowd workers more effectively. After this instruction, two images and five options appear. These options are linked to the five-pt Likert scale; for example, *'the left image is definitely more [adjective] than the right image'* is for option 1, and the complete opposite is option 5. Option 3 is *'these two images are equally [adjective], or are equally not [adjective]'.*

Estimating Goodness Values of Sampling Points. Given the relative scores, the next goal is to obtain the absolute goodness values $\mathbf{y} = [\, y_1 \, \cdots \, y_M \,]^T$ at the sampling points $\mathbf{x}_1, \ldots, \mathbf{x}_M$. Note that inconsistency exists in the data from crowds; thus, a solution that satisfies all the relative orders does not generally exist. We want to obtain a solution that is as reasonable as possible. In this work, this problem is solved by being formulated as optimization. Specifically, the system solves the optimization:

$$\min_{\mathbf{y}} \left\{ E_{\text{relative}}(\mathbf{y}) + \omega E_{\text{continuous}}(\mathbf{y}) \right\}, \tag{6.9}$$

where $E_{\text{relative}}(\cdot)$ is a cost function that reflects the relative scores data provided by crowds, $E_{\text{continuous}}(\cdot)$ is a cost function that regularizes the resultant values so as to be distributed smoothly and continuously, and $\omega > 0$ is a hyperparameter that defines the balance of these two objectives.

Fitting a Goodness Function. Now, the goal is to obtain a continuous goodness function from the goodness values at the discrete sampling points obtained in the previous step. For this purpose, this work adopted the radial basis function (RBF) interpolation technique (Bishop, 1995), which can be used to smoothly interpolate the values at scattered data points.

6.4.3 Applications

This method was applied to four applications from different design domains. In this experiment, each microtask contained ten unique pairwise comparisons, and 0.02 USD was paid for it. For the photo colour enhancement (6D), material appearance design (8D), and camera and light control (8D) applications, we deployed 200 tasks. For the facial expression modelling (53D) application, we deployed 600 tasks.

6.4.3.1 Photo Colour Enhancement

Here we selected six popular parameters for photo colour enhancement: brightness, contrast, saturation, and colour balance (red, green, and blue). In the crowdsourced microtasks, we asked crowd workers to choose the photograph that would be better to use in a magazine or product advertisement. Examples of VisOpt Slider visualizations with typical parameter sets are shown in Figure 6.8. These visualizations provide assorted useful information; for example, the photo at left needs to have higher contrast, the centre photo can be improved by making the brightness slightly higher and the red balance slightly lower, and the right photo is already good and does not require any dramatic improvements.

6.4.3.2 Material Appearance Design

Material appearance design is often difficult for novices to understand and tweak. The problem is that shaders often have unintuitive parameters that affect the final look in a way that is difficult for casual users to predict (e.g., 'Fresnel Reflection'). For this experiment, we used a shader for photo-realistic metals provided in a popular shader package called Hard

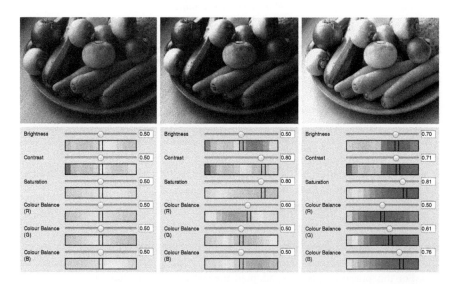

Figure 6.8 Designs and visualizations of goodness distributions in the photo colour enhancement application.

Surface Shaders[7], which has eight parameters. We applied this shader to a teapot model. We asked crowd workers to choose the one that was the most realistic as a stainless steel teapot. Figure 6.9 (Left) shows typical parameter sets with their visualizations. From these visualizations, we can learn, without any trial and error, that the 'Reflection' parameter (the fifth parameter in Figure 6.9 (Left)) performs the most important role in this application.

6.4.3.3 Camera and Light Control

Secord, Lu, Finkelstein, Singh, and Nealen (2011) presented a computational perceptual model for predicting the goodness of viewing directions for 3D models; however, their model is limited to the view direction and does not consider any other factors. We feel that good views will change according to other conditions, such as perspective and lighting. In this scenario, we chose a camera and light control task in a simple 3D scene consisting of a 3D model, a perspective camera, and a point light. Eight parameters are to be tweaked in total, including camera position (x, y, z), camera field of view, light position (x, y, z), and intensity of light. We used the dragon model. The orientation of the camera is automatically set such that it always looks at the centre of the model. We asked crowd workers to choose the better one with the same instruction. The results indicate a highly nonlinear relationship between the camera and light parameters. See Figure 6.9 (Right). When the camera comes to the left side (i.e., camera.$z < 0.0$) from the right side (i.e., camera.$z > 0.0$) of the dragon model, the visualization tells the user that he or she should also move the light to the left side (i.e., light.$z < 0.0$) so that the model is adequately lit.

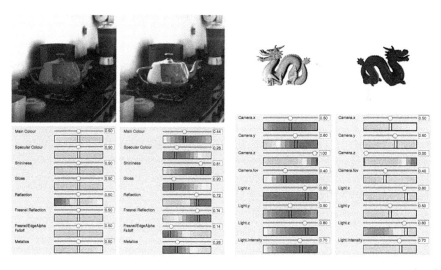

Figure 6.9 Designs and visualizations of goodness distributions in the shader application (Left) and the camera and light application (Right).

---

[7] https://www.assetstore.unity3d.com/#/content/729

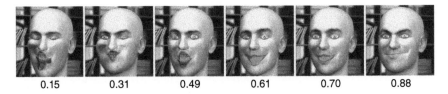

| 0.15 | 0.31 | 0.49 | 0.61 | 0.70 | 0.88 |

Figure 6.10 Designs and estimated goodness values in the facial expression modelling application. The values shown below the pictures are the estimated goodness values.

6.4.3.4 Facial Expression Modelling

Blendshape is a standard approach to control the facial expressions of virtual characters (Lewis, Anjyo, Rhee, Zhang, Pighin, and Deng, 2014), where a face model has a set of predefined continuous parameters and its expression is controlled by them. The space of 'valid' expressions is actually quite small in most cases, which means that careful tweaking is required to ensure natural, unbroken expressions. For this experiment, we used a head model parametrized by fifty-three parameters. We suppose that the goodness in this design scenario is the validity of the facial expression, so we asked crowd workers to choose the better 'natural (unbroken)' expression. Figure 6.10 shows some designs and their estimated goodness values. It is observed that the constructed goodness function successfully provides reasonable values even for this high-dimensional application.

6.5 Design Optimization with Crowds

This section illustrates a computational design method of *optimizing* visual design parameters by crowdsourced human computation (Koyama, Sato, Sakamoto, and Igarashi, 2017). This work defines a concept of *crowd-powered visual design optimizer* as a system that finds an optimal design that maximizes some perceptual function from a given design space and, to enable this, bases its optimization algorithm upon the use of crowdsourced human computation. This work offers an implementation of this concept, where the system decomposes the entire problem into a sequence of one-dimensional slider manipulation microtasks (Figure 6.4 (Right)). Crowd workers complete the tasks independently, and the system gradually reaches the optimal solution using the crowds' responses. Figure 6.11 illustrates this concept.

6.5.1 Interaction Design

This work envisions the following scenario: the user can push a 'Crowdsource' button in design software for running the crowd-powered optimization process, and then he or she can obtain the 'best' parameter set without any further interaction, as shown in Figure 6.11. The provided parameter set can be used, for example, as a final product or a good starting point for further tweaking. This work investigates how to enable this function in general design applications without relying on domain-specific knowledge.

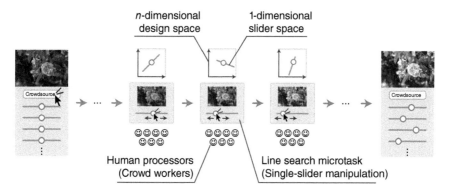

Figure 6.11 Concept of the method. This work envisions that the design software equips a 'Crowdsource' button for running the crowd-powered search for the slider values that provide the perceptually 'best' design. To enable this, the system decomposes the n-dimensional optimization problem into a sequence of one-dimensional line search queries that can be solved by crowdsourced human processors.

6.5.2 Maximizing the Objective Function

To build a computational framework for optimizing design parameters by crowds, this work extends *Bayesian optimization* techniques (Shahriari, Swersky, Wang, Adams, and de Freitas, 2016). Standard Bayesian optimization techniques are based on *function-value* oracles; however, with crowds and perceptual objective functions, it is not realistic to query function values as discussed in Section 6.3. Brochu, de Freitas, and Ghosh (2007) extended Bayesian optimization so that it could use pairwise-comparison oracles instead of function values; however, the information from a pairwise comparison task is limited, and so the optimization convergence is impractically slow. This work presents an alternative extension of Bayesian optimization based on *line search* oracles instead of function-value or pairwise-comparison oracles. The line search oracle is provided by a *single-slider manipulation* query; crowds are asked to adjust a single slider for exploring the design alternatives mapped to the slider and to return the slider value that provides the best design (see Section 6.3.3 for the the discussion on this microtask design).

6.5.2.1 Slider Space for Line Search

The system lets human processors adjust a slider; that is, find a maximum in a one-dimensional continuous space. We call this space the *slider space*. Technically, this space is not necessarily linear with respect to the target design space $\mathcal{X}$ (i.e., forming a straight line segment in $\mathcal{X}$); however, in this work, the case of a straight line is considered for simplicity and for the sake of not unnecessarily confusing crowd workers during the task.

At the beginning of the optimization process, the algorithm does not have any data about the target design space $\mathcal{X}$ or the goodness function $g(\cdot)$. Thus, for the initial slider space, we simply choose two random points in $\mathcal{X}$ and connect them by a line segment.

For each iteration, we want to arrange the next slider space so that it is as 'meaningful' as possible for finding $\mathbf{x}^*$. We propose to construct the slider space $\mathcal{S}$ such that one end is at the *current-best* position $\mathbf{x}^+$ and the other one is at the *best-expected-improving* position $\mathbf{x}^{EI}$. Suppose that we have observed t responses so far, and we are going to query the next oracle. The slider space for the next iteration (i.e., $\mathcal{S}_{t+1}$) is constructed by connecting

$$\mathbf{x}_t^+ = \arg\max_{\mathbf{x} \in \{\mathbf{x}_i\}_{i=1}^{N_t}} \mu_t(\mathbf{x}), \tag{6.10}$$

$$\mathbf{x}_t^{EI} = \arg\max_{\mathbf{x} \in \mathcal{X}} a_t^{EI}(\mathbf{x}), \tag{6.11}$$

where $\{\mathbf{x}_i\}_{i=1}^{N_t}$ is the set of observed data points, and $\mu_t(\cdot)$ and $a_t^{EI}(\cdot)$ are the predicted mean function and the *acquisition function* calculated from the current data. $\mu(\cdot)$ and $a^{EI}(\cdot)$ can be calculated based on an extension of *Bayesian optimization* techniques; see the original publication (Koyama, Sato, Sakamoto, and Igarashi, 2017) for details.

Example Optimization Sequence   Figure 6.12 illustrates an example optimization sequence in which the framework is applied to a two-dimensional test function and the oracles are synthesized by a machine processor. The process begins with a random slider space. After several iterations, it reaches a good solution.

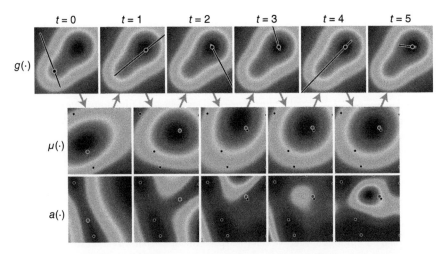

Figure 6.12 An example sequence of the Bayesian optimization based on line search oracle, applied to a two-dimensional test function. The iteration proceeds from left to right. From top to bottom, each row visualizes the black box function $g(\cdot)$ along with the next slider space $\mathcal{S}$ and the chosen parameter set $\mathbf{x}^{chosen}$, the predicted mean function $\mu(\cdot)$, and the acquisition function $a(\cdot)$, respectively. The red dots denote the best parameter sets $\mathbf{x}^+$ among the observed data points at each step.

6.5.2.2 Implementation with Crowds

Each crowd worker may respond with some 'noise,' so averaging the responses from a sufficient number of crowd workers should provide a good approximation of the underlying common preference. To take this into account, in each iteration, the system gathers responses from multiple crowd workers by using the same slider space, and then the system calculates the median of the provided slider tick positions and uses it for calculating x^{chosen}.

6.5.3 Applications

We tested our framework in two typical parameter tweaking scenarios: photo colour enhancement and material appearance design. All the results shown in this section were generated with fifteen iterations. For each iteration, our system deployed seven microtasks, and it proceeded to the next iteration once it had obtained at least five responses. We paid 0.05 USD for each microtask execution, so the total payment to the crowds was 5.25 USD for each result. Typically, we obtained a result in a few hours (e.g., the examples in Figure 6.13 took about sixty-eight minutes on average).

6.5.3.1 Photo Colour Enhancement

Here, we used the same six parameters as in the previous section. First, we compared our optimization with the auto-enhancement functions in commercial software packages. We

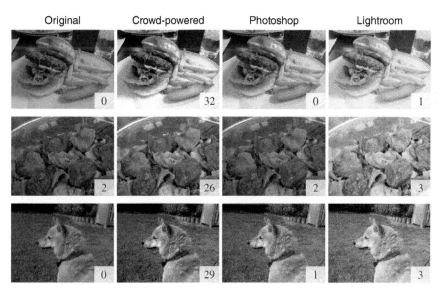

Figure 6.13 Comparison of photo colour enhancement between our crowd-powered optimization and auto-enhancement in commercial software packages (Photoshop and Lightroom). The number on each photograph indicates the number of participants who preferred the photograph to the other three in the study.

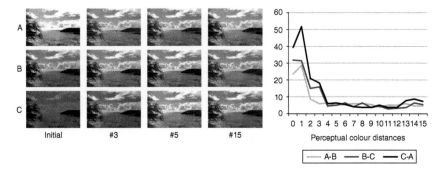

Figure 6.14 Comparison of three optimization trials with different initial conditions in photo colour enhancement. (Left) Transitions of the enhanced images. (Right) Transitions of the differences between each trial, measured by the perceptual colour metric.

compared the results of our enhancement (with fifteen iterations) with Adobe Photoshop CC[8] and Adobe Photoshop Lightroom CC[9]. Figure 6.13 shows the results. To quantify the degree of success of each enhancement, we conducted a crowdsourced study in which we asked crowd workers to identify which image looks best among the three enhancement results and the original image. The numbers in Figure 6.13 represent the results. The photos enhanced by our crowd-powered optimization were preferred over the others in these cases. These results indicate that our method can successfully produce a 'people's choice.' This represents one of the advantages of the crowd-powered optimization.

Next, we repeated the same optimization procedure three times with different initial conditions (Trial A, B, and C). Figure 6.14 (Left) shows the sequences of enhanced photographs over the iterations. We measured the differences between the trials by using a *perceptual colour metric* based on CIEDE2000; we measured the perceptual distance for each pixel in the enhanced photographs and calculated the mean over all the pixels. Figure 6.14 (Right) shows the results. It shows that the distances become small rapidly in the first four or five iterations, and they approach similar enhancement even though the initial conditions are quite different.

6.5.3.2 Material Appearance Design

In this experiment, 'Standard Shader' provided in Unity 5 was used as the target design space, where the material appearance was parametrized by albedo lightness, specular lightness, and smoothness. The number of free parameters was three in monotone and seven in full colour.

The presented framework enables the automatic adjustment of shader parameters based on a user-specified reference photograph; it minimizes the perceptual distance between the appearance in the photograph and the produced appearance by the shader. In the microtasks, crowd workers were showed both the reference photograph and a rendered

---

[8] http://www.adobe.com/products/photoshop.html
[9] http://www.adobe.com/products/photoshop-lightroom.html

Figure 6.15 Results of the crowd-powered material appearance design with reference photographs. In each pair, the top image shows the reference photograph and the bottom image shows the resulting appearance. Some photographs were provided by Flickr users: Russell Trow, lastcun, and Gwen.

'Mirror-like reflective' 'Dark blue plastic' 'Gold'

Figure 6.16 Results of the crowd-powered material appearance design with textual instructions.

image with a slider, side by side, and asked to adjust the slider until their appearances were as similar as possible. Figure 6.15 shows the results for both monotone and full colour spaces.

Another usage is that the user can specify textual instructions instead of reference photographs. Figure 6.16 illustrates the results of this usage, where crowd workers were instructed to adjust the slider so that it looks like 'brushed stainless,' 'dark blue plastic,' and so on. This is not easy when a human-in-the-loop approach is not taken.

6.6 Discussions

6.6.1 Usage of Computation: Estimation vs. Maximization

We have considered two usages involving computational techniques. The first approach, that is the estimation of the goodness function $g(\cdot)$, has several advantages compared to the other approach:

- The user can maintain control in terms of how to explore the design space $\mathcal{X}$. That is, he or she is not forced to follow the computational guidance by the system.

- The chosen solution $\mathbf{x}^*$ is always ensured to be optimal for the target user, as the 'true' goodness function used for deciding the final solution is owned by the user, which can be different from the 'estimated' goodness function used for guidance.
- Even if the estimation is not perfect, it can still guide the user to explore the design space $\mathcal{X}$ effectively. In Section 6.4, it was observed that the estimated goodness function was often useful for providing a good starting point for further exploration and for eliminating meaningless visits of bad designs.
- This approach can be seamlessly integrated in existing practical scenarios because it does not intend to replace existing workflows but does augment (or enhance) existing workflows.

In contrast, the second approach, that is the maximization of the goodness function $g(\cdot)$, has different advantages:

- The user does not need to care about the strategy of how design exploration should proceed. This could enable a new paradigm for aesthetic design and solve many constraints with respect to user experience. For example, users are released from the need to understand and learn the effects of each design parameter.
- The user no longer needs to interact with the system, enabling fully automatic workflows. This further broadens the possible usage scenarios.
- The found solutions by this approach can be used as either final products or good starting points for further manual refinement. In Section 6.5, it was observed that most of the results were not necessarily perfect but quite acceptable as final products.
- This approach aims to find the optimal solution as efficiently as possible, based on optimization techniques. For example, the second illustrative example uses Bayesian optimization techniques so as to reduce the number of necessary iterations. Compared to the approach of estimating the goodness function $g(\cdot)$ everywhere in the design space $\mathcal{X}$, whose computational cost is exponential with respect to the dimensionality, this approach may ease this problem in high-dimensional design spaces.

A hybrid approach between these two approaches is also possible. For example, partially estimating the goodness function $g(\cdot)$ around the expected maximum may be useful for supporting users to effectively explore the design space. Investigating this possibility is an important future work.

6.6.2 Advantages and Disadvantages of Crowds as a Data Source

We have discussed the use of microtask-based crowdsourcing as a data source for computation. Other possibilities for obtaining preference data include utilizing user's editing history (Koyama, Sakamoto, and Igarashi, 2016), relying on activities in an online community (Talton, Gibson, Yang, Hanrahan, and Koltun, 2009), and inserting an explicit training phase

(Kapoor, Caicedo, Lischinski, and Bing Kang, 2014). Here, we summarize the advantages and disadvantages of this data source.

Application Domain. The use of microtask-based crowdsourcing limits its application to the domains where even unskilled, non-expert crowd workers can adequately assess the quality of designs. An example of such domains is photo colour enhancement; it can be a valid assumption that most crowd workers have their preference on photo colour enhancement, since enhanced photographs are ubiquitously seen in daily lives (e.g., in product advertisements). However, some design domains exist where only experts can adequately assess the quality of designs; in such cases, asking crowds may not be a reasonable choice.

Whose Preference? Asking many people is advantageous in that the system can reliably understand 'people's choice' and utilize it. The illustrative examples described in the previous sections assume the existence of a 'general' (or universal) preference shared among crowds and ask multiple workers to perform microtasks to observe the general preference. However, in some design domains, crowds from different backgrounds can have clearly different preferences (Reinecke and Gajos, 2014). In such cases, it is necessary to take each worker's preference into account in the computation; otherwise, the computed preference would be less meaningful. It is also notable that the user's personal preference is not reflected in computation when crowdsourcing is the only source of data; to incorporate the user's preference, other data sources such as the user's editing history have to be used in combination with crowdsouring.

Data Gathering. Microtask-based crowdsourcing enables on-demand and stable generation of new data, which is a large advantage of this approach. One of the limitations in this approach is the latency for data generation; although there are techniques for enabling real-time crowdsourcing (e.g., Bernstein, Brandt, Miller, and Karger, 2011), it is generally difficult to obtain necessary responses interactively. Another limitation is that crowds may provide poor-quality data due to mistaking or cheating, which requires to use computational techniques that are robust for such 'noisy' data. The monetary cost is also an inevitable limitation.

6.6.3 Remaining Challenges

We have discussed computational design methods under many assumptions. To ease the assumptions and develop more practical methods, a number of possible challenges remain as next steps.

Design Space Parametrization. We have assumed that the target design space is appropriately parametrized in advance. It is important to seek appropriate parametrization techniques to broaden the applications of crowd-powered computational design. For example, it is difficult to directly handle very high-dimensional design spaces. We consider that dimensionality reduction techniques could be helpful for many problems with high-dimensional design spaces. However, this is still non-trivial because, unlike typical problems in data science, the resulting space in this case has to be either designer-friendly or optimization-friendly (or both) for maximizing aesthetic preference. Recently, Yumer, Asente, Mech, and Kara (2015) showed that autoencoder networks can be used for converting a high-dimensional, visually discontinuous design space to a lower-dimensional, visually continuous design space that is more desirable for design exploration. Incorporating human preference in dimensionality reduction of design spaces is an interesting future work.

Discrete Parameters. We focused on continuous parameters, and did not discuss how to handle discrete design parameters, such as fonts (O'Donovan, Lībeks, Agarwala, and Hertzmann, 2014) and web design templates (Chaudhuri, Kalogerakis, Giguere, and Funkhouser, 2013). The remaining challenges to handle such discrete parameters include how to represent goodness functions for design spaces including discrete parameters and how to facilitate users' interactive explorations. Investigating techniques for jointly handling discrete and continuous parameters is another potential future work.

Locally Optimal Design Alternatives. In some scenarios, totally different design alternatives can be equally 'best,' and it can be hard to determine which is better. For example, in Adobe Colour CC,[10] which is a user community platform to make, explore, and share *colour palettes* (a set of colours usually consisting of five colours), there are a number of (almost) equally popular colour palettes that have been preferred by many users, as shown in Figure 6.17. In this case, if we assume the existence of a goodness function for colour palettes, the popular palettes can be considered as local maximums of the goodness function. Considering that the goal is to support design activities, it may not be effective to assume that there is a sole global maximum in this design space and to guide the user toward the single maximum; rather, it may be more desirable to provide a variety of good design alternatives. There is a room for investigation about how computation can support such design scenarios.

Evaluation Methodology. One of the issues in computational design driven by aesthetic preference is the lack of an established, general methodology of evaluating each new method. Validation of methods in this domain is challenging for several reasons. The first reason is the difficulty of defining 'correct' aesthetic preference, which can be highly dependent on scenarios. Also, as the ultimate goal is the support of design activities, the effectiveness needs to be evaluated by designers. Methods in this domain are built on many

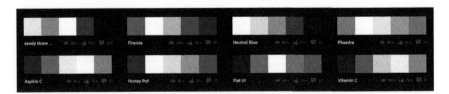

Figure 6.17 'Most Popular' colour palettes in the user community of Adobe Colour CC. Though visually different from each other, they are (mostly) equally popular and preferred by many users.

---

[10] https://color.adobe.com/

assumptions, each of which is difficult to validate. We consider that an important future work would be to establish general evaluation schemes.

More Sophisticated Models of Crowd Behaviours.   The two examples described in Sections 6.4 and 6.5 were built on an assumption of crowd workers: crowd workers share a common goodness function, and each crowd worker responds based on the function with some noise. Thus, it is assumed that the common goodness function is observed by asking many crowd workers and then averaging their responses. This assumption may be valid in some scenarios, but may not be in many other scenarios; for example, crowds may form several clusters with respect to their aesthetic preference. Modelling such more complex properties of crowds is an important future challenge.

Incorporating Domain-Specific Heuristics.   We have tried to use minimal domain-specific knowledge so that the discussions made in this chapter are as generally applicable as possible. However, it is possible to make computational design methods more practical for certain specific scenarios by making full use of domain-specific heuristics. For example, if one builds a software program to tweak the viewpoints of 3D objects, the heuristic features and the pre-trained model in (Secord, Lu, Finkelstein, Singh, and Nealen, 2011) could be jointly used with the methods described in the previous sections.

Combining General and Personal Preference.   We discussed how to handle crowds' *general* preference. However, it would also be beneficial if we could handle users' *personal* preference; Koyama, Sakamoto, and Igarashi (2016) presented a method for learning personal preference to facilitate design exploration and reported that this approach was appreciated by professional designers. Both approaches have advantages and disadvantages; to complement the disadvantages of each approach, we envision that the combination of these two approaches may be useful and worth investigating.

6.6.4 Future Directions

Finally, we conclude this chapter with discussions of several future research directions on computational design methods powered by crowds.

6.6.4.1 From Design Refinement to Design Generation

We focused on parametric design, where the design space is reasonably parametrized beforehand. This is often performed for the *refinement* of a design. On the other hand, the *generation* of a design from scratch is also an important step of an entire design process. It is an open question whether we can handle such free-form designs as an extension of parameter tweaking.

Some class of design generation processes can be described as a sequence of executable commands (or operations). In this case, the design space can be modelled as a tree structure whose leaves and edges represent visual designs and executable commands, respectively, and the design goal can be formulated to find the best leaf node from this tree. For this, tree search optimization techniques (e.g., the branch and bound method) might be useful. It is also notable that interactive evolutionary computation (IEC) can be used to generate designs while accounting for human evaluation in the loop. For example, Sims (1991) showed that IEC can generate interesting designs beyond predefined parametric design spaces.

6.6.4.2 More Complex Design Objectives

In practical design scenarios, designers may have to solve complex problems with more than one design objective. For example, when a graphic designer designs an advertisement targeted at mainly women, he or she has to bias the objective toward women's aesthetic preference. In this case, it is possible to formulate the design problem as

$$\mathbf{x}^* = \arg\max_{\mathbf{x} \in \mathcal{X}} \{w_{male}g_{male}(\mathbf{x}) + w_{female}g_{female}(\mathbf{x})\}, \tag{6.12}$$

where $g_{male}(\cdot)$ and $g_{female}(\cdot)$ are the goodness functions owned by men and women, respectively, and w_{male} and w_{female} are the weights for adjusting the bias, which can be $w_{male} < w_{female}$ in this case. With crowdsourced human computation, this could be solved by utilizing the demographic information of crowd workers (Reinecke and Gajos, 2014). Another complex scenario is a case in which some additional design criteria are expected to be at least satisfied, but do not have to be maximized. For example, a client may want a design that is as preferred by young people as possible and at the same time is 'acceptable' by elderly people. In this case, the problem can be formulated as a constrained optimization. Under these complex conditions, it should be difficult for designers to manually explore designs. We believe that this is the part that computational techniques need to facilitate.

6.6.4.3 Computational Creative Design with Crowds

We have considered aesthetic preference as the target criterion in design activities. Another important aspect of design is *creativity*. One of the keys to provide creative inspirations to designers is *unexpectedness* (Cohen-Or and Zhang, 2016). Some researchers have interpreted such unexpectedness as *diversity* in design alternatives and have explicitly formulated optimization problems for finding the most diverse set of design alternatives (e.g., Won, Lee, O'Sullivan, Hodgins, and Lee, 2014). We believe that there are many interesting opportunities to investigate computational frameworks for achieving creative designs by making use of crowds' creativity.

6.7 Summary

In this chapter, we discussed the possible mechanisms, illustrative examples, and future challenges of computational design methods with crowds. Especially, we focused on the facilitation of parametric design (i.e., parameter tweaking) and then formulated the design process as a numerical optimization problem, where the objective function to be maximized was based on perceptual preference. We illustrated the ideas of using crowdsourced human computation for this problem, either for the estimation of the objective function or for the maximization of the objective function.

....

REFERENCES

Allen, B., Curless, B., and Popović, Z., 2003. The space of human body shapes: Reconstruction and parameterization from range scans. *ACM Transactions on Graphics*, 22(3), pp. 587–94.

Bailly, G., Oulasvirta, A., Kötzing, T., and Hoppe, S., 2013. Menuoptimizer: Interactive optimization of menu systems. In: *UIST '13: Proceedings of the 26th Annual ACM Symposium on User Interface Software and Technology*. New York, NY: ACM, pp. 331–42.

Bell, S., Upchurch, P., Snavely, N., and Bala, K., 2013. Opensurfaces: A richly annotated catalog of surface appearance. *ACM Transactions on Graphics*, 32(4), pp. 111:1–111:17.

Bernstein, M. S., Brandt, J., Miller, R. C., and Karger, D. R., 2011. Crowds in two seconds: Enabling realtime crowd-powered interfaces. In: *UIST '11: Proceedings of the 24th Annual ACM Symposium on User Interface Software and Technology*. New York, NY: ACM, pp. 33–42.

Bernstein, M. S., Little, G., Miller, R. C., Hartmann, B., Ackerman, M. S., Karger, D. R., Crowell, D., and Panovich, K., 2010. Soylent: A word processor with a crowd inside. In: *UIST '10: Proceedings of the 23rd Annual ACM Symposium on User Interface Software and Technology*. New York, NY: ACM, pp. 313–22.

Bishop, C. M., 1995. *Neural Networks for Pattern Recognition*. Oxford: Oxford University Press.

Blanz, V., and Vetter, T., 1999. A morphable model for the synthesis of 3d faces. In: *SIGGRAPH '99: Proceedings of the 26th Annual Conference on Computer Graphics and Interactive Techniques*. New York, NY: ACM, pp. 187–94.

Brochu, E., de Freitas, N., and Ghosh, A., 2007. Active preference learning with discrete choice data. In: *NIPS '07: Advances in Neural Information Processing Systems 20*. pp. 409–16.

Bychkovsky, V., Paris, S., Chan, E., and Durand, F., 2011. Learning photographic global tonal adjustment with a database of input/output image pairs. In: *CVPR '11: Proceedings of the 24th IEEE Conference on Computer Vision and Pattern Recognition*. pp. 97–104.

Chaudhuri, S., Kalogerakis, E., Giguere, S., and Funkhouser, T., 2013. Attribit: Content creation with semantic attributes. In: *UIST '13: Proceedings of the 26th Annual ACM Symposium on User Interface Software and Technology*. New York, NY: ACM, pp. 193–202.

Cohen-Or, D., and Zhang, H., 2016. From inspired modeling to creative modeling. *The Visual Computer*, 32(1), pp. 7–14.

Gajos, K., and Weld, D. S., 2004. Supple: Automatically generating user interfaces. In: *IUI '04: Proceedings of the 9th International Conference on Intelligent User Interfaces*. New York, NY: ACM, pp. 93–100.

Gingold, Y., Shamir, S., and Cohen-Or, D., 2012. Micro perceptual human computation for visual tasks. *ACM Transactions on Graphics*, 31(5), pp. 119:1–119:12.

Howe, J., 2006a. Crowdsourcing: A definition. Available at: http://crowdsourcing.typepad.com/cs/2006/06/crowdsourcing_a.html, 2006. Accessed: October 23, 2016.

Howe, J., 2006b. The rise of crowdsourcing. Available at: https://www.wired.com/2006/06/crowds/. Accessed: October 23, 2016.

Huber, B., Reinecke, K., and Gajos, K. Z., 2017. The effect of performance feedback on social media sharing at volunteer-based online experiment platforms. In: *CHI '17: Proceedings of the 2017 CHI Conference on Human Factors in Computing Systems*. New York, NY: ACM, pp. 1882–6.

Ipeirotis, P. G., Provost, F., and Wang, J., 2010. Quality management on amazon mechanical turk. In: *HCOMP '10: Proceedings of the ACM SIGKDD Workshop on Human Computation*. New York, NY: ACM, pp. 64–7.

Kapoor, A., Caicedo, J. C., Lischinski, D., and Kang, S. B., 2014. Collaborative personalization of image enhancement. *International Journal of Computer Vision*, 108(1), pp. 148–64.

Kittur, A., Chi, E. H., and Suh, B., 2008. Crowdsourcing user studies with mechanical turk. In: *CHI '08: Proceedings of the SIGCHI Conference on Human Factors in Computing Systems*. New York, NY: ACM, pp. 453–56.

Koyama, Y., Sakamoto, D., and Igarashi, T., 2014. Crowd-powered parameter analysis for visual design exploration. In: *UIST '14: Proceedings of the 27th Annual ACM Symposium on User Interface Software and Technology*. New York, NY: ACM, pp. 65–74.

Koyama, Y., Sakamoto, D., and Igarashi, T., 2016. Selph: Progressive learning and support of manual photo color enhancement. In: *CHI '16: Proceedings of the 2016 CHI Conference on Human Factors in Computing Systems*. New York, NY: ACM, pp. 2520–32.

Koyama, Y., Sato, I., Sakamoto, D., and Igarashi, T., 2017. Sequential line search for efficient visual design optimization by crowds. *ACM Transactions on Graphics*, 36(4), pp. 48:1–48:11.

Koyama, Y., Sueda, S., Steinhardt, E., Igarashi, T., Shamir, A., and Matusik, W., 2015. Autoconnect: Computational design of 3d-printable connectors. *ACM Transactions on Graphics*, 34(6), pp. 231:1–231:11.

Lewis, J. P., Anjyo, K., Rhee, T., Zhang, M., Pighin, F., and Deng, Z., 2014. Practice and theory of blendshape facial models. In: *Eurographics 2014 - State of the Art Reports*. pp. 199–218.

Little, G., Chilton, L. B., Goldman, M., and Miller, R. C., 2010. Turkit: Human computation algorithms on mechanical turk. In: *UIST '10: Proceedings of the 23rd Annual ACM Symposium on User Interface Software and Technology*. New York, NY: ACM, pp. 57–66.

Matusik, W., Pfister, H., Brand, M., and McMillan, L., 2003. A data-driven reflectance model. *ACM Transactions on Graphics*, 22(3), pp. 759–69.

Miniukovich, A., and Angeli, D. A., 2015. Computation of interface aesthetics. In: *CHI '15: Proceedings of the 33rd Annual ACM Conference on Human Factors in Computing Systems*. New York, NY: ACM, pp. 1163–72.

Morishima, A., Amer-Yahia, S., and Roy, B. S., 2014. Crowd4u: An initiative for constructing an open academic crowdsourcing network. In: *HCOMP '14: Proceedings of Second AAAI Conference on Human Computation and Crowdsourcing – Works in Progress Abstracts*. New York, NY: ACM.

Nielsen, J. B., Jensen, H. W., and Ramamoorthi, R., 2015. On optimal, minimal brdf sampling for reflectance acquisition. *ACM Transactions on Graphics*, 34(6), pp. 186:1–186:11.

O'Donovan, P., Agarwala, A., and Hertzmann, A., 2011. Color compatibility from large datasets. *ACM Transactions on Graphics*, 30(4), pp. 63:1–63:12.

O'Donovan, P., Agarwala, A., and Hertzmann, A., 2014. Learning layouts for single-page graphic designs. *IEEE Transactions on Visualization and Computer Graphics*, 20(8), pp. 1200–13.

O'Donovan, P., Lībeks, J., Agarwala, A., and Hertzmann, A., 2014. Exploratory font selection using crowdsourced attributes. *ACM Transactions on Graphics*, 33(4), pp. 92:1–92:9.

Prévost, R., Whiting, E., Lefebvre, S., and Sorkine-Hornung, O., 2013. Make it stand: Balancing shapes for 3d fabrication. *ACM Transactions on Graphics*, 32(4), pp. 81:1–81:10.

Quinn, A. J., and Bederson, B. B., 2011. Human computation: A survey and taxonomy of a growing field. In: *CHI '11: Proceedings of the SIGCHI Conference on Human Factors in Computing Systems*. New York, NY: ACM, pp. 1403–12.

Reinecke, K., and Gajos, K. Z., 2014. Quantifying visual preferences around the world. In: *CHI '14: Proceedings of the SIGCHI Conference on Human Factors in Computing Systems*. New York, NY: ACM, pp. 11–20.

Secord, A., Lu, J., Finkelstein, A., Singh, M., and Nealen, A., 2011. Perceptual models of viewpoint preference. *ACM Transactions on Graphics*, 30(5), pp. 109:1–109:12.

Shahriari, B., Swersky, K., Wang, Z., Adams, R. P., and de Freitas, N., 2016. Taking the human out of the loop: A review of Bayesian optimization. *Proceedings of the IEEE*, 104(1), pp. 148–75.

Sigal, L., Mahler, M., Diaz, S., McIntosh, K., Carter, E., Richards, T., and Hodgins, J., 2015. A perceptual control space for garment simulation. *ACM Transactions on Graphics*, 34(4), pp. 117:1–117:10.

Sims, K., 1991. Artificial evolution for computer graphics. *SIGGRAPH Computer Graphics*, 25(4), pp. 319–28.

Stava, O., Vanek, J., Benes, B., Carr, N., and Měch, R., 2012. Stressrelief: Improving structural strength of 3D printable objects. *ACM Transactions on Graphics*, 31(4), pp. 48:1–48:11.

Streuber, S., Quiros-Ramirez, M. A., Hill, M. Q., Hahn, C. A., Zuffi, S., O'Toole, A., and Black, M. J., 2016. Bodytalk: Crowdshaping realistic 3d avatars with words. *ACM Transactions on Graphics*, 35(4), pp. 54:1–54:14.

Talton, J. O., Gibson, D., Yang, L., Hanrahan, P., and Koltun, V., 2009. Exploratory modeling with collaborative design spaces. *ACM Transactions on Graphics*, 28(5), pp. 167:1–167:10.

Todi, K., Weir, D., and Oulasvirta, A., 2016. Sketchplore: Sketch and explore with a layout optimiser. In: *DIS '16: Proceedings of the 2016 ACM Conference on Designing Interactive Systems*. New York, NY: ACM, pp. 543–55.

Umetani, N., Koyama, Y., Schmidt, R., and Igarashi, T., 2014. Pteromys: Interactive design and optimization of free-formed free-flight model airplanes. *ACM Transactions on Graphics*, 33(4), pp. 65: 1–65:10.

von Ahn, L., 2005. *Human Computation*. PhD thesis, Carnegie Mellon University, Pittsburgh, PA. AAI3205378.

von Ahn, L., and Dabbish, L., 2004. Labeling images with a computer game. In: *CHI '04: Proceedings of the SIGCHI Conference on Human Factors in Computing Systems*. New York, NY: ACM, pp. 319–26.

von Ahn, L., and Dabbish, L., 2008. Designing games with a purpose. *Commun. ACM*, 51(8), pp. 58–67.

von Ahn, L., Maurer, B., McMillen, C., Abraham, D., and Blum, M., 2008. reCAPTCHA: Human-based character recognition via web security measures. *Science*, 321(5895), pp. 1465–8.

Weber, J., and Penn, J., 1995. Creation and rendering of realistic trees. In: *SIGGRAPH '95: Proceedings of the 22nd Annual Conference on Computer Graphics and Interactive Techniques*. New York, NY: ACM, pp. 119–28.

Won, J., Lee, K., O'Sullivan, C., Hodgins, J. K., and Lee, J., 2014. Generating and ranking diverse multi-character interactions. *ACM Transactions on Graphics*, 33(6), pp. 219:1–219:12.

Yumer, M. E., Asente, P., Mech, R., and Kara, L. B., 2015. Procedural modeling using autoencoder networks. In: *UIST '15: Proceedings of the 28th Annual ACM Symposium on User Interface Software and Technology*. New York, NY: ACM, pp. 109–18.

Yumer, M. E., Chaudhuri, S., Hodgins, J. K., and Kara, L. B., 2015. Semantic shape editing using deformation handles. *ACM Transactions on Graphics*, 34(4), pp. 86:1–86:12.

PART III
Systems

7

· · • · ·

Practical Formal Methods in Human–Computer Interaction

ALAN DIX

7.1 Introduction

One might feel that the very association of the terms 'formal methods' and 'human' is an oxymoron; how can anything that is formal make any sense when faced with the complexity and richness of human experience? However, little could be more formal than computer code, so in that sense *everything* in Human–Computer Interaction (HCI) is formal. Indeed, all the chapters in this book are about practical formal methods, in the sense that they involve a form of mathematical or symbolic manipulation. From Fitts' Law to statistical analysis of experimental results, mathematics is pervasive in HCI.

However, in computer science 'formal methods' has come to refer to a very specific set of techniques. Some of these are symbolic or textual based on sets and logic, or algebraic representations. Others are more diagrammatic. All try to specify some aspect of a system in precise detail in order to clarify thinking, perform some sort of analysis, or communicate unambiguously between stakeholders across the design and engineering process.

The use of such methods is usually advocated in order to ensure the correctness, or more generally, the quality of computer systems. However, they are also usually regarded as requiring too much expertise and effort for day-to-day use, being principally applied in safety-critical areas outside academia. Similarly, in HCI, even when not dismissed out of hand, the principal research and use of formal methods is in safety-critical areas such as aerospace, the nuclear industry, and medical devices.

However, this chapter demonstrates that, in contrast to this perception, formal methods can be used effectively in a wider range of applications for the specification or understanding of user interfaces and devices. Examples show that, with appropriate choice and use, formal methods can be used to allow faster development and turnaround, and be understood by those without mathematical or computational background.

We will use two driving examples. One is from many years ago and concerns the development of simple transaction-based interactive information systems. The other is more recent

Computational Interaction. Antti Oulasvirta, Per Ola Kristensson, Xiaojun Bi, Andrew Howes (Eds).
© Oxford University Press 2018. Published 2018 by Oxford University Press.

and relates to the design of smart-devices where both physical form and digital experience need to work together.

In both cases, a level of appropriation is central: the adaptation of elements of specific formal methods so that their power and precision is addressed at specific needs, while being as lightweight and flexible as possible in other areas. Because of this, the chapter does not introduce a particular fixed set of notations or methods, but rather, through the examples, demonstrates a number of heuristics for selecting and adapting formal methods. This said, it is hoped that the specific methods used in the two examples may also themselves be of direct use.

The rest of this chapter is structured as follows. First, Section 7.2 looks at some of the range of formal methods used in computer science in general, and then at the history and current state of the use of formal methods in HCI. Sections 7.3 and 7.4 look at the two examples, for each introducing a specific problem, the way formalism was used to address it, and then the lessons exposed by each. Finally, we bring together these lessons and also look at emerging issues in HCI where appropriate formalisms may be useful or, in some cases, essential for both researcher and practitioner as we attempt to address a changing world.

7.2 Being Formal

7.2.1 Formalism in Computing: Theoretical and Practical

Formal methods in computer science is primarily about specifying aspects of computer systems in some mathematical or symbolic form, in order to better communicate, understand, or verify their behaviour and properties. The roots of this can be found in the work of the early giants of computer science, for example, Dykstra's use of assertions to prove program correctness.

Although they have diverged somewhat in recent years, formal theory has been part of practical computing since the beginning, as Alan Turing's early contributions make very clear. However, currently, theoreticians tend to deal more with abstract questions about the nature of computation, and the formal methods community is more connected with software engineering and developing formally based tools, notations, and methods that could, in principle, form part of system development processes. Indeed, while the particular notations used often get named and become the 'brand', an important issue is always how these fit into broader engineering processes.

One class of formal methods is concerned with specifying the data structures of the state of the system and the way these change during (typically atomic) actions. This form of specification is almost always textual using sets, logic, and functions, although in different mixes depending on the particular notation and methods. The most widely known of these is probably Z (Spivey, 1992), which uses a codified and strongly typed form of standard set theory (Figure 7.1). Note that mathematicians are often fairly free in their use of notation, modifying it to fit the particular theorem or problem area, but computing prefers more fixed notations, especially if these are to be subject to automatic analysis or verification.

The other use of formal methods focuses more on the overall order in which actions are performed. Early examples of this include state transition networks (STNs) and flowcharts for more sequential operations, both of which will be seen later in this chapter. STNs are

```
state ────────────────────────────────────────
  │ total: Nat              - running total (accumulator)
  │ disp: Nat               - number currently displayed
  │ pend_op: {+, −,*,/,none}        - pending operation
  │ typing: Bool                      - true/false flag
```

Figure 7.1 Example of Z to specify the internal state of a four-function calculator.

used extensively, including in the specification of communication protocols where it is essential that equipment produced by different manufacturers works together. Note that STNs are effectively a diagrammatic form of finite state machines, described in detail in Chapter 8.

Figure 7.2 shows an example of an STN specifying the behaviour of a caching protocol. The circles represent states, and the arrows potential transitions between the states. Note how the arcs, drawn differently, represent different kinds of transitions (in this case, whether they are initiated by activity on the system bus or internally by a processor).

Simple STNs only allow sequential, one state at a time, processes, but variants, such as Harel Statecharts (Harel, 1987), have been developed that allow concurrent activity, alongside a number of notations specialized for this, including Petri nets and process algebras (mostly variants of CCS and CSP). In some cases, temporal logics (that is, logics that reason about time) are used, primarily as a way to specify properties that must be satisfied by a system fully specified using other formalisms.

In fact, this last point demonstrates two slightly different uses of formal notations:

(i) specification of desired properties of a system; and

(ii) precise and detailed specification of a particular system.

Effectively, the first is about formalizing requirements and the second formalizing the detailed (technical) design. These can be used alone, i.e., (i) can be used on its own to create test cases or simply clarify requirements; (ii) can be used to analyse the behaviour or to verify that code does what the specification says it should. Alternatively, the two kinds may be used together where the detailed specification (ii) is verified to fulfil the formal requirements (i). Where using both, these may use the same formal notation, or two different ones, as noted with the use of temporal logics.

Simpler diagrammatic formalisms have always been well used, and many, including Statecharts, have found their way into Unified Modeling Language (UML) (Booch et al., 1999). There have been classic success stories of formal methods used in industrial practice dating back many years, notably, a large-scale project to specify large portions of IBM Customer Information Control Systems (CICS) in Z (Freitas et al., 2009). However, on the whole, more complex formal methods tend to require too much expertise and are perceived as taking too much effort. Hence, adoption is very low except for a few specialized safety-critical fields where the additional effort can be cost effective.

One suggestion to deal with this low adoption has been to develop *domain-specific notations*, designed explicitly for a very narrow range of applications using representations

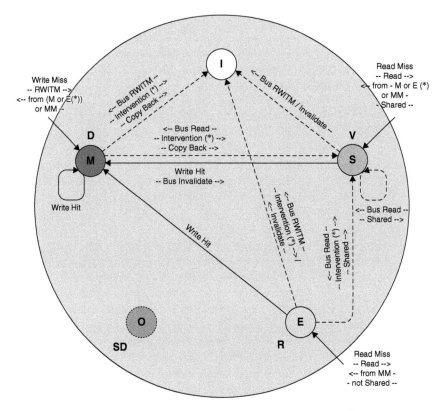

Figure 7.2 Example state transition network of MESI caching protocol. (from Wikipedia, by Ferry24.Milan—Own work, CC BY-SA 3.0, en.wikipedia.org/wiki/Cache_memory#/media/File:MESI_State_Transaction_Diagram.svg)

that are more likely to be comprehensible by domain experts, but which are built over or can be connected back to some form of semantic core that allows analysis and reasoning (Polak, 2002). The use of formal methods in HCI can be seen as one such specialization, as can the examples later in this chapter.

7.2.2 Why Formal Methods in HCI—History and Utility?

The use of formal methods in HCI dates back to the earliest days of HCI itself as a defined discipline. Much of this use was driven by strong practical concerns. Reisner's (1981) use of Backus-Naur form (BNF) to specify what we would now call the *dialogue* of interactive systems was driven by the desire to understand the properties and potential problems of alternative designs prior to the expensive process of creating systems prototypes. The choice of BNF was suggested by the successful use of formal grammars elsewhere in computing, notably in compiler construction, which itself was inspired by the lexical–syntactic–semantic decomposition from linguistics.

Early designers of User Interface Management Systems wanted to be able to create systems more rapidly and reliably, but found the user interface code increasingly complex. They also turned to dialogue specifications using a number of formalisms from grammars to production rules, and turned the linguistic triad into the distinction between presentation, dialogue and (programmer's interface to) functionality, embodied in the Seeheim Model (Pfaff and Hagen, 1985). Although the Seeheim Model itself is now all but forgotten, the presentation–dialogue–functionality distinction is explicit or implicit in many aspects of user interface design, for example, in the separation of web interface style information into the Cascading Style Sheet (CSS) (presentation layer).

In parallel, arising from cognitive science, was a growing interest in how the same or similar formalisms could be used to specify the way humans cope with interactions. Sometimes this involved models primarily of the human, Card, Moran, and Newells's (1983) Model Human Processor (MHP) being the most well-known example; and sometimes modelling both human and system in order to understand the interactions, including Cognitive Complexity Theory (Kieras and Polson, 1985), which used production rules as a cognitive model alongside a state model of the system in order to explore issues such as *closure* (the way one sometimes forgets 'finishing off' actions, such as picking up a receipt, when one's primary goal, say buying a ticket, is completed).

The interest in formal methods more broadly in computer science also turned to user interfaces, both because of their complexity, and also because any systems specified ultimately ended in some form of user interface. Sufrin's (1982) specification of a display editor is the first complete example of this using Z to specify the effects for editing actions (such as insert a character) on the internal state of an editor (text, cursor position, etc.).

The 'York Approach' arose primarily from the latter stream, but with a particular focus on specifying and analysing *generic properties* of user interfaces (such as the ability to predict and observe the system's behaviour when you perform an action). The idea of this was to be able to talk about these properties independently of the specific system that embodied them. The most well-known output of this was the PIE model (Dix and Runciman, 1985; Dix, 1991), which took a black-box view of the interactive system, describing only the inputs (e.g., keystrokes, mouse movements) and outputs (e.g., display, printouts).

The complexity of human interaction and user interface systems always limited the kinds of analysis possible, and this stream of work, rather like Seeheim, is now represented most strongly in the vocabulary of formal system properties developed during that time (observability, predictability, reversibility, etc.).

However, the strong algebraic properties of *undo* made it particularly suitable for abstract analysis, with early results (Dix and Runciman, 1985; Dix, 1991) showing that it was fundamentally impossible to have any undo system where the undo button perfectly reversed any action, including itself, which was a common claim at the time. This work was later extended, first to multi-user undo (Abowd and Dix, 1992) exposing potential problems and solutions before the first such systems were built, and then later using *category theory* (Mancini, 1997) to prove that any undo system that obeyed fairly simple properties fell into one of two camps: flip undo (where one previous state is stored and undo toggles between this and the most recent state), and stack undo (where undo/redo traverses back and forth through previous states, but any action freezes the process and discards actions back to that point).

During this same period there was also work on formally based architectural description such as PAC (Coutaz, 1987) and ARCH-Slinky (Bass et al., 1991), computational abstractions for construction of particular kinds of user interface such as Dynamic Pointers (Dix 1991, 1995), and a number of dedicated user interface formalisms that are still used today, including Interactive Cooperative Object, or ICO (Navarre et al., 2009), a variant of Petri Nets, and ConcurTaskTrees, or CTT (Paterno, 1999), a more formally based variant of hierarchical task analysis (Shepherd, 1989).

As a final word in this section, note again that while some of this early work arose from more theoretical concerns, the majority had roots in practical problems that arose when either trying to understand or build interactive user interfaces.

More information about the early development of this area can be found in a number of monographs and collections (Thimbleby and Harrison, 1990; Dix, 1991; Gram and Cockton, 1996; Palanque and Paterno, 1997; Paterno, 1999; Weyers et al., 2017).

7.2.3 Where We Are Now: Current Use and Research in HCI

Another recently published Springer volume, *The Handbook of Formal Methods in Human-Computer Interaction* (Weyers et al., 2017), captures the state of the art in this area, so this section will summarize this very briefly and the interested reader is referred to the full volume for further details.

While there is some work on state modelling, including continued use of Z (e.g., Bowen and Reeves, 2017), the largest volume of current work is on aspects of dialogue modelling, and indeed, the extended examples in this volume are also forms of dialogue modelling, albeit addressing slightly different levels. Some are based on longstanding techniques such as StateCharts, ICO (see Chapter 9), and CTT, although labelled transition systems (LTS) have also become common, either used directly or derived automatically from other notations. LTS are a form of state transition network where the arcs carry labels, usually from a finite set.

Part of the reason for the popularity of LTS, at least as a target notion, is that there are a number of tools that allow verification of properties of LTS. Automatic verification has always been a stated aim of formal methods, and in some cases (for example, in the analysis of some consumer devices and medical instruments (Thimbleby and Gow, 2008)), it has been possible to exhaustively analyse properties of the graph of possible dialogue states. However, the combinatorial state space explosion has often made this form of exhaustive analysis impossible. Developments in tool support for automatic verification, developed for other application domains, have increasingly been used to verify user interface properties (e.g., Masci et al., 2014; Bolton and Bass, 2017; Harrison et al., 2017).

A different form of tool support is found in model-based user interfaces (e.g., Manca et al., 2017). In this context, model-based is often used in a stronger sense than the models in UML, as the models are expected to be suitable for automatic transformation or execution. The models may be based on reverse engineering of existing systems or developed by hand, but are then used to automatically generate (for example, to enable plasticity) interfaces that change their appearance and behaviour depending on the device and user characteristics (e.g., Coutaz, 2010). As well as representing a long-term research effort, summarized in

Meixner et al. (2011), it has also led to a W3C standardization effort (Meixner et al., 2014).

Another development has been the work on domain specific notations (DSNs). These are notations designed for a specific application domain, e.g., chemical plants. The visualizations and vocabulary are created to more easily express the particular requirements and properties of the domain, and also be meaningful to domain experts. Chapter 8 argues strongly for the need for appropriate languages so that coders and designers can more easily express their intentions and understand the computer's semantics, hence improving both productivity and reliability.

There are elements of this in early work, for example, dynamic pointers (Dix 1991, 1995), which were designed to specify and construct systems that included complex changing structures and required locations or parts to be marked (e.g., cursors for editing, current scroll location in text). This was effectively a bespoke, handcrafted DSN. More recent work has focused on creating abstractions, tools, and methods that make it easier for a formal expert to construct a DSN (Weyers, 2017; Van Mierlo et al, 2017).

7.3 In Practice: Transaction-based Information Systems

As we have seen in the preceding section, there are a range of methods and domains being studied by formal methods in HCI. However, it is still the case, as for formal methods in general, that the vast majority of applications are in safety-critical areas such as aerospace (e.g., Chapter 9), the nuclear industry, and medical devices (e.g., Chapter 8).

This section looks at two case studies, spanning over 30 years, that demonstrate successful applications of formal methods outside the safety-critical area.

7.3.1 The Problem

This first case study dates from the early 1980s and the design and development of interactive transaction processing systems (for more details of this case study see Dix, 2002). For those unfamiliar with this kind of system, the easiest parallel is a web server, except each application effectively functions like a dedicated web server in order to offer high throughput. The particular systems were ICL-based, but similar to the better-known IBM CICS, which is still heavily used today for cashier terminals in shops and banks and as the backend of enterprise-scale web services, albeit currently more often programmed in Java than COBOL.

The author was working in a local government IT department, which used ICL/TP for interactive information systems. The end-users were principally council staff. They interacted with the information systems using semi-smart terminals, very like a web browser that can display simple web forms. Just like with a web-form interface, the user would enter some values into a form, for example, the name of a person to search for in a personnel database, send the form, and the system would respond with a screen of information.

There were known problems with the systems deployed in the council at the time, for example, if the response were a paged list, occasionally if two users submitted queries, one might get a second page corresponding to the second user's query. While this was annoying, it was infrequent enough to be acceptable for purely information access. However, the author was tasked with creating the council's first systems to also allow interactive update of data, and so it would be unacceptable to have similar issues.

The reason for this occasional bugginess was evident in the code of the existing applications, which was spaghetti-like due to complex decisions primarily aimed at working out the context of a transaction request. Similar code can indeed often be seen today in poorly structured web-server code that tries to interpret input from different sources, checking for the existence of variables to distinguish a submit from a cancel on a web form. In fairness to the programmers, this was very early in the development of such systems, and also the individual application did a lot of the work now done by web servers such as Apache, marshalling variables and directing requests to the appropriate code.

7.3.2 Technical Solution

Part of the solution was technical. A small non-editable identifier was placed on each form, which then functioned rather like the 'Referrer' field in a web transaction, telling the application what screen the request had come from. In addition, the ICL/TP system allowed information to be attached to each terminal, rather like a web cookie or session variable, which was used to keep track of context for each application transaction.

The first of these eased some of the spaghetti-code problems as it was now simply a matter of checking the non-editable field, and the second eased the odd problems on list-screens, which had been due to state being 'mixed up' between different users' transactions.

Although the particular form of the last issue is less likely on current web code, other kinds of mixed-up state are common as state is often spread between URL parameters, hidden fields in forms, cookies, server variables, and client-side JavaScript data structures.

These technical fixes made the code cleaner and more reliable; however, it was still effectively event-based and hard to interpret and construct.

In order to deal with this, a variant of flowcharts were used.

7.3.3 Standard Formal Notation: Flowcharts

Flowcharts had been heavily used for specifying computer program behaviour since the 1960s, with multiple standards including BSI/ISO (BSI, 1987), and ECMA (1966), who used to produce useful plastic templates. The use of flowcharts for computer program specification has been largely superseded, and the ECMA standard withdrawn, but flowchart-like activity diagrams are still used in UML for workflow modelling.

Flowcharts continue to be used extensively in other non-computing areas as evidenced by the number of desktop and web-based flowchart-drawing applications, the presence in PowerPoint symbol gallery, and indeed, numerous Facebook memes, like the example in Figure 7.3, except normally far more elaborate. Note also that the fact that they are effective social media memes is due to the ease with which non-experts can read them and understand what they represent.

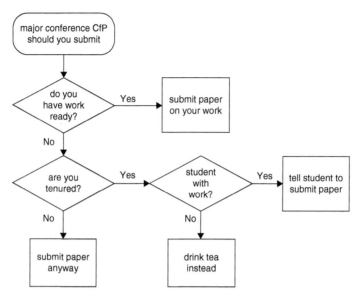

Figure 7.3 Example flowchart showing decisions (diamonds), activities (rectangles), and control flow (arrows).

Flowcharts developed rich vocabularies of shapes denoting different forms of action, but the basic elements are rectangular blocks representing activities, diamonds representing choices, and arrows between them representing control flow, one activity following another (see Figure 7.3).

Flowcharts have many limitations, not least in that they only deal with sequential activity, and do not deal with concurrency. There are extensions, such as UML activity diagrams, which add features, but part of the ongoing popularity of flowcharts is undoubtedly the simplicity that makes them work so well as a communication tool.

7.3.4 Flowcharts for User Interactions

While the normal use for flowcharts at the time was for describing the internal algorithms of a computer program, here the issue was to be able to describe the overall flow of user interaction. Flowcharts were therefore used to describe and specify the structure of interactions between the user and the computer system; that is, they were used as a user interaction specification notation.

Figure 7.4 shows an example of this for a standard delete dialogue. The diagram has two main kinds of blocks distinguishing user activity at the screen and backend processing.

The rectangles with corner inserts represent the on-screen forms that the user has to fill in. The shape was meant to suggest a screen, and a shortened version of the screen contents included in order to make them self-explanatory, rather like wireframe sketching tools today such as Balsamiq (https://balsamiq.com/).

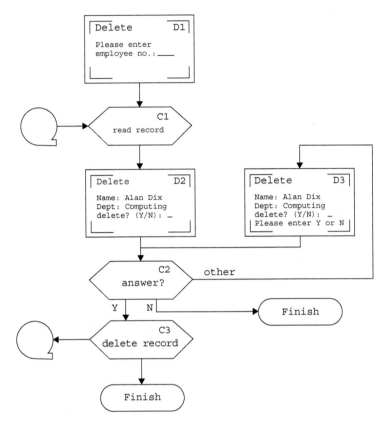

Figure 7.4 Flowchart of user interaction.

The lozenge shapes represented computer activity. This was chosen as it was available in flowchart templates, and was part way between the diamond (choice) and rectangular block (actions), as typical computer processing combines the two. Under the ECMA standard this shape had a specified meaning, but it was rarely used and so deemed unlikely to cause confusion. Quite complex internal processing would be represented as a single block, with the internal breakdown only being shown if there was an external difference (e.g., the record only being deleted if the confirm response was 'Y').

The small tape symbols were used to represent interactions with stored data—recall that this was the early 1980s, when personal computers used cassette tapes for storage, and, in mainframe computer centres, tapes were still used alongside disk storage for large data files.

Finally, note that each user and computer activity has an identifier at the top right. The computer ones corresponded to internal labels in the code and the user ones were displayed as the non-editable id at the top right of the display.

It is also worth noting what the user interaction flow charts *did not include*. There was little description of the internal code, for example, the way records would be read from disk. This was because this level of detail was 'standard programming', the thing the developer could easily do anyway, and which was pretty much self-documenting in the code. Neither did it give a complete description of the contents of the screens, merely enough to make the intention clear; again, it was often fairly obvious which fields from a record should be displayed and how, but if not, then this would be described separately. The formalism focused on doing the things that were hard to understand from the code alone.

These flowcharts were used in several ways.

- as a **design tool**, to help think about the flow of user interactions.

- as a way to **communicate with clients** (other departments in the council) on the behaviour of the planned systems, or alongside demos of constructed systems.

- to facilitate **rapid coding**; although the flowcharts were simply drawn on paper, there was a semi-automatic process of converting the diagrams into boilerplate code. Crucially this meant that turnaround times for changes, which were often in the order of weeks for other systems, could be accomplished in hours.

- As a structure for **testing**, as it was easy to verify that one had tried each path through the interaction.

- as aid to **debugging**, as users could easily report the id of the screens where problems were occurring.

In short, this led to systems that were more reliable, were more easily understood by the clients, and were produced more than ten times faster than with conventional methods at the time.

7.3.5 Lessons

It was only some years later that it became apparent just how unusual it is to see use of formal methods that was so clearly effective. In analysing this in a short report (Dix, 2002) on which the previous description is based, a number of features were identified that contributed to this success:

- *useful*—the formalism addressed a real problem, not simply used for its own sake, or applied to a 'toy' problem. Often, formalisms are proposed because of internal properties, but here it is the problem that drove the formalism.

- *appropriate*—there was no more detail than needed—what was *not* included was as important as what *was*. Often formal notations force you to work at a level of detail that is not useful, which both increases the effort needed and may even obfuscate, especially for non-experts.

- *communication*—the images of miniature display screens and clear flow meant that it was comprehensible to developers and clients alike. The purpose of formal methods has often been phrased in terms of its ability to communicate unambiguously, but if the precision gets in the way of comprehension, then it is in vain.

- *complementary*—the formalism used a different paradigm (sequential) than the implementation (event driven). There is often a temptation to match formalism and implementation (e.g., both object based), which may help verification, but this means that the things difficult to understand in the code are also difficult to understand in the specification.

- *fast payback*—it was quicker to produce applications (by at least 1000 per cent). It is often argued that getting the specification right saves time in the long term as there are fewer bugs, but often at the cost of a long lead time, making it hard to assess progress. The lightweight and incremental nature of the method allowed rapid bang-for-buck, useful for both developer motivation and progress monitoring.

- *responsive*—there was also rapid turnaround of changes. Often, heavy specification-based methods can mean that change is costly. This is justified, if the time spent at specification means you have a 'right first time' design, but for the user interface, we know that it is only when a prototype is available that users begin to understand what they really need.

- *reliability*—the clear boilerplate code was less error-prone. While the transformation from diagram to code was not automated, the hand process was straightforward, and the reuse of code fragments due to the boilerplate process further increased both readability and reliability.

- *quality*—it was easy to establish a test cycle due to the labelling, and to ensure that all paths were well tested.

- *maintenance*—the unique ids made it easy to relate bugs or requests for enhancements back to the specification and code.

In summary, the formalism was used to fulfil a purpose, and was neither precious nor purist.

7.4 In Practice—Modelling Physical Interaction

The second case study is set more than 25 years later, in the context of DEPtH, a cross-disciplinary project investigating the way digital and physical design interact (for more details of this case study see Dix et al., 2009; Dix and Ghazali 2017).[1]

7.4.1 The Problem

In the 1980s, the devices used to interact were largely determined by the size and shape that was technically possible. Now personal devices from smart watches to kitchen appliances embody aspects of digital behaviour set in a wide range of physical form factors. Effective

[1] We acknowledge that Parts of section 7.4 were supported by the AHRC/EPSRC funded project DEPtH 'Designing for Physicality' (http://www.physicality.org/).

design is not just about the abstract flow of actions and information, but the way these are realized in pressable buttons or strokeable screens.

Furthermore, maker and DIY electronics communities have grown across the world, enabled by affordable 3D printers, open-sourced hardware such as Arduino and RaspberryPi, and digital fabrication facilities, such as FabLabs, in most cities. This means that the design of custom electronics devices has moved from the large scale R&D lab to the street. Items produced can be frivolous, but can include prosthetics (Eveleth, 2015), reconstructive surgery (Bibb et al., 2015), community sensing (Balestrini et al., 2017), and prototypes for large-scale production through platforms such as Kickstarter. We clearly need to understand user interaction with these devices and find ways to make the resulting products safe, usable, and enjoyable.

There are many ways to describe the internal digital behaviour of such devices. DIY-end users may use graphical systems such as variants of Scratch, or data flow-based systems; professionals may use appropriate UML models, and researchers may use various user-interface formalisms, as discussed in section 7.2.1. However, all start with some form of abstract commands (such as 'up button pressed') or numerical sensor input, as it is available once it hits the computer system.

Similarly, there are many ways to describe the 3D form itself including standard formats for point clouds, volume and surface models; affordable devices to scan existing objects or clay formed models into these formats; and tools to help design 3D shapes including the complexities of how these need to be supported during printing by different kinds of devices. However, these focus principally on the static physical form, with occasional features to make it easy, for example, to ensure that doors open freely.

The gap between the two is the need to describe: (i) the way a physical object has interaction potential in and of itself, before it is connected to digital internals (buttons can be pressed, knobs turned, a small device turned over in one's hands); and (ii) the way this intrinsic physical interaction potential is mapped onto the digital functionality.

This issue has been considered in an informal way within the UI and design community, not least in the literature on affordance (Gibson, 1979; Gaver, 1991; Norman, 1999), where issues such as the appropriate placing and ordering of light switches and door handles has led to a generation of HCI students who are now unable to open a door without confusion. At a semi-formal level Wensveen et al.'s (2004) Interaction Frogger analyses some of the properties that lead to effective physical interaction.

Within the more formal and engineering literature in HCI, the vast majority of work has been at the abstract command level, including virtually all the chapters in a recent state-of-the-art book (Weyers et al., 2017), with a small amount of research in studying status–event analysis (Dix, 1991; Dix and Abowd, 1996) and continuous interaction (Massink et al., 1999; Wüthrich, 1999; Willans and Harrison, 2000; Smith, 2006).

There are some specialized exceptions. Eslambolchilar (2006) studied the cybernetics of control of mobile devices, taking into account both the device sensors and feedback, and the human physical motor system. Zhou et al. (2014) have looked at detailed pressure-movement characteristics of buttons, which is especially important when a button has to be easy to engage when an emergency arises, but hard to press accidentally (such as emergency cut-off, or fire alarm). Thimbleby (2007) has also modelled the physical layout of buttons on a VCR, to investigate whether taking into account Fitts' Law timings for inter-button movement was helpful in assessing the overall completion time of tasks, and similar techniques can also be seen in Chapter 9.

In order to address this gap, physigrams were developed, a variant of state-transition networks (as discussed in Section 7.2.1), but focused on the physical interactions.

7.4.2 Physigrams: STNs for the Device Unplugged

Figure 7.5 shows the simplest example of a physigram, the states of a simple on/off switch. It has two states, UP and DOWN, which the user can alter by pushing the switch up or down. At first this looks like a typical user interface dialogue specification. However, this is not about the state of the thing controlled by the switch (light, heating, computer power) with abstract on/off actions, but rather about the actual physical switch.

Imagine unscrewing the switch from the wall, removing the wires behind, and then screwing it back to the wall. It now controls nothing, but still has interaction potential—you can flick the switch up and down—and if you look at it, you can see there are two (stable) states: one with the switch pointing up, and one with the switch pointing down. The physigram captures this physical interaction potential of the device 'unplugged' from the electronic or digital functionality that it normally controls.

For a more complex example of a device unplugged, imagine giving a TV remote control to a small child to play with. You have removed the batteries; so that the child cannot change the actual channel, but they can still play with it in their hands, and press the various buttons.

Of course, the relationship between this physical interaction potential and the thing it controls is crucial. Figure 7.6 shows the physigram of the switch, on the left, connected to the states of the controlled electronic system (a light bulb), on the right.

In this case, the mapping between physical device states and the states of the underlying system are one-to-one, the simplest mapping and very powerful when possible, especially if there is any delay (as with a fluorescent tube) or the thing controlled is not visible

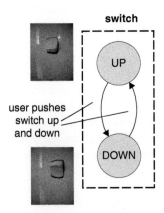

Figure 7.5 Physigram states of a switch.

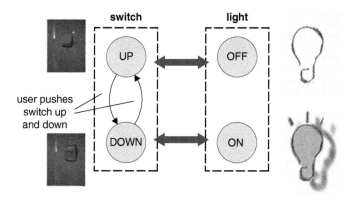

Figure 7.6 Logical states of an electric light map 1–1 with physigram states.

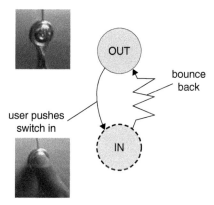

Figure 7.7 Physigram of a bounce-back button.

(e.g., outside light controlled from inside). In these cases, assuming there is no fault, the state of the light can be observed from the state of the switch.

More generally, this one-to-one mapping is not always possible, and in many cases the physical device controls some form of transition. In these cases, the link between the physical and logical sides of the system ends up more like the classic user specification with abstract commands, except in this case, we have a model of how the commands are produced, not just how they are used. In some ways, the ICO model of input device drivers in Chapter 9 fulfils a role similar to physigrams, albeit less focused on the actual physical behaviour. However, the way these are annotated with events and event parameters shows one way in which device behaviour can be linked to more abstract system models.

This connection between the physigram and underlying system states is very important, but for the purposes of the current discussion, we will focus entirely on the physigram itself, as it is the more novel aspect.

Figures 7.7 and 7.8 show two more examples of two-state devices.

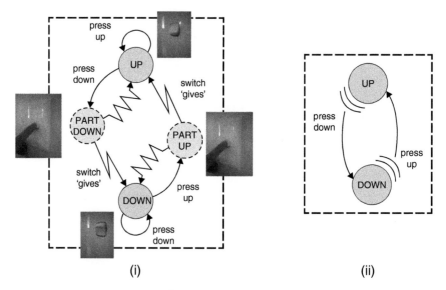

Figure 7.8 Switch with 'give' (i) detailed physigram; (ii) 'shorthand' physigram with decorated transition.

Figure 7.7 is a button with 'bounce-back'. These are common in electronic devices; indeed, there are seventy-nine on the laptop keyboard being used to type this chapter. Whereas most light switches stay in the position you move them to, when you press a key on a keyboard, it bounces back up as soon as you take your finger off the key. Notice that the IN state has a dashed line around it, which shows that it is a temporary tension state—unstable without pressure being applied. The arrow from OUT to IN is smooth, denoting a user action of pressing in, but the arrow from IN to OUT is a 'lightning bolt' arrow, denoting the physical bounce-back of the button.

In fact, even a typical up/down light switch has a small amount of bounce-back. If the switch is up and you press very lightly down, it moves a little, but if you release it before it gets to halfway it would pop back to its original position. When it gets to the halfway position it will suddenly 'give' snapping to the down position.

This can be represented by adding part-in/part-out states with bounce-back transitions, as shown in Figure 7.8(i). This detailed representation would be useful if the digital system had some sort of response to the partly moved states (perhaps an audio feedback to say what will get turned on/off). However, mostly it is sufficient to know that they have this feel for the user, and so the shorthand in figure 7.8(ii) was introduced; the 'bounce' marks where the arrow exits the state are intended to represent this small amount of resistance, bounce-back, and give.

Tables 7.1 and 7.2 summarize the symbols we have seen so far for states and transitions respectively. A more complete list can be found in Dix and Ghazali (2017) and online at http://physicality.org/physigrams/.

Table 7.1 Physigram states (from Dix and Ghazali, 2017)

Symbol	Meaning
OUT	**state**—physical state of the device.
IN	**transient tension state**—physical state which can only be maintained by some sort of continuous user pressure or exertion.

Table 7.2 Physigram transitions (from Dix and Ghazali, 2017)

Symbol	Meaning
press OUT → IN	transition—this may be labelled by the user action that causes this, or this may be implicit. It may also have a label to connect it with logical state.
OUT ← IN	bounce-back—when the device spontaneously returns from a transient tension state to a stable state when user pressure is removed.
UP → DOWN	**give**—where a button or other control moves slightly but with resistance before 'giving' and causing state change. If the user stops exerting pressure before the 'give' point, it will return to the initial state.

7.4.3 Handing Over

So far, the analysis described was all performed by the computing members of the DEPtH team. It was then handed over to the product designers on the project, who were, at the time, looking at prototypes of three variants of a media player: one with a protruding knob, one with a flat dial, and one with a round touch-sensitive pad, each used to control a hierarchical menu system with maximum seven items at each level. In each design, a press or push would activate the currently selected menu item. The product designers created physigrams for each design (see Figure 7.9).

The first thing to note about the designers' physigrams is the aesthetics. Whereas the physigrams shown previously were all flat, two-dimensional representations, the product designers used three dimensions, with the states drawn on gently curving disks. The third dimension was also used to highlight the correspondence of the position of the dial when pressed down or not pressed.

In designs 7.9(i) and 7.9(ii), the knob or dial was a bounce-back and this is clearly shown (albeit the bounce back arrow slightly hidden), but rather than have seven bounce-back arrows for each state, a single down and up transition is shown, so that UP and DOWN are sort of high-level states (there was an example of something like this in the documents the designers were given).

In contrast, in Figure 7.9(iii), the press down on the touchpad, while having a digital effect, had no tangible feel of being pressed, and there was no sense of being able to still twist it while it was pressed. That is, in Buxton's (1990) terms, Figure 7.9(iii) is a three-state (0–1–2) device, distinguishing internally not touching (state 0), touching/dragging (state 1), and pressing (state 2), although the press has no tangible feel, and hence does not distinguish Buxton's states 1 and 2 for the user. To represent this, the designers drew the DOWN state without separate selection sub-states, and the arc shown as a 'self-transition' (arrow

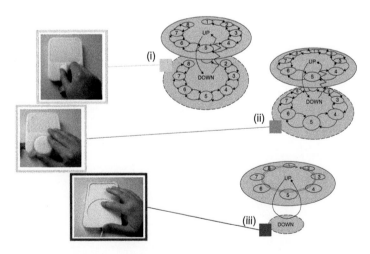

Figure 7.9 Product designers' use of physigrams.

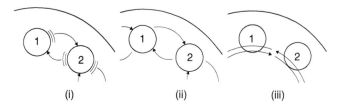

(i)   (ii)   (iii)

Figure 7.10 Detail of transitions in Figure 7.9.

from UP to itself, passing *through* the DOWN state, to denote that it was something that you know was happening, but without any physical feedback.

There were also detailed differences in the transitions when the knob, dial, or touchpad was rotated (see Figure 7.10). The knob had a resistance to movement and then gave, and hence was drawn with the 'give' arrows shown in Figure 7.8(ii). In contrast, the stops on the dial (Figure 7.10(ii)) had some tangible feel, but only slightly, and with no sense of resistance to motion; hence, the stats were drawn as simple transitions. Finally, the touchpad (Figure 7.10(iii)) had no tangible feedback at all. The designers 'knew' there were seven stops, but this was not at all apparent from the feel of the device. They felt they wanted to record the seven stops, but drew the transitions as simply passing through these; it would only be through visual or audio feedback that the user would be able to actually tell what was selected.

7.4.4 *Lessons*

First, this case study demonstrates the **complexity of physical interaction**. The specialized notation in the user interaction flowcharts in section 7.3 was developed once on a particular system design and then reused on other systems without any need for additional constructs. In contrast, the computer science side of the DEPtH team had analysed numerous devices in order to create a vocabulary for physigrams, and yet on the first use by others, new cases were found.

Of course, the good thing is that the designers were able to adapt the physigrams to model the unexpected physical properties. This demonstrated two things: **comprehensibility**, in that the notation was sufficiently comprehensible that they took ownership and felt confident to modify it, even though they were not mathematicians or computer scientists; and **openness to appropriation**, in that the notation had sufficient flexibility that there were obvious ways to extend or adapt it.

Of particular note in terms of appropriation, the fact the semantics of STNs only use connectivity, not layout, meant that the designers were free to use layout themselves, including 3D layout, in order to create the most meaningful version for human–human communication. This is an example of the appropriation design principle *openness to interpretation*, identified elsewhere (Dix, 2007): by leaving parts of a system or notation without formal interpretation, this makes it available for rich interpretation by users, or in Green and Petri's (1996) terms, *secondary notation*.

The downside of this ease of modification is that the **semantics were not fixed**, which would be problematic if we had wished to perform some sort of automatic analysis. In fact, for this purpose, the clarity for the product designers and the ability to communicate design intentions between designers and computer scientists was more important than having a computer readable notation.

7.5 Discussion

7.5.1 Critical Features

The first case study identified a number of features of interaction flowcharts that led to success: useful, appropriate, communication, complementary, fast payback, responsive, reliability, quality, and maintenance. Some of these, *reliability*, *quality* and ease of *maintenance*, would be familiar to anyone who has read arguments advocating formal methods, precisely where the formality and rigour would be expected to give traction. Others, notably, *fast payback* and *responsiveness*, would be more surprising as formal methods are normally seen as cumbersome with long lead times to benefit.

These additional benefits are effectively outcomes of the first four features, which can be summarized in two higher-level considerations, which are shared with the physigrams case study.

Tuned for purpose—The interaction flowcharts were *useful* and *appropriate*, i.e., they did what was necessary for a purpose and no more. Recall the way lower-level details were ignored, as these were already understood; only the high-level dialogue was represented and the way this attached to code and screens. Similarly, the physigrams focus on a specific aspect, i.e., the device unplugged and its interaction potential; all the digital features of the device are (initially) ignored. It is interesting to note that, while both specify interaction order and flow, one is at a higher level than most dialogue specifications, and the other a lower level.

Optimized for human consumption—In the case of the interaction flowcharts, the choice of a *complementary* paradigm (sequential rather than event based) helped the programmer understand aspects that were hard to comprehend in the code itself. Similarly, the physigrams specify an aspect of the device that normally is not represented in the code or standard diagrammatic interaction notations. Also, as noted in the first case study, while formal methods are often advocated as enabling communication, this is normally meant as unambiguous communication between highly trained members of a technical team. In contrast, both the interactive flowcharts and physigrams *focused on expressive communication*, enabling use by clients and non-formally trained designers respectively.

Early work emphasized the importance of bridging the *formality gap* (Dix, 1991), i.e., the need to be confident that a formal specification reflects the real world issue it is intended to express. That is, while it is relatively easy to ensure internal validity between formal expressions within a design process, it is external validity that is hard to achieve. It is precisely in establishing this external validity that expressive communication helps.

Both tuning and expressive communication were enabled by *appropriation*. This appropriation happened at two levels. In both case studies, an existing notation (flowcharts, state transition networks) was borrowed and modified to create a new lightweight notation *tuned* to the specific purpose. In both cases this extension included both features tuned to computational or analytic aims (overall flow of states), but also expressive communication (for example, the miniature screen images in interactive flowcharts and special arrows in physigrams). However, in the second case study we saw a further level of appropriation when the product designers themselves modified physigrams to express aspects beyond those considered by the notation's creators.

Some of this appropriation is possible because of the flexibility enabled by the uninterpreted aspects of the notations: the layout on the page, and the descriptive text annotating states and transitions; as noted previously, all classic ways to design for appropriation (Dix, 2007). However, in some cases, the appropriation may 'break' the formalism; for example, the 'parallel' states within the UP and DOWN high-level states in Figure 7.9 are clearly connected for the human viewer, but would not be so if the diagram were interpreted formally.

Achieving this flexible formalism is a hard challenge. The idea of domain specific notations, introduced in section 7.2.3, would certainly help in the first level of appropriation, as the formal expert effectively creates a rich syntactic sugar that allows the domain expert to use the DSN and have it transformed into a lower-level standard notation amenable to automated analysis or transformation.

The second level of appropriation requires something more radical. One option would be to allow *semantics by annotation*, where the user of the formalism has a lot of flexibility, but must map this back to a more restricted predetermined formalism (which itself may be domain specific). For example, in the product designers' physigrams in Figure 7.9(i), the arc between the UP and DOWN high-level states could be selected (either by the designers themselves or the formal experts) and then declared to represent the series of arcs between the low-level states. The primary diagram is still as drawn and, for most purposes, used for human–human communication, but if there is any doubt in the meaning, or if automated analysis is needed, then the expanded standard form is accessible. In many ways this is like Knuth's (1992) concept of *literate programming*; his WEB system allowed Pascal programmers to write their code and internal documentation in the order that suited them, with additional annotations to say how the fragments of code should be re-ordered and linked in the order needed for the Pascal compiler.

7.5.2 A Growing Need for Formal Methods in HCI

The 'Gaps and Trends' chapter of *The Handbook of Formal Methods in Human-Computer Interaction* (Weyers et al., 2017) suggests a number of challenges for formal methods, many of which are inherited directly from previously identified trends in the use of technology in the world and within HCI (Dix, 2016). Several of these are particularly relevant to this chapter.

First, the increasing use of digital systems in government, transport, and commerce has made the use of computers an essential part of being a citizen in the modern world. HCI has always recognized that it is important to take into account a *diversity of people*: different ages, different abilities, different social and cultural backgrounds. However, *digital citizenry* means this can no longer be an afterthought. Similarly, mobile access and digitally enabled household appliances mean that users encounter a *diversity of devices*, sometimes simultaneously, as with second-screen TV watching. Attempting to think through all the permutations of devices and personal characteristics and situations is precisely where automated analysis is helpful.

Looking at the technology itself, both the Internet of Things (IoT) and big data create situations where we encounter *complexity though scale* due to interactions of myriad small parts. This may lead to feature interactions or emergent effects that are hard to predict. Again, this is an area where more automated and formal analysis is helpful.

However, the above should be set in the context of digital fabrication and maker culture, where larger numbers of people are involved with hardware and software development and customization.

So, the circumstances in the world are making the use of formal methods more important, and yet also mean that those who would need to use them are likely to be less expert; the very same methods that many computer scientists find difficult. The need for practical formal methods is clear.[2]

....

REFERENCES

Abowd, G., and Dix, A., 1992. Giving undo attention. *Interacting with Computers*, 4(3), pp. 317–42.

Balestrini, M., Creus, J., Hassan, C., King, C., Marshall, P., and Rogers, Y., 2017. *A City in Common: A Framework to Orchestrate Large-scale Citizen Engagement around Urban Issues*. Proc. CHI 2017, ACM.

Bass, L., Little, R., Pellegrino, R., Reed, S., Seacord, R., Sheppard, S., and Szezur, M.R., 1991. The ARCH model: Seeheim Revisited, User Interface Developers' Workshop, April 26, Version 1.0.

Bibb, R., Eggbeer, D., and Paterson, A., 2015. *Medical Modelling: The Application of Advanced Design and Rapid Prototyping Techniques in Medicine*. 2nd ed. Kidlington: Elsevier.

Bolton, M., and Bass, E., 2017. Enhanced Operator Function Model (EOFM): A Task Analytic Modeling Formalism for Including Human Behavior in the Verification of Complex Systems. In: B. Weyers, J. Bowen, A. Dix, P. Palanque, eds. *The Handbook of Formal Methods in Human-Computer Interaction*. New York, NY: Springer. pp. 343–77.

Booch, G., Rumbaugh, J., and Jacobson, I., 1999. *The Unified Modeling Language User Guide*. London: Addison Wesley.

Bowen, J., and Reeves, S., 2017. Combining Models for Interactive System Modelling. In: B. Weyers, J. Bowen, A. Dix, P. Palanque, eds. *The Handbook of Formal Methods in Human-Computer Interaction*. New York, NY: Springer. pp. 161–82.

British Standards Institution, 1987. *BS 4058:1987, ISO 5807:1985: Specification for data processing flow chart symbols, rules and conventions*. Milton Keynes: BSI.

Buxton, W., 1990. A three-state model of graphical input. In: Proceedings of Human–Computer Interaction—INTERACT '90. Amsterdam: Elsevier, pp. 449–56.

---

[2] For additional links on the topics in this chapter, see: http://alandix.com/academic/papers/fmchap-2018/

Card, S., Moran, T., and Newell, A., 1983. *The Psychology of Human Computer Interaction*. Hillsdale, NJ: Lawrence Erlbaum Associates.

Coutaz, J., 1987. PAC, an object-oriented model for dialogue design. In: H-J. Bullinger and B. Shackel, eds. *Human Computer Interaction INTERACT '87*, pp. 431–6.

Coutaz, J., 2010. User Interface Plasticity: Model Driven Engineering to the Limit! In Engineering Interactive Computing Systems. Berlin, Germany, 19–23 June 2010.

Dix, A., 1991. *Formal methods for interactive systems*. New York: Academic Press. Available through: http://www.hiraeth.com/books/formal/.

Dix, A., 1995. Dynamic pointers and threads. Collaborative Computing, 1(3):191–216. Available through: http://alandix.com/academic/papers/dynamic-pntrs-95/.

Dix, A., 2002. Formal Methods in HCI: a Success Story—why it works and how to reproduce it. Available through: http://alandix.com/academic/papers/formal-2002/.

Dix, A., 2007. Designing for appropriation. In: D. Ramduny-Ellis and D. Rachovides, eds. HCI 2007...but not as we know it, Volume 2: People and Computers XXI, *The 21st British HCI Group Annual Conference*. Lancaster, UK, 3–7 September 2007. London: BCS. Available from: http://www.bcs.org/server.php?show=ConWebDoc.13347.

Dix, A., 2016. Human computer interaction, foundations and new paradigms, *Journal of Visual Languages & Computing*, in press. doi: 10.1016/j.jvlc.2016.04.001.

Dix, A., and Abowd, G., 1996. Modelling status and event behaviour of interactive systems. Softw Eng J 11(6), pp. 334–46, http://www.hcibook.com/alan/papers/SEJ96-s+e/

Dix, A., and Ghazali, M., 2017. Physigrams: Modelling Physical Device Characteristics Interaction. In: B. Weyers, J. Bowen, A. Dix, P. Palanque, eds. *The Handbook of Formal Methods in Human-Computer Interaction*. New York, NY: Springer, pp. 247–72.

Dix, A., Ghazali, M., Gill, S., Hare, J., and Ramduny-Ellis, S., 2009. Physigrams: Modelling Devices for Natural Interaction. *Formal Aspects of Computing*, 21(6), pp. 613–41.

Dix, A., and Runciman, C., 1985. Abstract models of interactive systems. In: P. Johnson and S. Cook, eds. *People and Computers: Designing the Interface*. Cambridge: Cambridge University Press. pp. 13–22. Available through: http://www.alandix.com/academic/papers/PIE85/.

ECMA International, 1966. Standard: ECMA 4, Flow Charts. 2nd ed. Geneva: European Association for Standardizing Information and Communication Systems.

Eslambolchilar, P., 2006. *Making sense of interaction using a model-based approach*. PhD. Hamilton Institute, National University of Ireland.

Eveleth, R., 2015. DIY prosthetics: the extreme athlete who built a new knee. *Mosaic*, 19 May 2015, [online] Available at: https://mosaicscience.com/story/extreme-prosthetic-knee.

Freitas, L., Woodcock, J., and Zhang, Y., 2009. Verifying the CICS File Control API with Z/Eves: An experiment in the verified software repository. *Science of Computer Programming*, 74(4), pp. 197–218. http://dx.doi.org/10.1016/j.scico.2008.09.012

Gaver, W., 1991. Technology affordances. In: *CHI '91: Proceedings of the SIGCHI conference on Human factors in computing systems*. New York, NY: ACM Press, pp. 79–84.

Gibson, J., 1979. *The Ecological Approach to Visual Perception*. New York, NY: Houghton Mifflin.

Gram, C., and Cockton, G., eds., 1996. *Design principles for interactive software*. London: Chapman & Hall.

Green, T., and Petri, M., 1996. Usability analysis of visual programming environments: a 'cognitive dimensions' framework. Journal of Visual Languages and Computing, 7, pp. 131–74.

Harel, D., 1987. Statecharts: A Visual Formalism for Complex Systems. *Science of Computer Programming*, 8(3), pp. 231–74.

Harrison, M., Masci, P., Creissac Campos, J., and Curzon, P., 2017. The Specification and Analysis of Use Properties of a Nuclear Control System. In: B. Weyers, J. Bowen, A. Dix, P. Palanque, eds. *The Handbook of Formal Methods in Human-Computer Interaction*. New York, NY: Springer. pp. 379–403.

Kieras, D., and Polson, P., 1985. An approach to the formal analysis of user complexity. *International Journal of Man-Machine Studies*, 22, pp. 365–94.

Knuth, D., 1992. *Literate Programming*. Stanford, CA: Stanford University Center for the Study of Language and Information.

Manca, M., Paternò, F., and Santoro, C., 2017. A Public Tool Suite for Modelling Interactive Applications. In: B. Weyers, J. Bowen, A. Dix, P. Palanque, eds. *The Handbook of Formal Methods in Human-Computer Interaction*. New York, NY: Springer. pp. 505–28.

Mancini, R., 1997. *Modelling Interactive Computing by Exploiting the Undo*. PhD. Università degli Studi di Roma 'La Sapienza'. Available through: http://www.hcibook.net/people/Roberta/.

Masci, P., Zhang, Y., Jones, P., Curzon, P., and Thimbleby, H., 2014. Formal Verification of Medical Device User Interfaces Using PVS. In: *Proceedings of the 17th International Conference on Fundamental Approaches to Software Engineering, Volume 8411*. New York, NY: Springer-Verlag. pp. 200–14. Available through: http://dl.acm.org/citation.cfm?id=2731750.

Massink, M., Duke, D., and Smith, S., 1999. Towards hybrid interface specification for virtual environments. In: *DSV-IS 1999 Design, Specification and Verification of Interactive Systems*. Berlin: Springer. pp. 30–51.

Meixner, G., Calvary, G., and Coutaz, J., 2014. *Introduction to Model-Based User Interfaces*. W3C Working Group Note, 7 January 2014. Available through: http://www.w3.org/TR/mbui-intro/.

Meixner, G., Paternò, F., and Vanderdonckt, J., 2011. Past, Present, and Future of Model-Based User Interface Development. *i-com*, 10(3), pp. 2–11.

Navarre, D., Palanque, P. A., Ladry, J-F., and Barboni, E., 2009. ICOs: a model-based user interface description technique dedicated to interactive systems addressing usability, reliability and scalability. *ACM Transactions on Computer-Human Interaction*, 16(4), pp. 1–56.

Norman, D., 1999. Affordance, conventions, and design. *Interactions*, 6(3), pp. 38–43, New York, NY: ACM Press.

Palanque, P., and Paterno, F., eds., 1997. *Formal Methods in Human-Computer Interaction*. London: Springer-Verlag.

Paterno, F., 1999. *Model-Based Design and Evaluation of Interactive Applications*. 1st ed. London: Springer-Verlag.

Pfaff, G., and Hagen, P., eds., 1985. *Seeheim Workshop on User Interface Management Systems*. Berlin: Springer-Verlag.

Polak, W., 2002. Formal methods in practice. *Science of Computer Programming*, 42(1), pp. 75–85.

Reisner, P., 1981. Formal Grammar and Human Factors Design of an Interactive Graphics System. *IEEE Transactions on Software Engineering*, 7(2), pp. 229–40. DOI=10.1109/TSE.1981.234520

Shepherd, A., 1989. Analysis and training in information technology tasks. In D. Diaper and N. Standton, eds. *The Handbook of Task Analysis for Human-Computer Interaction*. Mahweh, NJ: Lawrence Erlbaum. pp. 15–55.

Smith, S., 2006. Exploring the specification of haptic interaction. In: *DS-VIS 2006: Interactive systems: design, specification and verification*. Dublin, Ireland, 26–28 July 2006. Springer, Berlin. Available through: https://link.springer.com/chapter/10.1007/978-3-540-69554-7_14.

Spivey, J., 1992. *The Z Notation: a reference manual*. 2nd edn. Upper Saddle River, NJ: Prentice Hall.

Sufrin, B., 1982. Formal specification of a display-oriented text editor. *Science of Computer Programming*, 1, pp. 157–202.

Thimbleby, H., 2007. Using the Fitts law with state transition systems to find optimal task timings. In: *FMIS2007: Proceedings of the Second International Workshop on Formal Methods for*

Interactive Systems. Limerick, Ireland, 4 September 2007. Available through: http://www.dcs.qmul.ac.uk/research/imc/hum/fmis2007/preproceedings/FMIS2007preproceedings.pdf.

Thimbleby, H., and Gow, J., 2008. Applying Graph Theory to Interaction Design. In: J. Gulliksen, M. B. Harning, P. Palanque, G. C. van der Veer, and J. Wesson, eds. *Engineering Interactive Systems. Lecture Notes in Computer Science, Volume 4940*. Berlin: Springer.

Thimbleby, H., and Harrison, M., eds., 1990. *Formal Methods in Human-Computer Interaction*. Cambridge: Cambridge University Press.

Van Mierlo, S., Van Mierlo, Y., Meyers, B., and Vangheluwe, H., 2017. Domain-Specific Modelling for Human–Computer Interaction. In: B. Weyers, J. Bowen, A. Dix, P. Palanque, eds. *The Handbook of Formal Methods in Human-Computer Interaction*. New York, NY: Springer. pp. 435–63.

Wensveen, S., Djajadiningrat, J., and Overbeeke, C., 2004. Interaction frogger: a design framework to couple action and function. In: *DIS '04: Proceedings of the 5th conference on Designing interactive systems: processes, practices, methods, and techniques*. Cambridge, MA, 2–4 August 2004.

Weyers, B., 2017. Visual and Formal Modeling of Modularized and Executable User Interface Models. In: B. Weyers, J. Bowen, A. Dix, P. Palanque, eds. *The Handbook of Formal Methods in Human-Computer Interaction*. New York, NY: Springer. pp. 125–60.

Weyers, B., Bowen, J., Dix, A., and Palanque, P., eds., 2017. *The Handbook of Formal Methods in Human-Computer Interaction*. New York, NY: Springer.

Willans, J., and Harrison, M., 2000. Verifying the behaviour of virtual world objects. In: Proceedings of DSV-IS - Interactive Systems: Design, Specification, and Verification. Limerick, Ireland, June 5–6, 2000. Berlin: Springer.

Wüthrich, C., 1999. An analysis and model of 3D interaction methods and devices for virtual reality. In: Proceedings of DSV-IS - Interactive Systems: Design, Specification, and Verification. Braga, Portugal, 2–4 June 1999. Berlin: Springer.

Zhou, W., Reisinger, J., Peer, A., and Hirche, S., 2014. Interaction-Based Dynamic Measurement of Haptic Characteristics of Control Elements. In: Auvray, M., and Duriez, C., eds. *Haptics: Neuroscience, Devices, Modeling, and Applications: 9th International Conference*, EuroHaptics 2014, Proceedings, Part I, pp. 177–84. Versailles, France, June 24–26, 2014. Berlin: Springer.

8

. . • . .

From Premature Semantics to Mature Interaction Programming

PAUL CAIRNS,
HAROLD THIMBLEBY

8.1 Introduction

It is a truism that the only reason computers exist is for humans to use them—computers are not a natural phenomenon that 'just exist' (like rocks, flowers, or cats) but they and what they do are made by people *for* people. Better computers are easier to use.

Somehow the two concerns:

- Building computers and how to understand computers—programming, computer science
- How computers are used and how to understand how they are used—user-centred design, human factors

have become different specialities with few overlapping interests. University courses may study one and not the other. Web authoring systems mean that user experience (UX) people work on web site design and user experience, but the underlying services are done by completely separate teams of programmers, as are the tools that the UX people use. This separation misses out a lot of beneficial cross-fertilisation.

We believe that this disciplinary separation is premature and unnecessary. What is taught in user interface design or human-computer interaction courses raises deep computational problems. Conversely, what is taught as basic theoretical computer science has applications directly in user interface design. After all, a programmer understanding computers and getting them to do things correctly for them is an almost identical problem to users understanding computers and getting them to do things correctly for them. Pretending that one is about people and the other about computers over-simplifies.

This chapter explores the split and, specifically, we re-integrate basic computer science into the user-centred design arena.

Computational Interaction. Antti Oulasvirta, Per Ola Kristensson, Xiaojun Bi, Andrew Howes (Eds).
© Oxford University Press 2018. Published 2018 by Oxford University Press.

8.2 The Trouble with Programming

We all recognize that user interfaces are not always wonderful, but we often overlook the potentially very serious consequences of poor user interface design. In safety critical areas like aviation, what, in hindsight, look like quite simple design problems that should have been avoided have often led to planes crashing and death.

The conventional perspective is that computer software is built by programmers who do not really understand the needs of actual users and what they really do to achieve their tasks. Landauer (1995) is a classic exposition of this point of view; many have characterized the differences of opinion as 'trench warfare'—with programmers as the enemy (Gasen, 1995; Mulligan, Altom, and Simkin, 1991), etc.). Although there are some problems of communication between programmers and user-centred designers (Salah, Paige, and Cairns, 2014), it is not that simple.

In the years since HCI became established as a research field (and usability and UX as corresponding professional fields), it is has moved away from the basic details of programming and into more and more fields of human endeavour, from psychology through sociology into cultural heritage, gaming and art: supporting a huge variety of social experiences (Rogers, 2012). This move can in part be attributed to the fact that in the same period the technology itself has undergone radical transformations. Moore's law not only accounts for a growth in computing power, but there are similar exponential factors in economy, reduced screen size, increased screen resolution, increased power efficiency, and so on. The result of all of these changes is that technology has become more pervasive and ubiquitous, and hence it has reached into and affected more fields of human endeavour.

Alan Turing's famous result that any sufficiently powerful computer (and it does not have to be very powerful) can simulate *any* computer whatsoever has quietly moved from a theoretical insight into everyday life. Turing called it a Universal Computing Machine (Turing, 1936; Turing, 1938).

When we add high resolution displays, a universal computer can go beyond just simulating anything but can really *look like anything*. Since humans can't tell the difference by looks alone, we really mean *anything*, including non-computable things. We can, for instance, watch a realistic computer-generated science fiction animation—where anything that looks like it is working is in fact completely computer-generated and fictitious. Computer graphics used in popular animated films creates worlds that looks as good as and as realistic as the real world. Moreover, we can go beyond the merely visual: when we add robotic arms, sensors and other everyday features the computer *becomes anything*. These things look like they are computable, but our imagination is filling in the details (unaware that we are 'suspending disbelief')—we ignore the bugs that are the symptoms of implementing non-computable programs.

However, this move in both HCI and technology has somewhat left behind 'classic' usability problems and yet these are ones that are still important in terms of their impact on users, in some cases being literally a matter of life and death. The user experience is so powerful that less obvious problems, like errors, get less attention. Indeed, errors happen because they are *not* noticed—if we (whether designers, programmers or users) noticed errors, we would correct them. As computers have become more and more attractive, their underlying dependability has not improved as much as we think.

To understand these deep problems, it is necessary to go back to the very foundations of what it means to interact with a computer. When we interact with anything, we, at least implicitly, use a *language*. When we interact with humans we may use English or another natural language, and with programmed computers, whether web sites, PCs, or mobile phones and even door bells, we use much simpler languages. Language is the mechanism to convey meaning, be that a complex expression of our thoughts to a simple single 'I'm at your front door.'

No doubt linguists might object to pressing door bells being a language. It doesn't involve vocalisation or written sentences, certainly, but the physical actions are something like 'move finger to correct location' then 'press.' This *is* a language—and perhaps so seemingly trivial that a computer programmer would probably also overlook the obligation to think clearly about *the language* of interaction, even when it seems so obvious it can 'just be implemented'—which of course will give it premature semantics. Figure 8.1 gives an example of how pressing 'simple' buttons can go horribly wrong.

All computer programs implicitly define a language of either data or interactions (or both) that they can accept and give meaning to. Of course, they or their developers do not know they are giving meaning to the language but nonetheless they act according to the meaning understood by their developers. If we were building a system to understand English, this would be very obvious—you'd see things like 'verb' and 'noun' all over the program—but most of the time it is too easy to build systems without thinking clearly about the language and there is nothing visible to show for it. For a door bell, the language of interaction is so obvious that there is probably nothing left visible that specifies or defines the language, or even needs to.

Programmers are taught a lot about languages (regular languages, context free grammars, and so on). And then they promptly forget them because it is possible to program anything without going to the trouble of specifying a language clearly. The move of programming away from low-level details to using packages and complex APIs means that the languages actually being implemented by the computer are well-hidden from the programmer.

It follows that programmers typically build user interfaces *with the wrong languages*, because they never really thought about what the right languages might be. This, of course, creates the entire world of HCI: we need methods and processes to find out what the language should be, and we need ways to help programmers refine the programs to use the right languages, using iterative design and so on.

Design problems are often accompanied by tell-tale phrases that sound like language problems:

'I want to do this, but I don't know what to do or how to **say** it'	. . .	The system (or the user) has an insufficiently expressive language
'When I **told** it to do something, it did something else'	. . .	the system had a different semantics from the user

Figure 8.1 A very simple walk-up-and-use user interface. A UK Coast Guard phone (photographed in 2016) for the public to use to call the Coast Guard in the event of an emergency. In the UK, the standard emergency number is 999—as the sign makes very clear. But the phone itself does not have any way to dial 999, so what should you do? It is not very clear! Presumably only three buttons (labelled 1, 2, 3) were provided either to make it 'simpler' or to save money? Figure 8.2 shows the underlying FSM for this phone, and the FSM shows how to use the phone to correctly call the Coast Guard.

These problems often arise because the programmer has specified a simpler language than the user needs or expects. Part of the problem is that the right language is not obvious. On the other hand, if programmers carefully worked out the right language, they'd spend so much time planning and working with users they'd never get round to writing any useful programs—we are not blaming programmers, we are pointing out that implementing the wrong language is almost always inevitable because life is too short.

If programmers implement a simpler language something very interesting happens. The language they implement is easier for the computer (and for them to program) but probably at the expense of being harder for the human user. The computer program does do something, but it is not as powerful as users might wish. This is the what HCI is all about fixing. Yet because this problem is invisible, it remains a fundamental problem for HCI.

This chapter puts a name to the problem: *premature semantics*. Of course HCI tries to solve the problems caused by premature semantics, but it does so by 'fixes'—processes, such as iterative design, that come too late to avoid the *premature* part of the premature semantics. If we can recognise and know what premature semantics means, we can take steps to avoid it, and hence vastly improve normal HCI methods.

We will build up to our discussion of premature semantics by reviewing how user interfaces and languages intertwine—using regular languages and other fundamental computer science concepts—and then premature semantics will fall out of our discussion naturally. We will show that the idea exposes very clearly some serious issues in user interface design that have been widely overlooked, and certainly not attributed to a common factor.

8.3 Motivating Examples

In order to make our ideas concrete and meaningful to the reader, we will ground many of our examples in a very familiar user interface that has been around for more than fifty years, the calculator. Calculators were one of the first digital devices to have widespread ownership. Mechanical digital calculators gave way to electronic and then to computer-based calculators very rapidly. The basic design idea, defined in the 1970s, has hardly changed despite the radical changes that have occurred in computing over the years since their first introduction.

Calculators are simple, well-understood devices. We understand what they are supposed to do, namely arithmetic, better than many other tasks computers can do. Probably, we were all taught about them at school, and they haven't changed much. There is therefore no excuse for them to have poor user interfaces. We had thought of using a new user interface like WhatsApp (www.whatsapp.com) to illustrate our ideas about HCI, but interesting user interfaces tend to be complicated and any such choice for our example would leave some readers unfamiliar with critical details.

Calculators are a very simple technology we have had since before the start of HCI as a recognisable discipline, but which, despite briefly gathering some attention from HCI researchers (Thimbleby, 2000; Young, 1981), they are now ignored in mainstream HCI. Yet in 2000, Thimbleby noted that despite decades of use, development and research (Young, 1981), calculators still had horrible usability (Thimbleby, 2000). The problems persist to today (Thimbleby, 2015).

A cursory consideration might decide that they are too trivial to consider deeply— 'this is how they are.' Their persistence is a quirk of fate or history, like the QWERTY keyboard, and research in improving them is fraught with pointless difficulties. However, on the contrary, we show that there are subtle problems in their design. This is because of the dominance of **premature semantics** in their interfaces. This problem is not confined to calculators but can be seen in online forms, banking, health devices and more. Our analysis also shows that solving the problems of premature semantics is neither a simple matter of task redesign nor of better programming but requires substantial new approaches to thinking about interaction—and requires new approaches that have yet to be developed.

8.3.1 Calculators are Still Needlessly Bad

Being charitable, we might say that some of the problems identified were originally due to the physical construction of early calculators and then persisted because of their position as cheap, disposable consumer electronics. Thus, there were originally many physical constraints on the design of such devices and not enough profit to make substantial redesigns worthwhile. Of course, there has been decades since then to improve and, moreover, the 'mobile revolution' has occurred over the intervening time. Almost all smartphones have a calculator app so all of the physical constraints of older calculators have been removed and the investment in redesign is made in the move to software in any case. Yet remarkably, these entirely digital calculators are no better. And in fact, as we now demonstrate, they have unexpected problems. Something very strange is going on. It is even stranger that nobody else is noticing, or worried about the consequences of this.

We know users make mistakes, and almost all user interfaces provide features so that users can correct their mistakes. The delete key is the simplest example. In a word processor, web form, or even devices like car parking meters, the user types text (like their car registration number). If they make a mistake, they hit the delete key, and the last thing they typed disappears, so their error is corrected and they can carry on and try harder to do what they originally wanted. Let's say I want to type 'their' but I start to type 'thi. . .'—I missed out the e or typed the i too soon. I hit DEL (delete) and the text turns into 'th' and I can then carry on and type 'eir' with the final desired end-result of correctly typing 'their.' The delete key works when I type anything; you would not expect it to behave differently if the example was about correcting errors in typing a car registration number for instance rather than English words.

But now consider typing a number. If the delete key works the same way, when you make a mistake in typing a number, you can delete errors and hence correct them.

Strangely on almost every calculator, the delete key (when there is one) works in very strange ways.

1. On the Hewlett-Packard EasyCalc calculator, the delete key does not delete decimal points but only digits.

2. On the Apple iPhone calculator, the user interface does not allow numbers with more than one decimal point, so if you delete a second decimal point you keyed by mistake, doing this deletes the only decimal point, leaving you with no decimal points rather than one as you expected.

3. Many calculators have a limit on the number of digits they can display. For concreteness, suppose a calculator can display at most 8 digits. If you key 9 digits and delete the last accidentally excess digit, you will end up with 7 digits, not 8 as you expected.

We have found many people say, 'Well that's what they do!' But just because we are familiar with a problem does not mean it is harmless and that we should not try to solve it. Using computers and other complex devices may well be a form of hazing, which initiates users into the fraternity of experts; and once hazed, you disdain the naïvety of people who see problems rather than commit to learning the rituals that would save them and have saved you. (We will consider a more constructive way of talking about hazing in Section 8.6.4; more constructive in that it suggests some solutions.)

8.3.2 Entering Long Numbers

Obviously, there is no limit to the size of numbers in principle and so there is no limit on how many digits a person may wish to enter into a calculator. This of course causes a design problem for how many digits a calculator can display. Some calculators, following the tradition of the early calculators, simply prevent making numerals longer than the display of the device. So for instance, the Windows 10 calculator allows a user to enter 16 digits (in standard mode) after which no further keypresses are accepted.

However, the Apple iPhone calculator simply makes the font smaller and smaller to fit more in the display area of the calculator, and then at some point it starts to discard the user's digits without warning. On Apple Macs, the calculator makes the font smaller and smaller, so that it eventually becomes unreadable at about 1mm high, and then it starts discarding the most significant digits. These tricks show the programmers have made choices, premature choices, about the problem, but they have not made the calculator easier or more reliable to use. It seems strange: clearly the programmers thought about the problem, took steps to mitigate it, but yet failed to do it adequately.

There are boundary cases where, as the user approaches the limit of the display, the representation of the number becomes unstable. For example, on the iOS v7.1.2, the calculator that comes as standard on the iPhone allows users to enter up to 16 digits in scientific mode (which appears when you hold the phone on its side, in landscape). So if you enter fifteen 9s there is of course one last digit that can still be entered before the display is full. And this last, sixteenth, digit leads to very odd behaviour. If it is a 9, the display changes to exponent form and displays `1e+16`. Moreover, deleting the last digit results in 1 followed by 15 zeroes, which is not what you might expect from `DEL`. If the sixteenth keypress is a 3, the display becomes fifteen 9s followed by a 2. Similarly, entering a sixteenth digit of 5, 6, or 7 all results in the last digit in the display to being a 6.

Arguably, at such highly precise levels, a unit difference at the sixteenth significant digit is not often going to matter. But who knows? We certainly do not, but we think it is highly likely that the programmers of the calculator do not either. And the way `DEL` works is totally unlike the way it works on everything else. What this example implies is that the process of entering a number in this calculator is not simply one of entering a string of digits but is in some unfathomable way tied to meaning of the number (or something) as it is internally represented in the calculator. Even a six-year old child understands that the current behaviour of any calculator is peculiar (Patrick Cairns, personal communication).

These examples come from looking at specific boundaries prompted by our current concerns for number entry. It is impossible to know what other boundary cases arise in the multitude of other functions that calculators possess. What is very clear is that calculators are not simple user interfaces. Indeed, the way the way they are designed to handle errors (e.g., using delete keys) can make errors worse.

8.3.3 Why Calculators Should be Better

These problems illustrate that even the conceptually very simple task of entering a number into a device is not without usability problems. In some ways, this task is almost so small as to make it not worth considering because obviously it is easy to re-enter a number into a device when you make a mistake. But there are four responses to this.

1. The problems may be small but they are hugely widespread. Problems like these occur not only in the various designs we mentioned but in the design of all calculators that we have examined. Such ubiquitous problems may have small individual cost but have huge cumulative cost, that is, when multiplied up by the numbers of users of calculators and the number of times they are used by each user. For instance, nurses use calculators every day to work out drug doses for patients: one wonders how many design-induced errors happen with catastrophic results.

2. There is a secondary cost to this ubiquity in that we have to take time to teach our children what the problems are instead of solving them. Schools teach children not to trust calculators and to try performing calculations in various ways. It is like teaching people how to drive a car that doesn't have very good brakes instead of working out how to make safer brakes.

3. Calculators are only the most familiar representative of the type device that requires number entry; there are many variations on the number entry task in many other devices and we have found that these too have similar or related problems (Thimbleby and Cairns 2017; Thimbleby 2015). And when the devices considered are aircraft altimeters or medical infusion pumps, these fundamental problems become extremely important. People often die in hospitals from 'out by ten' errors where a drug dose is ten times (or more) too high. How often does it happen that correcting a number entered like `1..5` to be `1.5` gets mangled *by the bad design* to become 15? Nobody knows.

4. We have been using Arabic numerals in the West since Fibonacci published his bestseller *Liber Abaci* in 1202. Although there were a few issues sorting out decimals and negative numbers since then, by the twentieth century, certainly, Arabic numerals were perfectly well understood and, surely, there is now no excuse to program number entry systems improperly.

Something very interesting must be going on.

8.4 Finite State Machines and HCI

Whenever a user interacts with a system, there is the expectation that the system responds in some way; that is, on each user interaction, the system will normally change. To be precise, we can say it should change *state*.

In some cases, the change of state will be quite innocuous. For instance, pressing 1 on a calculator can make a 1 appear in the display. In some cases, the change of state is quite important such as pressing = on a calculator will lead to the display being cleared and the result of some calculation being presented, as well as getting the calculator ready to receive new numbers for further operations: the change of state here is quite complex. In some cases, a change of state may be very important, such as changing a setting on an autopilot in a commercial airliner can make the difference between setting a target altitude or setting the rate of descent, which can have very different end states (Degani, 2004).

From the earliest days of computer science, it has been recognized that many algorithms and interactions can be understood as the system moving through a serious of different states and this led to consideration of an important abstract idea called Finite State Machines (FSMs) or sometimes Finite State Automata (FSAs).

FSMs are very well established theoretical tools in computer science, though not always considered as practical tools. They have also been used in HCI to model interactions and to allow various sorts of analysis.

We can explain FSMs in many essentially equivalent ways:

- Pictorially, each state of a FSM can be drawn as a circle, and each transition from one state to the next as an arrow joining two circles. Typically the circles will be labeled with the states or modes they represent (like 'on' or 'off') and the arrows will be labeled with the names of the buttons or other actions that cause the changes of state. We'd expect, for instance, an off arrow to point to the off state circle. Note that there may be lots of arrows for the same action—many states can be switched off by pressing OFF so there may be lots of off arrows, one from each state (at least from those that can be switched off). However, there is only one circle for each state; there is usually only one Off circle, for instance.

  See figure 8.2 for an example. As shown in figure 8.2, normally one state will be marked as the starting state—typically the state when the device is off.

- Mathematically, a FSM can be understood as an abstraction of this pictorial representation in the form of an abstract graph, where circles correspond to elements of a set of states, called nodes, and arrows ordered pairs of nodes called edges that are mapped to labels via a labelling function. Graph theory is a substantial part of mathematics, though confusingly 'graph' is also used as the term for diagrams to plot functions like $y = x^2$.

- In software, an FSM can easily be represented by numbering each state, numbering each user action (e.g., each button), then using an array of state numbers T, to represent the FSM. When the user does action b in state s, the state is simply updated by doing the assignment s = T[b, s].

- Using algebra we can describe a FSM very abstractly. There is a set of states S and a set of transitions (typically user actions, button presses, hand waving, etc) T. Each transition t is a function that changes the current state to the next state: $t \in T : S \rightarrow S$. A FSM starts in an initial state $s_0 \in S$ and is operated on by a sequence of transitions $t_1; t_2; t_3 \ldots; t_n$ and it will then be in state $t_n(\ldots t_3(t_2(t_1(s_0)))\ldots)$. Typically a special

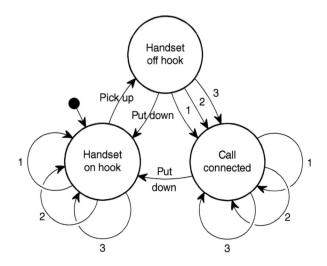

Figure 8.2 A drawing of the finite state machine for the Coast Guard phone shown in figure 8.1. The phone starts in the state indicated by the ➤ arrow (pointing to the bottom left circle, 'handset on hook'), then user actions follow arrows to the other two states. For example, in the start state, pressing any of the digit buttons (1, 2, 3) does not change state, so nothing happens—in this state the buttons do nothing. The user has to pick up the phone handset to start anything happening.

transition 'reset' (such as removing the batteries or unplugging it, or pushing in a paperclip into a special hole) will put the FSM back into the initial state s_0.

- Because FSMs are such basic yet ubiquitous things, there are many other alternative ways to represent and understand them including as algebras and as matrices (Thimbleby, 2004).

These different representations all support different forms of representing, understanding and hence analysing FSMs. It is an important fact that every computer system can be described as a FSM. Possibly some trivial additions may be required— e.g., a lottery computer will need to have some randomizing transitions to generate lottery ticket numbers— but *every* computer's user interface can be understood as state transitions caused by user actions. As *any* program represents a FSM, often the programmer will program 'how they like' and the FSM is then likely to be very hard to see— but a FSM is still there implicitly and can be "discovered" by special techniques (Thimbleby and Gimblett, 2010).

Despite their power and generality and their rigorous mathematical basis, FSMs have got a poor reputation.

We can easily draw a few circles and arrows and thus understand how FSMs work (they are no harder than the children's game of snakes and ladders), but then it is tempting to think that FSMs *have* to be simple enough to draw. If so, that would limit FSMs to a few states only— any more and they would get far too tedious to draw. In fact, FSMs work the same way even if they are so large we cannot sensibly draw them.

An analogy may help. We can 'draw' the number 6 by drawing : : :, and this familiar way of drawing numbers makes numbers very easy to understand. Adding one to six is easy to draw, and when we were children drawings like this helped us learn how numbers work. But we can't usefully draw 1,007 this way—it will look much like any other large number, like 999 for instance. Obviously, we can only sensibly draw relatively small numbers, but nevertheless we know that large numbers are still very useful even though we cannot draw them reliably.

Note that we can add 6 and 2 by simply putting our drawing of 6 next to a drawing of 2:

$$: : : + : = : : : :$$

We get 8 with no effort! In other words, we can add up *without consciously adding*. Indeed, if we *delete* the + symbol, the numbers 'just' add themselves.

Similarly, all programs are using FSMs, even if the FSMs cannot easily be drawn or visualized. A bit of program like if (x<0) x=-x is doing something an FSM can do, but you cannot see the FSM in the code—just as in : : : : you can't see the + sign.[1]

Another problem FSMs have is in the 'programmer's imagination,' which is that programmers think FSMs are technically limited compared to Turing Machines and general programming. This is true in infinite theory, but not in practice. Any real PC is a finite state machine—it is not an infinite machine like a Turing Machine. The practical truth is that FSMs do not have good ways to abstract them, so programmers tend to write in Java or some other convenient programming language. Their programs are strictly equivalent to (big) FSMs—not necessarily the same ones. Thus programmers 'think in' Java, not in FSMs, and the elegance and nice properties of the (correct) FSMs fail to be abstracted coherently.

8.4.1 An Example FSM

Figure 8.1 shows a UK Coast Guard phone near the sea. Imagine watching somebody getting into difficulty in the water: you run to this emergency phone to call the Coast Guard.

As you run towards it, the big writing on the sign primes you to press 999 (the UK emergency number, as opposed to 911, 112, etc, which are used elsewhere). But when you get closer and can see the details of the user interface, just *how* are you supposed to do that? One thing we can be certain of, is that priming you to do something impossible is going to make your emergency call harder.

This is a serious design issue that could have been prevented if the user interface had been represented as a finite state machine. As is clear from Figure 8.2 there is a transition between two states that has *three* buttons that are used nowhere else in the design—something very strange is going on in the design. In addition, giving the user unnecessary choice slows them

---

[1] One of us has a car whose user manual has the warning that its clever computer features do not help the driver overcome the laws of physics. In other words, the car obeys the laws of physics even though the driver cannot see them, and—as the manual tries to warn—even if the driver foolishly denies the laws, they are there anyway. Similarly, the laws of FSMs are obeyed even if they cannot be drawn or seen.

down (Hick's Law),[2] here further delaying calls to the Coast Guard—it'd be better to label all the buttons 999 anyway! (Notice the button labels shown in Figure 8.1 are blank and could have been filled in with 999—or, better, each button could have been labelled 999 instead of 1, 2 or 3.)

It would be easy to write a program to automatically find such errors, and many others, in the graphs of designs before they are built, but unfortunately here it is too late for the the Coast Guard to fix the problem easily.

8.4.2 Using FSMs for Interaction

It is easy to see how FSMs can represent many sorts of devices. Push button devices, such as DVD machines and calculators, move between states as a consequence of the user pressing buttons, the buttons provide the labels for the edges (arrows, state transitions). Simple websites display different pages, each page representing a different state, and move between pages/states as a consequence of a user clicking on links. Web sites can simulate any interactive device, so obviously since a web site is a FSM, then FSMs can simulate any device. It is a routine problem to use an FSM to see whether it is possible to navigate from any webpage in a website to any other, so it follows it is a routine problem to use an FSM to analyse accessibility for any interactive system. In fact, FSMs can be used with computer tools to analyse many interaction properties very easily—recall that a FSM is easy to represent in a program as an array, and we can automatically check that array for a large range of interaction properties (Gow and Thimbleby, 2005; Thimbleby, 2010).

Here are some typical questions that can be directly answered by analysing FSMs:

1. Can the user reach certain states?
2. Can a user always undo any action?
3. Is it possible to get into any state from anywhere?
4. Are there states that dispense chocolates following states where no coins have been inserted?
5. Can the device be switched off by pressing $\boxed{\text{OFF}}$ in any state?
6. If a burglar presses digits at random, how long do they take before guessing the code?

Even from thinking about simple examples like an oven temperature setting, it is clear that what state the system is in has a significant impact on what actions are possible or safe. Where a state is not otherwise visible, for instance the oven is above $40\,^\circ$C, it is important to indicate this to the user some other way such as a warning light or door lock. Again, we can automatically analyse FSMs to ensure they have such important properties.

---

[2] Hick's Law states that human choice time is proportional to $\log n + 1$ for a selection between n choices. In this example, the user interface provides three buttons when at most one would do hence, by Hick's Law (and ignoring other causes of delay), making the user $2 = \log 4 / \log 2$ times slower than need be.

Asaf Degani (Degani, 2004) uses state machines to consider the interaction with autopilots in airplanes. He shows how interactions with the autopilot can lead to unnoticed state transitions, particularly when the environment is providing inputs to the device such as the plane coming close to its target altitude. Where such transitions are not made visible to the pilots, it is impossible for the pilots to know what state the autopilot is in and therefore reliably predict the consequences of their interactions with it. Degani shows how this problem of hidden state transitions has led to fatal and expensive accidents.

With FSMs, it is also possible to add information to the transitions. For instance, if numbers between 0 and 1 are added to the edges to correspond to the probabilities of a particular button being pressed, then it is possible to calculate the probabilities of a system ending up in any particular state (in fact, we end up with a Markov model). We can then estimate how many steps it takes to get to any states of interest. We have previously used this idea to show that an error, say in setting a microwave to heat something up for a fixed time, can lead to users being unable to set the microwave at all. But, also, the introduction of a [Quit] key, and the knowledge to use it, can greatly help people from getting trapped when that happens (Thimbleby, Cairns, and Jones, 2001).

It can be seen that FSMs make a bridge between the theoretical tools of computer science and the ability to analyse interactive systems. It is probably also clear that effective analysis of real systems requires support from suitable tools that can manage the generally large sizes of real FSMs. Some such tools, like MAUI and others (Gow and Thimbleby, 2005; Thimbleby, 2010) exist and can help. However, analysing FSM models is one thing and building working programs is another. What is still needed is a way to move fluidly from the analytical power of FSMs and the actual systems being developed so that a programmer can do the job of programming but also exploit the analytical strengths of FSM for interaction design.

Unfortunately because programmers rarely use explicit FSMs (e.g., as simple as the array we illustrated above), even these simple questions are usually very difficult to answer. In fact, they are so hard to answer they are rarely even asked. It is arguable that major advances in HCI, such as the initial explorations of GOMS and KLM (Card, Moran, and Newell, 1980), floundered because what an HCI or UX professional is interested in is just too hard for a programmer to address. Thus GOMS was used for really very trivial systems, and still hasn't been used for anything of even ordinary complexity.

8.4.3 Regular Expressions

Another long-established tool in computer science is the regular expression. Regular expressions are a way to define formal languages—artificial languages with a clearly specified grammar. Regular expressions tend to be used with reference to problems like whether a given string of characters is a valid word in a particular language.

For example, YN16 AGY is a valid UK number plate for a new car, but YYYYX1 is not (for simplicity we will ignore the possibility of historical numbers that predate the current rules and 'vanity' numbers, like EGO 1, which can be bought at a price). Regular expressions can easily be used to specify the words (i.e., registration numbers) of the registration plate language.

A regular expression to capture the format of valid number plate registration numbers is:

```
L = 'A'|'B'|'C'|...|'Z'   L can be any letter, A or B or C...
D = '0'|'1'|...|'9'       D can be any digit, 0 or 1 or 2...
P1 = LLDD' 'LLL           A valid registration is letter, letter, digit, digit, space...
```

There are many other notations for regular expressions that can be used to say the same thing. Many readers will be more familiar with the Unix notation, which in this case would be

$$\text{[A-Z] [A-Z] [0-9] [0-9] [A-Z] [A-Z] [A-Z]}$$

and even then this is only one way Unix can express registration numbers. Our own notation used above has the advantage that we can *name* regular expressions—such as using L to represent letters—and then use the name L later to save rewriting the same idea multiple times (making it much less likely we make mistakes). For example, if we sorted out how to handle that the UK registration plate font makes the letters/digits I and 1, O and 0 identical, we only have to fix this in two places (in the definitions of L and D), rather than in seven where letters and digits are needed. Conversely, if there is a bug in our regular expression, then the same bug will reappear up to seven times: this might sound like a disadvantage, but we are also more likely to spot bugs in the first place, which is a huge advantage, and when we fix any bug we find, we actually fix seven. This is a very powerful advantage.

For real UK registration numbers there are actually more rules than this. For example, the pair of digits in the middle of the number plate represents the year of manufacture of the car, so for instance anything above 17 but below 50 is not currently valid (at the time of writing) but we did not specify this above. Ignoring such details, then, more or less P1 defines valid number plates and would, for instance, exclude many number plates from outside of the UK. Thus, regular expressions can be used to both define valid things and to check whether given things are valid or not.

The three basic operations permissible in regular expression are sequence, choice and iteration.

Sequence is the operation of being given two regular expression, you can have one expression follow on from another. This is precisely what is seen in defining P1; a valid registration is a letter *followed by* a letter *followed by* a digit...In most regular expression notations, there is no special symbol for sequence: thus, 'LD' means L followed by D.

Choice is that a new regular expression can be made out of two existing ones; it is either one or the other of them, that is for regular expression A and B, C = A | B means C is either A or B. Here the symbol "|" is the notation for choice. The expression L above is a short hand of listing the choice options that L[3] is one of the characters of the upper case roman alphabet.

---

[3] This example makes it look like choice allows twenty-six choices—more than two choices! In fact, if we write the choices out explicitly each with exactly two choices: (('A'|'B')|'C')|...|'Z' or as 'A'|('B'|('C'|...|'Z')), etc, these regular expressions are all the same, so the brackets are unnecessary. In other words, choice is associative.

Finally, a given expression can be iterated (repeated) a number of times to form a new expression, represented as $B = A^*$ which means B is any number of repetitions of A including no repetitions. If a $+$ is used instead of a $*$ then this means B is at least one repetition of A. Sometimes it is useful to be specific, and write A^n for repeating n times or A^{m-n} for repeating between m and n times. We did not use these ideas above because car registration numbers are too simple to need them—writing $P1 = L^2 D^2{}'\ 'L^3$ is more confusing that $P1 = LLDD'\ 'LLL$ which is what it means. In more complicated cases, though, the additional notation can be very useful (e.g., it is much easier to tell the difference between D^8 and D^9 than DDDDDDDD and DDDDDDDDD).

Regular expressions are the tool behind many familiar user interactions like making sure users enter a date in the correct format or enter a number when they should. However, even in these simple interactions where regular expressions are useful (and would help ensure user interfaces did what they were supposed to), they are often not applied when they might be.

Like FSMs, regular expressions also have a public image problem. They are fantastic for performing string operations, like finding car registration numbers in a big file of text. Many programming languages (e.g., JavaScript, PHP, etc) provide powerful built-in features for using regular expressions *for string operations*. But just because they are great at string operations does not mean that is all they can do, and in particular that they should not be used right across all aspects of user interface design.

Grete Fossbakk lost 50,000 Norwegian Krone (about US$60,000) due to a poorly programmed user interface (Olsen, 2008). Fossbakk entered an account number but accidentally pressed one digit twice. The resulting account number was of course then too long, but the bank's system truncated it, and the truncated number happened to be a valid account number but unfortunately the right number for another person. Fossbakk did not notice this error, and confirmed her money transfer—to the wrong account. Of course the bank argued Fossbakk had confirmed what she wanted to do, but she had confirmed a simple error that the bank should have—and could have—detected.

A regular expression in this case could have been used to validate Fossbakk's entry, and would have detected her error because it was too long. For example, D^8 would have done. The point is, had the programmer specified the user interface (here, using a regular expression), the problems would have been obvious, and a solution found (e.g., warning the user). In fact, using regular expressions to validate user input is an obvious professional decision. In this case, though, it seems the programmers did not specify anything, but rather 'it just happened' and then *nobody thought about it*.

The user interface (if designed properly) should have forced her or the bank to re-check the input more carefully. This may seem like a rare and unlikely feature of one particular bank but it is not. Figure 8.3 shows some code taken from the UK Lloyds Bank's current (2016) web pages for the same task. Lloyds Bank uses HTML to truncate account numbers to 8 digits, and it does so silently. Because the web browser (thanks to the HTML) truncates the number, the bank's servers have no idea that an invalid number has been entered.

Though we rarely think about it, Arabic decimal numbers (and indeed all number systems if they are reliable) have a well-defined structure that can be captured by a regular expression:

```
Account number:
<input
    type = "text"
    autocomplete = "off"
    id = "pnlSetupNewPayeePayaPerson:frmPayaPerson:stringBenAccountNumber"
    name = "pnlSetupNewPayeePayaPerson:frmPayaPerson:stringBenAccountNumber"
    maxlength = "8"
/>
```

Figure 8.3 HTML for a user to enter an account number, copied from a Lloyds Bank web site in 2016. Notice the code maxlength=`"8"` (on the penultimate line) which will *silently* truncate any account number to a maximum of 8 digits: neither the user nor the bank's server will know.

```
1 NZ = '1'|...|'9'        any non-zero digit
2 D = '0'|NZ              any digit, including zero
3 Pt = '.'               decimal point
4 Int = '0'|(NZ D*)      whole number part
5 Fr = D* NZ              fraction part
6 Num = Int|(Int Pt Fr)  a number is either an integer or a fractional number
```

These rules may seem unduly complicated (and we did not include any rules for signs, + and -) but they are not really complicated:

The final rule 6 is saying that a number is either a whole number (an integer) or an integer followed by a decimal fraction. Rule 4 is saying that a valid integer does not start with 0 unless it is actually 0, and rule 5 says that the decimal fraction of a number does not end in a 0. Actually, there are contexts where that is valid, for instance to show the number of significant figures but in general, if we are representing a precise value then rule 5 is necessary.

These rules make Num specify whole numbers (which do not have a decimal point) and fractional numbers (which do have a decimal point). We have not permitted a number to start with redundant zeros, and we have not allowed a fractional number to end with a zero: thus `00050` is not allowed to represent 50, and `0.50` is not allowed because of its trailing zero. Moreover, we do not allow 'naked decimal points'—so neither `.5` and `5.` are allowed. The naked decimal point rule is inspired by the Institute for Safe Medication Practices (ismp.org), which forbids naked decimals as they encourage errors— for instance, a nurse could misread `.5` as `5` and give somebody a drug dose ten times too high.

When it comes to a task like number entry, it seems unlikely that checking that a number is actually a valid number would make much difference to anyone—and few user interfaces check anyway. However, we found that in the possibility that users make errors when entering numbers, then simply checking if the result was a valid number reduced the risk of high impact errors by a half (where by high impact we mean when the number, perhaps a drug dose, is out by a factor of 10 from the correct value) (Thimbleby and Cairns, 2010). Unfortunately many programmers learn about regular expressions as a theoretical computer science curiosity and never realize they are very useful in user interface design!

8.4.4 Regular Expressions = FSMs

Though at first sight, regular expressions and FSMs look very different, in fact they are closely related.[4] Any FSM can be expressed as a regular expression and any regular expression can be transformed into a FSM (Aho, Sethi, and Ullman, 1986).[5] The basic idea is that if a regular expression defines which sets of characters define valid words or sentences, the FSM is able to check whether one is actually valid. It does this by starting in a specified state and then matching the letters of the word to labels on its edges. If, when it reaches the end of the word, it is in a special final state then the word is valid. If not, then the word is invalid. Thus, what looks like a complicated checking procedure of matching words to regular expressions becomes an entirely algorithmic process: just running a FSM. In this sense, regular expressions are a more humanly meaningful way to represent FSMs. A FSM may be hard to draw but its regular expression is usually much easier to write.

In fact, the operations of regular expressions (sequence, choice and iteration, described above) are *exactly* what FSMs do by using transitions. Thus, for instance, the regular expression choice $'x' \mid 'y'$ does just what a FSM in some state does when it makes one transition on the action x and another transition on y.

8.4.5 Programming with FSMs

Programming is complicated and is an activity that induces many well-known cognitive problems. We have brains of finite capacity, and the more work they do on a task it is inevitable that they have less spare capacity to work on other tasks or even consider all the peripheral issues. This problem is called loss of situational awareness or tunnel vision. Put in other words: getting a program to work at all is so hard that making it easy to use is likely to slip to second place, and, moreover, the programmer will be unaware this is happening— their brain is full. To be aware requires cognitive resources: loss of situational awareness by definition is unconscious.

One way to help is to use teamwork (so other people help you look out for things you are missing), but not the sort of teamwork that Landauer (1995) envisages of one team member (the UCD expert) telling the programmer what to do—which just makes the programmer's job harder—but means being present with them and helping them do it better.

Another way to help is to use programming techniques to help manage the complexity of programming. Software engineering is the discipline that studies this, and programmers should be trained in its techniques (Sommerville, 2015). One of the key techniques is *separation of concerns*, to split a programming problem into separate components with as little interaction between them as possible. Then the separate concerns can be addressed

---

[4] Technically, a FSM can end up in any state, but a regular expression can only end up either succeeding or failing to match its input; hence, regular expressions are exactly equivalent to special FSMs called finite state acceptors, which are FSMs with exactly two designated final states. Such final states can always be added to any FSM to make it into an acceptor.

[5] There are some easily addressed technical differences between FSMs (and non-deterministic FSMs) and REs but it is beyond the scope of this chapter to worry about it further.

independently. An example of successful separation of concerns happens on most web pages: the content, the activity, and the presentation are managed by separate parts of the site—in HTML, JavaScript and in CSS (to name a few). Certainly the boundaries are often blurred, but in principle the areas of concern can be separated, and systems become 'cleaner' and easier to develop and manage the sharper the separation—they also become easier to update in response to UCD requests. Note that these points apply to any interactive system, not just to web sites; indeed, web sites are a good way of prototyping any interactive system, and hence exploring the best separation of concerns.

A FSM provides an excellent separation of concerns, as it separates the 'machine' delivering the style of behaviour the user requires from the application and presentation details. For example, clicking buttons needs implementing (for example, so that a screen image changes as the mouse moves over it and when the mouse clicks on its active region), but what clicking a button does for the user is a different problem. As a useful side-effect, this approach makes the user interface more consistent for the user:

1. How do buttons work? What are the timing issues for double clicks? What is a long hold? Do buttons audibly click when pressed? What happens when the user clicks on a button and moves out of its active region before releasing the mouse?

2. What should the application do when a user clicks on a button? What are its modes, and how do buttons change their meanings in each mode?

3. How does the application achieve what it should do?

Step 2 above can often be done by a FSM, and doing so creates a useful wall—a separation of concerns—between steps 1 and 3, which makes those steps easier to implement reliably and consistently. Otherwise, there would be a temptation to implement particular buttons that do particular things one at a time, which would entwine the button and what it does, and hence each button would likely be implemented in a slightly different way.

A corollary of separation is that program code gets reused. Instead of every button being implemented in its own way all the buttons can share the exact same code. This means that any bugs in button design become apparent quickly—because testing any button is the same as testing all of them. In contrast, when buttons are implemented one at a time, then each button must be rigorously tested, and that is hard work. Separation of concerns concentrates design effort into a few important places, and those places get greater scrutiny than without the separation.

Not only does it make it easier for the programmer (and hence ultimately easier for the user because the program is better implemented) but the separation of concerns means the *meaning* of the interaction has been separated out and becomes a thing-in-itself. Once a FSM is used, it can be analysed.

For example, whatever a user interface looks like (step 1 above) and whatever it is doing (step 2 above) we probably do not want the user to get stuck. There are many ways of expressing this design requirement, but suppose it is expressed as 'whatever the user is doing, they always have the option to do anything else.' If this is the design requirement, it translates to a *trivial* test on the FSM—is it strongly connected? Another form of the requirement (with slightly different connotations) is 'the user can always undo whatever they have done.' If that is the design requirement, again it translates into a simple test on the FSM: is it symmetric?

Often, strict requirements like these simple examples are problematic or raise further design questions that need carefully exploring. For example, once you start using a fire extinguisher, you cannot go back to any state of not having used it—so fire extinguishers fail both of the properties above, but they are no less useful for failing them. On the other hand, activating a fire alarm, you might want to undo because it may be an accidental activation, and setting off a fire alarm is expensive (e.g., all staff have to stop work and leave the building).

Once a FSM is used: critical user interface design questions can be asked, questions can be answered, and the design trade offs are very easy to explore. These are advantages for programmers, designers and users that conventional programming rarely benefits from.

8.4.6 Going Beyond FSMs

FSMs are very good for designing simple systems (ones we can draw or express as regular expressions), but as we've emphasized they can become complex too quickly. Put more positively: FSMs therefore help keep designs simple because the effort of designing compli-cated ones hopefully dissuade designers from unnecessary complexity. Unfortunately, it's far more likely that UI designers will just start developing in completely *ad hoc* ways without using anything rigorous like FSMs. Programmers will be unlikely to correctly implement that which has been vaguely defined.

For the purposes of this chapter, though, FSMs highlight in a very clear way many user interface programming issues and trade-offs. FSMs are a type of *model*, in fact a very elegant and clean type of model, and their trade-offs are typical of trade-offs with any modelling approach.

Perhaps the most important and well-known bridge between the simplicity of FSMs and the intricacies of real life applications is Statecharts. Statecharts are a concise way of drawing interactive systems that designers can easily use, but they allow *much* more complex designs than can easily be handled with FSMs (Thimbleby, 2010). Yet Statecharts do not lose any of the technical advantages of FSMs. Furthermore, Statecharts have many design and analysis tools, such as those available to support UML (Statecharts are part of UML).

Unfortunately we do not have space to discuss Statecharts or UML further here—in some way, it would be like us telling you to use Java or C++ to program. It's an interesting choice, but the necessary discussion to understand the choices will divert us too much from user interface design and premature semantics.

There are others forms of model based programming for user interfaces, and their advantages and disadvantages are very similar. They all help programmers implement better programs and to reason about them. We recommend Jackson's *Software Abstractions* (2011) as an introduction to this substantial, big field.

8.5 Premature Semantics

Careful consideration of calculators makes it clear that a calculator, whether a mechanical device, electronic or entirely computerized, always displays a valid number in its display.

That is, the semantics of the input are forced to be a number *all the time*. For example, if you try to enter two decimal points in a calculator entry, the second one leads to no change because a valid number cannot have two decimal points. More generally, we call this issue *premature semantics*: the semantics of an input are fixed (to be a valid number) before the entry is finished. Note that the premature semantics affects the user—an input becomes a number before they have finished (they accidentally entered a non-number, but something was mangled to force it to be a number). That means the user's ability to correct their own error is compromised; for example, the DEL key won't work as they expect.

The reasons why calculators are like this are easy to imagine. Early electronic calculators would hold the input number in a register inside the calculator. The device could block any input that would lead to an incorrect number or to overflowing the size of the register. And, because the physical devices have a limited number of buttons, this was easy. In addition, the early devices did not allow delete, as we would understand it now, but only a Clear function which cleared the value in the register rather than remove individual digits.

Though they were almost certainly not programmed this way, it is straightforward to understand the interaction of entering a number in an early calculator through a FSM. With the underlying principle that the calculator always displays a valid number, there is (or there is in principle) an underlying FSM that accepts keypresses that lead to valid numbers and blocks keypresses that do not. So the display starts by showing 0 (a valid number even though the user has not even started entering a number) and as the user presses keys, the digits are accepted and appended to the display. A single keypress of a decimal point is a valid state transition in the FSM so the point is appended to the display. Having entered states with a decimal point, any further decimal point keypresses do not define valid state transitions so they are blocked. Pressing Clear resets the display and the FSM back to the initial state.

It is worth contrasting this with text entry. Because valid words in, say, English do not have a rigid structure that can be easily captured with a regular expression (or arguably any formal expression), it is not so tempting to enforce premature semantics in text entry. A spell checker can only identify an error once a word has been entered and even then, as we commonly experience, a correctly spelled word is not necessarily semantically rite. Sentence level checks on semantics are even more difficult. Certainly, there is no way to enforce semantics in text entry as the text is being entered.

Some systems, nonetheless, do impose premature semantics on text. As you write the space after, say, 'thankfull' it magically turns into 'thankful.' But if you are copy typing and not watching the screen, you would type 'thankfull# DEL DEL #' and you'd end up with 'thankfu'—since both you and the system deleted the extra 'l.'

We now consider how premature semantics leads to two specific types of problem: problems of construction and problems of representation.

8.5.1 Problems of Construction

Whenever a person enters information, be it digits, text, photographs or whatever else, into a system, there needs to be a process for the user to construct the input. But of course, people make mistakes and want to correct mistakes and for this reason, keys like Clear , C , DEL or 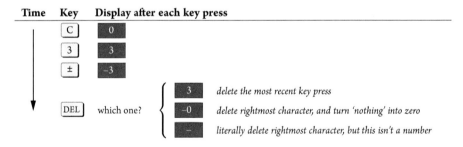 are useful functions. Clear is an all or nothing function which forces the user to re-start an entry from the beginning. This is of course frustrating if only the last keypress was incorrect. DEL is more convenient, as just it deletes individual keystrokes and is easier to control. Unfortunately, as we saw above, DEL is where a lot of problems of premature semantics come in and create strange special effects a user has to be aware of—and of course users probably are not aware of these special cases, especially when they are trying to correct their own errors.

The key DEL can have one of two meanings: delete the last (rightmost in Roman-based systems) character in the display or delete the last keypress pressed on the keyboard. In text entry, these two meanings almost always coincide. If we type A B C the display will show ABC. Clearly, here the last key pressed was C and the rightmost key displayed is the same, namely C. Pressing DEL will delete it, leaving AB in the display, which seems perfectly obvious.

Yet because of the premature semantics, this is not how things always happen.

When a calculator blocks a second decimal point, pressing DEL cannot delete the last keypress because the last keypress had no action visible in the display. Depending on how the calculator is implemented, it may delete the rightmost character or do nothing or delete a digit, or even something else. Premature semantics is the source of problems described in Section 8.3.1 of this chapter.

Or consider when a user presses the negation ± key on a calculator. When a number changes sign, the negative sign appears (or disappears) as a prefix in the display and so deleting the last keypress should remove the negative sign but deleting the last character shown in the display should remove the rightmost digit. You can't have it both ways. Also, if there is only one digit (possibly a zero), how can it be deleted when the calculator always displays a number? These choices have very different effects, as the following table makes the clear:

Time	Key	Display after each key press		
	C	0		
	3	3		
	±	-3		
	DEL	which one?	3	*delete the most recent key press*
			-0	*delete rightmost character, and turn 'nothing' into zero*
			−	*literally delete rightmost character, but this isn't a number*

And indeed, from the point of view of the calculator, it is not possible to know which is actually required.

A current example is the Apple iPhone calculator (early 2017): the following sequence of user keystrokes will make it crash AC ± DEL ± DEL. The sequence of keystrokes has a simple story: the user keyed ± by mistake and tries to correct it, but that doesn't work, so they try ± again (changing sign twice should cancel it out); that doesn't work either, so they hit DEL. Whoops, the calculator crashes. This is a bug—actually, it's the third bug we've seen in three keystrokes. Apple have some of the world's best programmers, but evidently they do not always make reliable interactive programs, even when they are this simple. We should not be blaming Apple; we should be wondering why it has taken us so long to notice that programming interactive systems is very hard. And the consequence of it being so hard is that it is rarely done well.

Now, summarizing this to pull out the morals:

- Programmers add simple features, like entering numbers.

- Programmers add more features. Decimal points and change sign are very simple examples. The DEL key is another example.

- Some features will be added implicitly. Most number entry systems impose a length limit on how long a number can be.

- Individually and separately, each of these features makes a lot of sense: indeed, they have sensible semantics. Unfortunately, *collectively* the individual semantics don't work together, and we now see that giving each feature, such as the decimal point, a semantics earlier was premature. Most design choices turn out to be inconsistent with later ideas—though the inconsistencies often lie unnoticed.

- The accepted wisdom of iterative design exacerbates these problems. Building a system and then evaluating it with users to see if it needs improving, and if so how, is conventional wisdom. But doing this creates many opportunities for premature semantics to cause problems. New features will be added (or earlier features modified), and the deep implementation, the premature assumptions, of the original features will come back and haunt the later design iterations.

8.5.2 Construction in Forms

These problems of incremental construction are not only seen in calculators of course. Online forms are a common and very useful means of gathering a rich set of data, for instance, name, payment and delivery details in online shopping. The data needed is structured but has several distinct components and online forms, by analogy with paper forms, indicate what is needed and essentially marks up what each part of the entered data should be (for instance, keeping your age and the number of tickets you want to buy as separate data items). Online forms increasingly facilitate correct entry by enforcing the correct semantics for each separate part of the data. For example, rather than entering a date which has many different and inconsistent formats, the user is asked to select it from a calendar. Or the user will at least be cued to enter the correct format by prompts such as 'DD/MM/YY.' And rather than entering an address which can have even more inconsistencies and ambiguities, people filling out the form can be asked to enter a postal code and then select their correct address from within that list.

However, large forms, such as tax returns, passport applications and so on, that go over several pages often require that each page is correct before allowing the user to proceed to the next page. Yet users may have perfectly valid reasons to move on before they have finished each page.

It is now possible in the UK to order a passport online. The form asks for several separate items of information before asking for a digital photograph. This must, understandably, have very specific formatting and styles which you are not informed of until you reach that page and have already entered half a dozen other items of information. But you cannot go past this page or save your form—because it is not yet correct—so if you do not have the photograph ready, you have to go away and start again when you come back (the form will have timed-out for security reasons).

This is premature semantics during construction. The form is requiring that it is *always* correctly filled out (and certainly must be if it is to be saved), including requiring that all fields that need completing have indeed been completed even though later pages still have completely unfilled sections. Paper forms, of course, cannot enforce such premature correctness, allowing users a much more flexible workflow.

It is worth noting that the UK Government has taken usability of its systems very seriously and has made a lot of effort to make all its online resources as accessible as possible to as wide a portion of the population as possible. Thus, even when usability is taken seriously, it is still possible to end up with problematic interactions because of premature semantics. As we've said, we think it is a shame that HCI (and UX in particular) has become quite separated from computer science. You cannot have good UX (or good HCI) without a foundation of good CS.

8.5.3 Problems of Representation

If an item of data must always be valid, there is also the problem of what to represent in the display. Early calculators solved this by having physical displays that necessarily had inflexible constraints. They could not display more than a fixed number of digits and often not even digits themselves very well (Thimbleby, 2013). Software calculators have no such obvious constraints. Once again, consideration of the semantics through FSMs helps to clarify the problems that arise.

Mathematically, there is no constraint on the size of a number so the representation can be literally any finite length. The FSM would therefore permit digits to be appended to the end of a number so long as users keep pressing them. This is one behaviour seen in Section 8.3.1 but of course it can result in an unreadable display—this is a logical necessity due to the finite limitations of any device together with the unbounded possibilities of what a user might enter.

The alternative is that the FSM prevents numerals from overflowing the display. That is, when a user reaches a certain length of number, no further digits are added at the end. Now however, the last digit displayed is not the same as the the the last key pressed, and so DEL becomes ambiguous causing problems in construction.

There is also the boundary case seen in Section 8.3.2 where the last key pressed in a long number does not result in the correct digit being displayed; this happens when the number displayed is almost at the maximum value the calculator's internal arithmetic can handle. What this makes clear is that there is no obvious FSM or regular expression underlying number entry in such a calculator. Instead, the number entered has been re-represented internally in some other format, probably a binary representation of the numerical value, and so results in rounding errors when displayed back to the user. This is premature semantics at its worst: the meaning of the number is *altered* even before the user has finished entering it!

In some cases, problems of representation can also become problems of construction. Modern calculators now have the capabilities to display numbers correctly in more sophisticated forms, such as standard exponent form, such as 6.022×10^{23}. Early calculators that used seven-segment displays could not represent this format correctly so instead they compromised with a notation like `6.022E23`, with E standing for Exponent (i.e., the exponent of a power of ten, so E23 means what we normally write as 10^{23}). In some early scientific calculators, a special key allowed users to enter this notation but not directly. Oddly, modern calculators, such as iOS calculators, display numbers in this historical and outmoded format: thus the iPhone (iOS v7.1.2) calculator displays `6.022e+23`. Not only is the representation a historical peculiarity, it interferes with construction. The `EE` key (not `e`!) in the same calculator allows users to enter numbers in this exponential form but acts like an operator (like `+`) and `=` has to be pressed to find out what it has done. This means `DEL` cannot be used conventionally: correction is not possible without a complete clear and re-entry! It looks like the programmers have not thought this through, yet they think 'it works' (and probably passes all their tests)—that is, it's premature semantics at work.

8.5.4 *Premature Semantics Through Strong Typing*

Typing is widely acknowledged to improve the quality of programming as it forces programmers to think about what data is and therefore can be used for. Any unusual uses of data, for instance using the middle two numbers of a car registration to represent a year, requires some further programming. It should not happen by accident. However, forcing all data into types before the data has been entered results in some of the problems already described. But this is a more general problem. For instance, suppose a user wants to enter their credit card security number. The program wants to implement this number so that the program can work; typically the programmer will declare a variable to hold this number, probably declared as an `int`, which is the common abbreviation for integer type in programming languages. Here, then, are some complications:

- Security numbers typically have three decimal digits, such as 479.

- The programmer will declare a variable, probably saying `int code` or similar to store the code. However the `int` type typically covers whole numbers from minus 2,147,483,647 to plus 2,147,483,648.

- Therefore the programmer *may* provide some sort of programming, formally called subtyping, to make their program check the user's number is exactly three digits. They probably won't do this, because 000 to 999 *obviously* fits within an `int` without special programming.

- The programmer will make some decisions over leading zeros. How will they handle 057, for instance? Is this a two digit number (equal to 57) or a three digit number with a leading zero? Unfortunately, in the program 057 and 57 are the same.

- The programmer will optimize their program, doing bit operations, writing in assembler, and more. Optimizations make programs more efficient, but they do so by relying on *assumptions*; and the more assumptions a programmer makes the more likely they are going to make premature assumptions further embedding in the premature semantics of those assumptions.

These sorts of issues are familiar to programmers, but if you agree with them you have already fallen into the trap of premature semantics!

- What do we do if the user does not enter a security code? This is *undefined*, and undefined is not a value an `int` can represent. Therefore the programmer must do a lot of work to handle this case, as no programming language helps directly. Many quality programming languages, Java being a good example, *force* the programmer to ensure that their variable `code` is defined—but it is possible that the user does not define it. If it is defined, it will have to be a number like zero (or 000) but that is not what the user did if the user has not entered it. This is a conflict.[6]
- What do we do it the user enters an invalid code, perhaps their credit card's expiry date 11/19 by mistake? This is an **error**, and error is not a value for an `int` either.[7]

These are both fundamental problems created by premature semantics. If either undefined or error occurs, what should the program do? Can the user still save their form they are entering the credit card details in? Even though saving a form makes perfect sense—especially when the user has made a mistake they want to think about—the program (as usually written) cannot offer the service, because undefined and error themselves cannot be saved as integers.

The programmer thought three digit security codes could obviously be implemented as an `int`, but—typically later, sometimes even after they have left for another job—somebody has to start hacking their program to handle 'special cases' to keep the usability professionals happy. These well-intentioned iterative 'improvements' are then likely to lead to further bugs.

> *Note.* When we explain a problem as we did above, not only did we choose a problem that was simple enough to explain but you have the privilege of hindsight: those errors we described seem very obvious and easy to avoid, don't they? But if you think you could correctly implement a three-digit security code (thanks to our lucid explanation), pause to think how many people in the world thought they could implement years—how hard could a four digit number be? Yet we ended up with one of the world's largest computer fiascos, the Y2K problem.

[6] Forcing variables to be defined reduces the risk that programs will crash, but it does not increase the chances the programs do what they should. Here, programming language designers (and their compilers) force premature semantics on users of their languages. Programming languages like Swift allow variables to be undefined, and they rigorously check how programmers managed undefined values; this helps.

[7] No programming language handles errors well—it is still a research problem. This is why many user interfaces say 'Unexpected error'—if they had correctly expected the error they would have fixed it!

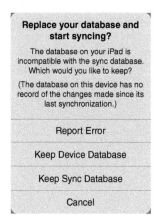

Figure 8.4 What the 'to do list' app Omnifocus does when it encounters an error it had not anticipated in its premature implementation. It successfully detects an 'error' but has no idea what to do. Note that the dialog box does not give the user sufficient information to make a wise decision either; whichever option they choose, they risk losing information. Ironically a 'to do list' is supposed to help users remember what to do, not help them forget things!

Figure 8.4 shows what still happens in 2017—almost two decades after Y2K. Here a programmer thought that a to do list was a simple database, a highly structure type of data. They then thought they would allow the user to run their to do list from several places (their desktop, their mobile phone, their tablet). And then they discovered that they had not implemented distributed error correctly. Their program just drops out in a panic, leaving the user an unanswerable question. Note the premature semantics: Omnifocus prematurely decided to program *perfect* databases (analogously to calculators implementing 'perfect' numbers but not supporting what users do). For whatever reasons, the programmer's utopian (premature semantics) databases do not exist in the real world of the user's actual tasks and activities.

Unlike a calculator, Omnifocus at least notices when its premature semantics fails, though it does not do this very gracefully, even though a brief consideration of what 'to do lists' are would suggest several options of what 'to do' with an inconsistent list including adding it to a list to sort out later. A user knowing they have a problem is a step better than a nurse using a calculator for a drug dose and *not knowing* there is a problem.

8.5.5 A Non-numeric Example

As discussed earlier, any user interface constrains the possibilities of interactions and so defines a language for interaction. Some of these constraints have become so familiar that we do not necessarily see them any more—earlier (Section 8.3.1), we speculated whether this was due or at least partly due to hazing.

For example, when you create a new blank document in a word processor, such as Microsoft Word, you are presented with a blank sheet of paper (well, a virtual one).

However, this sheet of paper does not work like real paper in that you cannot put your cursor wherever you like and start typing. In fact, there is only initially one place the cursor can be placed. It is only when text (including spaces) has been entered can the cursor be repositioned, but even then it has to be between characters and not in blank spaces where there are no characters. This is not necessarily bad premature semantics: we do not think many users would these days expect any different interaction. But at the same time, it is an unnecessary constraint where cursor position is inherently tied to the textual content of the document. This contrasts with new opportunities for interaction where with that very same document on a Microsoft Surface, it is possible to use the pen to make 'ink' marks anywhere on the page. So even if the semantics of the cursor language for the original Word are appropriate, they are not consistent with the pen language. Interestingly, this problem was solved in the 1980s (Thimbleby and Bornat, 1989), but hazing or other reasons meant the solution was never adopted.

8.5.6 The Tip of the Iceberg

It is possible to expand this list of premature semantics examples innumerably as problems of interaction are mapped to the meaning people are trying to convey through there actions. These examples include:

- an absence of an entry (literally nothing) in a drug dosing device being interpreted as zero (mathematically nothing) which has a different meaning
- a timetabling system ordering student-defined topics by pre-requisite knowledge before the students have defined their topics
- supermarket self-checkouts assuming shopping bags are almost no weight at all despite a change in UK law that encourages the use of robust, reusable and, consequently, quite heavy bags.

However, as our examples show, sometimes the problems arise because of premature oversight (the main cause, we think, of premature semantics), or the development of technology, sometimes because of contextual or cultural developments, and sometimes because the accumulation of otherwise sensible features that interact with each other incoherently. It is currently hard to imagine how to define a language involving multiple physical objects like a supermarket self-checkout. But if there were such a language, then it may be possible to formally analyse such systems to see how the changing world interacts with the changing language.

8.6 Solving the Problem of Premature Semantics?

Addressing premature semantics needs to detach the user interface, particularly user input, from the semantics that implements it. In many ways, this is the approach of many of the old-fashioned command style interfaces of early computers. A user could freely enter any command and its parameters. It is only when they pressed [↵] (i.e., enter, return, line feed, etc.) was the command interpreted; if it was invalid it was rejected, sometimes even with a helpful error message. This style of interaction has steadily been left behind because of the burden it puts on users to get things right all in one go (Sharp, Rogers, and Preece, 2007), something we know can be challenging even for the most diligent users (Li, Cox, Blandford, Cairns, Young, and Abeles, 2006). Instead, what is needed is a form of data entry that can be done alongside semantics but without constraining what users do—but also guiding them into correct semantics. Forms are an example of a user interface paradigm that does do this (to a varying extent, depending on the quality of the implementation) but they are not necessarily free from premature semantics (see Section 8.5.2).

In order to balance semantics and free-entry, Thimbleby and Gimblett (2011) implemented a system for number entry (and other forms of data entry) using a traffic light coding. A user is free to enter data however they wish but as each key is pressed the system also processes the input using an underlying FSM for the correct semantics. A user can press any keys but if it leads to a semantically invalid value, say if a key press adds a second decimal point, then the display turns red to indicate this has no meaning. Conversely, if the user has entered a sequence of keypresses leading to a semantically correct item then the display is green to indicate that what is currently displayed is semantically correct. Finally, the display will be orange to display that it could be the start of a semantically correct entry but needs further correct keypresses to make it so; for instance, if the display is 1. it needs some decimal digits before becoming a valid number (at least if we want to avoid 'naked decimals' (Institute for Safe Medication Practices, 2015)). Finally, the user interface can make sounds (or it could provide tactile feedback) when it transitions between traffic light colours: the user does not need to look at the display.

With this approach, the user is constantly aware of the potential or contingent semantics of their entry but without being constrained at all in their entry or correction. The interesting thing about this traffic light approach (and a range of related variations to better suit different sorts of user interface) is that the light colours can be automatically determined from the underlying FSM.

Such a traffic light system uses FSMs but does not work only with an FSM as the display itself acts as a buffer to store the user's actions, so [DEL] etc correctly work on the buffer regardless of its semantics. The system does not accept the user input, as represented on the display, until some form of commit key is pressed and that can only be pressed when the display is green.

8.6.1 Reengineering

If programming user interfaces causes so many problems for programmers, another approach is to consider if the designs themselves are faulty in some way, rather than the programs that implement them. Certainly, computers cannot correctly implement something that is inconsistent.

We should consider stepping back entirely from traditional user interfaces dictated by historic and outmoded technology. Why reproduce mechanical calculators, which inevitably were compromises when now computers can do anything? We should start by asking questions like 'what is the purpose of the system that is intended', in our particular examples 'what is the purpose of a calculator?'

A calculator is used to perform arithmetic calculations that arise in real situations with numbers or calculations that are difficult to do in the head or on paper. Some calculations fit well with entry into traditional calculators: how many oranges do I have if I have twenty-three crates with thirty-five oranges per crate? This problem can be translated into a sequence of key presses that look roughly like 23 × 35. However, many calculations we want to do are far less direct: if a worker works fifty minutes on and ten minutes off every hour for seven hours, and each of their data entry tasks takes on average thirty-five seconds, how many data entry tasks will they get through in a typical working day? Normally, you'd solve this sort of problem with a calculator helped by either using pencil and paper to write down the problem and then converting to a calculation or chancing your luck by a good guess as you work on the calculator. A better solution would be to represent the problem as you understand it in the calculator and then work with the calculator to get the answer. This is precisely the philosophy behind a novel gesture-based calculator (Thimbleby, 2004).

This novel calculator avoids the problem of premature semantics by allowing the user to write whatever they want on the calculating surface. The calculator was designed to allow the user to enter anything, even nonsense, and therefore does not have premature semantics—it does not require or force the user's input to be correct in any way, but uses another colour to correct the user's input. It turns out that correcting the user's input *also* provides the answer to the user's calculation. The relation between correction, error and premature semantics is profound and worth explaining in more detail.

You may want to know what to multiply 2 by to get 6 (you may well want to do something harder, but we are interested here in the principles not the actual problem). On a normal calculator, you might key $\boxed{AC}$ $\boxed{6}$ $\boxed{/}$ $\boxed{2}$ $\boxed{=}$ to get the answer you want, which here will be 3. However, note that you have had to convert the original question using multiplication into a question the calculator can handle, using division.

With the new calculator, typing '2× = 6' is not correct, but would be corrected to show the answer $\boxed{3}$ in the right place: 2 × $\boxed{3}$ = 6. In other words, the flexibility of correcting anything significantly increases the power and flexibility of the calculator.

Or if the new calculator was used like an old one, typing '6/2' is also not correct as it stands, so it would be immediately be corrected to '6/2 $\boxed{=3}$.' If the user continued typing '6/2 =' that is fine too, as it will be corrected to '6/2 = $\boxed{3}$'. Indeed, if the user typed '= 6/2' (i.e., the other way around) that would be corrected to ' $\boxed{3}$ = 6/2'.

See Figure 8.5. The calculator interprets whatever the user tries to enter so if the user cannot represent it, the calculator doesn't make it worse. And the result of the calculation and the calculation itself are co-present and persistent, which means that the user representation can be re-constructed as necessary and even the calculator representation can be re-constructed.

This is a specific solution to the problems of premature semantics that works with arithmetic calculations (which is really useful if that was all it did). However, it does show that really understanding what the user needs can lead to much better systems than the blind adherence to existing ways of doing things that computers, or at least programmers, may struggle with.

Figure 8.5 The classroom version of an intentionally *not* premature semantics calculator. The calculator also runs well on handheld tablets. A photograph of a user interface cannot do the interactive experience justice; the person shown using this calculator is Will Thimbleby, the implementer.

It is interesting how many applications—from mobile phones to word processors, spreadsheets to drawing programs—need numbers but cannot cope with arithmetic! How wide should your margins be is a simple question for a word processor but often needs a calculator to solve it: the calculation is something like the width of A4 paper is 21 cm, a good line length is 6.5 in, so the margin is $(21-6.5 \times 2.54)/2$—but very few apps allow such calculations. Apps prematurely want numbers, which is how they prematurely implement the user's problem, here, $(21-6.5 \times 2.54)/2 = 2.245$, so the programmer thinks 2.245 is good enough (why do something when the user can?) and all the user is allowed to do is enter the number, not an expression. Such 'programmer thinking'—premature semantics requiring numbers rather than calculations—makes the user's work harder.

We don't actually believe programmers *really* think of ways of making the user's life harder (except in some games). What they do is unconsciously make their own lives easier, by prematurely committing to the semantics of input, and that has consequences they are often unaware of. It is far easier to read a number than read an expression, and since a number *is* needed the programmer assumes that is all the user interface needs.

Clearly, the user interface ideas of this calculator are much more general than calculators. Usability studies of this calculator were very encouraging (Thimbleby, W. 2004; Thimbleby, W. and Thimbleby, H. 2005), so it is not just a theoretical discussion about premature semantics.

8.6.2 The Semantics of Interaction

It is well-known in mainstream computer science that compiler correctness is a critical problem; many compilers have subtle bugs, and finding and proving they are free of bugs is a hard research problem. However, once formal methods are used, one can create improved compiler construction processes that avoid entire classes of bugs, as well as construction processes that better match the capabilities of formal methods tools. The goal of such research is to make compilers more dependable, and hence ensure that hardware reliably does what programmers want it to do. In short, compilers are designed to be semantics preserving.

Similarly, a user interface makes hardware perform as the user intends, as expressed through a sequence of interactions with the computer. This is analogous to a compiler that makes hardware perform as the programmer intends—except a programmer inputs a static string (the program source code) whereas the user inputs a sequence of actions, including keystrokes and often two-dimensional gestures, such as taps and strokes, typically using their finger or a mouse (or even 3D in VR, speech and so on). A critical difference is therefore that a program is textual, and a programmer can think about it in various ways, for instance writing it down on paper and reasoning mathematically about it. In contrast, a user interface input almost always has no simple concrete representation, and certainly nothing that could be readily written down on paper and reasoned through.

When a bug is found in a compiler, it is usually very easy to reproduce the bug. A specific fragment of program source code does not do what it should, and it is generally possible to write a program where an assertion fails when the compiler bug causes an incorrect result, and so on. In contrast, when a bug is found in a user interface, reproducing it requires considerable attention to detail because it is not easy to represent and reproduce the interactions that revealed the bug. Indeed, the user who found the bug is unlikely to remember exactly what they did, since the effect of the bug cognitively interferes with their memory of what they are doing.

Seen from this perspective, any interaction with a device requires the preservation of semantics: the meaning that the user intends by their actions is correctly represented in and acted on by the device. At the same time, the fallibility of users needs to be recognized so that not everything a user does should be acted on immediately. In some contexts, such as text entry, this may not be a big concern but in other contexts, particularly ones that are mission critical or safety critical such as aircraft cockpits, it is.

However, historically, there has been little concern for examining the semantics of interaction. To really address semantics and reason about semantic correctness requires the use of what are known as formal methods, of which tools like FSMs and regular expressions form a central part. However, there is virtually no research in formal methods and user interfaces; it is very much a niche concern. In fact, formal methods are often considered counter-productive since even a formally correct user interface may not lead to one that is acceptable to users. Thus, much emphasis in evaluating interfaces is in the experience of users not the correctness of their interactions.

Another cause for the neglect of formal methods comes from a pragmatic view of what it takes to produce user interfaces. User interfaces are 'easy to program' and interaction is an emergent property of executing a program. The formal properties we might want to think about even for apparently simple devices like a calculator, such as display overflow and the regular expression for valid numbers, seems like a long way from the simple tasks that most users would encounter. Moreover, the list of formal properties have not ever been specified, even for calculators which in principle do have formal semantic foundations. Diligent user interface programmers would struggle to formally evaluate a user interface even if they wanted to.

And at the end of the day, much user interface design is about the acceptability of interfaces to users. Most users are tempted to say 'the user interface works'—why worry about a quirky case, which anyway can be avoided in a work-around if the bug ever affects a user (assuming the user notices the bug)? In addition it is well known that conventional informal user interface development (such as focus groups, scenarios, personas, etc) is a critical tool for user interface acceptance. Thus, even what we would identify as bugs in the semantic interpretation of an interaction, users frequently dismiss as not relevant.

8.6.3 Mature Semantics

Moving on from the current loose thinking about user interaction requires several changes that encompass both research and culture. First must come the recognition among programmers, but also more importantly among users, that the process of interacting with a system has meaning. And that meaning is perverted or lost in many existing systems. A person who engaged in such wilful neglect of meaning would be considered a sociopath but we accept such computer systems most often with rolling of eyes. There are many comedic sketches that capture the problem, like 'Computer says no!' (Walliams and Lucas, 2015).

Users need to recognize the importance of preserving meaning in interactions but also that, as with people, this may come with an overhead of interaction that is not quite so quick or occasionally requires a bit more effort on their part. To support this, programmers need to be able to develop interfaces, like the traffic light number entry system, that first are able to support semantics and secondly that can be reasoned about through the use of formal methods.

This last point leads to the third change that is needed, which is more research on what it means for interaction to be semantically correct. We know compilers have bugs; do user interfaces? Do user interface bugs matter? In other words, is research in user interface bugs useful? To address these questions we have the additional problem that user interfaces are not or very rarely formally specified, so the concept of preserving semantics is an awkward concept even before we start! In some cases, like number entry, we are beginning to understand some of the formal properties an interface needs (Cairns and Thimbleby, H, 2017; Thimbleby and Cairns, 2010) and to develop the tools to address them. With other areas like setting up an infusion pump or controlling a semi-autonomous vehicle, we are a long way from even specifying what the semantics should be but such devices already proliferate and are causing problems due to the breakdown of semantic correctness.

8.6.4 The Curse of Knowledge

A profound problem with premature semantics, the reason why it persists and has not previously been recognized, is that *it makes so much sense.* The programmer prematurely committing to a floating point number (calculators) or to an integer (credit card numbers) or to a perfect database (to do lists, web forms) all seem like very fine decisions—much like all the other decisions programmers have to make. If programmers did not make such decisions they would be paralysed and nothing would happen.

Steven Pinker's terrific book *The Sense of Style* (2015) on writing and how to understand writing well discusses the *curse of knowledge.* When we write, we know what we mean, so we tend to write complex sentences and complex paragraphs—what they mean is quite obvious to us, because we know what we are thinking. Our readers on the other hand, do not know what we mean and they have to decode (parse and interpret) what we write to find out. As writers we think this 'decoding' is easy—in fact, we already know what we mean so we don't need to do any decoding to find out! Why are our readers having trouble?

This is the same problem designers and programmers have; instead of writing English, they are programming interactive systems. They, too, have a curse of knowledge—they know what their systems are supposed to do, so their systems seem much easier to them than they really are. (HCI has developed techniques that programmers resist to fix this problem.) Figure 8.6 gives a simple example.

Premature semantics makes sense to programmers and, like the curse of knowledge, it is obvious that it makes sense. Note that 'making sense' is another way of saying 'it has the right semantics.' Hence, because of the curse of knowledge programmers, do not notice they are creating problems for users. So, Steven Pinker will help us write better English for readers; he, properly understood, will also help us design (i.e., write programs for) better interactive systems for users.

Figure 8.6 A familiar dialog box for users of iPhones, but what does it mean? Does pressing "Cancel" mean cancel undo, which means delete, or does pressing "Undo" mean undo undo delete, which probably means delete? So pressing either button means delete? We imagine—we hope—the programmer and other privileged people know what the choice means, and (presumably!) what these buttons means was obvious to them and (presumably!) they mean different things (otherwise why give a vacuous choice to users?). In any case, what exactly are we accused of deleting or undoing deleting that we might want to cancel or undo? Presumably (!) the programmer knows, but they haven't bothered to tell us to help us out of our confusion.

8.7 Conclusions—Moving Towards Mature Semantics

In this chapter, we have considered in some depth the apparently simple task of entering numbers into an interactive system and shown that it is still a surprisingly poorly understood task in interaction design. Premature semantics brings into relief the complexities of such seemingly simple tasks. This motivated our more general discussion of premature semantics, for it applies to all forms of user interface.

With modern user interfaces, data entry is no longer like writing with a pen on paper but is a dynamic, fluid, erroneous and correctable process. Until such processes are deemed complete by the user, it is very risky to assign semantics to what is being entered. Yet without guidance on the semantics, users may end up in a mess. We think our examples of numbers are so basic and widespread—even 'trivial'—that they convince us that they can't possibly be the only problem with user interfaces. They are typical of a whole range of poor user interface design—and why it happens. If something so trivial and apparently well-understood is broken, what else is?

Programmers do not have or prefer not to use tools to systematically identify and address these problems. User Experience practitioners did not (until this chapter) have the vocabulary to describe them, and virtually no vocabulary at all to talk in the same language as programmers need to understand them.

We hold that what is needed is systematic research on formal methods for interaction that allow all concerned to specify and reason about the semantic properties of interaction.

User interactions will change in the future in a way that will affect users (e.g., with implants) profoundly but we would hope that users and HCI workers will see the benefits of being able to avoid premature semantics that limit the user and induce complex errors they cannot fix. There is a better future.

· ·

REFERENCES

Aho, A. V., Sethi, R., and Ullman, J. D., 1986. *Compilers, Principles, Techniques*. Boston, MA: Addison Wesley.

Cairns, P., and Thimbleby, H., 2017. Interactive numerals. *Royal Society Open Science*, 4(160903).

Card, S. K., Moran, T. P., and Newell, A., 1980. The keystroke-level model for user performance time with interactive systems. *Communications of the ACM*, 23(7), pp. 396–410.

Degani, A., 2004. *Taming HAL: Designing interfaces beyond 2001*. New York, NY: Springer.

Gasen, J. B., 1995. Support for HCI educators: A view from the trenches. In: *Proceedings BCS HCI Conference*, Volume X, Cambridge: Cambridge University Press, pp. 15–20.

Gow, J., and Thimbleby, H., 2005. Maui: An interface design tool based on matrix algebra. In: *Computer-Aided Design of User Interfaces IV*. New York, NY: Springer, pp. 81–94.

Institute for Safe Medication Practices, 2015. *ISMP List of Error-Prone Abbreviations, Symbols, and Dose Designations*. Horsham, PA: ISMP.

Jackson, D., 2011. *Software Abstractions: Logic, Language, and Analysis*. 2nd ed. Cambridge, MA: MIT Press.

Landauer, T. K., 1995. *The trouble with computers: Usefulness, usability, and productivity*. Volume 21. Milton Park, UK: Taylor & Francis.

Li, S., Cox, A. L., Blandford, A., Cairns, P., Young, R. M., and Abeles, A., 2006. Further investigations into post-completion error: the effects of interruption position and duration. In: *Proceedings of the 28th Annual Meeting of the Cognitive Science Conference*. Mahweh, NJ: Lawrence Erlbaum, pp. 471–6.

Mulligan, R. M., Altom, M. W., and Simkin, D. K., 1991. User interface design in the trenches: Some tips on shooting from the hip. In: *CHI '91: Proceedings of the SIGCHI Conference on Human Factors in Computing Systems*. New York, NY: ACM, pp. 232–6.

Olsen, K. A., 2008. The $100,000 keying error. *IEEE Computer*, 41(108), pp. 106–7.

Pinker, S., 2015. *The Sense of Style: The Thinking Person's Guide to Writing in the 21st Century!* London: Penguin Books.

Rogers, Y., 2012. HCI theory: classical, modern, and contemporary. *Synthesis Lectures on Human-Centered Informatics*, 5(2), pp. 1–129.

Salah, D., Paige, R. F., and Cairns, P., 2014. A systematic literature review for agile development processes and user centred design integration. In: *Proceedings of the 18th international conference on evaluation and assessment in software engineering*. New York, NY: ACM, p. 5.

Sharp, J., Rogers, Y., and Preece, J., 2007. *Interaction design: beyond human-computer interaction*. Oxford: John Wiley.

Sommerville, I., 2015. *Software Engineering*. 10th ed. London: Pearson.

Thimbleby, H., 2000. Calculators are needlessly bad. *International Journal of Human-Computer Studies*, 52(6), pp. 1031–69.

Thimbleby, H., 2004. User interface design with matrix algebra. *ACM Transactions on Computer-Human Interaction (TOCHI)*, 11(2), pp. 181–236.

Thimbleby, H., 2010. *Press On: Principles of interaction programming*. Cambridge, MA: MIT Press.

Thimbleby, H., 2013. Reasons to question seven segment displays. In: *Proceedings of the SIGCHI Conference on Human Factors in Computing Systems*. New York, NY: ACM, pp. 1431–40.

Thimbleby, H., 2015. Safer user interfaces: A case study in improving number entry. *IEEE Transactions on Software Engineering*, 41(7), pp. 711–29.

Thimbleby, H., and Bornat, R., 1989. The life and times of Ded, display editor. In: J. B. Long and A. Whitefield, eds. *Cognitive Ergonomics and Human Computer Interaction*. Cambridge: Cambridge University Press, pp. 225–55.

Thimbleby, H., and Cairns, P., 2010. Reducing number entry errors: Solving a widespread, serious problem. *Journal of the Royal Society Interface*, rsif20100112.

Thimbleby, H., Cairns, P., and Jones, M., 2001. Usability analysis with Markov models. *ACM Transactions on Computer-Human Interaction (TOCHI)*, 8(2), pp. 99–132.

Thimbleby, H., and Gimblett, A., 2010. User interface model discovery: Towards a generic approach. In: G. Doherty, J. Nichols, and Michael D. Harrison, eds. *Proceedings ACM SIGCHI Symposium on Engineering Interactive Computing Systems — EICS 2010*. New York, NY: ACM, pp. 145–54.

Thimbleby, H., and Gimblett, A., 2011. Dependable keyed data entry for interactive systems. *Electronic Communications of the EASST*, 45, pp. 1/16–16/16.

Thimbleby, W., 2004. A novel pen-based calculator and its evaluation. In: *Proceedings of the third Nordic conference on Human-computer interaction*. New York, NY: ACM, pp. 445–8.

Thimbleby, W., and Thimbleby, H., 2005. A novel gesture-based calculator and its design principles. In: *Proceedings of the 19th BCS HCI Conference*. Volume 2. State College, PA: Citeseer, pp. 27–32.

Turing, A. M., 1936. On computable numbers, with an application to the entscheidungsproblem. *Proceedings of the London Mathematical Society*, 42, pp. 230–65.

Turing, A. M., 1938. On computable numbers, with an application to the entscheidungsproblem: A correction. *Proceedings of the London Mathematical Society*, 43, pp. 544–6.

Walliams, D., and Lucas, M., 'Computer says "no"', BBC, May 29, 2015.

Young, R. M., 1981. The machine inside the machine: Users' models of pocket calculators. *International Journal of Man-Machine Studies*, 15(1), pp. 51–85.

9

Performance Evaluation of Interactive Systems with Interactive Cooperative Objects Models

CÉLIA MARTINIE,
PHILIPPE PALANQUE,
CAMILLE FAYOLLAS

9.1 Introduction

Arguments to support validity of most contributions in the field of Human-Computer Interaction (HCI) are based on detailed results of empirical studies involving cohorts of tested users confronted with a set of tasks and an interactive prototype. Interestingly enough, the same approach is used by the industry when building new interactive applications, and by the academia when innovating with new interaction techniques. Based on iterative and User Centered Design processes as the ones promoted in (Göransson et al., 2003) or (Mayhew, 1999), these evaluations are conducted either on controlled conditions (i.e., usability labs) or on working environment (e.g., ethnographical studies). Such usability tests-driven contributions are both extremely empirical (forecasting of user tests results is not usually performed) and highly inefficient in terms of development costs (as several versions of systems have to be developed prior to run user tests in order to identify the ones that are possibly valuable).

Another way of handling the usability property problem is to base the work on models in order to be able to predict the overall performance (or the existence of properties in the resulting system). Such models can be used at design level and prior to implementation and their use is even required in the area of critical systems following development standards such as DO-178C (DO-178C, 2012) and more precisely, its supplement DO-333 (DO-333, 2011, p. 101). For instance, such standards state that high-level requirements should be modelled using (for instance) temporal logic (Emerson and Srinivasan, 1988), while low-level requirements should be modelled using state-based description techniques, e.g., Petri nets (Reisig, 2013). Compliance between these two models has to be done using

Computational Interaction. Antti Oulasvirta, Per Ola Kristensson, Xiaojun Bi, Andrew Howes (Eds).

model-checking techniques (Clarke et al., 2009). In that area, the term model corresponds to behavioural descriptions of software systems.

In the field of HCI, such model-based approaches have been used in two different directions. Models (in the meaning of **science** (Lee, 2016)) used to understand the world and to produce predictions (e.g., Fitts' law (Fitts, 1954) or Hick's law used in (Cockburn et al., 2007) to predict user performance on menus usage or (Lee and Oulasvirta, 2016) to predict error rates in temporal pointing). In that meaning, the quality of the model depends on its precision in representing the part of the world it is aimed at describing; there the goal is the proposition and the production of the *model*. Models (in the meaning of **engineering**) are used to produce a system that is supposed to carry the properties expressed in the model. Hence, the quality of the model lies in the information it contains and the quality of the system produced depends on how it covers what is expressed in the model; there the goal is the production of the *system*. Such approaches have been used in the area of engineering interactive systems (both for understanding what interactive systems are (e.g., the PIE model (see Dix, 1991)) and for building reliable, dependable, and usable multimodal interactive systems from formal models (Ladry et al., 2009) among many others.

This chapter presents an approach integrating both views presented here. More precisely, we present how a model (in the engineering meaning) can be enhanced with models (in the meaning of science) describing human (in terms of perceptive, motoric, and cognitive behaviour). This chapter thus presents a tool-supported generic framework for integrating user models into interactive systems engineering technologies. The performance evaluation techniques proposed aim at providing designers with data for comparing different designs of interactive systems. Therefore, this chapter does not present any contribution related to design aspects of interactive systems; new models of users nor provides means of calculating absolute values for usability or user experience properties.

9.2 Content and Objectives of the Chapter

This section provides an executive summary of the objectives of the chapter as well as its content. In order to do so, we first introduce the fundamental principles of interactive systems and, more precisely, their software and hardware architecture as we use these elements throughout the chapter. We then present the objectives of the paper and detail its content.

9.2.1 Principles of Interactive Systems

Interactive systems are a special class of computer systems that process (in real-time) inputs provided by users and produce outputs that are meant to be perceived and interpreted by users. Input and output are processed by the users exploiting dedicated physical devices such as keyboards and screens. Figure 9.1 presents a generic architecture for interactive systems where the main elements (at a coarse grain) are on the sides of the figure: physical interaction management (handling input and output devices and their respective drivers), logical interaction (that incorporates input and rendering management), and the

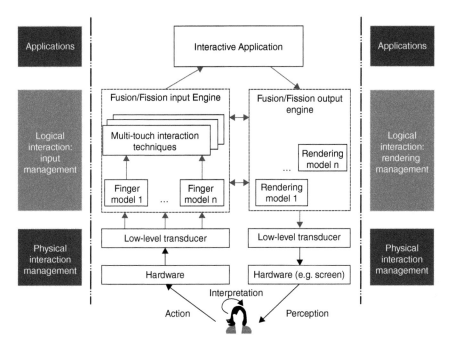

Figure 9.1 Generic architecture for interactive systems tuned for multi-touch applications.

interactive application at the higher level of abstraction. The middle part of the figure provides details on how this layered architecture can be refined and tuned for interactive systems offering multi-touch interactions. The flow of information is represented as a cycle from the user (bottom of the figure) exploiting input devices (and their associated interaction techniques), to the interactive application (top of the figure) and back to the user by means of information presentations (via the rendering engines) exploiting output devices and their drivers. As represented right in the middle of the figure, this loop may exhibit shortcuts (double-ended arrows) making it possible, for instance, to produce immediate feedback to the user (e.g., when displaying the new position of the mouse cursor when the user manipulates the mouse).

This architecture corresponds to a refinement of ARCH (Bass et al., 1991) architectural model proposed in the early 1990s. More importantly, this architecture offers a clear separation between hardware related elements and the other layers. Finally, it goes beyond ARCH by making explicit the role of input and output fusion and fission engines that are in charge of producing high-level events (and their associated interaction techniques) from low-level inputs produced by the users when they manipulate physically the input and output devices.

9.2.2 Objectives of the Chapter

The objective of this chapter is to present an integrated framework for both the predictive and summative performance evaluation of interactive systems. This framework is three-fold.

First, we present a formal modelling technique allowing the complete representation of the behaviour of interactive systems. This notation allows developers representing both hardware and software components of interactive systems going from input/output devices to interactive applications covering also the intermediate software layer of interaction techniques. This description technique is fully executable, making it possible to run the models as prototypes of the future system and amenable to formal verification to assess presence or absence of desirable properties (e.g., safety and liveness).[1] Second, we propose a generic approach to enrich those behavioural descriptions with human models including perceptive, cognitive, and motor information. These enriched models are then computed in order to perform predictive performance evaluation of the couple (human, interactive system). Lastly, we present a tool-supported process to perform systematic usability tests (on the final interactive system) based on precisely described scenarios and automatic logging of both user actions and evolutions of the interactive system models. Due to its connection to interactive system models, this information (gathered during user testing) supports the identification of the modification to be performed in order to improve the overall performance. Finally, we exemplify this three-fold approach on an industrial application in the area of interactive cockpits, demonstrating both its applicability and the benefits that can be brought by a model-based approach for interactive systems design, implementation, and evaluation.

9.2.3 Content of the Chapter

The chapter is structured as follows. Section 9.3 introduces a list of requirements for modelling interactive systems and presents the ICO[2] modelling technique for interactive application that is used throughout the chapter. We highlight the benefits of this modelling technique and demonstrate how it is able to model all the elements of an interactive system. Section 9.4 presents the approach to support predictive evaluation based on the calculation of the performance of 'engineering' models from computer science enriched with 'science' models from psychology. Section 9.5 presents the approach to support summative evaluation based on the logging of 'engineering' models at execution time. This supports activities of user testing and targets more specifically at the evaluation of interaction techniques. Section 9.6 presents PetShop, the environment for the editing, the verification, and the simulation of ICO models. This environment supports many aspects related to performance evaluation that go beyond what the notation alone can do. Section 9.7 presents the application of the approach described in Section 9.4 on a case study from the avionics domain. Enriched ICO models of this interactive application are used to predict the performance of the operators interacting with it. Section 9.8 presents the use of the summative evaluation approach from Section 9.5 on a case study of a multimodal interaction technique. Section 9.9 summarizes the lessons learned and concludes the paper.

---

[1] We refer here to the definition provided in (Pnueli, 1986) where safety is 'nothing bad will ever happen' and liveness 'something good will eventually happen'.

[2] Interactive Cooperative Objects (Navarre et al., 2009).

9.3 A Model-Based Approach for Complete and Unambiguous Description of Interactive Systems

This section presents the ICO (Interactive Cooperative Objects) modelling technique for interactive applications. It first introduces a list of requirements for modelling interactive systems and then presents the ICO notation, highlighting the benefits of this modelling technique and demonstrating how it is able to model all the elements of an interactive system. Finally, we highlight how the ICO modelling technique enables the properties assessment of interactive systems.

9.3.1 Describing Interactive Systems

The wide range of existing interaction techniques and associated input and output devices highlights the scientific community's effort and its recurring desire of increasing the bandwidth between the interactive system and users. For this reason, more sophisticated interaction techniques and previously unexplored interaction means are continuously being proposed. Furthermore, if the users' tasks are complex as, for instance, requiring the execution of multiple commands in a short period of time or the manipulation of large data sets (e.g., the pilot checking the weather radar implemented in the cockpit), it is likely that the new interaction techniques will significantly improve the overall performance of the operators, even though context might deeply influence the overall performance (Cockburn et al., 2017). A list of the requirements for these interaction techniques includes:

- Objects and values should be explicitly described and represented;
- States should be explicitly described and represented;
- Events should be explicitly described and represented;
- Qualitative time between two consecutive model elements should be made explicit for representing ordering of actions such as precedence, succession, and simultaneity;
- Quantitative time between two consecutive model elements should represent behavioural temporal evolutions related to a given amount of time (usually expressed in milliseconds);
- Quantitative time over non-consecutive elements for multi-input devices and fusion of interactions should be explicitly represented; and
- Concurrent behaviour should be explicitly described. It is necessary when the interactive systems feature multimodal interactions or can be used simultaneously by several users.

User interface (UI) components might be fully defined at design time (e.g., a set of user interface buttons in a window) or might be created and presented at runtime (e.g., a new icon is added on a Desktop application each time a new file is created). This creation of UI objects at runtime is the result of the dynamic instantiation of objects from classes (in the object-oriented programming paradigm). Being able to handle these new objects within the formalism is mandatory to be able to reason about them (for instance, to ensure that the number of dynamic instantiations is bounded). In the context of multi-touch interactions, touching the screen with a finger changes the interaction in a similar way as adding a new mouse in WIMP interactions requiring dynamic instantiation management for input and output devices that can be added or removed at runtime:

- Dynamic instantiation of widgets should be represented explicitly;
- Dynamic instantiation of devices should be represented explicitly;
- Reconfiguration of interaction technique should be represented explicitly;
- Reconfiguration of low level events should be represented explicitly.

9.3.2 Petri Nets as a Concurrent Behavioural Model for Describing Interactive Systems

9.3.2.1 Introduction to Petri Nets

C. A. Petri (1962) introduced Petri nets , which have been since then extensively used for the modelling of discrete event systems. Petri nets are a formalism that features a complete equivalence between a graphical and an algebraic representation thus making it possible to perform mathematical analysis of models. In few words, a Petri net is an oriented graph composed of a set of places (usually represented by ellipses), which symbolize state variables, holding tokens, which symbolize values, and a set of transitions (usually represented by rectangles), which symbolize actions and state changes. A set of arcs connect places to transitions (called input arcs) or transitions to places (called output arcs), and represents the flow of tokens through the Petri net model. The distribution of tokens across the set of places (called marking) represents the state of the modelled system. The dynamic behaviour of a marked Petri net is expressed by means of two rules: the enabling rule, and the firing rule. A transition is enabled if each input place (places linked to the transition with input arcs) contains at least as many tokens as the weight of the input arcs it is linked to. When an enabled transition is fired, tokens are removed from the input places of the transition and new tokens are deposited into the output places (the number of tokens is defined by the weight on the output arcs). These rules illustrate one of the main properties of Petri nets, called locality of enabling and firing of transitions, which makes, for instance, Petri nets enabled to model true concurrent systems. This is because the firing of a transition only impacts its input and output places, leaving the rest of the model unchanged.

9.3.2.2 Introduction to the Interactive Cooperative Objects Formal notation

Interactive Cooperative Objects (ICO) is a formal description technique based on Petri nets and dedicated to the specification of interactive systems (Navarre et al., 2009). It uses concepts borrowed from the object-oriented approach (dynamic instantiation, classification, encapsulation, inheritance, client/server relationship) to describe the structural or static aspects of systems, and uses high-level Petri nets (Genrich, 1991) to describe their dynamic or behavioural aspects.

ICOs are dedicated to the modelling and the implementation of event-driven interfaces, using several communicating objects to model the system, where both behaviour of objects and communication protocol between objects that are described by Petri nets. In the ICO formalism, an object is an entity featuring four components (Navarre et al., 2009):

- *Cooperative Object (CO)*: a cooperative object models the behaviour of an ICO. It states how the object reacts to external stimuli according to its inner state. This behaviour, called the Object Control Structure (ObCS) is described by means of high-level Petri net. A CO offers two kinds of services to its environment. The first one, described with Java software interfaces, concerns the services (in the programming language terminology) offered to other objects in the environment. The second one, called user services, provides a description of the elementary actions offered to a user, but for which availability depends on the internal state of the cooperative object (this state is represented by the distribution and the value of the tokens (called marking) in the places of the ObCS).

- *Presentation part*: the Presentation of an object states its external appearance. This Presentation is a structured set of widgets organized in a set of windows. Each widget may be a way to interact with the interactive system (user → system interaction) and/or a way to display information from this interactive system (system → user interaction).

- *Activation function*: the user → system interaction (inputs) only takes place through widgets. Each user action on a widget may trigger one of the ICO's user services. The relation between user services and widgets is fully stated by the activation function that associates to each couple (widget, user action) the user service to be triggered.

- *Rendering function*: the system → user interaction (outputs) aims at presenting to the user the state changes that occurs in the system. The rendering function maintains the consistency between the internal state of the system and its external appearance by reflecting system states changes.

More concretely, ICO models are Petri net in terms of structure and behaviour, but they hold a much more complex set of information. For instance, in the ICO notation, tokens in the places can hold a typed set of values that can be references to other objects (allowing, for instance, its use in a transition for method calls) or preconditions about the actual value of some attributes of the tokens. For instance, in Figure 9.2, the tokens in places 'p0', 'p1',

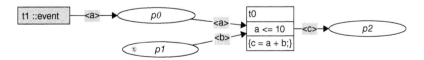

Figure 9.2 ICO model representing events and tokens with value.

and '*p2*' may hold an integer value respectively labelled '*a,*' '*b,*' and '*c.*' The Object Petri nets formalism also allows the use of test arcs that are used for testing presence and values of tokens without removing them from the input place while firing the transition (e.g., the arc connecting place '*p1*' to transition '*t0*' in Figure 9.2).

The ICO notation also encompasses multicast asynchronous communication principles that enables, upon the reception of an event, the firing of some transitions. For instance, the transition '*t1*' in Figure 9.2 is fired upon the receipt of an event named event that will result in the deposit of a new token in place '*p0*'.

9.3.2.3 On the Benefits and Need to use ICO as a Formal Model for Interactive Systems

Only Petri nets are able to cope with the explicit representation of concurrency as they embed a true concurrency semantics. Indeed, transitions firing in Petri nets only affect input and output places of a given transition. It is thus possible to make a Petri net evolve on a parallel computer and trigger multiple firing at a time. This make the use of Petri nets mandatory if users' behaviour (that is highly concurrent by nature) has to be described.

Petri nets make it possible to describe a system with an infinite number of states. Indeed, a state of a system is modelled as the distribution of tokens (and their value) in all the places of the net. This means that the tokens provide an implicit representation of the states. This is very different from Statecharts (Harel and Naamad, 1996) of Automata (Woods, 1970), where each state is represented by a graphical element in the model (e.g., a circle for automata). This makes these notations unable to deal with large or real-life systems having a large number of states. As in interactive systems, the states have to be presented to the user and as the number of states are usually huge, Petri nets are a very good candidate for modelling interactive systems as argued in (Bastide and Palanque, 1995). Figure 9.3 presents a Petri net describing the parenthesis language. At any time, a new parenthesis can be opened, but closing one can only be done when at least one parenthesis has previously been opened. In the current state of Figure 9.3, four parentheses have been opened (four tokens in place '*p0*'). Such behaviour cannot be represented with an automaton nor with a Statechart. The list of parentheses would have to be handled as an external data structure and thus, formal analysis will not take this into account.

The ICO notation fulfills all the requirements presented in Section 9.2.1. An ICO specification fully describes the potential interactions that users may have with the application. The specification encompasses both the 'input' aspects of the interaction (i.e., how user actions affects the inner state of the application, and which actions are enabled at any given time) and its 'output' aspects (i.e., when and how the application displays information relevant to the user).

ICO provides support for describing explicit representation of dynamic instantiation requires the notation to be able to explicitly represent an unbounded number of states, as

Figure 9.3 ICO model with an 'infinite' number of state representing the use of parenthesis.

the newly created objects will by definition represent a new state for the system. Most of the time, this characteristic is handled by means of code and remains outside the User Interface Description Languages (UIDL). Only Petri nets-based UIDLs can represent explicitly such a characteristic, provided they handle high-level data structures, or objects. So, the description language must be able to receive dynamically created objects. This dynamicity has also to be addressed at operation time (i.e., when the system is currently in use). An ICO specification is fully executable, which gives the possibility to prototype and test an application before it is fully implemented (Palanque et al., 2009). Multi-touch interactions are now widely available but their modelling remains a deep challenge. Indeed, fingers used on a multi-touch input device can be seen as dynamic instantiation and removal of input devices (e.g., one finger is similar to one mouse). ICOs are able to address this challenge, as demonstrated in (Hamon et al., 2013) going even to finger clustering interaction techniques as presented in (Hamon et al., 2014).

9.3.3 Properties Assessment of Interactive Systems

In addition to standard properties of computer systems (such as safety or liveness), interaction properties have been identified. Properties related to the usage of an interactive system are called external properties (Bass et al., 2004; Gram and Cockton, 1996), and characterize the capacity of the system to provide support for its users to accomplish their tasks and goals, potentially in several ways, and prevent or help to recover from errors. Although all types of properties are not always completely independent one from each other, external properties are related to the user's point of view and usability factor, whereas internal properties are related to the design and development process of the system itself (e.g., modifiability, run time efficiency). Interactive systems have to support both types of properties and dedicated techniques and approaches have been studied for this purpose, among which are formal methods. Formal languages have proven their value in several domains and are a necessary condition to understand, design, and develop systems and check their properties.

The use of formal description techniques can be greatly enhanced if they are supported by formal analysis techniques. In the area of Petri nets, such analysis techniques can be used for the detection of deadlocks (when no transitions are available/fireable in the Petri net model), the presence or absence of a terminating state, the boundedness of the model, the liveness of the model, the reversibility and home state, or to verify requirements, i.e., to verify properties of the system model such that a certain state can never be reached for example or that a given interface component is always enabled. Furthermore, certain analysis techniques can be used to extract scenarios of events leading to a particular state; this is useful for tracing history and for connecting interactive systems behaviour to incidents or accidents (Basnyat et al., 2006).

9.3.3.1 Structural Analysis

Petri nets provide a number of benefits for designers who wish to reason about the behaviour of an interactive system. Numerous formal analysis techniques exist which can be used to analyse and verify the correctness of the models. Methods of analysis include checking for service availability, which can be used to identify deadlocks and analyse the model liveness (i.e., for every widget, there will always be at least one sequence of events available on the user interface that will make that widget enabled). When modelling a system, it may be important to ensure that the initial state is always reachable (through a sequence of actions). This is particularly relevant for safety-critical interactive systems that may be required to reset/restart/shutdown quickly in an emergency situation. Such properties allow evaluation of the quality of the model before system implementation. A more detailed description on how to perform formal analysis of Petri nets models representing user interface behaviours can be found in (Palanque and Bastide, 1995).

The analysis on ICO models is performed on the underlying Petri net (a basic Place/Transition Petri net simplification of the original Petri net). The advantage of the underlying Petri net is that classical properties listed earlier are possible to prove with dedicated algorithms, but an important drawback is that properties verified by the underlying Petri Net are not necessary true on the original one. Thus, we usually use the result of classical property analysis as an indicator that highlights potential problems in the Petri net. Verifying these properties directly on the ICOs model is still a research challenge for the Petri nets community, which is still focusing on Petri nets with reduced expressive power as coloured Petri nets (Jensen et al., 2007). This chapter focuses on the use of formal methods (and more particularly of the ICO modelling technique) for the assessment of the efficiency of an interactive system through the predictive and summative evaluation of the performance of the couple (user, system). However, the ICO modelling technique can also be used of the verification of interactive systems properties (e.g., Palanque and Bastide, 1995; Palanque et al., 2006).

9.3.3.2 Reachability Analysis

Since our interest is in HCI, tracing scenarios of activities (both user and system) is particularly useful. Formal analysis technique based on marking graphs (called reachability analysis) may be used to identify the set of reachable states for a given model. The analysis starts from a known initial marking and identifies all the markings that a model can possibly reach, as well as the necessary conditions and event sequences that lead to each marking. As the state space might be huge, symbolic marking graphs (Chiola et al., 1997) may be constructed gathering in one symbolic state all the states that accept the same commands. ICO models are amenable to such verification technique, as demonstrated in (Silva et al., 2014).

The tools that are to be used for performing formal analysis of models require adequate user interfaces and should follow user-centered design. Petshop, the CASE tool supporting ICO modelling, has been designed in that way and details are available in (Fayollas et al., 2017).

9.4 Predictive Evaluation: Predictions through Enriching Behavioural Models with User Models

In the area of HCI, user performance evaluation has started in the early eighties with the work presented in (Card et al., 1980) and more detailed in (Card et al., 1983). Building on this early work, the Goals–Operators–Methods–Selections (GOMS) family has grown up, and a summary of this work can be found in (John and Kieras, 1996a; John and Kieras, 1996b). In Brumby et al., (2017), a chapter provides a deep related work on that topic. This section presents how to modify behavioural models in order to integrate human performance information.

9.4.1 User Models for Standard Behaviour and Deviations

Main user models, e.g., ACT-R (Anderson, 1993), EPIC (Kieras and Meyer, 1997), and the human model processor (Card et al., 1986) promote decomposition of user's behaviour in three main components. According to terminology used in (Card et al., 1986), these three components are: Motor Processor, Perceptual Processor, and Cognitive Processor.

In earlier work, we proposed to add temporal information (provided by those user models) to transitions in the system model represented using the ICO formalism (Navarre et al., 2009). Even though this approach works for generic performance evaluation, it does not allow for more complex and specific performance evaluation, taking into account, for instance, factors such as the impact of previous action on the performance of next action. In order to deal with such specific aspects that have a real impact on performance evaluation, we propose a different approach based on the extension and the transformation of the system model. With adequate modifications, we are able to represent temporal information relating to motoric user activity. Information related to user activity (both cognitive and perceptual) cannot be added to system model. Thus, we build a dedicated model for each of these elements that will be extended with temporal information.

9.4.1.1 Predictive Evaluation of Motoric Time

Human factors' resources have been investigated using two approaches: the keystroke-level model (Card et al., 1980), and Fitts' law (Fitts, 1954). The first approach has not been used in this study as it is more suitable for interaction with keyboard and mouse and only provides average values. We decided to use Fitts' law as more accurate, and its application to motor movements can be directly exploited. Fitts' law is presented in Formula (1) and is more general as it represents an index of difficulty for reaching a target (of a given size) from a given distance. Movement time for a user to access a target depends on width of the target (W) and the distance between the start point of the pointer and the center of target (A).

$$MT = a + b \log_2(2A/W) \qquad (9.1)$$

For predicting movement time on the systems under consideration constants are set as follows: a=0 and b=100ms (mean value for users).

In order to be able to estimate time movement using Fitts' law, we have to know where the movement starts and where it finishes. This is the reason why enriched ICO models contain transitions for representing all the possible movement on the interactive system. For instance, with a numeric keypad, estimated time when pressing button 1 immediately after pressing button 9 is different from pressing button 1 immediately after pressing button 2. Figure 9.4 presents the steps for enriching an ICO model with all possible motoric actions.

For each input interaction (represented by a transition in the ICO model):

For each possible movement
- ○ Add a transition that represents where the movement starts and where it finishes,
- ○ Place this transition between the incoming place and the outgoing place of the existing transition describing the currently targeted input interaction (in parallel with the described input interaction),
- ○ Add an action in the newly inserted transition to cumulate the estimated time to perform the possible motoric activity.

Figure 9.4 Steps for enriching an ICO model with motoric time predictions.

9.4.1.2 Predictive Evaluation of Cognitive Time

We use several user models to predict time performance of cognitive activities. Generic activities are quantified using work presented in (Card et al., 1986). In this work, mean cycle time for cognitive activity is set at 100ms [25~170ms]. When possible, we refine time predictions for specific cognitive activities for which more precise models exist. For example, Russo (1978) estimated that the cognitive activity of comparing two numbers is about 33ms. At decision level, the Hick–Hyman law (Hick 1952, Hyman 1953) describes human decision time as a function of the information content conveyed by a visual stimulus. These models are modelled using ICO notation in Section 9.3.2.2, and more precisely in Figure 9.13 and Figure 9.14.

For the sake of legibility, we show the use of simple user models in the evaluation process but our approach is compliant with complex cognitive models. Indeed, ICO notation provides supports for producing models that describe cognitive actions as well as for embedding time estimations in the models. Thanks to the notation, it is possible to describe concurrent actions as well as mutual exclusions between actions.

9.4.1.3 Predictive Evaluation of Perceptual Time

Here, again, temporal value comes from work described in (Card et al., 1986). Average time needed for the eye to capture information is about 100ms, but is subject to users' variability [50~200ms]. As for cognitive time we use the average value of 70ms, but, more complex temporal functions could be represented in models.

Figure 9.6(a) presents the sequence of stages as well are required and produced artefacts for the predictive performance evaluation of interactive systems.

In Figure 9.6(a), the process starts with the production of models that describe the behaviour of the interactive system. The output models serve as a basis for producing enriched dialog models with motoric actions by following the steps presented in Section 9.3.1.1. Cognitive and perceptive behaviour modelling stages aim at producing cognitive and perceptive behavioural models from human cognitive and perceptive performance laws. All the types of models are then the input for the predictive evaluation step. For this predictive evaluation stage, another input is required: evaluation scenarios. Evaluation scenarios describe the list of user actions that are relevant for the predictive evaluation (Figure 9.5). Dialogue models and enriched dialogue models are inputs to identify possible

```
Initialize time variable
For each user action in the scenario
        - If the user action is motoric
                ○ Search for the corresponding transition in the enriched dialog model
                ○ Increment time variable with time estimation produced in the transition
        - If the user action is cognitive
                ○ Search for the corresponding transition in the cognitive behaviour ICO model
                ○ Increment time variable with time estimation produced in the transition
        - If the user action is perceptive
                ○ Search for the corresponding transition in the perceptive behaviour ICO model
                ○ Increment time variable with time estimation produced in the transition
```

Figure 9.5 Steps for predicting time for one scenario.

sequences of actions as well as to identify sequences of actions that may decrease user performance. The predictive evaluation step consists in taking each scenario and performing the sum of action time for each action described in the scenario. Figure 9.6 presents in details the steps of the predictive evaluation stage.

In this process for predictive evaluation of user performance, it is important to note that real-time execution of the enriched dialogue models is not possible, in contrary to real-time execution of dialogue models. Furthermore, the predictive evaluation process suits to the application layer of the generic layered architecture for interactive systems (presented in Section 9.2 and in Figure 9.1). We enrich dialogue models of the application only, and not device driver models and interaction technique models. These other types of models are required for the summative evaluation.

9.5 Summative Evaluation: Predictions through Model-based User Study

User testing is a very well-known evaluation technique based on the observation of users performing tasks with a system. It can be used to assess the usability evaluation of interactive systems with respect to its effectiveness (i.e., users can perform their tasks), efficiency (i.e., tasks can be performed without any unnecessary delay), and user satisfaction. While specific questionnaires and interviews provide support for measuring user satisfaction, the execution of controlled tasks provide support for measuring efficiency and effectiveness. Users can be extremely fast so that it is often difficult to observe all events raised by them. The protocol for conducting user testing is out of the scope of this chapter. Our goal is just to demonstrate how it is possible to collect and trace back into interaction technique and device driver models the user actions. The summative evaluation process suits to the physical interaction and logical interaction layers of the generic layered architecture for interactive systems (presented in Section 9.1 and in Figure 9.1).

Figure 9.6(b) illustrates the general iterative approach for the assessment of interaction techniques. This chapter addresses the shaded parts of the process and we assume that early

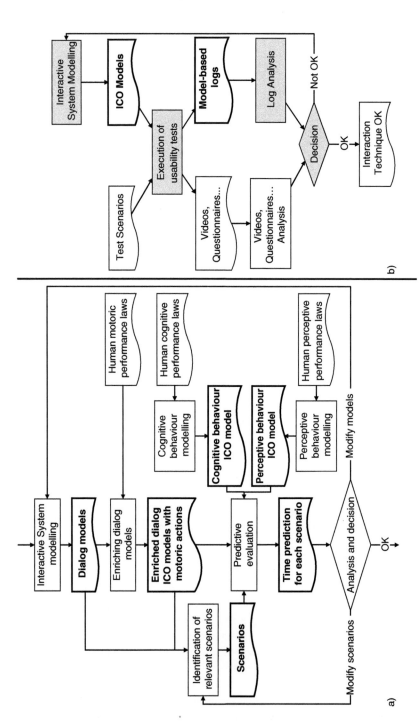

Figure 9.6 Processes for a) predictive evaluation of user performance with interactive systems and b) summative evaluation of interaction techniques.

steps such as requirements analysis, design, and low-fidelity prototyping have been carried out previously.

Figure 9.6(b) presents the process that starts with interactive system modelling. We use several types of artefacts including test scenarios, i.e., behavioural models of the interactive system (using the ICO description technique for describing both the general behaviour of the interaction technique and the treatment of low-level events from input devices). The prototype, running with ICO models, then follows a usability evaluation plan based on user testing. The output of the usability evaluation includes logs data that can be classical logs such as video or questionnaires, as well as model-based logs (that are related to the ICO models). These logs thus provide support for the assessment of the models of the interaction technique. They help in analysing whether or not the performance of these techniques meets the corresponding requirements and allows iterating (the rhombus box labelled 'Decision' in Figure 9.6(b)). The main idea is that usability problems discovered with the usability test can now point out these problems in the interactive system models themselves, making it easier for designer both to locate where changes have to be made and additionally how to make them.

The approach is quite generic but heavily dependent of a tool support and formalism able to support the main assumptions drew about models. In the present case, the approach exploits the ICO notation for describing the entire behaviour of the interaction techniques and relies on the tool support Petshop for executing ICO models.

9.6 Petshop: A CASE Tool Supporting the ICO Notation

PetShop (Petri net workshop) is a tool for creating, editing, simulating, and analysing system models using the ICO (Interactive Cooperative Objects) notation (Navarre et al., 2009).

9.6.1 Main Features of PetShop

Thanks to PetShop, an ICO specification is fully executable, which makes possible to prototype and to test an application before it is fully implemented (Palanque et al., 2009). Figure 9.7 presents a screenshot of a running ICO specification and the corresponding user interface. On this Figure, we highlighted the part of the ICO model (see Figure 9.7(a)) corresponding to the tilt selection part of the user interface (see Figure 9.7(b)). The state of this part of the user interface is defined by the state of the ICO model. First, the place AUTO holds a token, meaning that the tilt selection is automatic; this is visible on the user interface with the label 'TILT SELECTION: AUTO'. Second, the activation of interactive objects is directly connected to the activation of event handlers in the ICO model: the button 'Manual' is enabled as the transition 'switchManualcb ::switchManual' (supporting the 'switchManual' event handler) is fireable. On the contrary, the button 'Auto' is disabled as the transition 'switchAutocb ::switchAuto' (supporting the event handler 'switchAuto') is not fireable.

The PetShop tool provides the means to analyse ICO models by the underlying Petri net model (Silva et al., 2014) using static analysis techniques as supported by the Petri net

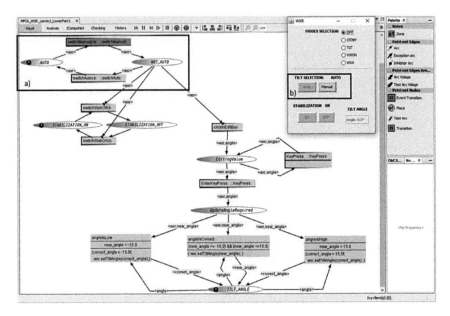

Figure 9.7 Screenshot of a running ICO specification in the PetShop tool and its associated user interface.

theory (Peterson, 1981). The ICO approach is based on high-level Petri nets. As a result, the analysis approach builds on and extends these static analysis techniques. The analyst must carefully consider analysis results as the underlying Petri net model can be quite different from the ICO model. Such analysis has been included in Petshop and can be interleaved with the editing and simulation of the model, thus helping to correct it in a style that is similar to that provided by spell checkers in modern text editors (Fayollas et al., 2017). It is thus possible to check well-formedness properties of the ICO model, such as absence of deadlocks, as well as user interface properties, either internal properties (e.g., reinitiability) or external properties (e.g., availability of widgets). Note that it is not possible to express these user interface properties explicitly—the analyst needs to express these properties as structural and behavioural Petri net properties that can be then analysed automatically in PetShop.

9.6.2 Model-based Logging

For summative evaluation of user performance, PetShop embeds a log tool for assisting evaluators by recording user interactions into a log file (Palanque et al., 2011). As models connect to the prototype, it is possible to record into log files the sequence of events occurring in the Petri net while the user is interacting with the prototype and the running models. In Petshop, the log tool records in a single row each basic Petri net event, like transition firing token movements (token added to a place, token removed from a place). The log tool produces only one log file even if more than one model is involved. Log data is stored in XML files and it is possible to transform and export it to spreadsheet tools for statistical analysis.

The structure of the log files is the following: the first field corresponds to the name of the model concerned by records, and the second field represents the type of the Petri net node (i.e., *place* or *transition*). The third field corresponds to the given *node name*. The fourth field represents the *action performed* associated to a node; for a transition, it can be *fire a transition* while for a place the actions are a token movement in the Petri net, such as *tokenAdded* or *tokenRemoved*. The fifth field represents the *time elapsed* from the start of the application in milliseconds. The last two fields (named *data 1* and *data 2*) represent additional data related to the node type. For a place, the field *data1* would represents the number of tokens *added* or *removed* at the same time, and the field *data2* would point out to the objects embed by the token. For a transition, the field *data2* represents the substitutions used for firing a transition.

9.7 Application of the Predictive Performance Evaluation to an Interactive Cockpit Application

This section presents the application of the proposed process, modelling technique, and associated tool to the development of an interactive cockpit application. This section focuses on the steps of the process that are related to the production of models and to their use for generating predictions of user performance.

9.7.1 Informal Presentation of the WXR Application

The weather radar (WXR) is an application currently deployed in many cockpits of commercial aircraft. It provides support to pilots' activities by increasing their awareness of meteorological phenomena during the flight journey, allowing them to determine if they may have to request a trajectory change, for example, in order to avoid storms or precipitation. Figure 9.8 shows, on the cockpit of the Airbus A380, the distribution of the various devices related to the weather radar.

Figure 9.8(a) presents a screenshot of the control panel of the weather radar used to operate the weather radar application. This panel provides two functionalities to the crew. The first one is dedicated to the mode selection of weather radar. The upper part of the panel contains radio buttons to change from one mode to another.

The second functionality, available in the lower part of the window in Figure 9.9(a), aims at adjusting the weather radar orientation (tilt angle). This adjustment can be automatic or manual (auto/manual buttons). Additionally, a stabilization function aims to keep the radar beam stable even in case of turbulences. Crewmembers use an input device named KCCU (Keyboard Cursor and Control Unit) to manipulate the control panel of the weather radar, depicted in Figure 9.9(c). It is composed of a keyboard (KBD part in Figure 9,9(c)) and of a rolling trackball (CCD part in Figure 9.9(c)).

Figure 9.9(b) presents a picture of the physical controls used to configure radar display, particularly to set up the range scale (right-hand side knob with ranges 20, 40, etc., nautical miles (NM)). Figure 9.10 shows screenshots of the navigation display according to two

Figure 9.8 WXR system positioned in the physical cockpit of an A380.

Figure 9.9 Image of a) the control panel of the weather radar; b) the radar display manipulation and, c) the input device Keyboard and Cursor Control Unit (KCCU).

different range scales (40 NM for the left display and 80 NM for the right display). Spots in the middle of the images show the current position, importance, composition, and size of the clouds.

This section focuses on the user tasks performed with the KCCU input device.

9.7.2 Behavioural Model of the Lower Part of the Control Panel of the Weather Radar

Figure 9.11 presents the ICO model of the behaviour of the lower part of the control panel of the weather radar. It describes how it is possible to handle the tilt angle of the weather radar application.

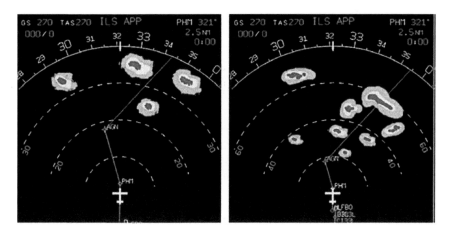

Figure 9.10 Screenshot of weather radar displays.

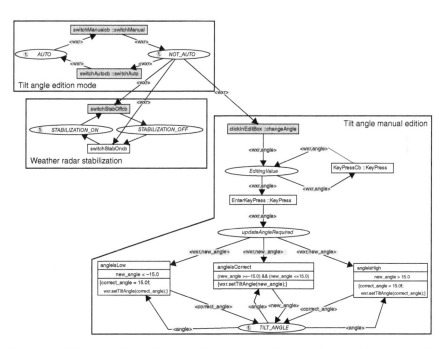

Figure 9.11 ICO model of the behaviour of the lower part of the control panel of the weather radar.

The top left part of Figure 9.11 describes the handling of the edition mode of the tilt angle, the bottom left part describes the handling of the weather radar stabilization, and the right part describes the behaviour of the manual editing of the tilt angle. In Figure 9.11, the place '*AUTO*' holds a token; this means that the edition mode of the tilt angle is set to automatic. If the user clicks on the button '*Manual*', the transition '*switchManualcb ::switchManual*' is fired and the token moves from the place '*AUTO*' to the place '*MANUAL*', thus setting the edition mode of the tilt angle to manual. This modification implies that the transition '*clickInEditBox*' becomes fireable, thus enabling the click on the corresponding editbox. If the user clicks on the editbox, the transition '*clickInEditBox*' is fired and a token is set in the place '*EditingValue*', thus enabling the user to use the keyboard in order to enter a new tilt angle value. When the user presses the key '*Enter*', the transition '*EnterKeyPress ::KeyPress*' is fired and the token is moved from the place '*EditingValue*' to the place '*UpdateAngleRequired*'. Finally, following the entered tilt angle value, one of the three transitions at the bottom is fired. If the entered angle is correct (included between -15.0 and 15.0), the value of the current tilt angle (value of the token held in the place '*TILT_ANGLE*') is set to the entered value (firing of the transition '*angleIsCorrect*'). Otherwise, if the entered value is too low, the tilt angle is set to its minimum (firing of the transition '*angleIsLow*') and if the entered value is too high, the tilt angle is set to its maximum (firing of the transition '*angleIsHigh*').

9.7.3 Behavioural Model Enriched with User Models

Figure 9.12 presents the ICO model of the lower part of the control panel of the weather radar enriched with possible user motoric actions. The number of places of the ICO model is the same, as the behaviour of the application does not change. Unlike the number of places, the number of transitions of the ICO model is higher, as there are several manners for the user to change the state of the application.

For example, as depicted in Figure 9.12, in the top left part between places labelled '*AUTO*' and '*NOT_AUTO*' (tagged 'a' in Figure 9.12), there are five new transitions in comparison with the behavioural model depicted in Figure 9.11. These transitions replace the '*switchManualcb ::switchManual*' transition in Figure 9.11. They represent the possible user motoric actions to change the mode of the weather radar. Starting from the top one labelled '*ParkingToManual ::switchManual*' to the bottom one labelled '*EditAngleToManual ::switchManual*', hereafter is the meaning of these added transitions:

- The transition '*ParkingToManual ::switchManual*' is fired if the user moves the cursor from the predefined parking point (initial position for the cursor, top left of the window) to the button '*Manual*' and clicks.
- The transition '*AutoToManual ::switchManual*' is fired if the user moves the cursor from the button '*Auto*' to the button '*Manual*' and clicks.
- The transition '*ONToManual ::switchManual*' is fired if the user moves the cursor from the button '*ON*' to the button '*Manual*' and clicks.
- The transition '*OFFToManual ::switchManual*' is fired if the user moves the cursor from the button '*OFF*' to the button '*Manual*' and clicks.

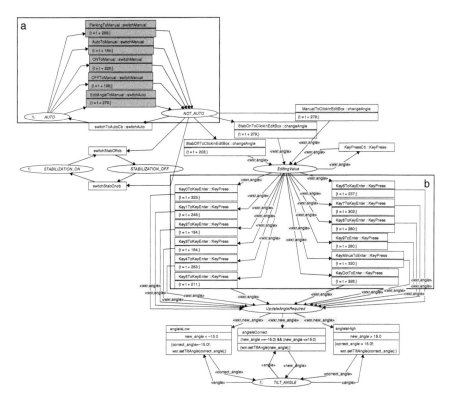

Figure 9.12 ICO model of the lower part of the control panel of the weather radar enriched with possible user motoric actions.

- Transition '*EditAngleToManual ::switchManual*' is fired if the user moves the cursor from the edit box to the button '*Manual*' and clicks.

In the same way, in the ICO model depicted in Figure 9.12, in the central part located around the places labelled '*EditingValue*' and '*UpdateAngleRequired*' (rectangle tagged 'b' in Figure 9.12), the transitions represent the possible user motoric actions to validate a value using the key '*Enter*' of the keyboard and replace the transition '*EnterKeyPress ::KeyPress*' in Figure 9.11. For example, in the top left of the rectangle 'b', the transition '*Key0ToKeyEnter ::KeyPress*' indicates that the user finger is located on the key '*0*' and that s/he has moved her finger towards the key '*Enter*' and to press it.

The aim of this presented model is to illustrate our approach and its main principles. It is not exhaustive, as the number of possible transitions would make the model not fully legible. However, the approach is scalable as the associated tool provides support for editing all the possible transitions (Navarre et al., 2009).

It is important to note that, as presented in the steps for enriching the system behavioural models (presented in Figure 9.4), all of the added transitions contain temporal information that will be used, when playing a scenario, to calculate the time needed to perform it. This time has been calculated, as presented in the Section 9.4.1.1, using Fitts' law (Fitts, 1954). The details about the interface elements enabling this calculation (e.g., the width of the different elements and the distance between them) are given in Section 9.7.5.

9.7.4 ICO Models for Time Prediction of Perceptual and Cognitive Actions

Figure 9.13 presents the ICO model for users' cognitive activity embedding temporal information. In Figure 9.13, as for the enriched interactive application model (see Figure 9.12), the important information is associated to the transitions. Therefore, each transition of the model is associated to a different cognitive activity and a mean time for accomplishing it (the rationale for the chosen mean times is explained in Section 9.4.1.2):

- An analysis cognitive activity is associated with the mean time 100ms and the transition 'Analyze_'.
- A comparison between two values' activity is associated with the mean time 33ms and the transition 'Compare2Values_'.
- A decision between several items' cognitive activity is associated with a calculation of the time using the Hick's law and the transition 'Decide_'. This transition is connected to the place 'NumberOfItems' that contains a set of values for the number of items to decide from. This transition is also connected to the place 'HickLawParameters' that contains the values of the Hick's law parameters that are necessary to perform the time calculation.

The ICO model presented in Figure 9.13 is rather simple as cognitive activity is quite limited for using the devices. However, models that are more complex could be considered for modelling information that must be remembered. For instance, as introduced in (Moher et al., 1996), due to memory overload some information might be lost in short-term memory. This would be modelled (in a user-cognitive model) using a time-out transition automatically removing information from the place representing information in short-term memory.

Figure 9.14 presents the ICO model for users' perceptual activity embedding temporal information. The model is very simple, as perceptual activity is quite limited for using the devices: we only consider here the perceptual activity of reading a value. This activity is

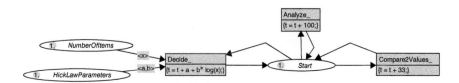

Figure 9.13 Simple ICO model of cognitive activities.

Figure 9.14 Simple ICO model of perceptive visual activities.

associated with the transition *'ReadValue_'* and the 100ms mean time (the rational for the chosen mean time is explained in Section 9.4.1.3).

9.7.5 Predictive Performance Evaluation

We exploit temporal information added in enriched behavioural models by applying scenarios to predict user temporal performances. Each action appearing in a scenario can be related to a transition in one of the models. In order to perform the predictive performance evaluation, we also need the following information: width of the interactive widgets, the distances between widgets of the control panel of the weather radar application, the width of the physical elements of the KCCU device, and the distances between the physical elements of the KCCU device.

In this example, we use the following scenario to make the predictive performance evaluation.

The pilot needs to check the weather on the flight path. S/he tests the status of the weather radar by clicking on the radio button TST. S/he then examine the Navigation Display to find out whether there are clouds containing thunderstorms or ice elements. As the Navigation Display pictures only a 2D layer of weather phenomenon in front of the plane, s/he has to change the tilt angle of the weather radar several times in order to display all the layers required for mentally building a 3D view of the weather phenomenon in front of the plane. The pilot then performs the following sequence of actions:

- click on the button 'Manual';
- click in the edit box, type the value '−5';
- validate the value (type key 'Enter');
- check that the entered value is displayed in the edit box;
- read the Navigation Display;
- type the value '−2.5' and validate it;
- check that the entered value is displayed in the edit box;
- read the Navigation Display, click on the edit box;
- type the value '0' and validate it;
- check that the entered value is displayed in the edit box;
- read the Navigation Display;
- type the value '2.5' and validate it;
- check that the entered value is displayed in the edit box;

Table 9.1 Interactive widgets width.

Widget Name	Button Auto	Button Manual	Button ON	Button OFF	Edit Box
Width (mm)	31	31	31	31	31

Table 9.2 Distances between the buttons (centre to centre) of the lower part of the control panel of the weather radar.

Widget Name	Button Auto	Button Manual	Button ON	Button OFF	Edit Box
Parking	95	99	131	134	170
Button Auto	0	40	46	59	106
Button Manual	40	0	59	46	92
Button ON	46	59	0	40	92
Button OFF	59	46	40	0	48
Edit Box	106	92	92	48	0

Table 9.3 KCCU keyboard keys width.

	0	1	2	3	4	5	6	7	8	9	.	+/−	Enter
Width (mm)	10	10	10	10	10	10	10	10	10	10	10	10	15

Table 9.4 Distances between physical elements in the KCCU.

	Trackball	0	1	2	3	4	5	6	7	8	9	.	+/−	Enter
Trackball	0	100	96	105	124	97	106	127	91	100	109	91	109	119
0	100		51	37	31	37	26	20	26	19	11	19	12	10	42
1	96	37	0	12	24	10	14	25	24	25	24	30	37	23
2	105	31	12	0	12	14	10	14	25	24	25	33	33	13
3	124	37	24	10	0	25	14	10	24	25	20	37	30	13
4	97	26	10	14	25	0	12	24	10	12	25	20	26	26
5	106	20	10	10	14	12	0	12	24	10	12	23	23	25
6	127	26	25	14	10	24	12	0	25	14	10	26	20	21
7	91	19	24	25	24	10	24	25	0	12	24	10	27	36
8	100	11	25	24	25	12	10	14	12	0	12	13	13	30
9	109	19	24	25	20	25	12	10	24	12	0	27	10	30
.	91	12	30	33	37	20	23	26	10	13	27	0	24	43
+/−	109	10	37	33	30	26	23	20	27	13	10	24	0	41
Enter	119	42	23	13	13	26	25	21	36	30	30	43	41	0

Table 9.5 Effective time for accomplishing the scenario.

Scenario Step	Type of Transition	Time (ms)
Click on button 'Manual'	Physical (transition 'switchManualCb ::switchManual')	288
Click in the edit box	Physical (transition 'ManualToClickInEditBox')	279
Press key '-'	Physical (transition 'TrackballToKeyMinus')	451
Press key '5'	Physical (transition 'MinusToKey5')	248
Press 'Enter'	Physical (transition 'Key5ToEnter')	211
	System (WXR radar)	3000
Perceive value	Perceptive (transition 'ReadValue')	100
Verify value	Cognitive (transition 'Compare2Values')	33
Read navigation display	Perceptive (transition 'ReadValue') + Cognitive (transition 'Analyze')	133
Press key '-'	Physical (transition 'KeyEnterToKeyMinus')	320
Press key '2'	Physical (transition 'KeyMinusToKey2')	292
Press key '.'	Physical (transition 'Key2ToKeyDot')	292
Press key '5'	Physical (transition 'KeyDotToKey5')	248
Press 'Enter'	Physical (transition 'Key5ToKeyEnter')	211
	System (WXR radar)	3000
Perceive value	Perceptive (transition 'ReadValue')	100
Verify value	Cognitive (transition 'Compare2Values')	33
Read navigation display	Perceptive (transition 'ReadValue') + Cognitive (transition 'Analyze')	133
Press key '0'	Physical (transition 'KeyEnterToKey0')	323
Press 'Enter'	Physical (transition 'KeyOToKeyEnter')	323
	System (WXR radar)	3000
Perceive value	Perceptive (transition 'ReadValue')	100
Verify value	Cognitive (transition 'Compare2Values')	33
Read navigation display	Perceptive (transition 'ReadValue') + Cognitive (transition 'Analyze')	133
Press key '2'	Physical (transition 'KeyEnterToKey2')	184
Press key '.'	Physical (transition 'Key2ToKeyDot')	292
Press key '5'	Physical (transition 'KeyDotToKey5')	248
Press 'Enter'	Physical (transition 'Key5ToKeyEnter')	211
	System (WXR radar)	3000
Perceive value	Perceptive (transition 'ReadValue')	100
Verify value	Cognitive (transition 'Compare2Values')	33
Read navigation display	Perceptive (transition 'ReadValue') + Cognitive (transition 'Analyze')	133
Press key '5'	Physical (transition 'KeyEnterToKey5')	211
Press 'Enter'	Physical (transition 'Key5ToKeyEnter')	211
	System (WXR radar)	3000
Perceive value	Perceptive (transition 'ReadValue')	100
Verify value	Cognitive (transition 'Compare2Values')	33
Read navigation display	Perceptive (transition 'ReadValue')+ Cognitive (transition 'Analyze')	133
	Total	153 819 ms

- read the Navigation Display;
- type the value '5' and validate it;
- check that the entered value is displayed in the edit box;
- read the Navigation Display.

Time required by the system to execute an action has an impact on the user performance. In this example, the weather radar system takes approximatively 3000 ms to change from one tilt angle to another one. Depending on the type of weather radar, the time required by the weather radar to scan the airspace in front of the aircraft (getting a reliable image takes two or three scans) ranges from 2000–4000ms.

Table 9.5 is the output of the predictive evaluation stage presented in Section 9.3.2. It highlights the results from the application of the steps for predicting time performance (presented in Figure 9.6) to the scenario of checking the weather on the flight path. From this table, we see that the total time performance for achieving the scenario is about 153 seconds and that system actions take 15 seconds in total (9.75 per cent of total time performance).

9.7.6 Identification of Relevant Improvements in Behavioural Models Based on Predictive Performance Evaluation

The first finding is that the system is not fully interactive as the pilot has to wait for the system response around ten per cent of the time. This issue would have to be studied in order to find ways to increase interactivity. The second finding is at the interactive application level, where we see that the pilot spends quite a lot of time in editing tilt angle value. A redesign option could be to change the edit box to a slider or to a scrollable edit box (as the range slider). The scenario could then be used to perform a new predictive performance evaluation in order to check whether time performance increases with this design option.

Finally, we could envision automation design options in order to increase global human-system performance. The redesign option of the range slider is equivalent to the automate user motoric task of entering the digits of the tilt angle value. Another automation option is to implement a timed mechanism in the weather radar that periodically changes the tilt angle so that the pilot only reads the navigation display. Further examples of dealing with automation design are available in (Martinie et al., 2011).

9.8 Application of the Summative Performance Evaluation to a Multimodal Interaction Technique

This section demonstrates the use of the process presented in Section 9.5 for summative performance evaluation of a multimodal interaction technique. More precisely, we use an interaction technique based on a multimodal click using two mice. When this interaction is performed, a specific command of the interactive application is triggered. Which command is triggered is not relevant and thus not detailed. Even though we take the example of

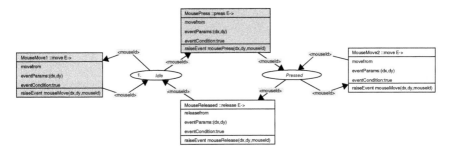

Figure 9.15 ICO model of the trackball input device driver (similar to a mouse device driver).

two-mice interaction, the approach is generic and could be applied, for instance, when multi-touch interactions are concerned, each finger playing the role of a mouse. The same interaction can also be performed by two users, each of them using one mouse. This could take place, for instance, in new modern civil aircraft, where interaction takes place by means of the KCCUs.

This section focuses on the application of the stages of the process to the production of systems models and to their use for summative performance evaluation.

9.8.1 Input Device Drivers

Figure 9.15 presents the ICO model of the trackball input device driver. This model is similar to a mouse input device driver and describes these input devices basic behaviour. The basic behaviour of this device is the following: the user can press and then release the button and s/he can move the cursor by moving the ball of the trackball (the button being either pressed or released). This is precisely described in the ICO model presented in Figure 9.15. This figure shows that the device can be in two different states: idle (when the place 'Idle' holds a token) and pressed (when the place 'Pressed' holds a token). In Figure 9.15, the ICO model describes the initial state of the device: the device is idle (the place 'Idle' holds a token) and waits for an event to occur. If the user press the device button, the device sends the event 'press' which fires the transition 'MousePress ::press'; setting the device in the pressed state and sending the event 'mousePress' that will be cought by the interaction technique model (see the following section). When the user then releases the device button, the device sends the event 'release' which fires the transition 'MouseReleased ::release'; setting the device in the idle state and sending the event 'mouseRelease'. If the user moves the device (either while being in the idle or the pressed state), the device sends the event 'move', which fires the transition 'MouseMove1 ::move' (if the device is in the idle state) or the transition 'MouseMove2 ::Move' (if the device is in the pressed state); sending in both cases the event 'mouseMove'.

9.8.2 Interaction Technique

Figure 9.16 specifies the behaviour of the physical interaction between the user and the system. This transducer takes mouse low-level events as inputs such as *mouseMove* or

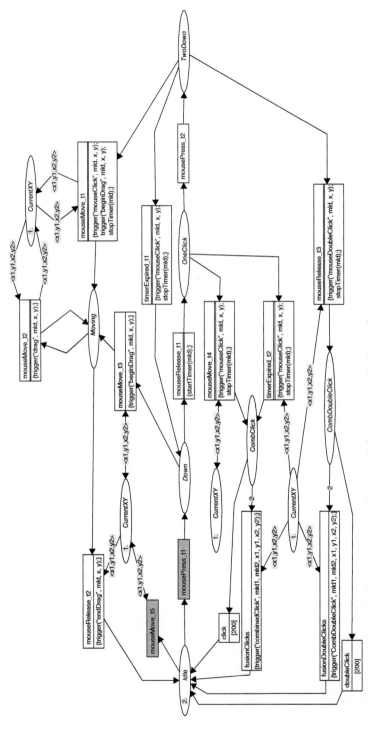

Figure 9.16 ICO model of the interaction technique with the KCCU trackball input device.

mousePress and triggers them as higher-level events, such as *combinedClick* that will be handled by the interactive application (for instance, the WXR application presented in Section 9.7). Place *currentXY* contains a token that keeps track of the mice target pointers' coordinates. For readability purpose, this place has been demultiplied into virtual places (functionality of the Petshop tool), which are clones of the initial one and are several views of this single place. It avoids overcrowding the figure. Each time a *mouseMove* event is caught (*mouseMove_t1, mouseMove_t2, mouseMove_t3, mouseMove_t4, mouseMove_t5*), the current coordinates are updated with the (x, y) deltas that have been done by the target pointers. In the initial state (2 tokens in place *Idle*, one for each mouse), the *mousePress_t1* and *mouseMove_t5* transitions are fireable (users can move or press their mouse). Once a *mousePress* event is caught, the *mousePress_t1* transition is fired and the corresponding mouse token is put into the place *Down*. If a *mouseRelease* event occurs, the transition *mouseRelease_t1* transition will be fired and a timer armed in case of a future double click. The token is put into the *OneClick* place. If a *mouseMove* event occurs, the *mouseMove_t4* transition will be fired. If the timer previously set expires, the transition *timerExpired_t2* will be fired. In both cases, the timer is stopped, a *mouseClick* event is triggered and the token put into the place *CombClick*.

- If all the previously described sequence of events happens for both mice, two tokens are in the *CombClick* place, and the transition *fusionClick* can be fired. It can be fired only in this case because the weight of the corresponding arc is 2. This *fusionClick* transition, when fired, triggers a *combinedClick* event (which will be caught by the interaction technique model, interactive application, for instance, the WXR application presented in Section 9.7) and then deposits the two tokens back to the place *Idle*.

- In other cases, for the place *CombClick*, if one token arrives in and that no other token arrives in within 200 milliseconds, the *click* transition will be fired and the token will go back to the place *Idle*.

The same principle is applied for the combined double click, which is not detailed here as ir was not used in our case study.

9.8.3 Log Analysis of User Testing

Any kind of interactive application may embed the multimodal click interaction technique. Figure 9.17 presents a short excerpt of the log recorded during a user testing session. This excerpt provides support to illustrate different usability problems found with the multimodal click interaction technique. In this excerpt, the combined click interaction technique triggers a file deletion in the system.

The log tool in PetShop records all the changes that occurs in the ICO models of device driver and interaction technique described in Figure 9.16 during the prototype execution (as well as in the ICO dialog model of the tested interactive application that we do not present here). The logged events include firing of each transitions, removal, and addition of a token in a place (with the complete print of all the values describing the content of

	class	type	name	action	time	data1	data2
606	mouse_transducer	transition	mousePress_t1	fire	8000		1*[evt:[mid=>1]]
609	mouse_transducer	transition	mouseRelease_t1	fire	9900		1*[evt:[mid=>1]]
613	mouse_transducer	transition	timerExpired	fire	10500		1*[evt:[mid=>1]]
617	mouse_transducer	transition	click	fire	10700		1*[evt:[mid=>1]]
640	mouse_transducer	transition	click	fire	10950		1*[evt:[mid=>2]]
752	mouse_transducer	transition	mousePress_t1	fire	11600		1*[evt:[mid=>1]]
758	mouse_transducer	transition	mousePress_t1	fire	12010		1*[evt:[mid=>2]]
761	mouse_transducer	transition	mouseRelease_t1	fire	12020		1*[evt:[mid=>2]]
774	mouse_transducer	transition	timerExpired	fire	12220		1*[evt:[mid=>2]]
781	mouse_transducer	transition	click	fire	12420		1*[evt:[mid=>2]]
794	mouse_transducer	transition	mouseRelease_t1	fire	13010		1*[evt:[mid=>1]]
1425	CombinedClick_Delete_File	transition	combinedClick	fire	20300		1*[evt:[x1=>40,x2=>400,y1=>40,y2=>400],presentationFrame=>javax...]
1426	CombinedClick_Delete_File	place	testIcon	tokenAdded	20300	1	w1, w2
1427	CombinedClick_Delete_File	place	Frame	tokenRemoved	20300		
1428	CombinedClick_Delete_File	transition	command1	fire	20300		1*(w1, w2)
1435	CombinedClick_Delete_File	transition	combinedClick	fire	22100		1*[evt:[x1=>40,x2=>400,y1=>80,y2=>400],presentationFrame=>javax...]
1436	CombinedClick_Delete_File	place	testIcon	tokenAdded	22100	1	w1, w2
1437	CombinedClick_Delete_File	place	Frame	tokenRemoved	22100		
1438	CombinedClick_Delete_File	transition	command1	fire	22100		1*(w1, w2)
1699	CombinedClick_Delete_File	transition	combinedClick	fire	23450		1*[evt:[x1=>290,x2=>400,y1=>40,y2=>400],presentationFrame=>javax...]
1700	CombinedClick_Delete_File	place	testIcon	tokenAdded	23450	1	null, w2
1701	CombinedClick_Delete_File	place	Frame	tokenRemoved	23450		
1702	CombinedClick_Delete_File	transition	command1	fire	23450		1*(null, w2)
2897	CombinedClick_Delete_File	transition	combinedClick	fire	40340		1*[evt:[x1=>120,x2=>400,y1=>120,y2=>400],presentationFrame=>javax...]
2898	CombinedClick_Delete_File	place	testIcon	tokenAdded	40340	1	w3,w2
2899	CombinedClick_Delete_File	place	Frame	tokenRemoved	40340		
2900	CombinedClick_Delete_File	transition	command1	fire	40340		1*(w3,w2)

Figure 9.17 Excerpt of the model-based log produced by PetShop.

the tokens). It is possible to know which model is in charge of the event by looking at the field class.

Two transitions are important to handle the correctness of the interaction technique multimodal click. If the transition '*command1*' is fired using two valid objects as parameter (visible in column data2 as (w1,w2)), it means that the user completed the launching of the command named '*command1*' using the CombinedClick interaction technique. If the transition '*command1*' has been fired with one missing object as parameter (visible in column data2 as (null,w2)), the user failed to launch the command, but managed to do a proper multimodal combine click. Figure 9.17 presents three successful combined clicks (lines 1425–1428, 1435–1438, 2897–2900), and one miss (lines 1699–1702).

We can calculate the time for completion of the task and the number of missed combined click by hands or with spreadsheet formulas. At this point, log data help to count the number of successful and failed tasks as well as the user performance. However, log data are also useful to understand complex sequences of events that may have led to unexpected user fails while trying to launch the command labelled '*command1*'. For that purpose, we should take a look on the events recorded at the transducer level.

In the ICO model of the interaction technique (see Figure 9.16) the transition '*click*' is fired only when the two clicks are not combined. The substitution contains the ID of a mouse. According to the log, the delay between click on mouse 1 (line 617) and click on mouse 2 (line 640) is 250ms. In fact, one of the main assumptions about this interaction technique is that a combined click is counted only if the user clicks on the two mice in an interval of less than 200ms. This makes it possible to count the number of failed combined clicks. Based on such an information, the evaluator can decide the means of delay or failure for combined clicks, and propose a better value for the trigger.

From the log data produced by our user while trying to perform her task, we can extract fine-grained information such as the time between the pressing the first mouse's button with the cursor on the widget labelled 'w1' and second mouse click on the widget labelled 'w2'. This time gives us the total time for completing the task of launching a command. The sequence of events described by the lines 752, 758, 761, 774, 781, and 794 are particularly revealing of a usability problem that would be very difficult to find without a model-based log environment. It shows that the user failed a combined click when s/he pressed the two mice at the same time but forgot to release the button of first mouse (see mid at column 'data2' in Figure 9.17) leading to a click after 200ms trigger on the second mouse.

9.8.4 Evolvability of Models

According to the performance evaluation obtained with the log analysis, some fine tuning can be applied in the model to increase the performance of the interaction technique. This fine tuning can either be done during or before the simulation as, in PetShop, models can be modified while being executed. The data collected during assessment steps, and in particular log data, can then be exploited to assess the performance of the interaction technique. If the performance does not fit the expectations, the log data can be used as input to modify or tune the model that will be simulated again.

As we have seen in our case study, the time of 200ms between two clicks with the two mice was too short in at least one situation. If this scenario is confirmed with more users, it would be reasonable to change the values used in the time interval. Such modification or fine-tuning of the interaction technique is made much easier as the information in the log is already related to the structure of the model.

The parameter used within the case study (time between two clicks) is just an example of what is possible, but the approach is generic enough to support the analysis of any parameter while the models explicitly highlight such parameters.

9.9 Conclusion, Limitations, and Perspectives

This chapter has proposed a unification of views around the notion of models in the domain of HCI. By differentiating the notion of 'science' model and 'engineering' model (according to Lee, 2016), we have presented how 'science' models from psychology can be used jointly with 'engineering' models from computer science, and exploited for designing, developing, and evaluating interactive systems.

For an 'engineering' model, we have presented the ICO modelling technique that is able to describe in a complete and unambiguous way all the elements of the interactive systems. For 'science' models, we have used several laws of human performance such as Fitts' law and the Hick-Heyman law. We have shown that enriching ICO models (of an interactive application) with human performance laws makes it possible to perform predictive performance evaluation, thus complementing standard HCI techniques for usability evaluation based on repetitive user testing. We have shown that, by exploiting ICO models of multimodal interaction techniques with a dedicated simulation tool, summative usability evaluation can be performed. These performance results can be used to identify locations in the models where fine-tuning is needed in order to increase the interaction technique performance and to reduce interaction errors.

This entire proposal relies on the production of ICO models for the interactive application under study. Producing such models would require time and knowledge from the engineers. While this is mandatory (imposed by standards such as DO-178C) in the area of critical systems, it is far from current practice in interactive systems engineering. One way of addressing this issue is to model only the part of the interactive system of which the performance must be carefully assessed. This means that some parts would be directly programmed, while other ones would be modelled. Integration of models with the code can be done following the approach presented by Fayollas et al. (2016).

ICO formal notation has been designed with the objective of being able to describe in a complete and unambiguous way interactive systems, even though they present complex interaction techniques (as stated earlier). This means that the expressive power is high and, for basic interactions techniques (as the ones on the infusion pumps only having one display and a couple of physical buttons (Cairns and Thimbleby, 2017)), its complexity is not fully exploited. This is the reason why, for these systems, standard automata are still used. Similarly, ICO models are meant to be executable, and are executed to bridge the 'classical' gap between models and implementations. For this reason, too, ICO models might appear complex and, if the analysis of models is the only goal, executability will add useless complexity in that context.

Further work would include integrating more complex models from psychology, especially those related to human error, such as cognitive or perceptive biases (Baron, 2000), but also to training, as this is an important element of the operations of critical interactive systems (DoDTD, 1975). Beyond that, integrating descriptions of the operators' tasks in such a usability evaluation framework would provide additional benefits, as described in (Barboni et al., 2010).

....

REFERENCES

Anderson, J. R., 1993. *Rules of the Mind*. New York, NY: Lawrence Erlbaum.

Barboni, E., Ladry, J-F., Navarre, D., Palanque, P., and Winckler, M., 2010. Beyond Modelling: An Integrated Environment Supporting Co-Execution of Tasks and Systems Models. In: *EICS '10: The Proceedings of the 2010 ACM SIGCHI Symposium on Engineering Interactive Computing Systems*. Berlin, Germany June 19–23 2010. New York, NY: ACM, pp. 143–52.

Baron, J., 2000. *Thinking and deciding*. 3rd ed. New York, NY: Cambridge University Press.

Bass, L., John, B., Juristo Juzgado, N., and Sánchez Segura, M. I., 2004. Usability-Supporting Architectural Patterns. In: *ICSE 2004: 26th International Conference on Software Engineering*. Edinburgh, Scotland, May 23–28 2004. pp. 716–17.

Bass, L., Pellegrino, R., Reed, S., Seacord, R., Sheppard, R., and Szezur, M. R., 1991. The Arch model: Seeheim revisited. *Proceedings of the User Interface Developers' Workshop Report*.

Basnyat, S., Chozos, N., and Palanque, P., 2006. Multidisciplinary perspective on accident investigation. *Reliability Engineering & System Safety*, (91)12, pp. 1502–20.

Bastide, R., and Palanque, P. A., 1995. Petri Net based Environment for the Design of Event-driven Interfaces. In: *International Conference on Application and Theory of Petri Nets*. Zaragoza, Spain 25–30 June 1995. pp. 66–83.

Brumby, D. P., Janssen, C. P., Kujala, T. D., and Salvucci, D. D., 2017. Computational Models of User Multitasking. In: A. Oulasvirta, P. O. Kristensson, X. Bi, and A. Howes, eds. *Computational Interaction*. Oxford: Oxford University Press.

Cairns, P., and Thimbleby, H., 2017. From premature semantics to mature interaction programming. In: A. Oulasvirta, P. O. Kristensson, X. Bi, and A. Howes, eds. *Computational Interaction*. Oxford: Oxford University Press.

Card, S. K., Moran, T. P., and Newell, A., 1980. The Keystroke-Level Model for User Performance Time with Interactive Systems. *Communications of the ACM*, 23(7), pp. 396–410.

Card, S. K., Moran, T. P., and Newell, A., 1983. The *psychology of human-computer interaction*. New York, NY: Lawrence Erlbaum.

Card, S. K., Moran, T. P., and Newell, A., 1986. The Model Human Processor: An Engineering Model of Human Performance. In: K. Boff and L. Kaufman, eds. *The Handbook of Perception and Human Performance: Sensory Processes and Perception*. Volume 1. pp. 1–35.

Chiola, G., Dutheillet, C., Franceschinis, G., and Haddad, S., 1997. A Symbolic Reachability Graph for Coloured Petri Nets. *Theoretical Computer Science*, 176(1–2), pp. 39–65.

Clarke, E. M., Emerson, A., and Sifakis, J., 2009. Model checking: algorithmic verification and debugging. *Communications of the ACM*, 52(11), pp. 74–84.

Cockburn, A., Gutwin, C., and Greenberg, S., 2007. A predictive model of menu performance. In: *CHI '07: The Proceedings of the SIGCHI Conference on Human Factors in Computing Systems*. New York, NY: ACM, pp. 627–36.

Cockburn A., Gutwin C., Palanque P., Deleris Y., Trask C., Coveney A., Yung M., and MacLean K., 2017. Turbulent Touch: Touchscreen Input for Cockpit Flight Displays. In: *CHI '17: The Proceedings of the 2017 CHI Conference on Human Factors in Computing Systems*. New York, NY: ACM, pp. 6742–53.

Dix, A., 1991. *Formal methods for Interactive Systems*. London: Academic Press.

DO-178C/ED-12C, 2012. *Software Considerations in Airborne Systems and Equipment Certification*. Washington, DC: RTCA, Inc.

DO-333, 2011. *Formal Methods Supplement to DO-178C and DO-278A*. Washington, DC: RTCA, Inc.

DoDTD, 1975. *U.S. Department of Defense Training Document*. Pamphlet 350–30.

Emerson, E.A., and Srinivasan, J., 1988. Branching Time Temporal Logic. *LNCS*, 354, pp. 122–72.

Fayollas, C., Martinie, C., Navarre, D., and Palanque P., 2016. Engineering mixed-criticality interactive applications. In: *EICS 2016: ACM SIGCHI symposium on Engineering Interactive Computing Systems*, pp. 108–19.

Fayollas, C., Martinie, C., Palanque, P., Barboni, E., Racim Fahssi, R., and Hamon, A., 2017. Exploiting Action Theory as a Framework for Analysis and Design of Formal Methods Approaches: Application to the CIRCUS Integrated Development Environment. In: B. Weyers, J. Bowen, A. Dix, and P. Palanque, eds. *The Handbook on Formal Methods for HCI*. Berlin: Springer, pp. 465–504.

Fitts, P. M., 1954. The information capacity of the human motor system in controlling the amplitude of movement. *Journal of Experimental Psychology*, 47, pp. 381–91.

Genrich, H. J., 1991. Predicate/Transitions nets. In: K. Jensen and G. Rozenberg, eds. *High-Levels Petri Nets: Theory and Application*. Berlin: Springer, pp. 3–43.

Göransson B., Gulliksen J., and Boivie, I., 2003. The usability design process—integrating user-centered systems design in the software development process. *Software Process: Improvement and Practice*, 8(2), pp. 111–31.

Gram, C., and Cockton, G., 1996. *Design principles for Interactive Software*. London: Chapman & Hall.

Hamon A., Palanque P., Cronel M., André R., Barboni E., and Navarre, D., 2014. Formal modelling of dynamic instantiation of input devices and interaction techniques: application to multi-touch interactions. In: *EICS '14: The Proceedings of the 2014 ACM SIGCHI Symposium on Engineering Interactive Computing Systems*. Rome, Italy, 17–20 June 2014. New York, NY: ACM, pp. 173–8.

Hamon A., Palanque P., Silva J-L., Deleris Y., and Barboni, E., 2013. Formal description of multi-touch interactions. In: *EICS '13: The Proceedings of the 2013 ACM SIGCHI Symposium on Engineering Interactive Computing Systems.* London, UK, 27–27 June. New York, NY: ACM.

Harel D., and Naamad A., 1996. The STATEMATE Semantics of Statecharts. ACM Transactions on Software Engineering and Methodology, 5(4), pp. 293–333.

Hick, W., 1952. On the rate of gain of information. *Journal of Experimental Psychology,* 4, pp. 11–36.

Hyman, R., 1953. Stimulus information as a determinant of reaction time. *Journal of Experimental Psychology,* 45, pp. 188–96.

Jensen, K., Kristensen, L., and Wells, L., 2007. Coloured Petri nets and CPN tools for modelling and validation of concurrent systems. *International Journal of Software Tools for Technology Transfer,* 9(3), pp. 213–54.

John, B., and Kieras, D., 1996a. The GOMS Family of User Interface Analysis Techniques: Comparison and Contrast. *ACM Transactions on Computer Human Interaction,* 3(4), pp. 320–51.

John, B., and Kieras, D., 1996b. Using GOMS for User Interface Design and Evaluation: Which Technique. *ACM Transactions on Computer Human Interaction,* 3(4), pp. 287–319.

Kieras, D., and Meyer, D., 1997. An Overview of the EPIC Architecture for Cognition and Performance with Application to Human-Computer Interaction. *Human Computer Interaction,* 12, pp. 391–438.

Ladry, J. F., Navarre, D., and Palanque, P., 2009. Formal description techniques to support the design, construction and evaluation of fusion engines for sure (safe, usable, reliable and evolvable) multimodal interfaces. In: *ICMI-MLMI '09 Proceedings of the 2009 international conference on Multimodal interfaces.* Cambridge, MA, 2–4 November 2009.

Lee, B., and Oulasvirta, A., 2016. Modelling Error Rates in Temporal Pointing. In: *CHI '16: The Proceedings of the 2016 CHI Conference on Human Factors in Computing Systems.* San Jose, CA, 7–12 2016. New York, NY: ACM, pp. 1857–68.

Lee, E. A., 2016. Fundamental Limits of Cyber-Physical Systems Modeling. *ACM Transactions on Cyber-Physical Systems,* 1(1), [online] 26 pages. Available from: http://dl.acm.org/citation.cfm?id=2912149&CFID=973113565&CFTOKEN=26116238.

Martinie, C., Palanque, P. A., Barboni, E., and Ragosta, M., 2011. Task-model based assessment of automation levels: Application to space ground segments. *In: Proceedings of the IEEE International Conference on Systems, Man and Cybernetics.* Anchorage, Alaska, 9–12 October 2011. Red Hook, NY: Curran, pp. 3267–73.

Mayhew D. J., 1999. *The Usability Engineering Lifecycle.* Burlington, MA: Morgan Kaufmann.

Moher, T., Dirda, V., Bastide, R., and Palanque, P., 1996. Monolingual, Articulated Modeling of Devices, Users, and Interfaces. In: *DSVIS'96: Proceedings of the Third International Eurographics Workshop.* Namur, Belgium, 5–7 June 1996. Berlin: Springer, pp. 312–29.

Navarre, D., Palanque, P., Ladry, J.-F., and Barboni, E., 2009. ICOs: a Model-Based User Interface Description Technique dedicated to Interactive Systems Addressing Usability, Reliability and Scalability. *Transactions on Computer-Human Interaction,* 16(4). DOI: 10.1145/1614390.1614393.

Palanque, P., Barboni, E., Martinie, C., Navarre, D., and Winckler, M., 2011. A model-based approach for supporting engineering usability evaluation of interaction techniques. In: *EICS '11: The Proceedings of the 3rd ACM SIGCHI symposium on Engineering Interactive Computing Systems.* New York, NY: ACM, pp. 21–30.

Palanque, P., and Bastide, R., 1995. Verification of an interactive software by analysis of its formal specification. In: *Interact '95: The Proceedings of the IFIP Human-Computer Interaction Conference.* Lillehammer, Norway, 14–18 July 1995. pp. 181–97.

Palanque, P., Bernhaupt, R., Navarre, D., Ould, M., and Winckler, M., 2006. Supporting usability evaluation of multimodal man-machine interfaces for space ground segment applications using Petri Net based formal specification. In: *SpaceOps 2006: The Proceedings of the 9th International Conference on Space Operations*. Rome, Italy, 19–23 June 2006. Available at: https://doi.org/10.2514/MSPOPS06.

Palanque, P., Ladry, J-F., Navarre, D., and Barboni, E., 2009. High-Fidelity Prototyping of Interactive Systems Can Be Formal Too. *HCI International*, (1), pp. 667–76.

Peterson, J. L., 1981. *Petri Net Theory and the Modeling of Systems*. New York, NY: Prentice Hall.

Petri, C. A., 1962. *Kommunikation mit Automaten*. Rheinisch-Westfaliches Institut fur Intrumentelle Mathematik an der Universitat Bonn, Schrift Nr 2.

Pnueli A., 1986. Applications of Temporal Logic to the Specification and Verification of Reactive Systems: A Survey of Current Trends. *LNCS*, (224), pp. 510–84. Berlin: Springer.

Reisig, W., 2013. *Understanding Petri Nets—Modeling Techniques, Analysis Methods, Case Studies*. Berlin: Springer.

Russo, J. E., 1978. *Adaptation of Cognitive Processes to Eye Movements. Eye Movements and Higher Psychological Functions*. New York, NY: Lawrence Erlbaum.

Silva, J. L., Fayollas, C., Hamon, A., Palanque, P., Martinie, C., and Barboni, E., 2014. Analysis of WIMP and Post WIMP Interactive Systems based on Formal Specification. *Electronic Communications of the EASST*, [online] 69(55): 29 pages. Available at: https://journal.ub.tu-berlin.de/eceasst/article/view/967.

Woods, W. A., 1970. Transition network grammars for natural language analysis. *Communications of the ACM*, 13(10), pp. 591–606.

PART IV
Human Behaviour

10

. . • . .

Interaction as an Emergent Property of a Partially Observable Markov Decision Process

ANDREW HOWES,
XIULI CHEN,
ADITYA ACHARYA,
RICHARD L. LEWIS

10.1 Introduction

A Partially Observable Markov Decision Process (POMDP) is a mathematical framework for modelling sequential decision problems. We show in this chapter that a range of phenomena in Human-Computer Interaction can be modelled within this framework and we explore its strengths and weaknesses. One important strength of the framework is that it embraces the highly adaptive, embodied and ecological nature of human interaction (Fu and Pirolli, 2007; Howes, Vera, Lewis, and McCurdy, 2004; Payne and Howes, 2013; Payne, Howes, and Reader, 2001; Pirolli and Card, 1999; Vera, Howes, McCurdy, and Lewis, 2004) and it thereby provides a suitable means of rigorously explaining a wide range of interaction phenomena.

Consider as an illustration a task where a user searches for an image in the results returned by a web search engine (Figure 10.1). Tseng and Howes (2015) studied a version of this task in which a person has the goal of finding an image with a particular set of features, for example to find an image of a castle with water and trees. A user with this task must make multiple eye movements and fixations because the relatively high resolution fovea is sufficient to provide the details of only about 2.5 degrees of visual angle. Eventually, after a sequence of these *partial observations* the user might find a relevant image (e.g. the one in the bottom right of the figure). Evidence shows that people do not perform a search such as this using a systematic top-left to bottom-right strategy; they do not start at the top left and then look at each image in turn. But, equally, they do not search randomly. Rather, the search is a rational adaptation to factors that include the ecological distribution of images

Computational Interaction. Antti Oulasvirta, Per Ola Kristensson, Xiaojun Bi, Andrew Howes (Eds).
© Oxford University Press 2018. Published 2018 by Oxford University Press.

Figure 10.1 Simulated results from a search engine. Reproduced with permission from Elsevier.

and the partial observations provided by the visual fixations. We show in this paper that rational strategies like these can be modelled as the emergent solution to a POMDP.

The approach that we take is heavily influenced by a long tradition of computational models of human behaviour (Card, Moran, and Newell, 1983; Howes and Young, 1996; Howes, Vera, Lewis, and McCurdy, 2004; Byrne, 2001; Gray, Sims, Fu, and Schoelles, 2006; Miller and Remington, 2004; Kieras and Hornof, 2014; Kieras, Meyer, Ballas, and Lauber, 2000; Halverson and Hornof, 2011; Hornof, Zhang, and Halverson, 2010; Zhang and Hornof, 2014; Janssen, Brumby, Dowell, Chater, and Howes, 2011). A key insight of this work has been to delineate the contribution to interactive behaviour of information processing capacities (e.g. memory, perception, manual movement times), on the one hand, and strategies (methods, procedures, policies), on the other. A contribution of the POMDP approach is that strategies emerge through learning given a formal specification of the interaction problem faced by the user where the problem includes the bounds imposed by individual processing capacities.

To illustrate the contribution of POMDPs, we examine two examples of their application to explaining human-computer interaction. The first is a model of how people search menus and the second of how they use visualizations to support decision making. Before describing the examples, we first give an overview of POMDPs. In the discussion, we explore the potential advantages and disadvantages of explaining interaction as an emergent consequence of a POMDP. The advantages include, (1) that the POMDP framing is a well-known and rigorous approach to defining stochastic sequential decision processes and there is a growing range of machine learning algorithms dedicated to solving them, (2) that POMDPs provide a means of defining and integrating theoretical concepts in HCI concerning embodiment, ecology and adaptation, and (3) that POMDPs provide a means to make inferences about the consequences of theoretical assumptions for interaction. The disadvantages concern tractability and the existing scope of application to human tasks.

10.2 Partially Observable Markov Decision Processes

Originally conceived in operations research (Papadimitriou and Tsitsiklis, 1987), POMDPs have been influential in Artificial Intelligence (Kaelbling, Littman, and Cassandra, 1998). They provide a mathematical framework for formalizing the interaction between an agent and a stochastic environment, where the state of the environment is not fully known to the agent. Instead, the agent receives observations that are partial and stochastic and that offer evidence as to the state. The problems faced by the agent are therefore to (1) generate a good estimate of the state of the environment given the history of actions and observations, and (2) to generate actions that maximize the expected reward gained through interaction.

POMDPs have also been used in cognitive science to explain human behaviour. For example, in one contribution to explaining human vision, a target localization task was framed as a POMDP problem by Butko and Movellan (2008), who studied a task in which a visual target was present in one position in a grid and participants had to localize the target by moving their eyes to gather information. The information received at each time step, a partial observation, was from the fixated point (with high reliability) and surrounding points (with lower reliability). Butko and Movellan's model learned a series of eye movements, a strategy, that maximized the reward gained from performing the task (it performed fast and accurate localization). The authors showed how this learned strategy could generate human-like behaviour without assuming ad-hoc heuristics such as inhibition-of-return to previous locations. They also showed that the learned strategy could sometimes contradict what might seem intuitively good strategies. For example, the model did not always fixate the location with the highest probability of containing the target. Instead, it sometimes it preferred to look just to the side of the target so as to gather more information about multiple potential targets with peripheral vision.

POMDPs have also been used to explain the behaviour of non-human species. A random dot motion discrimination task was framed as a POMDP problem by Rao (2010). In this task, primates were shown a visual display containing a group of moving dots. A fraction of the dots moved in one of two fixed directions (left or right) and other dots moved in random directions. The primates were rewarded for determining the direction in which the majority of dots moved, where the number of random dots was manipulated. Rao's (2010) model showed that primate decision times could be modelled as a reward maximizing solution to a POMDP. The model determined the optimal threshold for switching from information gathering to decision.

10.2.1 A Technical Overview

A POMDP defines a problem in which an agent takes a sequence of actions under uncertainty to maximize its reward. Formally, a POMDP is specified as a tuple $< S, A, O, T, Z, R, \gamma >$ (Figure 10.2), where S is a set of states; A is a set of actions; and O is a set of observations. At each time step t the agent is in a state $s_t \in S$, which is not directly observable to the agent. The agent takes an action $a_t \in A$, which results in the environment moving from s_t to a new state s_{t+1}. Due to the uncertainty in the outcome of an action, the next state s_{t+1} is modelled as a conditional probability function $T(s_t, a_t, s_{t+1}) = p(s_{t+1}|s_t, a_t)$, which gives the probability that the agent lies in s_{t+1}, after taking action a_t in state s_t (long dashed arrows in Figure 10.2). The agent then makes an observation to gather information about the state. Due to the uncertainty in observation, the observation result $o_{t+1} \in O$ is also modelled as a conditional probability function $Z(s_t, a_t, o_{t+1}) = p(o_{t+1}|s_t, a_t)$ (dotted arrows in Figure 10.2). Some agents are programmed to keep a history of action-observations pairs $h = < a_0, o_0, a_1, o_1, ... >$ that are used to inform action selections (small dashed arrows in Figure 10.2). In other agents, the history is replaced by a Bayesian Belief B distribution over possible states of the world and the observations are used to update this belief.

In each step t, the agent receives a real-valued reward $r_t = R(s_t, a_t, s_{t+1})$ if it takes action a_t in state s_t and results in s_{t+1} (small squares arrows in Figure 10.2). The goal of the agent is to maximize its expected total reward by choosing a suitable sequence of actions. A discount factor $\gamma \in [0, 1)$ is specified so that the total reward is finite and the problem is well defined. In this case, the expected total reward is given by $\sum_{t=0}^{\infty} \gamma^t R(s_t, a_t)$, where s_t and a_t denote the agents state and action at time t. The solution to a POMDP is an optimal policy (what to do when) that maximizes the expected total reward.

Applied to the visual search problem studied by Tseng and Howes (2015) (Figure 10.1) the problem is to maximize a reward function R in which finding images with a higher number of task-matching features than images with fewer matching features gains a higher

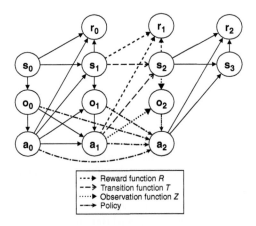

Figure 10.2 General representation of a POMDP.

reward. However, eye-movements and fixations incur a negative reward (a cost) that is proportional to the time taken. Therefore, maximizing reward means finding a sequence of action that trades more matching features against time. Each state s in this task might consist of a representation of the thirty-six images on the display and the location of the current fixation. The images might be represented as a bitmap or in terms of a more abstract symbolic feature vector. The actions A might include eye movements, mouse movements, and button presses. Again these might be abstracted to just include fixation locations and selections. An observation O would encode information from the fixated location (to 2.5 degrees of visual angle) with high reliability and information from the periphery with lower reliability according to the observation function Z. The transition function T models consequences of actions in A such as changing the fixation location. The transition function also models the reliability of action. For example, users might intend to fixate the second image from the left in the third row, but with a small probability fixate an adjacent image.

The usefulness of the assumption that users can be modelled with POMDPs rests on the ability of researchers to find psychologically valid definitions of $< S, A, O, T, Z, R, \gamma >$ and the use of machine learning algorithms to find approximately optimal strategies. Finding optimal strategies is computationally hard and often requires the application of the latest machine learning methods. Lastly, the usefulness of POMDPs also rests on demonstrating some correspondence between the behaviour generated from the learned optimal strategies and human behaviour.

10.2.2 Using POMDPs to Predict Interaction

What should be clear from the previous section is that defining a user's interaction problem as a POMDP is not in-and-of-itself sufficient to predict human behaviour. What is also required is a solution to the POMDP. The solution is a policy that makes use of the available resources to efficiently move through the state space to a desired goal state. While POMDPs often define very large and sometimes intractable state spaces, machine learning methods can sometimes be used to find efficient policies (Littman, Cassandra, and Kaelbling, 1995).

A concern in machine learning is with finding approximately optimal policies. These are policies that come close to maximizing the reward signal through task performance. Following Chen, Starke Sandra, Baber, and Howes (2017), we assume here that what is known in machine learning as a policy corresponds to what in HCI is often known as a strategy. In HCI it is often observed that users make use of a wide range of strategies and much HCI research has been aimed at uncovering these strategies and explaining why some are used in some circumstances and other elsewhere (Charman and Howes, 2001; Kieras, Meyer, Ballas, and Lauber, 2000). One finding is that users find strategies that are finely tuned to the particulars of the context and the bounds imposed by their own individual embodiment (Payne and Howes, 2013). In fact, users might be so good at finding efficient strategies that, which strategies they find might be predicted by the approximately optimal policies that solve well-defined POMDPs.

In tasks such as the visual search task in Figure 10.1 adaptation occurs within the bounds imposed by the human visual system (Kieras and Hornof, 2014), which are part of the problem definition. While the performance is bounded by these constraints, it is possible for people to find highly efficient strategies that trade the minimal number of eye movements for the highest quality image. Tseng and Howes (2015) found that when people performed this task in a laboratory they appeared to be computationally rational (Lewis, Howes, and Singh, 2014; Howes, Lewis, and Vera 2009). In other words, people were as efficient as they could given the computational limits of their visual system.

There has been much research in HCI and cognitive science demonstrating computationally rational adaptation (Fu and Pirolli, 2007; Payne and Howes, 2013; Lewis, Howes, and Singh, 2014; Trommershäuser, Glimcher, and Gegenfurtner, 2009; Sprague, Ballard, and Robinson, 2007; Hayhoe and Ballard, 2014; Nunez-Varela and Wyatt, 2013; Russell, Stefik, Pirolli, and Card, 1993; Russell and Subramanian, 1995). These analyses take into account the costs and benefits of each action to the user so as to compose actions into efficient behavioural sequences. One prominent example of this approach is Card's cost of knowledge function (Card, Pirolli, and Mackinlay, 1994). In addition, there are models of multitasking in which the time spent on each of two or more tasks is determined by their relative benefits and time costs (Zhang and Hornof, 2014). This literature supports the general idea that finding reward maximizing policies that solve well-defined POMDPs is a promising approach to modelling interaction.

10.2.3 A Caveat: Solving POMDPs is Difficult

The POMDP formalism is very general and is applicable to a diverse range of problems (Shani, Pineau, and Kaplow, 2013; Mnih, Kavukcuoglu, Silver, Graves, Antonoglou, Wierstra, and Riedmiller, 2013a). Unfortunately, the generality of POMDPs can result in high computational cost for deriving optimal control policies. As a consequence research on POMDPs is often focused on general methods for finding approximate solutions (Shani, Pineau, and Kaplow, 2013). Recent work on Deep Q-Networks is also a promising avenue for application to POMDPs. For example, Mnih, Kavukcuoglu, Silver, Graves, Antonoglou, Wierstra, and Riedmiller, (2013a) have shown that Deep Q-Networks are capable of learning human-level control policies on a variety of different Atari 2600 games.

10.3 Menu Search as a POMDP

Imagine that a goal for a user who is experienced with menus, but who has never used Apple's OS X Safari browser before, is to select 'Show Next Tab' from the Safari Window menu. A user might solve this goal by first fixating the top menu item, encoding the word 'Minimize'; rejecting it as irrelevant to the target, moving the eyes to the next group of items, that begins 'Show Previous Tab', noticing that this item is not the target but is closely related and also noticing, in peripheral vision, that the next item has a similar word shape and length to the target; then moving the eyes to 'Show Next Tab', confirming that it is the target and selecting it.

This section shows how interactive behaviours such as these can be predicted by solving a POMDP. Importantly, the aim is not to predict the interactions that people learn with specific menus and the location of specific items, rather the aim is to predict how people will perform interactive menu search for newly experienced menus. The requirement is that the model should learn, from experience, the best way to search for new targets in new, previously unseen, menus.

Chen, Bailly, Brumby, Oulasvirta, and Howes (2015) hypothesized that a key property of the menu search task is that human search strategies should be influenced by the distribution of relevance across menus. If highly semantically relevant items are rare then the model should learn to select them as soon as they are observed, whereas if they are very common then they are less likely to be correct, and the model should learn to gather more evidence before selection. The goal for the model, therefore, is not just to learn how to use a single menu, but rather it is how to use a new menu that is sampled from an experienced distributions of menus.

To achieve this goal Chen, Bailly, Brumby, Oulasvirta, and Howes (2015) built a computational model that can be thought of as a simple POMDP. In the model an external representation of the displayed menu is fixated and an observation is made that encodes information about the relevance of word shapes ('Minimize' and 'Zoom', for example have different lengths) and semantics (word meanings). This observation is used to update a vector representing a summary of the observation history (a belief about the state). This vector has an element for the shape relevance of every item in the menu, an element for the semantic relevance of every item in the menu, and an element for the current fixation location. The vector elements are null until estimates are acquired through observation. An observation is made after each fixation action, e.g. after fixating 'Minimize' in the above example. After having encoded new information through observation, the policy chooses an action on the basis of the current belief. The chosen action might be to fixate on another item or to make a selection, or to exit the menu if the target is probably absent. Belief-action values are updated incrementally (learned) as reward feedback is received from the interaction.

10.3.1 POMDP Formulation

A state s is represented as a vector consisting of n elements for the shape, n for the semantic relevance, and 1 for the fixation location. The semantic/alphabetic relevance had 5 levels [Null, 0, 0.3, 0.6, 1]. The shape relevance had 2 levels [0 for non-target length; 1 for target length]. The fixation was an integer representing one of the menu item locations [1..n]. From each state there were $n + 2$ actions in A, including n actions for fixating on n menu item locations, an action for selecting the fixated item, and an action to exit the menu without selection (target absent). It was assumed that the consequences of actions were entirely reliable and, therefore, the transition function T had probability 1.

An observation o_t modelled human vision by encoding information from the fovea with high reliability and information from the periphery with lower reliability according to the observation function $\mathcal{Z}$. Chen, Bailly, Brumby, Oulasvirta, and Howes (2015) modelled the observations with which people determine the semantic relevance of items by matching them to the goal specification. To implement this assumption, they used relevance ratings gathered from human participants and reported by Bailly, Oulasvirta, Brumby, and Howes (2014). They give the following example: if the model sampled the goal Zoom and foveated the word Minimize then it could look-up the relevance score 0.75 which was the mean relevance ranking given by participants. Chen, Bailly, Brumby, Oulasvirta, and Howes's (2015) model also observed the length of each menu item (0 for non-target length; 1 for target length). Observations of alphabetic relevance were determined using the distance apart in the alphabet of target and fixated first letters. This was then standardized to a four-level scale between 0 and 1, i.e., $[0, 0.3, 0.6, 1]$. Further details are reported in Chen, Bailly, Brumby, Oulasvirta, and Howes (2015).

Visual acuity is known to reduce with eccentricity from the fovea (Kieras and Hornof, 2014). In Chen and colleagues' (2015) model, the acuity function was represented as the probability that a visual feature was recognized. Semantic information was available with probability 0.95 at the fovea and probability 0 elsewhere. The model made use of semantic features and shape features but could easily be enhanced with other features such as colour. These parameter settings resulted in the following availability probabilities: 0.95 for the item fixated, 0.89 for items immediately above or below the fixated item, and 0 for items further away. On each fixation, the availability of the shape information was determined by these probabilities.

Chen and colleagues (2015) defined rewards for saccades and fixations in terms of their durations as determined by the psychological literature. Saccades were given a duration that was a function of distance. Fixations were given an average duration measured in previous work on menus. A large reward was given for successfully finding the target or correctly responding that it was absent.

10.3.2 Belief Update

The belief-state B was a vector with the same number of elements as the state S, but these elements initially had null values. These values were updated through observation.

10.3.3 Learning

Chen and colleagues' (2015) model solved the POMDP using Q-learning. The details of the algorithm are not described here but they can be found in any standard Machine Learning text (e.g. Sutton and Barto (1998)). Q-learning uses the reward signal, defined above, to learn state-action values (called Q values). A state-action value can be thought of as a prediction of the future reward (both positive and negative) that will accrue if the action is taken. Before learning, an empty Q-table was assumed in which all state-action values were zero. The model therefore started with no control knowledge and action selection was entirely random. The model was then trained until performance plateaued (requiring 20 million trials). On each trial, the model was trained on a menu constructed by sampling randomly from the ecological distributions of shape and semantic/alphabetic relevance. The model explored the action space using an ϵ-greedy exploration. This means that it exploited the greedy/best action with a probability $1 - \epsilon$, and it explored all the actions randomly with probability ϵ. q-values were adjusted according to the reward feedback. The (approximately) optimal policy acquired through this training was then used to generate the predictions described below.

10.3.4 Predicting Menu Search

The purpose of this first study was to examine the model's predictions on commonly used computer application menus. The task was to search for specific target items in a vertically arranged menu. How items were organized in the menu was varied. Items could be unorganized, alphabetically organized, or semantically organized. To determine the statistical properties of a menu search environment we used the results of a previous study (Bailly and Malacria, 2013) in which the menus of sixty applications from Apple OS X were sampled. Together these applications used a total 1049 menus, and 7802 menu items. Chen and colleagues (2015) used these to determine the ecological distribution of menu length, item length, semantic group size and first letter frequencies (for alphabetic search). The probability of each length (number of characters) observed by Chen and colleagues (2015) is reproduced in Figure 10.3 right panel. The distribution is skewed, with a long tail of low probability longer menu items.

Chen, Bailly, Brumby, Oulasvirta, and Howes (2015) then ran a study in which participants rated how likely two menu items were to appear close together on a menu. Each participant rated pairs sampled from the Apple OS X Safari browser menus. The probability of each semantic relevance rating is shown in Figure 10.3 left panel. These ratings were used by Chen and colleagues (2015) both to construct example menus and to implement the model's semantic relevance function.

The first set of results reported by Chen, Bailly, Brumby, Oulasvirta, and Howes (2015) were for the approximately optimal strategy (after learning), unless stated otherwise. The

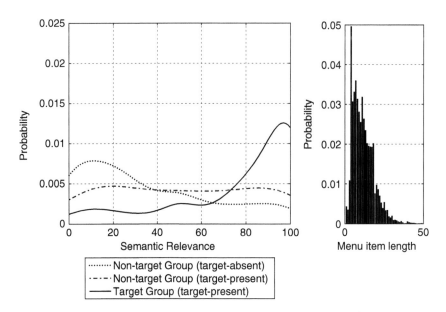

Figure 10.3 Menu ecology of a real-world menu task (Apple OS X menus). Left panel: The distribution of semantic relevance. Right panel: The distribution of menu length. Reproduced with permission from ACM.

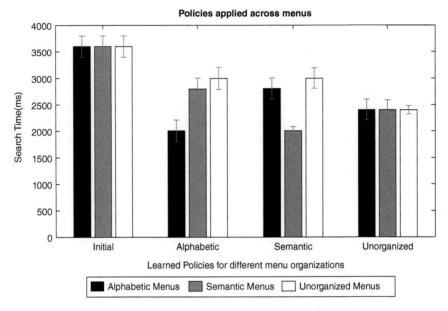

Figure 10.4 The search duration taken by the optimal strategy for each type of menu (95% confidence intervals (C.I.s)). Reproduced with permission from ACM.

optimal policy achieved 99 per cent selection accuracy. The utility of all models plateaued, suggesting that the learned strategy was a good approximation to the optimal strategy.

Figure 10.4 is a plot of the duration required for the optimal policy to make a selection given four types of experience crossed with three types of test menu. The purpose of this analysis is to show how radically different patterns of behaviour emerge from the model based on how previously experienced menus were organized. Prior to training (the far left *Initial* set of three bars in the figure), the model offers the slowest performance; it is unable to take advantage of the structure in the alphabetic and semantic menus because it has no control knowledge. After training on a distribution of *Unorganized* menus (far right set in the figure), performance time is better than prior to training. However, there is no difference in performance time between the different menu organizations. After training on a distribution of semantically organized menus (middle right set in the figure), the model is able to take advantage of semantic structure, but this training is costly to performance on alphabetic and unorganized menus. After training on a distribution of alphabetically organized menus (middle left set in the figure), the model is able to take advantage of alphabetic ordering, but this training is again costly to the other menu types. The optimal policy must switch the policy depending on the menu type.

Figure 10.5 shows the effect of different semantic groupings on performance time (reported by Chen and colleagues (2015). It contrasts the performance time predictions for menus that are organized into three groups of three or into two groups of five. The contrast between these kinds of design choices has been studied extensively before (Miller

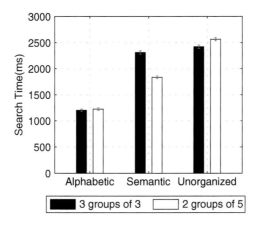

Figure 10.5 The effect of semantic group size (95% C.I.s). Reproduced with permission from ACM.

and Remington, 2004). What has been observed is an interaction between the effect of longer menus and the effect of the number of items in each semantic group (See Miller and Remington's (2004) Figure 8). As can be seen in Figure 10.5 while the effect of longer menus ($3 \times 3 = 9$ versus $2 \times 5 = 10$) is longer performance times in the unorganized and alphabetic menus, the effect of organization (three groups of three versus two of five) gives shorter performance times in the semantic condition. This prediction corresponds closely to a number of studies (See Miller and Remington's (2004) Figure 8).

The results show that deriving adaptive strategies using a reinforcement learning algorithm, given a definition of the human menu search problem as a POMDP, bounded by the constraints of the human visual systems (embodiment) and the ecology of the task environment (ecology), can lead to reasonable predictions about interactive behaviour.

10.3.5 Testing the Model Against Human Data

Chen and colleagues (2015) also tested the model against human data (Bailly, Oulasvirta, Brumby, and Howes 2014; Brumby, Cox, Chung, and Fernandes, 2014). These data were collected using laboratory menus with different distributions to those in the other study. The model was trained on these distributions and the optimal policy was then used to generate the predictions described in the following results section.

10.3.5.1 Target Location Effect on Gaze Distribution

Figure 10.6 shows the effect of target position on the distribution of item gazes for each menu organization. The model is compared to human data reported in (Bailly et al., 2014). The adjusted R^2 for each of the three organizations (alphabetic, unorganized, semantic) were reported as 0.84, 0.65, 0.80. In the top left panel, the model's gaze distribution is a consequence of both alphabetic anticipation and shape relevance in peripheral vision.

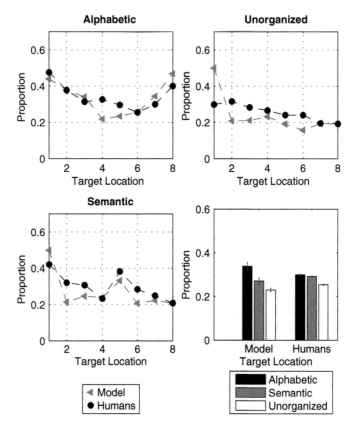

Figure 10.6 The proportion of gazes on the target location for each of the three types of menu (95% C.I.s). Reproduced with permission from ACM.

Interestingly, both the model and the participants selectively gazed at targets at either end of the menu more frequently than targets in the middle. This may reflect the ease with which words beginning with early and late alphabetic words can be located. In the top right panel, there is no organizational structure to the menu and the model's gaze distribution is a consequence of shape relevance only in peripheral vision. The model offers a poor prediction of the proportion of gazes on the target when it is in position 1, otherwise, as expected, the distribution is relatively flat in both the model and the participants. In the bottom left panel, the model's gaze distribution is a function of semantic relevance and shape relevance. Here there are spikes in the distribution at position 1 and 5. In the model, this is because the emergent policy uses the relevance of the first item of each semantic group as evidence of the content of that group. In other words, the grouping structure of the menu is evidence in the emergent gaze distributions. The aggregated data is shown in the bottom right panel; the model predicts the significant effect of organization on gaze distribution, although it predicts a larger effect for alphabetic menus than was observed.

10.3.6 Discussion

Chen and colleagues (2015) reported a model in which search behaviours were an emergent consequence of an interaction problem specified as a POMDP. The observation function and state transition function modelled the cognitive and perceptual limits of the user, and the reward function modelled the user's preferences for speed and accuracy. Predicted strategies were generated using machine learning to infer an approximately optimal policy for the POMDP. The model was tested with two studies. The first study involved applying the model to a real world distribution of menu items and in the second study the model was compared to human data from a previously reported experiment.

Unlike in previous models, no assumptions were made about the gaze strategies available to or adopted by users, Instead, a key property of the approach is that behavioural predictions are derived by maximizing utility given a quantitative theory of the constraints on behaviour, rather than by maximizing fit to the data. Although this *optimality* assumption is sometimes controversial, the claim is simply that users will do the best they can with the resources that are available to them. Further discussions of this issue can be found in (Howes, Lewis, and Vera, 2009; Lewis, Howes, and Singh, 2014; Payne and Howes, 2013).

10.4 Interactive Decision Making as a POMDP

The previous example of how a POMDP can be used to model interaction focused on a relatively routine low-level task. In this section we look at a model reported by Chen, Starke, Baber, and Howes (2017) of a higher-level decision making task. The model shows how decision strategies are an emergent consequence of both the statistical properties of the environment (the experienced cue validities, different time cost for extracting information) and of the constraints imposed by human perceptual mechanisms. For a decision making task that is supported by visualization, this theory can be written precisely by formulating the decision problem as a POMDP for active vision and solving this problem with machine learning to find an approximately optimal decision strategy (emergent heuristics). The model offers an alternative theory of decision making to the heuristic model of Gigerenzer and Todd (1999).

In the resulting model, eye movement strategies and stopping rules are an emergent consequence of the visualization and the limits of human vision (modelled with an observation function) (Chen, Bailly, Brumby, Oulasvirta, and Howes, 2015; Tseng and Howes, 2015; Butko and Movellan, 2008). The assumption is that people choose which cues to look at and when to stop looking at cues informed by the reward/cost that they receive for the decisions they make. Better decisions will receive higher rewards, which will reinforce good eye movement strategies.

Before introducing Chen, Starke, Baber, and Howes's (2017) POMDP theory of decision making through interaction, we briefly described the credit card fraud detection task that they used to illustrate the theory. The task is motivated by a real-world scenario that is known to be extremely difficult for people. Credit card fraud detection analysts attempt to identify fraudulent patterns in transaction data-sets, often characterized by a large number of samples, many dimensions, and online updates (Dal Pozzolo, Caelen, Le Borgne, Waterschoot, and Bontempi, 2014). Despite the use of automated detection algorithms, there continue to be key roles for people to play in the analysis process. These roles range from defining and tuning the algorithms that automatic systems deploy, to triaging and screening recommendations from such systems, to contacting customers (either to query a transaction or to explain a decision). In terms of triaging and screening, we assume that an automated detection process is running and that this process has flagged a given transaction (or set of transactions) as suspicious and a user will engage in some form of investigation to decide how to respond to the flag. Based on pilot interviews and discussions with credit card fraud analysts and organizations, we believe that there are several ways in which the investigation could be performed. In some instances, the investigation could involve direct contact with the card holder, in which the caller follows a predefined script and protocols that do not involve investigative capabilities. In some cases, these are passed to the analyst who needs to make a decision as to whether or not the credit card is blocked (this is the approach assumed in this paper). In this instance, the analyst would take a more forensic approach to the behaviour of the card holder and the use of the card, relative to some concept of normal activity. In some cases, investigation could be at the level of transactions, in which the analyst seeks to identify patterns of criminal activity involving several cards. In this instance, the analysis would be looking for evidence of stolen details or unusual patterns of use of several cards, say multiple transactions in different locations within a short timeframe. Other functions that people can perform in the fraud detection process include: risk prioritization, fast closure of low risk cases, documentation of false positives (Pandey, 2010), and identification of risk profiles and fraud patterns (Sáanchez, Vila, Cerda, and Serrano, 2009; Jha and Westland, 2013).

Chen, Starke, Baber, and Howes (2017) used a simplified version of fraud detection in which the task was to decide whether a transaction should be blocked (prevented from being authorized) or allowed. Participants were provided with nine sources of information (cues) and these were presented using one of four display designs (visualizations). The cues differed in the reliability with which they determine whether or not a transaction is a fraud and the participants must discover these validities with experience and decide which cues are worth using to make a decision.

10.4.1 POMDP Formulation

At any time step t, the environment is in a state $s_t \in S$. A state represents a true information pattern presented on the user interface. As shown in Figure 10.7, nine cues associated with credit card transactions are presented on the interface. The value of each cue was discretized into two levels, representing 'fraudulent (F)' and 'normal (N)' respectively. Therefore, for example, one of the states is a nine-element vector $[F,N,N,F,F,F,N,F,N]$, each item of which represents the value for one of the cues ('F' for fraudulent and 'N' for normal). Hence, the size of the state space is $2^9 = 512$.

An action is taken at each time step, $a_t \in A$. The action space, A, consists of both the information gathering actions (i.e., which cue to fixate) and decision making actions (i.e.,

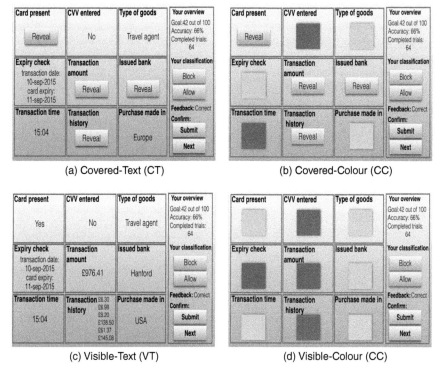

Figure 10.7 Four interface variants for credit card fraud detection. The information cues are represented with text (left panels) or light and dark grey shaded (right panels) and the information is either immediately available (bottom panels) or revealed by clicking the 'Reveal' buttons (top panels). Reproduced with permission from ACM.

Block/Allow transaction). Therefore, the size of the action space is eleven (nine cues plus two decision actions).

At any moment, the environment (in one of the states s) generates a reward (cost if the value is negative), $r(s, a)$, in response to the action taken a. For the information gathering actions, the reward is the time cost (the unit is seconds). The time cost includes both the dwell time on the cues and the saccadic time cost of travelling between cues. The dwell durations used in the model were determined from experimental data. In the experiment to be modelled (described below), the participants were asked to complete 100 *correct* trials as quickly as possible, so that errors were operationalized as time cost. In the model, the cost for incorrect decisions is based on participants' average time cost (Seconds) for a trial (CT:17 ± 15; CC:24 ± 7;VT:20 ± 8; VC:13 ± 3). That is, the penalty of an incorrect trial is the time cost for doing another trial.

In addition to the reward, another consequence of the action is that the environment moves to a new state according to the transition function. In the current task the states (i.e. displayed information patterns) stay unchanged across time steps within one trial. Therefore, $T(S_{t+1}|S_t, A_t)$ equals to 1 only when $S_{t+1} = S_t$. $T(S_{t+1}|S_t, A_t)$ equals 0 otherwise. That is, the state transition matrix is the identity matrix.

After transitioning to a new state, a new observation is received. The observation, $o_t \in O$, is defined as the information gathered at the time step t. An observation is a 9-element vector, each element of which represents the information gathered for one of the cues. Each element of the observation has three levels, F (fraudulent), N (normal), and U (unknown). For example, one observation might be represented as [F,N,U,F,U,U,U,N,N]. Therefore, the upper bound on the observation space is $3^9 = 19683$.

For the observation function $p(O_t|S_t, A_t)$ The availability of information about a cue is dependent on the distance between this cue and the fixation location (eccentricity). In addition, it is known that an object's colour is more visible in the periphery than the object's text label (Kieras and Hornof, 2014). In our model, the observation model is based on the acuity functions reported in (Kieras and Hornof, 2014), where the visibility of an object is dependent on, for example, the object size, the object feature (colour or text), and the eccentricity.

The observation obtained is constrained by a theory of the limits on the human visual system. The model assumed that the text information was obtained only when it was fixated. The colour information was obtained based on the colour acuity function reported in (Kieras and Hornof, 2014). This function was used to determine the availability of the colour information for each cue given the distance between the cues and the fixated location (called *eccentricity*), and the size of the item. Specifically, on each fixation, the availability of the colour information was determined by the probabilities defined in Equation (10.1).

$$P(available) = P(size + X > threshold) \qquad (10.1)$$

where *size* is the object size in terms of visual angle in degrees; $X \sim \mathcal{N}(size, v \times size)$; *threshold* $= a \times e^2 + b \times e + c$; e is eccentricity in terms of visual angle in degrees. In the model, the function were set with parameter values of $v = 0.7, b = 0.1, c = 0.1, a = 0.035$ as in (Kieras and Hornof, 2014).

10.4.2 Belief Update

At each time step, the environment is in a state s_i, which is not directly observed. The model maintains a belief b about the state given the sequence of observations. Every time the agent takes an action a and observes o, b is updated by Bayes' rule. At each time t, a belief b_t vector consists of a probability for each of the states, $b_t(s_i)$, where $i \in 1, 2, 3, ...N_s$ and N_s is the total number of states.

10.4.3 Learning

Control knowledge was represented in Chen, Starke, Baber, and Howes's (2017) model as a mapping between beliefs and actions, which was learned with Q-learning (Watkins and Dayan, 1992). Further details of the algorithm can be found in any standard Machine Learning text (e.g., Watkins and Dayan, 1992; Sutton and Barto, 1998).

Before learning, a Q-table was assumed in which the values (Q-values) of all belief-action pairs were zero. The model therefore started with no control knowledge and action selection was entirely random. The model was then trained through simulated experience until performance plateaued. The model explored the action space using an ϵ-greedy exploration.

Q-values of the encountered belief-action pairs were adjusted according to the reward feedback. The idea is that, Q-values are learned (or estimated) by simulated experience of the interaction tasks. The true Q-values are estimated by the sampled points encountered during the simulations. The optimal policy acquired through this training was then used to generate the predictions described below (last 1000 trials of the simulation).

While Chen, Starke, Baber, and Howes (2017) used Q-learning, any reinforcement learning algorithm that converges on the optimal policy is sufficient to derive the rational adaptation (Sutton and Barto, 1998). The Q-learning process is not a theoretical commitment. Its purpose is merely to find the optimal control policy. It is not to model the process of learning and is therefore used to achieve methodological optimality and determine the computationally rational strategy (Lewis, Howes, and Singh, 2014). Alternative learning algorithms include QMDP (Littman, Cassandra, and Kaelbling, 1995) or DQN (Mnih, Kavukcuoglu, Silver, Graves, Antonoglou, Wierstra, and Riedmiller, 2013b).

10.4.4 A Typical Decision-making Task

Participants in Chen, Starke, Baber, and Howes's (2017) study were asked to take on the role of a credit card fraud analyst at a bank. The task was to decide whether a given transaction should be blocked (prevented from being authorized) or allowed. As shown in each panel of Figure 10.7, nine information sources were laid out in a 3×3 grid. An operation panel was presented on the right side of the interface, including Block/Allow decision buttons and a feedback window. The nine cues were selected as relevant to the detection of credit card fraud based on the literature and discussions with domain experts. For example, one cue was called 'Transaction Amount'. For a particular transaction, this cue signalled either 'Fraud' or 'Not-fraud' with a *validity* of 0.60. The validity was the probability that the cue indicated fraud given that the ground truth of the transaction is fraudulent. Validities were arbitrarily assigned to the nine cues and reflected the observation that high quality cues are relatively rare in many tasks. The cues had validities [0.85, 0.70, 0.65, 0.60, 0.60, 0.60, 0.55, 0.55 and 0.55], The location of each cue on the interface was assigned randomly for each participant and stayed constant across all trials. Participants were asked to complete one hundred correct trials as quickly as possible. As trials in which an error was made (e.g., blocking a non-fraudulent transaction) did not reduce the total number of correct trials required, errors resulted in time costs.

The experiment manipulated three independent factors: *validity, format* and *availability*. *Validity* had nine levels (grouped into high, medium, and low levels of validity). *Format* had two levels: text vs. colour. *Availability* had two levels: visible vs. covered. Format and availability give four user interfaces (Figure 10.7).

- Covered-Text (CT) condition (Figure 10.7a): The cue information was presented in covered text. In order to check each cue, the participants had to click on the associated button on each cue and wait for 1.5 seconds while a blank screen was shown.

- Covered-Colour (CC) condition (Figure 10.7b): The cue information was presented by colour (light grey shade for possibly normal, dark grey shade for possibly fraudulent). As with CT, the information was covered until clicked.
- Visible-Text (VT) condition (Figure 10.7c): The cue information was presented in text. The information was visible immediately (no mouse-click was required).
- Visible-Colour (VC) condition (Figure 10.7d): The cue information was presented in colour and no mouse-click was required to reveal it.

10.4.5 Behaviour of the Model

Chen, Starke, Baber, and Howes (2017) were interested in explaining each individuals' interactive decision making behaviour as an approximate solution to a POMDP. The first step in the analysis therefore involved calibrating action dwell times to the empirical data and on average the calibrated dwell time was 0.66 ± 0.10 seconds across the cues.

Having calibrated the model, Chen, Starke, Baber, and Howes (2017) then used Q-learning to find a predicted (approximately) optimal strategy for each participant. This strategy was used to predict how many cues should (ideally) be fixated in each condition. This prediction and the human data are reproduced in Figure 10.8. The model correctly predicts that participants should fixate on more cues in the Visible-Text condition (VT: 6.21 ± 1.32) than in the other three conditions. It also correctly predicts that participants should fixate fewer cues in the Visible-Colour condition (Visible-Colour: 3.08 ± 1.32) and it learns to be relatively economical in the 'covered' conditions (Covered-Text: 3.95 ± 1.97; Covered-Colour: 3.84 ± 1.21).

Intuitively, these findings can be explained in terms of adaptation to information cost and limits of peripheral vision. In the Visible-Text condition, information is cheap and

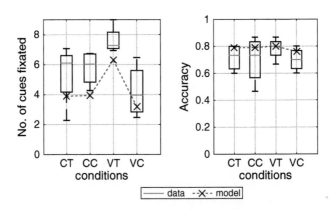

Figure 10.8 The number of cues (left) and accuracy (right) predicted by the model across four experimental conditions (x-axis). Model predictions (grey crosses) are plotted with the participant's data (boxplots). The figure shows that the model predicts that an elevated number of cues will be fixated by participants in the Visible-Text condition and a reduced number in the Visible-Colour. Reproduced with permission from ACM.

foveated vision is required to read text, and therefore more cues are used. In contrast, in the covered conditions (Covered-Text and Covered-Colour), information access is expensive, thus reducing the number of cues used. Lastly, in the Visible-Colour condition, peripheral vision, rather than only foveated vision, can be used to access information and it appears that, as a consequence, fewer cues are used, at least by being directly fixated.

10.4.6 Implications for Decision Strategies

Chen, Starke, Baber, and Howes (2017) also provides evidence about the use of decision heuristics such as Take-the Best (TTB) and Weighted Additive (WADD). TTB would be indicated by the participants selecting just the very best cue (which in our interface always discriminates) and then making a Block/Allow decision. However, participants did not only use the highest validity cue. Further, WADD would be indicated by the participants using all of the available cues. However, it is clear that this is not happening, with participants preferring to use only a subset of the best cues. While there is plenty of evidence in other tasks that people use TTB, they do not seem to do so in Chen and colleagues (2017) task, and may not do so exclusively.

TTB and WADD have been extensively studied in the human decision making literature, but more recent work has suggested that people exhibit a more flexible range of strategies. Instead of assuming TTB or WADD, Chen and colleagues (2017) model derived the optimal strategy given a POMDP problem formulation; this optimal strategy involved using a weighted integration of the best cues. These cues provide information that optimizes the trade-off between time and accuracy imposed in the experiment. This result is consistent with work that emphasizes the adaptation of strategies to a cognitive architecture in inter-action with a local task (Gray, Sims, Fu, and Schoelles, 2006; Howes, Duggan, Kalidindi, Tseng, and Lewis, 2015; Payne and Howes, 2013). Further work is required to determine whether TTB emerges as a consequence of different task scenarios.

10.5 Discussion

This chapter has reviewed two models, previously presented by Chen, Bailly, Brumby, Oulasvirta and Howes (2015) and Chen, Starke, Baber and Howes (2017), and shown that POMDPs permit a rigorous definition of interaction as an emergent consequence of constrained sequential stochastic decision processes. Theories of human perception and action were used to guide the construction of partial observation functions and transition functions for the POMDP. A reinforcement learning algorithm was then used to find approximately optimal strategies. The emergent interactive behaviours were compared to human data and the models were shown to offer a computational explanation of interaction. In the following paragraphs we summarize the ways in which embodiment, ecology, and adaptation constrain the emergence of interaction.

Embodied interaction. In the models, interaction was both made possible by and con-strained by the way in which cognition is embodied. A key element of embodiment concerns the constraints imposed by the biological mechanisms for encoding information from the environment. In both the menu and the decision model, the limitations of the observation function were key factors that shaped the cognitive strategies determining interaction. The observation function modelled human foveated vision. In menu search, foveated vision was the primary determinant of beliefs about the semantic relevance of items and in the decision task it was a primary determinant of beliefs about whether or not a transaction was fraudulent. However, peripheral vision also played a role. In the menu search model, peripheral vision provided an extra source of eye-movement guidance through the detection of items with similar or dissimilar shapes to the target. In the decision model, peripheral vision encoded cue validities without direct fixation, but only when cues were displayed with colour, and thereby played a substantive role in distinguishing the properties of the different visualizations.

Ecological interaction. The ecological nature of interaction was most evident in the menu search model, where menus were sampled from distributions that determined the proportions of high, medium, and low relevance distractor items. These ecological distributions were critical to the structure of the emergent cognitive strategies. While we did not report the analysis, it is obvious that the more discriminable these distributions (the greater the d' in signal detection terms) then the more it should be possible for the agent to adopt strategies that localize fixation to areas where the target is more likely to be found. Ecological constraints on the cognitive strategies were also evident in the decision model where the adaptive strategies were dependent on the distribution of cue validities. Here, high validity cues were rare and low validity cues relatively common resulting in behaviours that emphasized fixating high validitiy cues.

Adaptive interaction. In both the menu model and the decision model, the strategies for information gathering and choice, and consequentially the behaviour, were an adaptive consequence of embodied interaction with an ecologically determined task environment. The strategies emerge from the constraints imposed by ecology and embodiment through experience. They are adaptive to the extent that they approximate the optimal strategies for the user; that is, those strategies that maximize utility.

Chen, Starke, Baber, and Howes (2017) report that the key property of the model, that it predicts interactive strategies given constraints, is evident in the fact that it generates a broad range of strategies that are also exhibited by humans. For example, in addition to those described earlier, it also predicts a well-known strategy called *centre-of-gravity* (also called *averaging saccades* or *the global effect*) (Findlay 1982; Vitu 2008; Van der Stigchel and Nijboer 2011; Venini, Remington, Horstmann, and Becker, 2014), which refers to the fact that people frequently land saccades on a region of low-interest that is surrounded by multiple regions of high-interest. Figure 10.9 shows that this 'centre-of-gravity' effect is an emergent effect of our model. The model also predicts inhibition-of-return.

The fact that the model is able to predict the *strategies* that people use is a departure from models that are programmed with strategies so as to fit performance time. This is important because it suggests that the theory might be easily developed in the future so as to rapidly evaluate the usability of a broader range of interactions. For example, in the near future it should be possible to consider multidimensional visualizations that not only make use of colour, but also size, shape, grouping, etc. It should be possible to increment the observation functions, for example, with a shape detection capacity, and then use the learning algorithm to find new strategies for the new visualizations.

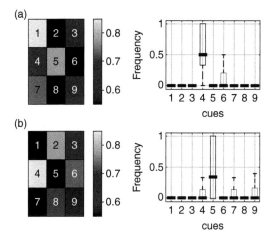

Figure 10.9 In each row of the figure, the frequency of the model's cue fixations (right panel) is shown for a different spatial arrangement of cue validities (left panel). The validity of ROIs in the left panels is represented as a heat map (high validity is a lighter colour). The frequency of model fixations is represented as a box plot. The column numbers in the box plot correspond to the numbers of the ROIs (1..9). In the top row, ROI number 4 has a low validity but is surrounded by relatively high validity ROIs (1, 5, and 7). In contrast, in the bottom row, ROI number 5 has a low validity and surrounding ROIs 2, 4 and 6 have high validity. In both rows, the model fixates frequently on the ROI that is surrounded by high validity ROIs. This is known as a centre-of-gravity effect. Reproduced with permission from ACM.

Before concluding, we briefly summarize the advantages and disadvantages of the POMDP approach to explaining interaction that have been discussed in this chapter. The advantages include:

- The POMDP framing is a well-known and rigorous approach to defining stochastic sequential decision processes and there is a growing range of machine learning algorithms dedicated to solving them.
- POMDPs provide a means of defining and integrating theoretical concepts in HCI concerning embodiment, ecology, and adaptation.
- POMDPs provide a means to make inferences about the consequences of theoretical assumptions for behaviour.

The disadvantages include:

- POMDPs are often computationally intractable and careful design is required to define tractable but useful problems.
- Modern machine learning algorithms do not yet provide a good model of the human learning process. Typically, it requires people many fewer trials to acquire rational strategies than are required to solve a POMDP for the same problem.

- Despite the fact that POMDPs are a universal formalism for representing sequential decision processes, the scope of which human behaviours have been modelled, to date, is quite limited. Mostly, the existing models are variants of visual information gathering tasks. The continued expansion of the scope of POMDP models of humans rests on the ability of researchers to find psychologically valid definitions of $< \mathcal{S}, \mathcal{A}, \mathcal{O}, \mathcal{T}, \mathcal{Z}, \mathcal{R}, \gamma >$.

In conclusion, evidence supports the claim that POMDPs provide a rigorous framework for defining interaction as constrained sequential stochastic decision processes. POMDPs can offer a computational explanation of interactive behaviour as a consequence of embodiment, ecology, and adaptation.

....

REFERENCES

Bailly, G., and Malacria, S., 2013. MenuInspector: Outil pour l'analyse des menus et cas d'étude. In: *IHM '13 Proceedings of the 25th Conference on l'Interaction Homme-Machine*. New York, NY: ACM.

Bailly, G., Oulasvirta, A., Brumby, D. P., and Howes, A., 2014. Model of visual search and selection time in linear menus. In: *ACM CHI'14*. New York, NY: ACM, pp. 3865–74.

Brumby, D. P., Cox, A. L., Chung, J., and Fernandes, B., 2014. How does knowing what you are looking for change visual search behavior? In: *ACM CHI'14*. New York, NY: ACM, pp. 3895–8.

Butko, N. J., and Movellan, J. R., 2008. I-POMDP: An infomax model of eye movement. In: *2008 IEEE 7th International Conference on Development and Learning*. New York, NY: ACM, pp. 139–44.

Byrne, M. D., 2001. ACT-R/PM and menu selection: Applying a cognitive architecture to HCI. *International Journal of Human-Computer Studies*, 55(1), pp. 41–84.

Card, S. K., Moran, T. P., and Newell, A., 1983. The Psychology of Human-Computer Interaction. Hillsdale, NJ: Lawrence Erlbaum.

Card, S. K., Pirolli, P., and Mackinlay, J. D., 1994. The cost-of-knowledge characteristic function: display evaluation for direct-walk dynamic information visualizations. In: *Proceedings of the SIGCHI Conference on Human Factors in Computing Systems*. New York, NY: ACM, pp. 238–44.

Charman, S. C., and Howes, A., 2001. The effect of practice on strategy change. In: *Proceedings of the Twenty-Third Annual Conference of the Cognitive Science Society*. London: Psychology Press, pp. 188–93.

Chen, X., Bailly, G., Brumby, D. P., Oulasvirta, A., and Howes, A., 2015. The Emergence of Interactive Behaviour: A Model of Rational Menu Search. In: *Proceedings of the 33rd Annual ACM Conference on Human Factors in Computing Systems*. New York, NY: ACM, pp. 4217–26.

Chen, X., Starke, S., Baber, C., and Howes, A., 2017. A Cognitive Model of How People Make Decisions Through Interaction with Visual Displays. In: *Proceedings of the ACM CHI'17 Conference on Human Factors in Computing Systems*. New York, NY: ACM, pp. 1205–16.

Dal Pozzolo, A., Caelen, O., Le Borgne, Y.-A., Waterschoot, S., and Bontempi, G., 2014. Learned lessons in credit card fraud detection from a practitioner perspective. *Expert systems with applications*, 41(10), pp. 4915–28.

Findlay, J. M., 1982. Global visual processing for saccadic eye movements. *Vision Research*, 22(8), pp. 1033–45.

Fu, W.-T., and Pirolli, P., 2007. SNIF-ACT: A cognitive model of user navigation on the World Wide Web. Human–ComputerInteraction, 22(4), pp. 355–412.

Gigerenzer, G., and Todd, P. M., 1999. Fast and frugal heuristics: The adaptive toolbox. *Simple Heuristics That Make Us Smart*. Oxford: Oxford University Press, pp. 3–34.

Gray, W. D., Sims, C. R., Fu, W.-T., and Schoelles, M. J., 2006. The soft constraints hypothesis: a rational analysis approach to resource allocation for interactive behavior. *Psychological Review*, 113(3), p. 461. doi: 10.1037/0033-295.113.3.461

Halverson, T., and Hornof, A. J., 2011. A computational model of "active vision" for visual search in human–computer interaction. Human–ComputerInteraction, 26(4), pp. 285–314.

Hayhoe, M., and Ballard, D., 2014. Modeling Task Control of Eye Movements. *Current Biology*, 24(13), pp. R622–R628.

Hornof, A. J., Zhang, Y., and Halverson, T., 2010. Knowing where and when to look in a time-critical multimodal dual task. In: *Proceedings of the SIGCHI Conference on Human Factors in Computing Systems*. New York, NY: ACM, pp. 2103–12.

Howes, A., Duggan, G. B., Kalidindi, K., Tseng, Y.-C., and Lewis, R. L., 2015. Predicting Short-Term Remembering as Boundedly Optimal Strategy Choice. *Cognitive Science*, 40(5), pp. 1192–223.

Howes, A., Lewis, R. R. L., and Vera, A., 2009. Rational adaptation under task and processing constraints: implications for testing theories of cognition and action. *Psychological Review*, 116(4), p. 717.

Howes, A., Vera, A., Lewis, R. L., and McCurdy, M., 2004. Cognitive constraint modeling: A formal approach to supporting reasoning about behavior. In: *Proceedings of the Cognitive Science Society*. Austin, TX: Cognitive Science Society, pp. 595–600.

Howes, A., and Young, R. M., 1996. Learning Consistent, Interactive, and Meaningful Task-Action Mappings: A Computational Model. *Cognitive Science*, 20(3), pp. 301–56.

Janssen, C. P., Brumby, D. P., Dowell, J., Chater, N., and Howes, A., 2011. Identifying optimum performance trade-offs using a cognitively bounded rational analysis model of discretionary task interleaving. *Topics in Cognitive Science*, 3(1), pp. 123–39.

Jha, S., and Westland, J. C., 2013. A Descriptive Study of Credit Card Fraud Pattern. *Global Business Review*, 14(3), pp. 373–84.

Kaelbling, L., Littman, M. L., and Cassandra, A., 1998. Planning and Acting in Partially Observable Stochastic Domains. *Artificial Intelligence*, 101(1–2), pp. 99–134.

Kieras, D., and Hornof, A., 2014. Towards accurate and practical predictive models of active-vision-based visual search. In: *Proceedings of the SIGCHI Conference on Human Factors in Computing Systems*. New York, NY: ACM, pp. 3875–84.

Kieras, D., Meyer, D., Ballas, J., and Lauber, E., 2000. Modern computational perspectives on executive mental processes and cognitive control: where to from here? In: S. Monsell and J. Driver, eds. *Control of cognitive processes: Attention and performance XVIII*. Cambridge, MA: MIT Press, pp. 681–712.

Lewis, R., Howes, A., and Singh, S., 2014. Computational rationality: linking mechanism and behavior through bounded utility maximization. *Topics in Cognitive Science*, 6(2), pp. 279–311.

Littman, M. L., Cassandra, A. R., and Kaelbling, L. P., 1995. Learning policies for partially observable environments: Scaling up. In: *Proceedings of the Twelfth International Conference on Machine Learning, tahoe city*. Burlington, MA: Morgan Kaufmann, p. 362.

Miller, C. S., and Remington, R. W., 2004. Modeling information navigation: Implications for information architecture. *Human-Computer Interaction*, 19(3), pp. 225–71.

Mnih, V., Kavukcuoglu, K., Silver, D., Graves, A., Antonoglou, I., Wierstra, D., and Riedmiller, M., 2013a. Playing âtari with Deep Reinforcement Learning. *arXiv preprint arXiv:1312.5602*.

Mnih, V., Kavukcuoglu, K., Silver, D., Graves, A., Antonoglou, I., Wierstra, D., and Riedmiller, M., 2013b. Playing Atari with Deep Reinforcement Learning. *arXiv preprint arXiv: ...*, 1–9. Retrieved from http://arxiv.org/abs/1312.5602 doi: 10.1038/nature14236

Nunez-Varela, J., and Wyatt, J. L., 2013. Models of gaze control for manipulation tasks. *ACM Transactions on Applied Perception (TAP)*, 10(4), p. 20.

Pandey, M., 2010. Operational risk forum: A model for managing online fraud risk using transaction validation. *Journal of Operational Risk*, (5)1, pp. 49–63.

Papadimitriou, C. H., and Tsitsiklis, J. N., 1987. The Complexity of Markov Decision Processes. *Mathematics of Operations Research*, 12(3), pp. 441–50. doi: 10.1287/moor.12.3.441

Payne, S. J., and Howes, A., 2013. Adaptive Interaction: A Utility Maximization Approach to Understanding Human Interaction with Technology. *Synthesis Lectures on Human-Centered Informatics*, 6(1), pp. 1–111.

Payne, S. J., Howes, A., and Reader, W. R., 2001. Adaptively distributing cognition: a decision-making perspective on human-computer interaction. *Behaviour & Information Technology*, 20(5), pp. 339–46.

Pirolli, P., and Card, S., 1999. Information foraging. *Psychological Review*, 106, pp. 643–75.

Rao, R. P. N., 2010. Decision making under uncertainty: a neural model based on partially observable markov decision processes. *Frontiers in Computational Neuroscience*. https://doi.org/10.3389/fncom.2010.00146

Russell, D. M., Stefik, M. J., Pirolli, P., and Card, S. K., 1993. The cost structure of sensemaking. In: *Proceedings of the interact '93 and CHI '93 Conference on Human Factors in Computing Systems*. New York, NY: ACM, pp. 269–76.

Russell, S., and Subramanian, D., 1995. Provably bounded-optimal agents. *Journal of Artificial Intelligence Research*, 2, pp. 575–609.

Sénchez, D., Vila, M. A., Cerda, L., and Serrano, J.-M., 2009. Association rules applied to credit card fraud detection. *Expert Systems with Applications*, 36(2), pp. 3630–40.

Shani, G., Pineau, J., and Kaplow, R., 2013. A survey of point-based POMDP solvers. *Autonomous Agents and Multi-Agent Systems*, 27(1), pp. 1–51.

Sprague, N., Ballard, D., and Robinson, A., 2007. Modeling embodied visual behaviors. *ACM Transactions on Applied Perception (TAP)*, 4(2), p. 11.

Sutton, R. S., and Barto, A. G., 1998. *Reinforcement learning: an introduction*. Cambridge, MA: MIT Press.

Trommershéuser, J., Glimcher, P. W., and Gegenfurtner, K. R., 2009. Visual processing, learning and feedback in the primate eye movement system. *Trends in Neurosciences*, 32(11), pp. 583–90.

Tseng, Y.-C., and Howes, A., 2015. The adaptation of visual search to utility, ecology and design. *International Journal of Human-Computer Studies*, 80, pp. 45–55.

Van der Stigchel, S., and Nijboer, T. C., 2011. The global effect: what determines where the eyes land? *Journal of Eye Movement Research*, 4(2), pp. 1–13.

Venini, D., Remington, R. W., Horstmann, G., and Becker, S. I., 2014. Centre-of-gravity fixations in visual search: When looking at nothing helps to find something. *Journal of Ophthalmology*, 2014. http://dx.doi.org/10.1155/2014/237812.

Vera, A., Howes, A., McCurdy, M., and Lewis, R. L., 2004. A constraint satisfaction approach to predicting skilled interactive cognition. In: *Proceedings of the SIGCHI Conference on Human Factors in Computing Systems*. New York, NY: ACM, pp. 121–8.

Vitu, F., 2008. About the global effect and the critical role of retinal eccentricity: Implications for eye movements in reading. *Journal of Eye Movement Research*, 2(3), pp. 1–18.

Watkins, C., and Dayan, P., 1992. Q-Learning. *Machine Learning*, 8, pp. 279–92.

Zhang, Y., and Hornof, A. J., 2014. Understanding multitasking through parallelized strategy exploration and individualized cognitive modeling. In: *ACM CHI'14*. New York, NY: ACM, pp. 3885–94.

11

Economic Models of Interaction

LEIF AZZOPARDI,
GUIDO ZUCCON

11.1 Introduction

When interacting with a system, users need to make numerous choices about what actions to take in order to advance them towards their goals. Each action comes at a cost (e.g., time taken, effort required, cognitive load, financial cost, etc.), and the action may or may not lead to some benefit (e.g., getting closer to completing the task, saving time, saving money, finding out new information, having fun, etc.). Describing Human-Computer Interaction (HCI) in this way naturally leads to an economic perspective on designing and developing user interfaces. Economics provides tools to model the costs and benefits of interaction where the focus is on understanding and predicting the behaviour and interaction of economic agents/users within an economy/environment. By developing economic models of interaction, it is possible to make predictions about user behaviour, understand the choices they make and inform design decisions. When interaction is framed as an economic problem, we can examine what actions lead to accruing the most benefit for a given cost or incur the least cost for a given level of benefit, from which it is then possible to determine what is the optimal course of action that a rational user *should* take, given the task, interface, context, and constraints.

Let's consider a simple example:[1] your friend has just completed a marathon, and you are curious to know how long it took them to complete the race. You have arrived at the web page showing all the times and names of runners, ordered by time. You consider two options: (i) scrolling through the list, or (ii) using the *'find'* command.[2] The first option would mean scrolling through on average about half the list of names, while the second would require

---

[1] This example is based on a study conducted in Russell (2015), where people were challenged to undertake such a task.
[2] Note that we have assumed that you are familiar with using the *'find'* command (e.g. *CTRL-f, CMD-f*, etc.). Of course, not all users are familiar with this option, or even aware that it is available.

Computational Interaction. Antti Oulasvirta, Per Ola Kristensson, Xiaojun Bi, Andrew Howes (Eds).
© Oxford University Press 2018. Published 2018 by Oxford University Press.

selecting the find command, typing in their name, and then checking through the matches. Unless the list is very small, then the second option is probably going to be less costly (i.e., fewer comparisons) and more accurate.[3] In this example, it may seem obvious that using the *'find'* option would be preferable in most cases—and indeed it is reasonably trivial to develop a simple model of the costs and benefits to show at what point it is better to use the *'find'* option over the *'scroll'* option, and vice versa. However, even to arrive at such an intuition, we have made a number of modelling assumptions:

1. that the user wants to find their friend's performance (and that the said friend took part in the marathon);
2. that the user knows and can perform both actions;
3. the currency of the costs/benefit is in time, i.e., time spent/saved; and,
4. that the user wants to minimize the amount of time spent completing the task.

Such assumptions provide the basis for a formal model to be developed. The last assumption is common to most economic models. This is because they are a type of 'optimization' model (Lewis, Howes, and Singh, 2014; Murty, 2003; Pirolli and Card, 1999; Payne and Howes, 2013), which assumes that people attempt to maximize their profit given their budget (costs) or minimize their budget expenditure given some level of profit. The other assumptions serve as constraints which are a result of the environment, the limitations of the person, and/or the simplifications made by the modeller. By engaging such an assumption, the model can be used to consider the trade-offs between different strategies, reason about how users will adapt their behaviour as the costs and benefit change, and make predictions about their behaviour. Consequently, economic models go beyond approaches which just focus solely on cost (e.g. GOMS-KLM (Card, Moran, and Newell, 1980), Fitt's Law (Fitts, 1954), Hick's Law (Hick, 1952), etc.), as economic models also consider the benefit and profit that one derives from the interaction. This is an important difference, because not all tasks are cost/time driven where the goal is to reduce the time taken or minimize friction. For example, when should an author stop editing a paper, when should an artist stop photoshopping an image, when should a researcher stop searching for related works? In the above example, the different options have varying degrees of accuracy when employed to find the correct runner's name and subsequent time. This is because as the number of items in the list increases, the chance of missing or skipping over an item also increases, thus decreasing the accuracy. So, in this case, there is a trade-off between the speed (minimizing time taken to complete the task) and the accuracy (finding the correct time). Also when using the *'find'* option, there is another trade-off between the number of letters entered (typing cost) versus the number of matching names (scanning costs, and thus accuracy). In such tasks, it is clear that understanding the trade-off between the benefits and the costs of different interaction strategies can help predict user behaviour. Economic models can help to

---

[3] It is easy to skip over records when browsing through thousands of entries. Indeed, in the study conducted in Russell (2015), subjects that scrolled often reported the incorrect time.

draw insights into these trade-offs and understand when one strategy (sequence of actions) is better to perform than another or what strategy to adopt under different circumstances.

In economic models, it is commonly assumed that users are economic agents that are rational in the sense that they attempt to maximize their benefits, and can learn to evolve and adapt their strategies towards the optimal course of interaction. Thus the theory is normative, and gives advice on how a rational user *should* act given their knowledge and experience of the system. Going back to the example above, if a user is not aware of the *'find'* option, then they will be limited in their choices, and so they would select the *'scroll'* option (or, choose not to complete the task, i.e., the *'do nothing'* option). However, when they learn about the existence of the *'find'* option, perhaps through exploratory interactions or from other users, then they can decide between the different strategies. While assuming that users are rational may seem like a rather strong assumption, in the context of search, a number of works (Azzopardi, 2014; Pirolli, Schank, Hearst, and Diehl, 1996; Smith and Kantor, 2008; Turpin and Hersh, 2001) have shown that users adapt to systems and tend to maximize benefit for a given cost (e.g., subscribe to the utility maximization paradigm (Varian, 1987)) or minimize cost for a given level of benefit (e.g., subscribe to the principle of least effort (Zipf, 1949)).[4] So a user, knowing of the *'find'* option would select it when the list of items is sufficiently long such that employing the find command is likely to reduce the total cost incurred. Once we have a model, we can then test such hypotheses about user behaviour, e.g., given the cost of using the find command, the cost of scanning items, etc., then we may hypothesize that when the length of the list is over say two pages, it is more efficient to use the *'find'* option—and then design an experiment to test if this assertion holds in practice (or not) in order to (in)validate the model.

During the course of this chapter, we first provide an overview of economic modelling in the context of HCI where we will formalize the example above by developing two models that lead to quantitative predictions regarding which option a user should employ (i.e., *'find'* or *'scroll'*), and, how they should use the *'find'* command, when chosen. Following on from this finding example, we then consider three further search scenarios related to information seeking and retrieval, where we develop models of: (i) querying, (ii) assessing, and (iii) searching. The first model provides insights into query length and how to encourage longer or shorter queries. The next model provides insights into when to stop assessing items in a ranked list of results and how to design different result pages for different result types. The third model on searching examines the trade-off between issuing queries and how many documents to examine per query during the course of a search session. This will lead to a number of insights into where the system can be improved and how users will respond to such changes. While these models are focused on search and search behaviour, similar models could be developed to help describe how people browse products, play games, use messaging, find apps, enter text, and so on. In the next section, we describe a framework for building economic models of interaction that can be used to build your own models, that inform your designs, and guide your experimental research.

---

[4] Note that essentially these optimizations objectives are two sides of the same coin and arrive at the same optimal solution, i.e., if the maximum benefit is $10 for five minutes of work, then for a benefit of $10 the minimum cost is five minutes of work.

11.2 Economic Models

An economic model is an abstraction of reality, that is, a simplified description of the phenomena in question, designed to yield hypotheses about behaviour that can be tested (Ouliaris, 2012). There are two types of economic models: *theoretical* and *empirical*.

Theoretical models aim to develop testable hypotheses about how people will behave and assume that people are economic agents that maximize specific objectives subject to constraints (e.g., amount of time available for the task, knowledge of potential actions, etc.). Such models provide qualitative answers to questions such as, how does the cost of querying affect the user's behaviour, if the benefit of query suggestions increases, how will user's adapt?

Empirical models aim to evaluate the qualitative predictions of theoretical models and realise the predictions they make into numerical outcomes. For example, consider a news app that provides access to news articles for a small payment, and a theoretical model that says that if the cost of accessing news articles increases, then users will reduce their consumption of such articles. Then an empirical model would seek to quantify by how much consumption will drop given a price increase.

Economic models generally consist of a set of mathematical equations that describe a theory of behaviour, and according to Ouliaris (2012), the aim of model builders is to include enough detail in the equations so that the model provides useful insights into how a rational user would behave and/or how a system works. The equations, and their structure, reflect the model builder's attempt to represent reality in an abstracted form by making assumptions about the system, the user and the environment. Economic models range in complexity. For example, we may model the demand for news articles as inversely proportional to the cost of the article. The less expensive the news articles, the more they are demanded according to such model. Models, however, can be much more complex consisting of non-linear, interconnected differential equations that, for example, predict the flow and transmission of fake news through a social network (Jin, Dougherty, Saraf, Cao, and Ramakrishnan, 2013).

11.2.1 Building Economic Models

Varian (2016) has described how to approach the problem of building a useful economic model (which is similar to other model building approaches, see Box, 1979; Chater and Oaksford, 1999; Murty, 2003). The main steps involved when building economics models are:

1. Describe the problem context.
2. Specify the functional relationships between the interactions and the cost and benefit of those interactions.
3. Solve the model.

4. Use the model to generate hypotheses about behaviours.

5. Compare the predictions with observations in the literature and/or experimental data.

6. Refine and revise the theory accordingly, and iterate the procedure.

Step 1 - Describe the Problem Context: First off, outline what is known about the problem context, the environment, and the interface(s) in which the interaction is occurring. It may also help to illustrate the interface(s), even if hypothetical, that the user population will be using. For example, we may want to consider how facets, when added to a shopping interface, would affect behaviour, and so draw a faceted search interface from which we can consider different ways in which the user can then interact with it (Kashyap, Hristidis, and Petropoulos, 2010). According to Varian (2016), all economic models take a similar form, where we are interested in the behaviour of some economic agents. These agents make choices to advance towards their objective(s). And these choices need to satisfy various constraints based upon the individual, the interface, and the environment/context. This leads to asking the following questions:

– Who are the people making the choices?
– What are their constraints?
– How do they interact with the interface?
– What factors/constraints in the environment will affect the interaction?

Let's re-visit the scenario we introduced earlier, where we want to know our friend's performance in the marathon. Imagine we are at the page containing a list of names and their race completion times. And let's assume we are tech savvy individuals. We are aware of several choices: (i) search by scrolling, (ii) search via the find command, (iii) some combination of scrolling and finding. To make things simple we consider only the first two and assume that we only select one or the other. We would like to try and find out as quickly as possible our friend's race time because we'd like to see whether we ought to congratulate our friend or sympathize with them. So, in this case, the objective is to minimize the time taken to find their name. Since time is at a premium, we have a constraint such that we want to complete the search within a certain period of time (after which we may give up), or, if we believe we could not complete the task within the time constraint, then we may decide not to search at all. In this later case, where we decide not to search, we may take some other action, like asking our friend. Though, of course, we would like to keep the initiative in the conversation from which we will derive benefit. In terms of interaction with the page, if we (i) scroll, then we plan to look down the list, one by one, and see if we recognize our friend's name in the list, while if we (ii) use command find, we plan to type in a few letters of their name, and step through each matching name. In both cases, we also acknowledge that there is some chance of skipping over their name and so there is some probability associated with finding their name—such that as the list of names that has to be checked increases, the chance of missing also increases. We also can imagine that in case (ii) if we enter more letters the list of names to check decreases proportionally with each additional letter. We can now formalize the problem with a series of assumptions (like those listed in Section 11.1), and then start to model the process mathematically.

Step 2 - Specify the Cost and Benefit Functions: For a particular strategy/choice, we need to identify and enumerate the most salient interactions which are likely to affect the behaviour when using the given interface. At this point, it is important to model the interaction at an appropriate level—too low and it becomes unwieldy (i.e., modelling every keystroke), too high and it becomes uninformative (i.e., simply considering the aggregated cost/benefit of the scroll option vs. the cost/benefit of find option). Varian (2016) suggests to keep this as simple as possible:

> 'The whole point of a model is to give a simplified representation of reality. . .your model should be reduced to just those pieces that are required to make it work'.

So initially focus on trying to model the simplest course of action, at the highest level possible, to get a feel for the problem, and then refine. If we start at too high a level, we can then consider what variables influence the cost of the scroll option (i.e., the length of the list), and start to parameterize the cost function, etc. We can also reduce the complexity of the interaction space: for example, in the facet shopping interface, we might start with one facet, and then progress to two facets. Essentially, make the problem simple and tractable to understand what is going on. The simple model that is developed will probably be a special case or an example. The next important step is to generalize the model: e.g., how do we model f facets?

In our scenario, for option (i) we need to perform two main actions: scroll (scr) and check (chk), where we will assume that the cost of a scroll is per item (c_{scr}), and the cost of checking the name is also per item (c_{chk}). In the worst case, we'd need to scroll through and check N names, while in the average case we'd only need to examine approximately half of the names $N/2$, and in the best case our friend came first, so $N = 1$. Let's consider the average case, where then, the cost of option (i) would be:

$$C_{(i)}(N) = \frac{N \cdot (c_{scr} + c_{chk})}{2} \tag{11.1}$$

We also know that the benefit is proportional to our likelihood of success and that is conditioned on how many items we need to check through, so we can let the probability of successfully finding our friend's name be $p_{scr}(N)$. Thus, we can formulate an expected benefit function, i.e., the benefit that we would expect to receive on average:

$$B_{(i)}(N) = p_{scr}(N) \cdot b \tag{11.2}$$

where b is the benefit, e.g., the time saved from having to hear your friend going on and on about how you are not interested in them, and how you couldn't even find it on the computer, etc. Now we can create a profit function to denote how much time we expect to save/lose if we take this option. A profit function is the difference between the benefit function and the cost function:

$$\pi_{(i)} = B_{(i)}(N) - C_{(i)}(N) = p_{scr}(N) \cdot b - \frac{N(c_{scr} + c_{chk})}{2} \tag{11.3}$$

On the other hand, for option (ii), we need to perform a different sequence of actions: command find (cmd), type (typ), skip (skp), and check (chk), where we will assume that the cost to evoke command find is c_{cmd}, to type in a letter is c_{typ} and to skip to the next match is c_{skp}. For simplicity, we will assume the cost of a skip and the cost of a scroll be the same $c_{skp} = c_{scr}$. The course of interaction is press command find, type in m letters, and then skip through the results, checking each one. Since typing in m letters will reduce the number of checks, we assume that there is a function $f(N, m)$, which results in a list of M to check through (and as m increases, M decreases). Again we are concerned with the average case, if there are M matches, then we'd only need to examine approximately half, i.e., $M/2$. Putting this all together, we can formulate the following cost function, which takes in both the size of the list and the number of letters we are willing to enter:

$$C_{(ii)}(N, m) = c_{cmd} + m \cdot c_{typ} + \frac{M(c_{scr} + c_{chk})}{2} \qquad (11.4)$$

We can also formulate the benefit function, which also takes in N and m as follows:

$$B_{(ii)}(N, m) = p_{scr}(f(N, m)) \cdot b = p_{scr}(M) \cdot b \qquad (11.5)$$

where, since M will be typically much smaller than N, the expected benefit will typically be higher. Again we can formulate a profit function $\pi_{(ii)}$ by taking the difference between the benefit and cost function.

Step 3 - Solve the Model: The next step is to solve / instantiate the model in order to see what insights it reveals about the problem being studied. This can be achieved through various means: analytically, computationally or graphically. For example, we could determine which option would be more profitable, $\pi_{(i)}$ or $\pi_{(ii)}$, by taking the difference and seeing under what circumstances option (i) is better than (ii), and vice versa. We could achieve this analytically, i.e., if $\pi_{(i)} > \pi_{(ii)}$, then select option (i), else (ii). Alternatively, we could instantiate the model, with a range of values, and plot the profit functions of each to see when $\pi_{(i)} > \pi_{(ii)}$, and under what conditions. Or in the case of option (ii), we could consider the tradeoff between typing more letters and the total time to find the name—and find the optimal number of letters to type. Note that here we have not specified the form of the functions $f(N, m)$ or $p_{scr}(\cdot)$; so in order to solve or plot, we would need to make some further assumptions, or look to empirical data for estimating functional forms.

If we are interested in deciding which option to take, then we can try and solve the inequality $\pi_{(i)} > \pi_{(ii)}$, which we can reduce to:

$$c_{cmd} + m \cdot c_{typ} > (N - M) \cdot (c_{scr} + c_{chk}) \qquad (11.6)$$

where we have assumed that $p(N)$ is approximately equal to $p(M)$ for the sake of simplicity i.e., we are assuming that the two methods perform the same (even though this is probably not the case in reality). To plot graphically the model, we further assumed that $f(N, m) = \frac{N}{(m+1)^2}$, to reflect the intuition that more letters entered will reduce the number of names to check. Later we could empirically estimate the form based on a computational simulation, i.e., given a list of names, we could count how many names are returned, on average, when N and m are varied in order to gather actual data to fit a function. Next we have to provide some estimates of the different costs. Here, we have set c_{typ} to be one second

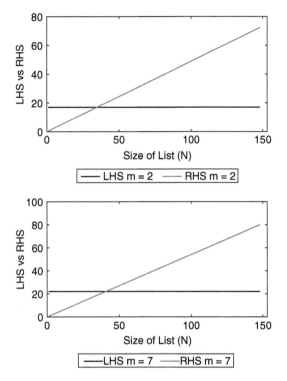

Figure 11.1 Top: Plot of the inequality when only two letters are entered. Bottom: Plot of the inequality when seven letters are entered, where if LHS > RHS then scroll, else use the find command. The plots suggest that once the size of the list is greater than thirty to forty items, using the find command is less costly. But as **m** increases, a longer list is required to justify the additional typing cost.

per letter, c_{cmd} to be 15 seconds, c_{scr} and c_{skp} to be 0.1 seconds per scroll/skip, and c_{chk} to be 0.5 seconds per name check. Of course, these values are only loosely based on the time taken to perform such actions—to create a more precise instantiation of the model, we would need to empirically ground these values. Part of the model building process involves iteratively refining the parameters and their estimates based on observed data. But, initially, we can get a '*feel*' for the model by using some reasonable approximations. Figure 11.1 shows a plot of the inequality when **m** = 2 (top) and **m** = 7 (bottom).

Now, focusing on option (ii), we can calculate the optimal way to interact when using the find command, i.e., how many letters should we type? To do this, we can consider maximizing the profit with respect to the number of letters we need to type (as this reduces the number of possible matches to skip through). To achieve this, we instantiate the profit function for option (ii), where we assume, for simplicity, that $p_{scr}(M) = 1$, such that:

$$\pi_{(ii)} = b - \left(c_{cmd} + m \cdot c_{typ} + \frac{N}{2 \cdot (m+1)^2}(c_{scr} + c_{chk}) \right) \qquad (11.7)$$

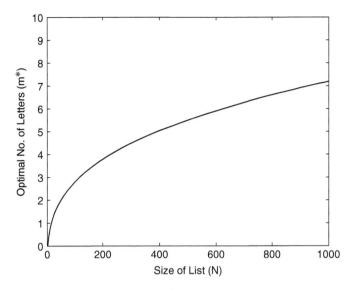

Figure 11.2 Top: Plot of $m^\star$ versus the size of the result list (N).

then we can differentiate the profit function with respect to **m** to arrive at:

$$\frac{d\pi_{(ii)}}{dm} = -c_{typ} + N \cdot (c_{scr} + c_{chk}) \cdot (m+1)^{-3} \tag{11.8}$$

Setting $\frac{d\pi_{(ii)}}{dm} = 0$, we obtain the following expression for $m^\star$, which is the optimal number of letters to enter for a list size of **N**:

$$m^\star = \left(\frac{N \cdot (c_{scr} + c_{chk})}{c_{typ}} \right)^{\frac{1}{3}} - 1 \tag{11.9}$$

Figure 11.2 shows a plot of the optimal number of letters $(m^\star)$ as **N** increases. As expected, more letters are required as **N** increases, but at a diminishing rate.

Step 4 - Use the Model and Hypothesise About Interaction: Given the models created above, we can now consider: how different variables will influence interaction and behaviour, find out what the model tells us about optimal behaviour, and see what hypotheses can be generated from the model.

From Equation 11.6 and Figure 11.1, we can see that if the cost of using the find command is very high, then the list will have to be longer before it becomes a viable option. Furthermore, there is a trade-off between the number of letters entered (**m**) and the reduction in **M**, which is, of course, proportional to *m*. From the plots, we can see that moving from **m** = 2 to **m** = 7 does not have a dramatic impact in changing when we'd decide to scroll or find, a longer list is needed to warrant the entry of more letters. Furthermore, from the graphs, we can see that, in these examples, once the list contains more than forty to fifty names, it is better to use the find command. Exactly where this point is depends on how we estimate the various costs and instantiate the functions used. However, it is possible to create hypotheses about how people would change their behaviour in response to different circumstances. For example, we could imagine a similar scenario where the cost of comparison is very high, because we are trying to match a long unique number that represents each runner instead (and so hypothesize that using the find command is preferable when lists are even shorter).

From Equation 11.9 and Figure 11.2, we can see that as the list size increases the optimal number of letters to enter (given our model) increases, such that four letters are optimal when the list is around 250 in size, while around seven letters are required when the list grows to 1000. Given these estimates, we can then hypothesise that for large lists (around 1000 in size), users will tend to enter, on average, seven letters, while for shorter lists (around 200–300), users will tend to enter, on average, four letters.

Step 5 - Compare with Observed Behaviour: The next step is to determine whether the hypothesis made using the model is consistent with empirical observations from the literature, and/or to validate the model by designing empirical experiments that explicitly test the hypotheses.

This is an important step in the process for two reasons: (a) the model provides a guide for what variables and factors are likely to influence the behaviour of users, and thus enables us to inform our experiments, and (b) it provides evidence which (in)validates the models, which we can use to refine our models. From the experimental data, we may discover that, for instance, users performed in a variety of ways we did not consider or that we ignored. For example, maybe a significant proportion of users adopted a mixed approach, scrolling a bit first, then using the find command. Or when they used the find command, they misspelled the name or couldn't remember the exact spelling, and so there is some probability associated with entering the correct partial string to match the name. As a consequence, we find that the model, or the estimates, need to be refined, and so the final step (6) is to iterate: refining and revising the model and its parameters accordingly. Once we have conduced an empirical investigation, we can better estimate the costs and benefits. Alternatively, they allow us to develop new models to cater for different interactions and conditions. With this respect, Box (1979) notes that:

'All models are wrong but some are useful'.

He points out that it would be remarkable if a simple model could exactly represent a real world phenomena. Consequently, he argues that we should build parsimonious models because model elaboration is often not practical, but adds increased complexity, without necessarily improving the precision of the model (i.e., how well the model predicts/explains the phenomena). This is not to say that we should be only building very simple models; instead, Box (1979) argues we should start simple, and then only add the necessary refinements based on our observations and data, to generate the next tentative model, which is then again iterated and refined, where the process is continued depending on how useful further revisions are judged to be. That is, there is a trade-off between the abstracted model and the predictions that it makes—the less abstracted, the greater the complexity, with perhaps increases model precision. Therefore, the refinements to the model can be evaluated by how much more predictive or explanatory power the model provides about the phenomena.

Following this approach helps to structure how we develop models, and crucially how we explain them to others and use the models in practice. The approach we have described here is similar to the methodology adopted when applying the Rational Analysis method (Anderson, 1991; Chater and Oaksford, 1999), which is a more general approach that is underpinned by similar assumptions. However, here we are concerned with building economic models as opposed to other types of formal models, e.g., Pirolli and Card, 1999; Murty, 2003; Payne and Howes, 2013; Lewis, Howes, and Singh, 2014. During the remaining of the chapter, we shall describe three different, but related economic models of human-computer interaction, where a user interacts with a search engine. Our focus is on showing how theoretical economics models can be constructed (i.e., steps 1–4) and discuss how they provide insights into observed behaviours and designs.

11.3 An Economic Model of Querying

We first consider the process of a user querying a search engine. The model that we will develop will focus on the relationship between the length of the query and the costs/benefits of the query given its length. This is because a user directly controls how long their query is, and query length is strongly related to performance (Jin, Dougherty, Saraf, Cao, and Ramakrishnan, 2013), as short queries tend to be vague, while long queries tend to be more specific. Of course, other factors also influence the performance of a query, i.e., the choice of terms, the type of search task, etc. For simplicity, however, we will only focus on length as the primary factor affecting performance and behaviour. Using the model we wish to answer the following questions:

- What is the trade-off between cost and benefit over length?
- What is the optimal length of a query?
- How does the length of a query change when the costs/benefits change?

11.3.1 Problem Context

Before answering these questions, let's first consider what we know about the length of queries, and how query length relates to performance. Typically, user queries tend to be short: in a typical web search scenario they have been measured to be around two to three terms in length (Arampatzis and Kamps, 2008). On the other hand, it has been shown on numerous occasions that longer queries tend to yield better performance (Azzopardi, 2009; Belkin, Kelly, Kim, Kim, Lee, Muresan, Tang, Yuan, and Cool, 2003; Cummins, Lalmas, and O'Riordan, 2011), but as queries get longer the performance increases at a diminishing rate (Azzopardi, 2009). This has led designers and researchers to develop interfaces that try to elicit longer queries from the user (Agapie, Golovchinsky, and Qvardordt, 2012; Hiemstra, Hauff, and Azzopardi, 2017; Kelly, Dollu, and Fu, 2005; Kelly and Fu, 2006). For example,

Agapie, Golovchinsky, and Qvardordt (2012) used a halo effect around the query box, such that as the user types a longer query the halo changes from a red glow to a blue glow. However, these attempts have largely been ineffectual and have not be replicated outside the lab (Hiemstra, Hauff, and Azzopardi, 2017). So can the model provide insights into why this is the case, why user queries tend to be short, and how we could improve the system to encourage longer queries?

11.3.2 Model

To create an economic model of querying, we need to model the benefit associated with querying and model the cost associated with querying. Let's assume that the user enters a query of length **W** (the number of words in the query). The benefit that a user receives is given by the benefit function **b(W)** and the cost (or effort in querying) defined by the cost function **c(W)**. Here we make a simplifying assumption: that cost and benefit are only a function of query length.

Now let's consider a benefit function which denotes the situation where the user experiences diminishing returns such that as the query length increases they receive less and less benefit as shown by Azzopardi (2009), and Belkin, Kelly, Kim, Kim, Lee, Muresan, Tang, Yuan, and Cool (2003). This can be modeled with the function:

$$\mathbf{b(W)} = \mathbf{k} \cdot \log_{\mathbf{a}}(\mathbf{W} + 1) \tag{11.10}$$

where k represents a scaling factor (for example to account for the quality of the search technology), and **a** influences how quickly the user experiences diminishing returns. That is as **a** increases, additional terms contribute less and less to the total benefit, and so the user will experience diminishing returns sooner. Let's then assume that the cost of entering a query is a linear function based on the number of words such that:

$$\mathbf{c(W)} = \mathbf{W} \cdot \mathbf{c_w} \tag{11.11}$$

where c_w represents how much effort must be spent to enter each word. This is, of course, a simple cost model and it is easy to imagine more complex cost functions. However the point is to provide a simple, but insightful, abstraction.

11.3.3 Optimal Querying Behaviour

Given the previous two functions, we can compute the profit (net benefit) π that the user receives for a query of length W:

$$\pi = \mathbf{b(W)} - \mathbf{c(W)} = \mathbf{k} \cdot \log_{\mathbf{a}}(\mathbf{W} + 1) - \mathbf{W} \cdot \mathbf{c_w} \tag{11.12}$$

To find the query length that maximizes the user's net benefit, we can differentiate with respect to W and solve the equation:

$$\frac{\partial \pi}{\partial \mathbf{W}} = \frac{\mathbf{k}}{\log a} \cdot \frac{1}{\mathbf{W} + 1} - \mathbf{c_w} = 0 \tag{11.13}$$

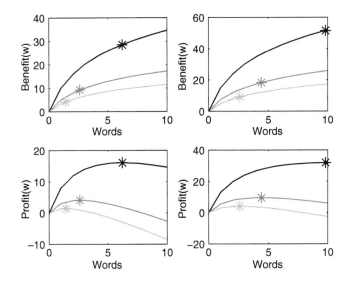

Figure 11.3 The top plots show the benefit while the bottom plots show the profit as the length of the query increases. Plots on the right show when the queries yield greater benefit (left **k=10**; right **k=15**). Each plot shows three levels of **a** which denotes how quickly diminishing returns sets in.

This results in:

$$W^\star = \frac{k}{c_w \cdot \log a} - 1 \tag{11.14}$$

11.3.4 Hypotheses

Figure 11.3 illustrates the benefit (top) and profit (bottom) as query length increases. For the left plots **k=10**, and for the right plots **k=15**. Within each plot we show various levels of **a**. These plots show that as k increases (i.e., overall the performance of the system increases), the model suggests that query length, on average, would increase. If **a** increases (i.e., additional terms contribute less and less to the overall benefit), then queries decrease in length. Furthermore the model suggests that as the cost of entering a word, c_w, decreases then users will tend to pose longer queries.

11.3.5 Discussion

This economic model of querying suggests that to motivate longer queries either the cost of querying needs to decrease or the performance of the system needs to increase (either by increasing **k** or decreasing **a**). The model provides several testable hypotheses, which provide key insights that inform the design of querying mechanisms and help explain various attempts to encourage longer queries. For example, the query halo does not reduce cost, nor increase benefit, and so is not likely to change user behaviour. On the other hand, the inline query auto-completion functionality now provided by most search engines, reduces the cost of entering queries (e.g., less typing to enter each query term), and also increases the quality of queries (e.g., fewer mis-spellings, less out of vocabulary words, etc.). Thus, according to the model, since the key drivers are affected, queries are likely to be longer when using query auto-completion than without.

While this model provides some insights into the querying process and the trade-off between performance and length, it is relatively crude. We could model more precisely the relationship between the number of characters, number of terms, and the discriminative power of those terms, and how they influence performance. Furthermore, depending on the search engine, the length of a query relative to performance will vary, and may even decrease as length increases. For instance, if our search engine employed an implicit Boolean AND between terms, then as the number of query terms increases the number of results returned decreases, and so fewer and fewer relevant items are returned (if any). In this case, we would need to employ a different benefit function to reflect and capture this relationship. It is only when we empirically explore, either through an analysis of query logs (Hiemstra, Hauff, and Azzopardi, 2017), user judgements and ratings (Verma and Yilmaz, 2017), or computational simulations (Azzopardi, 2009, 2011) that we can test and refine the model, updating the assumptions and cost/benefit functions/parameters.

11.4 A Model of Assessing

This section considers how people interact with a list of search results after they pose a query to a search engine. Intuitively, when examining search results a person decides to stop at some point in the ranked list and either stop searching altogether, being satisfied with what they have found (or not), or decide to issue a new query and continue searching. Here we will only consider a person's interaction with one list of results. From the literature, a number of studies have been conducted examining the question of when users decide to stop. The general finding is that users stop when they have found 'enough' (Dostert and Kelly, 2009; Prabha, Connaway, Olszewski, and Jenkins, 2007; Zach, 2005). Other research has suggested that people employ stopping rules, such as, stop after n non-relevant results (Cooper, 1973), or stop when the results do not provide any new information (Browne, Pitts, and Wetherbe, 2007). While these rules are reasonably intuitive, perhaps we can be more formal by modelling the process and considering the following questions:

- What is the trade-off between benefit over assessment depth?
- What is the optimal stopping point?
- How does the depth change in response to changes in costs and benefits?

11.4.1 Problem Context

Let's consider the interaction with the search engine. After a user poses a query, most search engines return a list of results, typically ranked in decreasing likelihood of being relevant to the user's query (Robertson, 1977). This implies that as the user goes down through the ranked list the benefit that they receive (or the expected benefit) decreases, and so at some point the cost outweighs the benefit of assessing a subsequent item. Of course, there are lots of factors that affect when people stop. For example, if a user types in a '*dud*' query, which retrieves no relevant items, they are likely to stop after only examining a few items, if any. If the user enters a '*good*' query, which retrieves many relevant items, then when they stop is probably more task or time dependent. If a user wants to find many relevant items, then presumably they would go deeper. But, of course, they don't want to waste their time assessing non-relevant items and so will stop at some point, or if they find enough information, then they will stop. On the other hand, if they only want one relevant item, then they will stop once they find one item. So the model we develop will need to be sensitive to these different conditions.

11.4.2 Model

To create an economic model of assessing, we need to formulate cost and benefit functions associated with the process. Let's start off by modelling the costs. A user first poses a query to the search engine and thus incurs a query cost c_q. Then for the purposes of the model, we will assume the user assesses items, one by one, where the cost to assess each item is c_a. If the user assesses A items, then the cost function would be:

$$c(A) = c_q + A.c_a \qquad (11.15)$$

Now, we need a function to model the benefit associated with assessing A items. Consider the scenario where a user is searching for news articles, and that they are reading about the latest world disaster. The first article that they read provides key information, e.g., that an earthquake has hit. The subsequent articles start to fill in the details, while others provide context and background. As they continue to read more and more news articles, the amount of new information becomes less and less as the same '*facts*' are repeated. Essentially, as they work their way down the ranked list of results, they experience diminishing returns. That is, each additional item contributes less and less benefit. So we can model the benefit received as follows:

$$b(A) = k.A^\beta \qquad (11.16)$$

where k is a scaling factor, and β represents how quickly the benefit from the information diminishes. If β is equal to one, then for each subsequent item examined, the user receives the same amount of benefit. However, if β is less than one, then for each subsequent item examined, the user receives less additional benefit. This function is fairly flexible: if $k = 0$ for a given query, then it can represent a 'dud' query, while $\beta = 0$ models when only one item is of benefit (e.g. $A^0 = 1$). So the benefit function can cater for a number of different scenarios.

11.4.3 Optimal Assessing Behaviour

Now, given these two functions, we can compute the profit (i.e., net benefit) π that the user receives when they assess to a depth of $\mathbf{A}$:

$$\pi = \mathbf{b(W)} - \mathbf{c(W)} = \mathbf{k.A}^\beta - \mathbf{c_q} - \mathbf{A.c_a} \qquad (11.17)$$

To find the assessment depth that maximizes the user's net benefit, we can differentiate with respect to $\mathbf{A}$ and solve the equation:

$$\frac{\partial \pi}{\partial \mathbf{A}} = \mathbf{k.\beta.A}^{\beta-1} - \mathbf{c_a} = \mathbf{0} \qquad (11.18)$$

This results in:

$$\mathbf{A}^\star = \left(\frac{\mathbf{c_a}}{\mathbf{k.\beta}}\right)^{\frac{1}{\beta-1}} \qquad (11.19)$$

11.4.4 Hypotheses

From Equation 11.19, we can see that the optimal depth is dependent on the cost of assessment $(\mathbf{c_a})$, and the performance surmised by $\mathbf{k}$ and β. Using comparative statics (Varian, 1987), we can see how a user should respond when one variable changes, and everything else is held constant. If the cost of assessing increases, and β is less than one (i.e., diminishing returns), then the model suggests that the user would examine fewer documents. For example, consider a news app that charges per article, while another does not. In this case, the model predicts that users would read fewer documents in the first app, when compared to the second.

Figure 11.4 shows how the profit of assessing changes as the cost of assessing is increased. If the performance increases, i.e., β tends to one, then the user would examine more documents. Similarly, as the performance increases via $\mathbf{k}$, then this also suggests that the user would examine more documents.

11.4.5 Discussion

Intuitively, the model makes sense: if the performance of the query was very poor, there is little incentive/reason to examine results in the list. And if the cost of assessing documents is very high, then it constrains how many documents are examined. For example, consider the case of a user searching on their mobile phone when the internet connection is very slow. The cost of visiting each page is high (i.e., it takes a lot of time to download the page, and may not even load properly), so the model predicts that users are less likely to click and assess documents. Alternatively, consider the case of a user searching for images. The cost of assessing thumbnails (and thus the image) is very low (compared to examining text snippets), and so the model predicts that a user will assess lots of images (but few text snippets). Interestingly, under this model, the cost of a query does not impact on user behaviour. This is because it is a fixed cost, and the analysis is only concerned

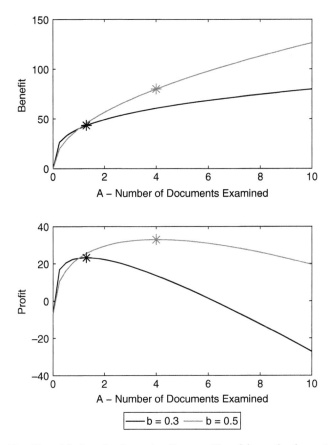

Figure 11.4 Top: Plot of the benefit of assessing. Bottom: Plot of the profit of assessing where the result list is of low quality (**b=0.3**) and higher quality (**b=0.5**). The model predicts users will assess more documents as the result list quality increases.

with the change in cost versus the change in benefit (i.e., stop when the marginal cost equals the marginal benefit). However, in reality, the cost of the query is likely to influence how a user behaves. Also, users are likely to issue multiple queries, either new queries or better reformulations which lead to different benefits. While this simple model of assessing provides some insights into the process, it is limited, and may not generalize to these other cases.[5] Next, we extend this model and consider when multiple queries can be issued, and how the trade-off between querying and assessing affects behaviour.

---

[5] As an exercise the reader may wish to consider a model where two queries are issued, and the benefit function is different between queries. See Azzopardi and Zuccon (2015) for a solution.

11.5 A Model of Searching

This section describes the process of searching over a session, where numerous queries can be issued, and the user examines a number of items per query. The model focuses on the different search strategies that users can undertake and how the costs and benefits affect the optimal search strategy; specifically, we explore the following questions:

- What is the trade-off between querying and assessing?
- What is the optimal search strategy?
- How does the search strategy change in response to changes in costs and benefits?

Essentially, given a particular context, we would like to know if a user should issue more queries and assess fewer items per query, or whether they should issue fewer queries and assess many items per query?

11.5.1 Problem Context

Let's first consider the standard search interface (much like a web search interface) consisting of a query box (or query area) and search button. When a user issues a query to the search engine, the search result page is shown and displays: (i) the number of search results, (ii) the current page number, (iii) a list of n result snippets (usually $n = 10$ result snippets per page), and (iv) a next and previous button, see Figure 11.5. Each search result has a title (often shown as a blue link), a snippet from the item, along with the URL/domain. This style of interface is usually referred to as the '*ten blue links*' (Kelly and Azzopardi, 2015).

Given this interface, the user can perform a number of actions: (i) (re)query, (ii) examine the search results page, (iii) inspect individual result snippets, (iv) assess items, e.g., click on the result and view the web page, image, news article, etc., and (v) visit subsequent results pages. Each of these actions have an associated cost and so are likely to affect search behaviour.

11.5.2 Model

Described more formally, during the course of a search session, a user will pose a number of queries (Q), examine a number of search result pages per query (V), inspect a number of snippets per query (S) and assess a number of items per query (A). Each interaction has an associated cost where c_q is the cost of a query, c_v is the cost of viewing a page, c_s is the cost of inspecting a snippet, and c_a is the cost of assessing an item. With this depiction of the search interface we can construct a cost function that includes these variables and costs, such that the total cost of interaction is:

$$c(Q, V, S, A) = c_q.Q + c_v.V.Q + c_s.S.Q + c_a.A.Q \qquad (11.20)$$

This cost function provides a reasonably rich representation of the costs incurred during the course of interaction. In modelling the interaction, we have assumed that the number

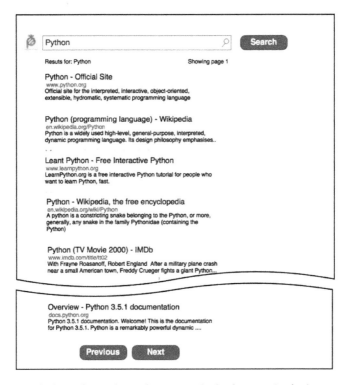

Figure 11.5 Standard Search Interface – showing results for the query '*python*'.

of pages, snippets, and items viewed is per query. Of course, in reality, the user will vary the number of pages, snippets, and items viewed for each individual query (see Azzopardi and Zuccon (2015) for how this can be modelled). So, **V**, **S**, and **A** can be thought of as the average number of pages, snippets, and items viewed, respectively. We thus are modelling how behaviour with respect to these actions changes, on average. Nonetheless, the cost function is quite complex, so we will need to simplify the cost function. To do so, we will need to make a number of further assumptions.

First, we shall ignore the pagination and assume that all the results are on one page, i.e., $V = 1$. Thus a user does not need to go to subsequent pages (i.e., infinite scroll).[6] The assumption is quite reasonable as, in most cases, users only visit the first page of results anyway (Azzopardi, Kelly, and Brennan, 2013; Kelly and Azzopardi, 2015).

---

[6]   However, it would be possible to encode the number of page views per query more precisely by using a step function based on the number of snippets viewed, representing the fixed cost incurred to load and view each page of results. The step function would be such that the number of pages viewed **V** would be equal to the number of snippets viewed, divided by the number of snippets shown per page (**n**), rounded up to the nearest integer, i.e., $\lceil \frac{S}{n} \rceil$.

Second, we shall assume that the number of items assessed is proportional to the number of snippets viewed, i.e., that users need to first inspect the result snippet, before clicking on and examining an item, thus $S \geq A$. Furthermore, we can associate a probability to a user clicking on a result snippet, p_a, and examining the item. The expected number of assessments viewed per query would then be $A = S.p_a$. Substituting these values into the cost model, we obtain:

$$c(Q, V, S, A) = c_q.Q + c_v.Q + c_s.\frac{A}{p_a}.Q + c_a.A.Q \qquad (11.21)$$

We can now reduce the cost function to be dependent only on A and Q, such that:

$$c(Q, A) = (c_q + c_v).Q + \left(\frac{c_s}{p_a} + c_a\right).A.Q \qquad (11.22)$$

Let's turn our attention to building the benefit function and characterising how much benefit the user receives from their interactions. Given the two main interactions: querying and assessing, we assume, as in the previous model, that as a user examines items, they obtain some benefit, but as they progress through the list of items, the benefit they experience is at a diminishing returns. As previously mentioned, when searching for news about the latest crisis, as subsequent news articles are read, they become less beneficial because they begin to repeat the same information contained in previous articles. In this case, to find out about other aspects of the topic, another related but different query needs to be issued. Essentially, each query issued contributes to the overall benefit, but again at a diminishing returns, because as more and more aspects of the topic are explored, less new information about the topic remains to be found. To characterize this, we shall model the benefit function using the Cobbs-Douglas function (Varian, 1987):

$$b(Q, A) = k.Q^\alpha.A^\beta \qquad (11.23)$$

where α represents returns from querying, while β represents the returns from assessing, and k is a scaling factor.[7] Let's consider two scenarios when $\alpha = 0$ and when $\alpha = 1$. In the first case, regardless of how many queries are issued $Q^0 = 1$, so issuing more than one query would be a waste as it would not result in more benefit. In the latter case, $Q^1 = Q$, there is no diminishing returns for subsequent queries. This might model the case where the user poses independent queries, i.e., the user searches for different topics within the same session, poses queries that retrieve different items for the same topic, or when there is a seemingly endless supply of beneficial/relevant items e.g., procrastinating watching online videos. Given the form in Equation 11.23 the benefit function is sufficiently flexible to cater for a wider range of scenarios. Azzopardi (2011) showed this benefit function to fit well with empirical search performance of querying and assessing.

11.5.3 Optimal Search Behaviour

Using the model of searching it is now possible to determine what the optimal search behaviour, in terms of Q and A, would be given the parameters of the model. To do this

---

[7] Note that if $\alpha = 1$ then we arrive at the same benefit as in the model of assessing, see Equation 11.16.

we assume that the objective of the user is to minimize the cost for a given level of benefit (or alternatively, maximize their benefit for a given cost). This occurs when the marginal benefit equals the marginal cost. We can solve this optimization problem with the following objective function (using a Lagrangian Multiplier λ):

$$\Delta = (c_q + c_v.v).Q + \left(\frac{c_s}{p_a} + c_a\right).A.Q - \lambda\left(k.Q^\alpha.A^\beta - b\right)$$

where the goal is to minimize the cost subject to the constraint that the amount of benefit is b. By taking the partial derivatives, we obtain:

$$\frac{\partial \Delta}{\partial A} = \left(\frac{c_s}{p_a} + c_a\right).Q - \lambda.k.\beta.Q^\alpha.A^{\beta-1} \qquad (11.24)$$

and:

$$\frac{\partial \Delta}{\partial Q} = c_q + c_v.v + \left(\frac{c_s}{p_a} + c_a\right).A - \lambda.k.\alpha.Q^{\alpha-1}.A^\beta \qquad (11.25)$$

Setting these both to zero, and then solving, we obtain the following expressions for the optimal number of assessments per query $A^\star$:

$$A^\star = \frac{\beta.(c_q + c_v.v)}{(\alpha - \beta).\left(\frac{c_s}{p_a} + c_a\right)} \qquad (11.26)$$

and the optimal number of queries $Q^\star$:

$$Q^\star = \sqrt[\alpha]{\frac{g}{k.A^{\star\beta}}} \qquad (11.27)$$

11.5.4 Hypotheses

Using this analytical solution we can now generate a number of testable hypotheses about search behaviour by considering how interaction will change when specific parameters of the model increase or decrease. From the model it is possible to derive a number of hypotheses regarding how performance and cost affect behaviour. Rather than enumerate each one below we provide a few examples (see Azzopardi (2016) for details on each).

Similar to the previous model, we can formulate an hypothesis regarding the quality of the result list, where as β increases, the number of assessments per query will increase, while the number of queries will decrease (as shown in Figure 11.6, top left plot). Intuitively, this makes sense because as β increases the rank list of results contains more relevant items: it is better to exploit the current query before switching to a new query.

Regarding costs, we can formulate a query cost hypothesis, such that as the cost of a query c_q increases, the number of items assessed per query will increase, while the number of queries issued will decrease (as shown in Figure 11.7, top, right plot). It should be clear from Equation 11.26 that this is the case because as c_q becomes larger, $A^\star$ also becomes larger. In turn, the number of queries issued will decrease, because as $A^\star$ becomes larger, $Q^\star$ tends to zero. Of course, to start the search session, there needs to be at least one query, e.g., Q must

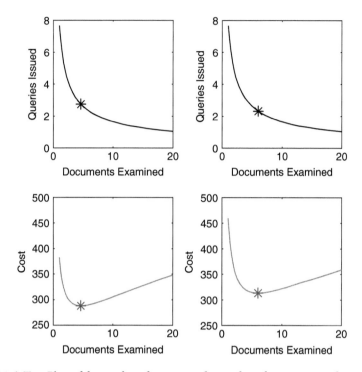

Figure 11.6 Top: Plots of the number of queries vs. the number of items examined per query for a given level of benefit. Any point yields the same amount of benefit. The asterisk indicates the optimal querying/assessing strategy, i.e., $(A^{\star}, Q^{\star})$. Bottom: Plots of the cost vs. the number of items examined per query. The asterisk indicates when the cost is minimized, i.e., at $A^{\star}$.

be equal to one or greater. A similar hypothesis can be formulated regarding assessment costs, where as the cost of an assessment increases, the number of items assessed per query will decrease, while the number of queries issued will increase. Since the assessment cost c_a appears in the denominator in Equation 11.26 then any increase will reduce the number of assessments.

Another hypothesis that the model produces is regarding the probability of assessing items. Here, as the probability of assessing increases, the number of items assessed increases, while the number of queries issued decreases (as shown in Figure 11.7, bottom, right plot). If a user examines every item in the ranked list, then p_a would equal one, meaning that for each snippet that they examine, they also examine the item. As a result, because more items are being examined, less queries are issued overall.

11.5.5 Discussion

This economic model of searching provides a useful representation of the interaction between a user and a search engine. The model provides a number of insights into

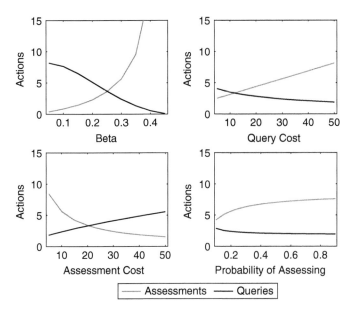

Figure 11.7 Top Left: Plot of A^* and Q^* as β changes. Top Right: Plot of A^* and Q^* as query cost changes. Bottom Left: Plot of A^* and Q^* as assessment cost changes. Bottom Right: Plot of A^* and Q^* as the probability of assessment changes.

different factors that are likely to affect behaviour, and serves as guide on how and where we could improve the system. For example, the search engine could focus on improving the quality of the results, in which case increases in performance should, according to the model, lead to changes in search behaviour. Or the search engine may want to increase the number of queries, and so may focus on lowering the cost of querying. Of course, the usefulness of the model depends on whether the model hypotheses hold in practice. These hypotheses were tested in two related studies. The first study by Azzopardi, Kelly, and Brennan (2013) explicitly explored the query cost hypothesis where a between groups experiment was devised where the search interface was modified to create different query cost conditions. They used a structured, standard and suggestion based search interface. Their results provided evidence to support the query cost hypothesis, such that when the query cost was high subjects issued fewer queries and examined more items per query, and vice versa. In a follow-up analysis on the same data, the other hypotheses above were explored, and it was shown that they also tend to hold in general (Azzopardi, 2014). In a study by Ong, Jarvelin, Sanderson, and Scholer (2017), they conducted a between groups study evaluating the differences in search behaviour when subjects used either a mobile device or a desktop device to perform search tasks. On mobile devices, the costs for querying and assessing are much higher due to the smaller keyboard (leading to slower query entry) and bandwidth/latency limitations (leading to slower page downloads). This resulted in subjects assigned to the mobile condition issuing fewer queries, but examining more snippets/items per query (Ong, Jarvelin, Sanderson, and Scholer, 2017). Again, this is broadly consistent with the model developed here.

While the model provides a number of insights into search behaviour for topic-based searches, there are a number of limitations and assumptions which could be addressed. For example, the model currently assumes that the user examines a fixed number of snippets/items per query, yet most users examine a variable number of snippets/items per query. Essentially, the model assumes that on average this is how many snippets/items are viewed per query. For a finer grained model, we would have to model each result list individually, so that the total benefit would be, for example, the sum of the benefit obtained from each result list over all queries issued. Then it would be possible to determine, given a number of queries, how far the user should go into each result list (see Azzopardi and Zuccon (2015) for this extension). Another aspect that could be improved is the cost function. We have assumed that the cost of different actions are constant, yet they are often variable, and will change during the course of interaction (e.g., a query refinement may be less costly than expressing a new query or selecting from among several query suggestions). Also a more sophisticated and accurate cost model could be developed which may affect the model's predictions.

11.6 Discussion and Conclusions

This chapter has described the process of building economic models and provided several examples in the context of information seeking and retrieval. In previous work (Azzopardi and Zuccon, 2016a,b) we have also enumerated a number of other models that analyse other aspects of search interface components, e.g., when should facets be used, when is it better to issue a new query or is it better to take a query suggestion, how many results should we put on a result page query, and so on. While such models are relatively simple, they provide useful abstractions which focus the attention on the main levers that are likely to affect the behaviour of users. Furthermore, we are able to derive testable hypotheses about user behaviour. This is particularly useful because it provides a guide for experimentation which is grounded by theory. If the hypotheses are shown to hold, then the model provides a compact representation of the phenomena which designers and researchers can use when developing interface innovations or improving the underlying systems. For example, in the last scenario, if it is difficult to formulate an effective query, say in the context of image search, then we would expect that users would examine many more result items, and so we could adapt the system to show more results per page. Indeed, search engines provide ten blue links for web pages but hundreds of results for images. While useful and informative, there are, however, a number of challenges in taking the theory and putting it into practice.

The first major challenge concerns the estimation of the costs and benefits. Firstly, we have only considered the costs and benefits as common, but abstract, units. However, if we wish to estimate the costs and benefits then we need to select some unit: this could be temporal, fiscal, physical, or cognitive based. Often, though, time is used as a proxy for the cost. However, it would be more realistic to consider multiple cost functions for the different aspects of cost, and the trade-offs between them, i.e., a user might prefer to expand physical effort over cognitive effort. Or to combine the different costs functions into an overall cost function, where the different aspects are weighted according to their impact on the user's preferences. For example, Oulasvirta, Feit, Lahteenlahti, and Karrenbauer (2017) created a benefit function that is a linear combination of several criteria (usefulness, usability, value, etc.) in order to evaluate which features/actions an interface should afford users. In this case, rather than having one possible optimal solution, instead, depending on what aspect(s) are considered most important, different solutions arise. On the other hand, what is the benefit that a user receives from their interactions with the system? Is it information, enjoyment, satisfaction, time, money? In our models, we have made the assumption that the cost and benefit are in the same units; however, if we were to assume time as the cost, then the benefit would be how much time is saved (as done by Fuhr, 2008). While this makes sense in the case of finding a name in a list, it does not make sense in all scenarios. For example, in the news search scenario, we could imagine that the amount of benefit is proportional to the new information found, and the benefit is relative to how helpful the information is in achieving their higher level work or leisure task. So, if we were to assume benefit as say, information gain (as done by Zhang and Zhai, 2015), or user satisfaction (as done by Verma and Yilmaz, 2017), then how do we express cost in the same unit? In this case, a function is needed to map the benefits and costs into the same units (as done by Azzopardi and Zuccon, 2015). Alternatively, the ratio between the benefit and the cost could be used instead, as done in Information Foraging Theory (IFT), see Pirolli and Card, 1999, or when performing a cost-effectiveness analysis. Once the units of measurement have been chosen, and instruments have been created to take such measurements, then the subsequent problem is how to accurately estimate the cost of the different interactions, and the benefit that is obtained from those interactions. This is very much an open problem.

A noted limitation of such models is the underlying assumption that people seek to maximize their benefit (e.g., the utility maximization paradigm). This assumption has been subject to much scrutiny, and shown to break down in various circumstances leading to the development of behavioural economics. Kahneman and Tversky have shown that people are subject to various cognitive biases and that people often adopt heuristics which result in sub-optimal behaviours (Kahneman and Tversky, 1979). In their work on Prospect Theory, they argue that people have a more subjective interpretation of costs and benefits, and that people perceive and understand risk differently (i.e., some are more risk-adverse than others). Whereas Simon argues that people are unlikely to be *maximizers* that relentlessly seek to maximize their benefit subject to a given cost (Simon, 1955), but rather *satisficers* who seek to obtain a satisfactory amount of benefit for the minimum cost. While the utility maximization assumption is questionable, there is opportunity to extend these economic models presented here, and create more behavioural economic models that encode these more realistic assumptions about behaviour. As pointed out earlier, though, it is best to start simple and refine the models accordingly.

Another challenge that arises when developing such models is to ensure that there has been sufficient consideration of the user and the environment in which the interaction is taking place. In our models, we have largely ignored the cognitive constraints and limitations of users, nor have we explicitly modelled the environment. However, such factors are likely to influence behaviour. For example, Oulasvirta, Hukkinen, and Schwartz (2009) examined how choice overload (i.e., the paradox of choice) affects search behaviour and performance, finding that people were less satisfied when provided with more results. While White (2013) showed that searchers would often seek confirmation of their a priori beliefs (i.e., confirmation bias), and were again less satisfied with the results that contradicted them. However within the Adaptive Interaction Framework (Payne and Howes, 2013) it is argued that the strategies that people employ are shaped by the adaptive, ecological, and bounded nature of human behaviour. And as such, these biases and limitations should be taken into account when developing models of interaction, that is, by using the economic modelling approach presented above it is possible to develop models that maximize utility subject to such constraints. Essentially, the economic models here could be extended to incorporate such constraints (and thus assume Bounded Rationality (Gigerenzer and Selten, 1999; Simon, 1955), for example). Furthermore, they could be incorporated into approaches such as Rational Analysis (Anderson, 1991) or the Adaptive Interaction Framework (Payne and Howes, 2013), whereby a model includes user and environmental factors as well. Imposing such constraints, not only makes the models more realistic, but they are likely to provide better explanations of behaviour and thus better inform how we design interfaces and systems.

On a pragmatic point, the design and construction of experiments that specifically test the models can also be challenging. In the models we have described above, we used a technique called comparative statics, to consider what would happen, when one variable is changed (i.e., as cost goes up), to behaviour (i.e., issue fewer queries). This required the assumption that all other variables were held constant. In practice, however, the manipulation of one variable will invariably influence other variables. For example, in the experiments performed examining the query cost hypothesis, one of the conditions contained query suggestions, the idea being that clicking on suggestions would be cheaper than typing in suggestions (Azzopardi, Kelly, and Brennan, 2013). However, this inadvertently led to an increase in the amount of time on the search result page for this condition, which was attributed to the time spent reading through the suggestions (Azzopardi, Kelly, and Brennan, 2013). However, this cost was not considered in the initial economic model proposed by Azzopardi (2011). This led to the revised model (Azzopardi, 2014), described above, which explicitly models the cost of interacting with the search result page as well as the cost of interacting with snippets. These changes subsequently led to predictions that were consistent with the observed data. This example highlights the iterative nature of modelling and how refinements are often needed to create higher fidelity models.

To sum up, this chapter has presented a tutorial for developing economic models of interaction. While we have presented several examples based on information seeking and retrieval, the same techniques can be applied to other tasks, interfaces, and applications, in particular where there is a trade-off between the cost and benefits. By creating such models, we can reason about how changes to the system will impact upon user behaviour before even implementing the said system. We can identify what variables are going to have the biggest impact on user behaviour and focus our attention on addressing those aspects, thus guiding the experiments that we perform and the designs that we propose. Once a model has been developed and validated, then they provide a compact representation of the body of knowledge, so that others can use and extend the model developed. While we have noted above a number of challenges in working with such models, the advantages are appealing and ultimately such models provide theoretical rigour to our largely experimental discipline.

....

REFERENCES

Agapie, E., Golovchinsky, G., and Qvardordt, P., 2012. Encouraging behavior: A foray into persuasive computing. In: *Proceedings on the Symposium on Human-ComputerInformation Retrieval*. New York, NY: ACM.

Anderson, J. R., 1991. Is human cognition adaptive? *Behavioral and Brain Sciences,* 14(3) pp. 471–85.

Arampatzis, A., and Kamps, J., 2008. A study of query length. In: *SIGIR '08: Proceedings of the 31st annual international ACM SIGIR conference on Research and development in information retrieval*. New York, NY: ACM, pp. 811–12.

Azzopardi, L., 2009. Query side evaluation: an empirical analysis of effectiveness and effort. In: *Proceedings of the 32nd international ACM SIGIR conference on Research and development in information retrieval*. New York, NY: ACM, ACM, pp. 556–63.

Azzopardi, L., 2011. The economics in interactive information retrieval. In: *Proceedings of the 34th ACM SIGIR Conference*. New York, NY: ACM, pp. 15–24.

Azzopardi, L., 2014. Modelling interaction with economic models of search. In: *Proceedings of the 37th ACM SIGIR Conference*. New York, NY: ACM, pp. 3–12.

Azzopardi, L., Kelly, D., and Brennan, K., 2013. How query cost affects search behavior. In: *Proceedings of the 36th ACM SIGIR Conference*. New York, NY: ACM, pp. 23–32.

Azzopardi, L., and Zuccon, G., 2015. An analysis of theories of search and search behavior. In: *Proceedings of the 2015 International Conference on The Theory of Information Retrieval*. New York, NY: ACM, pp. 81–90.

Azzopardi, L., and Zuccon, G., 2016a. An analysis of the cost and benefit of search interactions. In: *Proceedings of the 2016 ACM International Conference on the Theory of Information Retrieval*. New York, NY: ACM, pp. 59–68.

Azzopardi, L., and Zuccon, G., 2016b. *Two Scrolls or One Click: A Cost Model for Browsing Search Results*. In: *Advances in Information Retrieval: 38th European Conference on IR Research/i*. Padua, Italy: Springer, pp. 696–702.

Belkin, N. J., Kelly, D., Kim, G., Kim, J.-Y., Lee, H.-J., Muresan, G., Tang, M.-C., Yuan, X.-J., and Cool, C., 2003. Query length in interactive information retrieval. In: *Proceedings of the 26th ACM conference on research and development in information retrieval (SIGIR)*. New York, NY: ACM, pp. 205–12.

Box, G. E., 1979. Robustness in the strategy of scientific model building. In: R. L. Launer and G. N. Wilkinson, eds. *Robustness in statistics: Proceedings of a workshop*. New York: Academic Press, pp. 201–36.

Browne, G. J., Pitts, M. G., and Wetherbe, J. C., 2007. Cognitive stopping rules for terminating information search in online tasks. *MIS Quarterlyy,* 31(1), pp. 89–104.

Card, S. K., Moran, T. P., and Newell, A., 1980. The keystroke-level model for user performance time with interactive systems. *Communications of the ACM,* 23(7) pp. 396–410.

Chater, N., and Oaksford, M., 1999. Ten years of the rational analysis of cognition. *Trends in Cognitive Sciences,* 3(2), pp. 57–65.

Cooper, W. S., 1973. On selecting a measure of retrieval effectiveness part ii. implementation of the philosophy. *Journal of the American Society of Information Science*, 24(6), pp. 413–24.

Cummins, R., Lalmas, M., and O'Riordan, C. 2011. The limits of retrieval effectiveness. In: *European Conference on Information Retrieval*. Berlin: Springer, pp. 277–82.

Dostert, M., and Kelly, D., 2009. Users' stopping behaviors and estimates of recall. In: *Proceedings of the 32nd ACM SIGIR*. New York, NY: ACM, pp. 820–1.

Fitts, P. M., 1954. The information capacity of the human motor system in controlling the amplitude of movement. *Journal of Experimental Psychology*, 47(6), p. 381.

Fuhr, N., 2008. A probability ranking principle for interactive information retrieval. *Information Retrieval*, 11(3), pp. 251–65.

Gigerenzer, G., and Selten, R., 1999. *Bounded Rationality: The Adaptive Toolbox*. Cambridge, MA: MIT Press.

Hick, W. E., 1952. On the rate of gain of information. *Quarterly Journal of Experimental Psychology*, 4(1), pp. 11–26.

Hiemstra, D., Hauff, C., and Azzopardi, L., 2017. Exploring the query halo effect in site search. In: *Proceedings of the 40th International ACM SIGIR Conference on Research and Development in Information Retrieval*. New York, NY: ACM, forthcoming.

Ingwersen, P., and Järvelin, K., 2005. *The Turn: Integration of Information Seeking and Retrieval in Context*. New York, NY: Springer-Verlag.

Jin, F., Dougherty, E., Saraf, P., Cao, Y., and Ramakrishnan, N., 2013. Epidemiological modeling of news and rumors on twitter. In: *Proceedings of the 7th Workshop on Social Network Mining and Analysis*. New York, NY: ACM, p. 8.

Kahneman, D., and Tversky, A., 1979. Prospect theory: An analysis of decision under risk. *Econometrica: Journal of the Econometric Society*, 47(2), pp. 263–91.

Kashyap, A., Hristidis, V., and Petropoulos, M., 2010. Facetor: cost-driven exploration of faceted query results. In: *Proceedings of the 19th ACM conference on Information and knowledge management*. New York, NY: ACM, pp. 719–28.

Kelly, D., and Azzopardi, L., 2015. How many results per page?: A study of serp size, search behavior and user experience. In: *Proceedings of the 38th International ACM SIGIR Conference*. New York, NY: ACM, pp. 183–92.

Kelly, D., Dollu, V. D., and Fu, X., 2005. The loquacious user: a document-independent source of terms for query expansion. In: *Proceedings of the 28th annual international ACM SIGIR conference on Research and development in information retrieval*. New York, NY: ACM, pp. 457–64.

Kelly, D., and Fu, X., 2006. Elicitation of term relevance feedback: an investigation of term source and context. In: *Proceedings of the 29th ACM conference on research and development in information retrieval*. New York, NY: ACM, pp. 453–60.

Lewis, R. L., Howes, A., and Singh, S., 2014. Computational rationality: Linking mechanism and behavior through bounded utility maximization. *Topics in cognitive science*, 6(2), pp. 279–311.

Murty, K. G., 2003. Optimization models for decision making: Volume 1. *University of Michigan, Ann Arbor*.

Ong, K., Järvelin, K., Sanderson, M., and Scholer, F., 2017. Using information scent to understand mobile and desktop web search behavior. In: *Proceedings of the 40th ACM SIGIR*. New York, NY: ACM.

Oulasvirta, A., Feit, A., Lahteenlahti, P., and Karrenbauer, A., 2017. Computational support for functionality selection in interaction design. In: *ACM Transactions on Computer-Human Interaction*. New York, NY: ACM, forthcoming.

Oulasvirta, A., Hukkinen, J. P., and Schwartz, B., 2009. When more is less: The paradox of choice in search engine use. In: *Proceedings of the 32nd International ACM SIGIR Conference on Research and Development in Information Retrieval*. New York, NY: ACM, pp. 516–23.

Ouliaris, S., 2012. Economic models: Simulations of reality. Available at: http://www.imf.org/external/pubs/ft/fandd/basics/models.htm. Accessed: 30 April, 2017.

Payne, S. J., and Howes, A., 2013. Adaptive interaction: A utility maximization approach to understanding human interaction with technology. *Synthesis Lectures on Human-Centered Informatics*, 6(1), pp. 1–111.

Pirolli, P., and Card, S., 1999. Information foraging. *Psychological Review*, 106, pp. 643–75.

Pirolli, P., Schank, P., Hearst, M., and Diehl, C., 1996. Scatter/gather browsing communicates the topic structure of a very large text collection. In: *Proceedings of the ACM SIGCHI conference*. New York, NY: ACM, pp. 213–20.

Prabha, C., Connaway, L., Olszewski, L., and Jenkins, L., 2007. What is enough? Satisficing information needs. *Journal of Documentation*, 63(1), pp. 74–89.

Robertson, S. E., 1977. The probability ranking principle in IR. *Journal of Documentation*, 33(4), pp. 294–304.

Russell, D., 2015. Mindtools: What does it mean to be literate in the age of google? *Journal of Computing Sciences in Colleges*, 30(3), pp. 5–6.

Simon, H. A., 1955. A behavioral model of rational choice. *The Quarterly Journal of Economics*, 69(1), pp. 99–118.

Smith, C. L., and Kantor, P. B., 2008. User adaptation: good results from poor systems. In: *Proceedings of the 31st ACM conference on research and development in information retrieval*. New York, NY: ACM, pp. 147–54.

Turpin, A. H., and Hersh, W., 2001. Why batch and user evaluations do not give the same results. In: *Proceedings of the 24th Annual International ACM SIGIR Conference on Research and Development in IR*. New York, NY: ACM, pp. 225–31.

Varian, H. R., 1987. *Intermediate microeconomics: A modern approach*. New York, NY: W.W. Norton.

Varian, H. R., 2016. How to build an economic model in your spare time. *The American Economist*, 61(1), pp. 81–90.

Verma, M., and Yilmaz, E., 2017. *Search Costs vs. User Satisfaction on Mobile*. In: *ECIR '17: Proceedings of the European Conference on Information Retrieval*. New York, NY: Springer, pp. 698–704.

White, R., 2013. Beliefs and biases in web search. In: *Proceedings of the 36th International ACM SIGIR Conference on Research and Development in Information Retrieval*. New York, NY: ACM, pp. 3–12.

Zach, L., 2005. When is "enough" enough? modeling the information-seeking and stopping behavior of senior arts administrators: Research articles. *Journal of the Association for Information Science and Technology*, 56(1), pp. 23–35.

Zhang, Y., and Zhai, C., 2015. Information retrieval as card playing: A formal model for optimizing interactive retrieval interface. In: *Proceedings of the 38th International ACM SIGIR Conference on Research and Development in Information Retrieval*. New York, NY: ACM, pp. 685–94.

Zipf, G. K., 1949. *Human Behavior and the Principle of Least-Effort*. New York, NY: Addison-Wesley.

12

· · • · ·

Computational Models of User Multitasking

DUNCAN P. BRUMBY,
CHRISTIAN P. JANSSEN,
TUOMO KUJALA,
DARIO D. SALVUCCI

12.1 Introduction

Our world today is increasingly technological and interconnected: from smart phones to smart homes, from social media to streaming video, technology users are bombarded with digital information and distractions. These many advances have led to a steep increase in user multitasking (see, e.g., Mark, González, and Harris, 2005), as users struggle to keep pace with the dizzying array of functions at their fingertips. The field of human-computer interaction (HCI) has also struggled to keep pace, ever trying to understand how multitasking affects user behaviour and how new technologies might be better designed to alleviate the potential problems that arise from multi-tasking and distraction.

The world of user multitasking can be roughly characterized in terms of two broad categories that span a continuum of multitasking, in terms of the time interval that separates a switch from one task to another (see Salvucci and Taatgen, 2011). On one end of the continuum are pairs of tasks that are performed more or less concurrently, with very little (e.g., sub-second) time between task switches. Psychologists first studied concurrent multitasking many decades ago (e.g., Telford, 1931) to better understand why, in most cases, simultaneous tasks are more difficult than individual tasks. Studies of dual-choice phenomena (e.g., Schumacher et al., 2001), in which a user makes two different stimulus-response decisions in a rapid sequential order, have arguably been the most popular paradigm in which to study concurrent multitasking behaviour. These studies have yielded some interesting insights, showing that response times for a task generally increase as it is made to temporally overlap with the processing of another concurrent task. Studies of concurrent multitasking have broadened to more practical domains in recent years, especially those that involve performing an occasional short task while doing a continual primary task.

Computational Interaction. Antti Oulasvirta, Per Ola Kristensson, Xiaojun Bi, Andrew Howes (Eds).
© Oxford University Press 2018. Published 2018 by Oxford University Press.

Perhaps the best and most common example involves driving while interacting with an in-car entertainment system or smartphone, and researchers have identified many risks associated with driver distraction and inattention (see, e.g., Dingus et al., 2016). This is just one example of a large class of tasks in which a person does a continuous task while trying to perform a separate concurrent activity, such as interacting with a mobile computing device.

On the other end of the multitasking continuum, sequential multitasking describes those situations in which a user switches between two or more tasks, typically with a longer period of time dedicated to each task before switching. Psychology and HCI researchers have examined sequential multitasking in several forms using different terminology: 'task switching', in which each task is an isolated unit, and once the task is left it is typically not returned to at a later time (cf. Monsell, 2003); 'task interleaving', in which one task is temporarily suspended for another task, and the user later returns to the first task (e.g., Payne, Duggan, and Neth, 2007; Janssen, Brumby, and Garnett, 2012); and 'interruption tasks', in which the original task is disrupted by another task (e.g., Boehm-Davis and Remington, 2009). Everyday sequential multitasking has been found to be very common (González and Mark, 2004), and users can also adapt the time they spend between two tasks based on the reward rates of tasks (Duggan, Johnson, and Sørli, 2013; Janssen et al., 2011; Janssen and Brumby, 2015; Payne et al., 2007). Switching from one task to another task generally incurs a task resumption lag (Altmann and Trafton, 2002; Trafton and Monk, 2008) and increases the probability of making a resumption error (Brumby, Cox, Back, and Gould, 2013). The longer one is interrupted from working on a task, the longer it typically takes to resume that task later (Altmann and Trafton, 2002; Monk et al., 2008). Moreover, being interrupted at an inopportune moment can increase cognitive workload (e.g., Bailey and Iqbal, 2008), stress (Adamczyk and Bailey, 2004), and the likelihood of making an error (Borst, Taatgen, and Van Rijn, 2015; Gould, Brumby, and Cox, 2013).

This chapter surveys a number of recent approaches to understanding user multitasking using computational models. While strengths and weaknesses of the different approaches vary greatly, together they have shown great promise in helping to understand how users perform multiple tasks and the implications for task performance. Computational models are critical not only for scientific exploration of user behaviours, but also as computational engines embedded into running systems that mimic, predict, and potentially mitigate interruption and distraction.

12.2 Modelling Approaches for Simulating User Multitasking

A fundamental characteristic of user multitasking is that sometimes it seems effortless, whereas at other times it can seem excruciatingly difficult. What makes multitasking easy or difficult depends, of course, on the user, the tasks, and other contextual factors. Because these factors are so varied and plentiful, one of the most promising approaches to understanding multitasking is by simulating user behaviour via computational models. Such models enforce a rigorous specification of the factors being studied, and provide both quantitative and qualitative results for the impact of multitasking on behaviour and performance. A range of different modelling approaches have evolved to understand human multitasking behaviour. In this section, we summarize three different approaches: cognitive architectures, cognitive constraint modelling, and uncertainty modelling. These approaches are some of the most common and powerful approaches to computational models of user multitasking, and have complementary strengths. Later we discuss their benefits and drawbacks with respect to understanding and improving HCI, as well as illustrate the approach in the context of modelling various aspects of driver distraction.

12.2.1 Cognitive Architectures

One broad class of modelling approaches is that embodied by computational cognitive architectures (see Anderson, 1983; Newell, 1990). A cognitive architecture acts as a theory of human cognition, attempting to explain the workings of the components of the mind (e.g., memory, vision, movement) and how they interact. The architecture also provides a computational framework by which people can build models for particular tasks and run them in simulation to generate cognition and action. In some ways, then, a cognitive architecture is like a human-inspired programming language where the constraints of the human system are also embedded into the architecture. There have been a number of cognitive architectures developed over the past few decades, such as ACT-R (Anderson, 2007), Soar (Laird, Newell, and Rosenbloom, 1987; Laird, 2012), EPIC (Meyer and Kieras, 1997), and others.

While cognitive architectures have been used to model many general aspects of cognition, there have been several efforts to specifically address multitasking. Some prior work in this area (e.g., Meyer and Kieras, 1997; Byrne and Anderson, 2001) examined models of dual-task performance when applied to the laboratory dual-choice paradigms mentioned earlier. In these models, the multitasking 'strategy'—that is, the way in which two tasks were interleaved—were defined in the model itself, and was thus closely intertwined with the workings of the individual tasks. This approach produces refined and optimized models of performance, but does not necessarily generalize easily to other task domains.

More recently, within the context of the ACT-R cognitive architecture, the theory of threaded cognition has been proposed as a general mechanism for multitask interleaving (Salvucci and Taatgen, 2008; Salvucci and Taatgen, 2011). Threaded cognition posits that multitasking is achieved by cognitive 'threads,' each of which performs the cognitive processing for one particular task; as this processing spreads across multiple cognitive resources (vision, declarative memory, etc.), multiple threads can interleave and result in efficient multitasking behaviour. In theory, threaded cognition makes predictions about any two (or more) cognitive threads, and thus it serves as a general mechanism rather than requiring multitasking strategies to be specified for each task pairing.

Other recent developments in the cognitive architecture community have emphasized the role of the 'problem state' in multitask performance (e.g., Borst, Taatgen, and van Rijn, 2010, 2015). The problem state serves as temporary storage of information during the execution of a task, and when two or more tasks all require their own problem state, there can be interference among them, leading to a degradation in performance. These ideas can work hand in hand with threaded cognition: while the threads enable concurrent interleaving of processes, the problem state plays a central role in more sequential interleaving of tasks as task information is stored and later recalled.

12.2.2 Cognitive Constraint Modelling

We next describe cognitive constraint modelling as an approach that complements and extends the computational cognitive architecture approach to modelling multitasking described previously. Cognitive constraints models have been used to model human behaviour across a range of HCI activities (Payne and Howes, 2013). Here, though, we focus on models that have been used to understand human multitasking (Brumby, Salvucci, and Howes, 2009; Brumby, Howes, and Salvucci, 2007; Howes, Lewis, and Vera, 2009; Janssen and Brumby, 2010; Janssen, Brumby, and Garnett, 2012; Janssen et al., 2011; Janssen and Brumby, 2015). Before we do this, we first outline the key features of the cognitive constraint modelling approach and how it differs from other modelling approaches.

The cognitive constraint modelling approach seeks to explain behaviour given the range of possible strategies available to the user in a particular context. For example, in a multitasking situation, an important strategic dimension is how much time is given to a task before the user chooses to switch to another task. The choice of strategy in this situation will invariably have implications for how tasks are performed. The cognitive constraint approach embraces this element of strategic variability in human behaviour and attempts to understand the implications for performance outcomes. In doing so, it tries to understand why a particular strategy might be favoured over others, given a particular performance profile and an objective (or goal). To understand this approach, there are three critical features: constraints, strategy space, and objective function. We unpack each in turn.

Constraints. The first step in developing a cognitive constraint model is to explicitly define the factors that constrain performance. These constraints are determined by internal factors that limit the user's ability and external features from the environment. Internal factors are based on assumptions about the human cognitive architecture. For example, the time it takes to shift visual attention from one device to another, or the time it takes to press key on a device. In many cases, the assumptions that are made about the human cognitive architecture are consistent with other cognitive architecture frameworks, such as ACT-R and EPIC, introduced earlier. However, the unit of analysis has varied from very fine grained, such as an eye-brain lag (Lewis et al., 2014), to very coarse grained, such as the time interval between keypresses (Janssen and Brumby, 2015). Many more granularities are also possible (see Lewis, Howes, and Singh, 2014).

External factors are those from the task environment that affect behaviour. These can be experiences, encountered before taking part in a study, that shape the probabilities of specific actions (see Lewis, Howes, and Singh, 2014 for examples). However, they might also come from direct characteristics of the task or interface that a participant may encounter—for example, how the speed with which a button is pressed might depend on the size of that button.

Strategy space. Once the constraints are known, a model can be used to analyse what interaction strategies are possible. This is also illustrated using a Venn diagram at the bottom

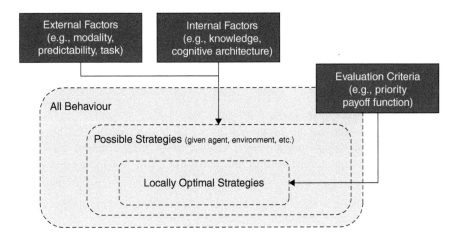

Figure 12.1 In the cognitive constraints-based approach, external and internal factors (top) narrow down what set of interaction strategies is possible, given the agent and the environment, out of all potential behaviours. Once an evaluation criterion is introduced, one can identify the set of local optimal strategies within the full set of possible strategies.

of Figure 12.1: the space of *all* possible behaviours is narrowed down to a space of possible behaviours for a *specific user* in a *specific task setting* once the external and internal constraints are known (top of figure).

Given the focus on understanding strategic variability, this approach contrasts sharply with the architecture-based approach that was described earlier, which typically looks to simulate only a small set of strategies for performing tasks, rather than the broader context of possible options. Instead, the cognitive constraint approach complements and extends previous HCI modelling approaches, such as a fast-man/slow-man approach (Card, Moran, and Newell, 1986) and performance bracketing (Kieras and Meyer, 2000). Whereas these previous approaches typically focus on performance in the extremes (i.e., predicting the fastest and slowest performance), the constraint-based approach aims to model a wider (and potentially, complete) range of strategies to understand why a particular strategy is chosen.

Objective function. A critical issue that cognitive constraint modelling brings into focus is the choice between strategies. The approach allows the modeller to predict the *range* of behaviours that are possible for an agent in a specific environment. A critical question that emerges from this approach is to consider the choice between strategies. An underlying assumption of this approach is that people will generally select strategies that maximize rewards (Howes, Lewis, and Vera, 2009). Such an evaluation criterion can take various forms. Ideally, there is an objective criterion, such as a score from an explicit payoff function, which allows identification of the overall best performing strategies (cf. Janssen et al., 2011; Janssen and Brumby, 2015), as illustrated in Figure 12.1. This allows one to assess how well people can optimize performance under constraints, which has been one of the focuses of this modelling approach (Howes, Lewis, and Vera, 2009; Janssen and Brumby, 2015; Lewis, Howes, and Singh, 2014; Payne and Howes, 2013).

An alternative approach is the use of a priority instruction. How people's multitasking performance changes with different priorities has been studied extensively (e.g., building on work such as Navon and Gopher, 1979; Norman and Bobrow, 1975). The role of constraint-based models is then to see whether a change in instructed priority results in a change of behaviour, and how well this performance compares with alternative ways of interleaving. As our example of driver distraction will later illustrate, this allows one to understand distraction from a speed-accuracy tradeoff perspective and to dissociate why instructed 'safe' performance might not always align with objectively assessed 'safe' performance.

12.2.3 Uncertainty Modelling

Successful allocation of users' limited attentional resources across different concurrent tasks at the time of demand is an important prerequisite for successful multitasking. There is a large class of models of human (focal) visual attention allocation in which uncertainty plays a central role (e.g., Johnson et al., 2014; Sullivan et al., 2012; Sprague and Ballard, 2003). Uncertainty can be interpreted as referring to numerous internal and external factors (e.g., memory decay, low contrast), but following Sullivan et al. (2012), we define the uncertainty determining visual attention allocation as 'the variance of the probability distribution associated with a belief that the world is in a particular state given a set of visual observations over time'. This section briefly discusses the role of uncertainty models of visual attention allocation in multitasking.

Uncertainty as a driving force behind attention allocation in automobile driving was first suggested by Senders et al. (1967), who suggested that drivers can maintain off-road glances until the level of uncertainty reaches each individual's preference threshold. Kujala et al. (2016) have shown that these individual preferences for off-road glance time (and distance) can vary at least by a factor of three. According to the original equation by Senders et al. (1967), the uncertainty accumulates over time while looking away from the road, proportionally to the instability of the vehicle and variability of the environment (e.g., speed of vehicle, information density of the roadway) as well as the individual differences in weighting and forgetting information. The equation predicts that if one's uncertainty of the road is below one's threshold, the driver can continue to look away from the road. Once the uncertainty increases over one's individual threshold, the driver will look back at the road. The model predicts long glances away from the road during secondary activities when the uncertainty grows slowly and/or when the individual threshold for the uncertainty is high. Lee et al. (2015) have utilized the model successfully in analysing and recognizing different off-road glancing patterns as well as task factors (number of screens, delay) affecting these while driving and concurrently reading messages at an in-car display. They concluded that the drivers who showed generally shorter glances off road were more intense but less capable of controlling the vehicle. This suggests that the observed individual differences in glance patterns off road may depend more on the rate of the growth of uncertainty rather than differences in tolerance of uncertainty.

Later, Kujala et al. (2016) introduced a simplified model of driver's uncertainty accumulation based on the event density of the road (i.e., environmental visual demands of driving):

$$\text{Umax}_k = D(x)OD(x)_k,$$

in which the constant Umax_k is the driver k's subjective uncertainty tolerance threshold, $D(x)$ is the event density of the road at point x, and $OD(x)_k$ is the preferred occlusion distance (the distance driven without visual information of the forward roadway) of the driver k starting at the road point x. The event density $D(x)$ is a discrete version of the information density of the road as defined by Senders et al. (1967). Each event represents an information-processing event of a task-relevant event state in the road environment by the driver. The model allows a prediction for driver behaviour to be made, that is:

$$OD(x)_k = \text{Umax}_k/D(x),$$

which can be used for predicting individual off-road glance durations if one's Umax_k and the event density of the road environment (e.g., curvature; see Tsimhoni and Green, 2001) are known. The metric of OD has been utilized as a baseline for acceptable off-road glance durations for in-car user interface testing in dynamic, self-paced driving scenarios (Kujala, Grahn, Mäkelä, and Lasch, 2016). Based on the findings of Lee et al. (2015), the constant Umax_k is likely to be determined by two individual factors instead of one, that is, of the uncertainty tolerance threshold as well as the rate of the growth of uncertainty. This complicates the interpretation of the OD measurements for a road environment, but for a sufficient driver sample, average OD can be taken as an estimate of the objective visual demands of the road environment.

An example of an alternative quantitative model of attentional control is SEEV (Saliency, Effort, Expectancy, Value; see Wickens et al., 2003), in which the operator's (internal) uncertainty does not play an explicit key role. SEEV's modifications have been utilized in modelling and predicting the allocation of visual (focal) attention of a human operator at areas of interest in aviation, driving, driving with secondary tasks, and visual workspaces in general (e.g., Steelman et al., 2011, 2016; Wortelen et al., 2013; Horrey et al., 2006). The SEEV model treats the eye as a single-server queue served by visual scanning (i.e., sampling). The SEEV model is based on optimal (prescriptive) models of information sampling, which rely on the product of expectancy (i.e., expected event rate) and value (i.e., relevance, priority) of information at a channel (Senders, 1964; Carbonell, 1966; Moray, 1986). SEEV adds the components of information saliency and effort (e.g., distance between displays) to the equation in order to provide a more accurate description on how (suboptimal) human operator shares visual attention in time between targets (Wickens et al., 2003). All of these components are quantified in the SEEV model(s) for evaluating the probability of gaze allocation at a task-relevant area of interest in time. SEEV can be applied to predict attention allocation between concurrent tasks, that is, task management in multitasking environments. Validation studies on SEEV have produced high correlations between predicted and observed percentage dwell times (PDTs) on areas of interest in the domains of aviation (Wickens et al., 2003) and driving (Horrey et al., 2006). An extension of the model (NSEEV, N for predicting *noticing* behaviour) is also capable of predicting the speed and probability with which human operators notice critical visual events (e.g., warning signals) in cockpits and in alert detection tasks while multitasking (Steelman et al., 2016, 2011). The SEEV-AIE (Adaptive Information Expectancy) model by Wortelen et al. (2013) is built upon the SEEV model with an advantage that it is able to derive the expectancy parameters automatically from a simulation of a dynamic task model in a cognitive architecture, whereas SEEV (and NSEEV) requires a human expert to provide an estimation of the operator's expectancies for the task-relevant event rates at the visual information channels in the task environment.

Also in SEEV, uncertainty is implicitly assumed to be a driver of attention allocation, but uncertainty is coupled tightly with the objective bandwidth of events in an information channel (Horrey et al., 2006). It is assumed that the higher the expected event rate in an information channel, the faster the operator's uncertainty about these events grows if the operator does not attend the channel. This is a sane assumption, but there are tasks and task environments in which uncertainty and expectancy are decoupled, and, in fact, uncertainty is coupled with the unexpected. For instance, a car driver feels a great demand to keep eyes on the road at the end of an unfamiliar steep hill because the driver does not know what to expect behind the hill (i.e., high uncertainty), not because of high expectancy of task-relevant events. Expectancy informs the human operator what the task-relevant channels are in the task environment and the expected event rates on the channels, but (individual) uncertainty of these expectations may add a significant (top-down) factor for explaining human attention allocation between the targets in unfamiliar and/or variable task environments. From the viewpoint of minimizing uncertainty, attentional demand for allocating attention to a source of information with an expected event and the related value of the sampled information can be actually rather low (Clark, 2013). From this perspective, SEEV and similar models are useful for predicting attention allocation for an experienced operator for a well-defined task and task environment (a prescriptive model), but are limited in their ability to describe or predict individual behaviours in uncertain tasks contexts (e.g., for operators with different uncertainty growth rates; see Lee et al., 2015, for a novice operator with under-developed expectancies, or for environments of high variability in task-relevant event rates). For instance, in the uncertainty model of Kujala et al. (2016), discussed earlier, the event density and visual demand is still very much coupled with the (objective) information bandwidth of the road, but overall, the uncertainty-based models of attention allocation seem to provide feasible solutions for predicting individual differences in the control of attention (of focal vision, in particular) in multitasking. Furthermore, these models are well in line with more general theories of brains as prediction engines (e.g., Clark, 2013, 2015).

12.3 Detailed Example: Driver Distraction

The ease of driving provided by modern cars and driving assistance systems together with mobile broadband and the numerous applications available on the road via drivers' smart-phones have led to a worldwide epidemic of driver distraction by secondary, non-driving related activities (Dingus et al., 2016; World Health Organization, 2011). Texting, instant messaging, tweeting, emailing, or browsing music are just some examples of secondary activities that some drivers want to do while driving, even if they are aware of the associated risks. Researchers, legislators, and the general public have all sought ways to understand, predict, and ultimately alleviate this growing problem.

All the current definitions of driver distraction are incomplete, as these do not define the activities necessary for safe driving, from which the driver is referred to be distracted (e.g., Foley et al., 2013; Regan et al., 2011). There are at least three forms of driver distraction: manual, cognitive, and visual (Foley et al., 2013). Manual distraction ('hands off the steering wheel') refers to *any physical manipulation that competes with activities necessary for safe driving*' and cognitive distraction ('mind off road') refers to *any epoch of cognitive loading that competes with activities necessary for safe driving*' (Foley et al., 2013, p. 62). Visual distraction, in short, refers to driver's eyes being off the road at the wrong moment. The act of driving requires visual attention, in particular, and visual distraction has been found to be the most significant type of distraction when associated with the safety-critical incident risk (Dingus et al., 2016). For this reason, optimizing driver's in-car user interfaces for minimizing visual distraction has been a major goal of HCI design efforts in the domain (e.g., Kun et al., 2016; Schmidt et al., 2010). This section provides examples of computational modelling on driver's time-sharing of visual attention between the task of driving and secondary mobile computing activities that are performed at the same time by the driver. We are interested in understanding the effects of driver multitasking on task performance and safety. As we shall see, a further concern is with visual distraction, which is often deeply entwined with cognitive distraction.

12.3.1 Modelling Driver Distraction in a Cognitive Architecture

The core idea of modelling driver distraction in a cognitive architecture can be broken down into three parts. First, we require a model of driving itself, particularly the aspects of driver behaviour that relate to basic control (steering and acceleration). Salvucci (2006) developed such a model, accounting for aspects of driving that included curve negotiation and lane changing as well as basic control; others have developed similar models (e.g., Liu, Feyen, and Tsimhoni, 2006). Second, we require models of some secondary task, such as dialling a phone or interacting with some other onboard system. Models of many such tasks are straightforward to build in cognitive architectures, although there has been less work on particular interactions (e.g., touchscreen swiping). Third, we need some way to integrate the two models, such that they can run together in a simulation architecture. Fortunately, as mentioned earlier, there are general mechanisms for integration, notably, threaded cognition in the ACT-R architecture.

Putting these parts together, there have now been a wide variety of efforts showing how cognitive architectures can account for driver distraction from secondary tasks. Some of the earliest work focused on cell-phone dialling as a common task (e.g., Salvucci, 2001a; Salvucci and Macuga, 2002). In later efforts, these models were expanded to other types of interaction, like tuning a radio or adjusting the climate controls (e.g., Salvucci, 2009). One important offshoot of this work was the development of rapid prototyping systems built explicitly for designers to prototype and evaluate possible interactions with respect to their potential for distraction. For example, the Distract-R system (Salvucci, 2009) allows for users to specify a new in-vehicle interface as well as sample tasks that can be performed on the interface; in doing so, the user specifies the architecture models not by explicit coding, but instead by demonstrating the task actions in sequence. Once the interface and tasks are specified, the user can run the system to simulate driver behaviour, checking how common measures of driver performance (e.g., deviation from the lane centre) might be affected by interaction with the proposed interface.

12.3.2 Modelling a Range of Driver Strategies using Cognitive Constraint Models

When people divide their time between two tasks, two interesting questions are what the best strategy is for dividing time between the two, and do people apply such strategies? In a driving context in particular, it is relevant to understand how different ways of dividing time between driving and other tasks impacts driving safety, given the frequent observation of such behaviour in everyday driving (Dingus et al., 2016). This section describes the results of a series of studies and models that has investigated peoples' efficiency for dividing time between two tasks in a dialling-while-driving paradigm using the cognitive constraint modelling approach (Brumby, Salvucci, and Howes, 2009; Brumby, Howes, and Salvucci, 2007; Janssen and Brumby, 2010; Janssen, Brumby, and Garnett, 2012). The value of the models has been to demonstrate that people adapt the pattern in which they interleave tasks based on the constraints of the tasks and how they choose to prioritize tasks. Moreover, the model gave a new interpretation for driver distraction: drivers try to optimize (subjective) speed-accuracy trade-offs. Sometimes, optimization of such trade-offs might result in behaviour that is irrational and sub-optimal when considered by an outside observer (i.e., it is not the safest possible). However, when described in the context of other strategies, such performance might be considered efficient.

The starting point of this work is that in goal-oriented tasks, people tend to interleave tasks at positions that are higher up in the task hierarchy (i.e., after the completion of subgoals). Interleaving here offers many advantages, such as a reduction in workload and the availability of cognitive resources for other tasks. These points are therefore also referred to as 'natural breakpoints' for interleaving (e.g., Bailey and Iqbal, 2008; Bogunovich and Salvucci, 2010; Janssen, Brumby, and Garnett, 2012; Miyata and Norman, 1986; Payne, Duggan, and Neth, 2007). When interleaving the manual dialling of a phone number with driving, people also tend to switch tasks at natural breakpoints (Salvucci, 2005). In this case, it is assumed that phone numbers are represented hierarchically in memory, where dialling the entire number requires one to retrieve and dial subsets of numbers (e.g., first '123', then '456', then '7890' for number 123–456–7890). Points where the next subtask starts (e.g., retrieving and dialling '456') form a natural breakpoint in the cognitive representational structure of task and so offer a natural opportunity for the driver to return their attention to the driving task.

We investigated under what circumstances people interleave at different positions than the chunk boundary (natural breakpoint) of the phone number. Specifically, we investigated the effect of task priorities (Brumby, Salvucci, and Howes, 2009; Janssen and Brumby, 2010) and motor cues (Janssen, Brumby, and Garnett, 2012). Participants were trained to memorize a phone number in a chunked manner. They were then required to dial the phone number while also steering a simulated car. While doing this, they were given an explicit task priority: either to prioritize the dialling of the phone number as fast as possible ('dialling focus' condition) or to prioritize keeping the car as close to the middle of the driving lane as possible ('steering focus' condition). Empirical results consistently showed that dialling and steering performance were affected by this manipulation of task priority instructions (Brumby, Salvucci, and Howes, 2009; Janssen and Brumby, 2010; Janssen, Brumby, and Garnett, 2012). A model was then used to investigate how efficient the performance was, by comparing it to predicted performance of a range of interleaving strategies.

The model developed for this purpose explored only sequential strategies in which a driver is either steering, dialling, or switching between dialling and driving (more details can be found in Janssen and Brumby, 2010). Each aspect of the model combines aspects of external factors (e.g., dynamics of the driving simulator) with internal factors (e.g., memory retrieval times). When the model is actively steering, it updates the heading (or lateral velocity) of the car every 250ms based on the current position of the car in the lane (lateral deviation (LD) expressed in m/s) as defined in this equation (Brumby, Howes, and Salvucci, 2007):

$$\text{Lateral Velocity} = 0.2617 \times \text{LD}^2 + 0.0233 \times \text{LD} - 0.022$$

The equation captures the intuition that steering movements are sharper when the car is further away from lane centre and are smaller when the car is close to lane centre. In the driving simulator, the position of the car was updated every 50ms and on each sample noise from a Gaussian distribution was added. As a consequence, during periods of driver inattention the car would gradually drift in the lane.

For the dialling task, the time to type each digit was calibrated based on single-task dialling time for each study. Typically, it was assumed that each digit required approximately the same amount of time to type. In addition, retrieval costs were added each time when a chunk needed to be retrieved from memory (i.e., before the first and sixth digit of the numbers, and after returning to dialling after a period of driving). Switching attention between tasks was assumed to take 200ms.

The model was used to make performance predictions for different dual-task interleaving strategies. This was done by systematically varying how many digits are dialled before the model returns to driving and how much time is spent on driving before returning to dialling. This approach meant that many different dual-task interleaving strategies were simulated and performance predictions made using the model. Figure 12.2 plots typical model results. Each grey dot indicates the performance of a particular strategy for interleaving the dialling task with driving. The performance of each strategy is expressed as total dialling time (horizontal axis) and the average lateral deviation of the car (vertical axis).

The modelling analysis demonstrates that the choice of dual-task interleaving strategy has a substantial impact on the performance of each task. In particular, for dialling time, the fastest and slowest strategy differ by more than a factor of 10 (note the logarithmic scale). For both dialling time and lateral deviation, lower values are better. More specifically, the closer that the strategy is to the origin, the better the strategy can be considered. Given a known criterion of performance on one task (e.g., a specific dialling time), the model can be used to predict the best possible performance on the other task (e.g., lateral deviation).

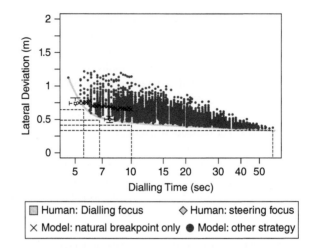

Figure 12.2 Typical model results of the cognitive constraint model of dialling-while-steering task. Human interleaving strategy changes based on the given priority focus. It typically lies on a performance trade-off outside curve. However, even when prioritizing steering, it is not applying the objectively safest strategy (far right), given the trade-off cost of the longer dialling time. Adapted from Janssen and Brumby (2010).

Examples are highlighted in the figure with the dashed grey lines. If one draws a line through the points on this lower-left outside edge of the model, a trade-off curve emerges (the solid light gray line in the figure).

Understanding the shape of the trade-off curve can give insights into why people might adopt particular dual-task interleaving strategies. To give an example, Figure 12.2 shows the dual-task performance of participants from Janssen and Brumby's (2010) dialling and driving study. Participants in this experiment were instructed to either prioritize the dialling task or the steering task. It can be seen that participants in these different task priority conditions made different dual-task tradeoffs: participants instructed to prioritize dialling were faster at completing the dialling task but maintained worse lateral control of the car, whereas participants instructed to prioritize steering were slower at completing the dialling task but maintained better lateral control of the car. The modelling analysis helps understand these tradeoffs: human performance falls at different points along the tradeoff curve. This result is important because it demonstrates the substantial impact that strategy choice can have on performance: people can choose to adopt quite different strategies and this has implications for how well each task is performed.

Another salient aspect is that participants in the steering focus condition did not apply the strategy that leads to the 'best possible' driving performance (i.e., they did not apply the strategy on the far right of the performance space). This behaviour can be understood given the broader context of the strategy space. The modelling analysis suggests that while better driving performance could be achieved by completing the dialling task very slowly, the improvements in driving are marginal relative to the additional time cost for completing the dialling task (i.e., the line flattens out after around 8s to complete the dialling task).

This suggests that participants were 'satisficing' by selecting a strategy that was good enough for the driving task while also completing the dialing task in a reasonable length of time. This insight is important because it suggests that satisficing could lead people to make decisions that seem good enough when compared to other multitasking strategies, but which are nonetheless worse for performance than a mono-tasking strategy.

12.3.3 Modelling Driver Visual Sampling Using Uncertainty Models

According to Horrey and Wickens (2007), the conditions likely to cause a motor vehicle crash do not occur under typical circumstances (i.e., at the mean of a distribution), but under atypical circumstances (i.e., at the tails of the distribution). They go on and demonstrate by an empirical study how an analysis of the average off-road glance durations to an in-car display might lead to inaccurate conclusions about the safety to use an in-car device while driving compared to an alternative analysis of the tail of the in-car glance distribution. In the failures in time-sharing visual resources between road and in-car devices, the occasional overlong off-road glances are rare, but are the most significant for crash risk (Dingus et al., 2016; Liang et al., 2012). This places challenges for computational modelling and prediction of driver behaviour, as instead of modelling average time-sharing behaviours, the models should be able to predict lapses of control in the visual sampling off road (i.e., the tails of the in-car glance distribution).

As one step toward understanding visual sampling, Kujala and Salvucci (2015) created a cognitive model that aims to represent a driver's basic visual sampling strategy when interacting with an in-car display and tried to predict, among other metrics, the effects of different user interface designs on the percentages of >2s in-car glances. The study was conducted in order to help in understanding these strategies as well as the effects of different unordered menu layouts on drivers' visual sampling while the driver is driving and searching for an item on an in-car display. Based on the early driver's visual sampling model by Wierwille (1993), the proposed visual sampling strategy assumes that drivers are aware of the passage of time during the in-car search task and they try to adjust their glances at the display to a time limit based on an uncertainty tolerance threshold, after which they switch back to the driving task. Furthermore, the drivers adjust their time limits based on their driving performance in the current driving environment. The time limit is reset to the lower 500ms limit of Wierwille's (1993) model if the driving is unstable after an in-car glance. If the driving is stable, the time limit is incremented by a smallest possible unit. This adjustment resembles a dynamic strategy in which the driver is trying to 'optimize' the time spent looking off road based on the dynamic visual demands of driving and the related uncertainty. A schematic of this basic visual sampling strategy is illustrated in Figure 12.3.

The modelling started with the most general visual sampling strategy based on existing empirical findings on driver behaviour with in-car tasks (Wierwille, 1993). In addition, the assumptions behind the model were based on existing research on visual search behaviours as well as the constraints provided by the ACT-R cognitive architecture (Anderson, 2007; Anderson et al., 2004). In general, the model followed the principles of the theory of threaded cognition (Salvucci and Taatgen, 2008, 2011) introduced earlier. The cognitive architecture (ACT-R) on which the model was built introduced certain constraints but, on the other hand, validated solutions, for modelling some of the details of the simulated behaviour. For example, the model benefited from ACT-R's embedded theory of time perception (Taatgen et al., 2007). The theory posits that time perception acts like a metronome that ticks slower as time progresses, with additional noise drawn from a logistic distribution. The end result is time estimates that match well to the abilities and limitations of real human time perception. The driving behaviour was based on the ACT-R driver model (Salvucci, 2006), and the ACT-R model of eye movements and visual encoding (Salvucci, 2001b). Model parameters were estimated to achieve the best overall fit to the empirical data gathered in two experiments.

The secondary search tasks simulated a situation in which the participant searches for a target song in an in-car music menu. The search tasks were performed on a screen with six different layouts, with six, nine, or twelve items per page, on a list or grid menu layout (3 × 2 design). For in-car visual search, the model assumes a random starting point, inhibition of return (Klein, 2000; Posner and Cohen, 1984), and a search strategy that always seeks the nearest uninspected item (Halverson and Hornof, 2007). A limitation of the search model was that it probably does not apply to semantic and alphabetic organizations of the in-car display items (Bailly et al., 2014). We decided to focus on the more general case in which there is no predetermined ordering for the menu items (e.g., sorting points of interest by proximity to the car). This served to minimize the potential effects of previous knowledge and practice on the visual search behaviours. Following Janssen et al. (2012), we assumed that the press of a scroll button after an unsuccessful search for a page would act as a natural break point for a task switch, and thus, the model returns eyes back to the driving environment after each change of a screen (Figure 12.3). Following the NHTSA in-car device testing guidelines (2013), the model driver was given the goal to drive at 80km/h on the centre lane of a three-lane road and to follow a simulated car that kept a constant speed of 80km/h. The model's predictions were validated with two empirical driving simulator studies with eye tracking ($N = 12$ each).

In terms of its results, the model accurately accounted for the increase in the total in-car glance durations as the number of display items, and the task time, increased (Exp 1: $r^2 = 0.843$, RMSSD $= 1.615$; Exp 2: $r^2 = 0.950$, RMSSD $= 1.108$). It also accounted generally for the number of in-car glances, although the model tended to overestimate the number

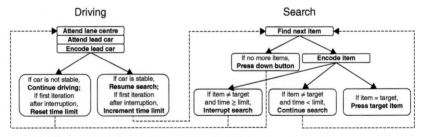

Figure 12.3 Schematic overview of the visual sampling model's flow of processing. Adapted from Kujala and Salvucci (2015).

of the glances. These metrics describe the model's (and architecture's) ability to model and predict the general visual demands (e.g., encoding times) of visual search tasks. However, here we were also interested in the model's ability to describe how drivers time-share their visual attention between the driving and the secondary task. In general, the model not only provided good predictions on mean in-car glance durations (Exp 1: $r^2 = 0.396$; Exp 2: $r^2 = 0.659$), but also indicated the challenges in predicting probabilities of the occasional long in-car glances. A major accomplishment of the model was its ability to predict that only the List-6 layout out of all the layout alternatives would (likely) pass the 15 per cent (max) NHTSA (2013) in-car device verification threshold for the percentage of >2s in-car glances. Another accomplishment was the model's ability to predict the in-car task length's increasing effect on the percentage of these long in-car glances. The work also provided a plausible explanation for this in-car task length effect observed in several studies (e.g., Lee et al., 2012; Kujala and Saariluoma, 2011). Due to the upward adjustment of the time limit after each in-car glance if the driving stays stable, the time limit is able to grow the higher the longer the task (i.e., the more in-car glances, the more upward adjustments can be made). The large time limit together with the inbuilt delay and noise in the human time perception mechanism (Taatgen et al., 2007) translate to a greater chance of risky overlong glances (i.e., lapses of control in visual sampling).

Besides the successes, there were significant limitations in the predictive power of the model. There could be alternative visual sampling models that could achieve similar or even better fits with the empirical data. In particular, our model overestimated the number of in-car glances in general, as well as the maximum in-car glance durations. There could be additional mechanisms in work in limiting the in-car glance durations that were absent in our model. For instance, there was no (explicit) internal uncertainty component in the model. On the other hand, it is possible the human drivers preferred to extend a glance to press a scroll button as a natural break point for a task switch, even if the time limit was close or passed (Janssen et al., 2012). Our model tended to move attention back to driving immediately after exceeding the time limit.

The most severe deficiencies of the model come clear if one studies individual time-sharing protocols at a detailed level. While the fits on the aggregate data are at a good level, at individual level one can see variations in the visual sampling strategies even in the behaviour of a single participant that are not taken into account in our original model. In Salvucci and Kujala, 2016, we studied the systematicities in the individual time-sharing protocols and modelled how the structural (e.g., natural breakpoints) and temporal constraints (e.g., uncertainty buildup for the driving task) of the component tasks interplay in determining switch points between tasks. The proposed computational model unifies the structural and temporal constraints under the notion of competing urgencies. The model was able to provide a good fit for the identified individual strategies, as well as for the aggregate data, comparable to the fit of our original model (Kujala and Salvucci, 2015). The findings give support for the computational model on the interplay between the subtask structure and the temporal constraints of the component tasks, and indicate how this interplay strongly influences people's time-sharing behaviour. More generally, the findings stress the importance of modelling individual time-sharing behaviours (including strategies and uncertainties) besides the aggregate behaviours.

12.4 Discussion

Throughout this chapter we have tried to emphasize the many benefits of computational models for understanding multitasking in the context of HCI. One of the most important overarching benefits of these models is that they capture fundamental characteristics of human behaviour and can be used to predict performance in novel settings. This is especially critical for the domain of multitasking, as humans are flexible in the ways that they combine multiple tasks. For example, new applications for smartphones and new types of technology are released continuously. Even when few empirical studies have been run on such novel settings, models can then be used to predict human performance. This is particularly relevant for the domain of driver distraction in the advent of automated and self-driving vehicles (Kun et al., 2016). As the capabilities of automated vehicles change, so will the role of the human driver. However, again, even though the requirements of the car change, the central characteristics of the human driver (i.e., as captured in a cognitive architecture or model) will not. For example, they might be used to predict how quickly drivers can recreate relevant driving context, or what might be an appropriate moment to request a human driver to take over control of the vehicle (see also, Van der Heiden, Iqbal, and Janssen, 2017). All the modelling approaches outlined here can be used to make predictions about how humans might perform in such changing circumstances, although each approach focuses on a different grain size of behaviour and/or different tradeoffs of aggregate behaviour vs. individual behaviours.

One important limitation of the modelling approaches presented here is that they are developed for goal-oriented tasks, whereas not all tasks in the world are goal-oriented. Recent efforts are being made on modelling less goal-oriented work, such as computational models of 'mind wandering' in a cognitive architecture (e.g., van Vugt, Taatgen, Sackur, and Bastian, 2015). Another limitation of the approaches is that in the construction and analysis of the models, we as modellers are often focused on the cognitive, perceptual, and motor aspects of behaviour, whereas other aspects of human behaviour—such as fatigue, arousal, mood, and emotion—also affect performance and experience (e.g., Dancy, Ritter, and Berry, 2012; Gunzelmann, Gross, Gluck, and Dinges, 2009), but are typically not addressed in these modelling efforts.

Although the main example illustrated in this chapter focused on driver distraction, the essential elements are captured in general constraints and characteristic of the human cognitive architecture, and therefore the approaches can also be applied to other settings. For example, the cognitive architecture approach of threaded cognition has been applied to study various combinations of tasks (Salvucci and Taatgen, 2011), and the constraint-based approach has been applied to study efficiency in desk-based dynamic tasks (e.g., Janssen and Brumby, 2015). Ideally, each of these approaches strives to account for as many known phenomena as possible, while simultaneously offering enough flexibility to predict and explain behaviour in novel situations and newly discovered phenomena.

12.5 Conclusion

This chapter introduces three approaches that have been used to model human multi-tasking: cognitive architectures, cognitive constraint modelling, and uncertainty modelling. The value of these modelling approaches lies in their detailed description and prediction of human behaviour, and each approach focused on slightly different aspects of behaviour. Given the diversity of situations in which multitasking occurs and the diversity in research approaches to study multitasking (Janssen, Gould, Li, Brumby, and Cox, 2015), the diversity in modelling approaches is extremely valuable. The diversity provides complementary strengths and applicability to different settings. The presented examples offer insights into how different task models can be combined in a cognitive architecture for providing estimates of aggregate measures of performance; how the space of task interleaving strategies can be explored by using cognitive constraint models; and how uncertainty models can predict occasional failures in visual sampling between tasks.

....

REFERENCES

Adamczyk, P. D., and Bailey, B. P., 2004. If not now, when? Proceedings of the SIGCHI Conference on Human Factors in Computing Systems, pp. 271–8.

Altmann, E., and Trafton, J. G., 2002. Memory for goals: An activation-based model. *Cognitive Science*, 26(1), pp. 39–83.

Anderson, J. R., 1983. *The Architecture of Cognition*. Cambridge, MA: Harvard University Press.

Anderson, J. R., 2007. *How Can the Human Mind Occur In The Physical Universe?* Oxford: Oxford University Press.

Anderson, J. R., Bothell, D., Byrne, M. D., Douglass, S., Lebiere, C., and Qin, Y., 2004. An integrated theory of the mind. *Psychology Review*, 111, pp. 1036–60.

Bailey, B. P., and Iqbal, S. T., 2008. Understanding changes in mental workload during execution of goal-directed tasks and its application for interruption management. *ACM Transactions on Computer-Human Interaction (TOCHI)*, 14(4), pp. 1–28.

Bailly, G., Oulasvirta, A., Brumby, D. P., and Howes, A., 2014. Model of visual search and selection time in linear menus. In: *CHI'14: Proceedings of the SIGCHI Conference on Human Factors in Computing Systems*. New York, NY: ACM, pp. 3865–74.

Boehm-Davis, D. A., and Remington, R. W., 2009. Reducing the disruptive effects of interruption: a cognitive framework for analysing the costs and benefits of intervention strategies. *Accident Analysis & Prevention*, 41(5), pp. 1124–9. Available at: http://doi.org/10.1016/j.aap.2009.06.029.

Bogunovich, P., and Salvucci, D. D., 2010. Inferring multitasking breakpoints from single-task data. In: S. Ohlsson and R. Catrambone, eds. *Proceedings of the 32nd Annual Meeting of the Cognitive Science Society*. Austin, TX: Cognitive Science Society, pp. 1732–7.

Borst, J. P., Taatgen, N. A., and van Rijn, H., 2010. The problem state: a cognitive bottleneck in multitasking. *Journal of Experimental Psychology: Learning, Memory, and Cognition*, (36)2, pp. 363–82.

Borst, J. P., Taatgen, N. A., and van Rijn, H., 2015. What makes interruptions disruptive? A process-model account of the effects of the problem state bottleneck on task interruption and resumption.

In: Proceedings of the 33rd Annual ACM Conference. New York, NY,: ACM, pp. 2971–80. Available at: http://doi.org/10.1145/2702123.2702156.

Brumby, D. P., Cox, A. L., Back, J., and Gould, S. J. J., 2013. Recovering from an interruption: Investigating speed-accuracy tradeoffs in task resumption strategy. *Journal of Experimental Psychology: Applied*, 19, pp. 95–107. Available at: <http://dx.doi.org/10.1037/a0032696>.

Brumby, D. P., Howes, A., and Salvucci, D. D., 2007. A cognitive constraint model of dual-task tradeoffs in a highly dynamic driving task. In: *Proceedings of the SIGCHI Conference on Human Factors in Computing Systems*. New York, NY: ACM, pp. 233–42.

Brumby, D. P., Salvucci, D. D., and Howes, A., 2009. Focus on Driving: How Cognitive Constraints Shape the Adaptation of Strategy when Dialing while Driving. In: Proceedings of the SIGCHI conference on Human factors in computing systems. New York, NY: ACM, pp. 1629–38.

Byrne, M. D., and Anderson, J. R., 2001. Serial modules in parallel: The psychological refractory period and perfect time-sharing. *Psychological Review*, 108, pp. 847–69.

Carbonell, J. R., 1966. A queuing model of many-instrument visual sampling. *IEEE Transactions on Human Factors in Electronics*, 7(4), pp. 157–64.

Card, S. K., Moran, T., and Newell, A., 1986. *The psychology of human-computer interaction*. New York, NY: Lawrence Erlbaum.

Clark, A., 2013. Whatever next? Predictive brains, situated agents, and the future of cognitive science. *Behavioral and Brain Sciences*, 36(3), pp. 181–204.

Clark, A., 2015. *Surfing Uncertainty: Prediction, Action, and the Embodied Mind*. Oxford: Oxford University Press.

Dancy, C. L., Ritter, F. E., and Berry, K., 2012. Towards adding a physiological substrate to ACT-R. In: *BRiMS 2012: 21st Annual Conference on Behavior Representation in Modeling and Simulation 2012*, pp. 75–82.

Dingus, T. A., Guo, F., Lee, S., Antin, J. F., Perez, M., Buchanan-King, M., and Hankey, J., 2016. Driver crash risk factors and prevalence evaluation using naturalistic driving data. *Proceedings of the National Academy of Sciences*, 201513271. Available at: <http://doi.org/10.1073/pnas.1513271113>.

Duggan, G. B., Johnson, H., and Sørli, P., 2013. Interleaving tasks to improve performance: Users maximise the marginal rate of return. *International Journal of Human-Computer Studies*, 71(5), pp. 533–50.

Foley, J. P., Young, R., Angell, L., and Domeyer, J. E., 2013. Towards operationalizing driver distraction. In: *Proceedings of the Seventh International Driving Symposium on Human Factors in Driver Assessment, Training, and Vehicle Design*, pp. 57–63.

González, V. M., and Mark, G. J., 2004. 'Constant, constant, multi-tasking craziness': managing multiple working spheres. In: *CHI '04: Proceedings of the SIGCHI Conference on Human Factors in Computing Systems*, pp. 113–20.

Gould, S. J. J., Brumby, D. P., and Cox, A. L., 2013. What does it mean for an interruption to be relevant? An investigation of relevance as a memory effect. In: *HFES 2013: Proceedings Of The Human Factors And Ergonomics Society 57th Annual Meeting*, pp. 149–53. Available at: <http://dx.doi.org/10.1177/1541931213571034>.

Gunzelmann, G., Gross, J. B., Gluck, K. A., and Dinges, D. F., 2009. Sleep deprivation and sustained attention performance: Integrating mathematical and cognitive modeling. *Cognitive Science*, 33, pp. 880–910.

Halverson, T., and Hornof, A. J., 2007. A minimal model for predicting visual search in human-computer interaction. In: *CHI'07: Proceedings of the SIGCHI Conference on Human Factors in Computing Systems*. New York, NY: ACM, pp. 431–4.

Horrey, W., and Wickens, C., 2007. In-vehicle glance duration: distributions, tails, and model of crash risk. *Transportation Research Record: Journal of the Transportation Research Board*, 2018, pp. 22–8.

Horrey, W. J., Wickens, C. D., and Consalus, K. P., 2006. Modeling drivers' visual attention allocation while interacting with in-vehicle technologies. *Journal of Experimental Psychology: Applied*, 12(2), pp. 67–78.

Howes, A., Lewis, R. L., and Vera, A., 2009. Rational adaptation under task and processing constraints: Implications for testing theories of cognition and action. *Psychological Review*, 116(4), pp. 717–51.

Janssen, C. P., and Brumby, D. P., 2010. Strategic Adaptation to Performance Objectives in a Dual-Task Setting. *Cognitive Science*, 34(8), pp. 1548–60. Available at: http://doi.org/10.1111/j.1551-6709.2010.01124.x.

Janssen, C. P., and Brumby, D. P., 2015. Strategic Adaptation to Task Characteristics, Incentives, and Individual Differences in Dual-Tasking. *PLoS ONE*, 10(7), e0130009.

Janssen, C. P., Brumby, D. P., Dowell, J., Chater, N., and Howes, A., 2011. Identifying Optimum Performance Trade-Offs using a Cognitively Bounded Rational Analysis Model of Discretionary Task Interleaving. *Topics in Cognitive Science*, 3(1), pp. 123–39.

Janssen, C. P., Brumby, D. P., and Garnett, R., 2012. Natural Break Points: The Influence of Priorities and Cognitive and Motor Cues on Dual-Task Interleaving. *Journal of Cognitive Engineering and Decision Making*, 6(1), pp. 5–29.

Janssen, C. P., Gould, S. J., Li, S. Y. W., Brumby, D. P., and Cox, A. L., 2015. Integrating Knowledge of Multitasking and Interruptions across Different Perspectives and Research Methods. *International Journal of Human-Computer Studies*, 79, pp. 1–5.

Jin, J., and Dabbish, L., 2009. Self-interruption on the computer: a typology of discretionary task interleaving. In: *Chi 2009: Proceedings of the SIGCHI Conference on Human Factors in Computing Systems*. New York, NY: ACM, pp. 1799–808.

Johnson, L., Sullivan, B., Hayhoe, M., and Ballard, D., 2014. Predicting human visuomotor behaviour in a driving task. *Philosophical Transactions of the Royal Society of London B: Biological Sciences*, 369(1636), 20130044.

Kieras, D. E., and Meyer, D. E., 2000. The role of cognitive task analysis in the application of predictive models of human performance. In: J. Schraagen, S. Chipman, and V. Shalin, eds. *Cognitive task analysis*. Mahwah, NJ: Lawrence Erlbaum, pp. 237–60.

Klein, R., 2000. Inhibition of return. *Trends in Cognitive Sciences*, 4, pp. 138–46.

Kujala, T., Grahn, H., Mäkelä, J., and Lasch, A., 2016. On the visual distraction effects of audio-visual route guidance. In: *AutomotiveUI '16: Proceedings of the 8th International Conference on Automotive User Interfaces and Interactive Vehicular Applications*. New York, NY: ACM, pp. 169–76.

Kujala, T., Mäkelä, J., Kotilainen, I., and Tokkonen, T., 2016. The attentional demand of automobile driving revisited—Occlusion distance as a function of task-relevant event density in realistic driving scenarios. *Human Factors: The Journal of the Human Factors and Ergonomics Society*, 58, pp. 163–80.

Kujala, T., and Saariluoma, P., 2011. Effects of menu structure and touch screen scrolling style on the variability of glance durations during in-vehicle visual search tasks. *Ergonomics*, 54(8), pp. 716–32.

Kujala, T., and Salvucci, D. D., 2015. Modeling visual search on in-car displays: The challenge of modeling safety-critical lapses of control. *International Journal of Human-Computer Studies*, 79, pp. 66–78.

Kun, A. L., Boll, S., and Schmidt, A., 2016. Shifting gears: User interfaces in the age of autonomous driving. *IEEE Pervasive Computing*, 15(1), pp. 32–8.

Laird, J. E., 2012. *The Soar cognitive architecture*. Cambridge, MA: MIT Press.

Laird, J. E., Newell, A., and Rosenbloom, P. S., 1987. Soar: An architecture for general intelligence. *Artificial Intelligence*, 33, pp. 1–64.

Lee, J. D., Roberts, S. C., Hoffman, J. D., and Angell, L. S., 2012. Scrolling and driving: How an MP3 player and its aftermarket controller affect driving performance and visual behavior. *Human Factors*, 54(2), pp. 250–63.

Lee, J. Y., Gibson, M., and Lee, J. D., 2015. Secondary task boundaries influence drivers' glance durations. In: *Automotive UI '15:* Proceedings of the 7th International Conference on Automotive User Interfaces and Interactive Vehicular Applications. New York, NY: ACM, pp. 273–80.

Lewis, R. L., Howes, A., and Singh, S., 2014. Computational Rationality: Linking Mechanism and Behavior Through Bounded Utility Maximization. *Topics in Cognitive Science*, 6(2), pp. 279–311.

Liang, Y., Lee, J.D., and Yekhshatyan, L., 2012. How dangerous is looking away from the road? Algorithms predict crash risk from glance patterns in naturalistic driving. *Human Factors*, 54, pp. 1104–16.

Liu, Y., Feyen, R., and Tsimhoni, O., 2006. Queueing Network-Model Human Processor (QN-MHP): A computational architecture for multitask performance in human-machine systems. *ACM Transactions on Computer-Human Interaction*, 13, pp. 37–70.

Mark, G., Gonzalez, V. M., and Harris, J., 2005. No task left behind?: examining the nature of fragmented work. In: CHI '05: Proceedings of the SIGCHI Conference on Human Factors in Computing Systems. New York, NY: ACM, pp. 321–30.

Meyer, D. E., and Kieras, D. E., 1997. A computational theory of executive cognitive processes and multiple-task performance: part 1. basic mechanisms. *Psychological Review*, 104(1), pp. 3–65.

Miyata, Y., and Norman, D. A., 1986. Psychological issues in support of multiple activities. In: D. A. Norman and S. Draper, eds. *User centered system design: New perspectives on human- computer interaction*. Hillsdale, NJ: Lawrence Erlbaum, pp. 265–84.

Monk, C. A., Trafton, J. G., and Boehm-Davis, D. A., 2008. The effect of interruption duration and demand on resuming suspended goals. *Journal of Experimental Psychology: Applied*, 14, pp. 299–313. [online] doi:10.1037/a0014402

Monsell, S., 2003. Task switching. *Trends in Cognitive Sciences*, 7(3), pp. 134–40.

Moray, N., 1986. Monitoring behavior and supervisory control. In K. R. Boff, L. Kaufman, and J. P. Thomas, eds. *Handbook of Perception and Performance, Volume II: Cognitive Processes and Performance*. New York, NY: Wiley Interscience, pp. 40–51.

Norman, D. A., and Bobrow, D. G., 1975. On Data-limited and Resource-limited Processes. *Cognitive Psychology*, 7, pp. 44–64.

Navon, D., and Gopher, D., 1979. On the Economy of the Human-Processing System. *Psychological Review*, 86(3), 214–55.

Newell, A., 1990. *Unified Theories of Cognition*. Cambridge, MA: Harvard University Press.

NHTSA (National Highway Traffic Safety Administration), 2013. Visual-Manual NHTSA Driver Distraction Guidelines for In-Vehicle Electronic Devices. NHTSA-2010-0053.

Payne, S. J., Duggan, G. B., and Neth, H., 2007. Discretionary task interleaving: heuristics for time allocation in cognitive foraging. *Journal of Experimental Psychology: General*, 136(3), pp. 370–88.

Payne, S. J., and Howes, A., 2013. *Adaptive Interaction: A utility maximisation approach to understanding human interaction with technology*. Williston, VT: Morgan & Claypool.

Posner, M. I., and Cohen, Y., 1984. Components of visual orienting. In: H. Bouma and D. Bouwhuis, eds. *Attention and Performance*. Volume 10. Hillsdale, NJ: Lawrence Erlbaum, pp. 531–56.

Regan, M. A., Hallet, C., and Gordon, C. P., 2011. Driver distraction and driver inattention: Definition, relationship and taxonomy. *Accident Analysis & Prevention*, 43, pp. 1771–81.

Salvucci, D. D., 2001a. Predicting the effects of in-car interface use on driver performance: An integrated model approach. *International Journal of Human Computer Studies*, 55, pp. 85–107.

Salvucci, D. D., 2001b. An integrated model of eye movements and visual encoding. *Cognitive Systems Research*, 1(4), pp. 201–20.

Salvucci, D. D., 2005. A Multitasking General Executive for Compound Continuous Tasks. *Cognitive Science*, 29(3), pp. 457–92.

Salvucci, D. D., 2006. Modeling driver behavior in a cognitive architecture. *Human Factors*, 48, pp. 362–80.

Salvucci, D. D., 2009. Rapid prototyping and evaluation of in-vehicle interfaces. *ACM Transactions on Computer-Human Interaction* [online], 16. doi:10.1145/1534903.1534906

Salvucci, D. D., and Kujala, T., 2016. Balancing structural and temporal constraints in multitasking contexts. In: *CogSci 2016: Proceedings of the 38th Annual Meeting of the Cognitive Science Society*. Philadelphia, PA, 10–13 August 2016. Red Hook, NY: Curran Associates, pp. 2465–70.

Salvucci, D. D., and Macuga, K. L., 2002. Predicting the effects of cellular-phone dialing on driver performance. *Cognitive Systems Research*, 3, pp. 95–102.

Salvucci, D. D., and Taatgen, N. A., 2008. Threaded cognition: An integrated theory of concurrent multitasking. *Psychological review*, 115(1), pp. 101–30.

Salvucci, D. D., and Taatgen, N. A., 2011. *The multitasking mind*. New York: Oxford University Press.

Schmidt, A., Dey, A. K., Kun, A. L., and Spiessl, W., 2010. Automotive user interfaces: human computer interaction in the car. In: *CHI'10: Extended Abstracts on Human Factors in Computing Systems*. New York, NY: ACM, pp. 3177–80.

Schumacher, E. H., Seymour, T. L., Glass, J. M., Fencsik, D. E., Lauber, E. J., Kieras, D. E., and Meyer, D. E., 2001. Virtually perfect time sharing in dual-task performance: Uncorking the central cognitive bottleneck. *Psychological Science*, 12, pp. 101–8.

Senders, J., 1964. The human operator as a monitor and controller of multidegree of freedom systems. *IEEE Transactions on Human Factors in Electronics*, 5, pp. 2–6.

Senders, J. W., Kristofferson, A. B., Levison, W. H., Dietrich, C. W., and Ward, J. L., 1967. The attentional demand of automobile driving. *Highway Research Record*, 195, pp. 15–33.

Sprague N., and Ballard D., 2003. Eye movements for reward maximization. In: S. Thrun, L. K. Saul, and B. Schölkopf, eds. *Advances in Neural Information Processing Systems*. Volume 16. Cambridge, MA: MIT Press, pp. 1467–82.

Steelman, K. S., McCarley, J. S., and Wickens, C. D., 2011. Modeling the control of attention in visual workspaces. *Human Factors*, 53(2), 142–53.

Steelman, K. S., McCarley, J. S., and Wickens, C. D., 2016. Theory-based models of attention in visual workspaces. *International Journal of Human–Computer Interaction*, 33(1), pp. 35–43.

Sullivan, B. T., Johnson, L., Rothkopf, C. A., Ballard, D., and Hayhoe, M., 2012. The role of uncertainty and reward on eye movements in a virtual driving task. *Journal of Vision*, 12(13). [online] doi:10.1167/12.13.19

Taatgen, N. A., Van Rijn, H., and Anderson, J., 2007. An integrated theory of prospective time interval estimation: the role of cognition, attention, and learning. *Psychological Review*, 114(3), pp. 577–98.

Telford, C. W., 1931. The refractory phase of voluntary and associative response. *Journal of Experimental Psychology*, 14, pp. 1–35.

Trafton, J. G., and Monk, C. M., 2008. Task interruptions. In D. A. Boehm-Davis, ed. *Reviews of human factors and ergonomics*. Volume 3. Santa Monica, CA: Human Factors and Ergonomics Society, pp. 111–26.

Tsimhoni, O., and Green, P., 2001. Visual demands of driving and the execution of display-intensive in-vehicle tasks. *Proceedings of the Human Factors and Ergonomics Society 45th Annual Meeting*, 45(14), pp. 1586–90.

Van der Heiden, R. M. A., Iqbal, S. T., and Janssen, C. P., 2017. Priming drivers before handover in semi-autonomous cars. In: *CHI '17*: Proceedings of the SIGCHI Conference on Human Factors in Computing Systems. Denver, Colorado, 6–11 May 2017. New York, NY: ACM, pp. 392–404.

van Vugt, M., Taatgen, N., Sackur, J., and Bastian, M., 2015. Modeling mind-wandering: a tool to better understand distraction. In: N. Taatgen, M. van Vugt, J. Borst, and K. Mehlhorn, eds. Proceedings of the 13th International Conference on Cognitive Modeling. Groningen: University of Groningen, pp. 252–7.

Wickens, C. D., Goh, J., Helleberg, J., Horrey, W. J., and Talleur, D. A., 2003. Attentional models of multitask pilot performance using advanced display technology. *Human Factors*, 45(3), pp. 360–80.

Wierwille, W. W., 1993. An initial model of visual sampling of in-car displays and controls. In: A. G. Gale, I. D. Brown, C. M. Haslegrave, H. W. Kruysse, and S. P. Taylor, eds. *Vision in Vehicles IV*. Amsterdam: Elsevier Science, pp. 271–9.

World Health Organization, 2011. Mobile Phone Use: A Growing Problem of Driver Distraction. Geneva, Switzerland: World Health Organization. Available at: http://www.who.int/violence_injury_prevention/publications/road_traffic/en/index.html.

Wortelen, B., Baumann, M., and Lüdtke, A., 2013. Dynamic simulation and prediction of drivers' attention distribution. *Transportation Research Part F: Traffic Psychology and Behaviour*, 21, pp. 278–94.

13

. . ● . .

The Central Role of Cognitive Computations in Human-Information Interaction

WAI-TAT FU,
JESSIE CHIN,
Q. VERA LIAO

13.1 Introduction

While Human-Information Interaction (HII) is dynamic and expresses itself in many different forms, information retrieval or search is almost always involved as an important component of HII. On the other hand, information retrieval is often not the final goal of most activities. Rather, information retrievals are often initiated and/or embedded as parts of a series of goal-directed actions that allow us to accomplish various tasks. As a result, optimizing information retrievals regardless of the cognitive context often does not help people to accomplish their tasks, and thus, will unlikely lead to a truly *intelligent* information system. A user-centred research theme may therefore benefit from conceptualizing information retrievals as parts of cognitive computations that allow users to accomplish a wide range of information tasks. By treating the user and the information system as a coupled cognitive system, we can also gain valuable insight into design guidelines for intelligent information systems that are more compatible with human cognitive computations.

Another benefit of adopting a cognitive science perspective is that it allows researchers to understand the nature of the acts of information retrievals in the broader context of how these cognitive computations are represented, selected, and executed to allow users to intelligently accomplish their tasks. The general idea is, by understanding the nature of these cognitive computations, researchers may have a better ability to more precisely characterize and predict how users will behave in certain information environments. With better understanding, researchers will have higher confidence in designing better information environments (or systems) that fit the cognitive computations of users, which allow them to more effectively accomplish their (information-rich) tasks.

Computational Interaction. Antti Oulasvirta, Per Ola Kristensson, Xiaojun Bi, Andrew Howes (Eds).
© Oxford University Press 2018. Published 2018 by Oxford University Press.

Cognitive science tends to focus on mechanisms and computations that explain intelligent behavior. By conceptualizing information retrievals as parts of the broader set of goal-directed cognitive computations, one can develop a more complete theoretical framework that encompasses cognitive computations that involve external (in the environment) and internal (inside the head of the user) information accesses (Newell, 1990) as they emerge during each goal-directed cognitive cycle. This framework may also be extended to account for how multiple users engage and (indirectly) interact with each other through the information environments (Fu, 2008, 2012).

One common concern about studies of human behaviour and HII is that it is influenced by many factors to variable extents in different situations, and thus is difficult, if not impossible to derive predictive principles. In HII, users may have different cognitive abilities, knowledge, experiences, or motivation, which all influence how they behave as they interact with sources of information. This is a real challenge, but a challenge that cognitive science has learned to embrace. One useful approach is to identify *invariants* at the right *level of abstraction*, such that *approximate but useful* predictions can be made (Simon, 1990). In fact, this approach is commonly adopted in many sciences to various degrees, as most invariant structures are approximate. For example, in chemistry, atomic weights of elements are approximately integral multiples of that of hydrogen; while the law of photosynthesis varies in details from one species to another, at some abstract level the law is an invariant that is useful for understanding the behaviours of plants in different environments. In human cognition, examples of these invariants with different granularities abound: the number of items one can remember is approximately seven (Anderson, 2002), and the movement time to a target is proportional to the log of the ratio of the distance and area of the target (Fitts, Paul, and Peterson, 1964). While these invariants are approximate, they are considered useful for various reasons. In the context of HII research, these invariants at least can help:

- characterize the general relations of variables related to the phenomena;
- predict behaviors as a function of these variables;
- highlight the boundaries of the level of abstraction under which the variables are measured and defined; and
- inspire new theories and methods.

The rest of the chapter is organized as follow. The next section discusses a few foundational concepts in cognitive science and how they can be applied to understand the nature of HII. After that, it covers the idea of levels of abstraction in cognitive science, and how they can be applied to understand the spectrum of HII. Finally, it discusses how these ideas derived from a cognitive science perspective can inform designs of information systems.

13.2 Foundation

We will first provide more concrete definitions of what we mean by cognitive computations, and how they are important for understanding the nature of intelligence in information systems. In fact, cognitive science emerged together with artificial intelligence around 1960s as researchers demanded a science of intelligent systems. Among existing theories of intelligent systems, the *physical symbol system* proposed by Newell and Simon (1972) is often considered the 'classical view' on how *knowledge* can be represented as symbol structures and how the *content* of knowledge is related to the states of the symbol structures by *semantic* relations,[1] such that intelligent actions can be produced by an artificial system (Newell, 1990). These ideas provide useful perspectives on how one can characterize and explain acts of information retrievals as parts of a cognitive task. We discuss some of the foundational concepts most relevant to HII in the next section.

13.2.1 Semantic and Algorithm Levels

Without a strong proposal of a formal definition, cognitive science research often conceptualizes intelligence loosely as *cognitive computations* that allow a person (or machine) to select a *better* set of operations to accomplish the goal (Newell and Simon, 1972). Cognitive computations involve processing of symbols in the specific contexts that the symbols are situated. For example, in the sentence 'Springfield is the capital of Illinois', each word is a symbol. However, processing each symbol individually is not enough to understand the meaning of the sentence, it also needs to consider how each word is put together in the sentence such that the meaning of the sentence can be extracted. Symbols are therefore situated in symbol structures that provide the context under which multiple symbols can be processed.

Generally speaking, the level of intelligence of a system (computer and human mind) is determined by the computations that specify *what* these symbol structures are, and *how* these symbol structures are processed. There are at least two distinct levels of computations and principles that apply to these levels that are most relevant to HII research. These levels provide important conceptual distinctions on how information systems can become *more intelligent* in different contexts, and therefore serve as useful references for providing design guidelines for these systems.

1. Computations at the Semantic or Knowledge Level

As this level, one describes and explains interactions based on information goals and knowledge of the users (or computers) and their relations. For example, when a person asks the question 'What is the capital of US?', a system will reply 'Washington' if it *knows* this fact, and understands how these pieces of knowledge of connected and used in different contexts. Note that this is often more than *retrieving* a fact. For example, a system can be programmed in multiple ways to *retrieve* the answer '4' when it is asked 'what is 2 plus 2?'. The semantic level, in addition, allows the system to also provide some explanations to *why* '4' is the answer. To do this, the system needs to know the number system, the meaning of the symbol and operations in the system, etc. To measure the intelligence of the system at this level, one may test how well it can provide answers that allow the user to *know* these facts and how these facts are relevant to the answers.

---

[1] While there has been opposition to the view that humans have symbol structures in their head, many (e.g., [43]) argue that there is no alternative theory that is capable of explaining how (human) intelligent behavior follows semantic principles while at the same time is governed by physical laws.

2. Computations at the Algorithmic or Symbolic Level

At this level, one describes the regularities and codes of the symbol structures and explains *how* the symbol structures are processed. For example, the system can *recognize* the 'plus' operation, which leads to a sequence of symbol processing to generate the answer—the system may first find the sum of the first digits of the numbers, then the second digits, and so on. Eventually these partial sums are weighted and added up to get the final sum. To measure the intelligence of the system at this level, one may test the accuracies and speeds of different operations. For example, information retrieval research mostly focuses on improving the *precision* and *recall* of a system by improving the algorithmic computations at this level.

Although the two distinct levels of explanation are often sought after by different method-ologies, they should both be equally relevant for understanding the nature of HII. Perhaps more importantly, we argue that the connection between the two levels of explanation is crucial to better inform the design of *intelligent* information systems that support the set of cognitive computations that emerge from the interaction between the user and the system. This point is elaborated in the next section.

13.2.2 HII as Coupled Cognitive Computations

At a general level, HII can be considered cognitive computations that allow the user to inter-act with the (technology-mediated) external information environment (see Figure 13.1). In the context of HII, the external interactions may involve technology-mediated infor-mation retrievals (e.g., Web search). The main idea is that for certain HII, the unit of analysis should include the coupled internal-external cognitive cycles. For example, when a user is engaged in an online learning task (e.g., learning about potential causes of a set of symptoms through Web searches), it will be more useful to analyse the patterns of behaviour that involve the coupling of the internal cognitive processes of the users and the external information search activities.

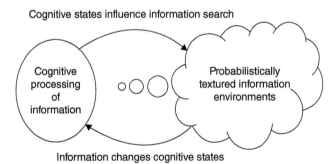

Figure 13.1 Human-Information Interaction as coupled external-internal cognitive computa-tions. Because of uncertainties, the external environment is often probabilistically textured. From Brunswik (1955).

Given that both internal and external cognitive computations can be characterized under the framework of a symbol system described earlier, an important advantage to study HII as coupled cognitive computations is the potential to provide explanations at both the algorithm and semantic levels, as well as how they are connected. This is useful because one can then provide more direct user-centred guidance for designing more intelligent information systems, as well as predicting changes in user behaviour in response to changes in information systems or tasks. For example, a better understanding of the changes of users' cognitive representations of information as they engage in online learning can inform how information systems can adapt to these cognitive representations, such that learning can be more effective.

13.2.3 Cognitive Search in Human Information Interaction

A process that is common to both internal and external cognitive computations is *search*. Given its central role, we need to provide a brief review of the central role of search in cognitive science below. The current focus is to provide a theoretical background that helps to understand the nature of the acts of information retrievals in the context of the broader set of cognitive computations in HII.

An important assumption of a cognitive computational system is that intelligence is achieved through processing of symbol structures, through which semantic relations of knowledge are utilized. In a particular context, for example, in a sentence, each word is a *symbol*[2], and the meaning of the sentence requires processing of each symbol in the specific context. However, processing each individual word is not enough to understand the sentence. It also needs knowledge about, for example, English grammar, the context under which the sentence is written, and other relevant general knowledge, which allows the system to understand how the words together represent the meaning of the sentence with respect to the general context that the sentence should be interpreted. The knowledge, however, is not contained in the symbols themselves, and therefore needs to be accessed from some other places. How the knowledge is being used is a function of both the local context and the knowledge itself, and the use can be determined only when that knowledge is acquired (Newell, 1990). More generally, each symbol always contains limited *local* information. To interpret the symbol, other symbol structures at *distal* locations need to be accessed. The distinction between local and distal symbol structures is general, so it applied to both internal and external computations.

The use of knowledge to guide the local-to-distal processing of symbol structures can be considered a part of a *cognitive search* process, because there is often some level of uncertainty about what and where to access the distal symbol structures. This *cognitive search* process is central to the intelligence of the system (Fu, 2015) because, except in some trivial tasks, the search process influences the extent to which the system can effectively (and efficiently) utilize its knowledge to generate a (good) response. *When we consider information search*

---

[2] Theoretically it should be called a symbol token as the symbol (a word) is situated in a particular context (the sentence). However, for the sake of simplicity we just call it a symbol here.

in this context, the goal of an intelligent information system should facilitate the cognitive search process in the coupled internal-external system, i.e., it should generate local structures that help the user to access distal structures most relevant to his/her goals.

There are a few properties that are worth highlighting, given their relevance to HII:

1. The context of each symbol structure plays a pivotal role in determining the search process. This is because the context determines what and how local cues should be processed, and guides the subsequent processing of distal structures. This context is defined by the task, the environment, as well as knowledge of the system (and user) (Simon, 1956).

2. Knowledge is always required to process the local cues to determine what and where to look for *relevant* symbol structures. This knowledge may vary across individuals and may change over time, and is represented through the relations of symbol structures.

3. Because of uncertainties, the search process involves detection of relevant *patterns of distal structures* that allow them to respond by *incrementally adjusting* the search process (Fu and Pirolli, 2013) as new symbol structures are processed.

13.2.4 Implication to Human Information Interaction Research

These properties about cognitive search provide interesting perspectives on HII research. Imagine a typical HII task, in which a user is engaged in some cognitive tasks that require the use of an information system (e.g., WWW) to retrieve relevant information to assist the task, such as when one is learning about a topic or collecting information to prepare for a talk. The initiation of external information retrievals can be cast as parts of the local-to-distal processing to fulfill the goals of the tasks. Similar to how one can measure the level of intelligence of a cognitive system (e.g., a chess program or a person), one can ask questions such as how the information systems can be designed to allow the user to accomplish the task more intelligently. The properties listed previously highlight a few features that are useful for this purpose.

The first property suggests that the initiation of information retrievals (e.g., generating or modifying queries) are highly context sensitive, and will therefore be dependent on the context defined by the combination of the task, the individual, and the environment. The second property suggests that knowledge is required not only to initiate the retrievals, but also interpret and evaluate the results of the retrievals. Finally, the third property suggests that the sequences of information retrievals can be conceived as a cognitive search process that are sensitive to the internal (cognitive) representation of the external information environments, to which the user incrementally adapts.

These features, followed from the properties of any cognitive (symbol) system, may help shed light on designs of more intelligent information systems, in the sense that the user can more efficiently accomplish a wider range of cognitive tasks (Marchionini, 2006). While these general observations are perhaps not entirely new ideas to the area of HII, the current purpose is to show how a cognitive science perspective can provide a useful perspective for improving our understanding of the nature of what and why certain properties can make HII more intelligent in general. This perspective may, for example, allow better synergies between cognitive science and HII research.

This classical view of cognitive science may also help to provide some new perspectives on future HII research. For example, by conceptualizing external information retrievals as parts of the cognitive computations, one can ask how to make the system more compatible with the cognitive processes and representations of the user. For example, a general observation shows that research on information retrieval (IR) systems often focuses on description or explanation at the algorithm level, whereas research on user experience of these IR systems often focuses on the knowledge level. A natural question one can ask is how we can design IR systems that operate at the knowledge level. In other words, how should the system be designed such that it does not focus on performance at the algorithmic level, but facilitate the cognitive computations involved the coupled internal-external system? Similarly, one can also ask how we can derive description of user behavior at the algorithm level to inform the design of user-centered IR systems. Research on these areas will perhaps lead to better theories and systems that make HII more *intelligent*.

To better illustrate this point, we can study, for example, how Web search engines operate. Normally, the user has to generate query keywords and the search engines try to match those keywords to a large set of documents according to some algorithms that calculate relevance. When we compare this process to, for example, how two persons communicate and exchange information, one can easily see how search engines often demand the user to convert knowledge-level representations to those at the algorithm level—i.e., the system is forcing the user to adapt to its level of description. While this by itself may not be too harmful, as people do adapt to technologies over time, it does limits the potential of a knowledge-level IR systems, which potentially can provide better support to higher level cognitive activities of the user, such as reasoning, hypothesis generation and testing, decision making, sense making, etc.

While extracting and representing (semantic) knowledge from large corpora of (online) documents has been an active area of research in IR, an equally important focus is perhaps on gaining more understanding on how humans represent and express ideas (or information needs) at their (natural) knowledge level *in the context* of the overall cognitive search process, such that the behavior of the information system can be described and expressed in ways that can adapt to the knowledge-level cognitive activities of the individual user. This is not an easy task, as it is a well-known challenge in artificial intelligence (AI). However, even with only incremental progress, a better synergy between research on systems and on users can potentially lead to important breakthroughs in developing more intelligent information systems.

In terms of having more description of user behavior at the algorithm level, one active area of research that can be useful is on the application of computational cognitive models to describe and predict user behavior in HII (Fu and Pirolli, 2007; Karanam, van Oostendorp, and Indurkhya, 2011; Kitajima, Blackmon, and Polson, 2000; Sutcliffe and Ennis, 1998; van Oostendorp and Goldman, 1999; van Oostendorp and Juvina, 2007). Because of their explicit representations and processes, these computational models of users can be used as cognitive agents that help to predict behavior, and potentially help IR systems to better evaluate relevance of information. Another possible application of computational cognitive models is to understand the possible impact of (wrong) mental models of IR systems on user behavior, an area that is more common in the traditional HCI research (e.g., see Jameson, 2003). Intuitively, the perception of how, for example, a Web search engine works will likely impact their strategies for query formulations and modification, as well as subsequent link-following actions. Cognitive models that capture the change in mental models can perhaps be used to better align the user's and the designer's mental models of IR systems.

13.3 Implication to Design

The spectrum of HII levels discussed earlier may also have important general implication to designs of information systems. First, to review, the 'success' of a system design can often be measured by the extent to which the system helps users to achieve their goals. Given the various levels of abstraction and the differences in the invariant structures of behavior at each level, the relevant *contexts* that influence those behavioral structures will likely be very different (e.g., from the visual context of a Web page that influence selection of links to the social context of an online community that influence the level of engagement of users), and thus the definition of 'success' may vary.

Design of information systems may need to pay more attention to the goal of the design to target how the systems can provide the right level of abstraction to the relevant contexts that facilitate the set of *desirable behavior* afforded by the design. For example, an IR system that works optimally for simple IR may assume the context of a well-defined information goal, under which the algorithm is optimized for these IR tasks (e.g., through measures such as precision/recall). When designing for HII at higher levels, for example, the context under which the system should be optimized may need to be adjusted (e.g., providing information in ways that help users to better formulate their information goals, learn, to make decisions, etc). Identifying the right level of abstraction, as well as the invariant structures at that level, could be useful for determining *what* and *how* the information systems should be optimized.

When determining the right level of abstraction for design, there are often two 'roads' that one can take. These are often associated with the Type 1 and Type 2 theories by Marr (1977). Marr proposed that when designing an information system, there are often two parts of the solution. The first part is an abstract formulation of *what* is being computed and *why*, and the second part consists of particular algorithms and thus specifics *how*. Marr advocated that designs of intelligent systems will benefit most from understanding the what and why part first—i.e., one should develop a Type 1 theory about what exactly an algorithm is supposed to be doing and why they should perform in a particular way, before one develops a Type 2 theory that specifies the details of how the algorithm works. Marr used Chomsky's notion of a *competence* theory for English syntax as an example of a Type 1 theory, which has little details about the computation involved but provide the reason why the English syntax should be computed. He used the example of protein folding as an example of Type 2 theory, in which there are too many interactions of factors that influence how protein will fold, and thus one can only derive specific mechanisms that *describe* the different protein folding processes.

When we look at the levels of activities in HII, one can think of two approaches that inform better designs that correspond to Marr's Type 1 and Type 2 theories. One can adopt a 'high road' to strive for discovering principles that characterize major variables at a certain level and abstract away details at lower level, and apply these principles to inform designs (e.g., apply foraging theory (Stephens and Krebs, 1986) to information search (Pirolli and Card, 1999)). One can also adopt the 'low road', by discovering a range of specific principles that characterize how people will behave in different contexts, and provide customized designs to support desirable behavior in these contexts.

Although Marr argued strongly for adopting the 'high road', one important question is whether these Type 1 theories exist for all (or any) of these levels of abstraction in HII. In fact, existing research will likely continue to have differences in the style of approach in HII research. There are researchers who are more concerned with searching for general principles of behaviour or IR algorithms, and there are some who are more concerned with predicting a certain level of abstraction of behaviour in specific contexts or improving IR algorithms for certain types of information environments. However, it is important to note that, even general principles may apply mostly *only* at their levels of abstraction, in which main variables and relations are defined. For example, although we are approaching general principles that optimize simple IR, they may not help HII at high levels. Or at least, the benefits across levels do not come automatically. An example from Marr may help to illustrate this point: if one wants to know how birds can fly, knowing the details of how their feathers are optimally structured is less useful than principles such as the law of aerodynamics.

To a large extent, perhaps research in HII will generate results that are at least generalizable to an extent that they are useful for designs and understanding. On the other hand, given the complex interactions factors in different contexts at multiple levels, generating a universal Type 1 theory for HII may be difficult, if not impossible. As Marr (1977) put it: the 'only possible virtue [of a Type 2 theory] might be that it works'.

13.4 Example of the use of a Computational Cognitive Model in Human Information Interaction

Developing computational cognitive models is a common way in cognitive science to understand intelligent systems. Recent research has applied this technique to understand information search behaviour. For example, computational cognitive models of Web navigation are developed to predict performance by taking into account cognitive theories that influence the information search process (Sutcliffe and Ennis, 1998). Examples of such cognitive theories include models of semantic memories (Anderson, 1991) and models of reading comprehension (Kintsch, 1998). Existing models of semantic memories have been applied to characterize how information cues (e.g., link texts, social tags, or text snippets of Web pages) are interpreted to reflect their semantic relevance with respect to the user's existing semantic knowledge (Juvina and van Oostendorp, 2008). The main goal of these computational cognitive models is to use well-tested cognitive mechanisms to characterize more complex information search behaviour. For example, CoLiDeS (van Oostendorp,

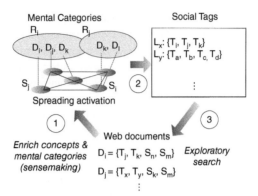

Figure 13.2 The rational model in Fu (2008). D=document, T=tags, S=semantic nodes, L=link/bookmark, R=mental categories. The model keeps tracks of growth of mental categories as new web documents are found and concepts extracted from them. The new mental categories led to use of new query terms and social tags in the next search cycle, which leads to new concepts learned. The model demonstrates the potential of using computational cognitive models to make information systems more intelligent by facilitating cognitive computations in the coupled internal-external system.

Karanam, and Indurkhya, 2012) is based on the well-tested Construction-Integration theory of text comprehension, whereas SNIF-ACT (Fu and Pirolli, 2007) was based on the ACT-R architecture (Anderson, Bothell, Byrne, Douglass, Lebiere, and Qin, 2004).

Figure 13.2 shows an example of the use of a computational cognitive model to characterize information search behaviour in a coupled internal-external computational system (Fu, 2008). The model was developed by combining the rational model of human categorization, spreading activation model of memories, and a rational model of information search behaviour. The model assumes a Bayesian updating of mental concepts (categories) based on new information they found during exploratory search. Based on the spreading activation model, the mental concepts will be used to generate query terms to search for new information online, which will be used to update the mental categories, and so on. This search-and-learn cycle allows the model to acquire new semantic concepts about a new topic through interaction with an information system. We discuss how this model can demonstrate how computational cognitive models can bridge the knowledge and algorithmic levels to potentially improve the intelligence of an information system.

Compared to previous computational cognitive models of information search (e.g., Fu and Pirolli, 2007; Juvina and van Oostendorp, 2008; van Oostendorp, Karanam, and Indurkhya, 2012), the main goal of this model is to capture the dynamic nature of information goals in exploratory search. In fact, users often do not know exactly what they are looking for initially, and their search behaviour will evolve as users gain more knowledge about the topics. The model therefore requires combination of knowledge (semantic concepts related to the domain) and algorithmic (choice of query terms and social tags) level description of the search and learning behaviour that emerges from the coupled internal-external system during iterative search-and-learn cycles.

The model was used to characterize search and learning behaviour over a period of eight weeks, during which eight users were asked to look for information related to two topics: 1. Independence of Kosovo, and 2. Anti-aging. Users were not familiar with both domains, and they were asked to search online to learn about the topics by using a social tagging system. The system allowed them to bookmark any Web pages that they found, and add social tags to these pages. Users were told that these social tags will be shared among the users, and that they will help them organize the Web pages that they found. At the end of the eight-week period, users were asked to organize their bookmarked pages into categories, and explain what they have learned about the topic based on the categorized pages.

Readers can find details of the model as well as its validation against experimental data in (Fu, 2008). To summarize the results, the model showed good fits to human behaviour. It predicted how users chose social tags and query terms to search, and what mental categories were formed as new information was found. The value of the model lies not only at its predictions of human behaviour, but also its potential to be integrated into an information system to enrich its knowledge level representations of information and learning processes that are more cognitively compatible with human users. For example, one can imagine that information systems can represent and organize documents by leveraging human categorization models, such that better local cues (e.g., search results returned from a query) can be presented to help users acquire new information that optimize learning of new concepts. In other words, a more cognitively compatible semantic representations and processes in information systems will likely optimize learning, as they will likely more directly facilitate cognitive computations in the coupled cognitive system.

13.5 General Discussion

The purpose of this chapter is to show how concepts, methodologies, and theories in cognitive science can be useful for HII researchers and developers. We propose that HII can be considered a coupled cognitive system involving the users and the systems, in which information retrievals are parts of the emergent cognitive computations that allow the system to produce intelligent behaviour. Given the general properties of a cognitive system, we derive some prescriptive guidelines for how these systems should be designed. While the guidelines may not be radically different from existing ones, our hope is that they provide at least a different perspective on this emerging research area.

Another important advantage is the development and use of computational cognitive models to predict HII, and to incorporate these models into information systems to enhance the knowledge-level representations and processes of the systems. These cognitive models can also facilitate personalization, as the learning mechanisms in these models can be used to capture effects of individual differences in cognitive abilities, domain-specific knowledge, and Internet experience on search and learning. For example, by comparing the simulated behaviour of different models, one can gain insight into how variations in cognitive abilities and knowledge will impact their search and learning performance (Chin, Fu, and Kannampallil, 2009; Chin and Fu, 2010, 2012; Liao and Fu, 2013; Liao and Fu, 2014a, 2014b; Liao, Fu, and Mamidi, 2015). In addition, given that computational programs are implemented as computer programs to simulate behaviour, they can be used to conduct automatic assessment of Web sites and simulation of Web behaviour by interacting with existing IR systems.

....

REFERENCES

Anderson, J. R., 1991. The adaptive nature of human categorization. *Psychological Review*, 98, pp. 409–29.

Anderson, J. R., 2002. Spanning seven orders of magnitude: a challenge for cognitive modeling. *Cognitive Science*, 26(1), pp. 85–112.

Anderson, J. R., Bothell, D., Byrne, M. D., Douglass, S., Lebiere, C., and Qin, Y., 2004. An Integrated Theory of the Mind. *Psychological Review*, 111, pp. 1036–60.

Chin, J., Fu, W.-T., and Kannampallil, T., 2009. Adaptive Information Search: Age-Dependent Inter-actions between Cognitive Profiles and Strategies. In: *CHI '09: Proceedings of the 27th ACM CHI Conference on Human Factors in Computing Systems*. New York, NY: ACM, pp. 1683–92.

Chin, J., and Fu, W.-T., 2012. Age Differences in Exploratory Learning from a Health Information Website. In: *CHI '12: Proceedings of the 30th ACM CHI Conference on Human Factors in Computing Systems*. New York, NY: ACM, pp. 3031–40.

Fitts, P., Paul, M., and Peterson, J. R., 1964. Information capacity of discrete motor responses. *Journal of Experimental Psychology*, 67(2), pp. 103–12.

Fu, W.-T., 2008. The microstructures of social tagging: A rational model. In: *Proceedings of the 17th ACM conference on Computer supported cooperative work & social computing*. New York, NY: ACM, pp. 229–38.

Fu, W.-T., 2012. From Plato to the WWW: Exploratory Information Foraging. In P. M. Todd, T. Hills, and T. Robbins, eds. *Cognitive Search*. Cambridge, MA: MIT Press, pp. 283–99.

Fu, W.-T., 2015. The Central Role of Heuristic Search in Cognitive Computation Systems. *Minds and Machines*, 1–2, pp. 103–23.

Fu, W.-T., and Pirolli P., 2007. SNIF-ACT: A cognitive model of user navigation on the World Wide Web. *Human–Computer Interaction*, 22(4), pp. 355–412.

Fu, W.-T., and Pirolli, P., 2013. Establishing the micro-to-macro link: Multilevel models of human-information interaction. In: J. Lee and A. Kirlik, eds. *The Oxford Handbook of Cognitive Engineering*. New York, NY: Oxford University Press, pp. 501–13.

Jameson, A., 2003. Adaptive Interfaces and Agents. In: *The Human-Computer Interaction Handbook: Fundamentals, Evolving Technologies and Emerging Applications*, J. A. Jacko and A. Sears, eds. Mahwah, NJ: Lawrence Erlbaum, pp. 305–30.

Juvina, I., and van Oostendorp, H., 2008. Modeling semantic and structural knowledge in Web navigation. *Discourse Processes*, 45(4–5), pp. 346–64.

Karanam, S., van Oostendorp, H., and Indurkhya, B., 2011. Towards a fully computational model of web-navigation. In: *Modern Approaches in Applied Intelligence*. Berlin: Springer, pp. 327–37.

Kintsch, W., 1998. *Comprehension: A paradigm for cognition*. Cambridge: Cambridge University Press.

Kitajima, M., Blackmon, M. H., and Polson, P. G., 2000. A comprehension-based model of web navigation and its application to web usability analysis. In: S. McDonald, S. Waern and G. Cockton. *People and Computers XIV—Usability or Else!* London: Springer, pp. 357–73.

Liao, Q., and Fu. W.-T., 2013. Beyond the filter bubble: Interactive effects of perceived threat and topic involvement on selective exposure to information. In: *Proceedings of the ACM CHI Conference on Human Factors in Computing Systems*. New York, NY: ACM, pp. 2359–68.

Liao, Q. V., and Fu, W., 2014a. Can You Hear Me Now? Mitigating the Echo Chamber Effect by Source Position Indicators. In: *Proceedings of the ACM conference on Computer supported cooperative work & social computing*. New York, NY: ACM, pp. 184–96.

Liao, Q. V., and Fu, W.-T., 2014b. Expert Voices in Echo Chambers: Effects of Source Expertise Indicators on Exposure to Diverse Opinions. In: *Proceedings of the ACM CHI Conference on Human Factors in Computing Systems*. New York, NY: ACM, pp. 2745–54.

Liao, Q. V., Fu, W.-T., and Mamidi, S., 2015. It Is All About Perspective: An Exploration of Mitigating Selective Exposure with Aspect Indicators. In: *CHI '15: Proceedings of the ACM CHI conference on Human Factors in Computing Systems*. New York, NY: ACM, pp. 1439–48.

Marchionini, G., 2006. Exploratory search: From finding to understanding. *Communications of the ACM*, 49, pp. 41–6.

Marr, D., 1977. Artificial Intelligence—A Personal View. *Artificial Intelligence*, 9, pp. 37–48.

Newell, A., 1990. *Unified Theories of Cognition*. Cambridge, MA: Harvard University Press.

Newell, A., and Simon, H. A., 1972. *Human problem solving*. Englewood Cliffs, NJ: Prentice-Hall.

Pirolli, P., and Card, S., 1999. Information foraging. *Psychological Review*, 106(4), pp. 643–75.

Pylyshyn, Z., 1989. Computing in Cognitive Science. In M. I. Posner, ed. *Foundations of Cognitive Science*. Cambridge, MA: MIT Press, pp. 49–92.

Simon, H. A., 1956. Rational choice and the structure of the environment. *Psychological Review*, 63(2), pp. 129–38. [online] doi: 10.1037/h0042769

Simon, H., 1990. Invariants of Human Behavior. *Annual Review of Psychology*, 41, pp. 1–20.

Stephens, D. W., and Krebs, J. R., 1986. *Foraging theory*. Princeton, NJ: Princeton University Press.

Sutcliffe, A., and Ennis, M., 1998. Towards a Cognitive Theory of Information Retrieval. *Interacting with computers*, 10, 321–51.

van Oostendorp, H., and Juvina, I., 2007. Using a cognitive model to generate web navigation support. *International Journal of Human-Computer Studies*, 65(10), 887–97.

van Oostendorp, H., Karanam, S., and Indurkhya, B., 2012. CoLiDeS+ Pic: a cognitive model of web-navigation based on semantic information from pictures. *Behaviour & Information Technology*, 31(1), 17–32.

14

. . • . .

Computational Model of Human Routine Behaviours

NIKOLA BANOVIC,
JENNIFER MANKOFF,
ANIND K. DEY

14.1 Introduction

User interfaces (UIs) that learn about people's behaviours by observing them and interacting with them are exemplars of Computational Interaction (CI). Such *human-data supported interfaces* leverage computational models of human behaviour that can automatically reason about and describe common user behaviours, infer their goals, predict future user actions, and even coach users to improve their behaviours. Computational models of behaviours already power technology that is changing many aspects of our lives (Stone et al., 2016). However, concerns remain about black box technologies that use large human behaviour data traces, but which inner workings cannot be examined to determine that they are not negatively impacting people for whom they make decisions (Pasquale, 2015; Stone et al., 2016). Understanding computational models of behaviours remains challenging because real-world behaviour data stored in behaviour logs and used to train these models is too heterogeneous to explore and too large to label.

Thus, to ensure that CI has a positive impact on people requires technology that can sense and model the underlying process behind people's behaviours and expose the source of its conclusions so that they can be used to describe, reason about, and act in response to those behaviours. Without such technology, interface designers are forced to hardcode limited knowledge, beliefs, and assumption about people's behaviours into their interfaces. Such user interfaces are ill suited to enable the future in which human-data supported interfaces aid people in real-world scenarios where they choose to perform many different activities to solve ill-defined problems in complex environments. Such interfaces cannot act autonomously to learn about people's behaviours and can only respond to a small subset of predefined commands in well-defined environments to accomplish specialized tasks.

Computational Interaction. Antti Oulasvirta, Per Ola Kristensson, Xiaojun Bi, Andrew Howes (Eds).
© Oxford University Press 2018. Published 2018 by Oxford University Press.

We take a step towards addressing this foundational challenge of CI by providing a probabilistic, generative model of high-level behaviours, such as routines, that can be used to describe, reason about, and act in response to people's behaviours (Banovic, et al., 2016). Our computational routine model describes behaviours and attempts to provide causal explanation for relationships between actions and situations in which people perform those actions, stored as event traces in large behaviour logs. To do so, we ground our model in our unified definition of human routine behaviour, which we express computationally as a Markov Decision Process (MDP) (Puterman, 1994). We then automatically estimate relationships between situations and actions from the data (i.e., train the model) using an algorithm based on the principle of Maximum Causal Entropy (Ziebart, 2010), which is a data mining algorithm grounded in statistical principles to ensure that the model finds explanations for behaviours that best fit the data. We use this algorithm because it trains models that can predict people's behaviours (Ziebart, et al., 2008; Ziebart, et al., 2009).

The model supports making sense of behaviour data, i.e., searching for salient representations in the data (Russell, et al. 1993), by identifying and encoding behaviours that are characteristic of a routine. We automate multiple aspects of the sensemaking process (Pirolli and Card, 2005) by automatically searching for relationships in the data (information foraging) to model (schematize) patterns of behaviours that form routines. The ability to generate behaviours from a model grounded in our unified definition of routine behaviour increases intelligibility of the model and allows stakeholders to search for evidence that the model matches empirical behaviour data. We implemented a custom visualization tool to support visual exploration of automatically detected and generated behaviours (Banovic et al., 2016).

The proposed probabilistic routine model and accompanying tools allow stakeholders to form hypotheses about behaviours (e.g., hypothesize that aggressive drivers are more prone to speeding) and test those hypotheses using statistical analysis methods (e.g., Bayesian inference). We leverage similar properties in the model to act in response to people's behaviours (e.g., automate tasks, prescribe behaviours), which we illustrated on an example UI that leverages driving routine models to automatically detect aggressive driving behaviour instances and coach drivers by simulating what non-aggressive drivers would do in the same situations (Banovic, et al., 2017). Our example shows how models of high-level human behaviour can inform the design and power human-data supported interfaces that showcase one aspect of Computational Interaction.

14.2 Background and Challenges in Modelling Human Behaviour

The ability to explore and understand human behaviour is important to all stakeholders that will influence the future of human-data supported interfaces. For example, enabling domain experts to explore and understand human behaviour will allow them to generate theory and models that will provide foundational knowledge that informs such interfaces (e.g., to understand and describe behaviours that are characteristic of aggressive drivers). Policy makers will use this knowledge and models to reason about behaviours and inform policies and guidelines that will ensure future interfaces have a meaningful and positive impact on people's wellbeing (e.g., to define responsibilities of virtual driving instructor interfaces). Interface designers will use such behaviour models to power their future interfaces that will act in response to people's behaviours (e.g., design interfaces that coach drivers to improve their driving and be safer in traffic). Enabling end users to understand their own behaviours could help them not only evaluate and change their behaviours to improve the quality of their lives, but also understand the decisions that future interfaces will make on their behalf (e.g., to understand what makes them aggressive drivers and dangerous in traffic).

Here, we first scope our discussion to goal-directed human routine behaviours. We then explore the implications that different data collection and analysis methods have on understanding data that captures such behaviours. We guide our discussion of different methods based on how they support the process of making sense (Pirolli and Card, 2005) of data. We contrast explanatory modelling (driven by statistical methods) and predictive modelling (driven by data mining) approaches (Friedman, 1997) and call out the challenges of both approaches.

14.2.1 Understanding Human Routine Behaviour Data

We refer to human behaviour as observable actions of individuals that are influenced by situations in which they find themselves. Although such behaviours result from low-level cognitive plans (Anderson et al., 2004), we focus on how people enact those plans to perform different activities (Kuutti, 1995) because this allows us to observe, record, model, and analyse such behaviour data. People perform goal-directed sequences of actions in different situations (Ajzen, 1991; Taylor, 1950), which we call *behaviour instances*, that they learn and develop through repeated practice (Ronis, Yates, and Kirscht, 1989). We refer to frequent sequences of actions people perform in different situations that cause those actions (Hodgson, 1997) as *routines*. To understand such behaviours thus means to identify routines and their *variations*—different frequent ways that people respond to the same situations. Variations are different from *deviations* and other uncharacteristic behaviours that occur rarely. Routines are ideal human behaviour data to support future interfaces because they define the structure of and influences almost every aspect of people's lives (e.g., daily commute, sleeping and exercising patterns, vehicle operation). We conduct a detailed review of routine behaviours in Section 14.3.

We can collect human behaviour data from various types of data collection studies, including lab, field, and log studies (Dumais, et al., 2014). Here, we focus on observational studies and collecting data to understand specific behaviours, as opposed to experimental studies, which compare and evaluate different user interfaces. Lab studies offer a controlled setting to collect data about a behaviour. However, such studies are often contrived and lack external validity (i.e., they do not generalize to behaviours outside of the experimental setting). Also, due to short time periods of such studies, they are not appropriate for studying routine behaviours that span long periods of time and different contexts. Field studies collect behaviour data from natural settings and over time. However, they are resource intensive and do not scale up. Furthermore, they often produce knowledge about behaviours that is difficult to operationalize.

We focus on log studies that collect traces of human behaviours in large behaviour logs. Such behaviour logs complement data from traditional lab and field observational studies by offering behaviour data collected in natural settings, uninfluenced by observers, over long period of time, and at scale (Dumais et al., 2014). Behaviour log data can be collected using various server- (Google, 2017) and client-side (Capra, 2011) software logging tools, and from sensors in the environment (Koehler, et al., 2014) and on people's personal or wearable devices (Ferreira, Kostakos, and Dey, 2015). Examples of behaviour logs include web use logs (Adar, Teevan, and Dumais, 2008), social network logs (Starbird and Palen, 2010), outdoor mobility logs (Davidoff et al., 2011), mobile device usage logs (Banovic, et al., 2014), and even vehicle operation logs (Hong, Margines, and Dey, 2014). Stakeholders can then use the trace data stored in behaviour logs to understand complex routine behaviours.

14.2.2 Making Sense of Data in Large Behaviour Logs

It is often challenging to explore and understand large amounts of heterogeneous and unlabelled data stored in behaviour logs. For example, behaviour logs contain information about what people did, but not why they did it (Dumais et al., 2014). Even when data contains information about what people did, individual activities may not be clearly segmented (Hurst, Mankoff, and Hudson, 2008). Stakeholders explore and understand behaviour logs through process of sensemaking, which Russell et al. (1993) define as 'the process of searching for a representation and encoding data in that representation to answer task-specific questions.'

We look at sensemaking about behaviours through the lens of Pirolli and Card's (2005) notional model of a sensemaking loop for intelligence analysis; in the information foraging loop, stakeholders first search for information and relationships in the data to find and organize evidence that supports their reasoning about behaviours patterns in the data. In case of human routine behaviours, this reduces to identifying salient patterns in behaviour data (representations) that describe routines. This process involves continued iterative search for relationship between situations and actions that form such behaviour instances.

Stakeholders then use the evidence to schematize their current understanding of behaviours and conceptualize it in a model of behaviour. Stakeholders then use this conceptual model in the sensemaking loop (Pirolli and Card, 2005) to create and support (or disconfirm) their hypotheses about behaviours and present their findings. Confirming or disconfirming hypotheses allows the stakeholder to form theories about behaviour. In turn, any of those theories could be challenged by considering new evidence. Such new evidence informs the conceptual model, which completes the loop.

14.2.3 Methods for Exploring and Understanding Data in Large Behaviour Logs

Sensemaking is associated with various costs, which can be reduced using various computer-supported methods. For example, Pirolli and Card (2005) suggest that automatically mining data (in our case, automatically detecting routine variations and rejecting deviations) reduces the cost of scanning the data for salient patterns in the foraging loop. A computational model of routines that encodes the probabilities of different variations reduces the cost of searching for evidence to confirm and disconfirm hypotheses, which in turn allows the stakeholder to consider more hypotheses and reduce confirmation bias. Here we consider two different methods for exploring and understanding data in large behaviour logs: 1) explanatory methods, and 2) predictive methods.

14.2.3.1 Explanatory Data Exploration Methods

Explanatory methods provide support for manually searching for salient patterns in the data. This is often done using Exploratory Data Analysis (EDA), which offers different descriptive statistics and data visualization techniques (Tukey, 1977) to manually explore and understand high-level patterns in behaviour logs. Note that EDA methods focus on observational data and differ from methods for analysing data derived in classical experimental setups (Good, 1983). Finding supporting evidence that describe people's behaviour from log data typically involves identifying meaningful variables on which to partition the data, and then comparing behaviours across the different partitions (Dumais et al., 2014). Finding such partitions is at the discretion of the stakeholder, but often includes variables that describe temporal properties in the data or characteristics of people. Temporal properties can reveal periodicity and recurrence of events and user characteristics allow stakeholders to compare behaviours across different populations.

Visualizing data from behaviour logs is another common way for stakeholders to identify salient patterns in the data. Such data is often visualized on a timeline as a sequence of events. The simplicity of this approach makes it applicable to a variety of domains, such as schedule planning to show uncertainty of duration of different events (Aigner, et al., 2005), visualizing family schedules (Davidoff, Zimmerman, and Dey, 2010), and representing events related to patient treatments (Plaisant, et al., 1996). More advanced timelines enable the user to specify properties of the timeline (e.g., periodicity) for easier viewing. For example, Spiral Graph (Weber, Alexa, and Müller, 2001) aligns sequential events on a spiral timeline using a user-defined period.

However, even advanced interactive visualizations have difficulty in visualizing behaviour patterns that depend on multiple heterogeneous variables, especially as the number of variables grows. For example, parallel coordinates visualization can clearly show relationships between different multivariate aspects of behaviour data (Clear et al., 2009), until the number of variables becomes too large. To address such challenges, stakeholders can manually highlight (Buono, et al., 2005) and aggregate common sequences of events based on features in the data (Jin and Szekely, 2010; Monroe, et al., 2013) until meaningful patterns emerge. The stakeholder is then able to judge the quality and saliency of the patterns by visual inspection. However, this can be painstakingly slow, making manual exploration challenging.

Both EDA and custom visualizations focus on isolated events, or temporal evolution of a particular state (e.g., sleep vs. awake) or variable (e.g., the number of steps walked per day). However, such partitions describe people's general dispositions using the principle of aggregation, which often 'does not explain behavioural variability across situations, nor does it permit prediction of a specific behaviour in a given situation' (Ajzen, 1991). Routines are characterized by both specific actions people perform in different situations (Hodgson, 1997) and variability of those actions across situations (Feldman and Pentland, 2003). This makes it difficult to manually find nuanced relationships in the data. Also, due to the complexity and size of behaviour logs, EDA methods do not guarantee that the stakeholder will be able to find patterns of behaviours (e.g., those that form routines) and not some other patterns in data that are unrelated to behaviours.

Conceptualizing routines using explanatory models can help ensure the patterns we find using EDA match the underlining processes that generate behaviour data through causal explanation and description (Shmueli, 2010). Past research shows that such models can explain people's low-level behaviours, e.g., pointing (Banovic, Grossman, and Fitzmaurice, 2013) and text entry (Banovic, et al., 2017). Such models perform well on behaviours that can be described with a few variables, e.g., some pointing models with as little as two variables: distance to and size of the target (MacKenzie, 1992). The main strength of such models is their support for the sensemaking loop where they provide a statistical framework for hypotheses generation and testing.

However, when applied to complex, heterogeneous, multivariate behaviour data, e.g., to explain how people adopt information technology (Venkatesh, et al., 2003), such explanatory models are often unable to explain most of the observed data. Such models have less predictive power than predictive models (Kleinberg, et al., 2015), even in some cases when they closely approximate the true process that generated the data (Shmueli, 2010). Thus, they may not be able to act in response to people's behaviours.

14.2.3.2 Predictive Data Exploration Methods

Data mining automates the process of identifying potentially useful patterns in data (Fayyad, Piatetsky-Shapiro, and Smyth, 1996) in a way that could automatically capture salient patterns that describe behaviours. Such methods alleviate manual exploration of data in the foraging loop that is characteristic of explanatory approaches discussed earlier. Data mining employs existing machine learning algorithms to detect (e.g., Bulling, Blanke, and Schiele, 2014), classify (e.g., Hong et al., 2014), predict (e.g., Krumm and Horvitz, 2006) and find structure of (e.g., Baratchi, Meratnia, Havinga, Skidmore, and Toxopeus, 2014; Rashidi and Cook, 2010) patterns in the data. Such methods can automatically create computational models that act in response to patterns in the data. Stakeholders can then explore the results of data mining algorithms using various visual analytics tools (Keim et al., 2008).

However, such general-purpose data mining methods may not be well suited to extract behaviour patterns. For example, such existing machine learning algorithms purposefully disregard variations in human behaviour to focus on classifying and predicting only the most frequent human activity. Some variations may happen infrequently in data and are difficult to detect using those existing algorithms. Some specific infrequent variations may be detectable, e.g., detecting when parents are going to be late to pick up their children (Davidoff, Ziebart, Zimmerman, and Dey, 2011). However, this requires a case-by-case approach to address each variation, which can be difficult to apply if all possible variations are not known a priori.

Most such models require labelled examples about which behaviour instances are characteristic of a routine, and those that are not. However, the lack of individually labelled behaviour instances in large behaviour logs makes it challenging to use those existing supervised machine learning algorithms to classify behaviour instances into routines. For example, to train a supervised machine learning algorithm to classify behaviour instances that lead parents to forget to pick up their children, Davidoff, Zimmerman, and Dey (2010) had to manually label each behaviour instance in the behaviour log they collected, and confirm this information with the participants in their next study (Davidoff et al., 2011). This places significant burden on stakeholders to properly label enough data to be able to train their data mining algorithms.

Unsupervised machine learning methods cluster behaviours without prior knowledge of labels. For example, algorithms based on Topic Models (Farrahi and Gatica-Perez, 2012) allow stakeholders to generate clusters of behaviour instances. However, the main limitation of general-purpose unsupervised methods is that they offer no guarantees that the resulting clusters group instances based on the routine they belong to (i.e., the clusters may not represent routines). Unsupervised anomaly detection algorithms (e.g., Mcfowland, Speakman, and Neill, 2013) could be used to find differences between behaviour instances. However, they detect if a behaviour instance is a deviation from a routine, but not whether it is part of the routine.

This highlights the major challenge with most traditional machine learning models: there is no easy way to inspect the model to ensure that it captures meaningful patterns of routine behaviour. Like any other black box predictive model, there is no easy way to inspect the model and ensure that it captures meaningful patterns of behaviour. Stakeholders can inspect generative models (Salakhutdinov, 2009) by generating behaviours from the model and comparing them with empirical behaviour instances in the data. However, this assumes that the stakeholder already understands behaviour instances characteristic of a routine, which is what the model is supposed to automatically extract for the stakeholder in the first place.

Unsupervised methods specifically designed to model routines from behaviour logs (Eagle and Pentland, 2009; Farrahi and Gatica-Perez, 2012; Li, Kambhampati, and Yoon, 2009; Magnusson, 2000) are designed to capture meaningful patterns of routine behaviour. Each offers a unique approach to modelling routines. The advantage of such specialized methods compared to general-purpose machine learning approaches is that each is grounded in theory about routine behaviours. Stakeholders can explore each model using various custom visualizations. For example, T-patterns (Magnusson, 2000), which model multivariate events that reoccur at a specific time interval, can be represented using arc diagrams (Wattenberg, 2002). This enables stakeholders to check that a model matches the actual patterns of behaviour in the data. Such models can then act in response to people's behaviour, e.g., predict their mobility (Sadilek and Krumm, 2012).

However, it remains unclear which aspects of routines those existing routine modelling approaches are able to capture. The next section explores different aspects of routine behaviours and the implications they have on the ability of each of those models to explain routine behaviours.

14.3 Operationizable Definition of Human Routines

A definition of routines conceptualizes high-level knowledge about behaviours (i.e., schematizes existing knowledge about routines). Such conceptual models encode high-level real-world processes that generate behaviours data across different routines (e.g., daily routine, exercising routine, driving routine) of both individuals and populations. This allows stakeholders to compare salient patterns they identified in the data with this conceptual model of routines and ensure they found patterns that are representative of a routine and not some other patterns in the data. This is particularly important for data mining methods that automate the foraging loop to create computational models of routines from patterns of behaviours automatically extracted from the data. Such a conceptual model provides constraints on computational models of routines to favour salient patterns in the data that match properties and structure of real world behaviours. A computational model of routine behaviours grounded in a definition of routines combines the power of explanatory models to describe behaviours with the power of predictive models to automatically find salient behaviour patterns in the data, and even act in response to those behaviours afterwards.

However, current definitions of routines focus on different aspect of behaviours that make up routines, which makes it difficult to reconcile them into a single unified definition that can be operationalized in a holistic computational model. We focus primarily on operationalizing routines of individuals, including routines of homogenous populations of people. Although such routines share similarities with organizational routines (see Becker, 2004 for a review), we only broadly explore how individuals perform in the context of organizational routines, i.e., the performative aspect of organizational routines (Feldman and Pentland, 2003), and do not focus on operationalizing organizational routines per se. Also, the goal here is not to define the processes that people use to generate mental plans that manifest themselves as routines. Instead, we focus our analysis on physical activity in a given context (Kuutti, 1995). Our goal is to provide a definition of routine behaviours as people enact them in action.

Focusing on how people enact their mental plans allows us to broadly include habitual behaviours into an operationalizable definition of routines. Habits represent people's tendency to act in largely subconscious ways (Hodgson, 2009) that are different from other planned behaviours that require deliberation (Ajzen, 1991). Although there exist qualitative differences between subconscious and deliberate behaviours (Hodgson, 1997), which may impact the outcome of those behaviours (Kahneman, 2011), when enacted both deliberate routines and subconscious habits form similar patterns. Note that, although we consider routines that may include bad habits and other behaviours that could negatively impact people, we exclude a discussion on pathological behaviours, such as addiction, which require special consideration.

14.3.1 Unified Definition of Human Routine Behaviour

At the highest level, we can define routines as rules: actions Y that people perform when in situation X that is the cause of action Y (Hodgson, 1997). Such a definition is too high level and is missing many aspects that define routines, and thus does not give enough information to be operationalized into a computational model of routines. Instead, we use this definition as a starting point to define high-level structure of routines, and clarify or scope it by considering other routine definitions. Together they form a unified definition of routine behaviour that can be operationalized into a computational model of routines.

For example, Hodgson (1997) does not explicitly describe what makes up situations that influence people's actions. This is likely because such features will vary across different types of routines (e.g., features that describe situations and actions in a daily routine are different from those in a driving routine. However, many existing routine definitions include essential features of routine behaviours. For example, some existing definitions consider routine only those actions that repeat on a specific time interval (Brdiczka, Su, and Begole, 2010; Casarrubea et al., 2015). Other such commonly considered routine defining features include spatial context (Feldman, 2000), and social influences (Hodgson, 2009). However, it is more likely that different routines are defined by combinations of multiple different features of situations and actions.

One such influence that few existing definitions of routines explicitly consider are people's goals, which provide motivation to act. For example, Pentland and Rueter (1994) loosely define routine behaviours of individuals that are part of an organization as a 'means to an end;' and Hamermesh (2003) proposes that people perform routine actions to maximize utility, which implies an existence of a goal. However, this aspect of routines requires more considerations. People act with a purpose because they want to attain a goal, and they behave in a way that they think is appropriate to reach that goal (Taylor, 1950). Goals give people an intention to act (Ajzen, 1991) and given availability of requisite opportunities and resources (Ajzen, 1985), encoded as other situational features, can such intention result in an enacted behaviour that we attempt to model.

Hodgson (1997) also does not specify the granularity of situations and actions. However, behavioural theories, such as Kuutti's Activity Theory (1995), often consider activities people perform at different levels of granularity. Picking the right granularity depends on the activity we want to study. Pentland and Rueter's (1994) definition explicitly accounts for this by breaking down routines into different hierarchical levels made up of activities at different levels of granularity. Such activities are made up of sequences of actions people perform in different situations that are characteristic of the routine. Chaining different pairs of situations and actions in Hodgson's (1997) definition can broadly encompass the sequential nature of routine actions in such activities (Pentland and Rueter, 1994).

Hodgson's (1997) definition implies that if a situation reoccurs so will the action that the person performs in that situation. This gives rise to the idea of recurrence of behaviours that characterize routines as people repeatedly perform those behaviours (Agre and Shrager, 1990). Hodgson's (1997) definition further implies a rigid, one-to-one mapping between situations and actions, which suggests that repeated behaviour instances will also be characterized by same rigidity (Brdiczka et al., 2010). However, routines, like most other kinds of human behaviours, have high variability (Ajzen, 1991). Thus, a unified definition must consider that routines may vary from enactment to enactment (Hamermesh, 2003). Also, people adapt their routines over time (Ronis, Yates, and Kirscht, 1989) based on feedback from different enactments (Feldman and Pentland, 2003).

We combine different aspects of routines and propose our own unified definition of routine behaviour:

> *Routines are likely, weakly ordered, interruptible sequences of causally related situations and actions that a person will perform to create or reach opportunities that enable the person to accomplish a goal.*

Our unified definition strongly builds on Hodgson's (1997) definition to give structure and ordering to routine behaviour, while at the same time allowing for variability in behaviour. We leave the features of situations and actions unspecified because finding such features in the data is an essential part of exploring and understanding routines. We do not attribute recurrence and repetitiveness to routines directly, but to features of situations in the environment (i.e., if situations repeat, so will corresponding actions). We leave the granularity of such features unspecified for the same reasons. However, we specifically require that data features that describe situations and actions include information about people's goals and opportunities to accomplish those goals. Situations and actions and the behaviour structures they form are characterized by causal relations between features of situations and actions that help describe and explain routines.

14.3.2 Unified Routine Definition and Existing Computational Models of Routines

The existing routine models (Eagle and Pentland, 2009; Farrahi and Gatica-Perez, 2012; Li, Kambhampati, and Yoon, 2009; Magnusson, 2000) do not capture all aspects of our unified definition of routines. Also, none of the models clearly differentiate between situations and actions. They can either consider events that describe situations only (actions are implicit) or events that are a combination the two. This limits the ability of such models to describe and explain routines because they do not explicitly model the causal relationships between situations and actions that define and describe routines. Also, by treating situations and actions separately allows the stakeholders to understand their separate effects and target interventions at people or their environments. Each of the existing approaches focuses on modelling limited aspects of routine behaviours. For example, Li, Kambhampati, and Yoon's(2009) model of routines exactly matches Pentland and Rueter's (1994) definition of routines as grammars of behaviour. However, that means that their model is only able to encode routine activity hierarchy (sequences of activities at different granularities), but not the causal relationships that define routines.

Both T-patterns (Magnusson, 2000) and Eigenbehaviours (Eagle and Pentland, 2009) focus on temporal relationships between multivariate events. By considering time, they still implicitly model other aspects of the routines. For example, sequences of situations and actions can be expressed over a period of time, and recurrent situations are often periodic. However, this is a limited view of routines because there are clearly other forces that influence people's free choice to act (Hamermesh, 2003). Although time may be correlated with many aspects of routine behaviours, it may not necessarily have a causal effect on people's actions. For example, people will attend a scheduled weekly meeting because of social interactions and norms, but not simply because of a specific day of week and time of day (Weiss, 1996).

From this we conclude that while these algorithms are helpful for extracting routines from behaviour logs, they are not sufficient for providing a holistic understanding of a routine behaviour. Thus, we propose a new model that is grounded in our unified definition of routine behaviour.

14.4 Computational Model of Human Routine Behaviour

This section provides a quick overview of our computational model of human behaviour (Banovic et al., 2016), which captures all aspects of routines as detailed by our unified definition of routines. We model routines as *likely, weakly ordered, interruptible sequences of situations and actions* encoded as a Markov Decision (MDP) (Puterman, 1994) (Equation 14.1):

$$M_{MDP} = (S, A, P(s), P(s'|s, a), P(a|s), R(s, a))$$ (14.1)

In our model, we model a set of situations S, where each unique situation $s \in S$ is described by a set of features F_{s_t}, and a set of actions A, where each action $a \in A$ is defined by a set of features F_{a_t} which describe unique actions that the people can perform. We can automatically convert raw behaviour traces from behaviour logs into sequences of situations and actions that describe behaviour instances that we can use to train our routine model. A behaviour instance is a finite, ordered sequence of situations and actions $\{s_1, a_1, s_2, a_2, \ldots s_n, a_n\}$, where in each situation s_i, the person performs action a_i which results in a new situation s_{i+1}. Behaviour instances describe peoples' behaviours as they seek to accomplish a goal.

We express the likelihood of any of these sequences by capturing the probability distribution of situations $P(s)$, probability distribution of actions given situations $(P(a|s))$, and probability distribution of situation transitions $P(s'|s, a)$, which specifies the probability of the next situation s' when the person performs action a in situation s. This situation transition probability distribution $P(s'|s, a)$ models how the environment responds to the actions that people perform in different situations. Then, assuming that each situation depends only on the previous situation and action, we calculate the probability of any behaviour instance b, where the probability of the initial situation $s_0(p(s_0))$ and the conditional probability of actions given situations ($p\,(a_i|s_i)$) are specific to routine model M:

$$P\,(b|M) = p\,(s_0) \cdot \prod_i p\,(a_i|s_i) \cdot p\,(s_{i+1}|s_i, a_i) \tag{14.2}$$

A reward function $R\,(s, a) \rightarrow R$ defines the reward the person incurs when performing action a in situation s. To model peoples' *goal* states, we seek situations with high reward that characterizes situations in which people have an opportunity to accomplish their goals. In an MDP framework, the reward function is used to compute a deterministic policy ($\pi : S \rightarrow A$), which specifies actions agents should take in different situations. Traditionally, the MDP is 'solved' using the value iteration algorithm (Bellman, 1957), to find an optimal policy (with the highest expected cumulative reward). However, our goal is to infer the reward function from peoples' demonstrated behaviour.

We use MaxCausalEnt algorithm (Ziebart, 2010) to infer the reward function that expresses the preference that people have for different situations and actions. Our main contribution to training models of routines is our insight that the *byproducts* of Max-CausalEnt (Ziebart, 2010), a decision-theoretic Inverse Reinforcement Learning (IRL) algorithm typically used to train MDP models from data and predict people's activity (Ziebart, et al., 2008; Ziebart et al., 2009), encodes the preference that people have for specific goal situations, and the causal relationship between routine actions and situations in which people perform those actions. Such IRL algorithms (Ng and Russell, 2000; Ziebart, Bagnell, and Dey, 2013) assume a parametric reward function that is linear in $F_{S,A}$, given unknown weight parameters θ:

$$R\,(s, a) = \theta^T \cdot F_{s_t, a_t} \tag{14.3}$$

To compute the unknown parameters θ, MaxCausalEnt computes the probability distribution of actions given situations $P\,(a|s)$ which maximizes the causal entropy between situations and actions:

$$P\,(a_t|s_t) = e^{Q_\theta^{soft}(a_t, s_t) - V_\theta^{soft}(s_t)} \tag{14.4}$$

Where Q_θ^{soft} represents the expected value of performing action a_t in situation s_t , and V_θ^{soft} represents the expected value of being in situation s_t:

$$Q_\theta^{soft}(a_t, s_t) = \sum_{s_{t+1}} P\,(s_{t+1}|s_t, a_t) \cdot V_\theta^{soft}\,(s_{t+1})$$
$$V_\theta^{soft}\,(s_t) = \operatorname*{softmax}_{a_t} Q_\theta^{soft}\,(a_t, s_t) + \theta^T \cdot F_{s_t, a_t} \tag{14.5}$$

Incidentally, $V_\theta^{soft}\,(s_t)$ and θ represent the preference that people have for different situations and features that describe those situations respectively, which implies *goal states*.

Using MaxCausalEnt (Ziebart, 2010), we can build a probabilistic model of routines that, unlike models that extract only the most frequent routines, also captures likely variations of those routines, even in infrequent situations. Our approach does this by modelling probability distributions over all possible combinations of situations and actions using behaviour traces from large behaviour logs. Our approach supports both individual and population models of routines, providing the ability to identify the differences in routine behaviour across different people and populations. By Jaynes's Principle of Maximum Entropy (1955), the estimated probability distribution of actions given situations $(P(a|s))$ is the one that best fits the situation and action combinations from the sequences in the behaviour logs. Assuming that the actions a person performs only depend on the information encoded by the current situation (the Markovian property of the model) makes this approach computationally feasible. See Banovic et al. (2016) for more details on the routine model, and Ziebart (2010) for proofs and detailed pseudocode for the MaxCausalEnt algorithm.

Having our probabilistic, generative model of routine behaviour allows us to automatically classify and generate behaviours that are characteristic of a routine (Banovic, Wang, et al., 2017). Classifying behaviour instances often involves considering two competing routine and finding behaviour instances that are characteristic of one routine, but not the other. To classify a behaviour instance, we need to calculate the probability that it belongs to a particular routine:

$$P(M|b) = \frac{P(b|M) \cdot P(M)}{P(b)} \tag{14.6}$$

where $(P(b|M))$ is the probability of the instance in the routine M, $P(M)$ is the probability that the routine of the person whose behaviour we are classifying is M, and $P(b)$ is the probability that people, regardless of their routine, would perform behaviour instance b. Then, assuming two models of opposing routines M and M' with probabilities of all possible behaviour instances in the model, by law of total probability:

$$P(M|b) = \frac{P(b|M) \cdot P(M)}{P(b|M) \cdot P(M) + P(b|M') \cdot P(M')} \tag{14.7}$$

This allows us to create a classifier that can automatically classify (or detect) if behaviour instance b is in routine M, but not in routine M', for some confidence level :

$$h(b) = I\left(P\left(M'|b\right) < \alpha\right) \cdot I\left(\alpha \leq P(M|b)\right) \tag{14.8}$$

The probabilistic nature of the models allows us to automatically generate behaviour instances that are variations of a routine. This is unlike finding the sequence of situations and actions that maximizes expected reward based on a reward function (Bellman, 1957) because generating instances this way hides the inherent uncertainty and variance in human behaviour. Instead, we sample behaviour instances using the probability distributions in a routine model. We start by sampling a starting situation from the probability distribution of situations $(P(s))$ and follow the chain to sample from probability distribution of actions given situations $(P(a|s))$ and transition probabilities $P(s|s, a)$ until we encounter a stopping situation or reach a maximum behaviour instance length.

Our approach conceptualizes behaviours from data in behaviour logs into a computational model of routines. Different stakeholders, such as domain experts and end users, could use this model to explore and understand routine behaviours. Automatically detecting and generating behaviour instances automates a fundamental task of the behaviour sense-making process: finding evidence to support that the model captures patterns in the data that represent behaviours and not some other patterns in the data. It also enables a class of CI UIs that can automatically act in response to peoples' behaviours.

14.5 Routine Models as Computational Tools

This section summarizes our work showcasing our routine model as a computational tool that enables CI (Banovic, et al., 2016; Banovic et al., 2017). We illustrate this on an example in the driving domain. We train models of aggressive and non-aggressive driving routines using a naturalistic driving dataset (Hong, Margines, and Day, 2014). We use these models to power a User Interface that can automatically detect when a driver is driving aggressively and coach the driver by simulating and showing what a non-aggressive driver would do in the same situation (see Figure 14.1) (Banovic et al., 2017). This is an important and timely problem given that drivers who routinely engage in aggressive driving behaviours present a hazard to other people in traffic and are often involved in fatal collisions (American Automobile Association, 2009). However, it is often difficult to create models of driving behaviour that can detect aggressive driving behaviours because labelling individual instances may be time consuming and even domain experts may lack knowledge about nuanced aspects of this complex type of behaviour.

14.5.1 Naturalistic Driving Behaviour Dataset and Model

To train our models of driving routines, we used a naturalistic driving data set originally collected by Hong, Margines, and Day (2014), which contains driving behaviour traces of 13 aggressive and 13 non-aggressive drivers, labelled based on their aggressive driving traffic violation history. The original data contained raw readings from an On-board Diagnostic tool (OBD2) (e.g., car location traces, speed, acceleration, throttle position), which were recorded every 500 milliseconds. We extended the original data set using the Open Street Map API and automatically marked each intersection in the data with intersection type, speed limits, and traffic signs and signals.

We converted raw data into behaviour instances by separating behaviours by inter-section type (e.g., T-junction) and manoeuver type (straight, right turn, left turn), and then dividing intersections into four stages (approaching, entering, exiting, and leaving the intersection). At each position, we recorded details of the vehicle, such as its current speed and acceleration. Between each position, we added actions that represent how the driver operated the vehicle. We converted raw vehicle operation data (depressing the gas and brake pedals) into aggregated driver actions showing changes in pedal positions between stages.

We then weakly labelled instances into aggressive and non-aggressive routines using per-person labels from Hong et al. (2014), which they assigned based on drivers' self-reported driving violations and their answers to the driver behaviour questionnaire from (Reason et al., 2011). We trained the two models, one for each label, as described in the previous

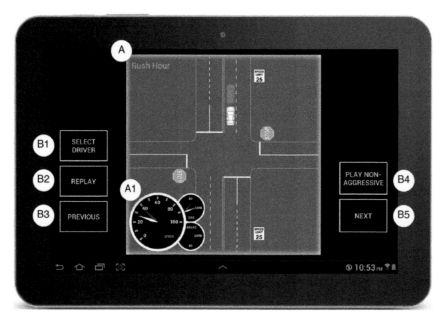

Figure 14.1 Driving behaviour detection and generation tool user interface from Banovic et al. (2017). The main animation region (A) shows a scenario in which a vehicle travels straight through an intersection. The simplified intersection consists of a main road with 25 miles per hour speed limit and a residential street with stop signs for opposing traffic. The current scenario depicts an automatically *detected* aggressive driving behaviour (speeding transparent vehicle) and an automatically *generated* non-aggressive behaviour (opaque vehicle, which drives within the posted speed limit). Dials (A1) show the vehicles' speed, and gas and brake pedal positions. The user can: B1) select a driver and a trip to review, B2) replay current driver behaviour, B3 & B5) load previous and next driving behaviour in the current trip, and B4) play or replay an automatically generated non-aggressive behaviour for the given driving scenario. Reproduced with permission from ACM.

section. We identified 20,312 different situations and 43 different actions in the dataset. The final models had 234,967 different situations, 47 different actions, and 5,371,338 possible transitions.

14.5.2 Detecting and Generating Driving Behaviour Instances

We used the two models (Agg and Non agg) to compute the probabilities of any driving behaviour instance in the model. The two models enabled automated classifiers that can detect if an instance is characteristic of an aggressive or non-aggressive driving routine:

$$
\begin{aligned}
h_{Agg}(b) &= I\left(P\left(NonAgg|b\right) < \alpha\right) \cdot I\left(\alpha \leq P\left(Agg|b\right)\right) \\
h_{NonAgg}(b) &= I\left(P\left(Agg|b\right) < \alpha\right) \cdot I\left(\alpha \leq P\left(NonAgg|b\right)\right)
\end{aligned}
\tag{14.9}
$$

Once the system detects an aggressive behaviour instance using the classifiers in Equation 14.9, it uses the non-aggressive driving routine model to sample behaviour instances that represent what a non-aggressive driver would do in the same situation. Generating behaviour instances for specific driving situations allows us to explore such 'what-if' scenarios for the two driver populations, even if our training data does not contain those exact scenarios.

14.5.3 Understanding and Acting in Response to Driving Routines

We leveraged the models and the UI in Figure 14.1 to explore and understand the driving routines we extracted from the data. Through our own analysis and with help from two driving instructors, we showed that our algorithm accurately detects aggressive behaviours and generates meaningful non-aggressive alternatives (Banovic et al., 2017). Our findings matched the summary statistics from Hong, Margines, and Day (2014), which we used as a benchmark. We also found nuanced aspects of aggressive driving behaviour, such as that in the most likely aggressive driving behaviour instances, the drivers exceeded the maximum speed limit by 20 mph. However, we also found that drivers do not always behave in a way that is characteristic of one driving routine or the other. Instead, both aggressive and non-aggressive drivers will engage in both kinds of behaviours, with aggressive drivers doing it more frequently.

Having evaluated the model, we tested the ability of our tool (see Figure 14.1) to raise people's awareness and help them understand their driving behaviours (Banovic et al., 2017). We conducted a user study in which twenty participants drove on a predefined route and reviewed their driving behaviours in two conditions: 1) *baseline*, in which they reviewed all of their behaviours, and 2) *intervention*, in which the tool detected their aggressive behaviour instances and coached them by simulating non-aggressive behaviours in the same situations. Our results showed that our tool raised awareness of more aggressive driving behaviours than status quo (no coaching in pre-test) and a baseline condition (unguided review). Our tool coached drivers to identify aggressive driving behaviours and contrast them with non-aggressive behaviours, which is a first step in helping them improve their driving behaviour.

Our use case illustrates one example of how we can leverage computational models of human behaviour as computational tools that can power CI. However, it is easy to see how it could generalize to other domains and applications. For example, a similar approach could be used to model routines of cancer patients to detect behaviour instances that could lead to re-hospitalization and coach those patients how to improve their routine by simulating behaviours of patients who have survived cancer. Such models could inform the design of future health monitoring CI that is based on and personalized for the patients based on their routines.

14.6 Conclusion and Future Work

This chapter presented a method for modelling complex human routine behaviours from large behaviour logs. One of the aspects that differentiate our model from black box alternatives is that it allows stakeholders to explore the model and the data used to train it. Our model allows stakeholders to generate knowledge about routines that will inform the design of human-data supported interfaces. We primarily focused on supporting stakeholders in the information foraging loop part of the sensemaking process (Pirolli and Card, 2005). We have shown how to automate the process of extracting salient patterns and searching for relationships in the data that describe routine behaviours.

We have shown how to schematize this collection of evidence into an automatically trained computational model of routines. We have verified that domain experts can inspect and search for relationships in the routine models to ensure the model captures meaningful patterns of behaviours in the data (Banovic et al., 2016). We also explored different aspect of the sensemaking loop in which stakeholders generate and test their hypotheses, and used various visual representations of the data to demonstrate the ability of our approach to present findings about human behaviours that gives stakeholders a holistic picture of this type of human behaviour (Banovic et al., 2017). Our probabilistic model allows the stakeholders to formalize the process by which they generate and test their hypothesis about behaviours using Bayesian Hypothesis Testing (Bernardo and Rueda, 2002). We have also show how the model can support interfaces that act in response to those behaviours to prescribe behaviour change (Banovic et al., 2017).

The ability of our proposed routine model to accurately encode behaviours is based on the assumptions that we can fully observe situations and actions, and that we can encode the world dynamics. The ability to collect information about situations and actions in behaviour logs satisfies the assumption that both are fully observable. However, the current model requires the stakeholders to manually specify how the environment responds to people's actions and other external factors that operate in and influence the environment. We can manually specify world dynamics when they are known ahead of time. This is often the case when people's actions fully describe situation transitions (e.g., when the model considers only factors that people have full control over in the environment). For example, it is easy to specify world dynamics in a routine model of people's daily commutes between different places that are all known ahead of time because the person always ends up at the place they indented to go to or stay at with 100 per cent probability. However, if we introduce more external factors into the model, we must also estimate the effect of those factors on the environment. The effects of such factors are often not known ahead of time, and even if they were, it may be tedious to encode such dynamics manually.

Learning world dynamics from the data is challenging because it requires large number of training examples to accurately model its complexity. For example, in a model where there are $|S|$ number of situations and $|A|$ number of actions, we need to estimate situation transition probability distribution ($P(s'|s, a)$) for $|S| \times |A| \times |S|$ number of transitions. This problem is compounded when modelling human behaviour from behaviour logs. In this case, transitions involving actions that represent deviations from a routine will be infrequent in the data (by definition). Some possible, but infrequent transitions will also not be well represented in the data. However, the nature of log studies prevents the stakeholders from asking people to go into their environment and perform such actions and hope they end up in situations that we have not observed. Even in situations when the stakeholders could contact people, asking them to perform specific actions might be cumbersome (e.g., if it requires time and resources), inappropriate (e.g., if they are unable to perform such actions), or unethical (e.g., if those actions could negatively impact them).

For future work, we propose a semi-automated method that learns complex world dynamics. We will begin by modifying the existing MaxCausalEnt algorithm (Ziebart, 2010) and to also estimate situation transition probabilities from the data. This will allow us to estimate the combined effects of situations and actions on situation transitions for situation transitions that are well represented in the data. Such improvements will bring us closer to a general purpose, generative model of routines that enables CI across domains and applications.

In our work, we illustrated a class of CI we define as Human-Data Supported Interfaces. However, the generalizable nature of the model makes it an ideal candidate for CI in the context of UI design. For example, such models can model interaction between the user and a class of devices, such as a mobile device, including the tasks and the goals that the user wants to accomplish. Such models can then be used to select the best design for the mobile device UIs that will streamline the user's interaction to complete tasks and accomplish the goals faster. Such examples offer a promise of a future in which computation drives UIs in ways that will help improve peoples' wellbeing and quality of their lives.

....

REFERENCES

American Automobile Association, 2009. Aggressive driving: Research update. Washington, DC: American Automobile Association Foundation for Traffic Safety.

Adar, E., Teevan, J., and Dumais, S. T., 2008. Large-scale analysis of web revisitation patterns. In: *CHI '08 Proceedings of the SIGCHI Conference on Human Factors in Computing Systems*. Florence, Italy, 5–10 April 2008. New York, NY: ACM, pp. 1197–206.

Agre, P. E., and Shrager, J., 1990. Routine Evolution as the Microgenetic Basis of Skill Acquistion. In: *Proceedings of the 12th Annual Conference of the Cognitive Science Society*. Cambridge, MA, 25–28 July 1990. Hillsdale, NJ: Lawrence Erlbaum.

Aigner, W., Miksch, S., Thurnher, B., and Biffl, S., 2005. PlanningLines: Novel glyphs for representing temporal uncertainties and their evaluation. In: *Proceedings of the 9th International Conference on Information Visualisation*. London, UK. 6–8 July 2005. Red Hook, NY: Curran Associates, pp. 457–63.

Ajzen, I., 1985. From intentions to actions: A theory of planned behavior. In: J. Kuhl and J. Beckmann, eds. *Action Control*. SSSP Springer Series in Social Psychology. Berlin: Springer.

Ajzen, I., 1991. The theory of planned behavior. *Organizational Behavior and Human Decision Processes*, 50(2), pp. 179–211.

Anderson, J. R., Bothell, D., Byrne, M. D., Douglass, S., Lebiere, C., and Qin, Y., 2004. An Integrated Theory of the Mind. *Psychological Review*, 111(4), pp. 1036–60.

Banovic, N., Brant, C., Mankoff, J., and Dey, A. K., 2014. ProactiveTasks: the Short of Mobile Device Use Sessions. In: *Proceedings of the 16th International Conference on Human-Computer Interaction with Mobile Devices & Services*. Toronto, ON, Canada, 23–26 September 2014. New York, NY: ACM, pp. 243–52.

Banovic, N., Buzali, T., Chevalier, F., Mankoff, J., and Dey, A. K., 2016. Modeling and Understanding Human Routine Behavior. In: *Proceedings of the 2016 CHI Conference on Human Factors in Computing Systems*. San Jose, CA, 7–12 May 2016. New York, NY: ACM, pp. 248–60.

Banovic, N., Grossman, T., and Fitzmaurice, G., 2013. The effect of time-based cost of error in target-directed pointing tasks. In: *Proceedings of the SIGCHI Conference on Human Factors in Computing Systems*. Paris, France, 27 April–2 May 2013. New York, NY: ACM, pp. 1373–82.

Banovic, N., Rao, V., Saravanan, A., Dey, A. K., and Mankoff, J., 2017. Quantifying Aversion to Costly Typing Errors in Expert Mobile Text Entry. In: *Proceedings of the 2017 CHI Conference on Human Factors in Computing Systems*. Denver, CO, 6–11 May 2017. New York, NY: ACM, pp. 4229–41.

Banovic, N., Wang, A., Jin, Y., Chang, C., Ramos, J., Dey, A. K., and Mankoff, J., 2017. Leveraging Human Routine Models to Detect and Generate Human Behaviors. In: *Proceedings of the 2017 CHI Conference on Human Factors in Computing Systems*. Denver, CO, 6–11 May 2017. New York, NY: ACM, pp. 6683–94.

Baratchi, M., Meratnia, N., Havinga, P. J. M., Skidmore, A. K., and Toxopeus, B. A. K. G., 2014. A hierarchical hidden semi-Markov model for modeling mobility data. In: *Proceedings of the 2014 ACM International Joint Conference on Pervasive and Ubiquitous Computing*. Seattle, WA, 13–17 September 2014. New York, NY: ACM, pp. 401–12.

Becker, M. C., 2004. Organizational routines: A review of the literature. *Industrial and Corporate Change*, 13(4), pp. 643–77.

Bellman, R., 1957. A Markovian decision process. *Journal of Mathematics and Mechanics*, 6, pp. 679–84.

Bernardo, J., and Rueda, R., 2002. Bayesian hypothesis testing: A reference approach. *International Statistical Review*, 70(3), pp. 351–72.

Brdiczka, O., Su, N., and Begole, J., 2010. Temporal task footprinting: identifying routine tasks by their temporal patterns. In: *Proceedings of the 15th international conference on Intelligent user interfaces*. Hong Kong, China, 7–10 February 2010. New York, NY: ACM, pp. 281–4.

Bulling, A., Blanke, U., and Schiele, B., 2014. A tutorial on human activity recognition using body-worn inertial sensors. *ACM Computing Surveys (CSUR)*, 46(3), pp. 1–33.

Buono, P., Aris, A., Plaisant, C., Khella, A., and Shneiderman, B., 2005. Interactive Pattern Search in Time Series. In: *Proceedings of the Conference on Visualization and Data Analysis (VDA 2005)*. San Jose, CA, 3 November 2005. Vol. 5669, pp. 175–86. http://doi.org/10.1117/12.587537

Capra, R., 2011. HCI browser: A tool for administration and data collection for studies of web search behaviors. In: A Marcus, ed. *Lecture Notes in Computer Science: Design, User Experience, and Usability*, Pt II. LNCS 6770, pp. 259–68.

Casarrubea, M., Jonsson, G. K., Faulisi, F., Sorbera, F., Di Giovanni, G., Benigno, A., and Crescimanno, G., 2015. T-pattern analysis for the study of temporal structure of animal and human behavior: A comprehensive review. *Journal of Neuroscience Methods*, 239, pp. 34–46.

Clear, A. K., Shannon, R., Holland, T., Quigley, A., Dobson, S., and Nixon, P., 2009. Situvis: A visual tool for modeling a user's behaviour patterns in a pervasive environment. In: H. Tokuda, ed. *Lecture Notes in Computer Science: Pervasive 2009*, LNCS 5538, pp. 327–41.

Davidoff, S., Ziebart, B. D., Zimmerman, J., and Dey, A. K., 2011. Learning Patterns of Pick-ups and Drop-offs to Support Busy Family Coordination. In: *Proceedings of the SIGCHI Conference on Human Factors in Computing Systems*. Vancouver, BC, Canada, 7–12 May 2011. New York, NY: ACM, pp. 1175–84.

Davidoff, S., Zimmerman, J., and Dey, A. K., 2010. How routine learners can support family coordination. In: *Proceedings of the 28th International Conference on Human Factors in Computing Systems*. Atlanta, GA, 10–15 April 2010. New York, NY: ACM, pp. 2461–70.

Dumais, S., Jeffries, R., Russell, D. M., Tang, D., and Teevan, J., 2014. Understanding User Behavior Through Log Data and Analysis. In: J. Olson and W. Kellogg, eds. *Ways of Knowing in HCI*. New York, NY: Springer, pp. 349–72.

Eagle, N., and Pentland, A. S., 2009. Eigenbehaviors: identifying structure in routine. *Behavioral Ecology and Sociobiology*, 63(7), pp. 1057–66.

Farrahi, K., and Gatica-Perez, D., 2012. Extracting mobile behavioral patterns with the distant N-gram topic model. In: *Proceedings of the 16th International Symposium on Wearable Computers (ISWC)*. Newcastle, UK, 18–22 June 2012. Red Hook, NY: Curran Associates, pp. 1–8.

Fayyad, U., Piatetsky-Shapiro, G., and Smyth, P., 1996. From Data Mining to Knowledge Discovery in Databases. *AI Magazine*, 17(3), pp. 37–54.

Feldman, M. S., 2000. Organizational Routines as a Source of Continuous Change. *Organization Science*, 11(6), pp. 611–29.

Feldman, M. S., and Pentland, B. T., 2003. Reconceptualizing Organizational Routines as a Source of Flexibility and Change. *Administrative Science Quarterly*, 48(1), pp. 94–118.

Ferreira, D., Kostakos, V., and Dey, A. K., 2015. AWARE: Mobile Context Instrumentation Framework. *Frontiers in ICT*, 2, pp. 1–9.

Friedman, H. J., 1997. Data mining and statistics: What's the connection? In: *Proceedings of the 29th Symposium on the Interface Between Computer Science and Statistics*. Houston, TX, 14–17 May 1997, pp. 1–7.

Good, I. J., 1983. The Philosophy of Exploratory Data Analysis. *Philosophy of Science*, 50(2), pp. 283–95.

Google. 2017. Google Analytics. Retrieved 10 April 2017, from http://www.google.com/analytics/

Hamermesh, D. S., 2003. Routine. *NBER Working Paper Series*, (9440). Retrieved from http://www.sciencedirect.com/science/article/pii/S0014292104000182

Hodgson, G. M., 1997. The ubiquity of habit and rules. *Cambridge Journal of Economics*, 21(6), pp. 663–83.

Hodgson, G. M., 2009. Choice, habit and evolution. *Journal of Evolutionary Economics*, 20(1), pp. 1–18.

Hong, J.-H., Margines, B., and Dey, A. K., 2014. A smartphone-based sensing platform to model aggressive driving behaviors. In: *Proceedings of the 32nd Annual ACM Conference on Human Factors in Computing Systems*. Toronto, ON, Canada, 23–26 September 2014. New York, NY: ACM, pp. 4047–56.

Hurst, A., Mankoff, J., and Hudson, S. E., 2008. Understanding pointing problems in real world computing environments. In: *Proceedings of the 10th International ACM SIGACCESS Conference on Computers and Accessibility*. Halifax, Nova Scotia, Canada, 13–15 October 2008, New York, NY: ACM, pp. 43–50.

Jaynes, E. T., 1955. Information Theory and Statistical Mechanics. *Physical Review*, 108(2), pp. 171–90.

Jin, J., and Szekely, P., 2010. Interactive querying of temporal data using a comic strip metaphor. In: Proceedings of the *2010 IEEE Symposium on Visual Analytics Science and Technology (VAST 2010*. Salt Lake City, UT, 25–26 October 2010. Red Hook, NY: Curran Associates, pp. 163–70).

Kahneman, D., 2011. *Thinking, fast and slow*. London: Penguin.

Keim, D., Andrienko, G., Fekete, J. D., Görg, C., Kohlhammer, J., and Melançon, G., 2008. Visual analytics: Definition, process, and challenges. In: A. Kerren et al., eds. *Lecture Notes in Computer Science: Information Visualization.* LNCS 4950, pp. 154–75.

Kleinberg, J., Ludwig, J., Mullainathan, S., and Obermeyer, Z., 2015. Prediction Policy Problems. *American Economic Review: Papers & Proceedings,* 105(5), pp. 491–5.

Koehler, C., Banovic, N., Oakley, I., Mankoff, J., and Dey, A. K., 2014. Indoor-ALPS: An adaptive indoor location prediction system. In: *Proceedings of the 2014 ACM International Joint Conference on Pervasive and Ubiquitous Computing.* Seattle, WA, 13–17 September 2014. New York, NY: ACM, pp. 171–81.

Krumm, J., and Horvitz, E., 2006. Predestination: Inferring destinations from partial trajectories. In: *Proceedings of the 8th international conference on Ubiquitous Computing.* Irvine, CA, 17–21 September 2006. Berlin: Springer, pp. 243–60.

Kuutti, K., 1995. Activity Theory as a potential framework for human- computer interaction research. In: B. Nardi, ed. *Context and Consciousness: Activity Theory and Human-Computer Interaction.* Cambridge, MA: MIT Press, pp. 17–44.

Li, N., Kambhampati, S., and Yoon, S., 2009. Learning Probabilistic Hierarchical Task Networks to Capture User Preferences. In: *Proceedings of the Twenty-First International Joint Conference on Artificial Intelligence.* Pasadena, CA, 14–17 July 2009. Menlo Park, CA: AAAI, pp. 1754–60.

MacKenzie, I. S., 1992. Fitts' law as a research and design tool in human-computer interaction. *Human-Computer Interaction,* 7(1), pp. 91–139.

Magnusson, M. S., 2000. Discovering hidden time patterns in behavior: T-patterns and their detection. *Behavior Research Methods, Instruments, & Computers,* 32(1), pp. 93–110.

Mcfowland III, E., Speakman, S., and Neill, D. B., 2013. Fast Generalized Subset Scan for Anomalous Pattern Detection. *Journal of Machine Learning Research,* 14, pp. 1533–61.

Monroe, M., Lan, R., Lee, H., Plaisant, C., and Shneiderman, B., 2013. Temporal event sequence simplification. *IEEE Transactions on Visualization and Computer Graphics,* 19(12), pp. 2227–36.

Ng, A., and Russell, S., 2000. Algorithms for inverse reinforcement learning. In: *Proceedings of the Seventeenth International Conference on Machine Learning.* San Francisco, CA: Morgan Kaufmann, pp. 663–70.

Pasquale, F., 2015. *The Black Box Society: The Secret Algorithms That Control Money and Information.* Cambridge, MA: Harvard University Press.

Pentland, B. T., and Rueter, H. H., 1994. Organizational Routines as Grammars of Action. *Administrative Science Quarterly,* 39(3), pp. 484–510.

Pirolli, P., and Card, S., 2005. The sensemaking process and leverage points for analyst technology as identified through cognitive task analysis. In: *Proceedings of the 2005 International Conference on Intelligence Analysis.* McLean, VA, May 2–6, 2005.

Plaisant, C., Milash, B., Rose, A., Widoff, S., and Shneiderman, B., 1996. LifeLines: visualizing personal histories. In: *Proceedings of the SIGCHI Conference on Human Factors in Computing Systems.* Vancouver, British Columbia, Canada, 13–18 April 1996. New York, NY: ACM, pp. 221–7.

Puterman, M., 1994. *Markov Decision Processes: Discrete Stochastic Dynamic Programming.* Oxford: Wiley Blackwell.

Rashidi, P., and Cook, D. J., 2010. Mining and monitoring patterns of daily routines for assisted living in real world settings. In: *Proceedings of the 1st ACM International Health Informatics Symposium.* Arlington, VA, 11–12 November 2010, New York, NY: ACM, pp. 336–45.

Reason, J., Manstead, A., Stradling, S., Baxter, J., and Campbell, K., 2011. Errors and violations on the roads: a real distinction? Ergonomics, 33(10–11), pp. 1315–32.

Ronis, David L., J., Yates, F., and Kirscht, J. P., 1989. Attitudes, decisions, and habits as determinants of repeated behavior. In: A. Pratkanis, S. J. Breckler, and A. C. Greenwald, eds. *Attitude Structure and Function*. Mahwah, NJ: Lawrence Erlbaum, pp. 213–39.

Russell, D. M., Stefik, M. J., Pirolli, P., and Card, S. K., 1993. The cost structure of sensemaking. In: *Proceedings of the INTERACT '93 and CHI '93 Conference on Human Factors in Computing Systems*. Amsterdam, Netherlands, 24–29 April 1993. New York, NY: ACM, pp. 269–76.

Sadilek, A., and Krumm, J., 2012. Far Out: Predicting Long-Term Human Mobility. In: *Proceedings of the Twenty-Sixth AAAI Conference on Artificial Intelligence*. Toronto, Ontario, Canada, 22–26 July 2012. New York, NY: ACM, pp. 814–20.

Salakhutdinov, R., 2009. *Learning Deep Generative Models. Annual Review of Statistics and Its Application*, 2, pp. 361–85.

Shmueli, G., 2010. To explain or to predict? *Statistical Science*, 25, pp. 289–310.

Starbird, K., and Palen, L., 2010. Pass it on?: Retweeting in mass emergency. In: *Proceedings of the 7th International ISCRAM Conference*. Seattle, WA, 2–5 May 2010.

Stone, P., Brooks, R., Brynjolfsson, E., Calo, R., Etzioni, O., Hager, G., Hirschberg, J., Kalyanakrishnan, S., Kamar, E., Kraus, S., Leyton-Brown, K., Parkes, D., Press, W., Saxenian, A., Shah, J., Tambe, M., and Teller, A., 2016. Artificial Intelligence and Life in 2030. *One Hundred Year Study on Artificial Intelligence: Report of the 2015–2016 Study Panel*. Stanford University, Stanford, CA, September 2016. Available at https://ai100.stanford.edu/2016-report

Taylor, R., 1950. Purposeful and non-purposeful behavior: A rejoinder. *Philosophy of Science*, 17(4), pp. 327–32.

Tukey, J., 1977. Exploratory data analysis. *Addison-Wesley Series in Behavioral Science*. New York, NY: Pearson.

Venkatesh, V., Morris, M. G., Davis, G. B., and Davis, F. D., 2003. User acceptance of information technology: Toward a unified view. *MIS Quarterly*, 27(3), pp. 425–78.

Wattenberg, M., 2002. Arc diagrams: Visualizing structure in strings. In: *Proceedings of the IEEE Symposium on Information Visualization*. Boston, MA, 28–29 October 2002. Red Hook, NY: Curran Associates, pp. 110–16.

Weber, M., Alexa, M., and Müller, W., 2001. Visualizing time-series on spirals. In: *Proceedings of the IEEE Symposium on Information Visualization (INFOVIS)*. San Diego, CA, 22–23 October 2001. Red Hook, NY: Curran Associates, pp. 7–14.

Weiss, Y., 1996. Synchronization of work schedules. *International Economic Review*, 37(1), pp. 157–79.

Ziebart, B., 2010. *Modeling Purposeful Adaptive Behavior with the Principle of Maximum Causal Entropy*. PhD. Carnegie Mellon University.

Ziebart, B., Ratliff, N., Gallagher, G., Mertz, C., Peterson, K., Bagnell, J. A., Hebert, M., Dey, A. K., and Srinivasa, S., 2009. Planning-based prediction for pedestrians. In: Proceedings of the *2009 IEEE/RSJ International Conference on Intelligent Robots and Systems*. St. Louis, MS, 10–15 October 2009. Red Hook, NY: Curran Associates, pp. 3931–6.

Ziebart, B. D., Bagnell, J. A., and Dey, A. K., 2013. The principle of maximum causal entropy for estimating interacting processes. *IEEE Transactions on Information Theory*, 59(4), pp. 1966–80.

Ziebart, B. D., Maas, A. L., Dey, A. K., and Bagnell, J. A., 2008. Navigate like a cabbie: Probabilistic reasoning from observed context-aware behavior. In: *Proceedings of the 10th international conference on Ubiquitous computing*. Seoul, Korea, 21–24 September 2008. New York, NY: ACM, pp. 322–31.

15

. . ● . .

Computational Methods for Socio-Computer Interaction

WAI-TAT FU,

MINGKUN GAO,

HYO JIN DO

15.1 Introduction

In the last two decades or so, various forms of online social media, forums, and networking platforms have been playing increasingly significant roles in our societies. Recent research by the Pew Research Center shows that 62 per cent of adults consider social media as their major sources of information about current events and social issues (Gottfried and Shearer, 2016). To understand how these online social platforms impact information consumption, researchers have conducted extensive research to investigate how the various features offered by these platforms may influence behaviour at the individual and collective levels. We call this general area of research Socio-Computer Interaction (SCI). This chapter starts with a few notable distinctions between SCI and traditional human-computer interaction (HCI), and provide examples of some of general computational methods used to perform analyses in SCI. Examples of these SCI analyses will be given to illustrate how these computational methods can be used to answer various research questions.

Our consideration of what SCI is and does implies a basic structure that emerges as a sequence of behaviour-artifact cycles, in which individual and social behaviour changes as new artifacts (e.g., online social platforms) are available. The focus of SCI is on analytic methods that investigate the interactions of humans and technologies at both the individual and social levels. As such, research methods on SCI have subtle differences from those commonly used in the area of social computing, as the latter focuses more on the design and characteristics of the technological systems that support social behaviour. In particular, this chapter focuses on computational techniques that are useful for characterizing and predicting the inherent structures of SCI. These techniques provide multiple measurements useful for understanding the dynamic interactions and their changes at multiple levels. These structures are dynamic because they often begin with people's desire to engage

Computational Interaction. Antti Oulasvirta, Per Ola Kristensson, Xiaojun Bi, Andrew Howes (Eds).
© Oxford University Press 2018. Published 2018 by Oxford University Press.

or share opinions with their friends, colleagues, or others. In the process of this, they sometimes encounter problems and sometimes make new discoveries. Capitalizing on the understanding of these social goals, new artifacts are developed to facilitate these social desires and to increase the satisfaction of the users. New artifacts, however, may (sometimes unintentionally) change the social interactions for which they were originally designed, and over time may even change the social norms of when and how people engage in these social interactions. This creates the need for further analysis of behaviour, which may prompt the development of new artifacts that satisfy the evolving social goals, and so on (Carroll et al., 1991). In short, SCI is the study of the emerging interactive ecology of social behaviour and technological artifacts.

15.2 Distinctions between SCI and HCI

When an individual user is using an online social platform (e.g., Reddit, Facebook, or Twitter), researchers can isolate the analysis by focusing solely on the individual user and the interface—i.e., traditional methods in HCI can be used to analyse how the user interacts with each interface object presented on his computer (or mobile phone) to characterize or predict his/her performance. However, given that the main goal of these social platforms is to allow users to interact with each other through the platforms, a more complete analysis should extend from the individual level to the broader set of interactions among users at different time scales. Broadening the analysis not only allows researchers to ask a wider set of research questions related to the impact of these social platforms on society, but it also provides opportunities to create new artifacts that address new social goals that emerge as technologies evolve. These analyses, however, often involve computational methods that go beyond traditional HCI research. We describe some of the distinction between SCI and HCI in this section, followed by a discussion of a few specific computational methods that are useful for analysis in SCI.

There are at least three important distinctions between SCI and traditional HCI. First, when analysing user behaviour in online social platforms, one should consider how the various cognitive and social processes may moderate the dynamics across multiple levels through various online social platforms—e.g., how individual choices percolate up to influence small groups, which influence the larger populations; and how 'mainstream' opinions from the larger population may have top-down influence on small groups and individual users. For example, it has been found that individuals with similar political opinions tend to interact more and discuss. In the online world, people with similar opinions can find each other through various dedicated 'threads', 'subgroups', or 'chatrooms' that allow them to create their own 'echo chambers' to reinforce similar opinions (Sunstein, 2009). This often allows individuals to more freely express their opinions, even when they might perceive that their own points of views are not widely shared among their friends or colleagues (sometimes refer to 'social desirability effect'). In contrast, when individuals perceive that an online social platform is dominated by opinions that differ from their own (e.g., certain platforms may highlight opinion leaders), there is a tendency for people to not speak up, leading to a 'spiral of silence' (Noelle-Neumann, 1974).

The second distinction between SCI and HCI relates to how people's beliefs, attitudes, and emotions may influence each other and impact their behaviour. The reason why these factors are particularly more important for SCI than HCI is that online social platforms provide multiple ways people can express *social signals* that influence other people's choices, beliefs, opinions, and behaviour. The influence is often magnified by the platforms as multiple social signals are aggregated or cascaded, or when the social signals 'resonate' with beliefs or emotional states of other users, which may reinforce the social signals or extend the social influence to more people. For example, research has shown that online content that leads to high arousal is more likely to be shared, suggesting that a causal impact of specific (emotional) responses is invoked by online contents on transmission (Berger and Milkman, 2012). Analysis in SCI therefore should include not only semantic or informational content, but also how people with different beliefs and attitudes may have different *responses or reactions* to the content, as these reactions play a pivotal role in predicting behaviour in SCI.

Finally, in SCI, the unit of analysis needs to be broader than in traditional HCI. In HCI, analysis tends to focus only on individual behaviour. In SCI, however, the main goal of the users is to interact with other users using the same platform, rather than interact with the interface itself. This distinction implies that the unit-of-analysis needs to be expanded to understand characteristics and patterns of *collective behaviour* that emerge at levels that involve multiple individuals, or how the *social networks* may predict or influence collective behaviour. We provide examples of computation methods for *network analysis* next, before we introduce examples of how it will be useful for SCI research.

15.3 Computational Methods in Socio-Computer Interaction

Given the characteristics of SCI discussed earlier, we now mention some general computational methods that are useful in analysing user behaviour. This list is not meant to be exhaustive. Rather, it highlights how these otherwise general methods can be combined to address the unique opportunities provided by the richness of data from SCI. In particular, we describe the general method of semantic analysis, sentiment analysis, and social network analysis.

15.3.1 Semantic Analysis

Social opinions often appear in a long series of synchronous or asynchronous (text) conversations. These conversations can be asynchronous as people communicate with each other at different times. Reading long sequences of texts is not an easy task, especially when comments coming from different people are staggered over each other. This has prompted researchers to develop computational methods to automatically create structures to help people understand these conversations.

15.3.1.1 Definition and Representation

Before any computational methods can be applied to texts, we need a convenient representation that computers can handle easily. A common representation is a *vector space model*, which represents text documents as vectors of identifiers in a 'bag-of-words' representation. First, using a large-text lexicon that contains all (common) words to be processed, one can represent each word with an index (i.e., a number) to this lexicon. To represent a document in which there are n words, for example, each word j in the document i can be represented with a weight w, such that each document d_i can be represented as a vector of weights $d_i = \{w_{i,1}, w_{i,2}, \ldots w_{i,n}\}$. With such representations, one can, for example, compare frequencies of different words between documents (or paragraphs), co-occurrences of words, or the similarities of two texts using various measures, etc.

15.3.1.2 Topic Segmentation

One important computation that is useful for SCI is to compute the *topics* of a document. In the area of natural language processing, a topic model is a statistical model that captures the latent structures, or 'topics', in a collection of documents. The general idea is that when a sequence of sentences is about a given topic, the distribution of word uses tends to be statistically similar, compared to when the sentences switch to a different topic. By analysing a large number of documents, these statistical properties that are lurking in the distribution of word uses can be captured and be used to detect abstract topical structures, which will be useful for automatically identifying topics in a document, as well as for detecting the boundaries of these topics in a document. Some common topic modelling methods include LDA (Latent Dirichlet Allocation) (Blei, Ng, and Jordan, 2003; Wei et al., 2010; Purver, Griffiths, Körding, and Tenenbaum, 2006; Eisenstein and Barzilay, 2008) and LSA (Latent Semantic Analysis) (Landauer and Dumais, 1997; Choi, Wiemer-Hastings, and Moore, 2001).

Topic segmentation is one basic step for further processing work of long conversation understanding. Good and accurate segmentation will make the further topic labeling or extracting work easier. Lexical features are important features in deciding whether adjacent sentences could be grouped together in similar topics. Similarity in lexical level reflects the similarity in topical level. For example, in a long piece of text that contains several topics, if there are multiple words or phrases repeated which occur in adjacent sentences or blocks of sentences, the possibility of being topically cohesive for the corresponding sentences or blocks is said to be high. Some approaches in topic segmentation such as TextTiling (Hearst, 1997) and LCSeg (Galley, McKeown, Fosler-Lussier, and Jing, 2003), rely on this hypothesis.

TextTiling (Hearst, 1997) is one early attempt at topic segmentation. Hearst and colleagues found that term repetition is a very good indicator of whether the adjacent sentences contain similar topics. They proposed a three-step algorithm:

1) Tokenization;
2) Similarity Evaluation; and
3) Segmenting,

The first step of the algorithm is to normalize term expressions by tokenizing, in which a text is broken up into words, phrases, or other meaningful units called tokens. After tokenizing, one can calculate the cosine-similarity between blocks of tokens. Each block is presented in the format of a feature vector. Based on the calculated similarities, one can decide where to split the blocks into different topics by checking whether the dissimilarity level between adjacent blocks reaches a threshold, which is set through empirical studies. Lexical cohesion is an important indicator of the similarity between two sentences or blocks. LCSeg (Galley, McKeown, Fosler-Lussier, and Jing, 2003) applies both text-based segmentation component features and conversational features into a machine learning approach. The text-based segmentation method uses lexical chains to reflect discourse structure based on term repetitions. Then, the lexical features are combined with conversational features, e.g., silences and cue phrases, and fed into the machine learning classifier.

The TextTiling algorithm may encounter problems as the calculations are based on raw terms frequency. For example, if two blocks contain the exact same terms, they will be considered similar. However, two similar sentences or two similar blocks don't have to contain exactly the same words. Different words could express similar meanings. Thus, Cho and colleagues (Choi, Wiemer-Hastings, and Moore, 2001) used LSA to measure similarity based on meanings, rather than term frequencies. In addition, instead of using a threshold to split blocks, they used clustering to perform topic segmentations.

Another approach is to use graph theory to perform segmentation. In graph theory, finding the minimum cut is a segmentation problem; one needs to split the graph into several connected components with the minimum removal of edges. This idea could be applied to topic segmentation if one could determine the graph structures of the texts in the corpus. For example, Malioutov and Barzilay (2006) built a weighted undirected graph representing a large text corpus. Each vertex in the graph represents one sentence and each edge presents the cosine similarity between two sentences in the TF.IDF format. With this graph structure of the corpus, partitioning the graph with minimum cut cost is equivalent to partitioning the corpus with maximized dissimilarity.

15.3.1.3 Topic Labelling

After topic segmentation, the subsequent step is to extract labels for different partitions. Mihalcea and Tarau (2004) proposed a topic labelling method called TextRank. This method could be used to extract key phrases from a piece of text. This method applies PageRank algorithm (Brin and Page, 2012) into the text mining process. They built a graphic structure for each document. In this graph, each vertex is a term which appears in the document. If any two terms have co-occurrence in a specific size of window, there will be an edge between those two corresponding terms. After PageRank has been conducted on this graph, it produces a ranked list of terms, with the most important keywords appearing at the top of the list. Later, to formulate the key phrases, the top keywords, say, the top one-third, are marked in the original text file. If any marked keywords are adjacent in the original text, these keywords could be used to formulate the corresponding key phrases.

Joty, Carenini, and Ng (2013) show an example of using topic modelling task on long conversations, such as long email conversations. First, they extract the conversation structure to form a graph called Fragment Quotation Graph (FQG) (Carenini, Ng, and Zhou, 2007). FQG is a directed graph where each vertex is one unit of text in the conversation and each edge (x, y), where vertex x is the reply unit to vertex y. The replying relationship is very important in a conversation, as usually similar topics continue to appear in the stream of replies. After the FQG graph is formulated, Carenini and colleagues applied the techniques mentioned previously on the FQG structure. They combined the LCSeg (Galley, McKeown, Fosler-Lussier, and Jing, 2003) and LDA (Blei, Ng, and Jordan, 2003) methods to the corresponding FQG structure of each conversation. Interested readers are referred to these studies for more detail on the mechanisms used in combining those methods.

15.3.2 Sentiment Analysis

In addition to semantic analysis, data from SCI often involves reactions or emotional content that contain useful information about user behaviour. For example, when the time has come to buy a new laptop, you probably want to read reviews and ask your friends about it. Sentiment analysis aims for capturing subjective information, including opinion and sentiment from natural language resources. Mining sentiment is challenging because it requires a deep understanding of syntactical and semantic characteristics of natural language, as well as of human behaviour and cultural/social context. Despite its difficulty, sentiment analysis is practically useful to many agents ranging from individuals to organizations. Individuals can effectively analyse a huge volume of opinionated data, reducing biases and mental burden. Sentiment analysis is also actively leveraged by companies to improve their marketing strategies or monitor consumer reviews of their products and services. Moreover, governments can automatically and rapidly conduct public polls for policy-making. In this section, we discuss the terminology, common tasks, and methodology of sentiment analysis.

15.3.2.1 Definition and Representation

How do we represent opinion in sentiment analysis? Liu and Zhang (2012) defined it as a quintuple, $[e_i, a_{ij}, oo_{ijkl}, h_k, t_l]$, where e_j is the name of an entity, a_{ij} is an aspect of e_i, oo_{ijkl} is an orientation of the opinion about the aspect a_{ij} of the entity e_i, h_k is an opinion holder, and t_l is a time when the opinion was expressed. For example, assume that Alice posted a review, 'the touch bar on the MacBook Pro is beautiful', in December 2016. The opinion quintuple will be $[MacBook Pro, touch bar, positive, Alice, Dec-2016]$.

15.3.2.2 Common Tasks of Sentiment Analysis

Sentiment analysis research can be considered a classification method, which classifies textual information into different orientations of opinion. This section explains the common tasks with regard to (i) level of information unit, (ii) granularity of opinion, (iii) domain, and (iv) language.

Level of Information Unit It is common to classify sentiment analysis tasks into three different levels of information units: document-level, sentence-level, and aspect-level analysis. The document-level sentiment analysis considers a document as a basic information unit that can express a major opinion on some main topics. The length can vary ranging from a short message like a Tweet or a movie review, to a long article like a blog post, as long as it expresses one major opinion on a general aspect.

The sentence-level sentiment analysis classifies a sentence to an associated sentiment. It assumes that a sentence expresses a single opinion, and thus, it is not appropriate for complex and compound sentences with multiple opinions. The analysis is often performed after subjectivity classification task (Wilson et al., 2005) that determines whether the given sentence contains subjective opinions. In this way, objective sentences are filtered out before analysing the sentiment. However, this task is easier said than done, since objective sentences can convey opinions and not all subjective texts have opinions. Moreover, recent research has dealt with conditional (Narayanan, Liu, and Choudhary, 2009), comparative (Ding, Liu, and Zhang, 2009), and figurative sentences (Davidov, Tsur, and Rappoport, 2010; Maynard and Greenwood, 2014).

The aspect-level analysis, or feature-level classification, is the most fine-grained analysis and focuses on individual aspects of an entity. For instance, given a review about a mobile phone, the sentiment for each aspect, including camera resolution, screen size, and voice quality, could be explored. Before recognizing sentiments, it is necessary to extract entities and aspects in a given corpus, collectively named as opinion target extraction. How to identify explicit or implicit entities and aspects is discussed in the literature (Liu, 2015), such as finding frequent noun phrases, exploiting syntactic patterns, supervised learning using sequential algorithms (e.g. hidden Markov models, conditional random fields), topic modelling, and co-occurrence rule mining (Hai, Chang, and Kim, 2011). The aspect-level analysis is especially valuable in analysing reviews and related works (Jo and Oh, 2011; Thet, Na, and Khoo, 2010; Xianghua, Guo, Yanyan, and Zhiqiang, 2013).

Granularity of Opinion   Classifying opinion into binary classes like positive and negative, thumbs up and thumbs down, like and dislike, is the simplest, and the most studied, task (e.g., Liu and Zhang, 2012). Simple extensions from binary opinions could consider a neutral class. Going further, a discrete numeric scale of opinion, such as five-star rating system, is also exploited in existing literature. Other binary classification tasks include agreement detection, i.e., whether the opinions are the same or different, and subjectivity detection, i.e., whether the sentence is subjective or objective. Binary classification is often too simple to analyse individuals' thoughts in detail. Thus, many recent works make efforts to incorporate fine-grained levels of opinion. Fine-grained emotions are widely perceived in two viewpoints: discrete and multi-dimensional emotion. The discrete emotion perspective argues that our emotion is based on distinct basic emotions. Paul Ekman's six emotion theory is the widely accepted emotion system that distinguishes sentiment into six basic emotions: happiness, sadness, anger, surprise, disgust, and fear. On the other hand, a few studies use a multi-dimensional viewpoint that depicts a sentiment in two dimensions: valence and arousal.

Domain   There is a broad spectrum of domains for sentiment analysis. Domains can be different in data sources, e.g., microblog, review, news, and blog, as well as in content, e.g., commodities, services, health, politics, education, and economics. Typically, each sentiment analysis task is attuned to one specific domain due to the difference in structures and words. To illustrate the difference in word use in different domains, consider some simple sentiment words used in product reviews and political discussions. Words that describe a product such as 'beautiful', 'malfunctioning', 'sturdy', and 'heavy' are likely to appear in product reviews, whereas 'support', 'disagree', 'prosper', 'secure', and 'progressive' are likely to be seen in the context of political discussions. Sentiment analysis tasks that are specialized for one domain often perform poorly in other domains. To cope with this issue, there have been several approaches that deal with cross-domain adaptation (Aue and Gamon, 1984; Glorot, Bordes, and Bengio, 2011; Pan, Ni, Sun, Yang, and Chen, 2010; Yang, Si, and Callan, 2006). For example, Glorot and colleagues performed domain adaptation using a deep learning technique. Pan and colleagues suggested the Spectral Feature Alignment (SFA) algorithm that exploits the relationship between domain-specific and domain-independent words.

There has been a considerable amount of research addressing both the temporal dynamics and rich network of social media. For example, Do, Lim, Kim, and Choi (2016) analysed emotions in Twitter to investigate the trend of public opinion during the Middle East Respiratory Syndrome (MERS) outbreak in South Korea. De Choudhury, Monroy-Hernández, and Mark (2014) examined sentiment in Spanish Tweets during the Mexican Drug War. Analysing the social media is a complicated task due to the unstructured and noisy nature with incorrect language usage. For instance, Twitter data should be used with caution because of its short length (less than 140 characters), novel features (e.g. mention, retweet, hashtag), and use of informal words including slang, profanity, and emoticons. Despite the difficulty in analysing Twitter data, the research will continue to gain its importance as a medium to evaluate SCI.

Language   Most sentiment analysis methods are dependent on emotion lexicons and training corpora, and thus, it is a language-dependent task. In comparison to the extensive research with textual data written in English and Chinese, there has been a limited research in other languages. The problem is aggravated by the very few non-English annotated datasets and resources that exists for sentiment analysis. Thus, many recent works focus on language adaptation (Abbasi, Chen, and Salem, 2008). A typical approach to cope with this language deficiency is to simply apply machine translation that translates existing corpus to English (Banea, Mihalcea, Wiebe, and Hassan, 2008). Also, in the efforts to construct non-English resources, Chen, Brook, and Skiena (2014) used graph propagation methods to generate emotion lexicons for 136 major languages.

15.3.2.3 Methodology

Most of the existing methodologies for sentiment analysis fall into two categories: supervised and unsupervised approaches. The supervised approach trains a classifier using an annotated dataset and classifies test instances into a finite set of sentiment classes, whereas unsupervised approaches do not require annotated data sets. In supervised approaches, manual tagging (Do and Choi, 2015a, 2015b) of sentences is mostly done in past literatures, although some scientists employed distant supervision (Go, Bhayani, and Huang, 2009) to reduce the burden. Moreover, the method represents the input instance into a set of features. Some of the widely used features are n-grams (typically bigrams and trigrams), parts of speech (especially adjectives and verbs), emotion lexicons, and parse structures, but it varies by domain and language characteristic. Classifiers are taught using the annotated training data and feature representations. Some of the most applied machine-learning classification algorithms are Support Vector Machine (SVM), Logistic Regression (LR), Random Forest (RF), and Naïve Bayes (NB). Ensemble methods that combine the existing classifiers for a single task are also actively leveraged in recent works.

On the contrary, the unsupervised approach does not require annotated training data. Instead, it determines the sentiment by the semantic orientation (SO) of the given information. The information is classified into an emotion class if the SO is above a threshold. The lexicon-based approach (Hu and Liu, 2004; Stone, Dunphy, and Smith, 1966) is the most representative way. It counts or aggregates the according values of predefined emotion lexicons that appear in the target textual data. For this reason, having good quality and abundant emotion lexicons is crucial for improving performance. It is known that the lexicon-based method performs better when it is combined with a machine-learning algorithm. An alternative unsupervised method is the generative models that deal with sentiment classification and topic modelling. The models simultaneously separate topics from a document and identify sentiments. Interested readers are referred to Jo and Oh, 2011; Lin and He, 2009; and Mei, Ling, Wondra, Su, and Zhai, 2007 for further information.

The most actively exploited machine-learning technique in the past few years is the deep learning approach (Giachanou and Crestani, 2016). The technique utilizes neural networks (NNs) with many hidden layers. Deep learning has demonstrated its successes in many fields of research including image recognition and natural language processing and it is also a promising direction for sentiment analysis. In 2016, during an international workshop on semantic evaluation (SemEval), multiple representative tasks were selected for evaluations of computational semantic analysis systems. One of the tasks was about sentiment analysis on Twitter. Forty-three teams participated in the task and most of the top-ranked teams used deep learning that included convolutional NNs, recurrent NNs, and word embedding. Among the methods used by these teams, the word embedding method was shown to be especially useful in learning continuous representation of words and phrases that can be leveraged as features for machine-learning classifiers instead of hand-crafting features. For instance, Tang et al. (2014) encoded the sentiment information into the representation of words so that positive and negative words are represented differently. Despite its high performance, the deep learning method requires a huge training corpus and high computational power to train the weights of the network. Comprehensive surveys of related papers can be found in Giachanou and Crestani, 2016.

Emotion lexicons are highly utilized in both lexicon-based and machine-learning based methods. Most of the literature in the past constructed the lexicons manually. However, it is not preferable as it takes too much time and laborious effort. A recent work by Hutto and Gilbert (2014) used crowd sourcing to manually create a large set of positive and negative lexicons for the purpose of Twitter sentiment analysis. Current sentiment analysis studies make effort to automatically construct the lexical resources. Typical approaches for automatic lexicon construction include statistical methods that investigate the frequency of lexicons in annotated corpus (Do and Choi, 2015a), or conjoined occurrence of existing emotion lexicon (Hatzivassiloglou and McKeown, 2009). Additionally, thesaurus-based methods use few emotional seed words and recursively expand lexicons by adding synonyms and antonyms using thesauruses, e.g. WordNet (Miller, 1995). Moreover, making lexicon sets for languages other than English can be achieved by the machine-translation-based method that simply translates existing English emotion lexicons to the target language. Furthermore, Du, Tan, Cheng, and Yun, 2010 studied transferring lexicons from one domain to another.

15.3.3 Social Network Analysis

Social network analysis (SNA) focuses on *relationships* of entities (e.g., people, organizations, posts, news items) instead of the entities themselves. The idea is to use patterns of this sets of relationships to as *predictors* of effects. For example, one might want to test to what extent past patterns of how a person's tweets on Twitter are shared in the social network (e.g., retweeted, forwarded, etc.) predict the likelihood that the same person will tweet again in the future about a particular candidate in the upcoming presidential election. In other words, in SNA, the unit of analysis is usually defined on the network by the relationships of the entities of interest, rather than any individual entity. While the theoretical foundation of SNA has a long history, the computational methods associated with it are relatively recent (e.g., see Freeman, 2004). Here, we focus on those methods more relevant to analysis of SCI.

15.3.3.1 Definition and Representation

A common way to represent social networks is the graphical method, in which each entity, or actor, is represented as a node or vertex in a graph, and each relation is represented as a connection between two nodes. While graphical representation is good for visualizing a social network, when the number of nodes increases, the network will become difficult to see. Besides, to facilitate computations, one needs a more generic representation such that tools can be developed to facilitate the analysis. Typically, social networks are also represented as matrices. For example, the social relations of four persons can be represented graphically and by a matrix (see Figure 15.1). Note that the social relations here are directional, but in general, they do not have to be. Also, a value can be assigned to each relation and be represented accordingly in the matrix.

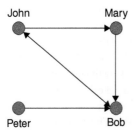

	John	Mary	Bob	Peter
John	--	1	1	0
Mary	0	--	1	0
Bob	1	0	--	0
Peter	0	0	1	--

Figure 15.1 Graphical (left) and matric (right) representation of a social network.

15.3.3.2 Computation Methods

By representing social networks as matrices, various computational methods can be applied to derive measures that inform the properties of the networks. We summarize a number of these measures based on current research topics.

Individual Nodes   Individual nodes (e.g., individual users, individual posts, etc.) play important roles in the network. For example, one may want to know who the most popular individual is, or who has the most influence, in a network. One may also want to identify whether there are different types of nodes based on the network structures. These questions can be answered by a combination of the following measures.

The simplest measure at the individual node level is a node's degree, which measures the number of edges connected to it. Degrees can be directional, so one can compute separate measures for in-degree (number of incoming edges) and out-degree (number of outgoing edges). Degrees in general represent the popularity of a node, such as the number of friends one has. It can also capture the number of incoming emails (or phone calls) one receives (in-degree) or sends out (out-degree). One can also compute the distribution of degrees in a network to visualize whether there are 'hub' nodes (with high degrees) in the network.

Another important measure is how often a node lies 'between' other nodes. This measure is computed by first locating the shortest paths between all possible pairs of nodes in the network, and calculating the percentage of these paths that contain a particular node. The higher the percentage, the more likely this particular node lies between the other nodes. This usually means that the node is more 'powerful' as it 'connects' the other nodes in the network. This measure also can indicate to what extent the network will be disrupted if a node is removed from the network.

Next, closeness is used to measure distance between nodes, i.e., how 'close' a node is to other nodes. It can be computed by the inverse of the average distance from that node to all other nodes. This measure reflects how long it will take to disseminate information from a node to the whole network. In general, a node with higher closeness will take less time to disseminate information to other nodes, and thus is more important for efficient spreading of information.

Overall Network Structures   One may be interested in the overall structures of the networks, such as the extent to which a group or subgroup of the nodes in the network are interconnected (i.e., how dense is the (sub)network?). One may want to know, for example, how many steps (or how long) it takes to go through all the nodes in the network (i.e., how easily information can diffuse in the network). While one can visualize the distributions of the individual node measures to get a sense of these general network properties, some general metrics can also be computed. We describe some of them next.

One may want to know the general interconnectivity in a network. Density can be computed by dividing the number of edges in the network by the number of possible edges if the network is fully connected (i.e., all nodes connect to all other nodes).

Next, the geodesic distance refers to the number of edges in a shortest path between two nodes (there could be more than one shortest path). The average geodesic distance measures the average number of 'hops' between two nodes in a network. The shorter this measure, the more connected is the network.

Additionally, one may want to know to what extent a network is hierarchical—i.e., how centralized the network is around a few key nodes (actors, posts, forums). One can compute the sum of differences between the node with the highest centrality (e.g., betweenness) and all the other nodes, and then divide this sum of differences by the maximum possible sum of differences. When this measure is close to 0, it means that the most central node is not much different from the other nodes—i.e., the network is not hierarchical. However, if this measure is close to 1, then the most central node is likely connecting all the other nodes, showing a hierarchical structure between the 'star' nodes and the rest of the nodes in the network.

15.4 Examples of Socio-Computer Interaction analysis

This section presents examples of SCI analysis to highlight how these computational methods are used to answer research questions related to how different online social platforms influence behaviour.

15.4.1 Social Opinions on Online Forums

We have been investigating how different social platforms shape social opinions (Liao and Fu, 2014a, b; Liao, Fu, and Mamidi, 2015). There has been an enormous amount of data on how people express their opinions about politics and other societal issues through platforms such as Facebook, Twitter, Reddit, and others. Given the massive amount of opinions, researchers have used various semantic analysis techniques to organize these opinions (e.g., Hoque and Carenini, 2016), such that people can more easily find, read, and appreciate the social opinions. This line of research uses many of the semantic analysis techniques discussed earlier, such that comments, conversations, and other user-generated texts are analysed and categorized into units that allow users to more easily access them. This line of research has led to many useful online social platforms that organize social opinions based on their semantic contents and topics, which allow users to more easily choose and access opinions about these topics.

One important issue currently garnering interest is to what extent these platforms allow people to appreciate opinions by others, even if these opinions are different from their own. This is important because there has been increasing research that shows that online social platforms often exacerbate selective exposure to information—i.e., people often selectively attend to information that is consistent with their own beliefs (e.g., Valentino, Banks, Hutchings, and Davis, 2009). In other words, more and more studies show that organizing social opinions based on semantic contents do not always lead to better exposure to opinions, as existing attitudes or beliefs of users may invoke different (strong) reactions to the opinions. Paradoxically, these kinds of organization may sometimes lead to even stronger selective exposure to information (Sunstein, 2009). Selective exposure is one main reason why social opinions become increasingly polarized, which is often considered harmful for deliberative democracy (Bessette, 1994; Sunstein, 2009).

In a series of studies (Liao and Fu, 2014a,b; 2015), we found that selective exposure is pervasive. To understand how to mitigate selective exposure, we designed interfaces and tested how they could encourage people to attend to information inconsistent with their beliefs. For example, in a recent study (Gao, Do, and Fu, 2017), in addition to semantic analysis, we included sentiment analysis techniques as discussed earlier to measure the emotional reactions to different social opinions by people with different existing beliefs.

Figure 15.2 shows the design of the new online social platform. We found that the addition of the sentiment analysis seems to help mitigate selective exposure much better than using only semantic analysis. On this platform, users see sentiments of social opinions related to a controversial social issue. These opinions were separately presented on two (or more) areas on the screen. These areas represent different perspectives on the issue by

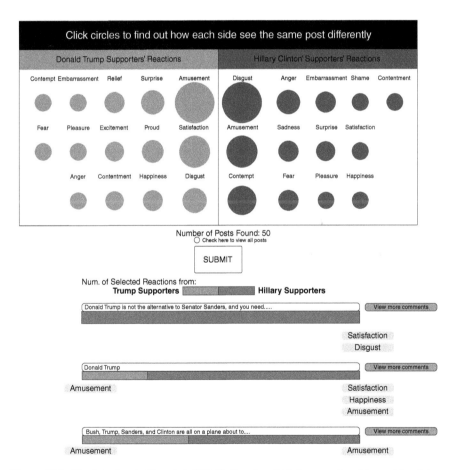

Figure 15.2 The interface in Gao et al. (2017). Emotional labels are assigned to social opinions about the 2016 US presidential election. These labels are then used to organize them into clusters for users to explore the opinions of supporters of both candidates.

different uses. For example, during the 2016 US presidential election, each box represents opinions from users who support one candidate. Inside each box, opinions are clustered as circles based on their sentiments, such as 'anger', 'surprise', 'pleasure', etc. These sentiments represent the *reactions* to each of the opinions by other users. Users can click on any of the circles to see the opinions in that sentiment category. The opinions will be displayed at the bottom. Reactions by other users (who also may have different perspectives) on each opinion will be displayed. Details of the setup of the platform can be found in Gao, Do, and Fu, 2017.

In a user study reported in Gao and colleagues (2017), we asked two groups of participants to explore a large set of user opinions of the two candidates of the 2016 US presidential election (Hillary Clinton and Donald Trump) from Reddit.com (the study was done before the election). This is a highly polarized topic, as supporters of either candidate tend to have extreme opinions about the other candidate. We recruited participants who were supporters of one or the other of the candidates and asked them to use the interface to understand the social opinions expressed on the platform. One group of the participants used the new interface, while the other group used the traditional Reddit interface (which organize opinions based on topics, i.e., semantic contents, only). We found that participants who used the new interface were more likely to read posts about the candidates that they did not support, whereas people who used the Reddit interface showed selective exposure, i.e., they tended to only check opinions about the candidates that they supported.

This example demonstrated an important characteristic of SCI—the emotional signals expressed through online social platforms are often magnified and indirectly influence behaviour at the individual and collective levels. While better organization at the semantic levels can facilitate cognitive processes that selectively attend to information that is semantically relevant to the social goals of users, they do not sufficiently address the emotional component of the social goals. In fact, in many controversial societal issues, the emotional component plays an important, if not stronger, role in determining user behaviour (e.g., which posts they will select, read, and share). A more complete analysis of SCI needs to consider other social factors that influence user behaviour, which may lead to development of better online social platforms.

15.4.2 Social Tagging

Social tagging systems allow users to annotate, categorize, and share Web content (links, papers, books, blogs, etc.) by using short textual labels called tags. Tags help users in organizing, sharing, and searching for Web content in shared social systems. The inherent simplicity in organizing and annotating content in these systems through 'open-ended' tags satisfies a personal and social function. At a personal level, customized tags can be added to a resource based on a specific information goal (e.g., mark up for future reading or identifying books for a history project) that will help in organization of resources or future search and retrieval. At the social level, the tags facilitate sharing and collaborative indexing of information, such that social tags act as 'way-finders' for other users with similar interests to search for relevant information.

But how do social tags contribute to social indexing of online information, and to what extent are they effective? One important question is whether the unconstrained, open-vocabulary approach is effective for creating indices in the long run. For example, if people use different words to index the same resources, over time these indices may not converge and its informational value may decrease. To study this, we performed a user study on how social tags grow when people can see other people's tags (the social condition), and compare them with a condition in which people cannot see other people's tags (the nominal condition). We hypothesized that, when a user can see existing tags created by others, these tags will serve as cues to invoke semantic representations of the concepts that the tags refer to, which in turn will influence the user to generate tags that are semantically relevant to the concepts. If this is true, then social tags may converge and their information value will not decrease over time. This is because, although people may use different words to represent similar concepts, the underlying semantic representations should remain relatively stable and thus, the information value should remain high (when measured at the semantic level, not the word level). The situation is similar to the growth of natural language—even though a child learns more and more words as they grow up, the informational value of each word does not decrease as the semantic content of each word is enriched by their connections to meanings in the real world through repeated interactions.

To answer the research question, Fu et al. (2010) represented a social tagging system as a network, and applied various computational methods from SNA to analyse the social tags. First, a social tagging system is represented as a tripartite network, in which there are three main components: a set of users (U), a set of tags created by the users (T), and resources (R) (URL, books, pictures, movies etc., see Figure 15.3). Resources can be different depending on the specific purpose of the social tagging system. By looking at any two of the sets, one can convert the bipartite set of connections into a graphical representation, in which each node is connected to the other if they shared the same connections (see Figure 15.4). The graphical representation allows the social network analysis that discussed earlier.

After representing the social tagging system as a network, SNA computational methods can be used to compare how tags grow as a network in a social group and in a nominal group. Figure 15.5 shows the node degree distribution of the two groups. Both groups show a *scale-free* distribution—i.e., there are a small number of nodes with high degrees (hub nodes connected to many other nodes), and a long tail of nodes that have few connections

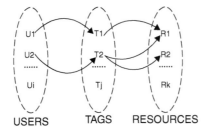

Figure 15.3 A Tripartite representation of social tagging.

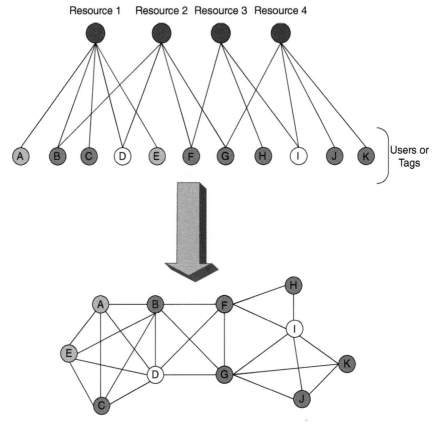

Figure 15.4 The top part shows a bi-partite set of connections. The bottom half shows the corresponding network obtained by linking nodes (tags or users) that are connected to the same resources.

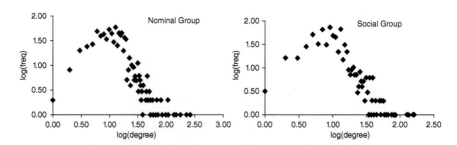

Figure 15.5 The node degree distributions in the nominal and social groups in the study by Fu et al. (2010). In the nominal group, participants could not see tags created by others. In the social groups, participants could see tags created by previous participants.

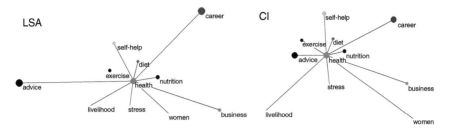

Figure 15.6 Graphical representation of a set of co-occurring tags for "health" in the social condition. LSA (Latent semantic analysis) scores measures the semantic similarities of two tags. CI (Co-occurrence index) score measures the distance between two tags based on co-occurrence.

(but still connected to the rest of the network through the hub nodes). More importantly, we found that average node degree of the social group (14.1) was significantly smaller than the nominal group (18.9), and that the social group had a higher clustering coefficient than the nominal group (0.86 vs. 0.76). This indicates that when people can see others' tags in the social group, the tags were more clustered than the nominal group. This finding was generally consistent with the hypothesis that social tags do converge as people can see tags by others.

We used two measures: Intertag Co-occurrence Index (CI) and Latent Semantic Analysis (LSA) scores to measure the usage similarity and semantic similarity respectively. The CI captures the likelihood of two tags being used together by the same user, whereas LSA is a statistical estimate of how semantically similar two words are (for more details, see Fu et al., 2010). Figure 15.6 shows an example of the CI and LSA score for the tag 'health'. Tags that are closer to 'health' have higher CI and LSA scores, and the sizes of the circles reflect the frequencies of uses. In general, the structures match well. However, there are notable exceptions. While 'health' and 'advice' had a higher likelihood of being used together, they had low semantic similarities. It is possible that 'advice' was frequently used together with 'health' because online information tends to have high frequencies of 'health advice', and thus the co-occurrence could have emerged as a common term.

15.5 Conclusion

We defined socio-computer interaction (SCI) as an emerging area of research that studies the ecology between social behaviour and online artifacts. We outlined distinctive characteristics of SCI research that demanded extension of analysis methods that are commonly used in traditional HCI research. We discussed a number of computational methods that can be utilized to analyse SCI behaviour, and demonstrated their uses in two research studies. These examples were chosen to demonstrate some of the uniqueness of the data collected from SCI research. In particular, we demonstrated how a combination of computational methods are often necessary to triangulate the important factors that influence behaviour at both the individual and social levels, and to what extent the analyses of these factors have implications to design of future online social platforms.

· ·

REFERENCES

Abbasi, A., Chen, H., and Salem, A., 2008. Sentiment Analysis in Multiple Languages: Feature Selection for Opinion Classification in Web forums. *Transactions on Information Systems*, 26(3), pp. 1–34.

Aue, A., and Gamon, M., 1984. Customizing Sentiment Classifiers to New Domains: A Case Study. *Educational Measurement: Issues and Practice*, 3(3), pp. 16–18.

Banea, C., Mihalcea, R., Wiebe, J., and Hassan, S., 2008. Multilingual Subjectivity Analysis Using Machine Translation. In: *Proceedings of the 2008 Conference on Empirical Methods in Natural Language Processing*. Red Hook, NY: Curran Associates.

Berger, J., and Milkman, K. L., 2012. What makes online content viral. *Journal of Marketing Research*, 49(2), pp. 192–205.

Bessette, J., 1994. *The Mild Voice of Reason: Deliberative Democracy & American National Government*. Chicago: University of Chicago Press.

Blei, D. M., Ng, A. Y., and Jordan, M. I., 2003. Latent dirichlet allocation. *Journal of Machine Learning Research*, 3(Jan), pp. 993–1022.

Brin, S., and Page, L., 2012. Reprint of: The anatomy of a large-scale hypertextual web search engine. *Computer Networks*, 56(18), pp. 3825–33.

Carenini, G., Ng, R. T., and Zhou, X., 2007. Summarizing email conversations with clue words. In: Proceedings of the 16th International Conference on World Wide Web. New York, NY: ACM, pp. 91–100.

Carroll, J. M., Kellogg, W. A., and Rosson, M. B., 1991. The Task-Artifact Cycle. In: J. M. Carroll, eds. *Designing Interaction: Psychology at the Human-Computer Interface*. Cambridge: Cambridge University Press.

Chen, Y., Brook, S., and Skiena, S., 2014. Building Sentiment Lexicons for All Major Languages. In: *Proceedings of the 52nd Annual Meeting of the Association for Computational Linguistics*. Red Hook, NY: Curran Associates.

Choi, F. Y. Y., Wiemer-Hastings, P., and Moore, J., 2001. Latent Semantic Analysis for Text Segmentation. In: *Proceedings of the Conference on Empirical Methods in Natural Language Processing*. New York, NY: ACM, pp. 109–17.

Davidov, D., Tsur, O., and Rappoport, A., 2010. Semi-Supervised Recognition of Sarcastic Sentences in Twitter and Amazon. In: *CoNLL '10: Proceedings of the 14th Conference on Computational Natural Language Learning*. New York, NY: ACM, pp. 107–16.

De Choudhury, M., Monroy-Hernández, A., and Mark, G., 2014. 'Narco' Emotions: Affect and Desensitization in Social Media during the Mexican Drug War. In: *Proceedings of the 32nd Annual ACM Conference on Human Factors in Computing Systems*. New York, NY: ACM.

Ding, X., Liu, B., and Zhang, L., 2009. Entity discovery and assignment for opinion mining applications. In: *Proceedings of the 15th ACM SIGKDD International Conference on Knowledge Discovery and Data Mining*. New York, NY: ACM Press.

Do, H. J., and Choi, H.-J., 2015a. Korean Twitter Emotion Classification Using Automatically Built Emotion Lexicons and Fine-grained Features. In: *Proceedings of the 29th Pacific Asia Conference on Language, Information and Computation*. Red Hook, NY: Curran Associates, pp. 142–50.

Do, H. J., and Choi, H.-J., 2015b. Sentiment Analysis of Real-life Situations Using Location, People and Time as Contextual Features. In: *Proceedings of the 3rd International Conference on Big Data and Smart Computing*. New York, NY: IEEE.

Do, H. J., Lim, C. G., Kim, Y. J., and Choi, H.-J., 2016. Analyzing Emotions in Twitter During a Crisis: A Case Study of the 2015 Middle East Respiratory Syndrome Outbreak in Korea. In: *Proceedings of the 3rd International Conference on Big Data and Smart Computing.* New York, NY: IEEE.

Du, W., Tan, S., Cheng, X., and Yun, X., 2010. Adapting Information Bottleneck Method for Automatic Construction of Domain-oriented Sentiment Lexicon. In: *Proceedings of the 3rd International Conference on Web Search and Data Mining.* New York, NY: ACM Press.

Eisenstein, J., and Barzilay, R., 2008. Bayesian unsupervised topic segmentation. In: *Proceedings of the Conference on Empirical Methods in Natural Language Processing.* Red Hook, NY: Curran Associates, pp. 334–43.

Freeman, L. C., 2004. *The development of social network analysis: A study in the sociology of science.* Vancouver: Empirical Press.

Fu, W.-T., Kannampallil, T. G., Kang, R., and He, J., 2010. Semantic imitation in social tagging. *ACM Transactions on Computer-Human Interaction,* 17(3), pp. 1–37.

Galley, M., McKeown, K., Fosler-Lussier, E., and Jing, H., 2003. Discourse segmentation of multi-party conversation. In: *Proceedings of the 41st Annual Meeting on Association for Computational Linguistics.*Volume 1. Red Hook, NY: Curran Associates, pp. 562–9.

Gao, M., Do, H. J., and Fu, W.-T., 2017. An intelligent interface for organizing online opinions on controversial topics. In: *IUI '17: Proceedings of the ACM conference on Intelligent User Interfaces.* Limassol, Cyprus, 13–16 March 2017.

Giachanou, A., and Crestani, F., 2016. Like It or Not: A Survey of Twitter Sentiment Analysis Methods. *ACM Computing Surveys,* 49(2), pp. 1–41.

Glorot, X., Bordes, A., and Bengio, Y., 2011. Domain Adaptation for Large-Scale Sentiment Classification: A Deep Learning Approach. In: *Proceedings of the 28th International Conference on Machine Learning.* New York, NY: ACM Press.

Go, A., Bhayani, R., and Huang, L., 2009. *Twitter Sentiment Classification using Distant Supervision. Technical Report,* Stanford. Available at: http://cs.stanford.edu/people/alecmgo/papers/TwitterDistantSupervision09.pdf.

Gottfried, J., and Shearer, E., 2016. News use across social media. Washington, DC: Pew Research Center. Available at: http://www.journalism.org/2016/05/26/news-use-across-social-media-platforms-2016/.

Hai, Z., Chang, K., and Kim, J. J., 2011. Implicit Feature Identification via Co-occurrence Association Rule Mining. In: *Proceedings of the 12th International Conference on Intelligent Text Processing and Computational Linguistics.* Tokyo, Japan, 20–26 February 2011. New York, NY: Springer.

Hatzivassiloglou, V., and McKeown, K. R., 2009. Predicting the Semantic Orientation of Adjectives. *ACM Transactions on Information Systems,* 21(4), pp. 315–46.

Hearst, M. A., 1997. Texttiling: segmenting text into multi-paragraph subtopic passages. *Computational Linguistics,* 23(1), pp. 33–64.

Hoque, E., and Carenini, G., 2016. Multiconvis: A visual text analytics system for exploring a collection of online conversations. In: *Proceedings of the 21st International Conference on Intelligent User Interfaces.* New York, NY: ACM, pp. 96–107.

Hu, M., and Liu, B., 2004. Mining and summarizing customer reviews. In: *KDD '04: Proceedings of the 2004 SIGKDD International Conference on Knowledge Discovery and Data Mining.* Seattle, Washington, 22–25 August 2004. New York, NY: ACM, pp. 168–77.

Hutto, C. J., and Gilbert, E., 2014. VADER: A Parsimonious Rule-based Model for Sentiment Analysis of Social Media Text. In: *Proceedings of the 8th International AAAI Conference on Weblogs and Social Media.* Ann Arbor, Michigan, 1–4 June 2014. Palo Alto, CA: AAAI Press.

Jo, Y., and Oh, A. H., 2011. Aspect and Sentiment Unification Model for Online Review Analysis. In: *Proceedings of the 4th ACM International Conference on Web Search and Data Mining.* New York, NY: ACM.

Joty, S., Carenini, G., and Ng, R. T., 2013. Topic segmentation and labeling in asynchronous conversations. *Journal of Artificial Intelligence Research*, 47, pp. 521–73.

Landauer, T. K., and Dumais, S. T., 1997. A solution to Plato's problem: The latent semantic analysis theory of acquisition, induction, and representation of knowledge. *Psychological Review*, 104(2), pp. 211–40.

Liao, Q. V., and Fu, W.-T., 2014a. Can you hear me now? Mitigating the echo chamber effect by source position indicators. In: *Proceedings of the 17th ACM conference on Computer Supported Cooperative Work and Social Computing*. New York, NY: ACM, pp. 184–96.

Liao, Q. V., and Fu, W.-T., 2014b. Expert voices in echo chambers: effects of source expertise indicators on exposure to diverse opinions. In: *Proceedings of the 32nd annual ACM Conference on Human Factors in Computing Systems*. New York, NY: ACM, pp. 2745–54.

Lin, C., and He, Y., 2009. Joint Sentiment/Topic Model for Sentiment Analysis. In: *Proceedings of the 18th ACM Conference on Information and Knowledge Management*. Hong Kong, China, 2–6 November 2009. New York, NY: ACM, pp. 375–84.

Liu, B., 2015. *Sentiment Analysis*. Cambridge: Cambridge University Press.

Liu, B., and Zhang, L., 2012. A Survey of Opinion Mining and Sentiment Analysis. In: Charu C. Aggarwal and C. Zhai, eds. *Mining Text Data*. New York, NY: Springer, pp. 415–63.

Malioutov, I., and Barzilay, R., 2006. Minimum cut model for spoken lecture segmentation. In: *Proceedings of the 21st International Conference on Computational Linguistics and the 44th annual meeting of the Association for Computational Linguistics*. Red Hook, NY: Curran Associates, pp. 25–32.

Maynard, D., and Greenwood, M. A., 2014. Who Cares About Sarcastic Tweets? Investigating the Impact of Sarcasm on Sentiment Analysis. In: *Proceedings of the 9th International Conference on Language Resources and Evaluation*. Reykjavik, Iceland, 26–31 May 2014. Red Hook, NY: Curran Associates.

Mei, Q., Ling, X., Wondra, M., Su, H., and Zhai, C., 2007. Topic Sentiment Mixture: Modeling Facets and Opinions in Weblogs. In: *Proceedings of the 16th International Conference on World Wide Web*. New York, NY: ACM Press.

Mihalcea, R., and Tarau, P., 2004. *TextRank: Bringing order into texts*. Stroudsburg, PA: Association for Computational Linguistics.

Miller, G. A., 1995. WordNet: A Lexical Database for English. *Communications of the ACM*, 38(11), pp. 39–41.

Narayanan, R., Liu, B., and Choudhary, A., 2009. Sentiment Analysis of Conditional Sentences. In: *Proceedings of the 2009 Conference on Empirical Methods in Natural Language*. New York, NY: ACM Press.

Noelle-Neumann, E., 1974. The Spiral of Silence: A Theory of Public Opinion. *Journal of Communication*, 24(2), pp. 43–51.

Pan, S. J., Ni, X., Sun, J., Yang, Q., and Chen, Z., 2010. Cross-Domain Sentiment Classification via Spectral Feature Alignment. In: *Proceedings of the 19th International Conference on World Wide Web*. New York, NY: ACM Press.

Purver, M., Griffiths, T. L., Körding, K. P., and Tenenbaum, J. B., 2006. Unsupervised topic modelling for multi-party spoken discourse. In: *Proceedings of the 21st International Conference on Computational Linguistics and the 44th Annual Meeting of the Association for Computational Linguistics*. Red Hook, NY: Curran Associates, pp. 17–24.

Stone, P. J., Dunphy, D. C., and Smith, M. S., 1966. *The General Inquirer: A Computer Approach to Content Analysis*. Cambridge, MA: MIT Press.

Sunstein, C. R., 2009. *Republic.com 2.0*. Princeton, NJ: Princeton University Press.

Tang, D., Wei, F., Yang, N., Zhou, M., Liu, T., and Qin, B., 2014. Learning Sentiment-Specific Word Embedding. In: *Proceedings of the 52nd Annual Meeting of the Association for Computational Linguistics*. Red Hook, NY: Curran Associates, pp. 1555–65.

Thet, T. T., Na, J.-C., and Khoo, C. S. G. K., 2010. Aspect-based Sentiment Analysis of Movie Reviews on Discussion Boards. *Journal of Information Science*, 36(6), pp. 823–48.

Valentino, N. A., Banks, A. J., Hutchings, V. L., and Davis, A. K., 2009. Selective exposure in the internet age: The interaction between anxiety and information utility. *Political Psychology*, 30(4), pp. 591–613.

Wei, F., Liu, S., Song, Y., Pan, S., Zhou, M. X., Qian, W., Shi, L., Tan, L., and Zhang, Q., 2010. Tiara: a Visual Exploratory Text Analytic System. In: *Proceedings of the 16th ACM SIGKDD international conference on Knowledge discovery and data mining*. New York, NY: ACM, pp. 153–62.

Wilson, T., Hoffmann, P., Somasundaran, S., Kessler, J., Wiebe, J., Choi, Y., Cardie, C., Riloff, E, and Patwardhan, S., 2005. OpinionFinder: A System for Subjectivity Analysis. In *Proceedings of HLT/EMNLP on Interactive Demonstrations*. Red Hook, NY: Curran Associates.

Xianghua, F., Guo, L., Yanyan, G., and Zhiqiang, W., 2013. Multi-aspect Sentiment Analysis for Chinese Online Social Reviews Based on Topic Modeling and HowNet lexicon. *Knowledge-Based Systems*, 37, pp. 186–95.

Yang, H., Si, L., and Callan, J., 2006. Knowledge Transfer and Opinion Detection in the TREC2006 Blog Track. In: *Proceedings of the 15th Text Retrieval Conference*. Gaithersburg, Maryland, 14–17 November 2006. Gaithersburg, MD: NST.

INDEX